ONE GOD, ONE PEOPLE, ONE FUTURE

ONE GOD, ONE PEOPLE, ONE FUTURE

Essays in Honor of N. T. Wright

Edited by John Anthony Dunne and Eric Lewellen

Fortress Press
Minneapolis

ONE GOD, ONE PEOPLE, ONE FUTURE
Essays in Honor of N. T. Wright

Fortress Press Edition © 2018
First published in Great Britain in 2018

Typeset by Fakenham Prepress Solutions, Fakenham, Norfolk, NR21 8NL

Print ISBN: 978-1-5064-4876-3
eBook ISBN: 978-1-5064-5067-4

Manufactured in the U.S.A.

Contents

Contents

ONE PEOPLE

Contents

ONE FUTURE

Abbreviations

1QH	*Thanksgiving Hymns*
1QM	*War Scroll*
1QS	*Community Rule*
1QSa	*Community Rule*, Appendix a
4Q504	*Words of the Luminaries*
4QMMT	*Miqsat Ma'ase ha-Torah* (*Some Precepts of the Law*)
Agr.	Philo, *On Agriculture*
AGSU	Arbeiten zur Geschichte des Spätjudentums und Urchristentums
An.	Tertullian, *The Soul*
Ann.	Tacitus, *Annals*
Ant.	Josephus, *Jewish Antiquities*
Apoc. Abr.	*Apocalypse of Abraham*
Apoc. Zeph.	*Apocalypse of Zephaniah*
Asc. Isa.	*Ascension of Isaiah*
b. Sanh.	*Sanhedrin* (Babylonian Talmud)
2 Bar.	*2 Baruch* (Syriac Apocalypse)
Barn.	*Epistle of Barnabas*
BDAG	Danker, Frederick W., Walter Bauer, William F. Arndt and F. Wilbur Gingrich. *A Greek-English Lexicon of the New Testament and Other Early Christian Literature.* 3rd edn. Chicago, 2000
BDF	Blass, F., A. Debrunner and R. W. Funk. *A Greek Grammar of the New Testament and Other Early Christian Literature.* Chicago, 1961
C. Ap.	Josephus, *Against Apion*
CD	Cairo Genizah copy of the *Damascus Document*
CD	Karl Barth, *Church Dogmatics.* Edinburgh: T&T Clark, 1936–69
CEB	Common English Bible
Cher.	Philo, *On the Cherubim*
Civ. Dei	Augustine, *City of God*
Comm. Eph.	Jerome, *Commentary on Ephesians*
Comm. Gal.	Chrysostom, *Commentary on Galatians*
Conf.	Philo, *On the Confusion of Tongues*

COQG	Christian Origins and the Question of God
CSEL	Corpus scriptorum ecclesiasticorum latinorum
Decal.	Philo, *On the Decalogue*
Det.	Philo, *That the Worse Attacks the Better*
Dial.	Justin, *Dialogue with Trypho*
Ebr.	Philo, *On Drunkenness*
Ep.	*Epistle*
Ep. Apos.	*Epistle to the Apostles*
Ep. Gal.	Victorinus, *Epistle to the Galatians*
2 Esd.	2 Esdras
ESV	English Standard Version
FC	Fathers of the Church
frag.	fragment
Gen. Rab.	*Genesis Rabbah*
Gig.	Philo, *On Giants*
GLAJJ	*Greek and Latin Authors on Jews and Judaism*, ed. M. Stern. 3 vols. Jerusalem, 1974–84
Haer.	Irenaeus, *Against Heresies*
Her.	Philo, *Who Is the Heir?*
Hist.	Tacitus, *Histories*
Hom. 2 Cor.	Chrysostom, *Homily on 2 Corinthians*
Hom. Eph.	Chrysostom, *Homily on Ephesians*
Hom. Gal.	Chrysostom, *Homily on Galatians*
IG	*Inscriptione graecae*. Editio minor. Berlin, 1924–
Ign. *Magn.*	Ignatius, *To the Magnesians*
Immut.	Philo, *That God Is Unchangeable*
Jub.	*Jubilees*
Kdms	Kingdoms
KJV	King James Version
L.A.B.	*Liber antiquitatum biblicarum* (Pseudo-Philo)
Leg.	Philo, *Allegorical Interpretation*
Legat.	Philo, *On the Embassy to Gaius*
Let. Aris.	*Letter of Aristeas* (Pseudo-Aristeas)
Lg.	Plato, *Laws*
LXX	Septuagint
m. B. Qam.	*Baba Qamma* (Mishnah)
m. Ber.	*Berakot* (Mishnah)
m. Hag.	*Hagigah* (Mishnah)
m. Tam.	*Tamid* (Mishnah)
4 Macc.	*4 Maccabees*

MAMA	*Monumenta Asiae Minoris Antiqua*. Manchester and London, 1928–93
Midr. Prov.	*Midrash on Proverbs*
Midr. Ps.	*Midrash on Psalms*
Migr.	Philo, *On the Migration of Abraham*
Mos.	Philo, *On the Life of Moses*
ms.	manuscript
MT	Masoretic Text
NA²⁷	Nestle-Aland, Novum Testamentum Graece (27th edn)
NA²⁸	Nestle-Aland, Novum Testamentum Graece (28th edn)
NETS	New English Translation of the Septuagint
NIV	New International Version
NJB	New Jerusalem Bible
*NPNF*¹	*Nicene and Post-Nicene Fathers*, Series 1
NRSV	New Revised Standard Version
NT	New Testament
OG	Old Greek
Opif.	Philo, *On the Creation of the World*
OT	Old Testament
Pasch.	Melito, *On the Pasch*
Pesiq. Rab.	*Pesiqta Rabbati*
PFG	N. T. Wright, *Paul and the Faithfulness of God*. London: SPCK; Minneapolis: Fortress, 1996
PG	Patrologica graeca, ed. J.-P. Migne. 162 vols. Paris, 1857–60
PGL	*Patristic Greek Lexicon*, ed. G. W. H. Lampe. Oxford, 1961
Phyl	Phylactery
Pirqe R. El.	*Pirqe Rabbi Eliezer*
PL	Patrologica latina, ed. J.-P. Migne. 217 vols. Paris, 1844–64
Plant.	Philo, *On Planting*
Pol. *Phil.*	Polycarp, *To the Philippians*
Post.	Philo, *On the Posterity of Cain*
PrAz	Prayer of Azariah
QE	Philo, *Questions on Exodus*
QG	Philo, *Questions on Genesis*
RSV	Revised Standard Version
RV	Revised Version
s.	*sōphronismos*
s. iv BC	fourth century BC
SBL	Society of Biblical Literature
Sib. Or.	*Sibylline Oracles*

List of abbreviations

Smyrn.	Ignatius, *To the Smyrnaeans*
Som.	Philo, *On Dreams*
Spec.	Philo, *On the Special Laws*
T. Mos.	*Testament of Moses*
Ta'an.	*Ta'anit*
Virt.	Philo, *On the Virtues*
War	Josephus, *Jewish War*
Yal.	*Yalqut*

Contributors

Richard Bauckham is Emeritus Professor of New Testament Studies at the University of St Andrews (UK).

Michael F. Bird is Lecturer in Theology at Ridley College (Australia).

J. Andrew Cowan holds a PhD from the University of St Andrews (UK).

S. A. Cummins is Professor of Religious Studies at Trinity Western University (Canada).

J. P. Davies is Tutor of New Testament, Trinity College, Bristol (UK).

James D. G. Dunn is Emeritus Lightfoot Professor of Divinity at Durham University (UK).

John Anthony Dunne is Assistant Professor of New Testament at Bethel Seminary (USA).

Crispin Fletcher-Louis is Visiting Fellow at the University of Gloucestershire (UK).

Andrew J. Goddard is Senior Research Fellow at the Kirby Laing Institute for Christian Ethics (KLICE), Cambridge, and Assistant Minister at St James the Less (London, UK).

Michael J. Gorman is Raymond E. Brown Professor of Biblical Studies and Theology at St Mary's Seminary & University (USA).

Scott J. Hafemann is Reader in New Testament at the University of St Andrews (UK).

Richard B. Hays is George Washington Ivey Professor of New Testament at Duke Divinity School (USA).

David G. Horrell is Professor of New Testament Studies at the University of Exeter (UK).

Edith M. Humphrey is William F. Orr Professor of New Testament at Pittsburgh Theological Seminary (USA).

Sylvia C. Keesmaat is Adjunct Professor of Biblical Studies at Wycliffe College and Trinity College, Toronto School of Theology, and Biblical Scholar in Residence at St James Anglican Church, Fenelon Falls (Canada).

Grant LeMarquand is Visiting Professor of New Testament, Trinity School for Ministry, Ambridge, PA (USA), Assistant Bishop in the Diocese of Egypt with North Africa and the Horn of Africa and Area Bishop for the Horn of Africa, retired (Egypt).

Eric Lewellen is Agency Engagement Specialist with the Evangelical Alliance Mission (USA).

Michael Lloyd is Principal of Wycliffe Hall, Oxford University (UK).

Bruce W. Longenecker is Professor and W. W. Melton Chair of Religion at Baylor University (USA).

Grant Macaskill is Kirby Lang Chair of New Testament Exegesis at the University of Aberdeen (UK).

Scot McKnight is Julius R. Mantey Chair of New Testament at Northern Seminary (USA).

Carey C. Newman is Director of Baylor University Press at Baylor University (USA).

Peter Oakes is Professor of New Testament at the University of Manchester (UK).

Oliver O'Donovan is Emeritus Professor of Christian Ethics and Practical Theology at the University of Edinburgh (UK).

Nicholas Perrin is Franklin S. Dyrness Professor of Biblical Studies at Wheaton College (USA).

Brian J. Walsh is Pastor of the Wine Before Breakfast Community at the University of Toronto, and Adjunct Professor of Theology at Wycliffe College and the Faculty of Divinity at Trinity College (Canada).

Ben Witherington III is Jean R. Amos Professor of New Testament at Asbury Theological Seminary (USA).

Stephen I. Wright is Vice Principal and Academic Director of Spurgeon's College, London (UK).

Introduction: Celebrating the Rt Revd Professor N. T. Wright

JOHN ANTHONY DUNNE AND ERIC LEWELLEN

It is with great joy and affection that we present this collection of essays to N. T. Wright on the occasion of his seventieth birthday (1 December 2018) in celebration of his illustrious career. As his former doctoral students at the University of St Andrews, we (the editors) began working on this volume just before the 2014 Annual Meeting of the Society of Biblical Literature in San Diego. There we began soliciting contributors and secretly plotting to create a volume in his honour. After four years of private meetings, collecting and editing essays, and multiple emails reminding contributors that 'mum's the word', we are thrilled that we can finally present this volume to our esteemed honorand.

Much can be said about Tom's achievements, but the thing that stands out the most to his students is his accessibility. As we can all attest, Prof. Wright is a pastoral and gracious supervisor, eager to meet with his students and read through our chapters (at various stages of polish and coherence). For those of us from the States it was a tough lesson because he loved to give us a hard time for our 'Americanisms' – we have learned well to use the word *interpretative* over the 'barbarism' *interpretive*! Many of us from his St Andrews tenure remember fondly the semester when he coordinated a weekly reading group centred on the Septuagint of Isaiah. His willingness to connect with us also went beyond our studies. As an outgoing extrovert – an ENFJ (Myers-Briggs) and Enneagram 7 – he always had loads of wit and wisdom to contribute to any conversation. Being an active participant in the weekly seminars, he would happily join us on our lively post-seminar discussions down at the pub (usually The Whey Pat). These are just a handful of the fond memories that we have of Tom, and are part of the reason why we wanted to celebrate him in this way.

Of course, the reasons for celebrating Tom Wright are numerous. He has contributed to both the Church and the academy, holding academic posts at Oxford, Cambridge, McGill and St Andrews, as well as serving in ecclesial offices as Dean of Lichfield Cathedral, Canon of Westminster and Bishop of Durham. His scholarly and ecclesial output has also been unrivalled, being at the front lines of fresh academic debate and providing accessible biblical scholarship 'for everyone'.[1] It is not for nothing that Wright has been awarded 15 honorary doctorates (to date). As an academic, Wright has helped set the agenda for much of New Testament scholarship since the 1990s, most notably in relation to historical Jesus methodology and the so-called 'New Perspective on Paul'. As a churchman, Wright has helped to blaze a trail for twentieth- and twenty-first-century Christianity away from quasi-Gnostic tendencies, literalistic fundamentalism, easy believism and political withdrawal. Whether writing for the academy or the Church, Wright always has a knack for doing so in an engaging manner, drawing the reader in with a poetic prose that compels both mind and heart. As a big-picture synthetic thinker, Wright is truly more of an artist than a scientist, never coming across as mechanical or stale.

Over the years Wright's contributions have stimulated a considerable amount of critical engagement. Two of Wright's volumes in the Christian Origins and the Question of God series have received their own book-length evaluations from multiple contributors,[2] each of which concludes with a review essay by Wright himself.[3] There have also been book-length 'conversations' with Wright's work, including *Jesus, Paul and the People of God*[4] and, more recently, *Exile*,[5] which similarly contain multiple contributors. Some single-author book-length evaluations have also been written. For example, John Piper wrote a full-length critique of Wright's view of justification,[6] Samuel Adams wrote a charitable though trenchant evalua-

---

[1] For someone as prolific as N. T. Wright it would be difficult to list all of his many publications here in this introduction, but these have all been catalogued on his website (ntwrightpage. com). For a regularly updated list of Wright's publications, see <http://ntwrightpage. com/2017/04/30/updated-publications-list/> (accessed 12 December 2017).
[2] See the evaluation of *Jesus and the Victory of God* (Wright 1996) in Newman 1999, and the evaluation of *Paul and the Faithfulness of God* (Wright 2013a) in Heilig, Hewitt and Bird 2017.
[3] Wright 1999, 244–77; 2017a, 711–68.
[4] Perrin and Hays 2011. The volume contains two parts, one on the historical Jesus and the other on Paul, with four essays per part. Each part also includes responses by Prof. Wright to each of the contributors as well as two closing essays on the scholarly fields of research on Jesus and Paul respectively within the life of the Church (see Wright 2011a, 115–58; 2011b, 262–81).
[5] Scott 2017. The volume is framed initially by a fresh essay by Wright (2017b, 19–80) on his view of 'continuing exile' in the Second Temple period, and ends with Wright engaging the 11 contributors to the volume who assess his essay in the light of their specializations (Wright 2017c, 305–32).
[6] Piper 2007.

tion of Wright's use of critical-realist epistemology for historical research,[7] and Tom Holland recently wrote a challenge to Wright's whole theological project.[8] A few volumes have even been written to help explain Wright's work to lay audiences. For example, Stephen Kuhrt wrote a short overview called *Tom Wright for Everyone* (2011), which looks at Wright's output prior to his post at the University of St Andrews. Since that time, Derek Vreeland has written a few explanatory guides to *Paul and the Faithfulness of God* (Wright 2013a) and *The Day the Revolution Began* (Wright 2016).[9] Both Kuhrt and Vreeland attempt to make Wright's work more accessible to laypeople and non-specialists.

Each of the aforementioned books highlights, in various ways, the sweeping impact of Wright's work, yet none can be categorized as a proper Festschrift. The present volume is offered to Tom as a token of appreciation from students, colleagues and friends who have been inspired and challenged by his stimulating scholarship and pastoral insights. The perceptive reader will of course recognize that certain essays pose various challenges to Wright's work, but all of the essays were written in a spirit of celebration. The volume is structured in three parts, according to the three categories of classic Jewish theology that Wright identifies as starting points for discerning the shape of New Testament theology: monotheism, election and eschatology. When writing about these 'basic beliefs' of Second Temple Judaism, Wright notes that the categories are ultimately inseparable. He speaks of the three topics as 'closely interrelated',[10] a 'tightly integrated whole',[11] and states further that 'Each is kept in place by the others, and each is partly defined in relation to the others.'[12] The fact that several of the essays in this volume could be placed in multiple categories provides tacit support to this affirmation.

The title we have chosen, *One God, One People, One Future*, is a shortened form of a line Wright repeats throughout his works, with some variation in wording, to describe the categories of monotheism, election and eschatology: 'one God, one people of God, one future for Israel and the world'.[13] Wright has famously argued that Paul redefined, reworked

7 Adams 2015.
8 Holland 2017.
9 Vreeland 2015; 2017.
10 Wright 2005, 84.
11 Wright 2013a, 611.
12 Wright 2013a, 611.
13 Wright 2013a, 611. Cf. 'one God, one people of God, one future for God's world' (Wright 2005, 84). This structure is so pervasive in Wright's work that it can even be seen in subtler ways. For example, in his recently reprinted popular book, *Small Faith, Great God* (Wright

and reimagined these categories in the light of the Messiah and the Spirit, so it should come as little surprise that many of the essays, though not all, focus on matters of Pauline interpretation.[14] Of course, such an emphasis represents the bulk of Wright's work throughout his career.[15] As a whole, we hope that this collection offers fitting tribute.

The volume begins with an introductory essay by Michael F. Bird that marks some of the enduring qualities that Bird sees in Wright's work which makes him worth celebrating. In his essay – 'N. T. Wright and the promise of New Testament theology' – Bird compares and contrasts the theological projects of Bultmann and Wright. He then offers his assessment of whose legacy will benefit church communities most. Considering a vast array of sources from each scholar's *oeuvre*, Bird elucidates Bultmann's and Wright's areas of individual brilliance, hermeneutics, views of Judaism, treatments of Jesus, accounts of the resurrection, and understandings of Paul. He concludes that whether it is exegesis or theology, it is Wright rather than Bultmann who holds out a more promising way of reading the New Testament, a better promise for constructing theology for the

---

2010 (1978)), there is a three-part structure to the book that maps on to the tripartite structure he advocates elsewhere. The three parts are 'Faith in a Great God', 'Faith to Live and Love' and 'Faith to Walk in the Dark' (this last one is about faith in the midst of adversity in the light of God's future for the world, including chapters on death, new creation and resurrection).

14 Cf. Part III of *Paul and the Faithfulness of God* (Wright 2013a), chs 9–11, which is dedicated to 'Paul's Theology'. Each chapter is focused on Paul's new understanding of these Jewish beliefs in the light of Christology and pneumatology (Wright 2013a, 609–1266; cf. also pp. 179–93). In *Paul: In Fresh Perspective* (Wright 2005), there are also three consecutive chapters that address these three themes (chs 5–7). This understanding of Paul's theological innovations can be seen as far back as *Climax of the Covenant* (1991), although in that book Wright was concerned to address 'the twin heads of Jewish theology' which he identifies as 'monotheism and election'. Eschatology is left aside because, as he explains elsewhere, monotheism and election are 'the main two', and he adds that 'When you put monotheism and election together, and then look at the present state of the world and of God's people, you will quickly come up with a third, namely eschatology' (Wright 2005, 83). Thus, as Wright states later, 'eschatology is the inescapable corollary of monotheism and election' (Wright 2005, 135; cf. Wright 1992, 247).

15 Wright's doctoral dissertation at Oxford was on the Christology and ecclesiology of Romans (Wright 1981). His recent two-volume magnum opus, the fourth part of the Christian Origins series, was on Paul (Wright 2013a). Each of his extended commentaries (outside the For Everyone series) has been on Paul's letters; see his commentary on Colossians and Philemon (Wright 2008 (1997)), and his commentary on Romans (Wright 2002). There are plans at the moment for extended commentaries on Galatians (in the Two Horizons series) as well as Philippians (in the International Critical Commentary series). Finally, he has written more books and articles on Paul than anything else in New Testament theology and interpretation, and many of those have been gathered and reprinted in his *Pauline Perspectives* (Wright 2013b).

4

Church, and a more promising method for how to shape the Christian life with biblical theology. As such our volume proceeds from here, exploring the categories of monotheism, election and eschatology which Wright maintains are constructive ways forward for New Testament theology.

The first major section of the volume is 'One God'. The bulk of the essays in this portion of the volume address some facet of the redefinition of monotheism in the light of Christology; however, the section begins with an essay on the problem of evil. For Wright, each of the three beliefs – monotheism, election and eschatology – 'are, at one level, all about the problem of evil',[16] but it is ultimately monotheism that makes the problem of evil so pronounced.[17] And so, fittingly, the section begins with an evaluation of Wright's theodicy by Michael Lloyd. The section is then bookended by Nicholas Perrin's Christologically focused essay on the Gospel of John, which deals with exile and restoration – the specific way in which Wright contends that the Jewish problem of evil was addressed.[18]

In his explanation and critique of 'N. T. Wright's theodicy', Michael Lloyd categorizes responses to the problem of evil within Christian theology 'according to whether they see suffering as [1] instrumental to the purposes of God, [2] inevitable within those purposes or [3] inimical to them'. He situates Wright's view in the third category and suggests that Wright's proposal (that human idolatry calls into being an anti-God, anti-creation force) is a distinctive contribution to inimical theodical positions. Lloyd then poses several questions that aim to clarify and challenge aspects of this contribution. He concludes with a provocative hypothesis which combines some of the insights of Wright's position with a traditional understanding of angels and demons as independent of humans for their existence. He argues that this has more exegetical coherence, explanatory power and internal consistency than Wright's proposal.

As stated above, the remaining essays in the 'One God' section focus on matters of Christology. James Dunn helpfully provides a framework for the following essays, exploring the weighty question of how the earliest Christology affects Christian understanding of God ('The human face of God: God and the Christology of the New Testament'). He begins by sketching an outline of the progression of the earliest Christology, elucidating several building blocks that emerge from the texts of the New Testament. Next, Dunn examines one of the building blocks, the

---

[16] Wright 2005, 88.
[17] Wright 2005, 26, 87; 2013a, 611.
[18] E.g. Wright 2005, 88.

application of 'Wisdom' and 'Word' terminology to describe Jesus, against the wider backdrop of speech about God in early Jewish sources. He suggests that this context provides a clearer lens for understanding how the earliest Christians developed their Christologies than the theories that emerged in the fourth and fifth centuries. Just as Wisdom and Word are portrayed as the self-expressions of God, so the man whom the Word became is portrayed as a self-expression of God – the human face of God.

The following two essays by Richard Bauckham and Grant Macaskill, in their own way, address the background of the Shema for 1 Corinthians. Together their essays provide further support for the argument that 1 Corinthians 8.6 is a Christological reworking of the Shema (Bauckham), and develop the implications of such a reworking for thinking about God's relationship with his people through the covenant (Macaskill). Bauckham's essay, 'The Shema and 1 Corinthians 8.6 again', revisits the question of whether Jews in the first century CE recited the Shema twice daily. Bauckham begins with a review of references to and interpretations of Deuteronomy 6.4 during the Second Temple period, concluding that the evidence provides ample reason to suppose that Paul would be familiar with Deuteronomy 6.4 and was deliberately reformulating this text in 1 Corinthians 8.6. He then considers an important piece of evidence that has yet to be discussed in the debates about twice-daily recitations of the Shema: the LXX version of Deuteronomy 6.4–9. Bauckham identifies several textual cues that suggest that the twice-daily recitation of the Shema, based on a literal interpretation of Deuteronomy 6.7 and 11.19, began as early as the third century BCE. Bauckham's essay also includes a valuable Appendix, in which he catalogues texts from the Hebrew Bible, the Septuagint, other Jewish literature from the Second Temple period and the New Testament that use the words 'one' or 'only/alone' to characterize the uniqueness of God as the only God.

Grant Macaskill, in his essay 'The way the One God works: covenant and ethics in 1 Corinthians', explores elements of Paul's moral teaching in 1 Corinthians, with a view to offering qualified support to Wright's assertion that Paul's understanding of the gospel is governed by God's covenantal relationship with Israel. Macaskill examines two texts to demonstrate that the theme of covenant is woven into the way Paul frames his ethical consideration. He begins by explaining the programmatic significance that the Shema, which Paul invokes in 1 Corinthians 8.6, has for Paul's argument throughout 1 Corinthians 8—13; then he unpacks the covenantal language of election that Paul employs in 1 Corinthians 1.27–29. With Wright, Macaskill affirms the importance of covenant in Paul's thought and the continuity between the story of Israel and the life of the Church under the gospel. He suggests, however, that this continuity is constituted principally through identification with God who is the single agent of salvation across stories, rather than a sweeping underlying narrative that unites them.

Our final two essays in the 'One God' section further develop a Christological monotheism, though in a way that provides a fitting transition into 'One people'. This is fitting because, as Wright explains, '[C]hristology is, for Paul, a means of redefining the people of God, and also a means of redefining God himself.'[19] Such overlap can be readily seen in the essays by Crispin Fletcher-Louis and Nicholas Perrin.[20]

Crispin Fletcher-Louis offers an exegetical study of 1 Kings 3—4 that complements Wright's claim that Paul uses the term *Christos* to communicate an incorporative messianism ('King Solomon, a new Adam and incorporative representative of God's people (1 Kings 3—4): a text that supports N. T. Wright on Paul and the Messiah'). He avers that the primary protagonist of 1 Kings 3—4, the wise and virtuous King Solomon, serves as God's representative, experiences a recovery of the identity Adam lost in the garden, and sums up in himself the interests and aspirations of the people of God. In doing so, Solomon brings partial completion to plans that began, but were eventually frustrated, in Genesis. Fletcher-Louis's essay offers fresh observations that support one of Wright's most controversial claims about Paul's use of messiah terminology.

To close out the 'One God' section, Nicholas Perrin's 'Reading *Climax of the Covenant* with John: return from exile, monotheism and the one people of God in the Fourth Gospel', offers an exegetical consideration of John 8.12–59 and John 10.1–21 that complements Wright's reading of Galatians 3.10–20 (developed programmatically in *Climax*). First, Perrin suggests that the seemingly inconsistent collage of images and scriptural stories in John 8.12–59 are best understood as a series of sub-arguments within a larger disagreement over the terms of exile, return and functional monotheism. Second, he posits that John 10.1–21 contains a depiction of Jesus as the Davidic restorer and revealer of a Christologically modified monotheism. Perrin's essay aims to demonstrate that John, like Wright's Paul, also develops an implicit connection between the themes of return from exile, monotheism and ecclesial unity.

Our volume now transitions to its largest portion – 'One people'.

---

[19] Wright 1991, 266.
[20] These essays can also be seen to overlap in how they address, sometimes implicitly, the way that God has dealt with the problem of evil through regal figures.

This section begins with a framing essay by Michael J. Gorman on the traditional marks of the Church: one, holy, catholic and apostolic. The remaining essays can be seen as unpacking these marks further in various ways. David G. Horrell, Scot McKnight and Grant LeMarquand reflect on topics related to race and ethnicity, unity and diversity, and identity within the early Church; Peter Oakes and Ben Witherington III address matters of education and ministry in the Church today; and Brian J. Walsh, Andrew J. Goddard, Oliver O'Donovan, Bruce W. Longenecker and Sylvia C. Keesmaat ruminate on issues pertaining to ethics and virtue.

Beginning this section, Michael J. Gorman's essay 'First Corinthians and the marks of God's *ekklēsia*: one, holy, catholic and apostolic' utilizes the four traditional marks of the Church as a framework for examining Paul's ecclesiology in 1 Corinthians. In the course of his examination, Gorman unpacks Wright's explicit emphases on 'unity' and 'holiness' in his discussions of the *ekklēsia* in *Paul and the Faithfulness of God* (Wright 2013a). He also draws attention to the ways in which Wright highlights the 'catholic' and 'apostolic' character of the *ekklēsia* without specific reference to either term. Gorman's analysis demonstrates that Paul's ecclesiology read through the lens of the marks and Wright's own understanding of the *ekklēsia* in Paul cohere in remarkable, theologically enriching ways.

Turning then to three essays on race and ethnic identity, David G. Horrell begins with his essay, 'Grace, race and the people of God', which focuses on the risks of comparing Jewish 'racial' identity and Christian trans-ethnic universalism. After analysing some of Wright's early works to introduce this topic, Horrell considers three recent strategies for avoiding such risks: (1) abandoning the language of race and changing the terminology we use to discuss the issue, (2) resituating Paul within Judaism in ways that reject the established conviction that Paul reconfigures both Jewish and Gentile identities around Christ, and (3) stressing how Paul's articulation of the early Christian movement is 'particular' within its own boundaries and patterns of inclusion and exclusion. He then identifies fruitful insights related to the third strategy, the most promising option in his view, in Wright's *Paul and the Faithfulness of God*. Horrell concludes with a brief consideration of patterns of inclusion in Jewish and early Christian groups, suggesting, provocatively, that the former may, from a modern perspective, appear more 'tolerant' and 'inclusive' than the latter.

Following from Horrell, the following two essays on race and ethnicity focus on some patterns of gentile inclusion in early Christianity centred on Christ as a regal figure over the people of God. In 'Saints re-formed:

the extension and expansion of *hagios* in Paul', Scot McKnight examines the way that Paul incorporates gentiles into the one holy family of Israel. More specifically, he elucidates the ways in which Paul freshly re-forms the description 'saints' through a grid of monotheism, election and eschatology. McKnight argues that the *q-d-sh* terminology that Paul adopts points to God's electing grace to locate Israel in his presence, and that gentiles become saints through their incorporation into the new covenant and the eschatological indwelling of the Holy Spirit. Moreover, 'saints' are defined by their life under the cosmic rule of Christ and God's transformative work to make them a people of love, justice, peace and reconciliation.

To round out this discussion on race, ethnicity and identity, Grant LeMarquand presents a reading of Matthew 21.14 that highlights the reconstitution of Israel as a multi-ethnic community united in the Messiah ('The healing of the blind and the lame in the Temple: David, "Canaanites" and the reconstitution of Israel in Matthew 21.14'). He provides thorough reviews of Matthew's use of terminology and themes related to David and kingship, then unpacks Matthew's specific, and underappreciated, focus on Canaanites as a subset of gentiles. LeMarquand posits that Jesus' healing of the blind and the lame at the Temple functions as the climactic scene in Matthew's presentation of Jesus as an 'anti-Davidic' figure, a figure who brings mercy to those previously thought to be beyond redemption, even archetypal enemies of God's people like the Canaanites. In doing so, Matthew portrays Jesus as a new king of a new people of God, newly constituted by God's mercy.

From here the essays in the 'One people' section address matters related to ministry in the Church, specifically theological education for laypeople and the role of women in leadership. In 'Tom (aka N. T.) Wright on Galatians', Peter Oakes addresses Wright's contribution to lay education. His essay pays tribute to Wright's ability to distil weighty academic discourse into accessible prose for a popular audience. In order to demonstrate Wright's skill, he offers snapshots of Wright's treatment of Galatians 1—3 in his popular For Everyone commentary series, noting the breadth of scholarly conversations and views that Wright engages and presents for devotional readers. Oakes contends that Wright's uncanny knack for connecting with these readers can be attributed to his immense skill as a writer, his sustained commitment to address concerns that non-academics in churches find valuable and his broadly inclusive ecumenical tone.

Following in the same vein of church ministry, Ben Witherington III's essay addresses the 'source' of the problem when it comes to controversies surrounding the role of women in the Church – 'The source of the problem: source arguments and the role of women in the world and in the Church'. The pun pertains to foundational issues at play as well as the text that some have, in Witherington's view, misinterpreted to arrive at wrong conclusions: Genesis 1—3. Witherington begins with an exegesis of these chapters that highlight divine intent for man and woman in creation and the effects of the fall on humanity; he then turns his attention to Jesus' and Paul's appeals to the creation accounts in Mark 10 and 1 Corinthians 11. He argues that gender difference is a part of God's original intention, but gender hierarchy is an effect of sin brought about by the fall. Such conclusions complement Wright's strong support of the role of women in ministry, as can be seen in, for example, *Surprised by Scripture* (Wright 2015).

The section on 'One people' concludes with essays on ethical issues within the Church, including homosexuality, obedience, moral instruction, poverty and justice. To start, Brian J. Walsh's essay 'Sex, Scripture and improvisation' serves as both a testimony to the creative and redemptive potential of Wright's improvisatory hermeneutic and a challenge to Wright's position on homosexuality. Drawing from Wright's conception of biblical authority as an unfinished five-act drama, Walsh revisits the parameters Wright sets for faithful improvisation to take place and argues that the experiences of the LGBTQ+ members of the Church need to be part of the equation. He then revisits the scriptural texts to which Wright appeals in his discussions of homosexuality and presents an exegetical case for affirming faithfulness, justice and covenant love – not heteronormativity – as the fundamental criteria for marriage. This is an impassioned plea from one pastor to another to reconsider his stance on this weighty and relevant topic.

Andrew J. Goddard's essay 'Paul and obedience' focuses on the underappreciated theme of obedience in Paul's writings. After noting the paucity of attention to this topic, both in Wright's work and in biblical scholarship more generally, Goddard provides thorough examinations of the passages in which Paul explicitly employs *hypakoē* terminology. He endeavours to demonstrate that obedience is a crucial component of several key aspects of Paul's thought and teaching – his missiology, Christology and ethics. Goddard delivers an appeal for the Church to recognize that God calls his people to a life of obedience within the reality he has made and restored in the Messiah.

Oliver O'Donovan then focuses directly on the pastoral injunction in 2 Timothy 1.7 ('Neither sober nor of sound mind: Timothy's spirit of *sōphronismos*'). English translations oscillate between 'soberness' and 'sound mind' as the interpretation for *sōphronismos*. After an analysis of 140 uses of *sōphronismos* in pagan and Christian texts from the end of the first century BCE to the end of the fifth century CE, O'Donovan makes two observations on the term's semantic spectrum: (1) in most occurrences the term refers to an event that makes a moral difference to one who experiences or perceives it; (2) most uses from the first two centuries speak of moral direction, warning and restraint. This evidence suggests a different interpretation of 2 Timothy 1.7: the spirit given to the Church is one 'of power, love and *moral instruction*'.

The final two essays of 'One people', by Bruce W. Longenecker and Sylvia C. Keesmaat, provide a fitting transition into the final section, 'One future', highlighting the vital roles of empathy and solidarity within the people of God as expressions of new creation that combat evil. Bruce W. Longenecker's essay – 'Paul, poverty and the powers: the eschatological body of Christ in the present evil age' – examines the relationship between poverty and Paul's conception of the cosmic powers. He begins by relating Paul's bleak anthropological discourse to 'social Darwinism', suggesting that there is a discernible link between the powers of Sin and Death on the one hand, and the competitive covetousness that characterizes humanity separated from Christ on the other. Longenecker then argues that a key Pauline instruction to the Jesus-groups he founded (groups composed of individuals from various economic levels) is that these communities bolster the most economically disadvantaged among them, as one among many 'gifted' means of building up 'the body of Christ'. Practising this 'other-concern' brings about pragmatic restorations of healthy relationships between distinct identities within Jesus-groups, and functions as a sign of God's triumph over the powers that promote chaotic self-interestedness.

Following from here, and concluding the 'One people' section, Sylvia C. Keesmaat's essay, 'Walking with the oppressed: lament and new-creational hope', addresses additional matters of justice, drawing a fundamental link between the pathos of suffering and the people of God's new-creational hope. She suggests that the Paul who emerges from Wright's academic work, while rooted in the hope of new creation, is removed from the daily injustices felt by those in the first century who longed for that new creation. Engaging in an act of historical imagination, Keesmaat introduces two fictive hearers of Romans – a gentile slave named Iris and a Judean freedperson named Nereus – and considers which parts of Paul's correspondence would have resonated most deeply with each, given their daily hardships. This exercise functions as a summons to the people of

God to name injustice, in Paul's day and our own, and mourn with those who experience its effects. By embracing suffering love, the Church can imagine new-creational hope with increased clarity and embody it with greater compassion.

The volume now turns to the final segment – 'One future'. In this portion of the volume we have essays on *how* and *when* the One God secures his One Future for Israel and the world. The first two essays, by Edith M. Humphrey and J. Andrew Cowan, explore atonement and justification respectively. These are then followed by an essay from S. A. Cummins on the eschatological 'newness of life' that results from God's provision. From here we have two essays by Carey C. Newman and J. P. Davies that address the framework of apocalyptic theology in the early Church, and the degree to which such a theology inherently disrupted continuity between promise, expectation and fulfilment. This leads nicely into the final three essays of the section. Scott J. Hafemann addresses the delay of the *parousia* in 2 Peter, and then Richard B. Hays and Stephen I. Wright address the future of the people of Israel in Romans 11, and the question of whether and how God will keep his promises to them.

Leading off, Edith M. Humphrey focuses on the atonement, which shows us how God's One Future for the world is achieved. In her essay 'Reclaiming all Paul's Rs: apostolic atonement by way of some Eastern Fathers', Humphrey focuses on how key Pauline texts were read by fourth- and fifth-century interpreters as a way to recapture a holistic view of the atonement. Humphrey argues that a full picture of the atonement needs to emerge that incorporates – with the clarity of alliteration – redemption, reparation, representation, righteousness, rescue, recapitulation, reconciliation and revolutionary recreation. This full picture is drawn from the entirety of what Christ was, is and did *pro nobis*, without being limited strictly to his death, and with some surprises for those who draw too strict a line between 'Western' and 'Eastern' interpretations of Paul. The Pauline texts upon which Humphrey focuses are Colossians 1, Galatians 3 and 2 Corinthians 5, exploring their meaning in dialogue with the interpretation found in patristic commentaries. Over against N. T. Wright's insistence that atonement needs to be *reimagined*, Humphrey argues rather that it needs to be *retrieved*. In the patristic commentators, Humphrey demonstrates, we can find such a holistic vision of the atonement.

Within that broader conception of all that Christ accomplished through the atonement is providing the means for justification. In Wright's configuration, justification is primarily a matter of ecclesiology, typically addressed as part of how Paul redefined the people of God.[21] Yet, in his essay 'N. T. Wright and justification revisited: a contrarian perspective', J. Andrew Cowan provides an appreciative though critical analysis of Wright's conclusions about the meaning of justification in Paul. He argues that many of the charges Evangelicals levy against Wright on this topic miss the mark because they fail to grasp the way Wright relates justification to covenant membership. Closely following Wright's hermeneutical cues, Cowan surveys early Jewish (including Pauline) texts to assess whether the link between covenant membership and *dikaiosynē* terminology is as pronounced as Wright maintains. Contrary to Wright, Cowan concludes that these terms never function as equivalents to 'covenant membership'; Paul does not use justification and righteousness language to declare that someone is in the covenant, but rather to describe just actions and a person's judgement before the bar of divine justice with respect to sin and right behaviour.

Following from this understanding of *dikaiosynē* to describe just actions, S. A. Cummins, in his essay 'Newness of life: gospel, Church and the common good in Romans 12—13', provides an exegetical and theological study of Romans 12—13, understood as an expansive call for the people of God to embody and enact 'newness of life' (Romans 6.4, NRSV). He begins by noting N. T. Wright's contribution to developing the theme of new creation in Paul and Romans in particular. He then contends that Romans 12.1–2 and 13.11–14, which highlight aspects of the eschatological new life, frame and sustain Paul's wide-ranging and compelling remarks throughout Romans 12—13. In these chapters Paul draws on key Old Testament themes and expectations, now realized in Jesus and the Spirit, in relation to God's gospel, the Church and the common good. In the end, Cummins elucidates the ways in which Paul advances a theological vision for the kind of life that ought to characterize the new creation.

The following two essays by Carey C. Newman and J. P. Davies address the framework of early Christian theology, which has been entrenched in false binaries. For example, is it 'covenantal' or 'apocalyptic'? Is it characterized by continuity or discontinuity? In his essay 'Narrative cross, apocalyptic resurrection: Ephesians and reading Paul', Carey C. Newman highlights the collision of narrative and apocalyptic elements in the

---

21 '*Justification, for Paul, is a subset of election*, that is, it belongs as part of his doctrine of the people of God' (Wright 2005, 121, emphasis original). Of course, for Wright, justification is not devoid of eschatological implications or dimensions. Cf., e.g., Wright 1997, 117–19.

letter to the Ephesians. Two mutually exclusive ways to read Paul now dominate. One school of thought construes Paul as a covenant theologian who is gripped by a singular narrative about Israel and Jesus. The other school of thought sees Paul as an apocalyptic theologian who focuses on God's dramatic intrusion into and disruption of the cosmos in Jesus. The former privileges continuity, while the latter emphasizes discontinuity. This article uses Ephesians as a sounding board for how Paul was first received. The essay discovers the presence of both apocalyptic and narrative in Ephesians. Both apocalyptic and narrative fund the theological, scriptural, symbolic and rhetorical world of Ephesians. But Newman's essay also retraces the ways that Ephesians consciously uses apocalyptic to interpret, reframe and restage covenant. Ephesians does so, particularly, by employing non-biblical cosmic myths about a primal, cosmic *anthrōpos*. Finally, the essay explores how Ephesians can conjoin both narrative and apocalyptic in its theological enterprise. Ephesians capitalizes on the implications inherent in the enchained symbols of cross and resurrection – one narrative, one apocalyptic – to describe God's purposes for Jesus, the Church and the world.

J. P. Davies then approaches the question of apocalyptic thought in the New Testament through the lens of apocalyptic epistemology in the Gospel of Mark ('Apocalyptic and the history of God: possibilities from Mark's epistemological *inclusio*'). Davies explores two texts, Mark 1.9–11 and Mark 15.38–39, in which Mark employs 'open heaven' motifs in connection with salvation-historical statements about the kingdom of God. He argues that Mark's juxtaposition of these themes demonstrates an apocalyptic epistemology that, in contrast to much recent interpretation, links revelation and expectation; in the second Gospel, Jesus is both the apocalypse of God and the long-expected king foretold in the story of Israel. Davies suggests that this Markan epistemology might provide a pathway towards transcending the false dichotomies that have come to characterize discussions of 'apocalyptic' and 'the history of God'.

As a conclusion to 'One future', the final three essays, by Scott J. Hafemann, Richard B. Hays and Stephen I. Wright, show how early Christian eschatology was rooted in a deep reflection upon Israel's Scriptures. Scott J. Hafemann – in his essay '"One day as a thousand years": Psalm 90, humility and the certainty of eschatological judgement in 2 Peter 3.8' – examines the significance of the maxim 'one day is as a thousand years' (Psalm 90.4) in 2 Peter 3.8. He suggests that the broader context of Psalm 90 provides the key for understanding the eschatological conclusion in 2 Peter 3.9. This context, he argues, merits reading the maxim as a truth about God's unwavering commitment to judge regardless of the time-span in view rather than as a statement about the transience of humanity or the timeless 'eternality' of God. Hence, the fact that the Messiah has not yet returned cannot be considered a 'delay', but rather an intentional act of the sovereign Lord for whom time is not a determining factor. Hafemann identifies the purpose of that intention to be the repentance of God's people, which, in the context of 2 Peter, is inextricably linked to a posture of Christian humility, characterized by the thoughtful evaluation of one's circumstances from the perspective of God's certain, impending judgement.

Richard B. Hays then offers an appreciative but critical engagement with Wright on a passage the latter has written about extensively throughout his academic career: Romans 11.25–27 ('Hope for what we do not yet see: the salvation of all Israel in Romans 11.25–27'). Hays carefully summarizes the strongest points of Wright's reading, identifies questions that require further critical exploration, and offers constructive exegetical suggestions, based primarily on his understanding of how the Psalms function in the intertextual network that underlies these verses. Of particular interest for Hays are the occurrences of the phrase *ek Siōn* in the Greek Psalter, which point to God's help coming 'from Zion' for the rescue or salvation of Israel. He argues that these occurrences, along with Isaiah 59.20, are part of the 'intertextual reservoir' from which Paul drew in his appeal to the coming of the Deliverer from Zion in Romans 11.26. As such, this verse should be understood to refer not only to the mission of the Church, as Wright maintains, but also to the eschatological *parousia* of the Lord.

Finally, to conclude the 'One future' section, we have an essay from Tom's brother. In his essay '"Beloved for the sake of their ancestors" (Romans 11.28b): God's covenant love in Romans and some Old Testament backgrounds', Stephen I. Wright explores the concept of God's covenant love for historical Israel to shed light on Paul's assertion that Israel is 'beloved for the sake of the ancestors'. After noting Luther's anti-Jewish reading of these verses and its lingering effects on Protestant scholarship, he unpacks Romans 11 to demonstrate Paul's affirmation of Israel's continuing place in God's purposes. He then examines the particularity of God's love for Israel in the Old Testament, giving special attention to Hosea. He finally concludes that Paul's description of this group as 'beloved' suggests a divine love that can endure the most profound trauma, a divine love that is particular, passionate and personally experienced, and a divine love that is meant to inspire its recipients to demonstrate that same love to other peoples.

In this manner the volume comes to an end. Throughout the volume we have chosen to transliterate all usage of Greek and Hebrew in keeping with Prof. Wright's preferred mode of academic writing. The one exception to this is found in the Appendix to Richard Bauckham's essay, which, given the volume of Greek and Hebrew terms utilized, would be ineffective unless the terms catalogued were provided in the biblical languages directly.

Finally, we wish to offer our sincere thanks to all of the contributors for their collegiality throughout the editorial process and for keeping things close to the chest during these past four years. We also want to thank those involved in the covert process of putting this volume together on the publishing side. Special thanks are due to Philip Law, Alexandra McDonald and Rima Devereaux of SPCK, Will Bergkamp of Fortress Press and to Mollie Barker for the copy-editing. With a volume like this there are a lot of moving parts, and so we are grateful for all of the help and support along the way from our publishers. We are also grateful to Adam Schalter, my (JAD) TA at Bethel Seminary, for compiling the indices. Thanks as well to Dianne White for her help at proof stage. Of course, this volume is ultimately dedicated to Tom, and we wish to extend our deep gratitude to him as someone who, through service and scholarship, has pointed us all to the One God for the building up of his One People with hope for his One Future.

John Anthony Dunne and Eric Lewellen

Bibliography

Adams, Samuel V. (2015). *The Reality of God and Historical Method: Apocalyptic Theology in Conversation with N. T. Wright.* New Explorations in Theology. Downers Grove, IL: IVP.

Heilig, Christoph, J. Thomas Hewitt and Michael F. Bird (2017) (eds). *God and the Faithfulness of Paul: A Critical Examination of the Pauline Theology of N. T. Wright.* Minneapolis, MN: Fortress.

Holland, Tom (2017). *Tom Wright and the Search for Truth: A Theological Evaluation.* London: Apiary.

Kurht, Stephen (2011). *Tom Wright for Everyone: Putting the Theology of N. T. Wright into Practice in the Local Church.* London: SPCK.

Newman, Carey C. (1999) (ed.). *Jesus and the Restoration of Israel: A Critical Assessment of N. T. Wright's Jesus and the Victory of God.* Downers Grove, IL: IVP.

Perrin, Nicholas, and Richard B. Hays (eds) (2011). *Jesus, Paul and the People of God: A Theological Dialogue with N. T. Wright.* Downers Grove, IL: IVP.

Piper, John (2007). *The Future of Justification: A Response to N. T. Wright.* Wheaton, IL: Crossway.

Scott, James M. (ed.) (2017). *Exile: A Conversation with N. T. Wright.* Downers Grove, IL: IVP.

Vreeland, Derek (2015). *Through the Eyes of N. T. Wright: A Reader's Guide to Paul and the Faithfulness of God.* Doctrina Press.

—— (2017). *N. T. Wright and the Revolutionary Cross: A Reader's Guide to The Day the Revolution Began.* Doctrina Press.

Wright, N. T. (1981). 'The Messiah and the People of God: A Study in Pauline Theology with Particular Reference to the Argument of the Epistle to the Romans.' DPhil Diss., Oxford University.

—— (1991). *The Climax of the Covenant: Christ and the Law in Pauline Theology.* Edinburgh: T&T Clark.

—— (1992). *The New Testament and the People of God.* Christian Origins and the Question of God 1. London: SPCK / Minneapolis, MN: Fortress.

—— (1996). *Jesus and the Victory of God.* Christian Origins and the Question of God 2. London: SPCK / Minneapolis, MN: Fortress.

—— (1997). *What St. Paul Really Said: Was Paul of Tarsus the Real Founder of Christianity?* Grand Rapids, MI: Eerdmans.

—— (1999). 'In Grateful Dialogue: A Response.' In *Jesus and the Restoration of Israel: A Critical Assessment of N. T. Wright's Jesus and the Victory of God*, edited by Carey C. Newman, 244–77. Downers Grove, IL: IVP.

—— (2002). 'The Letter to the Romans.' In *The New Interpreter's Bible Commentary*, Volume X, edited by Leander Keck, 393–770. Nashville, TN: Abingdon.

—— (2005). *Paul: In Fresh Perspective.* Minneapolis, MN: Fortress.

—— (2008 (1997)). *Colossians and Philemon.* Tyndale New Testament Commentaries. Downers Grove, IL: IVP.

—— (2010 (1978)). *Small Faith, Great God.* Downers Grove, IL: IVP.

—— (2011a). 'Whence and Whither Historical Jesus Studies in the Life of the Church?' In *Jesus, Paul and the People of God: A Theological Dialogue with N. T. Wright*, edited by Nicholas Perrin and Richard B. Hays, 115–58. Downers Grove, IL: IVP.

—— (2011b). 'Whence and Whither Pauline Studies in the Life of the Church?' In *Jesus, Paul and the People of God: A Theological Dialogue with N. T. Wright*, edited by Nicholas Perrin and Richard B. Hays, 262–81. Downers Grove, IL: IVP.

—— (2013a). *Paul and the Faithfulness of God.* Christian Origins and the Question of God 4. London: SPCK / Minneapolis, MN: Fortress.

—— (2013b). *Pauline Perspectives: Essays on Paul, 1978–2013.* London: SPCK / Minneapolis, MN: Fortress.

—— (2015). *Surprised by Scripture: Engaging Contemporary Issues.* San Francisco, CA: HarperOne.

—— (2016). *The Day the Revolution Began: Reconsidering the Meaning of Jesus' Crucifixion.* San Francisco, CA: HarperOne.

—— (2017a). 'The Challenge of Dialogue: A Partial and Preliminary Response.' In

God and the Faithfulness of Paul: A Critical Examination of the Pauline Theology of N. T. Wright, edited by Christoph Heilig, J. Thomas Hewitt and Michael F. Bird, 711–68. Minneapolis, MN: Fortress.

—— (2017b). 'Yet the Sun Will Rise Again: Reflections on the Exile and Restoration in Second Temple Judaism, Jesus, Paul, and the Church Today.' In *Exile: A Conversation with N. T. Wright*, edited by James M. Scott, 19–80. Downers Grove, IL: IVP.

—— (2017c). 'Responding to Exile.' In *Exile: A Conversation with N. T. Wright*, edited by James M. Scott, 305–32. Downers Grove, IL: IVP.

N. T. Wright and the promise of New Testament theology

MICHAEL F. BIRD

Introduction

Many years ago Norman Perrin wrote a booklet called *The Promise of Bultmann* which outlined the theological vision of the famous German New Testament theologian Rudolf Bultmann (1884–1976)[1] and what promise it held for the contemporary mainline churches of the 1960s and 1970s.[2] Perrin had by this time moved on from appropriating the insights of his earlier teachers T. W. Manson and Joachim Jeremias, was yet to become enamoured of Paul Ricoeur and was at the height of his theological man-crush on Bultmann.[3] So much so that in the Foreword to the 1978 printing his wife Nancy Perrin said that he 'considered Bultmann to be the greatest New Testament scholar of the twentieth century, and perhaps the greatest of any century'.[4] The genius of Bultmann, according to Perrin, is that Bultmann found a way to marry together the Christian theological tradition and the radical secularity of the modern world.[5] For Perrin, what Bultmann did was accept the challenge of the modern view of the world, including its view of history and natural processes, and reinterpret biblical categories in order to make faith possible in the age of electricity.[6] Or, to offer another accolade, in the words of John Barclay: 'I am not sure there is anyone alive who can match him [Bultmann] in offering a reading of the NT that is at once historically responsible,

---

1   On Bultmann's life, see Hammann 2009.
2   Norman Perrin 1969.
3   See esp. Norman Perrin 1974a; 1974b; 1976. See on Norman Perrin's development, Mercer 1986.
4   Norman Perrin 1969, 4. Similarly, Sandmel (1966, 211) said: 'It is my opinion that Rudolf Bultmann is not only the great New Testament scholar of our day, but also one of the truly great of all time.'
5   Norman Perrin 1969, 83.
6   Norman Perrin 1969, 84–90.

textually comprehensive, hermeneutically sophisticated, theologically relevant, and of contemporary kerygmatic significance.'[7]

Today, unlike the 1950s and 1960s, one might say that there are no towering giants who dominate the theological scene in the way that Karl Barth and Rudolf Bultmann did in their heyday. One might opine the absence of such scholarly heroes in our own time or else lament, with Bertolt Brecht's Galileo, 'Unhappy a land that needs a hero.' Suffice to say, it is almost impossible today for anyone to rise up and become a scholarly giant. Contemporary biblical scholarship is characterized by a mass fragmentation into dozens of niche clubs of critical enquiry which together produce a gargantuan volume of secondary literature. The mass of literature creates a cacophony of conversations with the result that most articles and monographs do little more than add to the deafening white noise of academia. In such a setting it is almost impossible for any single voice to be heard, let alone to dominate, but one man has certainly come close.

If there is one scholarly figure who has arguably risen above his peers in his stature and accomplishments – on account of his sheer industry, recognizable contributions, academic and popular reach – it is surely the Rt Revd Prof. N. T. Wright. His 15 honorary doctorates (and still counting!) are testimony to his brilliance, acumen, and popularity in the academy and Church and among the general public. Like him or loathe him, he is a scholarly figure who can hardly be rivalled for influence. Indeed, I would go so far as to say that Wright is to this generation of Evangelical-Orthodox-Catholic-esque believers what Rudolf Bultmann was to the more liberal churches of the mainline: an inspiration to take Scripture seriously, to wrestle with its challenges and to come away with a sense of theological renewal in one's faith.

All things considered, Wright and Bultmann are natural dialogue partners. Although their methods and contexts as biblical scholars are obviously very divergent, Bultmann and Wright are both trying to solve problems in Christian origins and address the question of God. Indeed, not since Bultmann has anyone attempted the 'full hermeneutical, historical, literary, and theological task' as Wright has undertaken it.[8] Also, both men are driven by their ambition to retrieve and reinterpret the kerygma of the early Church. Bultmann pursued the kerygma for its existential mileage whereas Wright pursues the kerygmatic worldview for the ecclesial vocations it generates.

---

[7] Barclay 2015, 209.
[8] Newman 1999, 9.

In the light of that, my objective is quite simple: I wish to engage in a modest contrast between the theological projects of Bultmann and Wright.[9] Further, I hope to demonstrate that Wright has a much more promising vision for New Testament theology in the life of the Church than the old Marburger. The way I intend to do that is by outlining the respective contributions of both Bultmann and Wright and then offering my own assessment as to whose legacy will benefit the church community the most. More precisely, I will note their particular areas of individual brilliance before looking more closely, albeit briefly, at their hermeneutics, view of Judaism, treatment of Jesus, account of the resurrection and understanding of Paul, and then offer an evaluation of both figures.

Rudolf Bultmann: demythologizing the New Testament

The brilliance of Bultmann

Bultmann is easy to admire as a Christian theologian. Despite his infamy for everything from form criticism to demythologizing, even those out of a conservative and Evangelical stable like F. F. Bruce insisted that Bultmann's name 'ought never to be mentioned without profound respect',[10] and George Beasley-Murray said:

> However absurd it may sound, in his desire to make men see their only hope of redemption in the Cross, Bultmann shares the evangelistic aim of a Billy Graham, even though the methods of the two men have no contact.[11]

It was a unique blend of piety and scholarship that made Bultmann what he was.[12] We should draw attention to four particular areas that exemplify his brilliance.

First, Bultmann was a master at source criticism with a particular gift for identifying the tell-tale signs of sources that had been stitched together. Bultmann's thesis about a signs source underlying John's Gospel, though not original to him, has largely been retained in scholarship.[13] In some cases, however, this penchant to discover disparate seams of materials that were fused together or secondary additions to a text verges on the

---

9 I am not the first to make this comparison. Daniel Boyarin praises Wright in a blurb for *Paul and the Faithfulness of God* as the 'Bultmann for our age' on the very first page of the first volume! See also Schliesser 2016, 23–31.
10 Bruce 1988, 332.
11 G. Beasley-Murray 1955, 601, cited in P. Beasley-Murray 2002, 144.
12 See also Ladd 1964.
13 Bultmann 1971, 6–7 (by Walter Schmithals but indebted to Bultmann) and see discussion in Porter 2015, 64–7.

ridiculous. For instance, his rearrangement of materials in John into their 'original order', like claiming that the light discourse originally ran in the sequence John 9.1–41; 8.12; 12.44–50; 8.21–29; 12.34–36 and 10.19–21, with John 8.41–47, 51–53, 56–59 as a fragment which concludes a hereto lost section, is simply fanciful and should make every narrative critic cringe with horror.[14] Similarly, Bultmann is notorious in *History of the Synoptic Tradition* for making bold and bald declarations about materials being obviously 'secondary' with no argumentation other than the force of his own pronouncement. Even so, Bultmann had a detective-like mind for identifying a text that did not quite gel with its context and would propose creative ways of explaining its disparity.

Second, Bultmann had almost unrivalled skill among his peers as a philologist. His entries in the *Theologische Wörterbuch des Neuen Testament* are among the best of the volumes. One thinks particularly of his lengthy article on *pisteuō* and cognates as evidence of his ability to confidently handle Hebrew and Greek sources and to offer insights into the theological employment of such words in the New Testament.[15] Of course, Bultmann also wanted to see authors like Paul and John using these key theological terms in dialogue with and in distinction to Gnosticism, a comparison which has proved to be the mother of all *religionsgeschichtlich* fallacies.[16] Despite that misstep, these were learned studies, trying to link Greek words with key theological ideas.

Third, Bultmann was a genius at capturing the theological texture of Paul and John. Bultmann admired Paul and John not as tradents of a tradition, but as genuine theological interpreters. That is what Bultmann himself aspired to be: an interpreter; not trying to think the thoughts of Paul and John after them, not organizing their ideas into a new system, but restating afresh what they had to say. It is in engaging these two apostolic figures that Bultmann was in his element. For example, Bultmann's brief exposition of 'grace as event' in Pauline thought wonderfully accents that God's grace is not a divine quality or attitude, namely graciousness, but God's eschatological deed towards humanity in Jesus Christ, something bestowed entirely as a gift.[17] Even when Bultmann rides his hobby horse of the Gnostic Redeemer Myth as the source of Johannine incarnational

---

14 Bultmann 1971, 312–15.
15 Bultmann 1968, 174–82, 197–228.
16 A good example of this is Bultmann's articles (1925; 1986), where he gives a superb survey of *logos* in Jewish and Greek sources, but ultimately opts to map its meaning for John against the backdrop of Manichean and Mandean literature of the fifth century.
17 Bultmann 1952–5, 1:288–92.

Christology, he still waxes eloquently and with genuine insight about the connection between the earthly Jesus and the exalted Jesus in John's testimony. He wrote:

> Faith in Jesus, then, is faith in the exalted Jesus, but not as if he were a heavenly being who had stripped off the garments of earthly-human existence as the Gnostic Redeemer was conceived to do. Rather, the exalted Jesus is at the same time the earthly man Jesus; the 'glorified one' is still always he who 'became flesh.'[18]

Bultmann was a figure who breathed the theological world of the New Testament.

Fourth, I tend to think that Bultmann's primary talent was not history, or even theology; rather it was apologetics. Bultmann's collected essays in *Existence and Faith* and *Faith and Understanding* arguably gave the greatest apology for modernist Christianity since Friedrich Schleiermacher's *On Religion*.[19] Bultmann found in Martin Heidegger's existentialism a philosophical framework that made faith both possible and attractive to moderns. He translated Lutheranism into a glossy Christianized existentialism by contending that faith, aroused by the encounter with God through the kerygma, enabled one to attain 'authenticity' (*Eigentlichkeit*): the saving knowledge of God which is true in every age. Bultmann's modernist Christianity had no pretensions to historic orthodoxy; his liberal pedigree had eroded that prospect and there was no going back. But he constructed a revisionist theology that made Christian faith palatable and relevant to modern audiences in a way that few of his peers could.

Engaging Bultmann

Hermeneutics

Bultmann's overall hermeneutical strategy was shaped by a neo-Kantian disjunction between 'fact' and 'value' as viewed through a Kierkegaardian lens which prized self-involvement with a subject as the proper path to attaining authenticity. Consequently, for Bultmann, tying faith to historical events serves to objectify God, to domesticate him in historical human consciousness. The problem is that historical enquiry is limited. It will never tell you that Jesus is the Logos or that God was in Christ reconciling the world to himself. Pursuing a faith rooted in history is pursuing Christ according to the flesh, the temptation of inauthenticity, and the theological

---

18 Bultmann 1952–5, 2:49.
19 Bultmann 1961a; 1969.

equivalent of justification by works. In Bultmann's mind, God's revelation is not found in historical artefacts; rather, God's word is the event where one encounters God, where one knows him by faith, and this encounter results in a renewed understanding of the self, God and the world.[20] Thus, the believer looks upon the world as a closed system of cause and effect, but can confess that 'nevertheless' God remains immanent within the world since his word confronts him or her with the news of divine grace.

This background helps us understand what Bultmann called *Entmythologizierung* ('demythologizing'). This is Bultmann's infamous and notoriously misunderstood strategy for approaching the New Testament.[21] According to Bultmann, one must extricate the New Testament message from the mythical worldview that it is encased in. That is because myth is inadequate on account of its attempt to objectify God and domesticate the divine into cultural forms which create constricting thought-forms. In addition, one simply cannot make use of electric lights, radios and modern medicine and believe any more in Christ's descent to Hades and his Ascension to heaven. He states: 'Mythical eschatology is finished basically by the simple fact that Christ's Parousia did not take place immediately as the New Testament expected it to, but that world history continues and – as every competent judge is convinced – will continue.'[22] For Bultmann, myth is not the content of the kerygma, merely the device that carries it to us. Myth is not wrong but limited, and needs to be interpreted. If we are to avoid a wholescale rejection of biblical imagery/eschatology or reducing it to a social gospel, then the only option is to demythologize the New Testament, to translate its cosmological images into an anthropological message, and to situate that message in existentialist terms.

Demythologization is warranted, first, when one remembers that myth presumes a disconnect between its imagery and the underlying reality to which it points; so mythic materials invite demythologization in order to testify to a transcendent power which is not visible. Second, the New Testament similarly points to demythologizing since many of its authors prefer existential interpretations (e.g. Christ's death as a sacrifice) over and against mythic alternatives (e.g. Christ's death as a cosmic occurrence). Furthermore, for Bultmann, to know Christ is not to know his mythology, or even his history, but his benefits given to us in the gospel, how it transforms our existence. Bultmann is noticeably aware that demythologizing

---

[20] Bultmann 1952–5, 2:239.
[21] See esp. Bultmann 1984, 1–43, 95–130, 155–63; 1958a. See also Congdon 2015a, 101–11; 2015b.
[22] Bultmann 1984, 5; 1958a, 17.

can end up excoriating both myth and kerygma, or reducing Christianity to religious idealism, or even ethics. He wishes to avoid that by an existentialist interpretation of the encounter with God attained through the demythologized kerygma. Bultmann sees Paul and John as the first great demythologizers by the way they discarded Gnostic and apocalyptic myths through laying out the message that salvation has already dawned in Jesus through faith. The Pauline and Johannine theological achievement is the pronouncement that God's liberating act may be experienced in the plane of human existence where obedience, faith, love and authentic life finally become possible.

Responses to Bultmann's demythologizing proposal have been voluminous and often incendiary.[23] While many flirted with his hermeneutical strategy, it did not last much beyond the 1970s as a serious way of interpreting the New Testament. Even the sympathetic Norman Perrin could call demythologizing a 'crude hermeneutical method'.[24] Bultmann appears to have defined myth simply as a complex analogy, yet the problem is that all religious language is to some extent analogical. Consequently, even myth cannot be fully demythologized any more than ideas can be frayed of words. Elsewhere Bultmann excoriates myth as a primitive and pre-scientific account of reality, like a three-storeyed universe comprising heaven, earth and hell. But he fails to differentiate between myth as *Weltbild* (pictures of the physical universe) and myth as *Weltanschauung* (a worldview or frame of reference for understanding reality).[25] Myths in Greco-Roman, Jewish and Christian accounts include a mixture of both *Weltbild* for the world as the ancients perceived it, and also *Weltanschauung* understood as a theologically laden symbology and narrative about metaphysics, history, the future, politics, social identity and ethics. While Bultmann was quite right to reject a primitive *Weltbild*, he was naive in the least to think that the *Weltanschauung* of myth could be salvaged only by an autopsy and removal of its existential organs. According to Anthony Thiselton:

---

23 Theissen (2012, 146) provides a crucial insight into Bultmann's programme: 'He [Bultmann] developed his modernizing program for Christianity as an alternative to the program of the German Christians. His message was: we need not overcome Judaism, but mythology. He argued that modernized Christianity must not require dejudaization, but demythologization. The mythical elements in the Christian faith must not be eliminated, but must be interpreted because they contain an existential truth about the human situation in the world.'
24 Norman Perrin 1975, 14, cited in Hasel 1978, 95.
25 See on this distinction Pennington 2008, 33. Even Congdon (2015b, 594–6) acknowledges that Bultmann did not always make distinctions about the nature of myth clear. See esp. Bultmann 1960.

The NT is not like a code, when once decoded we discard the original, but more like a masterpiece, to which we constantly return. Admittedly he [Bultmann] claims *not to abolish myth*, but to *interpret* it. However, most of his critics agree that the price of this is too high to pay.[26]

One should stress as well that Bultmann's demythologization programme was a conscious attempt to reject worldviews other than the Westernized European Protestant modernist one, to de-storify the New Testament and in a sense even to de-Judaize the New Testament.[27] This is wrong because by demythologizing the New Testament one colonizes the ancient world with the epistemological hegemony of the present. In this programme one ends up screening out the stories which express the underlying worldview of a biblical text, the Jewish worldview which provides the matrix of meaning in which a text should be understood and appropriated. Demythologizing also conveniently whittles away the most Jewish elements of the New Testament, namely, the story of God's choice of Israel and God's promises to make it a light to the nations.[28] Bultmann's non-narratival account of the gospel reduces it to a mere existential challenge to hear God in the here and now, or worse, it remythologizes myth into a Gnostic narrative of human self-discovery.[29]

David Congdon has courageously attempted to defend Bultmann's demythologizing programme as an example of intercultural theology or a radical recontextualization where the gospel is unmoored from the cultural contingencies of local cosmologies, narratives, artefacts and creeds. The result is that the gospel is culturally liberated and the mission of the Church is invigorated by deconstantinizing the Christian message (i.e. resisting any *Volkstheologie* where theology is tied to ethno-nationalism).[30] Joshua Jipp applauds Congdon's advocacy of Bultmann's demythologizing as a way to uphold the freedom of the gospel and to translate the gospel into new cultures. However, Jipp rightly worries that Bultmann still engaged in a departure from 'the framework of Israel's Scriptures and ensuing apostolic history' since

26 Thiselton 2015, 171.
27 Wright 2013, 456–9.
28 In defence of Bultmann against Wright's (1996, 79; 2013, 443 n. 322, 458, 779, 1109, 1290) accusation that Bultmann was a Marcionite and was de-Judaizing Jesus and Paul, see Schliesser 2016, 30–1 and Theissen 2012, 146–7. I take the point that Bultmann did not deny that Jesus was Jewish nor was his Paul Marcionite (see esp. 1952–5, 1:188, 262). However, for Bultmann, Judaism is simply a cognitive presupposition to Jesus' message and does not shape his identity, and Paul is mostly definitely not for Bultmann a Jewish thinker.
29 Wright 2013, 457–8.
30 Congdon 2015b, esp. 503–686.

confession of Jesus as Israel's Messiah, crucified, buried, risen, and enthroned at God's right hand entails a commitment to a particular and normative tradition or worldview and this confession has indeed taken a *missionary* form in numerous diverse cultures, traditions, and places.[31]

I concur. If Bultmann's demythologization makes one 'free from all ecclesiastical and metaphysical constraints' then his theological project is merely a licence for theological anarchy.[32]

Judaism

It is quite unfortunate that Bultmann operated with a view of ancient Judaism jaundiced by the law–gospel antithesis of European Protestantism, misconstrued by the crude sociological analysis of Max Weber, and derivative of the distortions of Wilhelm Bousset, Emil Schürer and Paul Billerbeck.[33] It comes as no surprise, then, that in *Primitive Christianity* his chapter on Judaism has the first subheading 'Jewish legalism' as a summary of what Judaism was about. Bultmann then proceeds to narrate how the Old Testament faith degenerated into the sterile and puritanical religion of Judaism. The God of Israel's history morphed into the transcendent metaphysical and mythical power of the apocalypses. The Old Testament ceased to be a historical record of God's dealings with Israel and was reduced to divine precepts to be meticulously obeyed. Jewish education was nothing more than rote memorization, not proper intellectual enquiry after the truth. Judaism was a pathetic missionary religion demanding converts by way of ritual. The Jews failed to differentiate morality and purity and reduced the law to ritual. The Pharisees were particularly notorious in this regard as a zealous 'monastic order' committed to imposing their views of ritual on the laity. There was no possibility of advancing the Jewish religion, only adding to the proliferation of legal interpretations. These many legal interpretations, codified in the Mishnah, went into detail 'to the point of absurdity'. The Babylonian and Jerusalem Talmuds were 'defective' commentaries on the stale collection of legal sayings and anecdotes. The only motive for ethics was obedience, and this legalistic obedience was motivated by a desire for merit and to avoid divine retribution. Even then, there was no concept of assurance, since there was no standard of obedience that held out the prospect of certainty in salvation.[34]

---

[31] Jipp 2016, 452.
[32] Congdon 2015b, 568.
[33] Sanders 1977, 43–7.
[34] Bultmann 1956, 59–71; 1958b, 21–3.

Very clearly, for Bultmann, Judaism is simply the darkness against which the light of Christianity shines. For example, Bultmann contended that 'faith' in Judaism departs from the Old Testament motif of faith as believing in the faithfulness of God and faith as trust in God's future actions. The Old Testament perspective became displaced in Jewish thought by the notion of faith as obedience to the law. The result was that in Judaism faith became mixed with works to the extent that it even rendered faith as a meritorious act.[35] According to Bultmann, Paul's conception of faith was the acceptance of Christ's lordship, whereas in Judaism it is related to religious self-assurance. What Paul advocated was the antithesis to Jewish striving for righteousness.[36]

Bultmann's tendency, says Samuel Sandmel, was 'to create his own categories and to superimpose these on Judaism, or else to make Judaism fit into them'.[37] Whatever strengths and merits we attribute to Bultmann, he is not a fair commentator on Judaism, and his statements are now something of an embarrassment to contemporary scholars.[38]

Jesus

It is to Bultmann's credit that, despite his defective account of Judaism, he declared:

> The proclamation of Jesus must be considered within the framework of Judaism. Jesus was not a 'Christian,' but a Jew, and his preaching is couched in the thought forms and imagery of Judaism, even where it is critical of traditional Jewish piety.[39]

However, Bultmann immediately returns to his usual stereotypes that pit his Lutheran-existentialist Jesus against the dark vestiges of Jewish legalism. Bultmann's Jesus engaged in 'tremendous protest against contemporary Jewish legalism' and 'Jesus brought this ethical monotheism [of the Old Testament] into full light again by liberating it from legalism just as the prophets had liberated it from cultic piety'.[40]

Bultmann cut a precise path through much of twentieth-century Jesus scholarship. He acknowledged Jesus as teacher of the love commandment, but not in the liberal sense of Adolf von Harnack, as neither a

---

[35] Bultmann 1968, 201.
[36] Bultmann 1968, 219–20.
[37] Sandmel 1966, 219.
[38] See Bird 2016, 1–47.
[39] Bultmann 1956, 71–2.
[40] Bultmann 1956, 72; 1963, 10; 1952–5, 1:11–12.

'blueprint for society nor [as] a programme for Utopia'. Bultmann granted to Johannes Weiss that Jesus preached the imminence of the kingdom, but refused to go along with Albert Schweitzer in making Jesus a deluded apocalyptic seer since Jesus' account of God's will was insulated from his (erroneous!) view of God's kingdom.[41] Jesus affirmed the Old Testament view of God as creator, yet against his contemporaries, he did not put God in a 'remote' and 'false transcendence', but saw him as one who was near, to hear prayers, as much as to make demands.[42] On Jesus' self-understanding, Bultmann thought it imperative that Jesus did not think himself to be the Messiah or the heavenly Son of Man, as it would have tethered Jesus' self-understanding to a certain mythology.[43]

The place of the historical Jesus in Bultmann's theology has been controversial. What we have to appreciate is that for Bultmann the central node is not the 'what' of Jesus' person, but the 'that' – the fact that Jesus really was the crucified messenger of God, whom God had acknowledged as Messiah by his resurrection. So the historical Jesus is not part of faith, because Jesus confronts people in the kerygma, and nowhere else, certainly not in the contingencies of history. It would be illegitimate and inappropriate then to go behind the kerygma to try to uncover any consciousness, inner life or heroism on the part of Jesus – these are inaccessible and irrelevant. That would be merely 'Christ according to the flesh' (2 Corinthians 5.16), not the exalted Christ who is the subject of God's action, and the object of devotion. That is why it is not the historical Jesus, but Jesus the Christ, who is proclaimed as Lord.[44] Consequently, Jesus is the presupposition to New Testament theology, not part of its actual content. Christian faith begins with the kerygma, the proclamation that the crucified and risen one is the eschatological agent of salvation, a proclamation that began with the primitive Church, and not with the historical Jesus.[45]

We should not get the impression that Bultmann was utterly disinterested in the historical Jesus *in toto*. Although Bultmann was definitely in the 'No Quest for the Historical Jesus' camp,[46] he still made the crucifixion of Jesus the vital link between history and kerygma, and he still wrote one whole book about Jesus.[47] For Bultmann, Jesus the man was inaccessible,

---

[41] Bultmann 1956, 75–6.
[42] Bultmann 1956, 77–9; 1952–5, 1:11–26.
[43] Bultmann 1958a, 16; 1958b, 15; 1952–5, 1:26–32.
[44] Bultmann 1969, 238, 241.
[45] Bultmann 1952–5, 1:3.
[46] See Wright 1996, 21–5.
[47] Bultmann 1958b.

but fragments of his message could be uncovered. Accordingly, he sought to sort out the meagre deposit of Jesus' authentic teachings in the Gospels and was very much concerned with the implications of Jesus' eschatology and his idea of God. Bultmann conceded that the kerygma often mentioned Jesus' message and career in passing; thus the historical Jesus cannot be completely delineated from a theology of the New Testament.[48]

What is more, and to his credit, Bultmann was genuinely interested in the continuity between the historical Jesus and the early Church.[49] To that end, Bultmann discouraged the view that one should abandon the Pauline myth for the simple gospel, timeless truths and universal religion of love taught by the historical Jesus. That is because Jesus' proclamation of the kingdom still contained elements of mythology. What is more, Jesus and Paul had an affinity on eschatology where God addressed the world and made demands, Jesus' concern for outcasts mirrored Paul's doctrine of justification by faith, they both shared the ethical imperative in the love command, and both affirmed the divine given-ness of the law. On top of that, it is not strictly true that Jesus proclaimed the kingdom and the Church then proclaimed Jesus, since Jesus had an elevated estimation of himself as God's ultimate agent and Paul too had a high view of Jesus. According to Bultmann, Jesus believed that divine grace was encountered precisely in his word about God, he demanded faith in his word, and Jesus understood his coming as God's grace in its final hour. Jesus' call to decision implied a Christology about his ultimate role in God's purposes. Paul's view that Jesus is the forgiving word of God could be considered an extension of Jesus' own view of himself.[50] When it comes to Bultmann's account of Jesus, Wright's verdict is correct: 'Bultmann trod the fine line between having no interest in the historical Jesus and wanting to keep him on his own side just in case.'[51]

In the end, for Bultmann, Jesus Christ is important, but not as a historical person; rather his worth is as the crucified one who is proclaimed as risen, in whom God offers redemption. Jesus is not a teacher, an exemplar or a hero; instead, Jesus is God's Word, a gracious word to humanity. As Bultmann wrote:

> The message of the forgiving grace of God in Jesus Christ is not a historical account about a past event, but rather it is *the Word which the Church*

---

[48] Bultmann 1952–5, 1:3.
[49] Bultmann 1952–5, 1:33–53.
[50] Bultmann 1961b, 183–201; 1969, 220–46; 1952–5, 1:7, 9.
[51] Wright 1996, 22.

proclaims, which now addresses each person immediately as God's Word and in which Jesus Christ is present as the 'Word.'[52]

A number of criticisms can be made against Bultmann's approach to the historical Jesus and his place in the early Church.

First, the form-critical method that Bultmann deployed in *History of the Synoptic Tradition*, and which became the basis of all that he said about Jesus, is fraught with problems. It assumed that the Gospels are more about the Church's faith in Jesus than about Jesus – to the point where Bultmann famously claimed:

> I do indeed think that we can know almost nothing concerning the life and personality of Jesus, since the early Christian sources show no interest in either, are moreover fragmentary and often legendary; and other sources about Jesus did not exist.[53]

Form critics wrongfully correlated the 'forms' or sub-genres of Gospel material with a life-setting in the Church. They viewed the oral tradition as akin to folklore legends, transmitted loosely, endemically adulterated, with no role assigned to eyewitnesses or teachers in conserving the Jesus tradition. They made an artificial distinction between Palestinian and Hellenistic settings where the Jesus tradition was transmitted and manu-factured.[54] Plus, form critics believed that certain criteria of authenticity could be used to separate authentic from inauthentic materials about Jesus. In this last task, they were far too confident of their ability. Attempting to sort out the authentic traditions from the inauthentic traditions is not really so easy, simply for the fact that the history of Jesus has been thor-oughly welded together with the early Church's proclamation of Jesus at every point. Trying to separate the history from theology in the Gospels is like trying to separate red from blue in the colour purple.[55]

Second, one of Bultmann's own students, Ernst Käsemann, saw the dangers of mythicism and docetism if Jesus was not grounded in history.[56] Käsemann's contention was that Easter did not totally eradicate the con-tinuity between Jesus and the primitive Church. The primitive Church never lost its interest in the life history of Jesus as being properly basic for faith.[57] Käsemann argued that the eschatological *kerygma* presup-

---

52 Bultmann 1963, 30 (8–35) (italics original).
53 Bultmann 1958b, 14.
54 See Bird 2014a, 113–24; Dunn 2003, 73–8; Keith 2012, 25–48; Nicholas Perrin 2013, 288–94.
55 Bird 2014b, 50.
56 See Wright 1996, 23–4.
57 Käsemann 1964, 15–47.

posed the historical *karios* in which Jesus was revealed. So although, for the Evangelists, eschatology had for the most part effectively swallowed up history, nevertheless, the particularity of the eschatological event remained bound to *this* man from Nazareth. Furthermore, revelation is of such a nature that it invades history, but does not forsake it. Consequently the history of Jesus remained 'constitutive for faith, because the earthly and the exalted Lord are identical'.[58] Whereas Bultmann was ambivalent about connecting the historical Jesus with the early Church, Käsemann was adamant that a connection had to exist if one were to avoid docetism.[59]

Resurrection

Bultmann is alleged to have said that 'If the bones of the dead Jesus were discovered in some Palestinian tomb tomorrow, all the essentials of Christianity would remain unchanged.'[60] That is because for Bultmann the resurrection is not *Historie* (a mere happenstance), but *Geschichte* (an epochal event). The resurrection is, in particular, an eschatological-epochal event, inaccessible to history, and unaffected by history. So it does not matter that there was no empty tomb, and irrespective of what Easter experiences the disciples had, God has declared Jesus as risen in the word of preaching. So, according to Bultmann, the resurrection myth proves that the cross is efficacious, for 'faith in the resurrection is really the same thing as faith in the saving efficacy of the cross'.[61] Consequently: 'Christ meets us in the preaching as one crucified and risen. He meets us in the word of preaching and nowhere else. The faith of Easter is just this – faith in the word of preaching.'[62] The Easter truth is that 'Jesus has risen into the kerygma.'[63]

For Bultmann, the Easter narratives might as well have been replaced with a line like 'God's cause rocks on' (let the reader understand which heavily copyrighted musical by Stephen Schwartz I'm echoing).[64] Resurrection is simply about the continuing presence of Jesus in the gospel, not a statement about a post-mortem return to life – that is just mythology. Crossan

---

[58] Käsemann 1964, 35–6.

[59] Of course, as to whether historical criticism really can inoculate against docetism, see Adam 1996.

[60] This statement is widely attributed to Bultmann, who did deny the empty tomb (see 1994 (1921), 287, 290), but I have not been able to verify its precise source. It most likely derives from an interview with a UK magazine in the 1960s. See Kreeft and Tarecelli 1994, 176.

[61] Bultmann 1984, 39.

[62] Bultmann 1984, 41.

[63] Bultmann 1967, 469.

[64] A similar criticism is made by Wright 2003, 735.

prosecutes the Bultmannian agenda with a wonderful description when he writes: 'Emmaus never happened. Emmaus always happens.' By which he means that the narrative of Luke 24 is essentially a 'metaphoric condensation of the first years of Christian thought and practice into one parabolic afternoon'.[65] Crossan is of course echoing what the Roman historian Sallust wrote about myth: 'These things never happened, but always are.'[66] Resurrection is translated from crass myth to charming metaphor.

There are insurmountable problems with Bultmann's view of the resurrection. First, Bultmann's position has nothing to do with what the early Church meant when it spoke of Jesus' 'resurrection'. The physicality of the resurrection was stressed clearly by Luke and John.[67] In fact, the tendency of the tradition was to emphasize the resurrection of the 'flesh'.[68] Bultmann is thus forced to criticize Paul for citing witnesses to Jesus' resurrection, as if it were an actual event, which is odd since for the early Church that is precisely what the resurrection was thought to be.[69]

Second, the eschatology *or* history dichotomy is needless and obfuscating. The problem with Bultmann's approach is that, as Wright ably points out, eschatological significance does not mean that an event is historically inaccessible. The destruction of Jerusalem in 70 CE was eschatological, indeed *geschichtlich* in its full sense, for Jewish and Christian groups. Yet the apocalyptic visions in *4 Ezra* and the forecasting of portents and signs in Mark 13 do not prohibit us from investigating its historical circumstances even though it is depicted as an eschatological event.[70]

Third, there is a rabid reductionism going on in Bultmann's theologizing of resurrection. History collapses into eschatology, eschatology into Christology, and Christology is manifested in the Church's proclamation. Resurrection is really about something else, not the eschatological return to life that Jews and Christians believed God had promised.

Fourth, one wonders if Bultmann's demythologization of the resurrection is simply an instance of cognitive dissonance. If God does not conquer death as he claimed in the bodily resurrection of Jesus (see 1 Corinthians 15.55–56; Revelation 5.5), then what ground is there for believing that God conquers death at all? Bultmann's metaphorizing of the resurrection

65 Crossan 1991, xiii.
66 Sallust, *On the Gods and the World*, 4.
67 Luke 24.37–43; John 20.25–27.
68 See, e.g., Ignatius, *Smyrn.* 3.1; Justin, *Dial.* 80.5; Tertullian, *De resurrectione* 56.1; *Praescriptione* 36; *De virginibus velandis* 1.3.
69 Bultmann 1952–5, 1:299, 305; Wright 2003, 317, 639–40.
70 Wright 2003, 26–7.

is a theological consolation prize to compensate for the disappointment that God does not really raise the dead.

Paul

Bultmann never dedicated a volume to the study of Paul. However, he wrote an influential dictionary article on Paul for *Die Religion in Geschichte und Gegenwart* during, of all things, a stay at a health spa.[71] It was in his *Theology of the New Testament* in the immediate aftermath of the Second World War that Bultmann returned to Paul and engaged in his famous anthropological reading of the apostle. Bultmann focused on Paul as a Hellenistic Christ-believing Jew who saw his self-understanding, striving after righteousness in works of the law, condemned in the cross by God's judgement. While Bultmann majored on anthropology, he regarded theology, Christology and anthropology as intimately inter-twined together.[72] Despite an atomistic study of major words as windows into Paul's anthropology, Bultmann excelled in theological exposition, particularly in his account of justification as a forensic-eschatological event, grace as God's eschatological deed, the unity of Christ's death and resurrection, and the meaning of faith. Bultmann's depiction of Paul is frustrating because it certainly does not produce a believable first-century Jewish figure, but it is brilliant as a theological exploration of how a figure like Paul could speak to an age that seeks a word from God about its own troubled existence.[73]

Benjamin Schliesser wonders if a rapprochement between Bultmann and Wright is possible at some level in the study of Paul. Wright's pursuit of 'Paul's world' and 'Paul's mindset' is analogous to Bultmann's account of 'Paul in his world' and 'man under faith'. Similarly, Wright's claim that there is 'an epistemological revolution at the heart of Paul's worldview and theology'[74] resonates with Bultmann's interest in Paul as leading believers into a new self-understanding.[75]

Evaluating Bultmann

There is no doubt that Bultmann was the dominating force in the second half of twentieth-century New Testament studies. Yet Bultmann, for all his brilliance, for his attempt to make Christian faith palatable in the modern

---

71 Bultmann 1930.
72 Bultmann 1952–5, 1:190–1.
73 Which is precisely Bultmann's stated aim in his *Theology* (1952–5, 2:251).
74 Wright 2013, 1355–6.
75 Schliesser 2016, 31.

world, despite his insights into source-critical questions, his penetration into the theological texture of Paul and John, and even taking into account his deep *evangelische* piety, despite all that, the scholarly edifices he built have turned out to be a sandcastle in the sky. Nothing Bultmann proposed has stood the test of time; everything he advocated is little more than debris in the history of New Testament studies. Some of his distinctive interests, like the constant appeal to the Gnostic Redeemer Myth, should even be taught as a morality tale to PhD students on how not to do biblical scholarship. I'm not saying that there is nothing to admire in Bultmann, or that there is nothing to learn from him; far from it. There is plenty to treasure here, but time has not vindicated his various proposals on Jesus, Paul and John, or his demythologizing project.

For a case in point, Martin Hengel, a late contemporary of Bultmann, ties the birth of his own formidable scholarly career to the desperate need to correct the aberrations and absurdities of the Bultmannian *Schule* which had intoxicated both German and American scholarship. According to Hengel:

> After I became *Stiftsrepetent* [i.e. a student instructor] in 1964, my colleagues at the instructors' table (with the exception of my friend Otto Betz, who had already then recognized the significance of the Qumran texts) appeared to me to be 'drunk from the sweet wine from Marburg.' In hearing the new theses I could time and again only shake my head: a radical synoptic criticism on the basis of 'form criticism,' an unmessianic Jesus of whom Paul knew hardly anything more than the 'that of his having come,' the radical separation between 'Palestinian' and 'Hellenistic' community, early Christianity as a 'syncretistic religion' profoundly influenced by a pre-Christian Gnosis and oriental mysteries, Paul and John as opponents of Jewish apocalyptic and as the first 'demythologizers,' Luke by contrast as a contemptible 'early catholic,' and above all a fundamental devaluation of all 'objectifying' historical knowledge and behind it all a latent Marcionism, for which the term 'Biblical theology' was almost already a swearword. Although I, being fascinated by the early church and ancient history, had more of an inclination to devote myself to church history, I began, to a certain extent as a protest against these 'new insights,' a New Testament dissertation which dealt with Judaism as the birthing ground of Christianity (*Die Zeloten* [AGSU 1], Leiden 1961). It was the then so fashionable theses of R. Bultmann, which dominated the field but were questionable in my judgment, that brought me to the New Testament.[76]

---

[76] Hengel 2012, 462.

If Hengel is right, it means that despite the apparent shine on Bultmann's apology for a modernist Christianity, in terms of evidence and lasting contribution there isn't much left. The most distinctive element of Bultmann's interpretation was his translation of theology into existential categories, a move which now seems utterly irrelevant to the postmodern world. Bultmann is proof of the axiom that anyone who marries the spirit of the age will be widowed within a single generation. If Bultmann's legacy is to endure, it will not be among *Neutestamentlers*, but among the *Theologen*.

N. T. Wright: telling the Jewish story of the New Testament

The wonder of Wright

The brilliance of N. T. Wright is that, as my doctoral co-supervisor Robert Webb told me, he paints with a thick brush on a big canvas. He is a big-picture thinker, and I mean big! Markus Bockmuehl once quipped:

> Tom Wright is not one to do things by halves. His is the high-octane, Grand Unified Theory approach to New Testament studies. Where lesser mortals may acquiesce in losing the wood for the exegetical trees, N. T. Wright deals in inter-galactic ecosystems – without neglecting in the process to footnote a surprising number of trees.[77]

Kevin Vanhoozer verbalizes the same thought:

> While many of us plod through the text word by word, phrase by phrase and paragraph by paragraph, Wright soars on the wings of narrative angels from Galatians to Genesis and back again, delighting his fans but sometimes occasioning interpretive motion sickness among his critics. For my own part, this is one of the features I most admire in his work. He is brilliant in connecting the textual and testamental dots, hitting home runs out of the park of theological interpretation with no need of allegorical steroids.[78]

Wright deals with how the various sub-stories of Scripture – creation, Abraham, Israel, exile, restoration, Jesus and the Church – are drawn together in a singular narrative web. All of Scripture is unified of course by 'the divine plan to put the world to rights'.[79]

The other thing about Wright is that he is not just a mapper of meta-narratives, but is truly interested in interpreting the New Testament for our time, and with applying its message for contemporary audiences. This

---

[77] Bockmuehl 2004, 489.
[78] Vanhoozer 2011, 240.
[79] See, e.g., Wright 2006a, *passim*.

is where Wright has a genuine affinity with Bultmann as one who wants to make sense of the New Testament for today and see how it speaks to us now. That is why Wright is fond of saying: 'We must stop giving nineteenth-century answers to sixteenth-century questions and try to give twenty-first-century answers to first-century questions.'[80] Wright makes a concerted effort to let first-century authors and texts speak to the conditions and situations of people in the twenty-first-century context. Like Bultmann, he's unwilling to let the constraints of dogmatics determine the rules of the exegetical game, and will break with tradition – on areas like justification – if necessary. Wright has that flexibility because he is conscious that the ultimate authority is not the Bible; rather, it is God himself.[81]

Engaging Wright

Hermeneutics

Wright exhibits a degree of epistemological and hermeneutical reflection that most exegetes rarely achieve. He is conscious that study of the New Testament involves a multidisciplinary exploration of literature, history and theology and this exploration needs to be undergirded with a particular theory of knowing. Wright propounds, with some affinity to Bernard Lonergan via Ben F. Meyer, a 'critical realist' epistemology which cuts a path through the Scylla of positivism and the Charybdis of phenomenalism. In Wright's presentation of critical realism, knowledge of objects, authors and the past is possible, but no one has a God's-eye view of reality because all perceptions of reality are conditioned. Thus, independent realities are knowable but never known independently of the knower.[82] I submit that his approach satisfies Bultmann's concern that we do not deny the role of 'pre-understanding' in our studies (i.e. we are necessarily self-involved with the subjects of our investigation and that is not necessarily a bad thing), nor succumb to the temptation to objectify a subject of enquiry (i.e. treat it as if it were reducible to cognitive knowledge, independent of our relationship to it, and act as if we behold it in a value-free vacuum), even while engaging in historical criticism as a form of scientific enquiry (i.e. the hard work of historical investigation).[83]

---

[80] Wright 2015, 26.
[81] Wright 2006b.
[82] Wright 1992, 32–7; see also Wright 1996, 55; 2003, 3–4; 2013, 48–56. See discussion in Moritz 2000; Denton 2004, 82–101, 210–25; Bird 2006; Wedderburn 2010, 7–13; Porter and Pitts 2015; Losch 2016; Bernier 2016.
[83] See Bultmann 1961c, 342–52.

Where Wright eclipses Bultmann is in his grasp of how our knowledge of things like history is shaped by story and worldview.[84] We are reminded by Wright that story is the most characteristic expression of worldview. All physical artefacts, as much as literary sources, are expressions of explicit and implicit narratives that tell us something about the symbols, praxes and questions of a given environment, that is, its worldview. So, in the first instance, any object of enquiry is shaped by the stories and world-view in which it was produced. Following on from that, the observer is in turn shaped by a larger framework of story and worldview around him or her which forms the basis of an observer's way of being in relationship to the world. Wright can even incorporate 'myth' into his construction, not as the embarrassing residue of a pre-scientific worldview as it was for Bultmann, but as 'the story element within worldview'. For Paul, his theology is undergirded by a myth, not things that never happened but always ring true, but rather a story about God's history with Israel and God's saving action in Jesus Christ.[85] Instead of neutering the narrative because of its archaic symbology, in Wright's mind the task of the inter-preter is to demonstrate how this story unifies creation and Israel, Israel and Jesus, Paul and Jesus, Paul and Israel, and Paul and the new creation. Wright's Paul is *the* anti-Bultmann in the sense that he was trying to tie together precisely what Bultmann's Paul loosened (Paul's Christ-devotion and its relationship to the historical Jesus) and what he allegedly brushed away as irrelevant (Paul's relationship with the empirical people and story of Israel).[86]

Wright is better equipped than Bultmann to grasp the storied world of Second Temple Judaism, the Roman Empire and the early Church, with a view to offering a successful explanatory story which explains the past, and which in turn authorizes a new set of symbols, tasks and praxes for the present.

Judaism

Bultmann never once visited Israel, but Wright has visited Israel some 15 times, and has trodden its terrain from top to bottom (I can say from experience that Wright makes a superb tour guide of the Holy Land). I would go so far as to say that for Bultmann, as long as Jesus was crucified in Jerusalem, the rest of the story could have been set in Narnia for all it

---

[84] Wright 1992, 38–46; 2013, 63–8.
[85] Wright 2013, 456–7.
[86] Schliesser 2016, 27.

matters. In contrast, Wright has been forthright that any serious interpreters really must get down into the nitty-gritty work of Judean texts
and history, diasporan socio-political realities, and mapping the Jewish
worldview in order to be taken seriously. Wright, just like Bultmann, finds
it vital to preface his account of Jesus and Paul with a study of ancient
Judaism. Yet, as we will see, the juxtaposition between Bultmann and
Wright on Judaism couldn't be sharper.

Whereas Bultmann reduced Judaism to 'legalism', Wright was part of –
and in some ways anticipated[87] – the E. P. Sanders revolution on the study
of Judaism which rejected the theologically inspired denigration of Jewish
merit theology as the plight to Jesus' and Paul's supposed solution. Wright
sees his task as indigenizing that revolution in the study of early Christian
movements as they stood in their complex relationship within Judaism.[88]
Wright also rejects features on Judaism embraced by Bultmann, the crass
bifurcation between a liberal Hellenistic Judaism and its more conservative counterpart in Palestinian Judaism, and reading post-135 CE Rabbinic
Judaism into the pre-70 CE period.[89] Furthermore, when Bultmann made
his brief forays into Judaism it was mostly as negative foil to the New
Testament. When it comes to theological context and cultural sources,
Bultmann sees Gnostic and Mandean literature as the primary coordinates
for mapping Pauline and Johannine thought. In diametric opposition to
Bultmann, Wright has relied heavily on Josephus, the Dead Sea Scrolls,
the Apocrypha and many pseudepigrapha for his investigation of the early
Church's thought, symbols and praxes. Judaism for Bultmann is merely
contrast, but for Wright it is background, foreground, colour and texture.
Consequently, Wright's Jesus, Paul and early Church are more authentic
as Jewish entities.

What I think is central to Wright, and worth remembering, is that
Wright studies Judaism as a multifaceted and diverse phenomenon within
the wider Greco-Roman world. He pays close attention to Judean ban-
ditry and revolutionary activity, first-century prophetic movements, and
obviously the Pharisees, with concerted attention to the interface between
religious beliefs and stories and the socio-political situation of Judea.
And then, later, grasping the manifold contours of Diaspora Judaism in
the wider Mediterranean theatre, he maps out the main stories (creation,
patriarchs, exodus, exile), symbols (Temple, land, Torah, ethnicity), praxes

---

[87] Wright 1978a.
[88] Wright 1992, 345.
[89] Wright 1992, 151–2, 342.

(cultic worship, festivals, Torah-study), beliefs (monotheism, election, covenant, eschatology) and hopes (apocalypses, end of exile, God becomes king, messianism, Adamic renewal, salvation).[90] In sum, what Wright does far better than Bultmann is to avoid reading non-Jewish ideas into Judaism, and he endeavours to achieve a 'critical-realist reading of first-century Judaism, including its beliefs and aspirations, in its own terms, which will then shed unexpected light on the rise of Christianity.'[91]

Where Wright is unique and controversial has been in his advocating that the Jewish worldview shared a particular construal of Jewish restoration eschatology. This eschatological configuration involved the hope for the final return of Israel from a protracted and punitive state of exile that did not end even after the return of a remnant of exiles from Babylon to Judea in the sixth century BCE. According to Wright:

> Most Jews of this period, it seems, would have answered the question of 'where are we?' in language which, reduced to its simplest form, meant: we are still in exile. They believed that, in all the senses which mattered, Israel's exile was still in progress. Although she had come back from Babylon, the glorious message of the prophets remained unfulfilled. Israel still remained in thrall to foreigners; worse, Israel's god (*sic*) had not returned to Zion.[92]

In the face of severe criticism, Wright has clarified his position, claiming:

> Be it noted, my case is not that *all Jews throughout the period* understood themselves to be living in a state of 'continuing exile', only that such an understanding was widespread, and was particularly likely to be true of zealous Pharisees.[93]

This is one of Wright's most notable and novel proposals, with obvious explanatory power for texts like Matthew 8.11–12 / Luke 13.28–29 and Galatians 3.13–14, but has received severe criticism for allegedly allegorizing the concept of exile.[94]

When compared with Bultmann's account of Judaism, Wright's account makes for better history, better theology, and arguably – though no doubt contestable – better interfaith relations between Jews and Christians.[95]

---

[90] Wright 1992, 147–338; 2013, 75–196.
[91] Wright 1992, 149–50.
[92] Wright 1992, 268–9.
[93] Wright 2013, 158 (italics original).
[94] See discussion of scholarship on Wright and exile in Evans 1999; Dunn 2003, 472–7; Bird 2015; White 2016; Scott 2017.
[95] On the critical side, see Fredriksen's (2015) review of *Paul and the Faithfulness of God*.

Jesus

The head-scratching thing about Bultmann is that his *Theology of the New Testament* dedicates a paltry 30 pages to Jesus and a massive 120 pages to some fictitious entity called the 'Hellenistic Community'. Even a sympathetic reader of Bultmann will have to concede that Bultmann misplaced his energies in this regard by swapping the real for the ephemeral. In contrast, study of the historical Jesus is no mere preface for Wright, but a vital first move for the serious theologian, and even a necessary task of discipleship.[96] If we don't study the historical Jesus, then the danger is that 'Jesus' can be reshaped into any number of images or made to sponsor any pernicious ideology. This was certainly true of the Aryan Jesus and it is just as true for any Marxist Jesus or pro-American Jesus. As Crossan said, the historical Jesus is a great place to 'do autobiography and call it biography [of Jesus]'.[97]

Wright's *Jesus and the Victory of God* catapulted him to the status of a leading Jesus researcher.[98] Wright engaged in a two-front contest against conservatives who only needed Jesus as an icon for the virgin birth and the atonement,[99] and the post-Bultmannian Jesus Seminar who touted their Jesus-the-Cynic-philosopher as the latest results of historical investigation.[100] The Jesus Seminar was an explicitly Bultmannian enterprise endeavouring to recover something of the historical Jesus by building upon Bultmann's view of the synoptic tradition and its transmission, though some of its members, like John Dominic Crossan, were very un-Bultmannian in trying to discover a historical Jesus who could anchor their theology and ethics.[101] Wright's critique of the Jesus Seminar was as brutal as it was apt:

> It is the Bultmannian picture, with variations: a deJudaized Jesus preaching a demythologized, 'vertical' eschatology; a crucifixion with no early theological interpretation; a 'resurrection' consisting of the coming to faith, some time later, of a particular group of Christians; an early sapiential/gnostic group, retelling the master's aphorisms but uninterested in his life story; a Paul who invented a Hellenistic Christ-cult; a synoptic tradition in which rolling aphorisms, as they slowed down, gathered the moss of narrative structure about themselves, and gradually congealed into gospels

---

96 Wright 2000, 1–17; 2011.
97 Crossan 1991, xxviii. See on the problem of bias, Allison 2009, 19–20.
98 See summaries in Witherington 1997, 219–32; Powell 1998, 159–77; Blomberg 1999.
99 Wright 1996, 14.
100 Wright 1996, 28–82.
101 Wright 1996, 34.

in which the initial force of Jesus' challenge was muted or lost altogether within a fictitious pseudo-historical framework. This modern picture, in fact, is the real fiction. For a time it seemed to be a helpful fiction. I suggest that that time has come to an end.[102]

Thanks to Wright, and others like Richard Hays, Gerd Theissen, Richard Burridge and John Meier, the Jesus Seminar's Jesus is now something of scholarly joke, openly mocked in publications as the 'California Jesus'.[103]

What Wright does in *Jesus and the Victory of God* is drive his British hatchback, with C. H. Dodd and G. B. Caird in the back seat, firmly down the *Schweitzer-bahn*, with consistent eschatology rather than consistent scepticism comprising the road upon which his scholarly journey proceeds. Thereafter comes Wright's analysis of Jesus' prophetic praxis, his stories–summons–symbols–statements about the kingdom, his enactment of his own version of Jewish restorationist eschatology which declared that through him Israel's exile was finally ending, all the while stressing how Jesus' words and deeds ultimately undermined the political status quo associated with the Temple and challenged competing accounts of Israel's story and future. On the aims and intentions of Jesus, Wright posits Jesus as making tacit messianic claims, identifying himself as Daniel's 'son of man', believing himself called to the vocation of Isaiah's 'servant' in dying to defeat Israel's true enemy, not Rome but the Satan, and returning to Jerusalem to announce and embody the return of Yahweh to Zion. In a nutshell:

> Jesus aimed to reconstitute Israel around himself, as the true returned-from-exile people; to achieve the victory of Israel's god over the evil that had enslaved his people; and, somehow, to bring about the great hope of all, the victorious return of YHWH to Zion . . . Jesus saw himself as the leader and focal point of the true, returning-from-exile Israel; he was the king through whose work YHWH was at last restoring his people. He was the Messiah.[104]

The juxtaposition of Wright with Bultmann could not be sharper. Bultmann would never have permitted, let alone engaged in, a study of Jesus' mindset, intentions and aims. Bultmann wanted Jesus insulated from messianic myths and apocalyptic visions about the restoration of Israel whereas Wright makes restoration eschatology absolutely central.[105] Bultmann could not imagine Jesus involved in petty disputes about cultic

---

[102] Wright 1996, 79–80.
[103] See Bird 2006, 293–7.
[104] Wright 1996, 473–4, 479.
[105] Bultmann 1952–5, 1:4, 25; Wright 1996, 297–301.

politics whereas Wright makes Jesus' confrontation with the Temple authorities a dominating theme.[106] Bultmann could not conceive of Jesus claiming to be the Messiah, and he thought Jesus looked forward to the coming of a 'Son of Man' as someone other than himself. In contrast, Wright makes messiahship vital to Jesus' sense of purpose, and the 'Son of Man' is Jesus' cryptic self-designation as the one called to be Israel-in-person.[107] These two Jesuses are antithetical, one is not like the other, and I find only one of them to be historically plausible.

The pay-off is that Wright's Jesus is a historically conceivable figure, who fits into first-century Judaism, and was understandably the most determinative influence on why the early Church began and why it took the shape that it did. Methodologically, Wright has turned Bultmann on his head by insisting that Jesus is both similar and dissimilar to Judaism and Christianity.[108] Historically, Wright's Jesus is more shaped by, speaks to and works out of a Jewish environment than does Bultmann's Jesus. Theologically, Wright's Jesus reshaped Jewish restoration eschatology around himself in such a way as to lead to a conception among his followers of themselves as the renewed Israel of the kingdom age, which in turn became the bedrock for a distinctively Christian hermeneutic and self-identity. For Bultmann, that role belongs to Paul and John.

Finally, on an anecdotal level, Wright's Jesus enables Christians to read the Gospels in a refreshingly new way. No longer reading the Gospels as the prolegomena to Paul, nor as an assorted catalogue of miracles, or loosely connected spiritual teachings, nor as Sunday school lessons; but as the story of the Messiah, who fulfils Israel's hopes, and who embodies in himself the identity of God and the destiny of his people. As my friend Dr Lynn Cohick once said in conversation, Wright gave back to Evangelicals the ability to read the Gospels. Or, as former Catholic Archbishop of Brisbane John Bathersby said on Wright's visit to Australia in 2006, reading *Jesus and the Victory of God* is like meeting Jesus for the first time.

Resurrection

Wright's book *The Resurrection of the Son of God* is not only a *tour de force* but might go down as the singularly greatest treatise on the resurrection in church history. No point Wright argues for is individually unique, but he prosecutes with rigour, originality and industry the point that resurrection

---

[106] Bultmann 1952–5, 1:17; Wright 1996, 339–67, 405–28.
[107] Bultmann 1952–5, 1:26–32; Wright 1996, 477–539.
[108] Contrast Bultmann 1994 (1921), 205, with Wright 1996, 131–3.

was something denied by pagans, believed by many Jews, and reaffirmed and redefined by the early Christians.[109]

Wright is fully aware of the trickiness about talking about 'resurrection' as 'history' when there are theological and naturalistic objections to treating the resurrection as history.[110] Yet he sticks to his guns that resurrection is *the* historical explanation for why the Church emerged and became the resurrection-movement that it was.[111] He goes to great lengths to prove that when the first Christians talked about 'resurrection' they did not mean it in a vague sense – that their recently departed friend Jesus of Nazareth had become an angel, was translated to heaven or was now comfortably seated at the bosom of Abraham. Rather, resurrection meant the reanimation of a dead body into a glorious and immortal life; it was life after life after death.[112] Resurrection was what God had promised to do for Israel at the end of history, to vindicate the nation from its sufferings, but he had now and mysteriously performed it for one man in the middle of history, vindicating him as Messiah and installing him as the Son of God in power. This meant reconfiguring the entire Jewish worldview around the risen Messiah, and it generated a whole constellation of new symbols and praxes.[113]

Along the way, Wright clinically demolishes the standard paradigm for resurrection held among the Bultmannians that the Jewish context was ambivalent about resurrection, Jesus' disciples had at most subjective visions of Jesus alive after his crucifixion, the early Church emphasized Jesus' exaltation over any resurrection, Paul believed in a spiritual resurrection body rather than a physical resurrection body, and the Easter narratives of an empty tomb and physical appearances are legendary developments.[114] On the Easter narratives, Wright makes an important point that the empty tomb *alone* and appearances *alone* would not have generated belief in Jesus' resurrection. That is because alternative beliefs about what happened to Jesus were readily available and easier to adjust to; it was only the empty tomb and appearances together that could have generated belief in Jesus' resurrection.[115] Wright has much to say about how resurrection generated a world of meaning for the early Church,

---

[109] Wright 2003, xvii–xviii.
[110] Wright 2003, 11–20.
[111] Wright 2003, 686–718 (esp. 710).
[112] Wright 2003, 199–206.
[113] Wright 1997, 36.
[114] Wright 2003, 7.
[115] Wright 2003, 686; affirmed by Allison 2005, 321–6.

not the least for their construal of Jesus' identity as Son of God, Messiah, and understanding him as 'the one in whom the living God, Israel's God, has become personally present in the world'.[116] Wright waxes eloquent about the fiercely political nature of resurrection hope since resurrection inaugurates a kingdom that inevitably will clash with the injustices and tyrannies of empires and their weapons, like crucifixion. Tyrants 'try to rule by force, only to discover that in order to do so they have to quash all rumours of resurrection, rumours that would imply that their greatest weapons, death and deconstruction, are not after all omnipotent'.[117]

For Wright, resurrection is part of a Jewish story about God acting in space and time to launch the new creation upon an unsuspecting world which is 'surprised by hope' in the face of God's life-giving power.

Paul

It is fair to say that Wright is a Paulinist at heart, or his theology is shaped by Paul more than by any other apostolic figure from the New Testament. Since his DPhil thesis – lamentably never published – Wright has argued that at the centre of Paul's thought is the notion of Jesus as the Messiah, a corporate figure who incorporates Jews and Gentiles into himself.[118] As a leading protagonist in the New Perspective on Paul, Wright has stressed that Paul was not responding to Jewish legalism, but to a 'national righteousness', the belief that ethnic descent guarantees covenant membership in God's people.[119] He has courted controversy with remarks like the following:

> Justification in this setting, then, is not a matter of *how someone enters the community of the true people of God*, but of *how you tell who belongs to the community*, not least in the period of time before the eschatological event itself, when the matter will become public knowledge.[120]

Similarly, he has sent Reformed critics into a spiral of salivating rage by denying the need for the imputation of Christ's righteousness,[121] and by emphasizing final justification as a verdict issued on the basis of 'an entire

---

[116] Wright 2003, 733.
[117] Wright 2003, 737.
[118] Wright 1981.
[119] Wright 1978a, 65, 83; 1991, 243–4.
[120] Wright 1997, 119 (italics original); and similarly Wright 2005, 122.
[121] Wright 1997, 98.

life'.[122] Subsequent criticisms were robust,[123] but Wright did subsequently clarify his position well, noting that covenantal categories are not inimical to forensic ones, union with Christ gets the same job done as imputation, and the final judgement is declarative rather than investigative.[124] His mature statement on the matter demonstrates a wonderful fusion of forensic, covenantal and participationist categories in explaining what it means to be 'justified in Christ', which should assuage any critic.[125] What Wright's critics rarely appreciate is that he has construed justification in a way that properly reflects the Jewish setting and polemical context of Paul's apostolic ministry, concerned as it was with the integrity of Christ-believing Gentiles *as* Gentiles, with their freedom from proselytism, and protecting them from forced acculturation to Judaism. In addition, theologically speaking, Wright has attempted to demonstrate how election and justification belong together, so that the latter is an expression of the former, which is a very Reformed theme if one thinks about it.[126]

The centrepiece of Wright's *Paul and the Faithfulness of God* volume has been demonstrating how Paul reworked the concepts of monotheism, covenant and eschatology around Jesus and the Spirit. Paul does this in a way that remains authentically Jewish even while speaking to some of the major concerns of Greek and Roman thinkers in the ancient world. Wright proposes that Paul invented the task of theology as something that congregations had to do as they strove to figure out how, in the Messiah, they were supposed to live and act. This 'theology' was a necessary venture to sustain the Church in its holiness and unity in a pagan world. Something seen in particular in the letter to Philemon where Paul urges Philemon to think messianically about how he should act towards Onesimus (see Philemon 6). In fact, family-language used in the letter to Philemon, between a master and a slave, was no doubt controversial, and it highlights that the united family of God was a key symbol of what Paul believed he was constructing by establishing clusters of *ekklēsia* rooted in the Messiah. Thus, Wright has done what few others have attempted: shown that Paul's idea of the Church as the socially diverse and multi-ethnic family of God, that is, ecclesiology, is the place where his Christology, ethics, soteriology and eschatology meet.

---

[122] Wright 1997, 129; 2001, 144; 2002, 440.

[123] See, e.g., Piper 2002; 2007.

[124] See esp. Wright 2006c; 2009.

[125] Wright 2013, 1026–32.

[126] In defence of Wright against his critics, see Bird 2007, 183–93; see a further appropriation of Wright in Anderson 2016. For the practical implications of the New Perspective, see McKnight and Modica 2016.

Evaluating Wright

One could score some points against Wright in many places. Has he over-cooked the still-in-exile motif he detects in Judaism? Is he too optimistic about recovering the historical Jesus from the Gospels? Is he not literal enough on eschatological imagery in places? Has he overplayed his hand at intertextuality by finding, for example, exodus allusions in Romans 6? Is he a little too eager to detect counter-imperial echoes in Paul's letters? Perhaps. Or else, one might complain about some of his rather broad blanket denials as to what justification is not about, or raise an eyebrow to the claim that no one these days has really figured out how kingdom and cross go together. Much grist for the mill can be found by Wright's critics.

Probably the harshest criticism that should be made against Wright is this (and I say it with typically Australian cheekiness to a Brit): he needs to be periodically reminded that between the years 100 and 1978 CE a couple of good things actually have been written. In particular, he is frequently guilty of overgeneralizing and caricaturing the Reformers (which is fiercely ironic since his first publication was on the English Reformer John Frith!).[127] Wright candidly concedes that he is not 'a specialist in the sixteenth and seventeenth centuries',[128] but that does not prevent him from engaging in rather cavalier dismissals of the Reformers. Something rather rampant for instance in his *Paul and His Recent Interpreters*. Such remarks are unfortunate because in conversation, Wright can demonstrate a clear familiarity and genuine respect for both the Church Fathers and Reformers. The problem is that this respect does not always manifest itself in his writings. I believe a penitential exercise for Wright would be for him to spend a year-long sabbatical in Wartburg castle in Germany with only the complete works of Augustine and Luther for company (though I panic to think about the number of books he could produce in that time!).

Those criticisms aside, the genius of Wright, his promise for New Testament theology – 'promise' here understood as both 'potential' and an 'anticipation' of what he is still to complete – is his ability to draw from the study of the early Church a normative narrative and a public truth, which authorizes a particular set of praxes for the Church centred around the God of Israel, Israel's Messiah and the Holy Spirit. Wright is developing a narrative theology of the New Testament which forces those in the Church to think theologically about their identity and mission, or, how to live out the divine drama as they anticipate the intended climax of the story

---

[127] Wright 1978b.
[128] Wright 2016, 32.

in which they find themselves.[129] Whereas Bultmann wanted theology to result in 'self-understanding' for the individual, Wright sees the task of theology as to enable the corporate Church to live out its elect vocation as part of God's plan to put the world to rights. To this end, I submit that Wright's account of New Testament theology is preferable and more promising than that of Bultmann.

Conclusion

When it comes to a comparison of Bultmann and Wright, I have to profess my unqualified preference for the historical description and theological vision of Wright. Wright's account of hermeneutics, Judaism, Jesus, the resurrection and Paul is to my mind infinitely superior to that of Bultmann. The only place where Bultmann betters Wright is possibly on John; a subject to which Wright has not expended much intellectual energy to date, so consequently I could not undertake a serious comparison of the two in the Johannine pastures.[130] Yet, whether it is exegesis or theology, I believe that Wright rather than Bultmann holds out a more promising way of reading the New Testament, a better promise for constructing theology for the Church, and a more promising method for how to shape the Christian life with biblical theology.[131]

This contest I have constructed between Wright and Bultmann in many ways mirrors the rivalry between British and German biblical scholarship in the nineteenth and twentieth centuries.[132] It is worth acknowledging that UK scholars did not take Bultmann hook, line and sinker as many of their American cousins did. In general, the British academy offered an appreciative yet critical appropriation of Bultmann's work (compare Austin Farrer, Vincent Taylor, C. H. Dodd, F. F. Bruce and George Beasley-Murray with R. H. Lightfoot and Dennis Nineham on the British reception of Bultmann). Wright entered the scholarly scene when academics were finally waking up from their Bultmannian slumbers and leaving the old Marburg master for fresher fields in narrative and post-liberal theology, exploring Jürgen Moltmann's theology of hope, still wrestling with Karl Barth's significance and exploring new frontiers in ideological criticism.

---

[129] See esp. Wright 1992, 139–43.

[130] See Wright 1992, 410–17; 2012, 135–47.

[131] As to what Wright's vision for theology looks like when indigenized in a local church, see Kuhrt 2011.

[132] I think here, for example, of J. B. Lightfoot vs F. C. Baur, C. H. Dodd vs A. Schweitzer, and C. K. Barrett vs E. Käsemann.

It was in this post-Bultmannian context that Wright emerged as a scholarly luminary. Despite a fairly modest beginning to his publishing career, due to heavy teaching and pastoral commitments, today Wright's Christian Origins and the Question of God (COQG) series is arguably the most exciting project in New Testament studies with its bold ambition to marry Christian origins and New Testament theology in a fresh new way. Notwithstanding his scholarly commitments, Wright has still found time for church ministry as an Anglican dean and bishop, writing a popular commentary on every book of the New Testament, composing dozens of pastoral and popular works, and keeping an international lecture schedule. The man is a powerhouse of scholarly energy and ecclesiastical industry that leaves most of his contemporaries in awe.

It is no surprise then that in the last three decades Wright has arguably influenced the study of Jesus, Paul and the Gospels in a way that few of his peers have done.[133] Along the way, he has attracted remarkably broad audiences in both the academy and the Church; people who identify as diversely as Evangelical, Mainline Protestant, Charismatic, Catholic and Orthodox can be counted among his many admirers. This is not an accident. The genius of Wright is his ability to map out the big picture as few can, to bring the threads of history and theology together with rare intelligence, engaging in feats of intertextual dialogue that if not always convincing are at least irrefutably elegant, to offer fresh readings of ancient sources that are provocative, to write paragraphs that are cathedrals of exegetical beauty, to make cogent pastoral insights that are as refreshing as they are challenging, and doing it all with some of the most enjoyable and refulgent prose one will ever read.

There have certainly been critics, some even quite ferocious, and most capable interpreters will have a valid bone or two of contention to pick with Wright. But even if Wright's scholarly accomplishments might not necessarily be made of marble, I am confident that the sculptures of Jesus, the resurrection and Paul that he has made will endure the test of time. Future excavators of New Testament studies will recognize the much-needed corrections he made, the value of his contributions, plus the overall acumen and artistry of his COQG project.

If I had to choose between sending the best and brightest of my students to 1920s Marburg or to 2010s St Andrews for their doctoral work, I would

---

[133] To be honest, I think it fair to say that Wright's scholarship is more significant when viewed as part of a scholarly triumvirate which includes E. P. Sanders and James Dunn as well; all three together have really dominated the questions and direction pertaining to the study of Jesus and Paul.

unhesitantly go for St Andrews. Many went to Marburg to sit at the feet of Bultmann, and behold, one greater than Bultmann is here.

Bibliography

Adam, A. K. M. (1996). 'Docetism, Käsemann, and Christology: Why Historical Criticism Can't Protect Christological Orthodoxy.' *Scottish Journal of Theology* 49: 391–410.

Allison, Dale C. (2005). *Resurrecting Jesus: The Earliest Christian Tradition and Its Interpreters*. London: T&T Clark.

—— (2009). *The Historical Christ and the Theological Jesus*. Grand Rapids, MI: Eerdmans.

Anderson, Garwood P. (2016). *Paul's New Perspective: Charting a Soteriological Journey*. Downers Grove, IL: IVP.

Barclay, John M. G. (2015). 'Interpretation Not Repetition: Reflections on Bultmann as a Theological Reader of Paul.' *Journal of Theological Interpretation* 9: 201–9.

Beasley-Murray, George (1955). 'Bultmann and "Demythologising."' *The Listener* 54 (13 October): 1389.

Beasley-Murray, Paul (2002). *Fearless for Truth: A Personal Portrait of the Life of George Beasley-Murray*. Carlisle: Paternoster.

Bernier, Jonathan (2016). 'A Response to Porter and Pitts' "Wright's Critical Realism in Context."' *Journal for the Study of the Historical Jesus* 14: 186–93.

Bird, Michael F. (2006). 'The Peril of Modernizing Jesus and the Crisis of Not Contemporarizing the Christ.' *Evangelical Quarterly* 78: 302–10.

—— (2007). *The Saving Righteousness of God: Studies in Paul, Justification, and the New Perspective*. Carlisle: Paternoster.

—— (2014a). *The Gospel of the Lord: How the Early Church Wrote the Story of Jesus*. Grand Rapids, MI: Eerdmans.

—— (2014b). 'Did Jesus Think He Was God?' In *How God Became Jesus: The Real Origins of Belief in Jesus' Divine Nature*, edited by Michael F. Bird, 45–70. Grand Rapids, MI: Zondervan.

—— (2015). 'Jesus and the Continuing Exile of Israel in the Writings of N. T. Wright.' *Journal for the Study of the Historical Jesus* 13: 209–31.

—— (2016). *An Anomalous Jew: Paul among Jews, Greeks and Romans*. Grand Rapids, MI: Eerdmans.

Blomberg, Craig (1999). 'The Wright Stuff: A Critical Overview of *Jesus and the Victory of God*.' In *Jesus and the Restoration of Israel: A Critical Assessment of N. T. Wright's Jesus and the Victory of God*, edited by Carey C. Newman, 19–39. Downers Grove, IL: IVP.

Bockmuehl, Markus (2004). 'Compleat History of the Resurrection: A Dialogue with N. T. Wright.' *Journal for the Study of the New Testament* 26 (2004): 489–504.

Bruce, F. F. (1988). *The Canon of Scripture*. Glasgow: Chapter House.

Bultmann, Rudolf (1925). 'Die Bedeutung der neuerschlossenen mandäischen und manichäischen Quellen für das Verständnis des Johannesevangeliums.' *Zeitschrift für Theologie und Kirche* 24: 100–46.

—— (1930). 'Paulus.' In *Die Religion in Geschichte und Gegenwart*, edited by Hermann Gunkel and Leopold Zscharnack, 4:1019–45. 2nd edition. Tübingen: Mohr Siebeck.

—— (1952–5). *Theology of the New Testament*. Translated by K. Grobel. 2 vols. London: SCM.

—— (1956). *Primitive Christianity in Its Contemporary Setting*. Translated by R. H. Fuller. New York, NY: Meridian.

—— (1958a). *Jesus Christ and Mythology*. London: SCM.

—— (1958b). *Jesus and the Word*. Translated by L. P. Smith and E. H. Lantero. London: Charles Scribner's Sons.

—— (1960). 'Mythos und Mythologie IV: Im Neuen Testament.' In *Die Religion in Geschichte und Gegenwart*, edited by Kurt Galling, 4:1263–84. 3rd edition. 6 vols. Tübingen: Mohr Siebeck.

—— (1961a). *Existence and Faith: Shorter Writings of Rudolf Bultmann*. Translated by S. M. Ogden. London: Collins.

—— (1961b). 'Jesus and Paul.' In *Existence and Faith: Shorter Writings of Rudolf Bultmann*, edited by S. M. Ogden, 183–91. London: Collins.

—— (1961c). 'Is Exegesis without Presuppositions Possible?' In *Existence and Faith: Shorter Writings of Rudolf Bultmann*, edited by S. M. Ogden, 342–52. London: Collins.

—— (1963). 'The Significance of the Old Testament for Christian Faith.' In *The Old Testament and Christian Faith*, edited by B. W. Anderson, 8–35. New York, NY: Harper & Row.

—— (1967). 'Das Verhältnis der urchristlichen Christusbotschaft zum historischen Jesus.' In *Exegetica*, edited by Erich Dinkler, 445–69. Tübingen: Mohr Siebeck.

—— (1968). 'πιστεύω κτλ.' In *Theological Dictionary of the New Testament*, edited by Gerhard Kittel and Gerhard Friedrich, 6:174–228. 10 vols. Grand Rapids, MI: Eerdmans.

—— (1969). 'The Historical Jesus and the Theology of Paul.' In *Faith and Understanding: Collected Essays*, translated by L. P. Smith, edited by R. W. Funk, 220–46. London: SCM.

—— (1971). *The Gospel of John: A Commentary*. Translated by G. R. Beasley-Murray et al. Philadelphia, PA: Westminster.

—— (1984). *New Testament and Mythology and Other Basic Writings*. Edited by Schubert Miles Ogden. Philadelphia: Fortress.

—— (1986). 'The History of Religions Background of the Prologue to the Gospel of John.' In *The Interpretation of John*, edited by John Ashton, 18–35. London: SPCK.

—— (1994 (1921)). *History of the Synoptic Tradition*. Translated by John Marsh. Peabody, MA: Hendrickson.

Congdon, David W. (2015a). *Rudolf Bultmann: A Companion to His Theology*. Eugene, OR: Cascade.

—— (2015b). *The Mission of Demythologizing: Rudolf Bultmann's Dialectical Theology*. Minneapolis, MN: Fortress.

Crossan, John Dominic (1991). *The Historical Jesus: The Life of a Mediterranean Jewish Peasant*. San Francisco, CA: HarperOne.

Denton, Donald L. (2004). *Historiography and Hermeneutics in Jesus Studies*. Journal for the Study of the New Testament Supplement Series 262. London: T&T Clark.

Dunn, James D. G. (2003). *Jesus Remembered*. Christianity in the Making 1. Grand Rapids, MI: Eerdmans.

Evans, Craig A. (1999). 'Jesus and the Continuing Exile of Israel.' In *Jesus and the Restoration of Israel: A Critical Assessment of N. T. Wright's Jesus and the Victory of God*, edited by Carey C. Newman, 77–100. Downers Grove, IL: IVP, 1999.

Fredriksen, Paula (2015). 'Review of *Paul and the Faithfulness of God*.' *Catholic Biblical Quarterly* 77: 387–91.

Hammann, Konrad (2009). *Rudolf Bultmann: Eine Biographie*. 2nd edition. Tübingen: Mohr Siebeck.

Hasel, Gerhard (1978). *New Testament Theology: Basic Issues in the Current Debate*. Grand Rapids, MI: Eerdmans.

Hengel, Martin (2012). 'A Young Theological Discipline in Crisis.' In *Earliest Christian History*, edited by Michael F. Bird and Jason Maston, 459–71. Wissenschaftliche Untersuchungen zum Neuen Testament 2/320. Tübingen: Mohr Siebeck.

Jipp, Joshua W. (2016). 'Review of David W. Congdon, *The Mission of Demythologizing*.' *Bulletin of Biblical Research* 26: 450–2.

Käsemann, Ernst (1964). 'The Problem of the Historical Jesus.' In *Essays on New Testament Themes*, trans. W. J. Montague, 15–47. London: SCM.

Keith, Chris (2012). 'The Indebtedness of the Criteria Approach to Form Criticism and Recent Attempts to Rehabilitate the Search for an Authentic Jesus.' In *Jesus, Criteria, and the Demise of Authenticity*, edited by Chris Keith and Anthony Le Donne, 25–48. London: T&T Clark.

Kreeft, Peter, and Ronald K. Tarecelli (1994). *Handbook on Christian Apologetics*. Downers Grove, IL: IVP.

Kuhrt, Stephen (2011). *Tom Wright for Everyone: Putting the Theology of N. T. Wright into Practice in the Local Church*. London: SPCK.

Ladd, G. E. (1964). *Bultmann*. Chicago, IL: IVP.

Losch, Andreas (2016). 'Wright's Version of Critical Realism.' In *God and the Faithfulness of Paul: A Critical Examination of the Pauline Theology of N. T. Wright*, edited by Christoph Heilig, J. Thomas Hewitt and Michael F. Bird, 101–14. Wissenschaftliche Untersuchungen zum Neuen Testament 2/413. Tübingen: Mohr Siebeck.

McKnight, Scot, and Joseph B. Modica (2016) (eds). *The Apostle Paul and the Christian Life: Ethical and Missional Implications of the New Perspective*. Grand Rapids, MI: Baker.

Mercer, Calvin R. (1986). *Norman Perrin's Interpretation of the New Testament:*

From 'Exegetical Method' to 'Hermeneutical Process'. Macon, GA: Mercer University Press.

Moritz, Thorsten (2000). 'Critical But Real: Reflecting on N. T. Wright's Tools for the Task.' In *Renewing Biblical Interpretation*, edited by C. Bartholomew, C. Greene and K. Möller, 172–97. Scripture and Hermeneutics 1. Grand Rapids, MI: Zondervan.

Newman, Carey C. (1999). 'Preface.' In *Jesus and the Restoration of Israel: A Critical Assessment of N. T. Wright's Jesus and the Victory of God*, edited by Carey C. Newman, 9–10. Downers Grove, IL: IVP.

Pennington, Jonathan T. (2008). 'Heaven, Earth, and a New Genesis: Theological Cosmology in Matthew.' In *Cosmology and New Testament Theology*, edited by Jonathan T. Pennington and Sean M. McDonough, 28–44. Library of New Testament Studies 355. London: T&T Clark.

Perrin, Nicholas (2013). 'Form Criticism.' In *Dictionary of Jesus and the Gospels*, edited by Joel B. Green, Jeannine K. Brown and Nicholas Perrin, 288–94. 2nd edition. Downers Grove, IL: IVP.

Perrin, Norman (1969). *The Promise of Bultmann*. Philadelphia, PA: Lippincott.

—— (1974a). *The New Testament: An Introduction*. New York, NY: Harcourt, Brace & Jovanovich.

—— (1974b). *A Modern Pilgrimage in New Testament Christology*. Philadelphia, PA: Fortress.

—— (1975). 'Jesus and the Theology of the New Testament.' Unpublished Paper, Catholic Biblical Association, 18–21 August.

—— (1976). *Rediscovering the Teachings of Jesus*. 2nd edition. New York, NY: Harper & Row.

Piper, John (2002). *Counted Righteous in Christ: Should We Abandon the Imputation of Christ's Righteousness?* Wheaton, IL: Crossway.

—— (2007). *The Future of Justification: A Response to N. T. Wright*. Wheaton, IL: Crossway.

Porter, Stanley E. (2015). *John, His Gospel, and Jesus: In Pursuit of the Johannine Voice*. Grand Rapids, MI: Eerdmans.

Porter, Stanley E., and Andrew W. Pitts (2015). 'Critical Realism in Context: N. T. Wright's Historical Method and Analytic Epistemology.' *Journal for the Study of the Historical Jesus* 2–3: 276–306.

Powell, Mark Allan (1998). *The Jesus Debate: Modern Historians Investigate the Life of Christ*. Oxford: Lion.

Sanders, E. P. (1977). *Paul and Palestinian Judaism*. Philadelphia, PA: Fortress.

Sandmel, Samuel (1966). 'Bultmann on Judaism.' In *The Theology of Rudolf Bultmann*, edited by C. W. Kegley, 211–20. New York, NY: Harper & Row.

Schliesser, Benjamin (2016). 'Paul and the Faithfulness of God among Pauline Theologies.' In *God and the Faithfulness of Paul: A Critical Examination of the Pauline Theology of N. T. Wright*, edited by Christoph Heilig, J. Thomas Hewitt and Michael F. Bird, 23–31. Wissenschaftliche Untersuchungen zum Neuen Testament 2/413. Tübingen: Mohr Siebeck.

Scott, James M. (ed.) (2017). *Exile: A Conversation with N. T. Wright.* Downers Grove, IL: IVP.

Theissen, Gerd (2012). 'Jesus within Judaism: The Political and Moral Context of Jesus Research and Its Methodology.' In *Soundings in the Religion of Jesus: Perspectives and Methods in Jewish and Christian Scholarship*, edited by Bruce Chilton, Anthony Le Donne and Jacob Neusner, 143–58. Minneapolis, MN: Fortress.

Thiselton, Anthony C. (2015). *The Thiselton Companion to Christian Theology.* Grand Rapids, MI: Eerdmans.

Vanhoozer, Kevin J. (2011). 'Wrighting the Wrongs of the Reformation? The State of the Union with Christ in St. Paul and Protestant Soteriology.' In *Jesus, Paul and the People of God: A Theological Dialogue with N. T. Wright*, edited by Nicholas Perrin and Richard B. Hays, 235–61. Downers Grove, IL: IVP.

Wedderburn, Alexander J. M. (2010). *Jesus and the Historians.* Wissenschaftliche Untersuchungen zum Neuen Testament 269. Tübingen: Mohr Siebeck.

White, Joel R. (2016). 'N. T. Wright's Narrative Approach.' In *God and the Faithfulness of Paul: A Critical Examination of the Pauline Theology of N. T. Wright*, edited by Christoph Heilig, J. Thomas Hewitt and Michael F. Bird, 181–204. Wissenschaftliche Untersuchungen zum Neuen Testament 2/413. Tübingen: Mohr Siebeck.

Witherington III, Ben (1997). *The Jesus Quest: The Third Search for the Jew of Nazareth.* 2nd edn. Downers Grove, IL: IVP.

Wright, N. T. (1978a). 'The Paul of History and the Apostle of Faith.' *Tyndale Bulletin* 29: 61–88.

—— (1978b). *The Work of John Frith.* Appleford: Sutton Courtney.

—— (1981). 'The Messiah and the People of God: A Study in Pauline Theology with Particular Reference to the Argument of the Epistle to the Romans.' DPhil Diss., Oxford University.

—— (1991). *The Climax of the Covenant: Christ and the Law in Pauline Theology.* Edinburgh: T&T Clark.

—— (1992). *The New Testament and the People of God.* Christian Origins and the Question of God 1. London: SPCK / Minneapolis, MN: Fortress.

—— (1996). *Jesus and the Victory of God.* Christian Origins and the Question of God 2. London: SPCK / Minneapolis, MN: Fortress.

—— (1997). *What Saint Paul Really Said.* Oxford: Lion.

—— (2000). *The Challenge of Jesus.* London: SPCK.

—— (2001). 'The Law in Romans 2.' In *Paul and the Mosaic Law*, edited by James D. G. Dunn, 131–50. Grand Rapids, MI: Eerdmans.

—— (2002). 'The Letter to the Romans.' In *New Interpreters Bible*, Volume X, edited by Leander E. Keck, 393–770. Nashville, TN: Abingdon.

—— (2003). *The Resurrection of the Son of God.* Christian Origins and the Question of God 3. London: SPCK / Minneapolis, MN: Fortress.

—— (2005). *Paul: Fresh Perspectives.* London: SPCK.

—— (2006a). *Simply Christian: Why Christianity Makes Sense.* New York, NY: HarperOne.

—— (2006b). *The Last Word: Scripture and the Authority of God*. New York, NY: HarperOne.

—— (2006c). 'New Perspectives on Paul.' In *Justification in Perspective: Historical Developments and Contemporary Challenges*, edited by Bruce L. McCormack, 243–64. Grand Rapids, MI: Baker.

—— (2009). *Justification: God's Plan and Paul's Vision*. Downers Grove, IL: IVP.

—— (2011). 'Whence and Whither Historical Jesus Studies in the Life of the Church?' In *Jesus, Paul and the People of God: A Theological Dialogue with N. T. Wright*, edited by Nicholas Perrin and Richard B. Hays, 115–58. Downers Grove, IL: IVP.

—— (2012). *How God Became King*. New York, NY: HarperOne.

—— (2013). *Paul and the Faithfulness of God*. Christian Origins and the Question of God 4. London: SPCK / Minneapolis, MN: Fortress.

—— (2015). *Surprised by Scripture: Engaging Contemporary Issues*. New York, NY: HarperOne.

—— (2016). *The Day the Revolution Began: Reconsidering the Meaning of Jesus' Crucifixion*. San Francisco, CA: HarperOne.

ONE GOD

N. T. Wright's theodicy

MICHAEL LLOYD

Introduction

It is an enormous privilege to be invited to contribute to this Festschrift for N. T. Wright. Tom and I have been friends for over 40 years, now – ever since he was my chaplain, hostel-keeper and supervisor at Downing College, Cambridge. And for all of that time, the problem of evil has been the major occupation of my intellectual life. I studied for my doctorate on 'The Cosmic Fall and the Free Will Defence' at Worcester College, Oxford, where Tom was Chaplain. Indeed, on one occasion, Tom was introducing me to a student from another college, and said to me, 'This is Nick. He's doing physics at Merton.' Then, to Nick, he said, 'This is Michael. He's doing evil at Worcester!' And evil is what I have continued to do. So, when I was asked to contribute to this Festschrift, it was an obvious choice to write about Tom's theodicy.

There is something unfair and anomalous about such an undertaking, as Tom is a biblical scholar rather than a systematic theologian or philosopher. So, in attempting to expound and critique Tom's theodicy, there is a danger of attempting to fit his thought into categories that are alien to it – a bit like trying to outline Einstein's view of Reader Response Theory. Indeed, Tom himself is critical of many theodicies for focusing on suffering as 'a philosophical or logical problem for a good creator, rather than having much to do with the story the Bible actually tells'.[1]

However, though there is a real danger of distorting Tom's thought by asking it to answer questions that are more at home in different disciplines, there is, conversely, much to be gained by bringing the resources – and the reticences – of biblical scholarship to bear on a vital question that cannot be the preserve of any one branch of academic pursuit. It is my hope that the engagement between philosophy, systematic theology and biblical studies that is involved in this critique may serve to bring these disciplines slightly closer together, to enable them to enrich and to

---

[1] Wright 2006, 65.

challenge each other, and to enable them together to shed more light on a question that has troubled not just scholars, but ordinary human beings throughout the millennia of human history.

An exposition of Tom's theodicy

If, as I have suggested elsewhere,[2] responses to the problem of evil within Christian theology may be categorized according to whether they see suffering as instrumental to the purposes of God, inevitable within those purposes or inimical to them, then Tom's writings strongly suggest that he falls in the third of those categories. He is explicitly critical of the view of suffering as instrumental to the purposes of God. In his only book-length (popular-level) treatment of the problem of evil, *Evil and the Justice of God* (Wright 2006), he writes:

> If you offer an analysis of evil which leaves us saying, 'Well, that's alright, then, we now see how it happens and what to do about it', you have belittled the problem. I once heard a leading philosophical theologian trying to do that with Auschwitz, and it was squirmingly embarrassing. We cannot and must not soften the blow; we cannot and must not pretend that evil isn't that bad after all.[3]

And later in the same book, he criticizes the justification of suffering that is characteristic of an instrumental view of suffering:

> We cannot get to the full solution of the problem of evil by mere progress, as though, provided the final generation was happy, the misery of all previous generations could be overlooked or even justified (as in the appalling line in a hymn, 'Then shall they know, they that love him, how all their pain was good', a kind of shoulder-shrugging acquiescence in evil which the New Testament certainly does not authorize).[4]

The New Testament does not – and could not – authorize it because of the divine assault on suffering in the mission and ministry of Jesus. If the One in whom the character of God is most fully seen, and who most fully performs the will of God, is the One through whom 'the blind receive their sight, the lame walk, the lepers are cleansed, the deaf hear, the dead are raised',[5] then Christian theologians have no authority to assert that suffering or death has any necessary, intended or positive place within the

---

2   Lloyd 2018a, 248ff.
3   Wright 2006, 20.
4   Wright 2006, 60.
5   Matthew 11.5, NRSV.

purposes of God. As a New Testament scholar – and, in particular, as a New Testament scholar who intends to allow 'the story the Bible actually tells' to shape our philosophical and theological responses to the problem of evil – Tom finds himself constrained by the contours of the ministry (and lordship) of Jesus. As a pastor, he is also aware of the pastoral dangers of pretending 'that evil isn't that bad after all'. Not only is such talk glib and 'squirmingly embarrassing', but it also tends to make God the inflictor of people's pain rather than its sharer and fellow victim. The view of suffering as instrumental to the purposes of God tends to make God seem the enemy of the sufferer. As Nicholas Wolterstorff writes in his *Lament for a Son*, after the death of his son in a climbing accident: 'What do you say to someone who is suffering? Some people are gifted with words of wisdom. For such, one is profoundly grateful. There were many such for us.' (Tom has been one such, for me, on countless occasions.)

> But not all are gifted in that way. Some blurted out strange, inept things. That's OK too. Your words don't have to be wise. The heart that speaks is heard more than the words spoken. And if you can't think of anything at all to say, just say, 'I can't think of anything to say. But I want you to know that we are with you in your grief.' Or, even, just embrace . . . But please: Don't say that it's not really so bad. Because it is. Death is awful. Demonic . . . I know: People do sometimes think things are more awful than they really are. Such people need to be corrected – gently, eventually. But no one thinks that death is more awful than it is. It's those who think it's not so bad that need correcting.[6]

This is Wolterstorff's pastoral protest against the instrumental view of suffering, and it is one that Tom clearly joins him in – on Christological and pastoral grounds.[7]

Tom nowhere, to my knowledge, comments upon the view of suffering as inevitable within the purposes of God. But his protest against the instrumental view of suffering, taken together with a strong eschatological conviction (and the high commitment to God's omnipotence that alone can sustain such a conviction), would find itself in great tension with any view of suffering as inevitable. Indeed, his attack on 'acquiescence in evil' fits more comfortably within a view of suffering as inimical to the

---

6   Wolterstorff 1989, 34–5.
7   At least, he joins in the protest against suffering, and against death *in its current form*. He leaves open the possibility that death might have had a natural and unproblematic occurrence within an unfallen context: 'Death, which we may be right to see as a natural and harmless feature of the original landscape, now assumes the unwelcome guise of the executioner' (Wright 2006, 28).

purposes of God than within a view of suffering as either instrumental or inevitable.

If suffering is inimical to the purposes of God, then it follows that he must have intended a world that was free of suffering. If, when we see him most clearly and personally at work, we see him assaulting suffering and death; and if he is committed to the ultimate overcoming and eradication of suffering and death, then it would be odd for him to have built them in to his creation in the first place.[8] In other words, Christology and eschatology commit one to a doctrine of the Fall, and this is what would appear to be Tom's position:

> I regard the main function of postmodernity, under God, to be the preaching of the doctrine of the Fall (the truth of a deep and fatal flaw within human nature) to the modernist, post-eighteenth century arrogance that supposes it has solved the world's problems.[9]

The doctrine of the Fall, however, is saying more than that there is 'a deep and fatal flaw within human nature'. It is saying that there is a gap between how creation is and how it was intended to be in the purposes of the Creator. If there is no such gap, then it would seem difficult to escape the conclusion that that deep and fatal flaw is a design fault for which the Creator bears some culpability.[10] And if there is no such gap, then the natural processes that are the occasion for the pain and suffering of sentient beings would seem to be so enmeshed with the purposes of God as to compromise the goodness of God. If the natural processes are largely as God intended them to be, then it is hard to account for the divine assault upon the suffering they occasion, which we see in the healing ministry of Jesus. And it would be correspondingly hard to defend the goodness of the

---

8   One attempt to resist this argument is the view that moral choice and character require pain and threat and danger in order to give opportunities for compassion, fortitude and courage. Tom (rightly, in my view) rejects this: 'Various writers have suggested . . . that God allows evil because it creates the special conditions in which virtue can flourish. The thought that God decided to permit Auschwitz because some heroes would emerge is hardly a solution to the problem' (Wright 2006, 11).

9   Wright 2006, 14.

10 It would, of course, be possible to come up with a purely anthropological account of how human beings developed a deep and fatal flaw within their own nature: as Tom suggests, postmodernity has done precisely that. But so interconnected are the physical, environmental, psychological and moral dimensions of the evolved human condition that it would be much harder to come up with such an account that was compatible with a Christian doctrine of creation, providence and the goodness of God.

God who deliberately set up those processes against the charge inherent within the atheologian's argument from evil.[11]

But if there is a gap between how creation is and how it was intended to be in the creational purposes of God, then by what event, events or processes did such a gap come about? And here, Tom is hesitant to give an answer. Here, his reticence as a biblical scholar holds him back. He points out that the *locus classicus* of the Fall story, Genesis 3, does not give us the help we need at this point:

> We all want to know what the story refuses to tell us: why there was a snake in God's beautiful creation in the first place, and why it wanted to use its cunning in that way. Instead of giving us an explanation for evil, the story gives us a brief analysis of it . . . The narrative then tells us once more what God does about it.[12]

In other words, he suggests that the purpose of the story is descriptive rather than explanatory, paradigmatic rather than aetiological. He reinforces this finding (or, rather, this *unfinding*) later in the book: 'I have also ruled out, to the disappointment (I fear) of some, any immediate prospect of finding an answer to the question of where evil came from in the first place, and what it's doing within God's good creation.'[13]

He mitigates that disappointment in two ways. First, he insists that the biblical narrative is more focused on what God does (and will do) about evil than on where it came from. As a good Wittgensteinian and a responsible biblical scholar, whereof he finds that he cannot speak, thereof he thinks it better to remain silent. And he defends his disappointing absence of answer at this point by reference to the contours of biblical theodicy. In contrast to the speculative tendencies of some philosophers and theologians, he considers it better to be constrained by 'the story the Bible actually tells'.

Second, he justifies this reticence by reference, not just to biblical reticence, but to our inability to understand any answer that might be given:

> We are not told, or not in any way that satisfies our puzzled questioning, how and why there is radical evil within God's wonderful, beautiful and essentially good creation. One day I think we shall find out, but I believe

---

11 This – and, indeed, the whole of this and the preceding paragraph – assumes, of course, that we are unconvinced (as I and, I think, Tom are unconvinced) by the views of suffering as instrumental and inevitable. See my two chapters in *Finding Ourselves after Darwin* (Lloyd 2018a; 2018b), and my doctoral thesis on 'The Cosmic Fall and the Free Will Defence' (Lloyd 1997) for a fuller critique of these approaches.

12 Wright 2006, 27.

13 Wright 2006, 88.

that we are incapable of understanding it at the moment, in the same way that a baby in the womb would lack the categories to think about the outside world. What we are promised, however, is that God will make a world in which all shall be well, and all manner of thing shall be well . . .[14]

Here, Tom's position is significantly in line with a mainstream movement in philosophical theodicy, namely what is known as 'Skeptical Theism'.[15] He develops this point in his more recent book, *Paul and the Faithfulness of God*, in the section on 'Jewish Monotheism and the Problem of Evil'. After a brief summary of different responses to the problem of evil within Second Temple Jewish monotheism, Tom writes:

> To repeat, none of these approaches attempts to explain why there is evil in the first place within the good creation of the wise creator. They are all ways of articulating the tension, not of resolving it. They are ways, in fact, of saying that there is something absurd about evil, something out of joint, something that doesn't fit. *The fact that one cannot really understand evil is itself an element of creational monotheism*, a demonstration that evil is an intruder, a force not only bent on distorting and destroying the good creation but also on resisting comprehension. If one could understand it, if one could glimpse a framework within which it 'made sense', it would no longer be the radical, anti-creation, anti-God force it actually is.[16]

Putting this side by side with a quotation from Alvin Plantinga will point up the similarities of thought between Tom and the Skeptical Theistic tradition here:

> Is there any reason to think that if God *did* have a reason for a given evil, we would be the first to know? Is there any reason to think we could even grasp His reason, if He proposed to tell us what it was? . . . Nothing much follows from the fact that some evils are inscrutable; if theism is true we would expect there would be inscrutable evil. Indeed, it is only *hubris* which would tempt us to think that we could so much as grasp God's plans here, even if He proposed to divulge them to us.[17]

---

[14] Wright 2006, 108. Note again how, though Tom finds that we cannot speak of where evil came from, and gives a reason as to why that may inevitably be the case, he finds that he can speak of what God has done, is doing and will do to rectify, reconcile and heal.

[15] I use the US spelling of 'skeptical' because I judge that this philosophical tradition is most adopted among American philosophers. It is fair to point out that most skeptical theists take the view of suffering as instrumental to the purposes of God. They see suffering as in some way necessary or beneficial but claim that we cannot know what that necessity or benefit is. Tom's skepticism falls, I suggest, within an overall view of suffering as inimical to the purposes of God.

[16] Wright 2013, 742 (emphasis original).

[17] This quotation is taken from the printed handout accompanying Alvin Plantinga's 1988

Thus far, we have seen that Tom's writing on the problem of evil coincides most easily with the view of suffering as inimical to the purposes of God. I have suggested that the inimical view of suffering requires a doctrine of the Fall. And we have noted that Tom is reticent about articulating such a doctrine, or, indeed, any account of where evil came from in the first place, and that he justifies that reticence both biblically and philosophically. Thus far, he fits into reasonably standard and recognizable traditions of theodical enquiry. However, he does not leave us with a complete absence of argument and articulation. He does offer his own version of (something like) a Fall narrative, which is original and intriguing. It centres around the Pauline concept of the Principalities and Powers. These are sometimes interpreted as references to demonic beings, and sometimes as references to unjust human structures. Tom's approach finds something of a middle way between these two interpretative traditions:

> When we humans commit idolatry, worshipping that which is not God as if it were, we thereby give to other creatures and beings in the cosmos a power, a prestige, an authority over us which *we*, under God, were supposed to have over *them*. When you worship an idol, whatever it is, you abdicate something of your own proper human authority over the world, and give it to that thing, whatever it is, calling into being a negative force, an anti-God force, a force which is opposed to creation . . .[18]

He seems to suggest that the Principalities and Powers, which interfere oppressively and destructively in human affairs, are the by-products of human idolatry. He seems to suggest that when 'Humans, instead of worshipping God as the source of their life, give allegiance to the non-human creation', two consequences follow. First, 'The earth, instead of being ruled wisely by God-fearing, image-bearing stewards, shares the curse for the sake of idolatrous humankind.' And second, 'Death, which we may be right to see as a natural and harmless feature of the original landscape, now assumes the unwelcome guise of executioner'.[19]

So our idolatry distorts the way we treat the world and the way we see the world, poisoning both our environment and our experience. That is the particularly distinctive contribution Tom has made to theodical discussion. What are we to make of it?

Wilde lectures.
[18] Wright 2006, 71–2.
[19] Wright 2006, 28.

A critique of Tom's theodicy

There is much to welcome. I have already argued that Tom's biblical and (therefore) Christological commitment and his pastoral sensitivity drive him to reject two broad approaches to the problem of evil which are commonly held and which have many significant academic advocates, but which raise serious intellectual difficulties for the goodness of God, and serious pastoral difficulties for the sufferer. His determination to address these age-old issues in the light of 'the story the Bible actually tells' lends his writing in this area a refreshingly confident Christocentricity at which many Christian philosophers and theologians tend to baulk.[20] Any attempt to give an account of evil and suffering that attributes their causality to a creature rather than to the Creator – and that is the task of any theodicy that sees suffering as inimical to the purposes of God – is going to have to be in narratival form, because creatures are historical and geographical beings; and Tom's narrative is the stronger for drawing on the original vocation of human beings to be image-bearing stewards of creation. Because of his robust trust in the historicity of the resurrection of Jesus,[21] Tom is happy to place weight upon God's soteriological, providential and eschatological assault upon evil and suffering, thus displaying an exemplary commitment to a necessary element in any satisfactory theodicy.

The clusters of questions that I wish to pose to Tom regarding his theodical writings are a testimony to the stimulating and provocative nature of his thinking in this area, as in so many others. The first cluster of questions is a request for clarification rather than a criticism: how does Tom's conception of the Powers relate to angels? Is it intended to replace all that was previously included within the category of the demonic? And if so, is the category of the angelic still operative or is it now defunct? Immediately after outlining his distinctive conception of how idolatry calls into being a negative force, Tom writes this:

---

20 Witness the chapter in the middle – and at the heart – of Wright 2006 entitled 'Evil and the Crucified God'. Tom, unlike many, is not afraid to give an explicitly and unapologetically Christian response to the problem of evil, and not a merely theistic one. Some Christian theodicists, especially philosophers, eschew any specifically Christian responses to the problem of evil on the grounds that Christian theism is more complex than 'mere' theism, and therefore logically less probable. I hope in my forthcoming book (with the working title, *The Evil of Suffering and the Goodness of God*) to argue that group conglomerations of propositions (such as make up a worldview) need to be weighed differently from single propositions probabilistically – or no worldview could ever be evaluated as being epistemologically warranted.

21 See Wright 2003.

This is why I think there is at least a grain of truth in the theory made famous by Walter Wink, that the inner or hidden forces latent within organizations, companies, societies, legislative bodies and even churches are the sum total of the spiritual energies which human beings have put into them, abdicating their own responsibility and allowing the organization, whatever it is, to have it instead. I believe there is more to it than that, but not less.[22]

In his trilogy on the Powers, Wink stated his belief that 'what people in the world of the Bible experienced and called "Principalities and Powers" was in fact real. They were discerning the actual spirituality at the center of the political, economic, and cultural institutions of their day.'[23] However, because they lacked the conceptuality and language which would have enabled them to identify that spirituality as the 'withinness' of power structures within their worldview, they projected it out into the heavenly realms as spiritual beings and cosmic forces. Now, we should 'withdraw that projection from on high and locate it in the institution in which it really resides.'[24]

Wink grounds his interpretation of the angelic upon the angels of the nations (based on Deuteronomy 32, Daniel 10—12 and Psalm 82), the angels of the churches (based on Revelation 1—3) and the angels of nature (about which he accepts that 'The Bible itself says very little').[25] On the whole phenomenon of angelophany, however, or the biblical narrative traditions of angel as messenger, comforter, interpreter, worshipper, intercessor or liberator/protector, Wink has nothing to say. To the extent that he is offering us an exegetical analysis of the biblical language of angels, his hypothesis will not be convincing until it can be shown to save all the phenomena. To the extent that he is offering us a reinterpretation or translation of that language into the worldview and thought forms of a different age, it will not be convincing until either he shows us that it can include all the different usages of that language, or he offers us a different way of understanding those usages that he has not so far addressed *and* gives us some indication as to why it is not arbitrary to offer different interpretations of the same language.

Tom seems to acknowledge the selectivity and limitation of Wink's exegesis when he (Tom) writes, 'I believe there is more to it than that, but not less.'[26] It seems churlish to ask someone who has already written

---

22 Wright 2006, 72.
23 Wink 1992, 6.
24 Wink 1992, 8.
25 See Wink 1986.
26 Wright 2006, 72.

a 1,700-page book on Paul to expand on anything, but, were he ever to revisit this area, it would be helpful to know the nature of that 'more', and how he thinks the negative force brought into being by idolatry relates to the evil spirits of the Gospels – and to the whole area of the angelic.

The second cluster of questions relates to the problem of natural evil *before* the evolution of human beings. If suffering is neither instrumental to the purposes of God nor inevitable within them but inimical to them, what account may we give of why suffering, death, disease, disaster and predation plagued the animal world prior to the emergence of hominids who were morally aware enough to be held morally accountable? The pain, suffering and destruction of the natural order is a significant moral issue for the Christian theologian because 'The cross reveals God as the one who lays down His life that others might live', whereas 'the natural world is one in which animals kill others that they themselves might live. The movement of the one in reckless self-giving is in a totally different direction from the movement of the other in ruthless self-preservation.'[27]

Now, it is, of course, perfectly acceptable for anyone to remain agnostic on this issue. And it is perfectly appropriate for a biblical scholar to be reticent at this point. However, if there were a different Fall narrative that were able to give an account of why a world created by the God we meet in the crucified Christ might operate on the principle of ruthless self-preservation, that different Fall narrative might, all other things being equal, be seen as a more explanatorily satisfactory hypothesis than one which remains silent at such a critical point. I want to argue that there is indeed such a Fall narrative, and that it is indeed more explanatorily satisfactory.

Third, and last, how, if the Powers are the product of an idolatrous worship of that which is not God, can Paul speak of them being reconciled? If a power is 'a negative force, an anti-God force, a force which is opposed to creation' brought into being by idolatry, we could understand why it might need to be defeated and disarmed (Colossians 2.15), but how could it be reconciled (Colossians 1.20)? What is there that is good about such an anti-God force? What would be left of an anti-God force if it were reconciled to God? There would seem to be nothing good about its engenderment (in idolatrous worship), nor about its (anti-God and anti-creation) operation. What is being posited here is not something created good that chose by its own free will to oppose the person and will of its Maker: what is being posited here is something that had no existence prior

---

to its being engendered by and into negativity. If a human being worships the moon, say, what he or she worships is of course something good. But there is nothing good about the idolatry, and there is nothing good about the negative power that is thereby brought into being. It is therefore difficult to see how a power (understood in the way Tom seems to understand it) would or could be reconciled to God.

Concluding remarks

I want, in closing, to suggest that there is a way of taking up some of the insights of Tom's position into a hypothesis that has exegetical coherence, explanatory power and internal consistency. I want to suggest that a more traditional understanding of the angelic and the demonic (as beings that are not dependent upon us for their existence) circumvents some of the difficulties inherent in Tom's position.

In Luke's temptation narrative, the devil shows Jesus all the kingdoms of the world, and says to him: 'To you I will give their glory and all this authority; for it has been given over to me'.[28] It is interesting that Jesus does not demur from that assertion. It is generally assumed that it is God who has handed over the kingdoms of the world and their glory to the devil. However, for God to have given over the kingdoms of the world into the hands of a malicious power would be problematic in the extreme. And here, Tom's insight that 'When we humans commit idolatry, worshipping that which is not God as if it were, we thereby give to other creatures and beings in the cosmos a power, a prestige, an authority over us which *we*, under God, were supposed to have over *them*'[29] comes into its own. We, by our idolatry and our sinfulness, have given these malicious forces an operational scope that they would not otherwise have had – but (I want to insist, *pace* Tom) we have not thereby given them existence.

To establish that this more traditional understanding of the angelic and demonic has exegetical coherence is clearly beyond the scope of this paper. I have not even answered the question I put to Tom as to the relation between these categories and that of the Principalities and Powers. It will have to suffice here to suggest that a traditional understanding of the angelic and demonic as spiritual beings created by God and not dependent upon us for their existence faces fewer challenges interpreting the Pauline passages regarding the Principalities and Powers than a Winkian or

---

[28] Luke 4.5–6, NRSV.
[29] Wright 2006, 71.

a Wrightian view has interpreting the full range of biblical traditions regarding angels and demons.

Second, I have claimed that this more traditional view (now incorporating Tom's insights) has greater explanatory power than does Tom's Powers Engendered by Human Idolatry hypothesis. If the Powers are the unintended by-products of human idolatry, then they cannot be held accountable for the violent competitiveness of the natural order that preceded the evolution of humanity. If, however, a more traditional view is taken of the creation and fall of the angelic realm, then it is possible that to the disruption of that angelic rebellion may be ascribed the disordered and divided state of the natural world.[30] Such a view enables us to see suffering as inimical to the purposes of God because it ascribes the cause of that suffering not to the will or incompetence of the Creator but to the will of creatures. It enables us to take full account of the fact of evolution, without requiring us to see the inherent suffering and violence of the evolutionary process as the divinely chosen means of creating. It enables us to help sufferers to see God, not as the inflictor, but as the sharer and antagonist of their suffering. It enables us to see the activity of God as consistent – instead of having to see God assaulting in Christ what he built in to his creation.

Third, I have claimed that this more traditional view has more internal consistency than Tom's Powers Engendered by Human Idolatry hypothesis. See the Powers as spiritual beings[31] created good and existing independently of us; see them as having voluntarily declined from that relationship with God (and that care for creation) for which they were made; see them as remaining ontologically good but becoming morally bad – and one can see why the God who hates nothing that he has made would die to achieve their reconciliation (*qua* ontologically good and loved creatures) and their disarming and defeat (*qua* their anti-God and anti-creation activity). In short, if they were the intended and loved and ontologically good creatures of God who have turned away from that Love and that Goodness, we may understand why he might labour to win them back. But if they were the unintended by-products of human idolatry, it is difficult to know what their reconciliation might mean.

---

[30] See my chapter (Lloyd 2018b) for a fuller exposition of this position.

[31] I do not intend to deny that Paul's term 'Principalities and Powers' may refer to human powers and forces as well as to 'spiritual' forces, any more than Tom's suggestion that the powers are engendered by human idolatry is intended to deny that they may include human powers and forces (not least of an imperial nature). It is merely intended to show that, in any mix of human and 'spiritual' powers, the latter are better understood as existing by divine intention, independently of human beings.

It may be that Tom has been moving slightly in this direction himself. In his more recent work on the problem of evil, Tom wrote with a different emphasis: 'Paul's robust monotheism allowed fully for the fact of rebellious non-human "powers", luring humans into idolatry and hence into collusion with their anti-creational and anti-human purposes.'[32] Here, the rebellious non-human powers are luring humans into idolatry, rather than being themselves the by-product of that idolatry. They pre-exist human idolatry, and are therefore available as potential causes of pre-human brokenness and suffering.

The questions I have asked of Tom's theodicy are minor: my debt to him theologically, pastorally and personally is immense. When I lived in the hostel of which he was hostel-keeper, I obtained an exciting theological education, and all Tom and Maggie got in return was an occasional chocolate mousse! I am deeply grateful to them both for four decades of friendship.

Bibliography

Lloyd, Michael (1997). 'The Cosmic Fall and the Free Will Defence.' DPhil Diss., Oxford University.

—— (1998). 'Are Animals Fallen?' In *Animals on the Agenda*, edited by Andrew Linzey and Dorothy Yamamoto, 147–60. London: SCM.

—— (2018a). 'Theodicy, Fall and Adam.' In *Finding Ourselves after Darwin: Conversations on the Image of God, Original Sin, and the Problem of Evil*, edited by Stanley P. Rosenberg. Grand Rapids, MI: Baker.

—— (2018b). 'The Fallenness of Nature: Three Non-Human Suspects.' In *Finding Ourselves after Darwin: Conversations on the Image of God, Original Sin, and the Problem of Evil*, edited by Stanley P. Rosenberg. Grand Rapids, MI: Baker.

—— (forthcoming). *The Evil of Suffering and the Goodness of God.*.

Wink, Walter (1986). *Unmasking the Powers: The Invisible Forces That Determine Human Existence*. The Powers 2. Philadelphia, PA: Fortress.

—— (1992). *Engaging the Powers: Discernment and Resistance in a World of Domination*. The Powers 1. Reprint edition. Minneapolis, MN: Fortress.

Wolterstorff, Nicholas (1989). *Lament for a Son*. London: Spire, Hodder and Stoughton (first published: Grand Rapids, MI: Eerdmans, 1987).

Wright, N. T. (2003). *The Resurrection of the Son of God*. Christian Origins and the Question of God 3. London: SPCK / Minneapolis, MN: Fortress.

—— (2006). *Evil and the Justice of God*. London: SPCK.

—— (2013). *Paul and the Faithfulness of God*. Christian Origins and the Question of God 4. London: SPCK / Minneapolis, MN: Fortress.

---

[32] Wright 2013, 771.

The human face of God: God and the Christology of the New Testament[1]

JAMES D. G. DUNN

Christology began with the impact made by Jesus of Nazareth on his disciples. The impact made by Jesus' resurrection – that is, the otherwise inexplicable conviction that God had not only vindicated the crucified Jesus but had begun the resurrection of the dead with Jesus – that was the most powerful impact. But Jesus had already made life-changing impact on his disciples during his mission. That was why they had left everything to follow him. That was why the memories of his life and teaching, the Jesus tradition which makes up the Synoptic Gospels, remained fundamental for their belief in the risen and exalted Christ.[2] The principal building blocks of this Christology can be sketched in fairly easily and perhaps in chronological sequence.

Probably the basic Christological conviction of the first disciples was that Jesus was *God's son*. The two principal contributory factors would have been:

- The growing belief that Jesus was God's Messiah, the son of David of whom God had said, 'I will be a father to him, and he shall be a son to me' (2 Samuel 7.14). Psalm 2.7 also provided the direct link: God says to his anointed, 'You are my son; today I have begotten you.' There is sufficient evidence in Hebrews and Acts[3] that these were texts which fed into earliest Christology. And the creedal confession on which Paul was able to draw at the beginning of his letter to Rome (Romans 1.3–4)

---

1 This lecture was originally delivered at the International Biblical Congress, in Seville, Spain, in September 2009. It had never been published, and I was wondering what to do with it when the invitation came to contribute to Tom Wright's Festschrift. Since the essay/lecture seemed to fit well with the planned volume, and since it accords so well with one of Tom's principal concerns in regard to the NT, it was an obvious solution to offer it to Tom with warmest congratulations and all good wishes.
2 This is one of the principal theses of my *Jesus Remembered* (Dunn 2003).
3 Hebrews 1.5; 5.5; Acts 13.33. Bible quotations in this chapter are either taken from the NRSV or are my own.

confirms that Jesus as both son of David and son of God was a firmly established belief among first-generation Christians.[4]

- Not to be neglected is the other contributory factor: that Jesus was remembered as distinctive in his prayer life by his address to God as 'Abba, Father'. The root within the Synoptic tradition of Jesus' mission could be stronger (Mark 14.36), but it is clear from Paul's letters[5] that the 'Abba' prayer was experienced by the first Christians as an echoing of the prayer so distinctive of Jesus and proof that they shared in his sonship before God.[6]

Now, of course, to describe someone as a son of God could be just a way of expressing the richness of the divine favour enjoyed by that person – a king, or a philosopher, or a righteous man.[7] But from the beginning Jesus' sonship was perceived to be something unique. Jesus' parable of vineyard tenants already spoke of a 'beloved son' in distinction from the earlier servants (Mark 12.6). The divine sonship which the believers shared with Christ was derivative, by adoption (Romans 8.15–17; Galatians 4.4–5). And the early talk that God sent his Son (Galatians 4.4) already carried the implication of the Johannine *monogenēs*, 'the one and only' Son of God.[8] It is hardly surprising, then, that the designation of Jesus as God's son, the Son of God, remained at the root of Christology, the most common way of conceptualizing and expressing the relation between God and Jesus, including the risen and exalted Jesus. Nor is it surprising that the classic Christian creeds made 'Son of God' the primary title for Jesus. It is just this extra implication, 'the one and only Son of God', to which Islam reacts so strongly in its insistence that 'God has no son.' It is just the extra implications of the talk of Jesus as Son of God, the implications for monotheism, for the fundamental dogma that God is one, which we will have to explore in this essay.

A second fundamental building block in the beginnings of Christology is the confession that 'Jesus is *Lord*', an assertion which may well have been the earliest baptismal confession (Romans 10.9). The conviction that Jesus had been exalted to heaven and had been seated at God's right hand, that

---

4 Note also the assumption in the record of Jesus' hearing before Caiaphas in the latter's question: 'Are you the Christ, the Son of the Blessed?' (Mark 14.61).
5 Romans 8.15–17; Galatians 4.6–7.
6 See further Dunn 2003, §16.2.
7 Details in Dunn 1989, §§3.2–3.
8 John 1.14, 18; 3.16, 18; 1 John 4.9. Jesus as the Son sent by the Father is a regular theme in John's Gospel.

is, presumably on the heavenly throne next to God's,[9] was certainly part of the impact of Jesus' resurrection. Here Psalm 110.1 undoubtedly played a significant role: 'The LORD said to my Lord, "Sit at my right hand, until I make your enemies your footstool."' The frequency with which this passage is quoted or referred to in the NT is clear enough evidence that it was one of the scriptures on which the earliest Christians most reflected;[10] it was the justification for their claim that God had made Jesus Lord (Acts 2.36).

Complications became apparent, since the word for 'Lord' was *kyrios*, and this was the Greek term used in the LXX when the reference of the Hebrew Bible was to YHWH. And the first Christians did not hesitate to use some of the YHWH texts in reference to Jesus. A notable instance is Romans 10.9–13, where the quotation from Joel 3.5 (LXX), 'Everyone who calls upon the name of the Lord shall be saved' (Romans 10.13), is referred to the Jesus confessed as Lord in the preceding verses (10.9). And more striking is Philippians 2.10–11, where one of the most emphatic asser-tions of monotheism, 'I am God, and there is no other . . . "To me every knee shall bow, every tongue shall swear"' (Isaiah 45.22–23), is drawn on to describe the heavenly acclamation of Jesus: 'At the name of Jesus every knee shall bend . . . and every tongue confess that Jesus Christ is Lord'.

So, even more than the description of Jesus as the Son of God, the confession that Jesus is Lord was bound to raise questions for the more fundamental confession that God is one. How quickly, we may wonder, did the first Christians realize that their beliefs about Jesus were becoming a challenge to the monotheism they had inherited from early Judaism?

A third building block was the application of language used of divine *Wisdom* in reference to Jesus. The clearest example is Hebrews 1.2–4, where God's Son is described as 'a reflection/radiance [*apaugasma*] of God's glory and an exact representation [*charaktēr*] of God's real being'. *Apaugasma* is used in only one other passage in biblical literature, in a description of Wisdom as 'a reflection/radiance of eternal light' (Wisdom 7.26). And *charaktēr* is one of the terms used by Philo in speaking of the divine Logos: 'the reasonable soul . . . [is] signed and impressed by the seal of God, the stamp [*charaktēr*] of which is the eternal Word' (Philo, *Plant.* 18).[11] For

---

9 The plural 'thrones' in Daniel's vision (Daniel 7.9) inevitably provoked speculation as to who the other throne was for.
10 Acts 2.34–35; Romans 8.34; 1 Corinthians 15.25; Ephesians 1.20; Colossians 3.1; Hebrews 1.3, 13; 8.1; 10.12; 12.2; 1 Peter 3.22. Mark 12.36 pars and 14.62 pars suggest that reflection on the significance of Psalm 110.1 began before Jesus' crucifixion, and may even have played a part in Jesus' condemnation. See further Dunn 2009, 218–21 (with Bibliography).
11 See the brief discussion and notes in Attridge 1989, 42–4.

Philo Word and Wisdom were alternative ways of saying that God acts upon his creation through or as Word/Wisdom, that the unknowable/unapproachable God is knowable through or as Word/Wisdom. The divine Wisdom/Word is God himself insofar as he may be known by humankind.[12] The writer of Hebrews draws on the same line of thought: God's Son is the climactic and clearest expression of God, the way in which God can be known as fully as it is possible for humankind to know God.

A distinctive feature of Wisdom language is talk of Wisdom as the divine agency through which God created the world. Proverbs, the Wisdom of Solomon and Philo all speak of Wisdom as the means by which God founded the earth, fashioned what exists and brought the universe to completion.[13] It is hardly surprising that Hebrews draws on the same thought in its acclamation of the Son in its opening sentence, the Son 'through whom he [God] also created the worlds' (Hebrews 1.2). Paul draws on the same Wisdom language when he speaks of the 'one Lord, Jesus Christ, through whom are all things and through whom we exist' (1 Corinthians 8.6). Similarly the letter to Colossae: 'all things have been created through him and for him' (Colossians 1.16). And in the prologue to John's Gospel the same is said of the divine Word: 'All things came into being through him, and without him not one thing came into being' (John 1.3). Although John focuses on the Word, it is generally recognized that the prologue draws more heavily on the traditions about Wisdom, including the echo of *1 Enoch* 42.2, that 'Wisdom went forth to make her dwelling among the children of men, and found no dwelling place' (cf. John 1.11).[14]

From where came the impulse to use Wisdom/Word language of Jesus? It is likely that Jesus referred to himself, on one occasion at least, as a child of Wisdom. In response to the criticisms made of the different lifestyles of himself and John the Baptist, Jesus evidently concluded that, 'Wisdom is justified by all her children' (Luke 7.35) – both the Baptist and Jesus as Wisdom's children. This is one of the points at which Matthew, taking up the same tradition, transformed it into what reads much more like an identification of Jesus as Wisdom (Matthew 11.19).[15] Is Matthew's transmutation of 'child of Wisdom' to Wisdom herself in reference to Jesus an indication of how earliest Christian thought about Jesus developed?

---

12 See further Dunn 1989, 220–8.
13 Proverbs 3.19; 8.27–30; Wisdom 8.4–6; Philo, *Det.* 54; *Her.* 188.
14 Dunn 1989, 164–5, 239–43.
15 'Yet Wisdom is justified by all her deeds' (Matthew 11.19), echoing Matthew's preface to the following group of sayings by referring to 'the deeds of the Christ' (11.2). See further Dunn 1989, 197–206.

Another factor may have been the natural progression that Jesus as the unique Son of God, and as the Lord at God's right hand, was, of course, also understood as God's representative, the one who represented God most fully. But that was precisely the function of Wisdom and Word language. It is not irrelevant here to note that in each of the principal expressions of earliest Wisdom Christology, it is taken for granted that there is a close link between these different Christological themes: the Wisdom language is explicitly used of the Son and of the one who now sits 'at the right hand of the Majesty on high' (Hebrews 1.2–13); it is 'the *Lord* Jesus Christ' through whom all things came to be (1 Corinthians 8.6); it is God's beloved Son through whom all things have been created (Colossians 1.13, 16); and the Fourth Gospel's Word Christology is wholly absorbed into the far more dominant Son Christology of the subsequent chapters.

We may deduce, then, that it was the growing realization that Jesus had revealed God to them in a unique and climactic way which caused his first disciples to reach for language adequate to express his significance. Jesus had not only been a messenger from God, a representative of God. It was not simply that God had been acting in and through Christ. It was much more: 'In him God in all his fullness dwells in bodily form' (Colossians 2.9). The language used most effectively to speak of God's knowability, of God's interaction with his creation and with his people, was quickly seen to be the appropriate language to use of Christ. Christ embodied God in saving outreach to his human creation; Christ had embodied what was knowable of God, making the invisible God visible.

If this suggested outline of the progression of earliest Christology is any-where near the mark, then a fourth factor or stage should be recognized. This is the emergence of the explicit thought of Jesus as the *incarnation* of God's *Word*: 'the Word became flesh and lived among us' (John 1.14). Whether we should speak of the thought of incarnation as implicit in earlier formulations, as in Colossians 2.9, is of little importance. What does matter, and what is clear in the Johannine prologue, is that before the end of the first century, within two generations of Jesus' mission, Jesus had been hailed as the incarnation of the Word, of the Word who 'was with God' and 'was God', through whom all things came into being (John 1.1–3).

Here, however, we must express ourselves carefully, particularly in ref-erence to the *pre-existence* of Jesus. John 1.14 states explicitly that Jesus was the man whom the Word *became*. The Incarnation was an event in history, to be dated to about 6 BCE. It would therefore not be accurate to say that the earlier verses of the Johannine prologue referred to Jesus as such. They refer to the Word which became flesh, which became the man

Jesus. Of course, it is quite natural for Jesus subsequently in the Gospel to speak in first-person terms of his pre-incarnation status, when, for example, in his prayer to the Father he speaks of 'the glory that I had in your presence before the world existed' (17.5). But to be accurate, that was the Logos speaking, not the incarnate Logos, not Jesus of Nazareth. We can of course speak of the pre-existent Logos, but we cannot so speak properly of Jesus as pre-existent, unless we mean that the Incarnation pre-existed the Incarnation. But the Incarnation was an event in time. So we cannot speak of the Incarnation as pre-existent.

The same is presumably true in reference to the earliest talk of Jesus as Lord. As there was a 'becoming' of what had not been the case before in regard to the Word becoming flesh, so we should speak of a 'becoming' in regard to Jesus as Lord. If the Incarnation can be dated historically to about 6 BCE, so Jesus' exaltation to the right hand of God should presumably be dated to about 30 CE. Of course the same casualness of language naturally results in talk of the *Lord* Jesus Christ as the one through whom God created all things. But a more accurate expression would be to say that it was that very creative, redemptive action and outreach of God which came to bodily expression in Jesus Christ.

And the same is probably true in regard to the earliest talk of Jesus as God's Son. Both Wisdom and Word were thought of as God's 'firstborn',[16] the Word as God's Son, God's 'elder Son' as Philo described the Logos (*Immut.* 31–2). As such, the language of pre-existence could be used of both Wisdom and Word. They were the self-expression of the pre-existent God. But again in application to Jesus such language has to be used more circumspectly. The linguistic problem is that the imagery of giving birth only really works when the birth is an event in time. The early Fathers resolved the problem by speaking of the 'eternal generation' of the Son. But the two words put together, 'eternal' and 'generation', extend the imagery of giving birth to breaking point. And the imagery of 'eternal generation' can only work in regard to the Word, the divine Logos. It can hardly be applied to the birth of Jesus of Nazareth, in effect provoking imagery of Mary in perpetual, eternal labour! So, once again, any talk of the son of Mary as such as pre-existent confuses rather than clarifies the thought of incarnation.

In short, pre-existence belongs only to God, because God alone is Creator, so God alone pre-exists creation. We should have no difficulty in speaking of divine Wisdom and Logos as pre-existent – because Wisdom/Logos are ways of speaking of God in action, in creation, in revelation, in

---

16 Proverbs 8.22, 25; Philo, *Agr.* 51; *Conf.* 146; *QG* 4.97.

redemption. Jesus, however, is the eternal Logos become flesh in time. To speak too lightly of Jesus as pre-existent is to undermine the very concept of 'incarnation', losing, indeed, something vital in the uniqueness of Jesus, the incarnate Word, as God's revelation of himself in a particular historical time and place.

How does all this bear on our overarching question, the question of God and Christology – the question of how the earliest Christology affects Christian understanding of God, the question of whether such Christology is or can be consistent with monotheism – the question, indeed, whether Christianity is really a monotheistic religion?

A good starting point in dealing with such questions is the recollection that Israel's and early Judaism's understanding of God was by no means simple in itself. The very basic assertion of Israel's faith, that idolatry is false worship, that God is not visible, not image-able, is beyond imagination, is sufficient to remind us that Israel's perception of God went well beyond mere imagery, mere words, recognizing that God is in the last analysis indescribable, or describable only in inadequate analogies and images. The very fact that the name by which God revealed himself to Moses in Exodus 3.14 is a name which we do not really know how to pronounce, the Tetragrammaton YHWH/Yahweh(?), tells us something about Israel's understanding of God's self-revelation which we should not ignore. Similarly, the fact that the Tetragrammaton was not pronounced, but substituted by the word Adonai, is a reminder that from very early days Israel instinctively felt that there was that of God which could not be expressed.

At the same time, Israel envisaged God as active in his creation and in humankind. The Spirit of God not only brooded over the cosmos (Genesis 1.2), but could quite naturally be imaged as God's breath, the breath of life, as in

- Job 33.4 – 'the Spirit of God has made me, and the breath of the Almighty gives me life';
- Psalm 104.29–30 – 'when you take away their breath, they die and return to the dust. When you send forth your spirit, they are created'.

God was indeed high and lifted up, inaccessible to human search and enquiry. But the Spirit of God, God as Spirit, was near, the creative breath, the breath of life. God as Spirit was inescapably present:

- Psalm 139.7 – 'Where can I go from your spirit? Or where can I flee from your presence?'

Whether this understanding of God should be described as 'binitarian' is neither here nor there. The fact remains that from earliest days Israel conceived of God as both transcendent and immanent, God unknowable but nevertheless making himself known.

Another early attempt to assert both aspects, God's hiddenness and his self-revelation, was the talk of 'the angel of the Lord' in patriarchal narratives, where 'the angel of the Lord' is also identified as the Lord himself. In Exodus 3 the self-revelation of YHWH is first introduced as 'the angel of the Lord' appearing to Moses in the burning bush (Exodus 3.2). And in other passages the conclusion drawn from an encounter with 'the angel of the Lord' is that it was the Lord who had revealed himself.[17] In other words, 'the angel of the Lord' was simply a way of speaking about YHWH himself but avoiding the too simplistic anthropomorphism of the garden of Eden narrative (Genesis 3.8–13). The God who could not be imaged could nevertheless manifest himself to his human creatures in a recognizable form – God, but not God as such.[18]

From early days, then, Israel's theologians and storytellers looked for ways of speaking of God which emphasized his nearness and knowability without compromising his transcendence and wholly otherness. Wisdom and Word were simply an extension of such attempts to speak of God acting in creation, in revelation, in redemption. To say that God created by or through Wisdom was to say that God created wisely, that in creation God's wisdom can be readily perceived, the wisdom which should guide humans and to which they should aspire. To say that God revealed his will through his Word was a way of saying that God acted rationally, communicated with his people through a prophet in the words spoken by the prophet. So, for example, when the Wisdom of Solomon says that Wisdom protected the patriarchs and prospered the children of Israel in their wilderness wanderings (Wisdom 9—10), this was hardly a denial of God's direct hand in it all, but a more vivid way of affirming the divine care which God lavished on his people. Likewise to attribute responsibility for the death of the firstborn in Egypt to God's 'all-powerful Word' leaping down from heaven, in Wisdom 18.14–16, was hardly a denial of God's responsibility in the plague, but simply a vivid way of describing God's action.

---

[17] E.g. Genesis 16.11–13; 21.17–18; 31.11–13; Judges 2.1; 6.12–16; 13.21–22; see also Dunn 1989, 150–1.

[18] The danger was seen in regard to visions of glorious angels who strictly forbid the visionary to worship them – as in *Apoc. Zeph.* 6.15; *Asc. Isa.* 7.21; Revelation 19.10; see particularly Stuckenbruck 1995.

The fact is that Wisdom and Word were the most striking examples of Israel's tradition of vigorous poetic imagery. 'Righteousness and peace' could be envisaged as kissing each other (Psalm 85.10); 'the trees of the field' could be envisaged as clapping their hands (Isaiah 55.12); in *Joseph and Asenath* 15.7–8 'Repentance' is depicted as 'the Most High's daughter . . . a virgin, very beautiful and pure and chaste and gentle'. So Israel's wisdom tradition, conscious that the word had a feminine gender, could portray Wisdom as a person, as a female figure of surpassing attractiveness (as particularly in Proverbs 1—9), far superior to the competing female deities of other religions. And Wisdom, in her first-person speech, could liken herself to the trees valued by Israel and her benefits to the shelter and fruits which such trees provided (Sirach 24.13–17). Similarly the more masculine Word could be likened to a fire or a hammer (Jeremiah 23.29). And Philo, as we have seen, does not hesitate to speak of the Logos as God's 'firstborn', but also as an 'ambassador', a 'judge', a 'prophet', 'the ruler and steersman of all'.[19]

Now, in a polytheistic culture Wisdom and Word might well have been regarded as other deities. But not within the context of Israel's belief in God as one. To be sure, Wisdom and Word could be spoken of as though they were personal beings, distinct from YHWH. But as we have seen, such language is much more appropriately to be regarded as poetic personification. Wisdom and Word were not other gods, or secondary gods; they were vivid poetic expressions of God in action. To envisage Wisdom was not to refer to a divine being different from the Logos – God, Wisdom, the Logos as three different divine beings. No, there was never any doubt that Wisdom was God's wisdom, that the Word was God speaking. God alone was the be all and end all. As Ben Sira says, 'Though we speak much we cannot reach the end, and the sum of our words is: "He is the all"' (Sirach 43.27, my translation).

Attempts have been made to find a middle ground between the alternatives that Wisdom and Word are either divine beings distinct from God, or personifications of God's actions. The most common alternative is to categorize Wisdom and Word as 'intermediaries', that is, as belonging to an in-between category, along with glorious angels and exalted human beings like Enoch. But the function of Wisdom and Word as ways of speaking about God's self-expression can hardly be reduced to the category of a mere intermediary. Equally unsatisfactory is the attempt to introduce the category of 'hypostasis' – Wisdom and Word as 'hypostatizations'.[20] To use

---

[19] *Her.* 205; *QE* 2.13; *Immut.* 138; *Cher.* 36.
[20] See, e.g., Ringgren (1947, 8), who quotes the definition of Oesterley and Box 1911, 195: a

that term in reference to Second Temple Judaism's reflections about God's self-revelation and activity would be entirely anachronistic. For the term 'hypostasis' has no use or meaning in modern usage except that which it acquired subsequently in the controversies of the third and fourth centuries CE over the ontological relation of the Logos–Son to the Father.[21] *Hypostasis* was at that time given a new meaning to distinguish it from its near synonym, *ousia*, 'being'. Consequently, to use the term 'hypostasis' in reference to Wisdom and Word is to attribute to the sages of Israel a metaphysical speculation about the nature of the Godhead, similar to the metaphysical wordplay of the Christian reflection of the third and fourth centuries, for which we have absolutely no trace in the literature of the period.

We can justifiably conclude, then, that in their reflection and speech-usage on divine Wisdom and Logos pre-Christian writers were quite content to use vivid poetic imagery about Wisdom and Word without any thought whatsoever that by doing so they were putting their fundamental belief that God was one in any kind of question or under any kind of threat. The fact that such vivid personifications could be used of Wisdom and Word, without such usage being seen as a threat to their monotheism, is a salutary lesson to us – a lesson which we should not forget when we examine the significance of similar language of divine agency used of Jesus Christ in the NT.

The key question is probably: what difference does or did the thought of the Incarnation, of the Word becoming flesh, make? And what are we to say about the one who was the incarnate Word? If the Word is the self-expression of God, what are we to say of the man whom the Word became? We have already noted that whereas it is entirely proper to speak of the pre-existence of the Word, it does not follow that we should speak of the pre-existence of the *man* whom the Word became. But should we now say, that since the Word is a way of speaking about God, so the man Jesus is a way of speaking about God; as the Word is the self-expression of God, so the man whom the Word became is a self-expression of God – the human face of God?

Philo might be of some assistance here, since he evidently felt able to speak of the Logos in grandiose terms. He could speak of the Logos as 'God' and 'the second God' (*Som.* 1.230; *QG* 2.62) without any evident

---

'quasi-personification of certain attributes proper to God, occupying an intermediate position between personalities and abstract beings'. See also Pfeifer 1967, 14–15.

21 I echo Moore 1922, 41–85 (here 55); also Marböck 1971, 65–6, 129–30.

sense that he was infringing his monotheism. He could speak of 'right reason' (*orthos logos*) as our 'father',[22] without any thought that he was thereby challenging the fatherhood of God – itself, of course, a metaphor. But while Philo clearly understood the Logos to be the self-expression of God, and that to attain to the Word is the means of attaining to God, he was also careful to observe that even when the Word has been attained, it only brings the realization that God in his very being (*ton kata to einai theon*) is still far beyond the Word (*Post.* 16–20). Here the Logos is asserted to be the self-revelation of God to the fullest extent possible. But it is also asserted that even if the Logos is the knowability of God to the fullest extent possible, there is still much more to God.

But does the thought of the Logos become flesh make a major difference? The Logos known through the artifice of creation, through the power of right reason, yes; but the Logos known through incarnation? How much of a step did the Johannine prologue take? After all, the wisdom tradition had already identified Wisdom with the Torah. Ben Sira completes the hymn in which Wisdom praises herself by adding, 'All this is the book of the covenant of the Most High God, the law that Moses commanded us as an inheritance for the congregation of Jacob' (Sirach 24.23). And Baruch similarly completes its paean of praise of Wisdom: 'She is the book of the commandments of God, the law that endures for ever' (Baruch 4.1). This tradition evidently found no theological problem in seeing Wisdom as embodied in Torah, in seeing Wisdom, we may say, as inscripturated in the law of Moses. Was it such a profound further step to speak of the Logos incarnated in the man Jesus? It was evidently not a great advance to move from speaking of the Torah as inspired by God, by the Spirit of God, to saying that the Torah embodied the self-revelation of God. Was it any more of an advance to move from speaking of Jesus as inspired by God's Spirit to saying that he incarnated the Word of God?

Whether it was such a great step in the logic of Hebrew poetic talk of God, it may well have proved a step too far for most Jews. To be sure there is no indication at all that the Jews of Paul's time found his use of Wisdom language in reference to Jesus objectionable.[23] We know well enough from his several allusions and protests what it was that his fellow Jews, including his fellow Jewish believers in Jesus, objected to in his preaching and teaching. They objected to his teaching on circumcision and on the laws of clean and unclean (Galatians 2.1–14; Romans 4; 14.1—15.6). So

---

[22] As in *Post.* 68, 91; *Ebr.* 68, 80–1, 95; *Conf.* 43; *Spec.* 2.29.
[23] I develop the point in Dunn 2010, 113–16, in response to Hurtado 1999.

far as his Christology was concerned, the non-believers among his fellow Jews found his preaching of a crucified Messiah to be a 'stumbling block' (1 Corinthians 1.23). For them Deuteronomy 21.23 proved that a crucified man fell under the curse of God (Galatians 3.13). Such objections we can well understand. But Paul shows no awareness that his reference to Jesus as 'wisdom from God' (1 Corinthians 1.30) or his attributing to Christ the role of Wisdom in creation (8.6) was causing offence or might undermine his gospel in the eyes of his fellow Jews. And given the rich variety of imagery and poetic licence in Israel's talk of Wisdom, it can be justly asserted that the lack of Jewish objection to Paul's Wisdom Christology is equally understandable.

The earliest Jewish objection to such Christology that we can trace is indicated by John's Gospel, which achieved its enduring written form probably in the closing years of the first century. It is generally recognized that John's Gospel attests the way in which Jesus was being presented in these final decades of the first century, and reflects also the response by Jewish leaders to that presentation. We see both facets most clearly in two passages:

- John 5.18 – 'For this reason the Jews were seeking all the more to kill him [Jesus], because he was not only breaking the sabbath, but was also calling God his own Father, thereby making himself equal to God.'
- John 10.30–33 – Jesus said, '"The Father and I are one." The Jews took up stones to stone him . . . [saying,] "It is not for a good work that we are going to stone you, but for blasphemy, because you, though only a human being, are making yourself God."'

What the Jews of John's Gospel were objecting to was in effect the identification of Jesus with the divine Word and Wisdom, that is, to the thought of Word or Wisdom having become incarnate in Jesus. They saw all too well that Word and Wisdom were ways of speaking about God, God in action towards his earthly and human creation. So, to identify Jesus with Word and Wisdom was to claim that Jesus was equal to God, or was God. This was not an objection that had been brought against the identification of Wisdom with the Torah, or to Philo's vivid personification of the Logos. These could be seen as quite consistent with their monotheism. But to use such language of a man was evidently perceived in the period following the catastrophe of the failure of the first Jewish revolt (70 CE) as, yes, a step too far.

But was it? Did the identification of Jesus with the Logos mean that the first Christians ceased to be monotheists? Did the Incarnation mean that Christians no longer believed that God was one? Christian theologians wrestled with the issue for centuries, and still do so today. They resolved the issue in the classic creeds of the fourth and fifth centuries. But the talk of God as three persons, Father, Son and Holy Spirit, arguably has made it more difficult to maintain Christian monotheism – for the simple reason that the term 'person' has lost the technical sense that it had in these early centuries and now more naturally signifies a person as you and I are persons, or indeed as Jesus of Nazareth was a person. So to speak of God as three persons invites the belief to be characterized as tritheism. If, however, we return to the Wisdom and Logos Christologies of the first two centuries we may be able to escape the problems of the later creedal Christologies. For the whole point in Wisdom and Logos reflection, whether Jewish or Christian, is to assert the immanence of God, the reality of the divine presence even of the wholly transcendent God. To understand Wisdom and Logos as persons, whether in the classic or modern sense of 'person', is to misunderstand what motivated the imagery and what the imagery was intended to assert. For Wisdom and Word are intended less to assert the otherness of Wisdom and Word from God as to assert that Wisdom and Word are precisely God's wisdom and God's word. Indeed they assert the oneness of God – 'very God of very God' – Son of God, not as a being distinct from God but Son of God as an image of the Word which is God.

Such a mesh of imagery is hard for the human mind either to disentangle or to hold together. But the first Christians show that it could be done, so perhaps we simply have to be content to juggle the imagery and hold to it firmly even when it goes beyond the reach of our comprehension. Christ as the Wisdom of God, as the Word of God become man. Christ as the love of God in saving expression for humankind. Christ as the one who makes the invisible God visible as never before. Christ as the human face of God.

Bibliography

Attridge, H. W. (1989). *Hebrews*. Hermeneia. Philadelphia, PA: Fortress.

Dunn, James D. G. (1980). *Christology in the Making*. London: SCM. Second edition; Grand Rapids, MI: Eerdmans, 1989.

—— (2003). *Jesus Remembered*. Grand Rapids, MI: Eerdmans.

—— (2009). *Beginning from Jerusalem*. Grand Rapids, MI: Eerdmans.

—— (2010). *Did the First Christians Worship Jesus?* London: SPCK.

Hurtado, Larry W. (1999). 'Early Jewish Opposition to Jesus-Devotion.' *Journal of Theological Studies* 50: 35–58.

Marböck, J. (1971). *Weisheit im Wandel: Untersuchungen zur Weisheitstheologie bei ben Sira*. Bonner Biblische Beiträge 37. Bonn: Hanstein.

Moore, G. F. (1922). 'Intermediaries in Jewish Theology: Memra, Shekinah, Metatron.' *Harvard Theological Review* 15: 41–85.

Oesterley, W. O. E., and G. H. Box (1911). *The Religion and Worship of the Synagogue, an Introduction to the Study of Judaism from the New Testament Period*. 2nd edition. London: Pitman.

Pfeifer, G. (1967). *Ursprung und Wesen der Hypostasenvorstellungen im Judentum*. Stuttgart: Calwer Verlag.

Ringgren, H. (1947). *Word and Wisdom: Studies in the Hypostatization of Divine Qualities and Functions in the Ancient Near East*. Lund: Ohlssoms.

Stuckenbruck, Loren T. (1995). *Angel Veneration and Christology*. Wissenschaftliche Untersuchungen zum Neuen Testament 2/70. Tübingen: Mohr Siebeck.

The Shema and 1 Corinthians 8.6 again

RICHARD BAUCKHAM

Introduction

In his important essay on 1 Corinthians 8, N. T. Wright argued that in 1 Corinthians 8.6 Paul reformulated the Shema in such a way as to include Jesus Christ in his understanding of the one God of Jewish monotheism, thus defining a kind of 'christological monotheism'.[1] Others, including myself, have developed this argument in greater exegetical detail and discussed its implications in a variety of ways.[2] It has become clear that 1 Corinthians 8.6 is one of the key texts for 'divine Christology' in Paul. But the discussions of this text have taken it for granted that the Shema was well known as a confession of monotheistic faith in first-century Judaism. Thus Wright asserted that the '*Shema* was already, at this stage of Judaism, in widespread use as *the* Jewish daily prayer'.[3] At the time of writing (1991) this was an uncontroversial statement.[4]

For example, E. P. Sanders, in his account of Judaism in the late Second Temple period, states that the Shema was recited twice daily by the priests in the Temple and that, among other Jews, this practice was 'very widespread'. He cites the Mishnah (priests in the Temple: *m. Tam.* 4.3; 5.1; *Ta'an.* 4.3; generally: *m. Ber.* 1.1–3) as well as the Qumran *Community Rule* (1QS 10.10). He holds that daily prayers accompanied the recitation of the Shema, taking Josephus's reference to morning and evening thanksgivings (*Ant.* 4.212) to mean that prayers were said along with the Shema. (Others have thought Josephus refers to the Shema itself.[5]) Sanders does

---

[1] Wright 1991, 120–36; de Lacey 1982, 191–203; Hurtado 1988, 97–8.
[2] Fee 2007, 16–17, 89–94, 562–4, 599–601; Bauckham 2008, 210–18; Waaler 2005, 262–446; Tilling 2012, 76–94; Lincicum 2010, 138–40; Nicholson 2010, 35–70; Fletcher-Louis 2015, 32–56. A connection with the Shema is denied by Cox 2007, 145.
[3] Wright 1991, 129. See also Wright 2013, 84: 'At the heart of Pharisaic Judaism . . . stood prayer; at the heart of daily prayer stood the *Shema*'.
[4] I still took the point for granted in Bauckham 2014, 176–200: the Shema 'was recited daily in the Temple and individually by devout Jews' (191).
[5] E.g. Feldman 2000, 406.

not cite the passage in Pseudo-Aristeas (*Let. Aris.* 160) that others have taken to refer to the twice-daily Shema.[6] He does point out that, outside the Temple, Jews would have said the Shema at home, on rising and on going to bed, not in a synagogue.[7]

However, more recently, at least three scholars (Paul Foster,[8] Jeremy Penner[9] and Sarit Kattan Gribetz[10]) have argued that we do not have good evidence for the claim that the Shema was already recited twice daily in the Second Temple period.[11] I shall discuss this issue later in this essay, but first I shall discuss the evidence from Second Temple Jewish literature that shows Deuteronomy 6.4 to have been very important, whether or not it was part of a twice-daily recitation.

The interpretation and importance of Deuteronomy 6.4

There is abundant evidence that Deuteronomy 6.4 was well known as a confession of Jewish monotheistic faith in the late Second Temple period, especially but not exclusively in the diaspora (see the collections of texts in the Appendix). This evidence has its own value and importance, whether or not the Shema was already being recited twice daily in this period. Because for the time being I leave aside the question of daily recitation, it will be inappropriate in this section to use the term Shema (which included Deuteronomy 6.4–5 and other, related passages). I am concerned here only with the one verse: 'Hear, O Israel, YHWH our God, YHWH is one' (Deuteronomy 6.4, my translation).

Since there is no verb 'is' in the Hebrew text, there are several possible ways of construing this sentence. The issue has been much debated.[12] There is much to be said for the translation I have just given, but, whatever the 'original' meaning of this text, it is clear that the translation I have just given is the way it was usually understood in the later Second Temple period. For a start, there is the evidence of the Nash Papyrus (from Egypt, *c.*150–100 BCE). It modifies the text of Deuteronomy 6.4 in such a

---

6   E.g. Falk 1995, 296; Cohn 2008, 82.
7   Sanders 1992, 196–7.
8   Foster 2003, 309–33.
9   Penner 2012, 73–100.
10 Gribetz 2015, 58–84.
11 Also, with reference only to Josephus, *Ant.* 4.212, Jonquière 2007, 45–50, does not see a reference to the Shema in this passage.
12 Janzen 1987, 280–300; Moberly 1992, 75–81; Orel 1997, 614–17; Veijola 1992, 528–41; Bord and Hamidović 2002, 13–29; Kraut 2011, 582–602; Block 2004, 193–212.

way as to make it unambiguous: *yhwh ʾĕlōhênû yhwh ʾeḥād hûʾ* (line 24).[13] The addition of *hûʾ*, used here as equivalent to the verb 'to be',[14] requires the meaning: 'YHWH our God, YHWH is one.' This is also very likely the meaning of the Septuagint Greek translation: *kurios ho theos hēmōn kurios heis estin*. This could be read as: 'The Lord our God is one Lord' (so NETS and some translations of Mark 12.29), and the translator of Daniel 3.17 LXX may have understood it in that way, since this Greek version adds to the Hebrew text the phrase 'our one Lord' (*heis kurios hēmōn*).[15] But when the Septuagint is quoted in Mark 12.29, it is clearly understood as 'The Lord our God, the Lord is one', since the scribe responds to Jesus, 'You have truly said that "he is one"' (*heis estin*, v. 32).[16]

A reading of the Hebrew as 'YHWH our God, YHWH is one' is probably evidenced within the Hebrew Bible itself at Zechariah 14.9: 'YHWH will be one and his name one' (followed by LXX). Another Hebrew text that reflects this reading is the Masada manuscript of Ben Sira: 'from eternity he is one' (*ʾeḥād hûʾ mēʿôlām*) (42.21) (note the parallel with the Nash Papyrus's use of *hûʾ*).

There are a number of clear or very probable allusions to Deuteronomy 6.4 in Jewish literature of the period, which indicate how it was understood. For example:

1 Josephus says that Moses 'represented him [God] as one, uncreated and immutable to all eternity' (*hena . . . auton apephēne kai agenēton kai pros ton aidion chronon analloiōton*) (*C. Ap.* 2.167). Like Ben Sira (42.21, quoted above), Josephus sees God's singularity as entailing his eternity. That it entails both eternity and immutability is a claim that Greek philosophers had made about the one God,[17] but in attributing it to Moses Josephus clearly associates it with Deuteronomy 6.4.

2 Josephus also says that 'the first word [of the Decalogue] teaches us that God is one and that he only must be worshipped' (*theos estin heis kai*

---

13 For the text, see Burkitt 1903, 392–408. For a photograph and information in the Cambridge Digital Library, see <https://cudl.lib.cam.ac.uk/view/MS-OR-00233/1> (accessed 23 March 2017).

14 I see no need, with Weinfeld 1991, 332, to postulate a connection with other uses of *hûʾ* with reference to God (such as Deuteronomy 32.39; Isaiah 43.10).

15 It is possible that *L.A.B.* 6.4 ('we know one Lord [*unum dominum*] and him we worship') attests a reading of Deuteronomy 6.4 as 'YHWH our God is one YHWH', though it is also possible that the Latin text reflects an original that meant, 'We know only YHWH, and him we worship.' Cf. Jacobson 1996, 358.

16 Unless otherwise noted, Bible quotations in this chapter are my own translations.

17 Staudt 2012, 68.

touton dei sebesthai monon) (*Ant.* 3.91). This is a combination of Exodus 20.3/Deuteronomy 5.7 and Deuteronomy 6.4.[18]

3 Probably another example of the combination of Deuteronomy 6.4 with the first commandment of the Decalogue is in *L.A.B.* 6.4: 'we know one Lord and him we worship' (*unum dominum novimus et ipsum adoramus*).

4 Philo says that Moses taught that 'God is one' (*theos heis esti*) (*Opif.* 171). Although Philo considers this one of the things Moses taught through his account of the creation of the world, it is likely that he also has Deuteronomy 6.4 in mind.

5 Philo refers to 'the belief' of the Hebrews 'about the one God' (*hē tou henos theou doxa*) (*Virt.* 35), which accounts for their solidarity as a people.[19]

6 Paul twice alludes to Deuteronomy 6.4 with the words 'God is one' (Romans 3.30: *heis ho theos*; Galatians 3.20: *ho . . . theos heis estin*).

7 The letter of James says that its readers 'believe that God is one' (*pisteueis hoti heis estin ho theos*) (2.19).

8 In 2 Maccabees 7.37, one of the martyrs calls on God to make King Antiochus 'confess that he alone is God' (*monos autos theos estin*).

9 In the *Letter of Aristeas*, the high priest Eleazar begins his exposition of the teaching of the Torah 'by demonstrating that God is unique' (*monos ho theos esti*) (132).

Many of the other texts listed in the Appendix (under 'God is one' and 'Only God' or 'God alone') are certainly also echoes of Deuteronomy 6.4. Clearly it is understood in these texts to mean that God is unique. He is the only God. Therefore *monos* ('only'), as well as *heis* ('one'), is a good translation of *'eḥād* in this context.[20] Occasionally the meaning 'God is the only God' is reinforced by the addition of another standard phrase of monotheistic rhetoric: 'there is no other' (e.g. Mark 12.32: 'he is one, and besides him there is no other').[21] A similar variation is used by Paul in 1 Corinthians 8.4: 'there is no God but one' (*oudeis theos ei mē heis*).

---

[18] Cf. Waaler 2005, 168–71.

[19] The association of one God with one people and one Temple – made by both Josephus and Philo – is important, but in the present context I am limiting the discussion to 'one God'. For the relevance to 1 Corinthians of the connection between one God and one people, see Byers 2016.

[20] For the rare combination of the two words – 'one and only' – see Philo, *Gig.* 64; *Sib. Or.* 3.11–12; frag. 3.3.

[21] This phrase (in several variations) is used in Deuteronomy 4.35, 39; 32.39; 1 Samuel 2.2; 2 Samuel 7.22; 1 Kings 8.60; 1 Chronicles 17.20; Isaiah 44.6; 45.5, 6, 14 (*bis*), 18, 21 (*bis*), 22;

Considering these texts and the others listed in the Appendix as a whole, several general features are notable. First, the words of Deuteronomy 6.4 are reduced to the simple formula 'God is one.' It is notable that virtually all the texts that use this formula were written in the diaspora (and in some cases Gentile readers could be expected). The Jewish confession that YHWH, the God of Israel, is the only God is transformed into the more universalistic declaration that there is only one God. These writers would have been aware that the formula *heis theos* ('one God') was also in pagan use.[22] Philo even quotes the Pythagorean philosopher Philolaus referring to the one God (*Opif.* 100: *theos heis aei ōn*). But that does not mean that they borrowed the phrase from its pagan use; rather they are exploiting the coincidence.[23] In pagan, as distinct from Jewish or Christian, usage the formula was fully consistent with the recognition and worship of all the gods. In Jewish usage it excluded the existence of other beings worthy of worship (though not, of course, the existence of otherworldly creatures such as angels).[24] In various ways, Jewish writers take care to clarify this, for example by using the formula 'there is no other' or by the addition of 'true' or 'truly' to the word 'God' (see examples in the Appendix).

Second, in many cases the words 'God is one' (with variations) are treated as a confession or declaration of belief. There is undoubtedly an intellectual content to the assertion. But very often belief entails also the obligation to worship this one and only God. Philo speaks of 'the honour due to the one God' (*Spec.* 1.52; 3.29). According to Josephus, following Elijah's demonstration that the God of Israel, not Baal, is the true God, the people 'fell upon the earth and worshipped the one God, whom they acknowledged as the almighty and only true God' (*Ant.* 8.343). In prayer to God, following biblical precedent (1 Kings 19.19; Nehemiah 9.6; Psalm

---

46.9; Joel 2.27; cf. 2 Samuel 22.32 = Psalm 18.32; Isaiah 64.4; Wisdom of Solomon 12.13; Judith 8.20; 9.14; Bel and the Dragon 41; Sirach 18.2; 36.5; 1QH 15.32; 18.9; 20.11, 31; 1Q35 1.6; 4Q377 frag. 1r 2.8; 4Q504 frag. 1–2 5.9; *Sib. Or.* 3.629, 760; 8.377; *Apoc. Abr.* 19.3–4; *Orphica* 16; Philo, *Opif.* 23, 46; *Leg.* 3.4, 82.

22 The classic study of the formula is Peterson 1926, reprinted with additions and commentary in Peterson and Markschies 2012. See also Dupont 1949, 330–41; Van der Horst 1978, 151–2; Di Segni 1994; Horbury and Noy 1992, 232–3; Chaniotis 2010; Belayche 2010; Staudt 2012, 22–70.

23 According to the table of examples in Staudt 2012, 66–8, the formula was used by Greek philosophers of the sixth to fourth centuries BCE, but then not much in pagan sources until the first to second centuries CE, when it appears in cultic use. It is possible that Jewish and/ or Christian influence contributed to its popularity in that period. But cf. Bohak 2000, who concludes that Jewish monotheism made little impact.

24 Staudt 2012, 78: 'Für die Juden war der Akzent *einer allein*, für die Griechen: der eine, des alles umfasst.'

86.10), the word 'alone' is preferred to 'one'. 'You alone are God' (PrAz 22; *4 Ezra* 8.7; 4Q504 1–2 5.8–9) amounts to an acknowledgement that worship is due to the only God. The frequent reference to worship as the implication of acknowledging only the one God is not only rooted in the Torah, but also especially relevant in the diaspora context, where the really distinctive feature of Jewish monotheism was monolatry.

Third, it is notable that in none of these contexts is there an explicit allusion to Deuteronomy 6.5, a feature that distinguishes these allusions to Deuteronomy 6.4 from the twice-daily recitation of the Shema (cf. Mark 12.29).[25] There may be two reasons for this. One is that, as we have noted, these allusions to Deuteronomy 6.4 often function as declarations of true belief. Whereas Deuteronomy 6.5 is a command of God, requiring response to God's uniqueness, these passages focus on the 'creedal' formula of Deuteronomy 6.4 and usually omit even the characterization of God as Israel's God in that verse ('Hear, O Israel: The Lord our God . . .').

On the other hand, as we have also noted, some of these passages do relate the confession of the one God closely to worship. It may well be that these references to worship sometimes, at least, carry an implicit reference to Deuteronomy 6.5. It is notable that in three cases (Josephus, *Ant.* 3.91; Philo, *Decal.* 65; Pseudo-Philo, *L.A.B.* 6.4) the first commandment of the Decalogue (Deuteronomy 5.6–7) is conflated with Deuteronomy 6.4. Probably, such writers observed a parallelism between Deuteronomy 5.6–7 and Deuteronomy 6.4–5. In both passages God is identified as unique and a devotional response is required (expressed only as a prohibition in Deuteronomy 5.7, but as a positive command to worship by Josephus, Philo and Pseudo-Philo). What we may well have in these three first-century authors is a conflation between the two parts of the first commandment and the two parts of Deuteronomy 6.4–5:

'God is one and he only must be worshipped' (*Ant.* 3.91);
'to acknowledge and honour one God who is above all' (*Decal.* 65);
'we know one Lord and him we worship' (*L.A.B.* 6.4).

In that case the command to 'love' God is interpreted as requiring worship of the one God (though worship need not be understood as all it requires). These three key passages can be understood as paraphrases of Deuteronomy 5.6–7 (which is how Josephus and Philo represent their words) or as paraphrases of Deuteronomy 6.4–5 or as both at once.

---

25 For allusions to Deuteronomy 6.5 without allusion to Deuteronomy 6.4, in late Second Temple period Jewish literature, see Waaler 2005, 181–94.

Fourth, and finally, there are several passages in which the singularity of God is juxtaposed with 'all things' or 'the universe'. This relates to a major feature of Jewish monotheism in the later Second Temple period: defining the one God as the sole Creator of all things and the sole Sovereign Ruler of all things.[26] Here are some examples with allusion to Deuteronomy 6.4:[27]

1 Writing of Abraham's conversion to worship of the one God, Josephus says that Abraham was 'the first boldly to declare that God, the creator of the universe, is one [*dēmiourgon tōn holōn hena*]' (*Ant.* 1.155).

2 Recounting the same event, *Jubilees* has Abraham pray: 'you alone are God to me. And you created everything, and everything which is was the work of your hands' (12.19).

3 According to Philo, Abraham discovered 'the One who alone is eternal and Father of the universe' (*tou henos . . . hōs estin aidios monos kai holōn patēr*) (*Virt.* 214).

4 According to Josephus, King Darius praised Daniel's God, 'saying that he alone was the true [God] and had the power over all things' (*monon auton einai legōn alēthē kai to pantōn kratos echonta*) (*Ant.* 10.263).

5 Pseudo-Aristeas says that Jews worship 'the only God, who is powerful over all creation' (*ton monon theon kai dunaton . . . par' holōn tēn ktisin*) (*Let. Aris.* 139).

6 Philo says that Moses continually repeats his teaching against idolatry, 'sometimes saying that God is one and the Framer and Maker of the universe [*heis esti kai ktistēs kai poiētēs tōn holōn*], sometimes that he is Lord of created beings' (*Spec.* 1.30), or, summing it up, that God is 'the Father and Ruler of all things [*ho patēr kai hēgemōn tōn sumpantōn*]' (*Spec.* 1.32).

7 Philo speaks of 'one, God, who alone can rightly claim that all things [*panta*] are his possessions' (*Cher.* 83).

8 Philo has Moses say that there is 'one [God], the Ruler of the universe [*hena ton hēgemona tōn holōn*]' (*Mos.* 2.168).

9 According to Philo, 'there is one sovereign and ruler and king [*heis archon kai hegemon kai basileus*], who alone [*monǭ*] may direct and dispose of all things [*ta sumpanta*]' (*Conf.* 170).

10 In the Jewish Pseudo-Orphic poem, we read: 'He is one, self-generated; all things have been brought forth as the offspring of this one [*heis est', autogenēs, henos hekgona panta tetuktai*]' (line 10). These words are

26 Bauckham 2008, 8–9, 154–7, 183–4.
27 See also *Sib. Or.* 3.11–12; frag. 1.7–8; frag. 3.3; PrAz 22; Josephus, *Ant.* 20.90; Philo, *Gig.* 64; *Cher.* 119; *Spec.* 1.14; *Mig.* 62; *Leg.* 115.

attributed to 'an ancient saying' (line 9), which may well be a reference to Deuteronomy 6.4.[28]

There was evidently a conventional association between 'one God' and 'all things'. This conclusion is plainly relevant to Paul's adaptation of the Shema in 1 Corinthians 8.6, where the term 'all things' occurs in relation both to the one God and to the one Lord. Since Paul there refers to the one God as 'the Father, from whom are all things', it may also be relevant to note that Philo describes God as 'the one Father of all things' (*Spec.* 1.14: *henos tou pantōn patros*), meaning the Creator of all things (cf. *Spec.* 1.32, quoted above; *Decal.* 51; *Spec.* 2.256; 3.178; *Leg.* 115; *Virt.* 179, 214). Elsewhere I have argued that in 1 Corinthians 8.6 Paul combines the words of Deuteronomy 6.4 with a formula like that in Romans 11.36: 'From him [God] and through him and to him are all things.'[29] This combination can be seen to be a natural one in view of the conventional association between 'one God' and 'all things'.[30]

From the evidence discussed in this section (together with the lists in the Appendix), we can conclude that in the later Second Temple period Deuteronomy 6.4 was well known and important as a statement of Jewish monotheistic faith, to which frequent allusion was made, often in the form 'God is one.' Such allusions are especially frequent in the literature of the western diaspora. So, even apart from a twice-daily recitation of the Shema, the evidence provides ample reason to suppose that Paul would be very familiar with Deuteronomy 6.4 and was deliberately reformulating that text in 1 Corinthians 8.6.

Daily recitation of the Shema

In the rabbinic period the passages recited twice daily were Deuteronomy 6.4–9, Deuteronomy 11.13–21 and Numbers 15.37–41 (*m. Ber.* 2.2), and the recitation of these passages was accompanied in the morning by three benedictions and in the evening by four (*m. Ber.* 1.4). According to the Mishnah, the priests in the Temple also recited the Decalogue preceding

---

28 The phrase *palaios logos* is used of a saying in Plato, *Lg.* 715E–716A, that is later identified as Orphic. But, although the themes of 'one God' and 'all things' can be paralleled in Orphic traditions, here the Jewish author will have been aware of the parallels in Jewish tradition too. See Holladay 1996, 159–60, 176–7.

29 Bauckham 2008, 213–16.

30 Note also Ephesians 4.6: 'one God and Father of all things, who is over all things and through all things and in all things' (*heis theos kai patēr pantōn, ho epi pantōn kai dia pantōn kai en pasin*).

93

these passages (*m. Tam.* 4.3—5.1), and rabbis offered explanations of why the Decalogue was later dropped.[31] For inclusion in *tefillin* (phylacteries) the rabbis prescribed Exodus 13.1–10; 13.11–16; Deuteronomy 6.4–9 and 11.13–21, while rabbinic *mezuzot* (on doorposts) contained only Deuteronomy 6.4–9 and 11.13–21.

The rabbinic practice of the twice-daily Shema depended on two points of exegesis of Deuteronomy 6.4–9. The first is a literal interpretation of the words 'when you lie down and when you rise' (6.7; also in 11.19). Originally this was probably a merism, a way of saying 'at all times',[32] just as the preceding words 'when you are at home and when you are away' mean 'wherever you are'. But it came to be interpreted literally as requiring a practice of recitation on going to bed and on getting up, just as 6.8–9 was understood literally, referring to *tefillin* and *mezuzot*. But, second, what were 'these words' (6.6) that were to be recited? The rabbinic practice presupposes that the reference is to the immediately preceding verses (4–5). So Deuteronomy 6.4–9 was recited, along with the parallel passage 11.13–21, which expands on Deuteronomy 6.4–5 and more or less repeats Deuteronomy 6.6–9, adding promises of the blessings that will follow obedience to these commands. It is not entirely clear why Numbers 15.37–41 was added as a third passage: it commands the wearing of fringes (*ṣiṣit*), a practice with the same purpose as those required in Deuteronomy 6.7–9, but the main point may have been to end the series of three readings with the identification of YHWH as the one who gives all the commandments (15.41).

From the *tefillin* and *mezuzot* that have been found in caves in the Judean desert, we know that in the late Second Temple period, at least in Palestine, there was considerable variation in the texts written on the leather scrolls in these objects.[33] Only four clearly conform to the rabbinic selection of texts.[34] Most include longer passages from Deuteronomy, often including the Decalogue. A few include longer passages from Exodus. Almost all of the longer passages from Deuteronomy are from the sections of the book immediately preceding those prescribed by the

---

[31] Oppenheimer 2011; Vermes 1975; Kimelman 2001, 68–80.
[32] Weinfeld 1991, 333; Gribetz 2015, 76.
[33] See especially the tables in Lincicum 2010, 203–8; also Penner 2012, 63; Cohn 2008, 65–7. For a more detailed account of the variations, see Cohn 2008, 68–73.
[34] 4QPhyl C, 8QPhyl, MurPhyl, XHev/SePhyl. Foster (2003, 330) notes that there are no fragments of Numbers 15.37–41, but this passage was not among the texts included in *tefillin* and *mezuzot* by the rabbis. It was only included in the Shema.

rabbis (i.e. from 5.1—6.3 and from 10.12—11.12).[35] They presumably reflect different understandings of the referent of the phrase 'these words' in Deuteronomy 6.6 and 11.18. The scrolls are fragmentary and so it is not easy to tell exactly what portions of Deuteronomy were included, but at least eight contain Deuteronomy 6.4–5.[36] The evidence of these *tefillin* and *mezuzot* has some bearing on the question of which texts were included in the twice-daily recitation of the Shema in this period (if it existed). But it is worth remembering that textual material that had to be memorized and recited at the beginning and the end of each day would preferably be short. The longer contents of many of the *tefillin* and *mezuzot* may therefore not have been recited in full.

Whether there was such a twice-daily recitation depends on whether the words 'when you lie down and when you rise' (6.7; 11.19) were understood literally. Almost all scholars agree that at least *Let. Aris.* 160 and Josephus, *Ant.* 4.212, do reflect such an understanding.[37] (*Let. Aris.* 160 cites the words *verbatim* from LXX, while both passages refer to a twice-daily practice in a context of referring also to *tefillin* and *mezuzot*.) More controversial is 1QS 10.10, 13–15, but the majority of scholars see a literal interpretation of Deuteronomy 6.7 here too.[38] Also controversial is Philo, *Spec.* 4.141, where he takes the whole of 6.7 to refer to education in the law.[39]

However, in none of these four texts is it unambiguous that the twice-daily practice to which they refer is a recitation of Deuteronomy 6.4–9 (with or without the Decalogue).[40] Those who doubt that our evidence supports the view that the Shema was recited in the Second Temple period argue that these passages reflect different interpretations of Deuteronomy

---

[35] 4QPhyl N contains Deuteronomy 32.14–20, 32–33. On this, see Cohn 2008, 75–7.

[36] 4QPhyl B, 4QPhyl C, 4QPhyl H, 4QPhyl M, 8QPhyl, MurPhyl, XHev/SePhyl. Also 1QPhyl probably contained these verses. Given that the manuscripts are fragmentary, I am not sure we can draw any conclusions from the 'rare occurrence of Deuteronomy 6.4–5 in the Qumran phylacteries' (Penner 2012, 64).

[37] In the case of Josephus, Jonquière 2007, 48, denies any reference to Deuteronomy 6.7.

[38] Gribetz 2015, 69–71, is not convinced of this. According to Penner 2012, 87–97, the language of Deuteronomy 6.7 is echoed, along with other biblical allusions, but not in order to specify fixed times of prayer. Foster 2003, 329, does not find an allusion to Deuteronomy 6.7 in 1QS 10.10, but does not consider 10.13–15. For the view that the reference is to the recitation of the Decalogue and the Shema, see Falk 1998, 112–19.

[39] For this as the meaning of the LXX, see Wevers 1995, 116. Gribetz 2015, 72, thinks Philo reads the time references in the verse as a merism, meaning 'all the time'. But for an alternative reading of the passage, as referring to recitation of the Shema, see Cohen 1995, 129–77. The passage is surprisingly rarely mentioned in discussions of the Shema.

[40] Another relevant passage is *Sib. Or.* 3.591–2, though it refers only to a morning ritual.

6.7 and even that the way they describe the twice-daily practice in each case cannot refer to the Shema.[41] In my view, all these passages take for granted a practice of reciting the Shema, but have in each case specific reasons for referring to it in rather indirect ways. There is no space here to discuss these passages in detail. Nor can I discuss here the important question of whether the rabbinic passages (especially *m. Ber.* 1.1–3) are reliable memories of the Second Temple period.[42] I shall confine myself to one issue that has not been adequately discussed before now.

The Shema in the Septuagint

In the debate about the Shema in the Second Temple period, an important piece of evidence has gone almost unmentioned: the LXX version of Deuteronomy 6.4–9. Between 6.3 and the words 'Hear, O Israel: The Lord our God the Lord is one', the Septuagint inserts a whole sentence that is not in any known Hebrew text (other than the Nash Papyrus, which we shall discuss below):

> *Kai tauta ta dikaiōmata kai ta krimata, hosa eneteilato kurios tois huiois Israēl en tēi erēmǭ exelthontōn autōn ek gēs Aiguptou.*
> And these are the statutes and the judgments, which the Lord commanded to the sons of Israel in the wilderness as they were coming out from the land of Egypt.
>
> (Deuteronomy 6.4a, NETS)

Whether the translator found this in his Hebrew *Vorlage* or added it himself, it is certain that it was not in the original Hebrew text of Deuteronomy, since 6.1–3 already form a full introduction to what follows, making 6.4a(LXX) not only redundant but an intrusion that interrupts the natural flow of the text.[43] In the MT Moses' speech to the Israelites in the second person runs without interruption from 5.1 to 26.19. So it does in the LXX apart from 6.4a. This half-verse does not address the Israelites and is not spoken by Moses. It is third-person narration about the Israelites, like the introduction to the whole book (1.1–4) and like 4.45–49, which probably forms an introduction to Moses' account of the Decalogue (5.1–33).

---

[41] Thus, on Pseudo-Aristeas, see Penner 2012, 75–81; Gribetz 2015, 65–7; on Josephus, see Penner 2012, 81–7; Gribetz 2015, 67–9; on 1QS 10, see Penner 2012, 87–97; Gribetz 2015, 69–71; Foster 2003, 329.

[42] For the view that *m. Ber.* 1.1–3 does provide reliable information from the time when the Temple was standing, see Instone-Brewer 2004, 41–5.

[43] Weinfeld 1991, 337.

In fact, 6.4a(LXX) is closely modelled on 4.45–46, but with some differences. Most of the differences serve to abbreviate the text. Thus 'the testimonies and the statutes and the judgments' (4.45) becomes just 'the statutes and the judgments' (6.4a), while 'in the wilderness' (6.4a), which looks at first sight like an expansion of 4.45, actually serves to give a brief indication of geographical location in place of the more extensive one in 4.46 (cf. 1.1–2). Thus 6.4a supplies what would be lacking if the following passage were taken out of context and provided with no indication of who is speaking where and when.

But another difference from 4.45 is important: in place of 'Moses spoke' (4.45), 6.4a has 'the Lord commanded'.[44] Generally, in Deuteronomy, it is Moses who voices the commandments, though he is understood to have received them from God. The only commandments that are directly reported as the words of God to the people are those of the Decalogue (5.6–21). The effect of 6.4a is to put the commandments that follow on a level with the Decalogue and to invite them to be heard as directly spoken by God. Whereas in the MT the speaker of 'these words that I command you' (6.6) is Moses, in the LXX the emphatic 'I' in this verse (*egō entellomai soi*) is the Lord God.

A further effect of 6.4a is to give 6.4–9 the character of a self-contained unit. Verse 6 refers to 'these words that I command you today', and verses 7–9 continue to refer to the same 'words'. In the MT the referent is not obvious. It could be verses 4–5, but it might pick up 'these words' from 5.22 and so refer to the Decalogue or perhaps to the Decalogue and 6.4–5 together. Or, following 6.1–3, it might refer to all the commandments in the whole speech of Moses in chapters 6—26.[45] The addition of 6.4a(LXX) has the effect of closing down these options and confining the reference to verses 4–5. With this narrative introduction in place, 'these words' cannot refer to anything that precedes it. The passage at 6.4a–9 is a narrative unit that gives remarkable prominence to 6.4b–5, represented as the direct words of God, and commands that Israel take *these words* to heart, teach them to their children, talk about them, bind them on hands and heads, and write them on doorposts.

Deuteronomy 6.4a–9(LXX) is evidently designed to be excerpted from its larger context and read as a self-contained unit, presumably for the purpose of fulfilling the commands of verses 6–9. It seems unlikely that

---

44 Some manuscripts of LXX have *eneteilato Mōysēs*, probably a correction to accord with usage elsewhere in Deuteronomy.
45 Cf. Cohn 2008, 42.

6.4a would have been added only for the purpose of providing text for *tefillin* and *mezuzot*. So far as we know, the manuscripts placed in these were never actually read. The point was simply to bind the words to hands and to heads and to affix them to doorposts. But the narrative introduction (6.4a) is there to contextualize the words for readers who read them as an excerpted unit. The purpose of such reading could be to memorize them or to meditate on them, depending on how 6.6 is understood. In the LXX, this verse is rendered literally as: 'these words . . . shall be in your heart and in your soul' (*estai ta rhēmata tauta . . . en tēi kardias sou kai en tēi psuchēi sou*).[46] But it is worth noting that, in the parallel in 11.18, the LXX, again translating the Hebrew literally, has 'you shall put these words in your heart and in your soul' (*embaleite ta rhēmata tauta eis tēn kardian kai eis tēn psuchēn humōn*), which more strongly suggests memorization. The text would be memorized by repeated recital aloud and, since individuals did not possess copies of Deuteronomy, it is easy to see how an excerpt of Deuteronomy 6.4a–9 or just Deuteronomy 6.4a–5 could be copied and used for that purpose.

Another possibility (not necessarily alternative) is that an excerpted text could be used for teaching children. The whole of Deuteronomy 6.7 LXX (like MT) could be understood to refer to the education of children, who will learn the text by the constant recital of the text to them by their parents. Alternatively, only the opening words ('and you shall teach them to your sons') could be understood as referring to education of children and the remaining part of the verse be understood as a separate requirement for adults to constantly 'talk about' the words (*laleseis en autois*).

However, we should take note of the LXX version of the parallel passage in Deuteronomy 11.19. Here a major difference of meaning from the MT results from a literal translation. The MT reads: 'Teach them to your children, talking about them [*lĕdabbēr bām*] when you are at home and when you are away, when you lie down and when you rise.' Clearly the whole verse is about teaching children, and the infinitive phrase (*lĕdabbēr bām*) means 'by talking about them'. But in the LXX we find: 'And you shall teach your children to say them when they are sitting at home and going on the way and lying down and rising' (*kai didaxete auta ta tekna humōn lalein auta kathēmenous en oikǭ kai poreuomenous en hodǭ kai koitazomenous kai dianistamenous*). Here, not only is the whole verse related

---

46 MT lacks 'in your soul'. The LXX addition *en tēi psuchēi sou* conforms to usage elsewhere in Deuteronomy (e.g. 4.29) but may be assimilation specifically to the parallel passage Deuteronomy 11.18.

to the children, but also what they are taught is a practice of recital of the words, presumably so that they should continue such a practice as adults. Whereas in 6.7 Jews are to 'talk about' the words, which need not mean reciting a text, in 11.19 they are to teach their children to 'say' the words, which strongly suggests reciting a text. Since *reciting a text* can hardly be done 'at all times', the most obvious way of reading Deuteronomy 11.19 is that children are to be taught to recite the words at specific times each day. Whether they are at home or travelling, they are to recite the words on going to bed and on getting up.

Thus if Deuteronomy 6.7 and 11.19, in the LXX, are read together, as they certainly would have been by Jewish exegetes,[47] their most likely interpretation is that Jews should recite Deuteronomy 6.4a–5 twice daily. (Deuteronomy 6.6–9 could but need not be part of the recitation.) This has gone unnoticed by previous scholars, perhaps because they assumed that the LXX was no clearer than the MT or because they focused on Deuteronomy 6.4–5 without taking account of the parallel but differently worded 11.19.

That the translators themselves already understood the texts in this sense is likely because this interpretation coheres with the addition of 6.4a to the Hebrew text. Indeed, the practice of excerpting the text of 6.4a–5 or 6.4–9 must already have been well established when the translation was made, since 6.4a is included despite the fact that for continuous reading of the whole book it is an awkward intrusion. (Of course, it is possible that 6.4a is a secondary addition to the LXX text.) An excerpted text, consisting of 6.4a–5 or 6.4–9, would have been used for memorization, ideally in childhood, with the purpose of twice-daily recitation. Memorization, education and regular recitation are not different possible uses of such an excerpt but aspects of the same use, since the text (especially 11.18–19) would be understood to mean that children should be taught to memorize the text in order to be able to recite it twice daily.

Outside the LXX, the earliest reference to a twice-daily practice based on Deuteronomy 6.7 is in the *Letter of Aristeas* (160), which cites the words of Deuteronomy 6.7/11.19 LXX *verbatim* (*koitazomenos kai dianistamenos*). Though it is difficult to date the *Letter of Aristeas* with any confidence, it certainly derives from Egypt and may have been written about a century after the Greek translation of Deuteronomy was made. It supports the

---

47 Philo, *Spec.* 4.141, seems to put the two verses together, understanding 6.7 to refer to the teaching and 11.19 to the result of the teaching. He expands the circle of those who are taught beyond children, probably by taking 'your sons' (6.7) to mean 'pupils', as attested in wisdom literature.

probability that twice-daily recitation of the Shema was practised initially in Egypt and represents an interpretation of Deuteronomy that is incorporated in the Greek version, especially by the addition of Deuteronomy 6.4a and the translation of Deuteronomy 11.19.

The Nash Papyrus also derives from Egypt, where it was written around the middle of the second century CE,[48] perhaps contemporaneously with the *Letter of Aristeas*. The fragmentary Hebrew text has two parts: the Decalogue, in a version that is taken from Deuteronomy but has harmonistic additions drawn from Exodus,[49] and Deuteronomy 6.4a–5. The text of the latter begins with a close Hebrew equivalent to Deuteronomy 6.4a(LXX) but breaks off midway through verse 5, so that we do not know whether it continued to 6.9 or even beyond. Because the manuscript is narrow and shows evidence of having been folded several times, it is generally now thought to have been contained in a *tefillin* or *mezuzah*.[50] This does not contradict my argument that Deuteronomy 6.4a(LXX) was designed to introduce an excerpt that was to be read, not merely placed in a *tefillin* or *mezuzah*. If that was the form in which the excerpt was recited, then it would naturally also be the form in which it was copied for inclusion in a *tefillin* or *mezuzah*. It is quite possible that the papyrus was originally used for memorization, with a view to twice-daily recital, and was then folded for inclusion in a *tefillin* or *mezuzah*.

The Hebrew version of Deuteronomy 6.4a differs from Deuteronomy 4.45 MT in most of the ways in which Deuteronomy 6.4a(LXX) differs from Deuteronomy 4.45(LXX). It does not seem to me possible to tell whether it represents the *Vorlage* of Deuteronomy 6.4a(LXX) or a Hebrew text that derives from Deuteronomy 6.4a(LXX), though the latter seems more likely, since it is specifically the LXX version of Deuteronomy 11.19 that provides a clear basis for twice-daily recitation and thus the rationale for an excerpted text of this kind. There is one way in which Deuteronomy 6.4a in the Nash Papyrus differs from Deuteronomy 6.4a(LXX): it has 'Moses commanded' not 'YHWH commanded'. So Deuteronomy 6.4a evidently existed in these two rather significantly variant forms.[51] In the context of the Nash Papyrus, the effect of the difference is that, whereas the Decalogue is delivered directly by God, the Shema is mediated by Moses,

---

48 Albright 1937, 145–76.
49 Eshel 1991, 123 n. 36. She says that the text of the Decalogue in the Nash Papyrus is close to that in 4QDeut[n], 4QPhyl G and 8QPhyl. For harmonization in versions of the Decalogue in the Qumran *tefillin* and *mezuzot*, see also Cohn 2008, 71.
50 Eshel 1991, 123 n. 36; Cohn 2008, 68.
51 There are also LXX manuscripts that have *Mōysēs*: see Wevers 1977, 120–1.

like most of Deuteronomy.[52] But Penner's suggestion that the 'words' of Deuteronomy 6.6–9 could, in the context of the Nash Papyrus, have been interpreted as a reference to the Decalogue,[53] is ruled out by the inclusion of Deuteronomy 6.4a. Even if the Shema here is less clearly than in the LXX on the same level as the Decalogue, it stands as an important text in its own right, not just as an aid to reading the Decalogue.

Whereas an excerpted version of Deuteronomy 6.4–5 or 6.4–9 required an introduction (6.4a), the same was not true of the Decalogue, since its opening words (Exodus 20.2; Deuteronomy 5.6) make perfectly clear who is speaking to whom. If the Nash Papyrus provided a text for memorization and recitation, not merely for a *tefillin* or *mezuzah*, then it attests a practice of reciting the Decalogue as well as the Shema. (We recall the Mishnah's claim that the Decalogue was recited along with the Shema in the Temple (*m. Tam.* 4.3—5.1).) Probably both the Decalogue and the Shema were understood as summaries of the whole law. We noticed earlier that Josephus, Philo and Pseudo-Philo all appear to conflate Deuteronomy 6.4 with the first commandment of the Decalogue.

So far as it goes, the evidence we have examined suggests that the twice-daily recitation of the Shema, based on a literal interpretation of Deuteronomy 6.7 and 11.19, began, as early as the third century BCE, in the diaspora. This may help to explain our previous finding: that allusions to Deuteronomy 6.4 in Second Temple period Jewish literature (without reference to recitation) occur predominantly in literature from the diaspora, though not exclusively. Albert Baumgarten suggested that the recitation of the Shema, along with the Decalogue, in the Temple was an 'invented tradition' instituted by the Maccabees. It was, he proposed, 'intended to reinforce an identity which had been challenged at the time of the [hellenizing] reforms, while reminding Jerusalem priests in particular, of what their new rulers saw as the essentials of their faith.'[54] If this suggestion is correct, then, in the light of our reading of the Septuagint, the practice would have been imported by the Maccabees from the diaspora. While the suggestion is very speculative, it does at least explain how such an innovation in Temple ritual could have come about. The practice would then have been borrowed from Temple practice for use by individuals in Jewish Palestine.

---

[52] It could be that treating the passage as the direct words of God was thought inconsistent with 'our God' in Deuteronomy 6.4b.

[53] Penner 2012, 64.

[54] Baumgarten 1996, 207. Cf. also Cohn 2008, 88–9, 100–1.

Paul and the Shema

In view of the evidence of the Septuagint version of Deuteronomy, we can now say that Paul, as a Jew born in the diaspora, was probably taught to recite the Shema twice daily already as a child. The recitation, as he practised it, may have included also the Decalogue.[55] He will also have known of the prominence of Deuteronomy 6.4 as the key scriptural expression of Jewish monotheistic faith in diaspora Jewish literature and doubtless also in preaching in diaspora synagogues. For that reason, some members of his Corinthian church would have been aware of Deuteronomy 6.4, at least in the summary form 'God is one', already before they became Christians. So we can confirm that this text would have been as important to Paul and as relevant to the context of 1 Corinthians 8.6 as N. T. Wright and other recent scholars have supposed – and not only because of the twice-daily recitation, important as that must have been. We can also now see that, not only the words of Deuteronomy 6.4, but also the connection between the 'one God' and 'all things' that Paul makes, had a background in Jewish literature.

Appendix: The texts

In these tables I have collected texts from the Hebrew Bible, the Septuagint, Second Temple period Jewish literature and the New Testament.[56] I have not included Christian texts later than the New Testament. I have also excluded works in the category of Old Testament Pseudepigrapha that I consider to be certainly or probably Christian.[57] I have confined the list to texts that use the words 'one' or 'only/alone' to characterize the uniqueness of God as the only God (excluding texts that use these words of God to make a more limited point; e.g. Judith 9.14; Mark 13.32; James 4.12).[58]

---

[55] In my view, Paul as a Pharisee in Jerusalem would have been familiar with the recitation of the Shema by the priests in the Temple and probably by other Palestinian Jews too. But I have not demonstrated these points in the present essay.

[56] There are less extensive lists, confined to Jewish works in Greek, in Waaler 2005, 447–9.

[57] These include the *Testaments of the Twelve Patriarchs, Joseph and Aseneth*, the *Paraleipomena of Jeremiah, Sibylline Oracles* 2, the *Testament of Abraham*, the *Apocalypse of Elijah*. At the very least, these works cannot be used with any confidence as evidence of Second Temple period Judaism. I have also excluded *2 Enoch*, because, although I am convinced that it is substantially a Jewish work of the Second Temple period, it is very difficult to establish the original text. Staudt 2012, 185–9, treats all these as Jewish works; Waaler 2005, 447–9, treats some of them as Jewish.

[58] Staudt 2012, 185–9, 286–9, lists all texts that use 'one' or 'only/alone' and not only of God.

'God is one'

Zechariah 14.9: 'YHWH will be one and his name one' (יהיה יהוה אחד ושמו אחד)
= Zechariah 14.9 LXX: 'the Lord will be one and his name one' (ἔσται
κύριος εἷς καὶ τὸ ὄνομα αὐτοῦ ἕν);

Malachi 2.10: 'Did not one God [אל אחד] create us?' = Malachi 2.10 LXX:
'Did not one God [θεὸς εἷς] create us?';

Daniel 3.17 LXX: 'there is a God in heaven, our one Lord' (ἔστι . . . θεὸς ἐν
οὐρανοῖς εἷς κύριος ἡμῶν);[59]

Sirach 42.21 (Hebrew): 'from eternity he is one' (אחד הו מעולם);[60]
Sirach 1.8: 'One is wise' (εἷς ἐστιν σοφός);[61]
Pseudo-Philo, *L.A.B.* 6.4: 'one Lord' (*unum dominum*);
2 Bar. 48.24: 'we have received one law from the one';

Sib. Or. 3.11: 'God is one' (εἷς θεός ἐστι);
Sib. Or. frag. 1.7: 'there is one God' (εἷς θεός);
Sib. Or. frag. 1.32: 'there is one God' (εἷς θεός ἐστι);
Sib. Or. frag. 3.3: 'God is alone, one' (θεός μόνος εἷς);[62]
Sib. Or. 4.30: 'one God' (ἑνὸς θεοῦ);

Pseudo-Sophocles: 'God is one, in truth one' (εἷς ταῖς ἀληθείαισιν εἷς ἐστι
θεός);
Jewish *Orphica* 10: 'he is one' (εἷς ἔστ');
Pseudo-Phocylides 54: 'The one God is wise' (εἷς θεός ἐστι σοφός);

Philo, *Opif.* 171: 'God is one' (θεὸς εἷς ἐστι);
Philo, *Opif.* 172: 'he who really is is one' (εἷς ὁ ὢν ὄντως ἔστι);
Philo, *Leg.* 2.1: 'God being one' (εἷς ὢν ὁ θεός);
Philo, *Leg.* 2.51: 'the one God' (τὸν ἕνα θεόν);
Philo, *Leg.* 3.82: 'God being one' (θεός εἷς ὤν);
Philo, *Leg.* 3.105: 'God is one' (ὁ θεός εἷς);
Philo, *Cher.* 27: 'God being indeed one' (ἕνα ὄντως ὄντα θεόν);
Philo, *Gig.* 64: 'the one and only God' (τῷ ἑνὶ μόνῳ . . . θεῷ);
Philo, *Conf.* 170: 'there is one sovereign' (ἔστιν εἷς ἄρχων . . .);
Philo, *Conf.* 171: 'God being one' (εἷς ὢν ὁ θεός);
Philo, *Som.* 1.229: 'he that is truly God is one' (ὁ μὲν ἀληθείᾳ θεὸς εἷς
ἐστιν);

---

59 The words 'in heaven, our one Lord' are not in the Hebrew text or in Theodotion's version.
60 In the Greek version ὡς is probably a corruption of εἷς. In that case, the Greek would read:
εἷς ἔστιν πρὸ τοῦ αἰῶνος καὶ εἷς τὸν αἰῶνα.
61 This verse is not extant in Hebrew.
62 On these passages in *Sib.Or.* 3 and fragments, see Guerra 1992, 149–51.

Philo, *Mos.* 2.168: '[there is] one [God]' (ἕνα);
Philo, *Decal.* 65: 'one God' (ἕνα . . . θεόν);
Philo, *Decal.* 155: 'one ruler and king' (ἡγεμὼν καῖ βασιλεὺς εἷς);
Philo, *Spec.* 1.30: 'God is one' (θεὸς εἷς ἐστι);
Philo, *Spec.* 1.52: 'the one God' (τοῦ ἑνὸς θεοῦ);
Philo, *Spec.* 1.65: 'the one truly existing God' (τοῦ ἑνὸς θεοῦ καὶ ὄντως ὄντος);
Philo, *Spec.* 1.67: 'God is one' (εἷς ἐστιν ὁ θεός);
Philo, *Spec.* 3.29: 'the one God' (τοῦ ἑνὸς θεοῦ);
Philo, *Spec.* 4.159: 'one God' (εἷς θεός);
Philo, *Virt.* 35: 'the one God' (τοῦ ἑνὸς θεοῦ);
Philo, *Virt.* 213, 214, 215: 'the One' (τοῦ ἑνός);
Philo, *Virt.* 216: 'there is one Cause above all' (ἔστιν ἕν αἴτιον τὸ ἀνωτάτω);[63]
Philo, *Legat.* 115: 'one God' (ἕνα . . . θεόν);

Josephus, *Ant.* 1.155: 'God . . . is one' (θεὸν . . . ἕνα);
Josephus, *Ant.* 3.91: 'God is one' (θεός ἐστιν εἷς);
Josephus, *Ant.* 4.201: 'God is one' (θεὸς . . . εἷς);
Josephus, *Ant.* 5.97: 'one God' (θεός . . . εἷς);
Josephus, *Ant.* 5.112: 'the one God' (θεόν . . . ἕνα);
Josephus, *Ant.* 8.343: 'the one God' (ἕνα θεόν);
Josephus, *C. Ap.* 2.167: [God is] 'one' (ἕνα);
Josephus, *C. Ap.* 2.193: 'one God' (ἑνὸς θεοῦ);

Mark 2.7: 'the one God' (εἷς ὁ θεός);
Mark 10.18 = Luke 18.19: 'the one God' (εἷς ὁ θεός);
Mark 12.29: 'the Lord our God, the Lord is one' (κύριος ὁ θεὸς ἡμῶν κύριος εἷς ἐστιν);
Mark 12.32: 'he is one' (εἷς ἐστιν);
John 8.41: 'one Father' (ἕνα πατέρα);
Romans 3.30: 'God is one' (εἷς ὁ θεός);
1 Corinthians 8.4: 'there is no God but one' (οὐδεὶς θεὸς εἰ μὴ εἷς);
1 Corinthians 8.6: 'one God . . . one Lord' (εἷς θεός . . . εἷς κύριος);
Galatians 3.20: 'God is one' (ὁ δὲ θεὸς εἷς ἐστιν);
Ephesians 4.5–6: 'one Lord . . . one God' (εἷς κύριος . . . εἷς θεός);
1 Timothy 2.5: 'there is one God' (εἷς . . . θεός);
James 2.19: 'God is one' (εἷς ἐστιν ὁ θεός).

---

63 In *Virt.* 213–16, Philo is describing Abraham's discovery of monotheism.

'God is one' + 'there is no other'

Jewish *Orphica* 10, 17: 'he is one . . . and there is no other' (εἷς ἔστ᾽ . . . οὐδέ τις ἔσθ᾽ ἕτερος);

Philo, *Leg.* 3.82: 'for God, being one, is in heaven above and on earth beneath, and there is none beside him' (θεός εἷς ὢν ἐν τῷ οὐρανῷ ἄνω ἐστὶ καὶ ἐπὶ τῆς γῆς κάτω, καὶ οὐκ ἔστιν ἔτι πλὴν αὐτοῦ);[64]

Mark 12.32: 'he is one and besides him there is no other' (εἷς ἐστιν καὶ οὐκ ἔστιν ἄλλος πλὴν αὐτοῦ).

'Worship the one God'

Pseudo-Philo, *L.A.B.* 6.4: 'we know one Lord and him we worship' (*unum dominum novimus et ipsum adoramus*);

Philo, *Decal.* 65: 'honour one God' (ἕνα . . . τιμᾶν θεόν);
Philo, *Spec.* 1.52: 'the honour due to the one God' (ἡ τοῦ ἑνὸς θεοῦ τιμή);
Philo, *Spec.* 3.29: 'the honour due to the one God' (τὴν τοῦ ἑνὸς θεοῦ τιμήν);
Josephus, *Ant.* 3.91: 'God is one and . . . he only must be worshipped' (θεός ἐστιν εἷς καὶ τοῦτον δεῖ σέβεσθαι μόνον);
Josephus, *Ant.* 8.343: 'fell upon the earth and worshipped the one God, whom they acknowledged as the almighty and only true God' (ἔπεσον ἐπὶ τὴν γῆν καὶ προσεκύνουν ἕνα θεὸν καὶ μέγιστον καὶ ἀληθῆ μόνον ἀποκαλοῦντες).

'Only God' or 'God alone'

2 Kings 19.19: 'you, YHWH, alone are God' (אתה יהוה אלהים לבדך); = 4 Kdms 19.19 LXX: 'you alone are the Lord God' (σὺ κύριος ὁ θεός μόνος);
Nehemiah 9.6: 'you are YHWH, you alone' (אתה הוא יהוה לבדך); = 2 Esd. 19.6 LXX: 'you yourself are the Lord alone' (σὺ εἶ αὐτὸς κύριος μονός);
Psalm 86.10: 'you alone are God' (אתה אלהים לבדך); = Psalm 85.10 LXX: 'you alone are God' (σὺ εἶ ὁ θεὸς μόνος);
Isaiah 37.16: 'you are God, you alone . . .' (אתה הוא האלהים לבדך); = Isaiah 37.16 LXX: 'you alone are God . . .' (σὺ θεὸς μόνος εἶ . . .);

Sirach 24.24: 'the Lord Almighty alone is God' (κύριος παντοκράτωρ θεὸς μόνος ἐστιν);[65]

---

64 After the first three words, this is a quotation from Deuteronomy 4.39.
65 This verse is not in most manuscripts.

PrAz 22 (Daniel 3.45 LXX, Θ): 'you alone are the Lord God' (LXX: σὺ εἶ μόνος κύριος ὁ θεός; Θ: σὺ εἶ κύριος ὁ θεὸς μόνος);

2 Maccabees 7.37: 'he alone is God' (μόνος αὐτὸς θεός ἐστιν);

4 Macc. 5.24: 'the only existing God' (μόνον τὸν ὄντα θεόν);

Jub. 12.19: 'you alone are God to me [Abraham]';

T. Mos. 10.7: 'the only, eternal God' (*deus aeternus solus*);

2 Bar. 21.10: 'you alone live, immortal . . .';

4 Ezra 8.7: 'you are unique' (*solus . . . es*);

4Q504 1–2 5.8–9: 'you are a living God, you alone' (אתה אל חי לבדכה);

Let. Aris. 132: 'God is unique' (μόνος ὁ θεός ἐστι);

Let. Aris. 139: 'the only God' (τὸν μόνον θεόν);

Sib. Or. 3.629: 'he alone is God' (αὐτὸς . . . μόνος ἐστί θεός);

Sib. Or. 3.718: 'he alone is sovereign' (μόνος ἐστί δυνάστης);

Sib. Or. 3.760: 'he alone is God' (αὐτὸς . . . μόνος ἐστί θεός);

Sib. Or. 5.284: 'God who alone is preeminent' (θεὸν μόνον ἔξοχον ὄντα);

Sib. Or. 8.377: 'I alone am God' (μοῦνος . . . θεός εἰμι);

Sib. Or. frag. 1.7: 'who alone rules' (ὃς μόνος ἄρχει);

Sib. Or. frag. 1.15–16: 'him who alone is ruler of the world, who is alone from age to age' (αὐτὸν τὸν μόνον ὄντα . . . ἡγήτορα κόσμου, ὃς μόνος εἰς αἰῶνα καὶ ἐξ αἰῶνος ἐτύχθη);

Sib. Or. frag. 3.3: 'God is alone, one' (θεός μόνος εἷς);

Philo, *Gig.* 64: 'the only God' (μόνος ὢν θεός);

Philo, *Gig.* 64: 'the one and only God' (τῷ ἑνὶ μόνῳ . . . θεῷ);

Philo, *Mos.* 1.75: 'to whom alone existing belongs' (ᾧ μόνῳ πρόσεστι τὸ εἶναι);

Josephus, *Ant.* 8.335: 'who alone is God' (ὃς μόνος ἐστὶ θεός);

Josephus, *Ant.* 8.337: 'the only true God' (θεὸν ἀληθῆ καὶ μόνον);

Josephus, *Ant.* 8.343: 'only true God' ([θεὸν] ἀληθῆ μόνον);

Josephus, *Ant.* 8.350: 'the only God is the existing one' (μόνος εἴη θεὸς ὁ ὤν);

Josephus, *Ant.* 10.263: 'he alone is the true God' (μόνον αὐτὸν εἶναι . . . ἀληθῆ [θεόν]);

Josephus, *Ant.* 18.23: 'God alone is their leader and master' (ἐστὶν αὐτοῖς μόνον ἡγεμόνα καὶ δεσποτήν);

Josephus, *Ant.* 20.90: 'only rightful lord of all' (τῶν πάντων δικαίως μόνον . . . κύριον);

Josephus, *War* 7.323: 'he alone is the true and rightful lord of people' (μόνος . . . οὗτος ἀληθής ἐστι δίκαιος ἀνθρώπων δεσπότης);

Josephus, *War* 7.410: 'God alone as their lord' (θεὸν . . . μόνον . . . δεσπότην);

Luke 5.21: 'God alone' (μόνος ὁ θεός);
John 5.44: 'the only God' (τοῦ μόνου θεοῦ);
John 17.3: 'the only true God' (τὸν μόνον ἀληθινὸν θεόν);
Romans 16.27: 'the only wise God' (μόνῳ σοφῷ θεῷ);
1 Timothy 1.17: 'the only God' (μόνῳ θεῷ);
1 Timothy 6.15: 'only sovereign' (μόνος δυνάστης);
Jude 25: 'the only God' (μόνῳ θεῷ).

'God alone' + 'there is no other'

4Q504 1–2 5.8–9: 'you are a living God, you alone, and there is no other apart from you' (אתה אל חי לבדכה ואין זולתכה);

Sib. Or. 3.629: 'he alone is God and there is no other' (αὐτὸς . . . μόνος ἐστί θεός κοὐκ ἔστιν ἔτ' ἄλλος);
Sib. Or. 3.760: 'he alone is God and there is no other' (αὐτὸς . . . μόνος ἐστί θεὸς κοὐκ ἔστιν ἔτ' ἄλλος);
Sib. Or. 8.377: 'I alone am God and there is no other God' (μοῦνος . . . θεός εἰμι καὶ οὐκ ἔστιν θεὸς ἄλλος).

'Worship God alone'

Exodus 22.20: 'whoever sacrifices to any god … except to YHWH alone' (זבח לאלהים . . . בלתי ליהוה לבדו) = Exodus 22.19 LXX: 'the one who sacrifices to the gods except to the Lord alone' (ὁ θυσιάζων θεοῖς . . . πλὴν κυρίῳ μόνῳ);
1 Samuel 7.3–4: 'direct your hearts to YHWH and serve him only … they served YHWH only' (והכינו לבבכם אל יהוה ועבדהו לבדו . . . ויעבדו יהוה לבדו) = 1 Kdms 7.3–4 LXX: 'prepare your hearts towards the Lord and serve him only … they served the Lord only' (ἑτοιμάσατε τὰς καρδίας ὑμῶν πρὸς κύριον καὶ δουλεύσατε αὐτῷ μόνῳ . . . ἐδούλευσαν κυρίῳ μόνῳ);

4 *Macc.* 5.24: 'we worship the only existing God' (μόνον τὸν ὄντα θεὸν σέβειν);
Let. Aris. 139: 'worshipping the only God' (τὸν μόνον θεόν . . . σεβόμενοι);
Sib. Or. 3.593–4: 'they honour only the immortal one who always rules' (τιμῶσι μόνον τὸν ἀεὶ μεδέοντα ἀθάνατον);
Sib. Or. frag. 1.15: 'revere him who alone is ruler of the world' (αὐτὸν τὸν μόνον ὄντα σέβεσθ' ἡγήτορα κόσμου);

Philo, *Spec.* 1.42: 'to serve you alone' (μόνον σὲ θεραπεύειν);

Josephus, *Ant.* 1.156: 'to whom alone it is right to render our homage and thanksgiving' (ᾧ καλῶς ἔχει μόνῳ τὴν τιμὴν καὶ τὴν εὐχαριστίαν ἀπονέμειν);

Josephus, *Ant.* 3.91: 'he only must be worshipped' (τοῦτον δεῖ σέβεσθαι μόνον);

Josephus, *Ant.* 10.263: 'praising the God whom Daniel worshipped and saying that he alone was the true and almighty God' (ἐπαινῶν τὸν θεόν ὃν Δανίηλος προσκυνεῖ, καὶ μόνον αὐτὸν εἶναι λέγων ἀληθῆ καὶ τὸ πάντων κράτος ἔχοντα);

Matthew 4.10 = Luke 4.8: 'worship the Lord your God and serve only him' (κύριον τὸν θεόν σου προσκυνήσεις καὶ αὐτῷ μόνῳ λατρεύσεις).

Bibliography

Albright, William F. (1937). 'A Biblical Fragment from the Maccabean Age: The Nash Papyrus.' *Journal of Biblical Literature* 56: 145–76.

Bauckham, Richard (2008). *Jesus and the God of Israel: God Crucified and Other Studies on the New Testament's Christology of Divine Identity*. Milton Keynes: Paternoster / Grand Rapids, MI: Eerdmans.

—— (2014). 'Devotion to Jesus Christ in Earliest Christianity: An Appraisal and Discussion of the Work of Larry Hurtado.' In *Mark, Manuscripts, and Monotheism: Essays in Honor of Larry W. Hurtado*, edited by Chris Keith and Dieter T. Roth, 176–200. Library of New Testament Studies 528. London: Bloomsbury.

Baumgarten, Albert I. (1996). 'Invented Traditions of the Maccabaean Era.' In *Geschichte – Tradition – Reflexion: Festschrift für Martin Hengel zum 70. Geburtstag*, edited by Peter Schäfer, 197–210. Tübingen: Mohr Siebeck.

Belayche, Nicole (2010). '*Deus deum . . . summorum maximus* (Apuleius): Ritual Expressions of Distinction in the Divine World in the Imperial Period.' In *One God: Pagan Monotheism in the Roman Empire*, edited by Stephen Mitchell and Peter van Nuffelen, 141–66. Cambridge: Cambridge University Press.

Block, Daniel I. (2004). 'How Many Is God? An Investigation into the Meaning of Deuteronomy 4:4–5.' *Journal of the Evangelical Theological Society* 47: 193–212.

Bohak, Gideon (2000). 'The Impact of Jewish Monotheism on the Greco-Roman World.' *Jewish Studies Quarterly* 7: 1–21.

Bord, Lucien-Jean and David Hamidović (2002). 'Écoute Israël (Deut. VI 4).' *Vetus Testamentum* 52: 13–29.

Burkitt, Francis C. (1903). 'The Hebrew Papyrus of the Ten Commandments.' *Jewish Quarterly Review* 15: 392–408.

Byers, Andrew (2016). 'The One Body of the Shema in 1 Corinthians: An Ecclesiology of Christological Monotheism.' *New Testament Studies* 62: 517–32.

Chaniotis, Angelos (2010). 'Megatheism: The Search for Almighty God and the Competition of Cults.' In *One God: Pagan Monotheism in the Roman Empire*, edited by Stephen Mitchell and Peter van Nuffelen, 112–40. Cambridge: Cambridge University Press.

Cohen, Naomi G. (1995). *Philo Judaeus: His Universe of Discourse.* Beiträge zur Erforschung des Alten Testaments und des antiken Judentum 24. Frankfurt am Main: Peter Lang.

Cohn, Yehudah B. (2008). *Tangled up in Text: Tefillin and the Ancient World.* Brown Judaic Studies 351. Providence, RI: Brown University Press.

Cox, Ronald (2007). *By the Same Word: Creation and Salvation in Hellenistic Judaism and Early Christianity.* Beihefte zur Zeitschrift für die neutestamentliche Wissenschaft 145. Berlin: de Gruyter.

Di Segni, Leah (1994). 'Εἷς θεός in Palestinian Inscriptions.' *Scripta Classica Israelica* 13: 94–115.

Dupont, Jacques (1949). *Gnosis: La Connaissance Religieuse dans les Épitres de Saint Paul.* Louvain: Nauwelaerts / Paris: Gabalda.

Eshel, Esther (1991). '4QDeutⁿ – A Text That Has Undergone Harmonistic Editing.' *Hebrew Union College Annual* 62: 117–54.

Falk, Daniel K. (1995). 'Jewish Prayer Literature and the Jerusalem Church in Acts.' In *The Book of Acts in Its First Century Setting, Volume 4: The Book of Acts in Its Palestinian Setting,* edited by Richard Bauckham, 267–301. Grand Rapids, MI: Eerdmans / Carlisle: Paternoster.

——(1998). *Daily, Sabbath, and Festival Prayers in the Dead Sea Scrolls.* Studies on the Texts of the Desert of Judah 27. Leiden: Brill.

Fee, Gordon D. (2007). *Pauline Christology: An Exegetical-Theological Study.* Peabody, MA: Hendrickson.

Feldman, Louis H. (2000). *Josephus: Judean Antiquities 1–4.* Flavius Josephus: Translation and Commentary. Leiden: Brill.

Fletcher-Louis, Crispin (2015). *Jesus Monotheism, Volume 1: Christological Origins: The Emerging Consensus and Beyond.* Eugene, OR: Cascade.

Foster, Paul (2003). 'Why Did Matthew Get the *Shema* Wrong? A Study of Matthew 22:37.' *Journal of Biblical Literature* 122: 309–33.

Gribetz, Sarit Kattan (2015). 'The Shema in the Second Temple Period: A Reconsideration.' *Journal of Ancient Judaism* 6: 58–84.

Guerra, Anthony J. (1992). 'The One God Topos in Spec. Leg. 1.52.' In *The Society of Biblical Literature 1990 Seminar Papers,* edited by David J. Lull, 148–57. Atlanta, GA: Scholars.

Holladay, Carl R. (1996). *Fragments from Hellenistic Jewish Authors, Volume 4: Orphica.* Society of Biblical Literature Texts and Translations 14. Atlanta, GA: Scholars.

Horbury, William and David Noy (1992). *Jewish Inscriptions of Graeco-Roman Egypt.* Cambridge: Cambridge University Press.

Hurtado, Larry (1988). *One God, One Lord: Early Christian Devotion and Ancient Jewish Monotheism.* Philadelphia, PA: Fortress.

Instone-Brewer, David (2004). *Traditions of the Rabbis from the Era of the New Testament, Volume 1: Prayer and Agriculture.* Grand Rapids, MI: Eerdmans.

Jacobson, Howard (1996). *A Commentary on Pseudo-Philo's Liber Antiquitatum*

Biblicarum, Volume 1. Arbeiten zur Geschichte des antiken Judentums und des Urchristentums 31. Leiden: Brill.

Janzen, J. Gerald (1987). 'On the Most Important Word in the Shema (Deuteronomy VI 4–5).' *Vetus Testamentum* 27: 280–300.

Jonquière, Tessel M. (2007). *Prayer in Josephus*. Leiden: Brill.

Kimelman, Reuven (2001). 'The *Shema*' Liturgy: From Covenant Ceremony to Coronation.' In *Kenishta: Studies of the Synagogue World*, edited by Joseph Tabory, 9–105. Ramat-Gan: Bar-Ilan University Press.

Kraut, Judah (2011). 'Deciphering the Shema: Staircase Parallelism and the Syntax of Deuteronomy 6:4.' *Vetus Testamentum* 61: 582–602.

Lacey, Douglas R. de (1982). '"One Lord" in Pauline Christology.' In *Christ the Lord: Studies in Christology Presented to Donald Guthrie*, edited by Harold H. Rowdon, 191–203. Leicester: IVP.

Lincicum, David (2010). *Paul and the Early Jewish Encounter with Deuteronomy*. Wissenschaftliche Untersuchungen zum Neuen Testament 2/284. Tübingen: Mohr Siebeck.

Moberly, R. Walter L. (1992). '"YHWH Is One': The Translation of the Shema.' In *From Eden to Golgotha: Studies in Biblical Theology*, 75–81. South Florida Studies in the History of Judaism. Atlanta, GA: Scholars.

Nicholson, Suzanne (2010). *Dynamic Oneness: The Significance and Flexibility of Paul's One-God Language*. Eugene, OR: Pickwick.

Oppenheimer, Aharon (2011). 'Removing the Decalogue from the *Shema* and Phylacteries: The Historical Implications.' In *The Decalogue in Jewish and Christian Tradition*, edited by Henning Graf Reventlow and Yair Hoffman, 97–105. New York, NY: T&T Clark.

Orel, Vladimir (1997). 'The Words on the Doorpost.' *Zeitschrift für die Alttestamentliche Wissenschaft* 109: 614–17.

Penner, Jeremy (2012). *Patterns of Daily Prayer in Second Temple Period Judaism*. Studies on the Texts of the Desert of Judah 104. Leiden: Brill.

Peterson, Erik (1926). Εἶς Θεός: *Epigraphische, formgeschichtliche Untersuchungen*. Forschungen zur Religion und Literatur des Alten und Neuen Testaments 24. Göttingen: Vandenhoeck & Ruprecht.

Peterson, Erik and Christoph Markschies (2012). *Heis Theos: Epigraphische, formgeschichtliche Untersuchungen zur antiken 'Ein-Gott' Akklamation*. Würzburg: Echter.

Sanders, E. P. (1992). *Judaism: Practice and Belief 63 BCE–66 CE*. London: SCM.

Staudt, Darina (2012). *Der eine und einzige Gott: Monotheistische Formeln im Urchristentum und ihre Vorgeschichte bei Griechen und Juden*. Novum Testamentum et Orbis Antiquus 80. Göttingen: Vandenhoeck & Ruprecht.

Tilling, Chris (2012). *Paul's Divine Christology*. Wissenschaftliche Untersuchungen zum Neuen Testament 2/323. Tübingen: Mohr Siebeck.

Van der Horst, Pieter W. (1978). *The Sentences of Pseudo-Phocylides*. Leiden: Brill.

Veijola, Timo (1992). 'Höre, Israel! Der Sinn und Hintergrund von Deuteronomium VI 4–9.' *Vetus Testamentum* 42: 528–54.

Vermes, Geza (1975). 'The Decalogue and the Minim.' In *Post-Biblical Jewish Studies*, 169–77. Leiden: Brill.

Waaler, Erik (2005). *The Shema and the First Commandment in First Corinthians: An Intertextual Approach to Paul's Re-reading of Deuteronomy*. Wissenschaftliche Untersuchungen zum Neuen Testament 2/253. Tübingen: Mohr Siebeck.

Weinfeld, Moshe (1991). *Deuteronomy 1–11*. Anchor Bible 5. New York, NY: Doubleday.

Wevers, John William (1977). *Deuteronomium*. Septuaginta Vetus Testamentum Graecum III, 2. Göttingen: Vandenhoeck & Ruprecht.

—— (1995). *Notes on the Greek Text of Deuteronomy*. Atlanta, GA: Scholars.

Wright, N. T. (1991). *The Climax of the Covenant: Christ and the Law in Pauline Theology*. Edinburgh: T&T Clark.

—— (2013). *Paul and the Faithfulness of God*. Christian Origins and the Question of God 4. London: SPCK / Minneapolis, MN: Fortress.

The way the One God works: covenant and ethics in 1 Corinthians

GRANT MACASKILL

Introduction

Throughout his academic career, Tom Wright has argued that Paul's understanding of the gospel is governed by the story of God's covenantal relationship with Israel. The gospel is the fulfilment of that story, though its own dramatic elements continue to be performed in the life of the Church, so that the fulfilled story is not yet a completed one. His account of the relationship between gospel and covenant is essentially narratival and is deliberately opposed to those approaches that have set the two in opposition. This emphasis on an underlying narrative that makes sense of the particulars of Paul's writing has been one of Wright's most influential contributions to scholarship, and has also probably been the one for which he has been most widely criticized. Those unconvinced by his arguments will point to the apparently negative representations of Israel's story and the law in Paul, or to the absence of covenant language in the key texts; Wright's approach is considered to project back on to Paul a narrative that is not warranted by the words that are encountered, or is even explicitly excluded by language that suggests disjunction.

In this essay, I want to explore some elements of Paul's moral teaching in 1 Corinthians, with a view to offering some qualified support for Wright's claims and some reflection on the qualifications. These elements, I will suggest, make best sense when understood in terms of a relationship between God and his people that is assumed to be covenantal in character; they point to the diffuse influence of covenant as a framing or underlying concept for Paul's moral thought. As such, they establish a certain continuity between the story of Israel and the life of the Church under the gospel. Crucially, though, this continuity is not constituted principally by a metanarrative that unifies events or players, but rather by the identification of the God who is the single agent of salvation across stories. For Paul, it is characteristic of the God whose identity is now disclosed fully in the gospel to act in particular ways, and this characteristic can be traced through the testaments, allowing figural correspondences to connect characters who belong in different storylines.

The essay will fall into two sections: the first will consider the programmatic significance that the Shema – the classic statement of covenantal monotheism – has for Paul's thought throughout chapters 8—13, and the second will consider the language he uses of 'election' in 1.27. In both cases, the presence of covenantal imagery has been widely noted, but less attention has been paid to the way the language is used with reference to the identity of God.

One God, one body, one table

The Shema of Deuteronomy 6.4 is the classic expression of covenantal monotheism:

Hear, O Israel: The LORD our God, the LORD is one.[1]

This statement concerning the uniqueness of YHWH is the basis for the exhortation to give worship solely to him, and not to idols, and to do so in a disposition of love that unifies the different parts of our constitution: 'Love the LORD your God with all your heart, and with all your soul, and with all your might' (6.5). There is no room for a divided self, distributing love and worship partitively to an assortment of idols, for the LORD our God is One and not many. The surrounding chapters in Deuteronomy, which is essentially a covenant document, are dense with the language of divine jealousy (4.24; 5.9; 6.15), used repeatedly to warn the Israelites that they are to have nothing to do with idols and are to express their love for God by living out his commandments.

Much is debated about the character of covenantal monotheism in the history of Israel and in Second Temple Jewish thought, particularly with respect to the reality of other powers that might be labelled (in some sense) 'divine' or the rightness of showing veneration towards a personage other than YHWH.[2] There is certainly no room for the simplistic assumption that

---

1 This rendering is reflected in the NIV and several other modern versions. The NRSV modifies the significance of *heis* to the adverbial 'alone', which obscures the numerical emphasis of the text. All subsequent quotations are taken from NRSV.

2 See, for example, Boyarin 2010, 323–65; see also Boyarin 2001, 243–84; see also Litwa 2012 for an application of this different approach to monotheism to Paul. An excellent discussion of some of the salient issues is found in Alexander 2016. Having noted these, I am compelled to stress that I disagree with the conclusions each reaches about whether early Christology can really be accounted for within the framework of a looser concept of monotheism. I am

all Jews of the Second Temple period thought in the same way about these issues, or for the equally problematic assumption that the monotheism to which they subscribed was held in terms that correspond to modern definitions of the concept. What we can more safely say is that statements like the Shema indicate a conviction that there is a single centre of identity who is considered to be the maker and sustainer of all things, and that this One has a distinctive relationship to a particular people that is defined by the covenant between them. As Bauckham has argued,[3] the conviction articulated in the Shema does not primarily articulate *what* Jews considered God to be, but *who* he is: the One who made all things and cares for them providentially is YHWH, the LORD of Israel's covenant. This act of identification certainly invites reflection on matters of ontology, on what God is in distinction to what other things are, but the varying reflections on this – developed very differently in Philo and in apocalyptic or mystical texts, for example – are unified by this basic assertion of identity: YHWH is One.

Undoubtedly, this category of identity is narratival,[4] for YHWH is identified by the role he plays in the stories of the cosmos and of Israel. Here, though, we need to be careful not to assume that the storied dimension is best rendered in terms of a single unified metanarrative, as it would be in a standard modern novel. By way of analogy, we might compare the rendering of identities in the Star Wars series, where a single storyline is played out through the range of movies and spin-offs, to that in the Batman tales. In the former, characters are very specifically identified by the things they do (the roles they play) within a single linear timeline; the linearity of the narrative is vital to the characterization at work. In the latter, a range of stories have been told and retold – we have had multiple 'versions' of the Batman story – but there are certain elements that cannot be moved, and the character of Bruce Wayne and his relationship to Gotham has an accepted form. That character will always determine the content of the stories that are told about him.

---

broadly in agreement with Bauckham 1998 that Jesus is comprehensively identified with *who* God is.

[3] Bauckham 1998.

[4] This point underlies the category of identity in Bauckham 1998; he points broadly to the work of both Paul Ricoeur and Hans Frei. See Ricoeur 1992; 1985; 1988 (1984); 1995; and the posthumously published 2016. The works listed here are, of course, the English translations of French originals. Frei's key work is Frei 1975. The connection of narrative and identity is also explored fruitfully in Kelsey 2009. Kelsey's argument is interesting, for he explores the way that different narratives might have different governing metaphors and differing logics. As such, he is attentive to a plurality of narratives at work within Scripture and refuses to reduce these to a single governing narrative.

I use this analogy, not to reaffirm a form-critical account of folk story and the origins of Israelite belief, but rather to highlight the oversimplicity with which we often use words like 'narrative' and 'identity'. Once we allow that a character might play a role in multiple stories – even if those stories belong within a coherent conceptual 'universe', as in the contemporary Marvel adaptations – what becomes most striking is *how* a character acts. Wright has modified his own narrative approach to Paul to allow for greater complexity, using the structure of *A Midsummer Night's Dream* to furnish a less linear account of salvation history, but it is still one in which characters occupy specific roles in specific parts of the complex narrative that is nevertheless unified.[5] The biblical material, though, might be more constructively read to allow it to tell multiple stories about a God whose character is consistent in all of them. For example, it is not simply that YHWH is the Creator, that he acts to create at the beginning of the world story, but that his activity is performed in a particular way that reflects who he is. He creates in an orderly way that parallels the order of the covenant with Israel, in turn reflected in the arrangement of Temple and cult. There is no randomness to his creative activity, no risk that his unpredictable character will throw a tantrum of cosmic proportions, and those who meditate upon his commandments will acquire insight into what it means to live appropriately within the world that he has made to have a particular shape. Numerous scholars have traced the connections between the creation accounts of Genesis 1—2 and the covenant and cult of Israel.[6] While it may be tempting to understand these connections immediately in terms of a plot-line of fall and restoration, we should also consider whether they simply point to a consistency between the works of God's hands: he makes in a particular way, he relates in a particular way, he saves in a particular way. What is common between these is his character, *who* he is. In saying this, I am not ruling out the possibility of a plot-line connection between things, but simply indicating that there may be another explanation for correspondence that is traced to the identity of the principal agent at work. The task of reading wisely involves reflection on which kind of correspondence the text seems to suggest.

It is widely recognized that Paul invokes the Shema in 1 Corinthians 8.6, but incorporates into its assertion of the oneness of YHWH an identification of Jesus with the God of Israel:

---

5 See the chapter entitled 'The Plot, the Plan and the Storied Worldview' in Wright 2013 (457–537).
6 For an overview, see Brown 1999.

> Indeed, even though there may be so-called gods in heaven or on earth – as in fact there are many gods and many lords – yet for us there is one God, the Father, from whom are all things and for whom we exist, and one Lord, Jesus Christ, through whom are all things and through whom we exist.
>
> (1 Corinthians 8.5–6)

So much has been written on this that little needs to be said here, other than noting a few key (and well-established) points of detail. First, the text repeats the numerical *heis* that is used once in Deuteronomy 6.4 to indicate the uniqueness of YHWH: the same assertion of 'oneness' is made here, but is now made of two persons – God the Father and Jesus Christ – who are both identified and individuated by the conjunctive 'and' (*kai*). Second, the identification of these two 'persons'[7] is further developed by the similar doubling of the statement made of the Father, 'from whom are all things and for whom we exist', with respect to Jesus. These are classic statements of monotheism, ascribing creational priority and providential ultimacy to the singular figure of God, but now in a way that appears to individuate two identities within this one being. Those identities are further individuated by the different preposition used in each of the statements: all things are 'from' (*ex*) the Father, 'for' (*eis*) whom we exist, but they are 'through' (*dia*) Jesus, 'through' whom we exist. That is, both the Father and Jesus Christ are identified in parallel with respect to creation and providence (or, perhaps better, sustenance), but they are represented relative to different aspects of these activities. The Father is represented with respect to the origin and *telos* of all things, while Jesus is represented in rather more mediatorial terms, as the one through whom these activities are accomplished. Third, the common designation of Jesus as *kyrios* is encountered again here, but in a context where the divine connotations of such a title are unavoidable because of its occurrence in the source text: the term is encountered in the Greek translation of Deuteronomy 6.4 as the substitute for the divine name YHWH, apposed to the title 'our God'. Hence, where Deuteronomy speaks of the single entity designated 'the Lord our God' (*kyrios ho theos hēmōn*), 1 Corinthians 8.5–6 indicates that 'for us' (*hēmin*) there is 'one God' (*heis theos*) and 'one Lord' (*heis kyrios*). Fourth, this reassertion of monotheistic commitment is made in response to the reality of polytheistic opportunities or pressures: there are many things 'spoken of' (*legōmenoi*) as 'gods' and 'lords' in heaven and earth, but they

---

7 It is, of course, important to stress that the modern language and conceptuality of 'persons' is not identical to its ancient counterparts. I use it here to indicate that two centres of identity are present in the text, yet in a way that co-identifies them as the One God.

are to be considered as mere idols, void of true divinity. This is the driving concern behind Paul's articulation of Christological monotheism.

This Christological appropriation of the Shema at once speaks back to the discussion of idolatry that has preceded 1 Corinthians 8.6, and speaks forward into the discussion of idol feasts and Christian freedom that will follow. The point, of course, is quite obvious: the God of the gospel is the same one that led the people of Israel from Egypt and made a covenant with them, and he has not changed his disposition towards those who compromise his worship with idolatry. His identity is now disclosed more fully in the Christ event, and a new freedom comes with this, but it has not in itself changed. As Walter Moberly has argued, the wider context of 1 Corinthians mirrors the wider context of Deuteronomy 6.4: both texts are insistent that idolatry be purged from the community that exists in the presence of the holy God.[8]

Alongside this demand for singularity of worship, Paul extends the significance of the Shema to the demand for Christian unity. The connection between the two themes is nowhere seen more clearly than in 1 Corinthians 10.16–17, when read in its immediate context, and within the flow of Paul's thought leading up to his discussion of the body in 1 Corinthians 12:

> The cup of blessing that we bless, is it not a sharing in the blood of Christ? The bread that we break, is it not a sharing in the body of Christ? Because there is one bread, we who are many are one body, for we all partake of the one bread.
>
> (1 Corinthians 10.16–17)

Several elements within and around these verses reinforce the sense that we are dealing with covenant language and imagery. First, the reference to the 'cup of blessing' has been widely understood to echo the language used in Passover practices at the time (similar to later forms of the Seder) of the third cup taken during the meal; it indicates a strong identification of the Eucharist with the Passover, which is essentially a meal celebrating the covenant between God and Israel. Hence, the relationship between God and the Church is ritually represented in similarly covenantal imagery. Second, in the wider context (10.22), Paul warns of provoking God to jealousy. We have already seen that the language of divine jealousy is used in the chapters around the Shema, to indicate the singularity of worship expected of God's people; it is striking here, then, that it recurs in relation

---

8 Moberly 1999, 124–44.

to the expectation that those who sit at the Lord's table will not partake in idol feasts. The covenantal relationship retains its exclusivity, because God remains a jealous God. Third, the description of those who sit exclusively at this table emphasizes their unity by repeating the numeral *heis/hen/ henos*: 'Because there is one [*heis*] bread, we who are many are one [*hen*] body, for we all partake of the one [*henos*] bread' (1 Corinthians 10.17). It is noteworthy that the singularity of the body is emphasized by the placement of *hen sōma* ('one body') at the beginning of its clause, somewhat jarringly next to the plural *hoi polloi* ('the many'). It is also important that this singularity is sandwiched between two references to the singularity of the bread, the second of which involves a genitive construction, linked to the verb *metechō* ('to partake'). Leaving to one side the precise participatory overtones of this particular verb, we can still note that the construction makes the unity of the participants a function of the singularity of that in which they participate: Christ himself, represented in the bread.

This same move is elaborated in 1 Corinthians 12.12–13, where the unity of the body in Christ is reasserted (following, of course, a lengthy discussion of the Eucharist in chapter 11) and now developed with reference to the Spirit.

> For just as the body is one and has many members, and all the members of the body, though many, are one body, so it is with Christ. For in the one Spirit we were all baptized into one body – Jews or Greeks, slaves or free – and we were all made to drink of one Spirit.
>
> (1 Corinthians 12.12–13)

Again, the numeral 'one' is repeatedly deployed, and again in relation to a state that is derived from a single thing in which believers collectively participate. Just as the singularity of the body derives from the singularity of Christ, so it derives from the singularity of the Spirit.

The point is important: the unity of the body is not represented as a future state to be achieved dynamically through processes of fellowship or ecumenical activity, as many work to generate a solidarity, but as a basic quality of the corporate entity – the Church – that participates in the life of the One God. The oneness of God is the starting point, and not the endpoint, for reflection on Christian unity: its opposite – disunity – is a problem precisely because it constitutes a violation of the oneness of the God in whom we now participate. Were it not for the appropriation of the Shema in 1 Corinthians 8.6, we might feel free to trace this emphasis on unity to somewhere other than Deuteronomy 6.4; having recognized that appropriation, though, it is hard to ignore its reverberations through the chapters that follow. In a nutshell, the entire reality of Christian worship is represented as an outworking of the Shema, the classic statement not just of monotheism, but of monotheism rendered in covenantal terms.

All of this, I think, provides support for Wright's claims concerning the place of covenant in Paul's thought: covenant is present as a diffuse, associative concept, framing the way in which he represents Christian community. It also, I think, provides some support for his criticisms of those who would understand Paul's gospel to be radically separated from the story of Israel, particularly the period of that story governed by the Sinai narrative: the same God is at work in the same way now as then, and the same principles bear upon the relationship of his people with him.

Yet, interestingly, Paul does little in these chapters to prompt his readers to identify themselves with the *story* of Israel, as if the story*line* of YHWH's conflict with idolatry is reaching a stage of fulfilment in the life of the Church. If anything, he rather inverts this: Israel is represented as if, in some sense unknown to it at the time, it shared in the Church's experience:

> All were baptized into Moses in the cloud and in the sea, and all ate the same spiritual food, and all drank the same spiritual drink. For they drank from the spiritual rock that followed them, and the rock was Christ.
>
> (1 Corinthians 10.2–4)

Considered within the confines of a linear and progressive storyline of salvation history, it is difficult to read this as anything but metaphor: it is typological, at best. If we allow, however, that it may be informed not by a preoccupation with an overarching storyline, but rather with the character of the principal agent who works in multiple stories – a principal agent whose identity has now been disclosed more fully in Jesus Christ – then this statement can be read rather differently: now it involves a retelling of the wilderness story that sees the God-of-the-Gospel to be at work. Paul now identifies YHWH differently, as a result of the disclosure that is at the heart of the gospel, and the result is a richer acknowledgement that the benevolent activity of God is (and always was) mediated 'through' Jesus Christ. If there is a consistency to the way that God works, then he must have met his people's needs through Jesus; this is not metaphor, but reality understood in fresh ways.

There may be elements that Wright (or others) could point to that do seem to indicate some kind of storyline. The reference to 'our ancestors' at the beginning of chapter 10, for example, might be read in such a way. Certainly, there is something interesting by way of both identification and distinction that we see in the call to consider 'Israel according to the flesh'

(*Israēl kata sarka*) in 10.18, and this might be read in terms of a storyline that locates the Church in the fulfilment of the covenant with Israel, as Wright argues throughout his work. What seems to me to be most striking about all of the points made above, however, is that they do not require such a narrative dynamic to function: their ethical force is traced not to the story itself, but to the identity of the One God who works in consistent ways.

Electing to act wisely

Having seen one extensive example of the covenantal strand in Paul's moral thought in the middle chapters of 1 Corinthians, I turn back to a much more tightly focused example at the beginning of the letter, one that nevertheless has broad implications for the ethics of Christian community. In 1 Corinthians 1.27–29, Paul makes the character of divine 'election' the key to how Christians should ascribe value to each other, allowing this to speak to various practices involving social capital:

> But God chose what is foolish in the world to shame the wise; God chose what is weak in the world to shame the strong; God chose what is low and despised in the world, things that are not, to reduce to nothing things that are, so that no one might boast in the presence of God.
>
> (1 Corinthians 1.27–29)

In fact, the same basic concern is at work here in the wider context that we saw to be at work in chapters 10 and 12: Paul is concerned by disunity within the Corinthian body, generated by factions forming around particular people, and further connected to socio-economic distinctions. There are 'wise' and 'powerful' people, and the life of the church has come to revolve around these – as is typical of human society – resulting in multiple circles within the body, ordered by the tacit principles of economic stratification. For Paul, this is essentially at odds with the gospel, and he begins an argument about the nature of the Christian community that will lead through to his statements about the practices of the Eucharist in 1 Corinthians 11.

The verb that is used with respect to God's electing activity is *eklegomai*, and it is here deployed in a way that draws attention to the differences between God's rationale for choosing to show favour and native human attitudes that attach significance to social capital: we show favour to the wise and powerful, but God shows it to the weak and foolish. In fact, the language used in verse 28 is as basic a negation of any notion of capital that we can imagine: God chose 'the things that are not' (*ta mē onta*) to nullify 'the things that are'. The dynamic that is visible within the Corinthian church, where factions have formed around impressive teachers and where the 'have nots' are functionally separated from the wealthy at the Lord's Supper (1 Corinthians 11.22), is one that Paul considers to reflect the natural fleshly instincts that the gospel holds to account. If we are to participate in the gospel, our attitude to showing favour should reflect that of God himself.[9]

The verb *eklegomai* is widely found in Greek translation of the Old Testament, and while not all of the occurrences are obviously linked to the covenant between God and Israel, some are. Several of these are encountered in the chapters building up to and then moving on from the Shema, and when considered together they make a strikingly similar point to the one that Paul emphasizes in 1 Corinthians 1.27–29.

> And because he loved your ancestors, he chose [*exelexato*] their descendants after them. He brought you out of Egypt with his own presence, by his great power . . .
>
> (Deuteronomy 4.37)

> For you are a people holy to the LORD your God; the LORD your God has chosen [*proeilato*] you out of all the peoples on earth to be his people, his treasured possession. It was not because you were more numerous than any other people that the LORD set his heart on you and chose [*exelexato*] you – for you were the fewest of all peoples.
>
> (Deuteronomy 7.6–7)

> Yet the LORD set his heart in love on your ancestors alone and chose [*proeilato*] you, their descendants after them, out of all the peoples, as it is today.
>
> (Deuteronomy 10.15)

These chapters of Deuteronomy are closely connected to the Shema and are embedded within a retrospectively narratival portion of the book that establishes the character of the covenantal relationship between God and his people and therefore frames the subsequent legal requirements. Given what we have seen of the importance of the Shema to Paul's ethical thought in 1 Corinthians, it is reasonable to see these verses from the context of the Shema to inform the way that he speaks of God's election,

---

9 The implications of this for pastoral theology and ethics are enormous. I probe this somewhat in my recent article, Macaskill 2017. I note there that our churches continue to embody the instinctive veneration of people perceived to be smart or successful and commonly marginalize those who do not fit with a particular pattern of interaction.

even if the verses actually quoted (in 1.18 and in 1.31) are from Isaiah 29.14 and Jeremiah 9.24. Those verses indicate that the natural tendency to glory in riches and wisdom, as humanly evaluated, will be shown for the hubris that it is. Paul therefore begins and ends this particular section of his argument with quotations that show the true folly of the standards at work in the Corinthian community and indicate the judgement that will befall these; in between, however, in a series of strikingly parallel statements, he points to the character of divine election as the explanation for this judgement. His particular description of God's electing activity is, at the very least, similar to what we find in Deuteronomy 7.6–7 and 10.14, where the same verb occurs, and this, I would suggest, allows us to speak in a modest way of Paul's description of divine election being informed or shaped by these verses, as he reflects on the character of those who make up the Church as mirroring the marginal or insignificant character of the Israel chosen by God (cf. 1.26).

This, moreover, is not a passing ethical matter in the broader sweep of 1 Corinthians. As I have noted already, the argument of 1 Corinthians 1.27–29 emerges from Paul's opening concerns about factionalism within the Corinthian church and runs as a thread through the chapters that follow until it again becomes the dominant issue of concern in chapters 11 and 12, with their linked accounts of Eucharist and the body of Christ. And, as we have seen, these chapters themselves are linked back through chapter 10 to the appropriation of the Shema in 1 Corinthians 8.6. They are also, of course, linked forward to his description of the practices of mutual love in 1 Corinthians 13, which should be recognized as embedded in the account of the body and its spiritual gifts (discussed in chapter 12 and mentioned immediately after the end of chapter 13, in 14.1). Paul's ethics of Christian unity and his understanding of how it must bear on the fellowship of the Church, across its socio-economic strata, seems to be grounded in his understanding of the character of divine activity, as expressed in the covenant with Israel.

Crucially, though, there is no narrative of the covenant visible in these verses. Instead, Paul simply seems to work with a recognition (or even a more tacit assumption) that God works in the same way now as he did with Israel, that his saving activity is best labelled with the covenantal language of election, and that the nature of that election – reflected in the composition of the Church – is the same as it has always been, attaching itself to those void of capital significance. As with the outworking of the Shema in chapters 8, 10 and 12, where the oneness of God is the basis for speaking of the unity of the Church, so here Paul's strategy is not so much to point to a narrative and to locate the Church within it, but rather to point to the identity and activity of God, whose agency is consistent in all that he does. The challenge that faces the Church is to participate in that character, to be holy as he is holy. This is less about fulfilling our place in the story, and more about being attentive to the identity of the central protagonist, after whom we are to pattern our behaviour.

Conclusion

What I hope has emerged from this study is that the theme of covenant is woven into the way that Paul thinks and the way that he frames ethical consideration, even in the light of his recognition that his old fleshly way of thinking was twisted by sin (cf. 2 Corinthians 5.16–21; Philippians 3.2–10). For all that the gospel has essentially disrupted his understanding of the world and the place within this of the law, he continues to approach moral matters in a way that is shaped by the category of covenant. Moreover, his understanding of covenant is informed particularly by Deuteronomy, especially the passages that are found in the vicinity of the Shema. So, we cannot allow ourselves to set the Abrahamic covenant (of promise) at odds with the Mosaic one (of law), with the latter understood in flatly negative terms.

All of this, I think, provides some support for Wright's claims about the place of covenant in Paul's thought and represents a response to those who have been critical of him in this regard because the actual terminology of covenant is not as widely found as might be expected on the basis of his account. At the same time, it seems to me that Paul's covenantal thinking is not necessarily tied to a single overarching narrative – even if a very complicated one – but is, rather, tied to the identification of the One who is the principal agent of multiple stories. While it is possible that an overarching narrative can be identified, it is not necessarily demanded by the way that he uses covenant conceptuality. This allows Paul to see figural relationships at work between stories: it is not simply that one story anticipates or points forward to the story of Jesus, typologically or prophetically, but the new identification of God that has been made possible in the apocalypse at the heart of the gospel allows Paul to reread the stories of Israel as 'gospel-shaped'. In certain regards, this conclusion is very similar to the one reached elsewhere by Francis Watson[10] (although I am less persuaded

---

[10] See Watson 2002, 231–9.

that the gospel can be described as 'essentially nonnarratable'),[11] but my version places a distinct emphasis on the category of covenant. As such, I also think that it remains important to Paul that Jesus was himself born within the context of the covenant, as a child of pious Jewish parents. All of this lends support to the emphasis on covenant in Wright's work, but invites reflection on whether it should be considered principally with respect to an overarching story, or rather with respect to the principal agent of multiple stories. Covenant is the way the One God works, with ordered, loving relationships properly mediated. There may or may not be a unified narrative of the covenant, but there is one God and one mediator between God and humanity.

Bibliography

Alexander, Philip (2016). 'The Agent of the King Is Treated as the King Himself: Does the Worship of Jesus Imply His Divinity?' In *In the Fullness of Time: Essays on Christology, Creation and Eschatology in Honor of Richard Bauckham*, edited by Daniel Gurtner, Grant Macaskill and Jonathan Pennington, 97–114. Grand Rapids, MI: Eerdmans.

Bauckham, Richard (1998). *God Crucified: Monotheism and Christology in the New Testament*. Carlisle: Paternoster.

Boyarin, Daniel (2001). 'The Gospel of the Memra: Jewish Binitarianism and the Prologue to John.' *Harvard Theological Review* 94.3: 243–84.

—— (2010). 'Beyond Judaisms: Metatron and the Divine Polymorphy of Ancient Judaism.' *Journal for the Study of Judaism* 41.3: 323–65.

Brown, William P. (1999). *The Ethos of the Cosmos: The Genesis of Moral Imagination in the Bible*. Grand Rapids, MI: Eerdmans.

Frei, Hans (1975). *The Identity of Jesus Christ: The Hermeneutical Bases for Dogmatic Theology*. Philadelphia, PA: Fortress.

Kelsey, David (2009). *Eccentric Existence: A Theological Anthropology*. Louisville, KY: Westminster John Knox.

Litwa, M. David (2012). *We Are Being Transformed: Deification in Paul's Soteriology*. Beihefte zur Zeitschrift für die neutestamentliche Wissenschaft 187. Berlin: de Gruyter.

Macaskill, Grant (2017). 'Autism Spectrum Disorders and the New Testament: Preliminary Reflections.' *Journal of Disability and Religion*. Published 11 October. Online: <http://www.tandfonline.com/doi/full/10.1080/23312521.2017.1373613>.

Moberly, R. Walter (1999). 'Towards an Interpretation of the Shema.' In *Theological Exegesis: Essays in Honor of Brevard Childs*, edited by Christopher Seitz and Kathryn Greene McCreight, 124–44. Grand Rapids, MI: Eerdmans.

---

[11] Watson 2002, 239.

Ricoeur, Paul (1984). *Time and Narrative, Volume 1.* Translated by Kathleen Blamey and David Pellauer. Chicago, IL: University of Chicago Press.

—— (1985). *Time and Narrative, Volume 2.* Translated by Kathleen Blamey and David Pellauer. Chicago, IL: University of Chicago Press.

—— (1988). *Time and Narrative, Volume 3.* Translated by Kathleen Blamey and David Pellauer. Chicago, IL: University of Chicago Press.

—— (1992). *Oneself as Another.* Translated by Kathleen Blamey. Chicago, IL: University of Chicago Press.

—— (1995). *Figuring the Sacred: Religion, Narrative and Imagination.* Translated by David Pellauer. Edited by Mark Wallace. Minneapolis, MN: Fortress.

—— (2016). *Philosophical Anthropology: Writings and Lectures, Volume 3.* Translated by David Pellauer. Edited by Johann Michel and Jérôme Porée. Cambridge: Polity Press.

Watson, Francis (2002). 'Is There a Story in These Texts?' In *Narrative Dynamics in Paul: A Critical Assessment,* edited by Bruce Longenecker, 231–9. Louisville, KY: Westminster John Knox.

Wright, N. T. (2013). *Paul and the Faithfulness of God.* Christian Origins and the Question of God 4. London: SPCK / Minneapolis, MN: Fortress.

King Solomon, a new Adam and incorporative representative of God's people (1 Kings 3—4): a text that supports N. T. Wright on Paul and the Messiah

CRISPIN FLETCHER-LOUIS

Paul's incorporative royal Messiah

Tom Wright has argued that when Paul uses the word '*Christos*' he means 'Messiah', a word that has representative connotations. The Messiah, as the true king, is an incorporative figure. He is both the true Adam and also the one 'in whom the true people of God are summed up and find their identity'.[1] To be 'in Christ' means to be in 'the Messiah and his people'.[2] Paul's expression '*in* Christ' sits within, and gathers up, the several layers of a storied worldview, as do related prepositional phrases. The word connotes a triple-layered narrative: Christ's role in the story of God's dealings with the cosmos, as bearer of God's love and justice; his role as the true Adam fulfilling the frustrated story of Adam and Eve's call to be God's image and likeness ruling in creation on God's behalf; and his role in completing the story of Israel, the people called to be the true Adam, who have been unable, in their own strength, to be God's means of completing the vocation of Adam. This aspect of Wright's understanding of Pauline theology has not been widely accepted.[3] However, it is one of the many ways that 30 years ago Wright's scholarship first stimulated my excitement and thinking about Jewish and early Christian messianisms. So it is

---

[1] Wright 1991, 46. A 'Messiah . . . draws on to himself the hope and destiny of the people itself' (Wright 1991, 25). 'It is endemic in the understanding of kingship, in many societies and certainly in ancient Israel, that the king and the people are bound together in such a way that what is true of the one is true in principle of the other' (Wright 1991, 46). See further Wright 1991, 18–49, cf. 162–8; 2003, 42–50, 248, 256, 395, 582, 655, 730; 2005, 16; 2013a, 17, 356, 517–37, 405, 529, 658, 815–16, 821, 823–35, 839, 865–6, 897; 2013b, 510–46 (esp. 534–8).

[2] Wright 2013a, 17. For helpful discussions of Wright's understanding of the representative function of the Messiah, see Lee 2016, and Hewitt and Novenson 2016.

[3] See, e.g., the criticisms of Barclay 2015, 238–40.

a pleasure to offer here this study of one Old Testament text in support of Tom's approach to Paul's '*Christos*' language.

Wright finds evidence for his claims for Paul's '*Christos*' in two literary corpora: in Paul's own letters and in the pre-Pauline history of the word and others that are related to it, especially biblical kingship texts. For the second of these Wright appeals to a few texts in the books of Samuel and Kings that have the phrase 'a portion *in David*', or similar language and ideas:[4]

And the men of Israel answered the men of Judah, 'We have ten shares *in the king* [*ḥammelek*; *en tō basilei*], and *in David* [*bᵉḏāwiḏ*, *en tō Dauid*] also we have more than you. Why then did you despise us? Were we not the first to speak of bringing back our king?' But the words of the men of Judah were fiercer than the words of the men of Israel.

(2 Samuel 19.43)

Sheba, the son of Bichri, a Benjaminite . . . blew the trumpet and said, 'We have no portion *in David* [*bᵉḏāwiḏ*; *en Dauid*], and we have no inheritance *in the son of Jesse* [*bᵉḇen-yišay*; *en tō huiō Iessai*]; every man to his tents, O Israel!' So all the men of Israel withdrew from David and followed Sheba the son of Bichri. But the men of Judah followed their king steadfastly from the Jordan to Jerusalem.

(2 Samuel 20.1–2)

And when all Israel saw that the king did not listen to them, the people answered the king, 'What portion do we have *in David* [*bᵉḏāwiḏ*; *en Dauid*]? We have no inheritance *in the son of Jesse* [*bᵉḇen-yišay*; *en huiō Iessai*]. To your tents, O Israel! Look now to your own house, David.' So Israel went to their tents.

(1 Kings 12.16; cf. LXX 1 Kings 12.24t and 2 Samuel 5.1–3)

In these texts being 'in David' or 'in the king' is certainly an expression that appears to give Israel's anointed king a representative function in relation to his people.

In his recent careful study of Paul's Christological language, Matthew Novenson is supportive of Wright's argument that *Christos* is not simply a personal name, but that for Paul it also connotes messiahship. However, Novenson considers Wright's claims for Paul's debt to an incorporative messianism problematic and his appeal to texts in 2 Samuel and 1 Kings unpersuasive. For one thing, these texts do not provide exact linguistic

---

4 Unless otherwise noted, Bible quotations in this chapter are taken from the ESV; any emphasis has been added.

parallels to Paul's 'in *Christ*'.[5] There is also the objection that 'the idiom is relatively obscure . . . and apparently without currency in Jewish literature of the Hellenistic and Roman periods'.[6]

Many Pauline specialists have also found Wright's multi-storied, incorporative, view of the Messiah unconvincing. Others, notably, A. J. M. Wedderburn, have appealed instead to the use of representative language for Abraham and his seed as a conceptual parallel to Paul's 'in Christ' and 'with Christ' language.[7] In the argument of Galatians 3 Paul makes linguistic and theological connections between being 'in Christ Jesus' (v. 14; cf. v. 16) and being in Abraham and in Abraham's seed. Those who are 'in Christ' constitute the fulfilment of God's promise to Abraham that '*in you* [*en soi*] shall all the nations be blessed [*eneulogēthēsontai*]' (Genesis 12.3 cited in Galatians 3.8; cf. Genesis 18.18); a statement that appears at the start of the story of Abraham and which both Genesis and Paul connect to subsequent promises that the nations, or tribes of the earth, are to be blessed in Abraham's seed (Genesis 22.18; 24.4; 28.14; cf. Galatians 3.16). For Paul 'the seed' of Abraham is 'Christ' (Galatians 3.16). So, at the very least, Galatians shows that for Paul the story of Abraham and the notion that Abraham was the kind of representative figure through whose seed God would act to bless the world provided a conceptual analogy to his understanding of Christ and Christ's representative relation to those who are blessed in him.

However, it is not necessarily the case that Galatians 3 provides any clear evidence that the Abraham story, or a first-century interpretation of it, or even Paul's own reading of it, was the conceptual *source* of Paul's ubiquitous 'in Christ' language.[8] 'In Christ' language is ubiquitous in Paul's letters and in the majority of cases has no obvious connection to the passages Paul evokes in the letter to the Galatians. And whereas Abraham is neither a king nor a messiah in Genesis and later Jewish interpretation, Wright's appeal to incorporative language for David and Israel's king provides a closer analogy to Paul's talk of being 'in *Christ*'.

Indeed, there is one scriptural kingship text, which until now has not figured in this discussion, that offers some support for Wright's arguments.

---

5 Novenson 2012, 124. See generally pp. 119–26, and also Hewitt and Novenson 2016, 399–401.
6 Novenson 2012, 124; cf. 126. For Wright's reasons to hold on to the incorporative sense of Messiah, see Wright 2013a, 825–35; 2013b, 534–7.
7 Wedderburn 1985; cf. Novenson 2012, 124–6, and Hewitt and Novenson 2016, 401–6.
8 Though see now Hewitt and Novenson 2016, 401–9, for a suggestive attempt to argue for that scenario.

In 1 Kings 3—4 (MT 3.1—5.14) there is biblical kingship material that expresses precisely the kind of relationship between Israel's king and the three stories that Wright thinks inform Paul's worldview. And 1 Kings 3—4 is sandwiched between the texts to which Wright appeals as background to the expression 'in Christ' (2 Samuel 19.41—20.2; 1 Kings 12.16), in a way that suggests sensitive first-century readers would naturally read the words 'in David/in the king/in the son of Jesse' the way Wright supposes Paul read them. These two chapters are also important because they show that, already in Israel's Scriptures, the ideal king's incorporative function was related to the fulfilment of the promises to Abraham that Paul treats in Galatians 3.

1 Kings 3—4

Chapters 1—11 of the first book of Kings form a distinct literary block covering the succession from David to Solomon and the new king's reign. It plays a central role in the overarching structure of the Deuteronomistic History and the Primary History (Genesis—2 Kings). Chapters 3—4 (MT 3.1—5.14) provide a glowing account of the early years of Solomon's reign, his achievements and glory, with hints at personal flaws that will mar his later reign. Its interpretative issues are many and fascinating. Several are hotly contested, but need not concern us here.

The account of the early phase of Solomon's life – when he is obedient, wise and faithful to God – ascribes to the young king a multilayered identity. These chapters proclaim the partial completion, in Solomon, of three stories:

1 The story of God's creative work in ordering an earth and cosmos abundant with life that is fit for human flourishing. A story, that is, that begins in Genesis 1—2, but that is incomplete before it is frustrated by human sin.
2 The story of humanity that is created to be God's image and likeness, but that has failed to be the bearer of his presence and action from the garden of Eden onwards.
3 Israel's story as the people called to be the solution to the problem of a disobedient Adam and Eve; the people to whom God promises a recovery of the conditions and identity lost in Eden.[9]

Each of these overarching stories is evoked and finds at least a partial completion in 1 Kings 3—4. But crucially, each of these metanarratives

---

9 For these stories see especially Beale 2011.

lies not far beneath the surface of the story told in 1 Kings. And although the primary actor in two of these stories – God and Israel – is present in 1 Kings 3—4, neither is the lead actor in the drama. Indeed, the three pro-tagonists of these three metanarratives – God, humanity and Israel – are each *represented* on the stage of history by another actor, namely Solomon, Israel's king. It is Solomon, the wise and virtuous ideal king, who, for much of the story, represents God to the people. It is Solomon who experiences a recovery of the identity Adam lost in the garden. And it is Solomon who sums up in himself the interests and aspirations of the people of God. Solomon is a representative of God, of the true Adam and of Israel (the truly human people). And in the early phase of his reign there is a kind of inaugurated eschatology. The way Solomon acts means he brings to partial completion the stories that were begun but frustrated in Genesis.

Solomon's role in representing each of these actors and their stories is not rigidly confined to discrete portions of the text. Although the Solomon-as-Adam theme predominates in 1 Kings 4, his identification with God and with Israel is a theme that runs through both chapters. In the rest of this essay I present the evidence for the Solomon-as-representative reading of 1 Kings 3—4 in three parts that approximate to the three stories outlined above. But given the complexities of the drama, my observations in each part sometimes pertain to more than one of the three stories.

1 Solomon is the tester and revealer of human hearts (1 Kings 3.16–28)

At first glance a prosaic description of the young king's reign, chapters 3—4 of 1 Kings are full of narrative and visual symbolism, as well as pro-found political theology. They also contain riddles that invite the reader to engage in careful reading and critical reflection. One of the riddles comes in 3.16–28: how does Solomon solve the apparently unsolvable case of a dispute between two prostitutes over one dead, and one still living, child?

There has been considerable scholarly discussion of the means by which Solomon solves this memorable case. Here are some observa-tions which ought to be matters of general agreement and a few fresh insights which deal with the story's most obvious questions and explain its primary purposes at this point in the account of Solomon's reign.

It would surely be obvious to the implied readers of the story that Solomon, like other Israelite kings and kings in the wider Ancient Near Eastern world, serves as the nation's highest judicial authority. Presumably, the reader imagines, the case has come to Israel's supreme court, over which Solomon presides, because it could not be solved in a lower one (cf. Deuteronomy 17.8–9). It is a difficult case. There were, presumably, no witnesses. Certainly, we are to assume that there was no father to act as head of the household. Today the case would be resolved easily: a DNA test would identify the mother of the living child. According to the account of Israel's history of which 1 Kings 3 is now a part, Solomon would have had a copy of the laws of Moses and the time necessary to study it diligently (Deuteronomy 17.18–19). But Moses does not stipulate a procedure to judge a case like this one. So it provides an opportunity for Solomon to demonstrate his supreme wisdom (see v. 28).

Solomon solves the case by a different kind of test, I propose. A DNA test finds the answer written in genetic code. Solomon's treatment of the two women shows that the truth of the matter is written elsewhere: it is recorded on the hearts and in the minds of the mothers. Mothers know their children and are not easily confused by circumstances that might lead to a mix-up between them. Each mother knows whose baby still lives. One mother is lying, and knows it; the other comes before the king hoping for justice. Whether his command – 'Bring a sword! Divide the living child in two and give half to each' (see vv. 24–25) – is a thoughtful stratagem arising from long reflection or, more likely as the story tells it, a moment of inspired genius, it is, I propose, a consciously conceived action that expects, or hopes for, the result it produces. *It proves to be an effective action because it exposes the hearts of the women whereupon the record of the identity of the true mother is written.* The heart of the living child's mother burns with compassion (v. 26). Her protestation reveals her heart, and Solomon is able to solve the legal case. As the child's mother, she would rather the child live with the other woman than see it die horribly. The other mother has no natural feelings for the living child and so is content to see it die.

The purpose of the account of Solomon's hearing of the case of the two women is to present David's successor as the ideal king who acts as God's representative on earth in his wise judgement. When 'all Israel heard of the judgement that the king had rendered . . . they perceived that the wisdom of God was in him to do justice'. Queen Elizabeth I of England is famously remembered as refusing to 'open windows into men's souls'. 1 Kings 3, by contrast, puts forward an ideal king who, as one in possession of divine wisdom, is able to do that very thing. For the discerning reader steeped in Israel's Scriptures the story is naturally interpreted in the light of the commonplace notion that it is the Lord God who tests and reveals human hearts (Jeremiah 12.3; 17.10; 20.12; Deuteronomy 8.2; 1 Kings 8.39; Psalms 26.2; 66.10; 139.1–3, 23; Job 7.17–18). Although the testing and seeing of the heart is usually a divine prerogative, the story of Samuel's choosing of David shows that, on occasion, those who represent God could mediate the divine discernment of the human heart (1 Samuel 16.7). In our text, Solomon possesses God's wisdom (v. 28) and he is Israel's king, a position in Ancient Near Eastern societies that typically entailed the bearing of the character of the gods. So it is fitting that he too is able to test and reveal hearts, the way God does, in his position as the highest judge of the land. Solomon is not just possessed of God's wisdom; he is the veritable bearer of the divine presence, and of truth and justice.

There are other features of the passage that show this is probably the way the story was intended to be heard and how later biblically literate readers would have naturally taken it. There are ways in which both the immediate literary context and the story's historical setting – in relation to competing accounts of the kings of Israel's neighbours – confirm the impression that Solomon tests hearts the way the living God tests hearts.

Before he hears the case of the two prostitutes, Solomon has a dream after sacrificing at Gibeon (3.5–14). In that dream Solomon is himself tested. The Lord asks him a question: 'What do you want me to do for you, Solomon?' (see 3.5). This is surely divine reassurance. It reveals that God is a present help to the young king. But it is also a test, one that Solomon passes with flying colours, by asking for wisdom to govern God's people, rather than for wealth, long life and the death of his enemies.

That the question functions as a test is especially clear when we compare the dream dialogue with the prayers of Ancient Near Eastern kings. For the form and content of Solomon's dream dialogue there are close parallels in Mesopotamian royal prayers. Except that in those prayers the king typically *does* ask his god for wealth, long life, territorial dominion and the death of his enemies. For example, the Babylonian king Nebuchadnezzar II (604–562 BCE) prays:

> O Lord Marduk, wisest of the gods, proud prince, it was you who created me and entrusted to me the kingship of all peoples, I love your lofty form as (my own) precious life. None of your holy places in the whole inhabited world did I render more renowned than your holy place, Babylon. Even as I love your divine splendour and have ever sought after your dominion, so accept my entreaty, hear my prayer! Let me be royal provider who pleases you, let me be your faithful shepherd who keeps your people safe, let me be a skilled governor who provides for all your holy places.
>
> At your command, O merciful Marduk, may the house I built long endure and may I enjoy its delights in full measure. May I reach old age and enjoy venerable years therein. May I receive therein the massive tribute

of the kings of the four world regions and of all humankind. From horizon to zenith, where ever the sun comes forth, may I have no opponents nor encounter those to affright me. Within it may my descendants hold dominion over the people of this land forever.[10]

Solomon's prayer dialogue echoes this kind of prayer closely. The opening lines, in which Nebuchadnezzar acknowledges his debt to the chief god of the Babylonian pantheon, Marduk, parallels Solomon's thanksgiving to YHWH for his putting him in the place of his father David (1 Kings 3.6–8). And in the closing lines of the first paragraph, Nebuchadnezzar's prayer that he be a faithful shepherd of the people and a skilled governor parallels Solomon's request for wisdom to govern Israel in 1 Kings 3.9. However, the second paragraph of the Babylonian king's prayer runs directly counter to the logic of the text in 1 Kings.

Solomon is commended by God for *not* asking for three things: for long life, for wealth and for the death of his enemies (3.11). These are precisely the things, in the very same order, for which Nebuchadnezzar *does* ask in his prayer (in its second paragraph). The parallels and differences between the two prayers mean that in the context of the patterns of Ancient Near Eastern royal piety, one reason Solomon is commended is that his prayers do not have the kind of self-oriented focus that (sometimes) character-ized the spirituality of pagan kings. We have preserved royal inscriptions on Mesopotamian public buildings that record similar prayers. They show that the form and content of Nebuchadnezzar's prayer was typical and would most likely have been well known.[11] That impression is con-firmed by one of Israel's own psalms, Psalm 72, where all the subjects of Nebuchadnezzar's prayer find expression in a prayer for the well-being of the king: long life (Psalm 72.5, 15a, 17a–b); dominion over enemies (vv. 8–11, 15b); material abundance (vv. 15b, 16; cf. vv. 3, 6–7); justice and true judgement in rule (vv. 1–4, 12–14). Psalm 72 is dedicated to Solomon and it shows that prayers for kings typically covered these topics.

The evidence of Psalm 72 and 1 Kings 3.10–11 shows Israelites knew that the topics covered in Nebuchadnezzar's prayer were typical of the royal cults of their neighbours. However, in the biblical psalm there are also points of contrast to Nebuchadnezzar's prayer. It is the psalmist who

---

10 Translation from Foster 2005, 843.

11 For similar Babylonian prayers see Foster 2005, IV.7, prayers (a) and (b) – for King Nabopolassar; IV.8, prayers (b), (c), (f), (g), (i) and (j) – all for Nebuchadnezzar II; and IV.10 – a prayer for King Neriglissar. The Nebuchadnezzar II prayer cited above and several of these other ones include a prayer for the king's role as a means of justice and right rule, a theme that also has a parallel in 1 Kings 3—4.

prays for the welfare of the king – rather than the king who asks for blessings for himself – and the king's blessings are bound up with blessings for
his people ('prosperity for the people' (vv. 3, 4), help for the poor, needy
and oppressed (vv. 12–14, 16) and for all the nations (v. 17)), rather than
the focus being on his own prosperity and exaltation.[12]

So, too, in 1 Kings 3 there are both similarities and differences between
the biblical text and comparable Mesopotamian royal prayers. In asking
for nothing for himself, save that he should have a 'listening heart' or
'mind' (*lēḇ šōmēa*ʿ) to govern God's people, and to discern between good
and evil (1 Kings 3.9), Solomon proves himself to be a worthy ruler of
God's people. He is so worthy because, *inter alia*, he is a king who, in
important ways, is unlike the kings among Israel's neighbours. God's invitation to Solomon in 1 Kings 3.5 – 'Ask what I shall give you' – amounts
to another, deeper, question: 'Do you want to rule my people the way the
kings of all the other nations rule theirs, with a self-serving pursuit of
power and wealth?' In his answer, which point for point echoes but subverts the preserved prayers of Babylonian kings, Solomon distinguishes
himself from the kings of the nations.

This also means that, from the perspective of the Deuteronomistic
historian, the early years of Solomon's reign addressed, at least in some
respects, anxieties surrounding kingship that appear prominently in other
parts of the account of Israel's history and her laws. In these earlier years of
his reign, Solomon was not a king like the kings among Israel's neighbours.
He does not act entirely in his own interests, treating his brothers and
sisters as slaves (see 1 Kings 8, esp. vv. 5, 17; cf. Deuteronomy 17.14–20).

This all means, also, that within the framework of the narrative of 1
Kings 3, *the young Solomon passes the test God sets for him at Gibeon*. It is
a test that calls to mind Psalm 17.3 – 'You have tried my heart, *you have
visited me by night*, you have tested me . . .' So the theme of the divine
testing and revealing of hearts is already to the fore before the judgement
of the two prostitutes. We are perhaps meant to conclude that Solomon is
uniquely suited to test and reveal the hearts of his subjects because, in his
own dealings with God – in worship and prayer – his own heart has been
tested and found to be faithful, righteous and upright.

Read this way, we can now see that the judgement story of the two prostitutes demonstrates a fulfilment of God's promise that Solomon would

---

[12] The prayer for the king in Psalm 72 can also be fruitfully compared with the Coronation
Prayer for Assurbanipal (669 BCE) in Foster 2005, 815–16. I take it that the superscription
for Psalm 72 means that this psalm is about, or for the benefit of, Solomon. It is not a psalm
that was spoken by Solomon.

receive the 'listening heart' for which he had asked in his dream (3.9; cf. vv. 10–14). Solomon hears the case of a deceased child and discerns, *by means of the test of the sword*, between the good and the evil hearts of the two mothers. *Solomon does as he has been divinely done by*. He was tested by God, and his heart's intentions were revealed (in the dream). Then he acts as God in testing the women, and their hearts are revealed.

As a chapter that depicts Solomon bearing the action and presence of God in the judicial sphere, 1 Kings 3 provides a fitting lead-in to 1 Kings 4, a chapter that functions as a kind of State of the Union address at the height of Solomon's kingdom. In chapter 4 the reader encounters more reasons to think that, as the true king, Solomon imitates or actualizes the character and presence of God. Only, in this portion of the story there are multiple connections to a story like the one with which the Hebrew Bible begins: the story of Adam and his role as God's image and likeness in creation, and in Eden (Genesis 1—2).

2 A new Adam, the image of the Creator (1 Kings 4)

Chapter 4 boasts of Solomon's administrative and economic skills, the bounteous provision he receives from a small empire that has expanded to include territories 'from the Euphrates to the land of the Philistines and to the border of Egypt' (vv. 7, 21–28), and of his superior wisdom that gives him worldwide fame (vv. 30–34). He is a philosopher king, a political and economic mastermind; accomplished in the arts, conversant in the sciences.

Beneath the obvious surface of the text there are more profound claims, and Solomon's glory evokes a story; the story of God's creation of humanity to bear his image and complete his own divine work. Following up the work of Greg Beale, Peter Leithart and John A. Davies, we can identify at least nine features of 1 Kings 4 that continue the theme begun in 1 Kings 3: Solomon, the anointed and true king, manifests something of the true image of God.[13] We can parse that identity further since in some respects he is all that Adam *the man* had been created to be, while in others he is much more – his achievements manifest the creativity of the Creator. He is truly human (according to the vision for human life in Genesis 1—2), but also more than simply human; in some ways he is divine.

In addition, what has not been noticed in modern discussion is the way in which here (and in the previous chapter) our author says that – to use Wright's words for Jesus as Messiah – Solomon is the one who 'sums up his

---

[13] Leithart 2006, 42–52; Beale 2011, 66–73; Davies 2011.

people in himself, so that what is true of him is true of them'.[14] I shall come to that in the next section. First, to Solomon as a restored Adam, who functions as a kind of co-creator, continuing or recapitulating the work of *the* Creator. In at least five ways his identity and activities mean that here, at a climactic moment in Israel's history, there is a king who fulfils Adam's original vocation.

(i) In Genesis 2 God creates a garden in Eden – a place of plenty and safety, which is to be guarded by human beings. Solomon's kingdom also has Edenic qualities. It is a place of prosperity and abundance, of biological variety and *shalom*; a place of safety for God's people that is protected by *Shelomoh* (an archaic Hebrew spelling of 'his peace'), and by *Shelomoh*'s chariots and horsemen.[15] All this comes in the course of Solomon's reign. The young king did not start (in 1 Kings 2—3) with this abundance.[16] Similarly, Adam was created outside Eden and then set in the garden of delights (Genesis 2.7–8). Other biblical and Ancient Near Eastern texts show that the association of the ideal king with gardens of plenty was traditional (e.g. Ecclesiastes 2.4–6).[17]

(ii) In Genesis 1.26 God makes humankind in his image and likeness and to have dominion (*rāḏāh*) in creation. He blesses them so that they might 'be fruitful and multiply [*pᵉrû ûrᵉḇû*], and fill the earth [*hā'āreṣ*] and subdue it and have dominion [*rᵉḏû*]' (1.28). Echoing this command to humankind, 1 Kings 4.24 says that Solomon 'had dominion [*rōḏeh*] over all the region west of the Euphrates from Tiphsah to Gaza, over all the kings west of the Euphrates'. And the description of Israel spread out in distinct territories, living in abundance, suggests God's people have achieved a partial fulfilment of the original command to be fruitful and multiply.

(iii) The sweep of the narrative of Genesis 1 builds to a climactic vision of humanity as God's image-idol (the *tselem elohim*), enshrined, as it were, in the central nave of the cosmic temple. Everything else is ordered to create

---

14 Wright 1991, 48.

15 The word *shalom* (1 Kings 4.24) does not appear in Genesis 1—3, but Davies (2011, 41) notes its appearance in other creational texts (Leviticus 26.6; Isaiah 45.7; Ezekiel 37.26).

16 For Genesis 2.7 – 'the Lord God formed the man of dust from the ground and breathed into his nostrils the breath of life' – as a description of the beginning of a king's rule, see Brueggemann 1972 (comparing esp. 1 Kings 16.2).

17 For Ancient Near Eastern texts and images that place the king in a (sacred) garden, see Stordalen 2000, 94–104; Callender 2000; Wyatt 2014.

a place fit for human flourishing.[18] And on the sixth day, God lays down humanity's dining rights (Genesis 1.29–30): 'Behold, I have given you every plant yielding seed that is on the face of all the earth, and every tree with seed in its fruit. You shall have them for food.' Not that humanity's needs compete with the needs of others (Genesis 1.30): 'And to every beast of the earth and to every bird of the heavens and to everything that creeps on the earth, everything that has the breath of life, I have given every green plant for food.'

A similar theme is prominent in 1 Kings 4. Almost everything in the Solomonic utopia is oriented to the flourishing of Solomon and his people: the arrangement of 12 officers over 12 districts is 'for the provision of food for the king' (v. 7). All his subject kingdoms bring tribute (v. 21) and the rich fare of his kitchen is laid out: 'Solomon's provision for one day was thirty cors of fine flour and sixty cors of meal, ten fat oxen, and twenty pasture-fed cattle, a hundred sheep, besides deer, gazelles, roebucks, and fattened fowl' (vv. 22–23).

The land ('āreṣ, v. 19) of greater Israel is the provider for Solomon, just as the whole earth ('āreṣ) is the provider for Adam in Genesis 1.30. (That there are seven types of meat on Solomon's table presumably signifies a fullness of the land's, or the earth's, provision.) And to the account of the food given to the beasts in Genesis 1.30 there corresponds the notice that barley and straw was prepared for the horses in 1 Kings 4.28.

(iv) At the climax of Genesis 1, humanity created as God's *tselem* and *demut* is exalted over the rest of creation: 'over all the earth' (v. 26).[19] At the climax of 1 Kings 4, Solomon – the new Adam – is twice exalted in his wisdom. He is master of the natural world by his science, and he is exalted over his peers – wiser than 'all other men' (v. 31).

(v) In his learning, Solomon 'speaks of' trees, beasts, birds, creeping things and fish (vv. 33–34). That surely means he knows their names. So in this mastery of the natural world we are bound to recall Adam's naming of all the animals (Genesis 2.19–20) and to hear a further echo of the original command to subdue and have dominion over beasts, birds, creeping things and fish (Genesis 1.26, 28).

In these and other ways Solomon is a new Adam. In other respects he

---

18 The notion that the world was created for the benefit of humanity was a commonplace at the dawn of the Christian era: see, e.g., Philo, *Opif.* 78–9; *4 Ezra* 6.46, 55; 8.44; *2 Bar.* 14.17; *2 Enoch* 65.3 [J].

19 The emphasis on the universal, even cosmic, scope of Adam's authority is conveyed by the ten 'all's in the Hebrew text of Genesis 1.26–30.

is so much the image and likeness of God that he imitates, or actualizes, God's own creativity.[20]

(vi) In 1 Kings 4.32 (MT 5.12) Solomon 'is the image of the creator God in . . . the creative impulse of his poetry and songs'.[21]

(vii) In Genesis 1, creation comes about through God's establishing of order. Days 1–3 comprise an ordered structure in space and time, with heavenly and earthly spheres then governed by a distinct entity (the sun and the moon, and human beings) on days 4 and 6. Solomon creates a well-ordered kingdom, defined *spatially* by 12 economic districts (4.7–19) and *temporally* by a monthly contribution to the king and his household (4.7). So he creates his own, well-ordered microcosm in space and time of the order of the whole cosmos that God has created.

The Hebrew text of Genesis 1 emphasizes the theme of order with an intricate web of numerical patterns: 3s, 7s, 10s and multiples of 7s. For example, 7 times God sees that what he has made is 'good'. There are 7 words in Genesis 1.1; 14 words in verse 2; and so on. The numerical order of the passage 'imparts a remarkable mathematical aesthetic, the quantifiable order of a fully stable, life-sustaining, differentiated world'.[22] Numerical patterns are used in a similar way in 1 Kings 4. There are several 12s: a 12-man cabinet (if we include Solomon, in 4.1–6), 12 officers over the 12 districts (and also 12,000 horsemen), following a monthly cycle of service of the centre. There are 7 animals served up on Solomon's table (v. 22), and in verses 32–33 the king's scientific and artistic interests cover 7 disciplines (proverbial wisdom, songs, dendrology, zoology, ornithology, herpetology and ichthyology).

(viii) Both God's and Solomon's *ordering* creativity is an expression of wisdom. In Proverbs 3.19 the Lord creates the heavens and the earth *by wisdom* and understanding. As a sequel to chapter 3, 1 Kings 4 invites the conclusion that it is by his wisdom that Solomon creates his ordered, life-giving, value-laden world.

(ix) The God of Genesis takes initiative in creating the world and there are hints already in Genesis 1 that he will be revealed, in due course, as *the king*

---

[20] Inasmuch as Solomon is the creator of his kingdom – by his economic, political and scientific wisdom – and that kingdom is Edenic (the first point, above), he is in fact like God who created a garden in Eden.

[21] Leithart 2006, 50.

[22] Brown 2010, 37, and cf., e.g., Cassuto 1961, 14–15.

of all creation and history.[23] But if he is a sovereign, he is no totalitarian tyrant. He gives freedom to his humanity and, before that, his creative work proceeds, in part, through a delegation of authority to other entities. He delegates creativity to the land (which brings forth both the vegetation and the living creatures, vv. 11 and 19) and to the seas (which bring forth swarming living creatures, v. 20). His own sovereignty is parcelled out to the sun and moon (over the day and the night in Genesis 1.16–18) and to humanity. In a similar way, 1 Kings 4 presents Solomon as a king, who in his wisdom rules by sharing power with an executive. He shares power with his high officials and with the officers over the land (1 Kings 4.1–20).

So, in all these ways Solomon is caught up into God's story and the story of the rediscovery of the truly human identity that God originally intended. In the context of all that goes before and that comes after these chapters, especially Solomon's building of the Temple as a place of divine habitation, *1 Kings 3—4 says that, in and through this wise and Torah-faithful king, the grand stories of God, humanity and Israel have now found an ending (of sorts).* (Though tragically, in time, any sense of arrival is frustrated by Solomon's failings and inability to cope with threats from outside his pristine world.)

3 Solomon as Israel's representative

Solomon is more than just an example of the truly human or ideal king. There are features of 1 Kings 4 that tie the fortunes of the people closely to Solomon and his success. At a casual reading, we could be forgiven for thinking that the nation only experiences prosperity because it is a passive beneficiary of the king's economic policies. But it is a mistake to conclude that the text espouses a cynical trickle-down economics – the promise of gleanings for the many from the table of the few. Even if we are bound these days to read any vision of empire through a hermeneutic of suspicion, the connections to Israel's story of the first humans and God's original creation invite us to discern a positive theological structure beneath the image of an economic and political utopia. After all, Solomon and the people have experienced a recovery of God's purposes *for humanity as a whole*. Furthermore, the relationship between Solomon and his people should not be interpreted through a lens that judges all hierarchical relationships as necessarily dysfunctional or tyrannical. In a way that challenges the abusive relationship between kings and their subjects, leaders and the led, *portions of 1 Kings 4 portray Solomon as a*

---

[23] For God's royal character in Genesis 1 see, e.g., Middleton 2005, 70–4.

representative leader who has had his people on his heart; as one who has drawn others into his own destiny.

In 1 Kings 4.20 we read: 'Judah and Israel were as many [*rabbîm*] as the sand by the sea [*kaḥôl 'ªšer-'al-hayyām*] in multitude [*lārōḇ*].' Here there is a fulfilment of the promises to Abraham, especially those made in Genesis 22.17: 'I will surely bless you, and I will surely multiply ['*ªḇārekkā wᵉharbā*] your offspring as the stars of heaven and as the sand that is on the seashore [*kaḥôl 'ªšer 'al-śᵉpaṯ hayyām*]' (cf. Genesis 15.5; 32.12; 33.22).

Of course, as N. T. Wright has shown, Genesis 22.17 is one of a string of texts in Genesis–Joshua that harks back to the commission to Adam in a way that says that Israel is called to be what Adam was created to be.[24] Given all the ways in which Adam is evoked in 1 Kings 4, our passage in the account of the life of Solomon now confirms Wright's reading of the patriarchial narratives. Here too it is not just the king; it is *the whole people of God* whose identity is defined by their place in a larger story. In the one verse (1 Kings 4.20) there is an echo of both Genesis 1.28 and the promise to Abraham in Genesis 22.17. The people of Judah and Israel in 1 Kings 4.20 are 'as many [*rabbîm*]' as the sand by the sea '*in multitude* [*lārōḇ*]' (literal translation) which, given all the other echoes of Genesis 1—2, implies that under Solomon Israel fulfils God's original command to Adam to be fruitful and *multiply* (*rᵉḇû*). The same verse (1 Kings 4.20) also claims a fulfilment of the promise that God would bless Israel in passages such as Genesis 22.17.

Under Solomon the chosen people experience the partial fulfilment of the original command to Adam to be fruitful and multiply; that had been their vocation since the calling of the Patriarchs. And this has happened because Solomon has been the true Adam. *He* has achieved abundance, multiplication and the subduing of Israel's enemies and so, says 1 Kings 4, have *they*, the people.[25]

Clearly, 1 Kings 4.20 (LXX 2.46a) is a stand-out verse in the chapter. In the midst of regular Hebrew prose, 4.20a is a syntactically independent noun clause:

yᵉhûḏāh wᵉyiśrā'ēl rabbîm kaḥôl 'ªšer-'al-hayyām lārōḇ
Judah and Israel [were] many, as the sand by the sea in multitude

---

24 Wright 1991, 25.
25 Israel now moves out beyond its own land (*'āreṣ*) to fill out a larger territory between the Euphrates and the border of Egypt. This should be seen as a step towards the completion of the original commission to Adam to move out from the garden in Eden to fill the whole earth with image-bearing human life and divine glory (cf., e.g., Beale 2004, 29–167).

Also, while the surrounding narrative is a matter-of-fact, carefully ordered, description, 4.20a employs (a traditional piece of) poetic simile. It is virtually the only such literary device in the chapter. The one other instance of similar language has the same simile, and a metaphor ('largeness of heart'). That is, verse 29 (MT 5.9) says: 'And God gave Shelomoh wisdom and understanding beyond measure [*harbê m^e'ōḏ*], and largeness of heart [*rōḥaḇ lēḇ*] like the sand on the seashore [*kaḥôl '^{a}šer 'al-ś^{e}paṯ hayyām*]' (literal translation).

The striking parallelism between verses 20 and 29 invites reflection.[26] What does it mean that Solomon's heart is enlarged to be like the sand on the seashore? The expression 'largeness of heart' is unusual and biblical parallels offer little interpretative help (cf. Isaiah 60.5; Psalm 119.32). And why is that enlargement described in a way that echoes the description of Judah and Israel a few verses earlier? Should the expression be taken literally ('largeness of heart'), or is it better translated 'breadth of understanding' (so NRSV)? The unparalleled and vivid image of an unnaturally large, pulsating heart in verse 29 should remind us of other references to the internal organs in the preceding episodes. Similar anatomical terms in the story of the two prostitutes indicate that the heart of the matter of Solomon's success in these two chapters is the matter of the heart, in both its cognitive and its affective faculties.

The drama of chapter 3 is, throughout, taken up with the affairs of the human heart and mind. There is an overarching interest in right understanding or wisdom and there is exploration of what it means to have proper affections for God and for others. Physiological terms are used at key points. David '*walked*' before God 'in faithfulness, in righteousness and in uprightness *of heart* [*lēḇāḇ*]' (3.6). Solomon asks for and is granted a listening '*heart*' or '*mind*' (*lēḇ*) (3.9, 12). The true mother burns with compassion, or, in '*her wombliness*' (*raḥ^{a}mêhā*), for her child (3.26). Modern readers are inclined to distinguish between the cognitive and the emotional, and the English versions typically direct readers down an interpretative path that forces a division between the two. So most translations say that Solomon asks for 'an understanding *mind*' (e.g. KJV, ESV, NRSV). But the cognitive and affective are intertwined throughout the story in a way that points to a distinctive claim for Solomon's relationship with his people in chapter 4.

To be sure, the mother's compassion for her child is emotional. But it is a morally proper compassion, not a narcissistic love, that directs her to

---

26 The parallelism is reinforced by the Hebrew of 4.29b (MT 5.9). The words 'breadth of heart as the sand that is *on the lips* [*śpaṯ*] of the sea' in the Hebrew at 5.9 picks up, if only subliminally, the talk of Israel 'eating and drinking' in 4.20b. Some Hebrew manuscripts and the Peshitta expand 4.20 to include the expression to match the language at 5.9 (Heb.): 'on *the lips* of the sea.'

a right judgement: she judges it better that her child live with the other woman rather than suffer a sudden death, despite the pain she herself will thereby suffer. In the case of Solomon, the language of verses 9 and 12 is probably ambiguous. The young king seeks both a listening heart and an understanding mind.[27] Obviously, there are good reasons to think he seeks a kind of intellectual knowledge. In the wider context he is praised for his wisdom in understanding the ways of the created world (4.29–34 (MT 5.9–14)). Solomon's understanding mind was proverbial (Proverbs 1.1; 10.1; 25.1). And, as we have seen, the summary comment in 3.26 that he has 'the wisdom of God' has in view especially his understanding of the ways of the human heart. It is a grasp of a mother's psychology that helps him solve the case of the two women.

On the other hand, there are other good reasons to think that 1 Kings 3 presents Solomon as the true king who has a kind of empathic feeling for his people. At the outset Solomon is portrayed as a man whose affections are fully engaged and properly directed. In the physical act of the offering of lavish sacrifices (3.3–4) he directs his wealth to God, the Creator of the creatures that he offers on the altar. In his dream dialogue his heart speaks in thankfulness for all that God had done for David, his father, and for his own succession to the throne (3.6–7). The literary context of the words of his request for divine help are revealing:

> [8]And your servant is in the midst of your people whom you have chosen, *a great people* [*'am-rob*], too many to be numbered or counted *for multitude* [*mērōb*]. [9]Give your servant therefore a listening heart [*lēb šōmēa'*] to govern your people, that I may discern between good and evil, for who is able to govern this your great [*kkābēd*, lit. 'heavy'] people [LXX: *laon sou ton baryn touton*]?

Both Solomon's words before (v. 8) and after (v. 9c) his request (v. 9a) show that what motivates the young king is not detached intellectual enquiry – wisdom simply for the love of learning. The nation is 'a great people, too many to be numbered' and, as such, they are a burden to Solomon. They are a '*heavy* people', weighing on his heart. He asks for help to govern them because he has their interests on his heart.

Solomon's faculties and attention in all their parts – the physical, the intellectual and the emotional – are directed outwards. He is not forgetful of his own position. He is grateful for it and is conscious of his vocation to serve as a good and effective king. But that vocation is defined by and

---

[27] The 1984 NIV captures the ambiguity nicely with the expression 'discerning heart'.

directed towards the needs, or interests, of others. He is concerned for the needs of the people. And he is concerned for God's interests. The people are God's ('*your* people' (three times in vv. 8–9)) and Solomon is the Lord's servant ('*your* servant' (twice in vv. 8–9)); they are not *his* people, that he would own them, as servants or slaves.

We have seen that there is continuity between chapters 3 and 4 insofar as both explore Solomon's identity as God's representative and the king's role in the restoration of the kind of conditions that God originally intended for humanity according to Genesis 1—2. These observations on Solomon's character and disposition at the start of 1 Kings 3 point to another connection between the two chapters and they help to explain the poetic parallelism of 4.20, 29. The linguistic echoes of 3.8–9 at 4.20, 29 suggest the former explains the latter:

> 3.8–9: Israel is 'a great [or '*many*'] people ['*am-roḇ*]', beyond counting '[*for multitude* [*mērōḇ*]', but, thankfully, they have a king who desires a 'listening *heart* [*lēḇ šōmēaʿ*]' to hear even their most difficult cases (3.16–25).

> 4.20, 29: Judah and Israel were *many* (*rabbîm*), as the sand by the *sea in multitude* (*lārōḇ*) but, thankfully, they are ruled by a king to whom God has given both wisdom 'beyond measure (lit. 'very *much*', *harḇê mᵉʾōḏ*)' and 'largeness *of heart* [*rōḥaḇ lēḇ*]'.

These linguistic parallels between 3.8–9 and 4.20, 29 invite us to reflect on the thematic connections between the two chapters.[28] Both chapters are concerned with the right ordering of relationships: between God, king and people (and the wider creation). In the previous sections, we have seen that in both the true king functions as God's representative. Now we have seen that in chapter 3 (esp. 3.8–9) the king has a particular kind of relationship to the people; he carries them on his heart. This, I propose, is the purpose of the poetic parallelism between verses 20 and 29. Solomon has a largeness of heart like the sand on the seashore because he carries the people, who are many – as the sand by the sea in multitude – on his heart. In its affective capacity to bear their interests, aspirations and human vocation (to be God's image-bearers) his heart is co-extensive with his people, in all their multitude. It may also be that verse 29 speaks of Solomon's extensive knowledge, a theme taken up in the verses that follow (4.32–33).

---

28 1 Kings 4.29–31 and 34 also reiterate the outcome of the story of the testing of Solomon's heart in 3.12–13. They record the fulfilment of the promise that God would give Solomon a wise and discerning heart (3.12a) and that he would be unsurpassed by all before and after him (3.12b–13).

However, the primary purpose of the expression 'largeness of heart like the sand on the seashore' is to articulate a distinctive relationship between king and people.

Perhaps the largeness of Solomon's heart can be explained by the phenomenon that psychologists today call empathic place-taking. In his dialogue with God, Solomon so identifies himself with the needs of his people that he puts himself in their position and so, not surprisingly, he ends up with a heart that is co-extensive with them (4.20, 29). Psychology today recognizes two kinds or aspects of empathy: the affective *feeling* of somebody else's pains or desires and a cognitive, imaginative, entry into their situation that enables one to see the world the way the other sees it. As we have seen, 1 Kings 3—4 is interested in both the affective and the cognitive dimensions of healthy human personhood. It may then do justice to the literary and poetic structure of the text (especially the relationships between 3.8–9 and 4.20, 29) to say that in 3.26 the child's mother is both cognitively and affectively empathic: she feels (in 'her wombliness') the pain of the child's imminent death and, in her desire to effect the best for the child, even at her own expense, she steps out (cognitively) from her own situation, needs and desires into those of the child. Similarly, in 3.8–9 Solomon has the needs, interests and aspirations of the whole people on both his mind and his heart.

Whatever we make of the text's psychological presuppositions, *literarily* the author or compiler of the sequence of texts in 1 Kings 3—4 connects Solomon and Israel in a way that makes the king a kind of representative of the people. The relatively weak heart that felt overwhelmed by the needs of the people and that God tested at Gibeon in chapter 3 is strengthened and enlarged so that at the height of his rule it has become co-extensive – physically, or metaphorically – with the people. The burdensome people have grown in number (in fulfilment of Genesis 1.28). But Solomon's heart has also grown, like muscles exercised by a load's resistance. There is probably an intellectual aspect to the heart in this case, inasmuch as Solomon's organizational – political and economic – leadership entails an understanding of his people in their physical environment. Solomon's organization of the people implies an analysis of Israel's geography and the nation's tribal histories. So, in a real sense, by setting his heart on the needs of his people (in prayer and worship before his God), by engaging with them both cognitively and affectively, and by then acting in their interests, Solomon has become the representative in whom the people are summed up. He has, as we would say, a 'big heart'. But not because he is generous. He has a big heart that has a representative, empathic, relationship to the people.[29] So these chapters express the belief in a kind of corporate personality. So focused is Solomon on the interests, aspirations and vocation of his people that it is fitting to use a bodily, *corporeal*, image to describe his being their representative.

Conclusion

In 1 Kings 3—4 King Solomon makes God present to the world. He is a new Adam and he is a representative of Israel. Apparently, a key to his success as king in a time of unprecedented prosperity, peace and cultural flourishing was his understanding of the ways of the human heart. But that understanding was not a matter of simply detached observation. Solomon bore the people on his heart in a way that means it made sense to use a bodily, corporeal image to speak of his representation of them. *He was their incorporative messiah.*[30] In a sense, he embodied them. He also, simultaneously, in many and various ways, represented God to the people.

According to the Deuteronomistic historian, this is what it means to be the true king, the royal Messiah. Not only does the passage illustrate very well the representative functions of kingship that Wright discerns behind Paul's *Christos*, it also leads us back to those texts that Wright adduced as background for the 'in Christ' language in his seminal 1991 study.[31] We note that 1 Kings 3—4 is sandwiched between the passages which speak of Israel being 'in David' and 'in the king':

2 Samuel 19.41—20.2
  1 Kings 3—4
1 Kings 12.16

The literary position of 1 Kings 3—4 implies that for the author or compiler of the Deuteronomistic history the meaning of the expression '(have a portion/inheritance) in David/the king' is meant to be defined by the

---

29 Perhaps this striking image is also a deliberate play on the depiction of kings of the Ancient Near East who are sometimes imagined as giants dwarfing those around them. See, e.g., the Victory Stele of Naram-Sin (in the Louvre) and the huge form of King Gilgamesh in his eponymous epic I 52–8 (Standard Babylonian version), for which see George 2003, 540–1, and the improved reconstruction in George 2007, 247–8. If the language at 1 Kings 4.20, 29 plays with this notion, then the image of Solomon's large heart is all the more poignant: instead of a gigantic form that signifies physical and military power *over* others (especially other peoples), Solomon has a disproportionately great size because he is identified *with* his people.

30 The king is an anointed one (see 1 Kings 1.34, 39, 45; 5.1).

31 Wright 1991, ch. 2.

vision of the son of David, the ideal king, in 1 Kings 3—4.[32] First-century Jews, like Paul, who were steeped in the Scriptures would probably have noticed these themes. Although there are no echoes or citations from these chapters of 1 Kings in Paul's extant letters, they are connected literarily, as we have seen, to some of his favourite passages in Genesis. It is especially significant that one of the Abrahamic texts (Genesis 22.18) which contributed, on at least one occasion, to Paul's understanding of his 'in Christ' language (see Galatians 3.7–20), immediately precedes one of the verses from Genesis that is echoed in 1 Kings 4 (Genesis 22.17 is echoed in 4.20). The use of that Abrahamic text in 1 Kings 4 suggests, therefore, that long before Paul wrote his letter to the Galatians, incorporative language (and imagery and stories about the nation's leaders) combined royal themes with passages from the patriarchal narratives. In any case, 1 Kings 3—4 provides good evidence that when Paul uses 'in Christ' language he means precisely the kinds of things that N. T. Wright has claimed he means.

Bibliography

Barclay, J. M. G. (2015). 'Paul and the Faithfulness of God.' *Scottish Journal of Theology* 68.2: 235–43.

Beale, G. K. (2004). *The Temple and the Church's Mission: A Biblical Theology of the Dwelling Place of God.* New Studies in Biblical Theology. Downers Grove, IL: IVP.

—— (2011). *A New Testament Biblical Theology: The Unfolding of the Old Testament in the New.* Grand Rapids, MI: Baker Academic.

Brown, W. P. (2010). *The Seven Pillars of Creation: The Bible, Science, and the Ecology of Wonder.* New York, NY: Oxford University Press.

Brueggemann, W. (1972). 'From Dust to Kingship.' *Zeitschrift für die Alttestamentliche Wissenschaft* 84.1: 1–18.

---

[32] This point could be reinforced by discussion of the likely relationship between 1 Kings 3—4 and the possible meanings of the names of Solomon's infamous successors, Jeroboam and Rehoboam. Both names figure prominently in the immediate literary context of the account of 'all Israel' telling Rehoboam that they have neither a 'portion in David' nor an 'inheritance in the son of Jesse' (1 Kings 12.16). (For 'Jeroboam' see 1 Kings 11.26–31, 40; 12.2–3, 12, 15, 20, 25–26, 32 and for 'Rehoboam' see 11.43; 12.1, 3, 6, 12, 17–18, 21, 23, 27). The name Jeroboam (*Yārāḇeʿām*) can be taken as a pun, with the last part the Hebrew word for people (*ʿam*) and the first three consonants a wordplay between the verb *rābā* or *rāḥaḇ*, 'to be, become, many' ('he multiples a people'; cf. Genesis 28.3; Exodus 1.20) and the verb *rîḇ*, 'to strive, contend' ('he strove, quarrelled' + 'a people'; cf. Exodus 17.2; Numbers 20.3). So, too, the name Rehoboam (*Reḥaḇ ʿām*) can be taken as a combination of 'people' (*ʿam*) and the verb *rāḥaḇ*, 'to be wide, grow large' ('he makes grow, enlarges, a people'). An attentive reader of the Hebrew is perhaps meant to hear in those names an ironic, and tragic, echo of the account of Solomon who truly enlarged his people and gave them prosperity, because he, unlike his son Rehoboam, had their interests in his inner being – on his enlarged heart. For a play on the word 'broad' in the name 'Rehoboam', see Ben Sira 47.23.

Callender, D. E. (2000). *Adam in Myth and History: Ancient Israelite Perspectives on the Primal Human.* Harvard Semitic Studies 48. Winona Lake, IN: Eisenbrauns.

Cassuto, U. (1961). *A Commentary on the Book of Genesis.* Jerusalem: Magnes Press, Hebrew University.

Davies, J. A. (2011). '"Discerning between Good and Evil": Solomon as a New Adam in 1 Kings.' *Westminster Theological Journal* 73.1: 39–57.

Foster, B. R. (2005). *Before the Muses: An Anthology of Akkadian Literature.* 3rd edition. Bethesda, MD: CDL Press.

George, A. R. (2003). *The Babylonian Gilgamesh Epic: Introduction, Critical Edition and Cuneiform Texts.* Oxford: Oxford University Press.

—— (2007). 'The Gilgamesh Epic at Ugarit.' *Aula Orientalis* 25.2: 237–54.

Hewitt, J. T., and M. V. Novenson (2016). 'Participationism and Messiah Christology in Paul.' In *God and the Faithfulness of Paul: A Critical Examination of the Pauline Theology of N. T. Wright,* edited by C. Heilig, J. T. Hewitt and M. F. Bird, 393–415. Wissenschaftliche Untersuchungen zum Neuen Testament 2/413. Tübingen: Mohr Siebeck.

Lee, A. H. I. (2016). 'Messianism and Messiah in Paul. Christ as Jesus?' In *God and the Faithfulness of Paul: A Critical Examination of the Pauline Theology of N. T. Wright,* edited by C. Heilig, J. T. Hewitt and M. F. Bird, 375–92. Wissenschaftliche Untersuchungen zum Neuen Testament 2/413. Tübingen: Mohr Siebeck.

Leithart, P. J. (2006). *1 & 2 Kings.* Brazos Theological Commentary on the Bible. Grand Rapids, MI: Brazos.

Middleton, J. R. (2005). *The Liberating Image: The Imago Dei in Genesis 1.* Grand Rapids, MI: Brazos.

Novenson, M. V. (2012). *Christ Among the Messiahs: Christ Language in Paul and Messiah Language in Ancient Judaism.* New York, NY: Oxford University Press.

Stordalen, T. (2000). *Echoes of Eden: Genesis 2–3 and Symbolism of the Eden Garden in Biblical Hebrew Literature.* Contributions to Biblical Exegesis and Theology 2. Leuven: Peeters.

Wedderburn, A. J. M. (1985). 'Some Observations on Paul's Use of the Phrases "in Christ" and "with Christ."' *Journal for the Study of the New Testament* 25: 83–97.

Wright, N. T. (1991). *The Climax of the Covenant: Christ and the Law in Pauline Theology.* Edinburgh: T&T Clark.

—— (2003). *The Resurrection of the Son of God.* Christian Origins and the Question of God 3. London: SPCK / Minneapolis, MN: Fortress.

—— (2005). *Paul: Fresh Perspectives.* London: SPCK.

—— (2013a). *Paul and the Faithfulness of God.* Christian Origins and the Question of God 4. London: SPCK / Minneapolis, MN: Fortress.

—— (2013b). 'Messiahship in Galatians?' In *Pauline Perspectives: Essays on Paul, 1978–2013,* 510–46. London: SPCK / Minneapolis, MN: Fortress.

Wyatt, N. (2014). 'A Royal Garden: The Ideology of Eden.' *Scandinavian Journal of the Old Testament* 28.1: 1–35.

Reading *Climax of the Covenant* with John: return from exile, monotheism and the one people of God in the Fourth Gospel

NICHOLAS PERRIN

Introduction

Almost as if it was yesterday, I remember how as a 20-something seminary student I was first introduced to N. T. Wright – not the person (that would come later) but the author. At the time, I was attending a week-long conference where author Jim Sire was the featured speaker. On one of the free afternoons, I found Jim sitting outside, where he was engrossed in a splendid, blue-covered book entitled *Climax of the Covenant*. When I asked him what he was reading, he excitedly began to explain that he was going through a series of essays written by a brilliant, rising-star scholar and that, especially since I was working on my MDiv, I myself should look into this promising author. Soon enough I did – and have never looked back. Of all the inspirations which have been brought to bear on my adult life (and of course there have been many), I dare say that none have surpassed the abiding influence of my mentor and friend Tom Wright. Little was I to know on that day that a near-stranger's off-the-cuff book tip would eventually serve to revolutionize my understanding of Scripture, and, no less importantly, sow the initial seeds for a deeply satisfying friendship which would endure for years.

Of all the chapters in *Climax*, two proved to be especially thought-provoking, even unsettling, for me in those days: 'Curse and Covenant: Galatians 3.10–14' (Chapter 7) and 'The Seed and the Mediator: Galatians 3.15–20' (Chapter 8).[1] In the first of these essays, Tom argues that the 'curse of the law' is not, as we have so often been told, the potential curse that hangs over individuals bent on securing their salvation by 'works',

---

[1] Wright 1991, 137–74. The essential argument of both these essays is reiterated with only minor adjustments in Wright 2013a, 860–76; 2013b, 522–33.

but rather the curse of the Deuteronomic covenant besetting Israel – in a word, exile. In the second piece, Wright maintains that the mysterious seed of Galatians 3.16, 20 is the one family of God (incorporated in Christ), and that this seed must necessarily be one, so Paul insists, because God is one. The text of Galatians 3.10–20, then, is not first and foremost about the soteriological pitfalls which works of the law posed for personal destinies, but rather the discursive space in which Paul works out the related themes of (return from) exile (vv. 10–13), ecclesial unity (vv. 14–19, 28–29) and monotheism (v. 20). For Wright's Paul, while the divine goal has always been to establish one people of God as a reflection of the one God, and this goal had been impeded by the 'traffic jam' of exile, Christ has now come to release believing Israel from that jam in order that this all-important unity might finally be accomplished. Though initially, I confess, all my built-in theological instincts were leading me to resist this seemingly novel (and therefore assuredly incorrect!) interpretation of Galatians 3.10–20, in the end I was persuaded that Wright's reading of this difficult passage provided more explanatory heft than the traditional Lutheran-*esque* readings have managed to muster. Of all the merits of Tom's reading, one of the most compelling is its ability to integrate the otherwise discordant pieces of Galatians 3.10–20 within a logical progression from restoration to a monotheistically grounded unity which embraces Jew and Gentile alike.

Yet if Tom is right about Galatians 3.10–20, then, unless the apostle stood strangely alone within apostolic Christianity, one might perhaps also expect to find glimpses of this same conceptual complex elsewhere. To put it differently, if Paul's argument in Galatians 3 really does depend on an implicit connection between return from exile, ecclesial unity and monotheism, then indications of the same conceptual chain in other early Christian texts would provide corroborating evidence for Wright's Paul. In this vein, I propose that when we closely examine John 8.12–59 and 10.1–21, two related passages each with its own appeal to divine unicity, we discover not only the convergence of these three concepts, but also an underlying framework that meshes them much in the manner of Wright's Paul.[2] As John saw it, so I shall argue, exile prevented the formation of one family of God and, consequently, compromised the unicity of the name;

---

[2] In Judaism divine unicity was never more crisply expressed than it was in the Shema. Within the scholarly literature, sightings of the Shema have occurred – beyond John 8.41 and 10.11 – at the following places: Matthew 4.1–11; 13.1–23; Mark 2.7; 10.18; 12.28–33 (par.); 1 John 4.20–21; James 2.8–11, 19; Romans 3.30; 1 Corinthians 8.4–6; Galatians 3.20; Ephesians 4.4–6; 1 Timothy 2.5; see the review in Waaler 2008, 206–61.

conversely, return from exile meant nothing less than a properly unified people of God and the restoration of divine oneness. This much, at any rate, is suggested by the Gospel's implicit assumptions.

Intimations of exile and return

The dialogue of John 8.12–59 touches on a broad-ranging collage of images and scriptural stories, at points seemingly inconsonant with one another. What are we to make of Jesus' initial claim to be 'light of the world' (v. 12),[3] attempts to discredit that claim (vv. 13–30), an ensuing discussion on Abrahamic and diabolical lineage (vv. 31–41a), disputes over faithfulness (vv. 41b–47) and finally an attempted stoning (vv. 48–59)? How do these elements advance John's narrative argument? In my judgement, the long scene is best understood as a series of sub-arguments within a larger disagreement over the terms of exile and return, with 'the Jews' as unwitting participants in the former and Jesus as the singular hope for the latter.

But it all begins with Jesus' controversial and – as we shall see – programmatic claim to be 'light of the world' (v. 12). Read alongside its Gospel co-text, this contention asks to be understood not only alongside the Prologue, where Jesus the Word is identified with the primordial light (1.4–5; cf. Genesis 1.3), but also within the more immediate Feast of Tabernacles (Sukkoth) setting (cf. John 7.2), complete – as John's first readers would have been aware – with its ritual involving massive, night-time torches in the Court of the Women.[4] As the 'light of the world' in this second ritualized sense, Jesus seems to embody that which the torches symbolized: retrospectively, the pillar of fire that accompanied Israel through the desert (Exodus 13.21; Psalm 78.14) and, prospectively, the perpetual light of the age to come (Zechariah 14.6–7). The first of these lights was of course the divinely sent agent tasked with leading Israel out of Egypt, through the wilderness and eventually into the land. The second, still-future light was expected to mark out the climactic, eschatological Feast of Tabernacles, when 'there shall be continuous day . . . and not night' (Zechariah 14.7), when, too, the Gentiles would converge on the Temple (vv. 16–17) and when, finally, 'the LORD will be one and his name one' (v. 9). Against this backdrop of the Sukkoth torch-lighting ceremony (*m. Sukkah* 5.2–4), designed as it was to memorialize the pillar cloud of

---

3   Unless otherwise noted, Bible quotations in this chapter are taken from the NRSV; any emphasis has been added.
4   See Yee 1989, 73–4; Kerr 2002, 226–7.

the past and dramatize Zechariah's eschatological glory of the future, Jesus' claim to be 'light of the world' suggests an association with both of these realities.

But let's take these one at a time. That the Evangelist intended a symbolic interface between Jesus and the pillar cloud is strengthened by several considerations, including the progress of the narrative up to this point.[5] In John 6.25–59, Jesus is presented as true bread from heaven. Then, in 7.37–38, he claims to be the source of living water (cf. 4.13–14). Finally, in this passage, he is identified as the light of the world (8.12). According to a rabbinic tradition, which was almost certainly current in the first century CE, God had given three gifts to the exodus generation: bread, water and light. By the time we come to 8.12, then, Jesus is poised to embody all three Sinaitic gifts, that is, so long as we also understand him as a human recapitulation of the pillar cloud of light.[6] Further reinforcement of the same point comes from not only the Sukkoth setting of 8.12–59 (recall that the Feast of Tabernacles was celebrated in commemoration of the exodus) but also the unmistakable traces of exodus within the same passage.[7] One of the most striking of these is the recurring language of slaves and households in verses 31–47, which inevitably invokes the 'house of slavery', better known as Egypt (Exodus 13.3, 14; 20.2; Deuteronomy 5.6; 6.12; 7.8; 8.14;13.6; Joshua 24.17; Judges 6.8; Jeremiah 34.13; Micah 6.4).[8] Through his claim to be the light of the world, Jesus' link with the pillar cloud is all but certain, implicating himself as a key accomplice in a new exodus.

Yet in designating Jesus as light of the world, John equally seems to have had Zechariah 14.6–7 in mind.[9] The hypothesis is supported not least by the Evangelist's interest in Gentile mission and the eschatological temple, coupled with the fact that both these concerns come together in Zechariah's vision of perpetual light, where the surviving nations make their way to Jerusalem for an eschatological Feast of Tabernacles (Zechariah 14.12–19). Already in the narrative, John's reader has gathered intimations of Jesus' co-identification with the eschatological temple (John 1.3–14; 2.19), which was also presumed to be the source of eschatological luminosity (Isaiah

---

5 The connection between 'light of the world' and the pillar cloud is supported by a number of commentators, including, e.g., Brown 1966–70, 344; Morris 1995, 388.

6 So too Glasson 1963, 62–3; Culpepper 1987, 189.

7 See Hoskins 2010, 47–63.

8 Hoskins 2010, 55.

9 This too is hardly controversial. Representative advocates include, e.g., Westcott 1950, 123; Glasson 1963, 60; Dodd 1968, 349.

60.1–13, 19–20). Even so, we learn soon enough that an hour is coming when Jesus 'will draw all people to myself' (John 12.32). By understanding Jesus *qua lumen mundi* within the context of Zechariah 14, we put our finger on the convergence of both concerns; John 8.12's appeal to Zechariah 14.6–7 confirms Jesus as the eschatological temple *and* as the focal point for the Gentiles' pilgrimage during Israel's last, great Sukkoth feast.[10]

The symbolic backdrops, exodus and Zechariahan eschaton, tee-up the ensuing conversation in two different ways. The 'new exodus' motif receives further elaboration as the narrative progresses, not least when Jesus tells certain Jews who had believed in him: 'If you continue in my word, you are truly my disciples; and you will know the truth, and the truth will make you free' (8.31–32). Focused on the abstract concepts 'truth' and 'freedom', this is a difficult saying. Thankfully we have some initial guidance from the co-text: John's reader has already been informed that Jesus is the repository of truth (1.14, 17), that truth is one and the same as Jesus' words (8.44–46; cf. 14.6; 18.37) and that these words also come from the Father (8.40). But then what are we to make of the statement 'the truth will make you free [*eleutherōsei hymas*]' (8.32)? Here our best step forward is to take a cue once again from the scene's Sukkoth setting, prompting us to understand the Son's offer of freedom primarily as a bid to restore Israel's autonomy, the very aspiration signified by the festive water and light rituals. According to Jesus, only those who remained in his word would experience an exodus-like deliverance.

Of course in the post-exilic literature, the biblical writers drew on images of exodus not to wax nostalgic about the past but to express a profound hope for the future – the hope of restoration. John's own interest in restoration has already been signalled earlier in the narrative. For example, when Jesus assures Nicodemus that his entering the kingdom of God is contingent on being born of water and the spirit, these two paired elements are best explained by the same metaphorical correlation in Ezekiel 36—37, where water and wind symbolize the regenerative Spirit who would free God's people from exile.[11] Borrowing two focal images from

---

10 Compare Tobit, where the eponymous hero speaks to the in-gathering of the Gentiles and a luminous 'rebuilt tent' in the same breath: 'Acknowledge the Lord, for he is good, and bless the King of the ages, so that his tent may be rebuilt in you in joy . . . A bright light will shine to all the ends of the earth; many nations will come to you from far away, the inhabitants of the remotest parts of the earth to your holy name, bearing gifts in their hands for the King of heaven' (Tobit 13.10–11).

11 So too, e.g., Schlatter 1975, 89; Brown 1966–70, 140; Beasley-Murray, 1987, 46–8; Carson 1991, 194–5; cf. Manning 2004, 186–9.

a key restoration text, John's Jesus is essentially inviting his night-time visitor to participate in his return-from-exile movement. This is no one-off within the Gospel. The Gospel writer's interest in restoration moves to the forefront as the narrative progresses, especially as we come to John 10 (see below), John 12 and beyond.[12]

By positing return from exile as the controlling sub-narrative for John 8.12–59, we are in better position to explain Abraham's prominence in the same passage. The relevant portion of the conversation starts with verses 31–32, where we find Jesus promising that those who hold to the truth will gain their freedom. On hearing this, the Jews take exception to the premise of Jesus' offer: 'They answered him, "*We are descendants of Abraham* [*sperma Abraam esmen*] and have never been slaves to anyone. What do you mean by saying, "You will be made free"?' (John 8.33). The central issue separating Jesus from his half-baked converts is – much as it was for Paul and his Galatian opponents – the question as to who belongs (and does not belong) to the Abrahamic trajectory.[13] According to Jesus, the Jews' perceptible bondage to sin (and therefore exile) decisively negates their claims to Abrahamic genealogy (vv. 39–41). Firing back, the Jews insist on their Abrahamic lineage and correlate this pedigree with their unbroken freedom.

That the Jews here are *not* claiming freedom in the fullest sense possible is apparent, I think, from the sheer facts of history: as those who languished under Roman rule, these same Jews presumably would have confessed along with Ezra to being, at least on some level, 'slaves in the land that you gave to our ancestors' (Nehemiah 9.36). Indeed, the Jews' claim to have *never* been slaves – not even in Egypt – only makes sense on the assumption that they are thinking of freedom much the way Rabbi Akiba did when he famously said, 'Even the poorest in Israel are looked upon as freemen who have lost their possessions, for they are the sons of Abraham, Isaac, and Jacob' (*m. B. Qam.* 8.6). For Akiba, as for Jesus' hearers in John 8, freedom is more a function of elective destiny than the present experience of political autonomy. For his part, Jesus does not disagree. Although he differs with his debate partners as to how one confirms their elective status within the Abrahamic seedline (that is, whether along genealogical or moral–spiritual lines), Jesus shares one of the Jews' basic assumptions: relationship to Abraham was *the* decisive predictor of future

---

12 On John 12, see Brendsel 2014, 187–211.
13 Hays 2016, 290, draws passing attention to the Abrahamic connection between John 8 and Galatians 3.

inheritance of the land. More than that, whatever perks accrued to those who called Abraham their father, the chief of these was return from exile.[14]

The Johannine connection between Abraham and re-inheritance is of a piece with long-standing biblical tradition, which likewise granted the patriarch and his offspring special eschatological significance. This significance arises out of the initial promise of land made to Abraham (Genesis 15.7; 13.14–17; 15.18–20), only to be reinforced in the prophetic corpus (Ezekiel 11.15; 33.23; Isaiah 51.2; 63.16), where consistently the primary benefit falling to the 'seed of Abraham' is return from exile back to the land.[15] Isaiah 41 provides a handy example:

> But you, Israel, my servant, Jacob, whom I have chosen, the offspring of Abraham [LXX: *sperma Abraam*], my friend; you whom I took from the ends of the earth, and called from its farthest corners, saying to you, 'You are my servant, I have chosen you and not cast you off' . . .
>
> (Isaiah 41.8–9)

Because Isaiah's vision of the new exodus drew its working terms and images from the first exodus, it is no surprise that the prophet's dream of return from exile was likewise anchored, much like the original exodus account (Exodus 3.5–6), in the promise made to the Abrahamic seed (cf. also Isaiah 51.2; 63.16). In ancient Judaism, therefore, to self-identify with the seed of Abraham was not to register an innocent point of purely historical interest, nor was it to express a strictly personal hope relating only to individual eschatology; rather to say '*sperma Abraam esmen*' was, above all, to assert oneself as legitimate co-claimant of the promised land. It is this claim and the claim of freedom on the part of the Jews – a double plea that virtually implied that return from exile was already unfolding within their own community quite apart from Jesus – that Jesus denies.

John 8.12–59's central concern with exile is further expressed through the query which Jesus poses to his dialogue partners: 'Why *do you not* understand my language [*tēn lalian tēn emēn ou ginōskete*]?' (v. 43).[16] While on the surface the question appears to be nothing more than an expression of frustration, I am almost certain that John's Jesus is in fact granting these words an added significance. In scriptural terms, when Israel encounters a

---

[14] As rightly emphasized by Williamson 2010, 68–78 (esp. 77–8).
[15] In this connection, we should also mention Nehemiah 9.7–8. For a survey of Abrahamic traditions in the biblical materials and their bearing on restoration, see also Tiemeyer 2008, 49–66; Köckert, 2006, 103–28; Calvert-Koyzis 2005, *passim*; Ego, 2005, 165–79; Gosse 2001, 421–7.
[16] The translation here is my own.

nation 'whose language you do not understand' (Deuteronomy 28.49) or when Yahweh speaks to his people with 'alien tongue' (Isaiah 28.11), this is always incontrovertible evidence of exile (cf. Isaiah 33.19; Jeremiah 5.15; also Psalm 114.1). Though John 8.43 undoubtedly has its own role within a larger theme of misunderstanding, the actual reason Jesus' hearers cannot understand him here is because they cannot *hear* (*akouein*), as the Shema requires, and therefore remain in the thrall of exile.[17] In asking his opponents to consider *why* they cannot understand his language, Jesus is inviting them to consider the possibility, first, that they are in fact much more part of the problem of exile than the solution, and, second, that this is evidenced even in their failure to comprehend.

Following the interlude of John 9 (to which we will return), John 10.1–21 again picks up the theme of exile through its imagery of shepherds and sheep. Here there's little denying Andreas J. Köstenberger's statement: 'Doubtless the most important OT passages for an understanding of Jesus' teaching in John 10, where Davidic typology and shepherd imagery intersect, are Ezekiel 34 (esp. vv. 23–24) and 37 (esp. vv. 24–25).'[18] These two, closely tied prophetic chapters are of course centrally concerned with exile and restoration; accordingly, John's appropriation of the Ezekielian imagery, together with his identification of Jesus as the 'good shepherd' (John 10.11), serves to present Jesus as the messianic agent divinely entrusted with leading the true sheep of Israel out of exile. Yet because Jesus is also the uniquely entrusted restorer of Israel, he must disqualify those who might otherwise seem to qualify for the role. Jesus sets himself *apart from* those who have climbed into the sheep pen by 'by another way' (v. 1), messianic impostors who proved to be no better than 'thieves and bandits' (v. 8).[19] Yet he is also to be distinguished from the 'hired hand' (v. 12). As to whom exactly Jesus has in mind with these metaphors, we perhaps cannot be finally certain.

We can be certain, however, that within the *Hirtenallegorie* the renewed Temple is not too far in the background. After all, Jesus' return-from-exile intentions have already been hinted at in his act of judgement against the Temple, where – with a verb regularly associated with Yahweh's displacement of disobedient Israel and the nations (Exodus 23.28–31 (4x); 33.2; 34.11, 24; Deuteronomy 11.23; 29.27; Psalm 44.2; Zechariah 7.14; etc.) – he *drove* (*exebalen*) all the sheep (representing Israel) and cattle (representing the Gentiles) out of the Temple.[20] Now in John 10 Jesus declares his

---

17 For treatment of this theme, see Carson 1982, 59–89.
18 Köstenberger 2002, 67–96 (76).
19 So also, e.g., Sanders 1968, 249; Johnson 2009, 2:124.
20 Tom recently remarked to me on the possible intertextual significance of the Temple livestock

messianic intention to *lead forth* (*exagei*) his own sheep; this time the verb predicated of Jesus matches Yahweh's actions in the exodus (Exodus 3.8–12 (4x); 6.6, 7, 26, 27; 12.7; Deuteronomy 1.27, 4.20; etc.) and restoration (Isaiah 42.7; 43.8; 65.9; Ezekiel 20.34; but most notably Ezekiel 34.13 and 37.1). The movement from expulsion to a redemptive *exagōgē* (leading out) has already been dramatized in John 9. In contrast to the Jewish leaders who 'drove out' (*exebalon*) the erstwhile blind man, much as Pharaoh had driven Israel out of Egypt (Exodus 6.1; 10.11; 11.1), Jesus now through the so-called parable of the good shepherd offers a safe haven of inclusion, with Jesus himself as 'the gate' (John 10.7, 9), the eastern gate of the Temple.[21]

For all Jesus' concern with the Temple elite, the parable also turns to face Rome. For just as the good shepherd sets himself *apart from* the hired hands, thieves and robbers, he also sets himself *in opposition to* the wolf (vv. 11–13), identifiable as the Roman interests embodied in Herod.[22] According to the parable, the wolf's presence has the effect of scattering (*skorpizei*) the sheep (v. 12), resulting in a scenario tantamount to exile (1 Kings 22.17; 2 Chronicles 18.16; Psalm 44.11; Jeremiah 10.21; 23.1–4). And while the hired hands run away from the wolf, the good shepherd lays down his life. Both elements find their fulfilment in John 19.15, when shortly before Jesus is turned over to be crucified, the chief priests insist, 'We have no king but the emperor.' John's point is simple enough: while the scattered sheep of exiled Israel have no reliable shepherds who might fend off the wolves of pagan powers, Jesus now comes as one good shepherd who will restore and unify the sheep through his death. Between John 8 and 10, the human fault-lines of exile and restoration have now been clearly elucidated.

Restoration and its implications for socio-political and divine unicity

Whether one thinks of biblical exile and restoration as absolutely distinct or potentially overlapping realities (a debated issue among scholars), if exile meant anything at all, it meant a disintegration of divine unicity

---

(John 2) and has since developed the point – in a slightly less allegorical direction than I have – in a Festschrift contribution of his own (Wright, forthcoming).

[21] If we accept with a number of commentators (e.g. Brown 1966–70, 1:394) that Jesus' co-identification with the gate leads us back to Psalm 118.19–20 (which would certainly make sense given the Sukkoth setting and Psalm 118's liturgical use during that festival), then Jesus is most likely identifying himself specifically with the eastern gate of the Temple, the portal through which Yahweh was expected to return – coinciding with the people's return from exile (Ezekiel 43.1–5). For details, see Brunson 2003, 317–50 (esp. 335–46).

[22] As Keener notes, wolves were regularly associated with Israel's enemies (Keener 2003, 816).

which corresponded to a fracturing of Israel's socio-political unity. As is abundantly clear from the Scriptures, Israel's prerogative to remain in the land essentially hinged on its adherence to the Shema, that is, its faithfulness to the name of the one God Yahweh, measured by its avoidance of idols. Therefore, its expulsion from the land presupposed not only a violation of the nation's monotheistic commitments but also a fragmenting of the divine name – not on an ontological level of course but on the practical level within the sphere of Israel's experience. By the same logic, again, eschatological restoration coincided with the reintegration of the name: 'on that day the LORD will be one and his name one' (Zechariah 14.9).

Because horizontal realities mirrored the vertical reality, the prospect of exile also threatened deleterious effects on Israel's social cohesion, as evidenced by recurring language of centrifugality and dispersal in scriptural descriptions of exile (Genesis 49.7; Leviticus 26.33; Deuteronomy 4.27; 28.64; 30.3; 32.26; 1 Kings 14.15; 22.17; 2 Chronicles 18.16; Nehemiah 1.8; etc.). Whether the scattering of the tribes is best understood as the divinely imposed acceleration of Israel's socio-political dissolution or as the appropriate response to the nation's diffuse spiritual allegiances, the interchange between horizontal and vertical realities remains ineradicable. The unity of the name and the unity of the covenantal people were made to hang in mutual balance, so that the violation of either one of these two poles constituted a violation of both. This was necessarily the case, simply because the unicity of God could only be actualized through the unity of God's people – and vice versa. All this, I think, provides an important point of reference for unpacking the declaration of Jesus' interlocutors: 'We are not illegitimate children; *we have one father, God himself [hena patera echomen ton theon]*' (8.41b). At first blush, the Jews' protestation appears to be little more than a standard, if not somewhat pedestrian, affirmation of Jewish orthodoxy in response to Jesus' insinuations. However, here I suspect John's irony is at work through the echoes of Malachi: 'Have we not all one father [*ouchi patēr heis pantōn hymōn*]? Has not one God created us [*ouchi theos heis ektisen hymas*]? Why then are we faithless to one another, profaning the covenant of our ancestors?' (Malachi 2.10).[23]

That Malachi 2.10 stands behind John 8.41b is hardly to be doubted.[24] Yet on the assumption that the context surrounding Malachi 2.10 is potentially no less relevant to the intended force of John 8.41b than the

---

23 Interestingly the LXX translators swap the order of the two questions as presented in the Hebrew text. This translation conveys the order of sentences in accordance with the MT but preserves the LXX rendering of the individual sentences.

24 For discussion, see Waaler 2008, 232–4.

prophetic verse by itself, I would suggest that the words of Malachi on the lips of the remonstrating Jews are meant to be ironically self-indicting. This is a natural inference given not just John's well-known penchant for irony but also the co-texts surrounding Malachi 2.10 and John 8.41b. Drawing attention to the contradiction between his contemporaries' professed monotheism and their intermarrying with the 'daughters of foreign gods', Malachi declares that both the covenant and the Temple have been profaned, even as the unicity of God has been compromised (see Malachi 2.10–11). Meanwhile, if the opposition to Jesus in John 8 is meant to be read as part and parcel of a more thoroughgoing – even Temple-profaning (John 2.13–22) – recalcitrance, then the Evangelist would certainly lump in the same opposition with Malachi's targets. True, while it is Malachi who asks, 'Have we not all one Father?', that he does so within a larger diatribe against the perpetrators of profanation commands our attention. The Jews' indignant appeal to Malachi 2.10 at John 8.41b is ironically belied by the narrative context of both texts.[25]

Yet it would be a mistake to regard the Jews' ironic invocation of Malachi 2.10 (John 8.41b) as merely the Evangelist's casual attempt to vilify the antagonists. More to the point, I suspect that the Evangelist uses Zechariah 14—Malachi 2 (three successive chapters in the canon) as a redemptive-historical grid on which these same apostate figures might be typologically mapped and explained. This begins to come into focus when we consider the way in which Malachi looks forward to the eschatological turn even as it looks back to Zechariah 14 in its framing of those eschatological expectations. In this connection, one observes that the charges of sacrilege at Malachi 2.10, issued in response to exogamy, are not the first of their kind: similar allegations of profanation have already been mooted, though in this case on account of priestly malfeasance (Malachi 1.6–8). Together these instances fit into Malachi's multiple-count indictment drawn up in response to various behaviours that dishonour the divine name. Even so, the prophet also announces another day – an approaching eschatological day – on which the name *will* be great among the nations (Malachi 1.11). The nature of that greatness is not entirely elusive. For if, as has been convincingly argued elsewhere, the author of Malachi 1—2 is self-consciously interpreting and extending the eschatological message of Zechariah 14, then the future greatness of the divine name must include the unicity of the

---

[25] John's use of Malachi 2.10 in the way I am arguing would certainly be strategic if, as we might well imagine, the Jewish communities of his day were claiming the theological 'high road' in professing adherence to a purer monotheism than their Christ-following confreres.

name.[26] In other words, whereas Malachi 1.6–11 and 2.10 together underscore a profound tension between the present-day profanation of the name and the community's stated allegiance to 'one Father', it is a tension which – especially when read in conjunction with Zechariah 14.9 – promises to be resolved in the eschaton, when the unity of the divine name would come into its full and proper expression. Sensitive to Malachi's redemptive-historical location, John seeks not so much to show up Jesus' resistant hearers as unusually wicked individuals, but to aggregate them alongside Malachi's targets as those who fall on the wrong side of the eschatological divide. Unless change of heart occurs, John seems to warn, they like their spiritual forebears are destined to remain in the state of profanation and continuing exile, a condition which the Mosaic economy had proven incapable of reversing (John 3.3–8; cf. Ezekiel 36—37).

Thus we come full circle in tracing the conflict between Jesus and his unbelieving audience. In John 8.12, Jesus declares himself 'light of the world'. In doing so, he declares himself – in the terms of Zechariah 14 – as the source of eschatological illumination, as well as the cultic space on which the nations would converge, signalling the coming of the kingdom and restoration of divine unicity. Appealing to the same tract of text (Zechariah 14—Malachi 2), the Jews stake a quite different claim, namely, that they presently confess one God who is also their 'one Father' (John 8.41b). Thus we come face to face with two irreconcilable and mutually competing accounts as to how (and when) Yahweh-monotheism is to be reinstated. The positions which Jesus and the Jews hold in respect to divine unicity is parallel to their respective positions in regard to exile. Whereas Jesus insists that his hearers remain slaves to sin and therefore in the bondage of exile, the Jews counter that they have no need of deliverance (vv. 31–33). Towards adjudicating the two sets of contested claims in John 10, Jesus makes the following statement in the midst of his allegorical disquisition on exile and restoration:

> My sheep hear my voice. I know them, and they follow me. I give them eternal life, and they will never perish. No one will snatch them out of my hand. What my Father has given me is greater than all else, and no one can snatch it out of the Father's hand. The Father and I are one.
>
> (John 10.27–29)

Jesus' final sentence, affirming his unity with the Father with terms typically reserved for the Shema, is as provocative as it is arresting. The claim

---

[26] Goswell 2013, 625–38 (629–33).

holds together with Jesus' earlier insistence that one day there would be – in fulfilment of Ezekiel 34.23 and 37.24 together with Ecclesiastes 12.1 – 'one flock', comprised partially of sheep 'not of this fold', all under 'one shepherd' (John 10.16, RSV), a redemptive-historical reality coinciding with the unification of the scattered tribes, inclusive of the Gentiles.[27] While it is perhaps the case that John's phrase 'one shepherd' refers to Jesus' role as Messiah as well as to his participation in the godhead, the latter point is by no means certain. But by verse 29 ambiguity has given way to univocality: Jesus' assertion of sharing oneness with the Father implies nothing less than outright co-identification with the divine – precisely in the Shema's terms of the 'one God'.

It is no accident that Jesus' self-revelation as one who shares in the divine unicity occurs within the very passage where the themes of exile and return are given their fullest treatment. If John 8 identifies two competing visions of return and functional monotheism (one represented by the Jews and the other by Jesus), now in John 10 Jesus is rendered as the Davidic restorer and the revealer of a Christologically modified monotheism. In this respect, we should think of Jesus' statement of divine unity in its redemptive-historical context. In declaring himself to be the Good Shepherd in these terms, Jesus is announcing return from exile and the restoration of the unicity of the name. Again for John, following suit with the prophets, return from exile logically entails a fully functional monotheism.

But neither restoration nor divine unicity (what we might perhaps call eschatological monotheism) can be separated from the unity of God's people, an especial point of interest in John's Gospel. In this connection, we should not miss the contrast drawn between the unity of the ideal community of disciples and the social instability of the human forces which oppose Jesus. On the one side, John calls attention to the internal dissent among members of Jesus' opposition, be it in the form of grumbling and arguing (6.41, 43, 52) or division (7.12–13, 40–44; 9.16; 12.42–43). On the other side, according to Jesus' eschatologically realizable ideal, the disciples are called to love another (John 13.34–35), enter into organic union with the true vine (15.1–7), and exhibit the degree and quality of unity that is exhibited in the person of God:

> I ask not only on behalf of these, but also on behalf of those who will believe in me through their word, that they may all be one. As you, Father, are in me

---

[27] So Thompson 2015, 227. For a recent strong defence for the Gentiles' inclusion in the restoration of the tribes, see Pitre 2015, 459–65. For an argument that the phrase 'one shepherd' retains messianic significance in Ecclesiastes 12.11, see Perrin 2001, 37–60 (48–57).

and I am in you, may they also be in us, so that the world may believe that you have sent me. The glory that you have given me I have given them, so that they may be one, as we are one, I in them and you in me, that they may become completely one, so that the world may know that you have sent me and have loved them even as you have loved me.

(John 17.20–23)

As the climactic epitome of John's ecclesiology, John 17.20–23 maintains that the unity between the Father and the Son, already asserted in 10.29, serves as both the model and the ground for the unity of the disciples. This implies that the Church's ecclesiological unity finds its rationale not in some ahistorical philosophical principle but in the eschatological (Christologically redefined) monotheism promised by the prophets. At the same time, the Evangelist would hasten to add, neither horizontal unity nor practical monotheism would be viable apart from the resurrection of Jesus and the imparting of the Spirit (15.1–17; 16.5–16). Because the conditions of this ecclesial unity are Spirit-wrought, such unity is inherently eschatological in character. For John, it is only this possibility of eschatological unity, occasioned by return from exile, that justifies Jesus' enfolding of 'other sheep', namely Gentiles (10.16). In fact, full recovery of monotheistic worship demands an all-inclusive community which brings together Jews and Gentiles, and exhibits the traits of mutual love and submission.

Conclusion

While Yahweh's kingship and unicity remained fundamental truths in Ancient Israel's religious thought, this did not hinder the tradition from envisaging either Yahweh's *becoming* king or Yahweh's *becoming* one. Again from the ancient Jewish point of view, both these transformations, Yahweh's full unicity and full kingship expressed through return from exile, would not be fully actualized until the eschatological Day of the Lord. For the late first-century writer John, who operated squarely within this framework, this implied that the contemporary confession of Jewish-style monotheism apart from Christ was necessarily self-qualifying – even self-undermining – on account of Israel's status of continuing exile. If John's narrative takes the correlation of restoration, unicity and ecclesial (Jew and Gentile) unity for granted, it is only because the Evangelist understood return from exile to be the necessary and sufficient condition for the oneness of both God's name and God's family. The triad of concepts in John has implications for our appraisal of Tom Wright's interpretation of Galatians 3.10–20, an interpretation, we recall, which would suggest an underlying logical sequence moving coherently from return-from-exile to an ecclesial unity grounded in divine unicity (Christological mono-theism). Given indications of precisely the same theological grammar underwriting John's narrative, we can confirm Wright's reading. The implications for our understanding of Galatians 3 are perhaps obvious enough. If we can all agree that verses 14–20 are centrally concerned with the eschatological one people of God and divine unicity, then we must also virtually agree that Paul is either tacitly presupposing return from exile as the notional basis for his discussion or explicitly addressing it ahead of time, much as Wright argues, in verses 10–13. In my view, the latter option is far preferable. *In fine*, for John and Paul alike, the unity of the one people of God and the corresponding unity of the name were not abstract ideals, but eschatological realities which could only follow – and indeed would necessarily follow – return from exile. For both apostles and probably for early Christianity as a whole, the people of God could not contemplate either divine unicity or ecclesial unity apart from their return-from-exile location in redemptive history.

Bibliography

Beasley-Murray, G. R. (1987). *John.* World Biblical Commentary. Waco, TX: Word, 1987.

Brendsel, Daniel J. (2014). *'Isaiah Saw His Glory': The Use of Isaiah 52–53 in John 12.* Beihefte zur Zeitschrift für die neutestamentliche Wissenschaft 208. Berlin: de Gruyter, 2014.

Brown, Raymond E. (1966–70). *The Gospel according to John.* 2 vols. Anchor Bible. New York, NY: Doubleday.

Brunson, Andrew C. (2003). *Psalm 118 in the Gospel of John.* Wissenschaftliche Untersuchungen zum Neuen Testament 158. Tübingen: Mohr Siebeck.

Calvert-Koyzis, Nancy (2005). *Paul, Monotheism and the People of God: The Significance of Abraham Traditions for Early Judaism and Christianity.* Journal for the Study of the New Testament Supplement Series 273. London / New York, NY: T&T Clark.

Carson, D. A. (1982). 'Understanding the Misunderstandings in the Fourth Gospel.' *Tyndale Bulletin* 33: 59–89.

—— (1991). *The Gospel According to John.* Pillar New Testament Commentary. Leicester: IVP / Grand Rapids, MI: Eerdmans.

Culpepper, Alan (1987). *The Anatomy of the Fourth Gospel: A Study in Literary Design.* Philadelphia, PA: Fortress.

Dodd, C. H. (1968). *The Interpretation of the Fourth Gospel.* Cambridge: Cambridge University Press.

Ego, Beate (2005). 'Interpreting the Exile: The Experience of the Destruction of the

Temple and Devastation of the Land as Reflected within the Nonpentateuchal Biblical Abraham Tradition.' In *Reading the Present in the Qumran Library: The Perception of the Contemporary by Means of Scriptural Interpretations*, edited by Kristin De Troyer and Armin Lange, 165–79. Atlanta, GA: Society of Biblical Literature / Leiden: Brill.

Glasson, F. T. (1963). *Moses in the Fourth Gospel.* Naperville, IL: Allenson.

Gosse, Bernard (2001). 'Les traditions sur Abraham et sur le jardin d'Éden en rapport avec Is 51,2–3 et avec le livre d'Ézéchiel.' In *Studies in the Book of Genesis: Literature, Redaction and History*, edited by André Wénin, 421–7. Leuven: Leuven University Press.

Goswell, Greg (2013). 'The Eschatology of Malachi after Zechariah 14.' *Journal of Biblical Literature* 132: 625–38.

Hays, Richard B. (2016). *Echoes of Scriptures in the Gospels.* Waco, TX: Baylor University Press.

Hoskins, Paul M. (2010). 'Freedom from Slavery to Sin and the Devil: John 8:31–47 and the Passover Theme of the Gospel of John.' *Trinity Journal* 31: 47–63.

Johnson, B. D. (2009). 'The Jewish Feasts and Questions of Historicity in John 5–12.' In *John, Jesus, and History: Aspects of Historicity in the Fourth Gospel*, edited by P. N. Anderson, F. Just and T. Thatcher, 2:117–29. Atlanta, GA: Society of Biblical Literature.

Keener, Craig S. (2003). *The Gospel of John.* 2 vols. Peabody, MA: Hendrickson.

Kerr, Alan R. (2002). *The Temple of Jesus' Body: The Temple Theme in the Gospel of John.* Journal for the Study of the New Testament Supplement Series 220. London: Sheffield Academic Press.

Köckert, Matthias (2006). 'Die Geschichte der Abrahamüberlieferung.' In *Congress Volume Leiden 2004*, edited by André Lemaire, 103–28. Leiden: Brill.

Köstenberger, Andreas J. (2002). 'Jesus the Good Shepherd Who Will Also Bring Other Sheep (John 10:16): The Old Testament Background of a Familiar Metaphor.' *Bulletin of Biblical Research* 12: 67–96.

Manning, Gary T. (2004). *Echoes of a Prophet: The Use of Ezekiel in the Gospel of John and in Literature of the Second Temple Period.* Journal for the Study of the New Testament Supplement Series 270. London / New York, NY: T&T Clark.

Morris, Leon (1995). *The Gospel According to John.* New International Commentary on the New Testament. Grand Rapids, MI: Eerdmans.

Perrin, Nicholas (2001). 'Messianism in the Narrative Frame of Ecclesiastes?' *Revue Biblique* 108: 37–60.

Pitre, Brant (2015). *Jesus and the Last Supper.* Grand Rapids, MI: Eerdmans.

Sanders, J. N. (1968). *A Commentary on the Gospel According to St. John.* Edited and completed by B. A. Mastin. New York, NY: Harper & Row.

Schlatter, Adolf (1975). *Der Evangelist Johannes: Wie er spricht, denkt und glaubt: Ein Kommentar zum vierten Evangelium.* Stuttgart: Calwer.

Thompson, Marianne Meye (2015). *John: A Commentary.* The New Testament Library. Louisville, KY: Westminster John Knox.

Tiemeyer, Lena-Sofia (2008). 'Abraham – a Judahite Prerogative.' *Zeitschrift für die alttestamentliche Wissenschaft* 120: 49–66.

Waaler, Erik (2008). *The Shema and the First Commandment in First Corinthians: An Intertextual Approach to Paul's Re-Reading of Deuteronomy.* Wissenschaftliche Untersuchungen zum Neuen Testament 2/253. Tübingen: Mohr Siebeck.

Westcott, B. F. (1950). *The Gospel According to John.* Grand Rapids, MI: Eerdmans.

Williamson, H. G. M. (2010). 'Abraham in Exile.' In *Perspectives on Our Father Abraham: Essays in Honor of Marvin R. Wilson,* edited by Steven A. Hunt and Marvin R. Wilson, 68–78. Grand Rapids, MI: Eerdmans.

Wright, N. T. (1991). *The Climax of the Covenant: Christ and the Law in Pauline Theology.* Edinburgh: T&T Clark.

—— (2013a). *Paul and the Faithfulness of God.* Christian Origins and the Question of God 4. London: SPCK / Minneapolis, MN: Fortress.

—— (2013b). 'Messiahship in Galatians?' In *Pauline Perspectives: Essays on Paul, 1978–2013,* 510–46. London: SPCK / Minneapolis, MN: Fortress.

—— (forthcoming). 'Son of Man – Lord of the Temple? Gospel Echoes of Psalm 8 and the Ongoing Christological Challenge.'

Yee, Gale A. (1989). *Jewish Feasts and the Gospel of John.* Wilmington, DE: Michael Glazier.

164

ONE PEOPLE

First Corinthians and the marks of God's *ekklēsia*: one, holy, catholic and apostolic

MICHAEL J. GORMAN

Introduction

It is a great honour and joy for me to contribute to this Festschrift for my good friend Tom Wright. We have known each other for the better part of two decades, and one of my great privileges as Dean of St Mary's Ecumenical Institute was to invite him to lecture for us on several occasions, including our 2012 commencement, when St Mary's awarded him an honorary doctorate. I have also had the privilege of reading a fair amount of Tom's work while it was in process, including his massive *Paul and the Faithfulness of God* (*PFG*).[1] This essay is, in part, a dialogue with aspects of that book as well as an amplification of a thesis I put forward in the second edition of *Apostle of the Crucified Lord*, which Tom graciously endorsed.[2]

I have chosen to focus on the *ekklēsia*, or Church, not least because for Tom in *PFG* the renewed people of God, or *ekklēsia*, is the 'key visible symbol' of the 'transformed worldview' Paul embraces,[3] its 'central symbol'.[4] Both the worldview and the *ekklēsia* itself are sustained, according to Tom, by the theology that Paul develops.[5] I have also chosen to focus on 1 Corinthians, in part because – not surprisingly – it does not figure as prominently in *PFG* as does the only other Pauline letter of comparable length, Romans.[6] One way of judging this prominence is to count index entries: the index for 1 Corinthians in *PFG* takes eight columns,

---

1. Wright 2013.
2. Gorman 2017. I do not mean to imply that Tom endorsed the specific thesis about 1 Corinthians.
3. Wright 2013, 369.
4. See, e.g., Wright 2013, 356, 358, 365, 389, 396, 401–6, 536, 563, 566–7, 1260, 1278, 1515; in fact, this point is the 'overall case' (1260; cf. 11) made in Part II (chs 6–8) of *PFG*.
5. Wright 2013, xvi, 11–12, 404, 447, 566–7, 1510; in addition, the Church's integrity sustains the worldview (387 n. 125).
6. According to Murphy-O'Connor (1995, 121), 1 Corinthians contains 6,829 words and Romans 7,111. Second Corinthians has 4,477 words.

while for Romans it takes more than 22 crowded columns.[7] That is, there are probably three times as many references to Romans as there are to 1 Corinthians.[8]

To be sure, 1 Corinthians does figure in Tom's discussions of the *ekklēsia* in Paul,[9] and essential to his understanding are two characteristics prominent in 1 Corinthians: unity and holiness.[10] Thus with these two features we are halfway to seeing in Paul the four traditional marks of the Church: one, holy, catholic and apostolic. We turn in this essay, then, to explore 1 Corinthians regarding the *ekklēsia*, assisted by the theological framework of those traditional marks.

The puzzle that is 1 Corinthians

For a long time, interpreters of Paul have wondered what to do with 1 Corinthians. On the surface it appears to be an annotated laundry list of a variety of problems in the Corinthian community fathered, and now remotely 'pastored', by Paul. Ambrosiaster, for instance, introduces the letter by listing ten reasons Paul wrote 1 Corinthians, stopping after reviewing only chapters 1 to 7. 'The other reasons', he adds, 'will be brought to light in the body of the commentary.'[11] At the same time, these various problems seem to be interrelated, manifesting at least one commonality: disunity. Many modern interpreters, often influenced in recent years by Margaret Mitchell, focus on 1.10 as the stated purpose of the letter.[12] These interpreters, consciously or not, echo the words of some of the letter's earliest interpreters, such as Clement of Rome (esp. *1 Clement* 47) and the author(s) of the Muratorian Fragment, which says that the purpose of 1 Corinthians is to prohibit the 'heresy of schism'.

Without discounting the significance of divisions at Corinth or of Paul's call to unity, some interpreters have perceived something more going on

---

[7] By comparison, the second edition of my *Apostle* (Gorman 2017, about half the length of *PFG*) has just over seven columns for 1 Corinthians and just under nine for Romans.

[8] Galatians, which has 2,230 words (Murphy-O'Connor 1995, 121), has about 6½ (once again, full) columns of index entries. That is, Galatians is one-third the length of 1 Corinthians but figures about as prominently in *PFG*.

[9] E.g. Wright 2013, 390–6, on unity; 711–13, on the Church (and each believer) as God's temple.

[10] See Wright 2013, 711, and, e.g., 387, 437, 450, 563–7, 667–8, 687, 1048, 1260, 1299, 1491–4, 1505, 1511, 1514–15.

[11] Cited in Kovacs 2005, 8–9.

[12] See Mitchell 1991, who finds 'factionalism' throughout 1 Corinthians (e.g. 67). Tom thinks unity is a central theme (Wright 2013, 390–6), which 'unlocks a good deal (not all) of the letter' (391).

in this letter. Raymond Collins, for instance, by paying attention to the letter's rhetorical features, agrees that 1.10 is the formal thesis but insists that, in context, the substantive issue is 'ultimately ecclesiological',[13] with two foci, unity and holiness:[14]

> These two aspects of the social identity of the Christian community at Corinth provide two foci of Paul's letter. How is the community one? How is the community distinct? How can it be one and distinct? . . . The statement of purpose that Paul expressed in 1.10 is that the community at Corinth be *united* as God's *holy* people (cf. 1.2).[15]

Stephen Chester, working within a sociological framework, comes to similar conclusions, contending that 'the Corinthians display neither the degree of internal *unity* nor the degree of *separation* from unbelievers desired by Paul'.[16]

A related approach to the letter appears in the anthropological work of J. Brian Tucker. Utilizing identity theory, he argues that the Corinthians lack a 'salient "in Christ" social identity' and that Paul's goal in 1 Corinthians is therefore precisely the formation of such an identity. This means the formation of an alternative community, distinct from other Greco-Roman ways of being in the world, that nonetheless recognizes the ongoing reality and value of pre-existing social identities.[17] Sin-pan Daniel Ho, likewise appealing to social-identity theory, writes about Paul's goal of creating a 'counter-cultural community' but, after examining Mitchell's work, finds no evidence of Corinthian factionalism in a large portion of the letter (5.1—11.1).[18] Ho, Tucker, Chester and others using the social sciences can summarize Paul's goal in terms like 'resocialization' while still employing the more theological language of 'conversion' or sanctification/holiness.[19]

Both rhetorical studies and the social sciences, then, have provided helpful lenses for viewing the nature and purpose of 1 Corinthians. Of course, more explicitly theological approaches have also provided significant

---

13 Collins 1999, 27.
14 Recall Tom's focus on these ecclesial traits, which he also associates with 1 Corinthians (Wright 2013, 390–6, esp. 394).
15 Collins 1999, 21 (emphasis added).
16 Chester 2003, 318 (emphasis added).
17 See Tucker 2010; 2011.
18 Ho 2015, 33–50. Ho argues that 5.1—11.1 actually witnesses to Corinthian unity 'in acting against Paul's teachings' (50). (I find certain strands of unity against Paul but also, contra Ho, clear signs of disunity.) Ho, obviously, does not focus on the entire letter, but he would affirm that issues that do involve factionalism also require a countercultural response.
19 E.g. Tucker 2010, 138–9.

insight. Anthony Thiselton, for instance, while allowing that 'discord colors nearly all of the issues' in the letter, claims it *'would be a very serious mistake to imply that internal unity as an aspect of ecclesiology* dominated' the letter's contents.[20] For Thiselton, Paul's agenda is seen in 1.26–31 – to place the whole community 'under the *criterion and identity of the cross of Christ*' in order to effect a *'reversal of value systems'*.[21] The re-proclamation of grace, the cross and the resurrection, leading to a new 'value system' characterized by love, is the community's need and Paul's message.[22]

Somewhat similarly, I have argued that we can summarize 1 Corinthians in the phrase 'Chaos, the Cross, and the Spirit at Corinth'.[23] With Thiselton, I suggest (appealing to both theological content and rhetorical structure) that love is as critical a theme as unity and, with the identity theorists, that holiness, or possessing a different identity/culture, is critical as well: 'First Corinthians is a well-crafted piece of deliberative rhetoric intended above all to strengthen, sanctify, and unify the community (1:8, 10) by urging all its members to "let all that you do be done in love" (16:14)'.[24] In that context, I have also suggested that creating *koinōnia*, both with the Lord and with one another (1.9; 10.16 (2x)), might be a good summary of Paul's intentions, and that this *koinōnia* will require holiness, which will in turn require 'resocialization' (in social-scientific terms) or 'ongoing conversion' (in theological terms).[25] This overarching goal can be expressed also in narrative terms:

> Their [the Corinthians'] previous personal and corporate stories had been rearranged by their encounter with God, Jesus, and the Spirit (6:11) in the message of Christ crucified, through whichever minister happened to be the agent.
>
> Now their lives needed to be rearranged once again. Their resocialization, as sociologists would say, had been incomplete. We might more appropriately say that their conversion had been incomplete and needed to be ongoing. The Corinthians' stories, ideologies, and spiritualities of wisdom and power needed to be deconstructed and reconstructed – reshaped by the story of Christ crucified.[26]

---

20 Thiselton 2000, 33 (emphasis original).
21 Thiselton 2000, 33 (emphasis original).
22 Thiselton 2000, 33–4, 40.
23 Gorman 2017, 273–341. One might argue, in fact, that Paul's agenda is to make a charismatic community countercultural by its becoming also cruciform (285).
24 Gorman 2017, 282.
25 On *koinōnia* in 1 Corinthians, see also Wright 2013, 251, 421, 428–9, 1277, 1345–8.
26 Gorman 2017, 282. As we will see below, even these key aspects of the letter can be understood within the framework of the four marks.

That is, 1 Corinthians is an exercise in *deconstruction* and *reconstruction*. Furthermore, the resulting requisite holiness is

> countercultural cruciformity in expectation of the coming day of judgment and salvation. It is participation in the life of Christ, the life of the Spirit, the life of God . . . It is such participation in the life of the triune God that will build unity – and make the community an appropriate witness to the gospel.[27]

In his *New Testament Ethics*, Frank Matera – anticipating some of the scholarship just reviewed – characterized the Corinthian correspondence as having three principal ethical themes: '(1) the moral implications of being God's chosen and *sanctified people*; (2) the importance of building up the *community* of the church through *love*; and (3) the moral example of *his own life*.'[28] Matera introduces a dimension of 1 Corinthians (as well as 2 Corinthians) that we have not previously noted: the significance of the apostle himself to his own argument; he wants the Corinthians to be 'apostolic'. Thus we have in Matera's three themes, essentially, three marks of the Church, all but 'catholic'. For that fourth mark, we can turn to Matera's *New Testament Theology*, in which he notes an implicit universal Church in 1 Corinthians.[29]

This confluence of suggested emphases in the letter, from various perspectives, suggests that the theological lens of the four marks should also prove useful.

The 'marks' as hermeneutical lens

At a session of the Theological Hermeneutics of Christian Scripture (now Theological Interpretation of Scripture) unit of the Society of Biblical Literature during the SBL's annual meeting in November of 2009, Richard Hays offered a paper entitled 'Spirit, Church, Eschatology: The Third Article of the [Niceno-Constantinopolitan] Creed as Hermeneutical Lens for Reading Romans'.[30] In commenting on that paper privately (if memory serves), Tom Wright asked whether the third article of the creed had really helped Richard interpret Romans, or whether Richard had just noticed what any astute, careful reader of the text like Richard would (or should) notice. Richard's response (again, if memory serves) was to claim that the

---

27 Gorman 2017, 282–3, with the last phrase about 'witness' added.
28 Matera 1996, 139 (emphasis added).
29 Matera 2007, 123–6.
30 21 November 2009. It was later published as Hays 2011, 35–48.

creed may help us see things and raise questions that we would otherwise not perceive or ask.

I will make basically the same point here by taking one part of that third article – specifically, a set of four descriptors generally called the 'marks' of the Church – and allow it to provide a framework for interpreting 1 Corinthians. Focusing on these four marks, represented by the English words 'one, holy, catholic and apostolic', helps us to name Paul's desire for the Corinthian community and, by extension, all Christian communities.

This does not mean that I think Paul had these marks in mind as he wrote the letter, or that perceptive interpreters might not come to similar interpretations without explicit reference to the creed and the marks of the Church. (It is clear from the discussion above that many of the creed's themes have emerged in scholarship on the letter.) It simply means that this normative Christian theological framework can provide a way of looking at and perhaps even structuring 1 Corinthians that *might* otherwise escape us, and that the results of reading the letter within this framework are theologically and exegetically both appropriate and illuminating. As we will see, none of these marks stands alone in 1 Corinthians; they are all interconnected, as any good work on ecclesiology would affirm.[31] For this reason, we shall treat certain aspects of the letter in more than one section below.

One: united

'Has Christ been divided?' (1.13).[32] As interpreters ancient and contemporary have observed, the most obvious, if not the only, need at Corinth according to 1 Corinthians is unity. Paul of course devotes chapters 1—4 to the existence of *schismata* (1.10),[33] a term that appropriately reappears in 11.18 (singular) and 12.25 (plural). In those later chapters, additional forms, or manifestations, of the Corinthians' factious spirit are addressed in what we might describe as evidence of 'liturgical chaos'.[34] In 11.18 Paul somewhat sarcastically admits that he actually believes the reports of

---

[31] In Gorman 2017, 283–4, I suggest that the four marks correspond more or less to four major divisions of the letter: 1.10—4.21 (one), 5.1—7.40 (holy), 8.1—14.40 (catholic) and 15.1–58 (apostolic). In this essay, I highlight the interconnectedness of the marks and their presence across the letter.

[32] All translations in this chapter are from the NRSV unless otherwise noted.

[33] NRSV (with other translations), 'divisions'; NJB, 'factions'; CEB, 'rival groups'.

[34] Gorman 2017, 284, 305–29.

divisions at the Lord's Supper. In 12.25 he pleads for mutual care within the community as a way to prevent *schisma*, doing so in the immediate context of spiritual gifts within a unified but diverse body (ch. 12), and in the larger context of the deployment of those gifts when the community assembles for worship (chs 12—14).

We should also think of the first reference to *schismata*, in its context, as a liturgical problem. One of Paul's central claims in chapters 1—4 is this: 'Do you not know that you [plural throughout] are God's temple and that God's Spirit dwells in [among] you? If anyone destroys God's temple, God will destroy that person. For God's temple is holy, and you are that temple' (3.16–17).[35] The Corinthian divisions are antithetical to the reality that the community is a single liturgical body, the locus of God's presence in Corinth.[36] It is this reality, rather than (say) a general political philosophy about corporate solidarity, that determines and drives Paul's emphasis on unity.

Paul's concern about liturgical division and chaos is not limited to the three discussions where the term *schisma* occurs. In proximity to 11.18 and 12.25, two such problems are addressed. The issue of meat-eating that occupies 8.1—11.1 is a liturgical matter since it involves the inappropriateness of believers who constitute the temple of God participating in activities related to pagan temples (idolatry; 10.7, 14). The Corinthians have not only permitted such activities to split the community (ch. 8),[37] but they have also failed to recognize that those activities are antithetical to participation in the Lord's Supper (10.1–22), which ought to be a public expression of the Corinthians' unity with one another and with the Lord.[38] The subsequent matter of proper hairstyle or headdress (11.2–16) at times of prayer and prophecy is obviously both a liturgical and also a 'contentious' matter (11.16).

Furthermore, the other issues in 1 Corinthians often classified as 'ethical' matters are also both liturgical and divisive, or potentially divisive,

---

35 On the Corinthians as God's temple and its significance for unity, see Levison 2006, 189–216. For Tom, the 'main locus of Paul's pneumatology is . . . Messiah's people as the new Temple' (Wright 2013, 378; cf., e.g., 402, 442, 712, 726–7, 1021–2, 1074–8). Indeed, 'Paul's aims and intentions could be summed up as the vocation to build and maintain *the new temple*' (Wright 2013, 1492; emphasis original).

36 As Paul makes clear in 1.2, the *ekklēsia* in Corinth is in fundamental ways 'one' with all others devoted to Jesus (i.e. all other *ekklēsiai*); we will discuss this 'macro-unity', as opposed to 'micro-unity' (local unity), under catholicity below.

37 *Pace* Ho 2015, 49.

38 That is, eating idol meat in the temple precincts, and potentially elsewhere, is not an *adiaphoron* but a temple-destroying, disunifying practice that is both 'unloving and idolatrous' (Cheung 1999, 109); cf. Gorman 2017, 305–14.

in nature. The situation of a man sleeping with his stepmother (5.1–11) is almost certainly divisive, on the plausible assumption – given Corinthian disunity and confusion about sexuality – that not all of the Corinthians approve of the relationship,[39] and it is also clearly liturgical, since it is a matter of who can and cannot be part of the assembly (5.4–5). The divisions involving siblings taking siblings (*adelphoi*) to court (6.1–11) split the Christian family and violate, for Paul, the transformation that has occurred in the liturgical event of washing, sanctification and justification, an implicit reference to baptism and its significance (6.11). The issue of visiting prostitutes (6.12–20) is, for Paul, liturgical as well, since one of the fundamental concerns is how believers are to glorify God in their bodies, that is, in the (individual) temple of the Holy Spirit (6.19–20) that is part of the larger temple (the *ekklēsia*), and how to appropriately express their union with Christ (6.15–17). And since undoubtedly only some, not all, of the Corinthians are committing this kind of *porneia*, it would most likely not be known to Paul or to us if the matter were not troubling to some and thus divisive. In addition, the various questions about marriage (ch. 7) are not merely about rules concerning sexual behaviour and marriage, but also about such liturgical concerns as prayer (i.e. private liturgy, 7.5), holiness (i.e. the danger of losing one's holy status and thus one's place in the community as the temple of God, 7.10–16), and 'devotion to the Lord' (7.35), as well as the dangerous divisions that can arise between spouses (7.1–16).

Finally, what about the theological problems concerning the resurrection in chapter 15? This is fairly obviously to some degree a divisive issue since only 'some' of the Corinthians 'say there is no resurrection of the dead' (15.12). Moreover, it is also fundamentally a liturgical matter since the 'creed' delivered to the Corinthians, and believed by them (15.1ff.), would have probably been recited – like the similar liturgical tradition of the Lord's Supper in 11.23–25 – in worship. The issue for Paul is whether the Corinthians' beliefs and practices (e.g. 15.29) are consistent with their liturgy, represented by the creed. In other words, are they embodying in daily life the gospel they profess in liturgy?

All of this discussion points to a significant Pauline perspective: as the one holy temple of God's Holy Spirit, the *ekklēsia* is called to be a sort of *harmonious living liturgy*. Paul makes this clear throughout the letter, though sometimes only implicitly. (The perspective is articulated more succinctly and explicitly in Romans 12.1–2.) The Church *must* be unified

---

[39] Again, *pace* Ho 2015, 48–9.

because it *is* unified – the one assembly and temple of the living God. This is more than a claim that 'indicative leads to imperative'; rather, the indicative actually *is* imperative. The *ekklēsia* cannot be the *ekklēsia* unless it is one. That is why the warning about those causing division is so dire (3.17). It is also why Paul claims that the supper being practised at Corinth is no longer the Lord's Supper (11.20), for the supper practices reveal that the one body is no longer functioning as one body – even if there are a few 'genuine' believers left (11.19).

The logical conclusion, one would think, is that the Corinthians have become a non-church. But Paul does not draw that conclusion: 'To the church of God that is in Corinth' (1.2). The Corinthians are on the brink of ecclesial extinction, but there is still time to reunite and re-become a harmonious living liturgy. That reunion will require a return to the gospel narrative that created, and that should define, the community. It is a narrative of cruciform, alter-cultural power, wisdom and love. Unity, in other words, is impossible without, and inseparable from, holiness – as we will see in a moment.

Paul's call to the Church, then, is that it actualize the liturgical reality that it is: one body/assembly/temple brought into being by Christ's death and resurrection, and into which those who have been washed, sanctified (made holy) and justified have entered (6.11). Divisions acceptable in a competitive, divided and litigious culture are not acceptable here. What is acceptable – indeed required – is cruciform love (ch. 13; 16.14), with special attention to the weak, that must be actualized in daily life and in a particular way at the meal that the one body/assembly/temple regularly shares (11.17–34).

Holy: alter-cultural

We have already noted that unity and holiness are fused for Paul in his understanding of the Church – the corporate body – and of each believer – the individual body – as the temple of God's Holy Spirit (3.16–17; 6.19–20). But what, more precisely, does Paul understand by 'holy'?

The basic understanding of holiness as set apart from common use by God, for God's service, is widely accepted.[40] This sort of language, when integrated with the work done by proponents of social-identity theory (and others with similar concerns), suggests that a holy person or community is an alternative to the 'normal' person or culture. That is, such a

---

40 See Milgrom 2007, 850–8.

person or community possesses an alternative 'social imaginary' (Charles Taylor) or 'worldview' (Tom Wright; 'what you look through, not at'[41]) that translates into an alternative way of being in the world – alternative practices that constitute an alternative politic. The Church, then, is an alter-culture.[42] It is not merely different, however; it is different by virtue of being, and becoming, Godlike – which means, in the New Testament, Christlike.[43]

Three members of the 'holiness' or 'sanctification' family of words (*hagiazō, hagiasmos, hagios*) appear in 1 Corinthians, totalling 17 occurrences, mostly of the adjective or noun *hagios*.[44] The centrality of holiness to the letter is evident from the start; Paul writes to 'those who have been made holy [*hēgiasmenois*] in Christ Jesus, the chosen holy ones [*hagiois*]' (1.2b, my translation).[45] Just as the Church must be one because it is one, so also it must be holy because it is holy.[46] This is, as Tom says, 'basically a Jewish-style "holiness", but redefined on the one hand and intensified on the other' in the light of Christ.[47]

It is clear throughout the letter that the *ekklēsia* as a whole and all of its 'members' are both already holy/set apart/alter-cultural and called to be holy/set apart/alter-cultural. Thus, as noted above, the Church as God's (single) temple is 'holy' (*hagios*, 3.17), and those who are in the Church/in Christ 'were made holy' (6.11, my translation; *hēgiasthēte*).[48] In both 1.2 and 6.11 there is a passive verb, for it is the work of God to call people and form them into an alter-culture. The result is transformation, from 'what . . . you used to be' into holy ones (6.11).[49]

According to 6.11, this alter-culture is called and formed by the activity of the triune God: Father (implied), Son and Spirit.[50] Its peculiar holy (Godlike) shape is given by the crucified Christ, who was the only Christ Paul preached to the Corinthians (1.2) and who, he says, 'became for us wisdom from God, and righteousness [or justice] and holiness [*hagiasmos*]

---

41 Wright 2013, 28, 404, 463, 536–7, 541, 710.
42 Writing about Acts, Rowe 2009 speaks similarly of a new 'culture'.
43 See Johnson 2007, 846–50.
44 Specifically, *hagiazō* 4x (1.2; 6.11; 7.14 (2x)), *hagiasmos* 1x (1.30) and *hagios* 12x (1.2; 3.17; 6.1, 2, 19; 7.14, 34; 12.3; 14.33; 16.1, 15, 20).
45 Most translations have 'sanctified' (or 'consecrated') rather than 'made holy', though cf. CEB, 'made holy'.
46 NRSV: 'to those who are sanctified in Christ Jesus, called to be saints'.
47 Wright 2013, 443.
48 NRSV and most translations have 'were sanctified'; CEB has 'were made holy to God'.
49 According to 5.9–13, the act of returning to one's previous way of life is a tacit decision to leave the *ekklēsia* that the body should in fact recognize in practice.
50 On the Trinity in Paul, see, e.g., Hill 2015; Gorman 2001, 63–74.

and redemption' (1.30, my translation).[51] That is, the resurrected crucified Messiah Jesus is the source and shape of holiness. Fundamentally, then, holiness in Paul is cruciformity.[52]

The Church's holiness is not only derivative, but it is also completely counter-intuitive, for that is precisely the character of the crucified Christ, as Paul makes clear in his elegant and eloquent account of Christ crucified as the definition and the revelation of divine wisdom and power (1.18–25, esp. vv. 23–24). As many interpreters have noted, this cruciform power in weakness and wisdom in folly was manifested to the Corinthians – indeed to the incredulous world – in the ministry of Paul (1.26–31) and in the make-up of the Corinthian community (2.1–5). This means that when God called, washed, justified and sanctified the Corinthians (and Paul before them; e.g. Galatians 2.15–21), God was bringing them into an alter-cultural narrative – or, more precisely, into an alter-cultural reality that was explicated in the narrative – that was the heart of the new social imaginary and the new social entity corresponding to the imaginary. This means that all regnant Corinthian understandings of wisdom and power, including imperial power, must be deconstructed and reconstructed to correspond to the new narrative and new reality of Christ crucified.[53]

What Paul does not say specifically in chapter 1 is that this cruciform wisdom and power was and is manifest as cruciform *love*. The succinct summary of the gospel – 'the crucified Messiah' – is filled out elsewhere in the Pauline correspondence, both explicitly and implicitly, as the revelation of God's love, of Christ's love.[54] As I have argued elsewhere, the poetic story in Philippians 2.6–11 is, among other things, a story of love.[55] Although the word 'love' does not appear in the poem itself, it is present in the immediate context (Philippians 2.2). Indeed, the preface to the poem is a superb summary of Paul's vision of the holy community, his vision of the cruciform alter-culture shaped by the reality and the narrative of the crucified Messiah:

If then there is any encouragement in Christ, any consolation from love, any

---

[51] Most translations have 'sanctification'; NIV and NJB have 'holiness'.
[52] See my discussion of cruciformity as holiness and theosis in Gorman 2009, 105–28. Cf. Wright 2013: the life of the justified is 'the Messiah-shaped cruciform life of holiness and suffering' (960) and may be characterized as theosis, but '*cruciform* "divinization"' (1023), for the Church is 'the *cross-and-resurrection-reshaped* people of God in the Messiah' (375); all emphasis is original.
[53] See, e.g., Finney 2005, 20–33.
[54] Romans 5.5–8; 8.35–39; 2 Corinthians 5.14; 13.13; Galatians 2.20.
[55] E.g. Gorman 2001, 164–9.

sharing in the Spirit, any compassion and sympathy, make my joy complete: be of the same mind, having the same love, being in full accord and of one mind. Do nothing from selfish ambition or conceit, but in humility regard others as better than yourselves. Let each of you look not to your own interests [*mē ta heautōn . . . skopountes*], but to the interests of others [*ta heterōn*].

(Philippians 2.1–4)

This is what it means to live together in Christ Jesus (Philippians 2.5), to be made holy in Christ Jesus (1 Corinthians 1.2). It is holiness understood as love, a cruciform, others-regarding love that unifies.[56]

We find clear echoes of these sentiments throughout 1 Corinthians, not least in the encomium to love in chapter 13, which uses essentially the same idiom we find in Philippians 2.4 – love 'does not seek its own interests [*ou zētei ta heautēs*]' (1 Corinthians 13.5, my translation). This sort of cruciform love becomes the criterion, explicitly or implicitly, for many of Paul's exhortations throughout the letter. It is this holy (alter-cultural) love that will care for the other and build unity where there is division.

For instance, Paul explicitly appeals to this criterion in 1 Corinthians 10.24 – 'Do not seek your own advantage, but that of others' (*mēdeis to heautou zēteitō alla to tou heterou*) – at the conclusion of his discussion of meat-eating in various social settings. And, as we will see further below, Paul offers himself as an example of this cruciform love, using the same sort of idiom in 10.33 (*mē zētōn to emautou symphoron*), which is essentially a summary of chapter 9. Although the immediate context of 10.24 is the question of eating meat in a private home, it is abundantly clear that the same criterion is operative for Paul in response to the meat-eaters noted in chapter 8 who seem to have no regard for their Christian siblings. Such dangerous disregard is an abject failure of love, which builds up others (8.1), especially the weak (8.7–13).

More implicitly, Paul applies the criterion of alter-cultural cruciform love – perhaps with a focus on the weak once again – in the matter of litigation: 'Why not rather be wronged? Why not rather be defrauded?' (6.7). These rhetorical questions are not only implicitly about love, but specifically about the kind of love revealed in the death of Jesus, the same sort of love advocated in 8.1—11.1.[57] Paul implies the same criterion of cruciform love in the discussion of unity and diversity within the body, this time being explicit about concern for those deemed weaker or inferior:

---

[56] The cluster of phrases expressing unity in v. 2 is impressive; cf. Philippians 1.27.
[57] So also, e.g., Thiselton 2000, 437.

[T]he members of the body that seem to be weaker are indispensable . . . But God has so arranged the body, giving the greater honour to the inferior member, that there may be no dissension within the body, but the members may have the same care for one another. If one member suffers, all suffer together with it; if one member is honoured, all rejoice together with it.

(1 Corinthians 12.22, 24b–26)

The weak appear again in Paul's strong words about the Lord's Supper, where the failure of unity is, implicitly but clearly, a failure of love: '[Do] you show contempt for the church of God and humiliate those who have nothing?' (11.22; cf. 1.26–27).[58]

At the same time, while cruciform love is at the heart of holiness according to Paul, it does not exhaust its meaning. The entirety of 1 Corinthians is a call to an alter-cultural life that challenges the received cultural wisdom not only about relations with other humans, but also about relations with God, and about the relationship between those two sorts of relations. The holy temple which is the human body cannot, as we saw above, be in right relationship with the holy God (including the Lord Jesus and the Holy Spirit) – or with the holy community – while engaging in improper sexual relations (5.1–11; 6.12–20). Nor can the justified, those who have been made just and incorporated into the community of the just, continue to practise acts of injustice, such as litigating others in the family of God (6.1–11).[59]

Paul's various exhortations to this alter-cultural life, marked especially by holiness understood as self-giving love for others and self-giving devotion to God, derive from Paul's fundamental understanding of the Church as the locus of God's holy presence and the 'place' into which formerly unholy persons have been transferred and, in that process, been transformed into holy persons (6.11). There they are empowered by the Holy Spirit to be the holy people of God in Christ that they are: a *holy*, harmonious living liturgy. As that holy assembly in Corinth, however, they are not alone, for they are part of a larger reality.

Catholic: universal

First Corinthians begins in typical Pauline epistolary fashion, with an identification of the correspondents, a greeting/benediction and a

---

[58] As Tom says, '[Paul] insisted (in 1 Corinthians 11) that corporate worship should not only be properly ordered but should model an integration, a reconciliation, which challenged the social and cultural divisions in the world outside' because the church is the primary symbol of 'the new reality that was called into being by the gospel' (Wright 2013, 1511).

[59] See Gorman 2015, 212–60.

thanksgiving (1.1–9). We expect the thanksgiving to preview the letter's contents, and we are not disappointed as we see special emphasis on spiritual gifts, eschatology and holiness. But these nine verses are more than an overture to the letter; in them we find a robust, if not fully developed, ecclesiology. Verse 2 alone is rich: among other characteristics of the Church, all four marks are present, either explicitly or implicitly. In addition to the explicit mention of holiness (v. 2; cf. v. 8), unity is implied (v. 2, 'the church', singular), as is apostolicity (by virtue of Paul's addressing the Corinthians in his role as 'apostle', v. 1). What is perhaps most striking, however, is the focus on the Church's catholicity: 'To the church of God that is in Corinth . . . together with all those who in every place call on the name of our Lord Jesus Christ, both their Lord and ours' (v. 2). The universality of Jesus' lordship and of those who call on him as Lord could hardly be clearer.

Despite the claims of some interpreters, then, Paul definitely has a sense of the Church catholic: a single, set-apart group of holy ones devoted to the one Lord Jesus: an 'ecumenical', empire-wide body (ch. 12) implicitly in continuity with the holy ones who have called on the name of the Lord throughout the centuries (cf. ch. 10) and implicitly in discontinuity with the unholy ones outside the Church (cf. 6.1–6) who call on the name of other lords and gods (8.4–6).[60] Perhaps an appropriate term for this worldwide entity would be the 'assembly of assemblies' – a single universal reality constituted by many local assemblies that happen to be 'in Corinth' or wherever.[61] We may speak of this sense of being universal as 'macro-catholicity'. But Paul also writes about the Church being catholic in a narrower sense, what we might call 'micro-catholicity' – universality, or inclusion, at the local level.

Clear indications of ecclesial macro-catholicity appear at various points in 1 Corinthians. For example, Paul avers that there is a universal practice, based on the teaching of Jesus, of supporting apostles financially

---

[60] Although 1 Corinthians 12 is clearly focused on specific issues at Corinth, its description of the Church is implicitly applicable both to other *ekklēsiai* and to all *ekklēsiai* as a whole (cf. 1.2) since the fundamental defining criterion of being part of the *ekklēsia* is confessing Jesus as Lord (12.3; cf. again 1.2). Matera (2007, 125 n. 17) contends that the body image 'implies the universal nature of the church inasmuch as there cannot be more than one body of Christ'. Although Tom does not use the word 'catholic', he refers repeatedly to the *ekklēsia* as the 'one people of the one God' and notes that 'the church of God' and similar phrases are both local and universal in scope (Wright 2013, 540), designating God's mission as Paul sees it: 'generat[ing] *a single worldwide people praising the God of Israel*' (Wright 2013, 399; emphasis original).

[61] Similarly, Hays 1997, 16–17.

and permitting them to bring their wives with them (9.3–14). Moreover, he implies that his basic teaching on marriage and (non-)divorce for believers is also a universal ecclesial stance, once again grounded in the teaching of Jesus (7.10) and in contrast to his own personal interpretations (7.11, 25), even if he considers them trustworthy and inspired (7.25, 40). Furthermore, 'let each of you lead the life that the Lord has assigned, to which God called you' is at least a quasi-catholic rule ('my rule in all the churches', 7.17), and whatever the conclusion of the discussion in 11.2–16 actually means, it implies a macro-catholic practice that needs to be implemented locally ('But if anyone is disposed to be contentious – we have no such custom, nor do the churches of God', 11.16). A concrete practice that demonstrates the universality of the Church for Paul is the collection for the Jerusalem holy ones, which involves not only the Corinthians but also 'the churches of Galatia' (16.1–4) and, as we know from elsewhere, 'the churches of Macedonia' too (2 Corinthians 8.1–6; 9.1–5).[62]

Especially important to Paul with respect to macro-catholicity are the two places where he cites Christian tradition that he has received and handed on: the traditions of the Lord's Supper, or 'sacrament' (11.23–25),[63] and of the Church's four-part Christological affirmation, or 'creed' (15.3–5). (Both of these texts will also figure in our discussion of apostolicity below.) Although Paul does not specify the precise source of the creedal tradition ('For I handed on to you as of first importance what I in turn had received', 15.3a), he implies that the content is both non-negotiable and universal, perhaps stemming from Jerusalem. As for the tradition of the Lord's Supper, Paul says he received it 'from the Lord', which could in theory mean by direct revelation (cf. Galatians 1.12), but is more likely a reference to the oral Jesus tradition (cf. esp. Luke 22.14–20) known throughout the churches.[64] Once again, Paul implies that the tradition's content is both non-negotiable and universal. In other words, the sacramental and Christological teaching we find in 1 Corinthians does not belong merely to the Corinthians or to their apostle. It is the 'property' of the Church catholic.

These traditions are not merely sacred texts to be remembered and recited, for they contain within them mandates for certain practices that are constitutive of the Church *qua* Church – the Church as living liturgy.

---

62 Cf. Romans 15.22–29.
63 I use 'sacrament' here in a very general sense as shorthand for a sign and means of divine beneficence.
64 Cf. Thiselton 2000, 866–9.

That is, the Church cannot be one or holy or apostolic if its practices are inconsistent with its catholic traditions. This is especially clear in Paul's excoriation of the Corinthians for their behaviour at the Lord's Supper (11.17–34). No matter what words they have received and (most likely) regularly recited together, their practices of 'show[ing] contempt for the church of God and humiliat[ing] those who have nothing' (11.22) invalidate their words and turn the Lord's Supper into something else (11.20). Ironically, in spite of their possessing a catholic tradition, the Corinthians have become a non-catholic church. That is, their reception of tradition has made them 'macro-catholic', but their practices of exclusion have prevented them from being 'micro-catholic', or locally universal, which also, in turn, prevents them from embodying their macro-catholic character.

For Paul, such uncatholic practices of humiliating those who have nothing (*kataischynete tous mē echontas*, 11.22) are not minor matters, as 11.17–34 makes abundantly clear. This is because the gospel of God, the character of God and the activity of God all centre precisely on such people, for

> God chose what is foolish in the world to shame [*kataischynē*] the wise; God chose what is weak in the world to shame [*kataischynē*] the strong; God chose what is low and despised in the world, things that are not [*ta mē onta*], to reduce to nothing things that are.
>
> (1 Corinthians 1.27–28)

The Lord's Supper, as a proclamation of the Lord's death (11.26), must, as an ecclesial practice, conform to the character of that death. Because Christ crucified is the wisdom and power of God (1.18–25) precisely in its identification with the foolish and weak (1.26—2.5), the remembering of that death at the Supper must be a faithful living exegesis of, and a harmonious living liturgy about, the divine wisdom and power manifested in foolishness and weakness. And inasmuch as Paul himself strove to be such a living exegesis of and liturgy about the gospel (e.g. 1 Corinthians 4.7–13; 9.1–27; 2 Corinthians 4), to be catholic, both micro-catholic (inclusive) and macro-catholic (universal), is to be both holy and apostolic. (We shall return to the catholic–apostolic connection below.)

Paul's concern for micro-catholicity at Corinth emerges throughout the letter, but especially in chapters 8 to 14. In addition to his exhortation to include the 'have-nots' noted in 11.17–34, a group that he could have labelled 'the weak' (non-elite; cf. 'what is weak in the world' (*ta asthenē tou kosmou*) in 1.27), we see an explicit concern for those he calls 'weak', or having a 'weak' consciousness (or self-awareness),[65] in the lengthy discussion about eating meat sacrificed to idols in 8.1—11.1 (8.7, 9, 10, 11, 12; 9.22). The burden of 1 Corinthians 8 is that the Church, especially the (self-identified?) 'non-weak', must act in ways that demonstrate love for the weak, prevent them from abandoning Christ/the *ekklēsia* by returning to idolatry, and thus remain included in the body of Christ that is comprised of strong and weak alike.

Similar concern appears in chapter 12, where once again the weak are to be treated as indispensable and honoured (12.22). There is no room, from Paul's perspective, for either feelings or practices of superiority that would essentially deny the micro-catholicity of the Church, which includes – and needs! – all kinds of persons and all kinds of gifts. The use of these various gifts in worship gives concrete expression to the micro-catholic reality: 'When you come together, each one has a hymn, a lesson, a revelation, a tongue, or an interpretation' (14.26). And this participation will naturally include the 'stronger' as well as the 'weaker' members, plus Jews and Greeks and slaves and free, for if they have the Spirit – and they do (12.13) – then they have gifts for the good of all.

But what about women? The exclusion of 'men and women' from the list of the baptized and gifted by the Spirit in 12.13 (i.e. an abridgement of Galatians 3.28) cannot mean that women are excluded from having and using *charismata*. The assumption of 11.5 is that women both pray and prophesy, that is, speak to God on behalf of the assembly and to the assembly on behalf of God.[66] The omission of the gender binary from 12.13 is quite possibly due to Paul's already having discussed men and women at length in 11.2–16.[67]

Apostolic: Pauline in belief and practice

Finally, we see in 1 Corinthians that Paul wants the community to be apostolic: the Corinthians should believe and practise what Paul has taught them, both with his words and with his life. Moreover, there is to be an intimate connection between the Corinthians' belief and their behaviour,

---

[65] See discussions in Thiselton 2000, 640–4; Collins 1999, 324–5.

[66] Thus whatever the meaning of 14.33b–35 (if it is original) – including its appeal to macro-catholicity ('As in all the churches of the saints', v. 33b) – it cannot be understood to prohibit prayer and prophecy by women.

[67] In 1 Corinthians 7, there is similar implicit regard for the equality of men and women (specifically in marriage, 7.2–5), of slaves and free (7.20–24), and of Jews and Gentiles (7.17–20) in the Church.

just as there was in Paul's life. We may say that Paul wants the Church to be apostolic in three interconnected ways: creedal, cruciform and missional.

As noted above, there are several indications in the letter that Paul passed on to the Corinthians certain shorter and longer creed-like texts that he affirmed but did not invent. Paul wants the Corinthians to be apostolic in a way that is Pauline but not merely Pauline; he means 'apostolic' in a broader, more catholic sense.

These creed-like texts include

- 8.6, widely recognized as an early Christian reinterpretation of the Shema;
- 11.23–25, the 'sacramental' tradition about the Lord's Supper;
- 12.3 ('Jesus is Lord'), the logical corollary of the reinterpretation of the Shema;
- 15.3–5, the four-part Christological creed;
- 16.22 (*marana tha*; 'Our Lord, come!'), an exclamation in Aramaic.

Each of these texts is apostolic in both the narrow (Pauline) and wider (agreed-upon early Christian) senses. As the community's father, Paul wants the Corinthians to adhere to 'his' teaching, which is – paradoxically but significantly – not merely his: 'Whether then it was I or they, so we proclaim and so you have come to believe' (15.11). Thus there is overlap, once again, between the marks: apostolicity implies catholicity, and vice versa. Furthermore, to the degree that these several affirmations have, for Paul, existential implications, he wants the Corinthians (and indeed all believers) to embody these affirmations in their individual and corporate lives. The one, holy and catholic Church actually embodies its beliefs in, for example, the death, resurrection, lordship and eschatological coming of Jesus – making it also apostolic.

That is, *creeds have concrete consequences*. Perhaps the clearest example of this Pauline connection between creed and conduct is related to the claim that Jesus is Lord. Paul avers that his claim to apostleship is grounded in and authenticated by the Lord's having appeared to him (9.1; 15.8–11). Yet the ultimate manifestation of his apostleship is not his having had this experience of the risen Lord, but his embodying the narrative of the *crucified* risen Lord in and among his communities, not least at Corinth. When he tells the Corinthians, 'Be[come] imitators of me, as I am of Christ' (11.1), he does so at the conclusion of the lengthy exposition of a problem at Corinth that can be solved, from his perspective, only by apostolic, Christlike, cruciform love. The self-centred, knowledge-based ethic of the meat-eaters (8.1–13) needs to be replaced with the loving, others-centred ethic that Paul constantly seeks to embody.[68] It is this – and nothing else – to which he draws attention when he points to himself:

- 'Therefore, if food is a cause of their falling, I will never eat meat, so that I may not cause one of them to fall' (8.13);
- 'Nevertheless, we have not made use of this right [to financial support; *exousia*], but we endure anything rather than put an obstacle in the way of the gospel of Christ . . . But I have made no use of any of these rights, nor am I writing this so that they may be applied in my case . . . What then is my reward? Just this: that in my proclamation I may make the gospel free of charge, so as not to make full use of my rights [*exousia*] in the gospel. For though I am free with respect to all, I have made myself a slave to all, so that I might win more of them' (9.12b, 15a, 18–19);
- 'just as I try to please everyone in everything I do, not seeking my own advantage [*mē zētōn to emautou symphoron*], but that of many, so that they may be saved' (10.33).

Essentially, Paul is saying that he, like love itself, like Christ himself, does 'not insist on its [his] own way' (13.5; *ou zētei ta heautou*) – and neither should the Corinthians, no matter the situation. This exhortation-by-example is grounded, finally, not in a hymn or encomium to love, however, but in the incarnation of love narrated in Philippians 2.6–8 and echoed throughout 1 Corinthians. The narrative pattern of Philippians 2 can be described as 'although [x] not [y] but [z]': although (x) possessing status and rights, not (y) using them for selfish gain, but (z) practising self-giving love. The pattern reappears most closely in the sentences from chapter 9 printed above and is thus the narrative of a sort of 'reincarnation' of that incarnate love.[69]

But Paul is not saying that he and Christ ignored, much less contradicted, their own identities – his status as an apostle or Christ's status as equal with God. Rather, if we translate Philippians 2.6 and 1 Corinthians 9.19 with a different nuance (in each case by interpreting the initial participle causally), we find that both Paul and Christ *expressed* their status by means of their self-giving love:

---

[68] Commenting on the creedal consequences of 8.6 for those mistreating the 'weak', and connecting the whole of ch. 8 with the scandal of a crucified Messiah (1.18–25), Tom notes, 'The cross at the heart of God means the cross at the heart of the worldview-symbol which is the united and holy family itself' (Wright 2013, 667).

[69] For the Philippians pattern, see, e.g., Gorman 2001, 90–2, 164–9, echoed in Wright 2013, 394.

- 'who, [*because*] he was [*hyparchōn*] in the form of God, did not regard equality with God as something to be exploited, but emptied himself, taking the form of a slave, being born in human likeness. And being found in human form, he humbled himself and became obedient to the point of death – even death on a cross' (Philippians 2.6–8);[70]
- 'For [*because*] I am [*ōn*] free with respect to all, I have made myself a slave to all, so that I might win more of them' (1 Corinthians 9.19).

So too, Paul tells the Corinthians, they will develop and express *their* true identity as those who have been 'washed . . . sanctified . . . [and] justified in the name of the Lord Jesus Christ and in the Spirit of our God' (1 Corinthians 6.11) when and as they love others apostolically – that is, in a Christlike, cruciform manner.[71] In addition to 8.13 and chapter 9, the rhetorically forceful text of 4.7–13 also implies the need for a similar *imitatio Pauli*, which is actually *imitatio Christi*, which is ultimately participation in Christ and he in us.[72] Such practices that manifest, for instance, strength in weakness and blessing in response to being cursed, are not limited to Paul and his apostolic colleagues, for they derive from the example and teaching of the crucified Lord.

The significance of 8.1—11.1 in this discussion of apostolicity points to another, related aspect of the Corinthians' being apostolic, namely their missional concern for the salvation of others. We see this especially within chapters 8 to 10, as well as earlier and later in the letter. For example, we may note the following:[73]

- 5.1–13: Paul implicitly condemns the Corinthians for their poor witness to the Gentiles. 'A Christian community whose conduct is indistinguishable from the basest human behavior cannot possibly hope to attract others. By invoking Gentile sensibilities Paul indicates that, for him, the evangelistic function of Christian behavior is a significant consideration in this situation.'[74]

---

[70] For this interpretation, see Gorman 2009, 9–39, as well as Wright 1991, 83–4, 90.

[71] Although Paul does not make an explicit connection between dying and rising with Christ in 1 Corinthians as he does in Romans 6, the basis of the spirituality of participation in Christ's death and resurrection (Romans 6) is the reality of that death and resurrection narrated in the creedal content of 1 Corinthians 15. There is no doubt already an implicit connection between Christ's death and resurrection and participation in it already being made in 1 Corinthians.

[72] This has been the strong emphasis of all my work. See also Wright 2013, 1104–5.

[73] For discussion of these and other passages in 1 Corinthians that exemplify this apostolic concern for others' salvation, see Barram 2006, 149–73; 2011, 234–46; Rosner 2011, 180–96.

[74] Barram 2006, 153–4.

- 7.12–16: Paul urges married believers not to initiate the option (presumed right?) of divorce but to remain with their unbelieving spouses, for 'you might save your husband/wife' (v. 16).[75]
- 8.7–13: Paul's exhortation to not exercise the right (*exousia*, v. 9) to eat meat is grounded in his concern that no one cause a brother or sister to stumble, fall or be 'destroyed' – the antithesis of salvation.
- 10.23–33: Paul's own concern for the salvation of all becomes the model for the Corinthians' interactions with unbelieving neighbours at meals with meat.
- 14.21–25: in a confusing passage, one thing is clear: whatever is done must be done with the welfare/salvation (potentially manifested in worship) of the 'unbeliever or outsider' in mind.

Michael Barram, in his analysis of 1 Corinthians 9.19–23 and 10.31—11.1, has referred to the disposition Paul encourages in these sorts of situations as a 'missional consciousness' and 'salvific intentionality'.[76] Barram makes several important points. First, these texts reveal that if we speak of Paul's 'mission', it should refer not merely to his evangelistic outreach to non-believers, but to his comprehensive vocation, including the ongoing formation of existing communities. Second, Paul provides himself as a model, specifically as a Christlike model, of 'behavioural flexibility' that is not an end in itself but has the salvation of others as its criterion and goal, and the self-giving death of Jesus (i.e. in my terms, 'cruciformity') as its content. In other words:

> [w]hatever else it may entail, mission involves behavioral flexibility and adaptability as the Christian community purposively and intentionally embodies Christ's salvific example for the sake of all people, Christian and non-Christian alike. In short, mission, for Paul, is best understood not in terms of evangelism, but rather as a comprehensive salvific intentionality.[77]

Barram assists us, then, in seeing that 'Be[come] imitators of me' is an invitation to an attitude of salvific intentionality towards all, believers (especially 8.1–13) and non-believers (chs 7, 10, 14) alike. That is, to be apostolic is to be like Paul, which is to be cruciform for salvific purposes, just as Christ's self-giving death was purposeful for salvific purposes. Furthermore, since this salvific purpose has, for Paul, a universal scope

---

[75] My 'optimistic' interpretation of this disputed text is due to the similar language of forgoing rights/options for the salvation of others in chs 8 and 9. Cf. Rosner 2011, 187–8.
[76] See Barram 2006; 2011.
[77] Barram 2011, 241.

(1 Corinthians 9.19–23), reflecting Christ's death for all, the Corinthians should also be committed to the salvation of all: weak and strong, believer and non-believer, slave and free, etc. Once again, marks overlap: cruciform holiness, apostolicity and catholicity.

This sense of apostolicity does not require that the believers in Corinth be physically 'sent' anywhere; they are, so to speak, apostolic simply by virtue of being in Christ, of being the one, holy, catholic *ekklēsia* of God in Corinth. I have argued elsewhere that the Pauline churches were much more apostolic or 'missional' – in many ways – than most interpreters recognize. Tom himself, while citing both Barram and myself on this topic with some approval, and even cautiously adding 'mission' to unity and holiness as essential to Paul's understanding of the *ekklēsia*, is more reluctant to see the Pauline churches as 'apostolic' in the third sense discussed here.[78]

Which leads us, finally, back to the place we began.

Conclusion: Paul, the four marks and Tom Wright

We have now seen, from many angles, the four interrelated marks of the Church – that it is one, holy, catholic and apostolic – in 1 Corinthians. At the beginning of this essay we also saw that Tom Wright focuses especially on two of these, unity and holiness. We have also seen, however (especially in footnotes), that although Tom does not name those four marks as such or use the words 'catholic' and 'apostolic', he does in fact concur with many of the claims made in this essay about all four marks.

I suggest that this is the case for several reasons. For one, Tom is a creedal Christian and knows that these four marks did not arise in a vacuum but are grounded in scriptural ecclesiology, not least Pauline ecclesiology; he cannot help but perceive the four marks in Paul. For another, Tom thinks that Paul 'saw the church as a microcosmos . . . the prototype of what was to come', which 'is why, of course, unity and holiness mattered'.[79] If 'microcosmos' and 'prototype' rightly characterize the Church, then it must be an alternative to that which is (the surrounding culture): 'a new sort of polis'.[80] Furthermore, if its life is defined by the crucifixion and resurrection of the Messiah, it will be a cruciform microcosmos, guided in belief and behaviour by the apostle of the crucified Lord (apostolicity). Moreover, since for

---

78 See Wright 2013, 436–7.
79 Wright 2013, 1492.
80 Wright 2013, 1492.

Tom the Abrahamic and prophetic promises of blessing to the nations are realized in Christ and the Church, the Church must be committed to the salvation and reconciliation of all (catholicity).

In other words, Paul's ecclesiology read through the lens of the four marks and Tom's own understanding of the *ekklēsia* in Paul cohere in remarkable ways. Although Tom and I interpret Paul's ecclesiology with slightly different emphases (I perhaps focusing a bit more on cruciformity, theosis and mission), reading both Paul in 1 Corinthians and Tom in *PFG* in the light of the marks can be exegetically and theologically enriching.[81]

Bibliography

Barram, Michael (2006). *Mission and Moral Reflection in Paul.* Studies in Biblical Literature 75. New York, NY: Peter Lang.

—— (2011). 'Pauline Mission as Salvific Intentionality: Fostering a Missional Consciousness in 1 Corinthians 9:19–23 and 10:31–11:1.' In *Paul as Missionary: Identity, Activity, Theology, and Practice,* edited by Trevor J. Burke and Brian S. Rosner, 234–46. Library of New Testament Studies 420. London: T&T Clark.

Chester, Stephen J. (2003). *Conversion at Corinth: Perspectives on Conversion in Paul's Theology and the Corinthian Church.* Studies of the New Testament and Its World. London: T&T Clark.

Cheung, Alex T. (1999). *Idol Food in Corinth: Jewish Background and Pauline Legacy.* Journal for the Study of the New Testament Supplement Series 176. Sheffield: Sheffield Academic Press.

Collins, Raymond F. (1999). *1 Corinthians.* Sacra Pagina. Collegeville, MN: Liturgical Press.

Finney, Mark T. (2005). 'Christ Crucified and the Inversion of Roman Imperial Ideology in 1 Corinthians.' *Biblical Theology Bulletin* 35: 20–33.

Gorman, Michael J. (2001). *Cruciformity: Paul's Narrative Spirituality of the Cross.* Grand Rapids, MI: Eerdmans.

—— (2009). *Inhabiting the Cruciform God: Kenosis, Justification, and Theosis in Paul's Narrative Soteriology.* Grand Rapids, MI: Eerdmans.

—— (2015). *Becoming the Gospel: Paul, Participation, and Mission.* Grand Rapids, MI: Eerdmans.

—— (2017). *Apostle of the Crucified Lord: A Theological Introduction to Paul and His Letters.* 2nd edition. Grand Rapids, MI: Eerdmans.

Hays, Richard B. (1997). *First Corinthians.* Interpretation. Louisville, KY: Westminster John Knox.

—— (2011). 'Spirit, Church, Resurrection: The Third Article of the Creed as Hermeneutical Lens for Reading Romans.' *Journal of Theological Interpretation* 5.1: 35–48.

---

81 I am grateful to Andy Johnson and Michelle Rader for feedback on a draft of this essay.

Hill, Wesley (2015). *Paul and the Trinity: Persons, Relations, and the Pauline Letters.* Grand Rapids, MI: Eerdmans.

Ho, Sin-pan Daniel (2015). *Paul and the Creation of a Counter-Cultural Community: A Rhetorical Analysis of 1 Cor. 5:1–11:1 in Light of the Social Lives of the Corinthians.* Library of New Testament Studies 509. London: Bloomsbury/T&T Clark.

Johnson, Andy (2007). 'Holy, Holiness, NT.' In *The New Interpreters' Dictionary of the Bible*, vol. 2, edited by Katharine Doob Sakenfeld et al., 846–50. Nashville, TN: Abingdon.

Kovacs, Judith L. (2005) (trans. and ed.). *The Church's Bible: 1 Corinthians; Interpreted by Early Christian Commentators.* General editor Robert Louis Wilken. Grand Rapids, MI: Eerdmans.

Levison, John R. (2006). 'The Spirit and the Temple in Paul's Letters to the Corinthians.' In *Paul and His Theology*, edited by Stanley E. Porter, 189–216. Pauline Studies 3. Leiden: Brill.

Matera, Frank J. (1996). *New Testament Ethics: The Legacies of Jesus and Paul.* Louisville, KY: Westminster John Knox.

—— (2007). *New Testament Theology: Exploring Diversity and Unity.* Louisville, KY: Westminster John Knox.

Milgrom, Jacob (2007). 'Holy, Holiness, OT.' In *The New Interpreters' Dictionary of the Bible*, vol. 2, edited by Katharine Doob Sakenfeld et al., 850–8. Nashville, TN: Abingdon.

Mitchell, Margaret (1991/1993). *Paul and the Rhetoric of Reconciliation: An Exegetical Investigation of the Language and Composition of 1 Corinthians.* Tübingen: Mohr Siebeck / Louisville, KY: Westminster John Knox.

Murphy-O'Connor, Jerome (1995). *St. Paul the Letter-Writer: His World, His Options, His Skill.* Collegeville, MN: Liturgical Press.

Rosner, Brian S. (2011). 'The Missionary Character of 1 Corinthians.' In *New Testament Theology in Light of the Church's Mission: Essays in Honor of I. Howard Marshall*, edited by Jon C. Laansma, Grant Osborne and Ray Van Neste, 180–96. Eugene, OR: Cascade.

Rowe, C. Kavin (2009). *World Upside Down: Reading Acts in the Graeco-Roman Age.* New York, NY: Oxford University Press.

Thiselton, Anthony C. (2000). *The First Epistle to the Corinthians: A Commentary on the Greek Text.* New International Greek Testament Commentary. Grand Rapids, MI: Eerdmans.

Tucker, Brian J. (2010). *You Belong to Christ: Paul and the Formation of Social Identity in 1 Corinthians 1–4.* Eugene, OR: Pickwick.

—— (2011). *'Remain in Your Calling': Paul and the Continuation of Social Identities in 1 Corinthians.* Eugene, OR: Pickwick.

Wright, N. T. (1991). *The Climax of the Covenant: Christ and the Law in Pauline Theology.* Edinburgh: T&T Clark.

—— (2013). *Paul and the Faithfulness of God.* Christian Origins and the Question of God 4. London: SPCK / Minneapolis, MN: Fortress.

Grace, race and the people of God

DAVID G. HORRELL

Introduction

In his astonishingly extensive and influential *oeuvre*, N. T. Wright has been remarkably consistent in pursuing the method and agenda set out programmatically in the opening volume of his series on Christian Origins and the Question of God (COQG), the series that stands at the heart of his scholarly project. Here he sets out the basic contours of what he calls Israel's worldview, and sketches the ways in which he sees the early Christian movement as both fulfilling and subverting the basic stories at the heart of that worldview. Paul, for example, 'subverts the Jewish story from within' along the following lines:

> The exile came to its cataclysmic end when Jesus, Israel's representative Messiah, died outside the walls of Jerusalem, bearing the curse, which consisted of exile at the hands of the pagans, to its utmost limit . . . [With the exile now finished] Israel's god had poured out his own spirit on all flesh; his word was going out to all the nations; he had called into being a new people composed of all races and classes, and both sexes, without distinction. These major features of Paul's theology only make sense within a large-scale retelling of the essentially Jewish story, seen now from the point of view of one who believes that the climactic moment has already arrived, and that the time to implement that great achievement is already present.[1]

While much has been added along the way, those familiar with Wright's subsequent work on Jesus and Paul will recognize here, *in nuce*, the key convictions that shape his interpretation. What I want to offer here, as a token of gratitude and appreciation, may initially appear as little more than tinkering at the edges of such a project, but does, I hope to show, bear wider significance for our construals of Christian origins and of Paul in particular.[2]

---

[1] Wright 1992, 406.

[2] I am indeed grateful for this occasion to honour Tom publicly, and to thank him for his kindness and generosity in our interactions across the years, not least in the Foreword he very

My initial point of focus is Wright's use of the language of race in some of his earlier works, and the risks of a contrast between Jewish 'racial' identity and Christian trans-ethnic universalism. Focusing primarily on Paul as a case study, I then go on to consider three possible strategies for avoiding such risks, finishing with the one that seems to me the most promising and that Wright presents (though not in explicit relation to this issue) in the latest volume in the COQG series, *Paul and the Faithfulness of God*.[3] Reaching that position in the argument – where both Jewish and early Christian groups are seen as representing some kind of 'ethno-social particularity' – leads, however, to a final step, a (brief) consideration of the patterns of inclusion evident in both groups.

Jewish 'racial identity' and the contrast with Christian universalism

In *The New Testament and the People of God*, Wright describes the central symbols of first-century Jewish identity as Temple, Land, Torah and 'Racial identity'.[4] Concerning the latter, he stresses the importance of a concern for 'racial purity', exemplified in Ezra's efforts to preserve the 'holy seed'; and he finds a consistent emphasis through 'the Hasmonean and Roman periods' on 'the race as the true people'.[5] This racially defined sense of the people of God stands, therefore, in contrast with the reworking of this symbol in the early Christian worldview: the Church is 'the new human family, called into being by the creator god, transcending all race and nationhood'.[6] Thus, in a typically pithy and memorable phrase in *The Climax of the Covenant*, Wright describes Israel's 'meta-sin', as Paul sees it in Romans 9—11, as 'the attempt to confine grace to one race'.[7] Paul, by contrast, is 'establishing a new view of the people of God', as 'a new people composed of all races and classes, and both sexes, without distinction'.[8]

There are, I think, serious risks in using such language to draw a comparison between Jewish and early Christian worldviews. In the present

kindly wrote to the new edition of my book on Pauline ethics: Horrell 2015. I appreciate this kind support all the more since, as he knows well, our perspectives are significantly different. I would also like to thank the Arts and Humanities Research Council of the UK for their support of the research project on which this essay draws (grant reference AH-M009149/1).
3 Wright 2013.
4 Wright 1992, 215–43.
5 Wright 1992, 231.
6 Wright 1992, 367.
7 Wright 1991, 240; cf. also 167.
8 Wright 1991, 14; Wright 1992, 406, respectively.

context, however, it is appropriate to signal immediately that I want to go on to suggest that Wright's depiction of the identity of the people of God in *Paul and the Faithfulness of God* offers a route by which we can avoid, at least potentially, the major difficulties.

The most obvious risk is connected with the depiction of Judaism as a particular, bounded, exclusive form of ('racial') identity set in contrast to an open, all-embracing, inclusive (non-racial) Christianity which thus marks the universalizing fulfilment of that to which Judaism pointed, but could not attain. This kind of contrast has all too often featured in the quasi-Hegelian narratives of Christianity's achievements that have characterized critical constructions of Christian origins from at least the time of Ferdinand Christian Baur.

For Hegel, the history of the world is a history of progress towards freedom: 'World history', he writes, 'is the progress of the consciousness of freedom', a process of history orientated towards and directed by *Geist*, or spirit.[9] Hegel sets out a history in which this movement towards freedom has three basic phases. The first is found in 'the Oriental World', in which the spirit, 'still immersed in nature', is not truly free, except in the one person of the despotic ruler. The second is found in the Greek and Roman worlds, where an awareness of the spirit's own freedom begins to emerge: some (those participating in democracy) are free. The third phase comes with Christianity and 'the Germanic age', in which the spirit can truly ascend to freedom.[10] It is important to stress, as Shawn Kelley has done, how thoroughly Hegel's is thus a racialized (and Orientalist) philosophy of history and of historical progress, articulating a narrative of Western European (and specifically Germanic) cultural, religious and racial superiority.[11] The specific connections between racial and religious superiority in the story of progress towards freedom are clear. In Hegel's words: 'The Germanic nations, with the rise of Christianity, were the first to realise that man is by nature free, and that freedom of the spirit is his very essence.'[12]

Judaism plays a particular role in this history, and a strictly limited one. As part of the Oriental world, and with its specific subservience to the law, it 'remains external, legalistic, ritualistic and ceremonial . . . Jewish monotheism and morality must be purged of its Jewish particularism and

---

[9] Hegel 1975 (1830), 54.
[10] Hegel 1975 (1830), 130–1; cf. 54.
[11] Kelley 2002, 33–63.
[12] Hegel 1975 (1830), 54. Cf. Kelley 2002, 49.

its Oriental despotism before it can become the foundation for Western culture and freedom.'[13]

This is precisely the narrative of history that Baur sees played out in earliest Christianity: both Jesus and Paul, in their different ways, with their spiritual insight and freedom, represent a stark contrast to their fellow Jews, with their outward rites and ordinances, legalism and lack of true spiritual freedom. Judaism's role in the story of religious progress by which Christianity comes to triumph is unique and important, but nonetheless particular and limited: 'Judaism is nothing more than the religion of the law in contradistinction to Christianity, which is the religion of the spirit.'[14] The profoundly Hegelian character of Baur's historical narrative is clear in his reflections on 'Christianity as a new principle in the world's historical development': 'Christianity is reached by the progress of the spirit to the freedom of its own self-consciousness, and humanity cannot arrive at this period till it has traversed that of unfreedom and servitude.'[15] Paul in particular claims a place of especial importance in Baur's view of this historical and theological development, because of the way in which he takes up key elements of his Jewish heritage yet purges them of the particularism that characterized them in their Jewish form and context, which lacked true spirituality and freedom.[16] While this particular articulation of the relationship between Judaism and Christianity is dated, and specific to its historical and philosophical context, more recent depictions of the process share some structural features in common with this influential early version.[17]

The key danger of such narratives, it should be clear, is that the categorical contrast between Jewish particularism and Christian universalism is woven deeply into a theory of both Christian and Western European superiority, a theory non-coincidentally related to the era of expansive and vigorous European imperialism and violent anti-Semitism. Not only is Jewish identity racialized, but also, conversely and ironically, the racialized character and particular location of Western European Christianity

---

[13] Kelley 2002, 58–9. Cf. also Gerdmar 2014, 125–6.
[14] Baur 1878–9, 1:58; cf. 1–43 (and on the superiority of Judaism to the 'heathen' religions, but also its particularism, see 17–18).
[15] Baur 1873–5, 2:214. The preceding phrase is the title of chapter 6 in *Paul the Apostle of Jesus Christ*, vol. II, from which this quotation is taken.
[16] Harris 1975, 195, notes that 'his book on Paul [published in 1845] was the work that he [sc. Baur] most prized . . . With this book Baur's representation of the Apostolic Church received its final form, and was never altered in any essential points.'
[17] See further Horrell 2016, 441–3.

are obscured behind the veil of universalism and claims to have attained humanity's true freedom.

Strategies to avoid the risks

Change the terminology

There are a number of strategies employed in attempts to avoid the dangers of reading Paul and other NT texts in the light of this kind of contrast between a racially particular Judaism and an inclusive, universal Christianity. One strategy is to reject the language of 'race' in particular, due to its enmeshment in the pseudo-scientific, biological theories that emerged from the seventeenth century onwards and were so important in legitimating European colonialism and Nazi anti-Semitism specifically.[18] This is the central argument in Calvin Roetzel's critique of Wright's work:

> The concept of race has its origins largely in the eighteenth and nineteenth centuries, and the concept of the 'race of Israel' is a product of racial theories of that recent period and not a historical product of the first century.[19]

The positive proposal associated with this critique is generally – as it is in Roetzel's essay – to propose the category of 'ethnicity' as a preferable alternative:

> More acceptable is the allusion to Israel as an ethnic people. Ethnicity is a cultural, sometimes even a religious, category that can be passed on from generation to generation and is not confined to, but may be related to, a physical place. So it would appear more appropriate to refer to Israel as an *ethnos*, a people, than as a race or a nationality.[20]

This kind of rationale goes back to the relatively recent origins of the word 'ethnicity'. Despite having etymological connections with one of the key ancient 'people' words (*ethnos*), 'ethnicity' as such is a modern concept, first used, apparently, in 1941 (though previous discussion in the 1930s had already begun to talk of 'ethnic groups').[21] In the 1950 UNESCO statement on 'the race question', for example, it is clear that one key reason why 'ethnicity' came to the fore in the period immediately after the Second World War is because of what the report describes as 'the injustices and

---

18 On these historical developments, see, e.g., Hannaford 1996; Kidd 2006.
19 Roetzel 1997, 239.
20 Roetzel 1997, 243.
21 See Miller 2012, 296.

crimes which give such tragic overtones to the word "race".[22] The report therefore proposes that 'it would be better when speaking of human races to drop the term "race" altogether and speak of *ethnic groups*.'[23] 'Ethnicity' thus came to displace 'race', though the phenomena the term seeks to capture remain essentially the same. Moreover, as Rogers Brubaker remarks, the concept of ethnicity was formed 'precisely by abstracting from the specificities of language, religion, and other ascriptive markers such as phenotype, region of origin, and customary mode of livelihood'.[24] It is a (modern) analytical and abstract category that seeks to encapsulate the variety of factors by which people are believed (or believe themselves) to belong to specific people-groups and are treated and judged as such.

The question, of course, is how much is solved by replacing one term with another. To be sure, there is considerable importance in continually reminding ourselves that people-group identities, whether we call them racial or ethnic, are constructed and maintained through discourse and practice, not biologically or physiologically determined. And given the history of the racialization of Jews there are particular reasons to be wary of applying the term 'race' to Jewish identity. But as Wright notes, in a brief response to his critics on this point, it may be possible to use such language in ways that make clear that 'what matters is not genetics, but the fact of a community that lives by certain customs and narratives, in which kinship is important but is blended in with all the other factors, including a relationship with a particular territory'. He also remarks that other terms – such as 'nation and family' – may be equally anachronistic, and that ethnicity itself is 'acquiring various unhelpful overtones in the contemporary western world'. As Wright quips: 'If this goes on we will soon only be able to converse in the decent obscurity of learned languages.'[25] We need, then, to be aware – and find ways to signal – that many of the terms we routinely use in historical analysis (including 'religion' and 'ethnicity') carry conceptual and ideological baggage that renders them open to critical suspicion. But replacing established terms (often with neologisms) is not necessarily a full solution, and can result in a never-ending quest for unproblematic alternative terminology.

Denise Kimber Buell has argued that there are good reasons to keep the term 'race' in play, not least in order to foreground (rather than evade)

---

[22] 'The Race Question. Text of the Statement Issued 18 July 1950', 1. Accessed 16 December 2015: <http://unesdoc.unesco.org/images/0012/001282/128291eo.pdf>.

[23] 'The Race Question', 6 (italics original).

[24] Brubaker 2015, 88.

[25] Wright 2013, 94 n. 78, from which all three of the adjacent quotations above are taken.

issues of racism.[26] She is, in my view rightly, 'suspicious of the ways that certain modern concepts seem to be viewed as unproblematic for analysis of antiquity – religion, ethnicity, and gender, for example – whereas others have become "off-limits" ("race" and increasingly also "sexuality")'.[27] In particular, 'replacing race with ethnicity', she insists, 'has obscured the racist aspects of using ethnicity to distinguish Jews from Christians . . . we need to confront the elusive elasticity of race, since racism persists even when race has been exposed as a construct'.[28] Philip Esler objects that this is akin to a decision to 'smack our misbehaving children in supermarkets rather than admonish them so as to alert others of (*sic*) the evil of smacking'.[29] However, the logic of Buell's argument is, I think, quite the opposite: one might say, to stay with Esler's illustration, that the issue of the physical abuse of children is not solved merely by avoiding the word 'smacking' and talking instead of discipline, or some other euphemism. In other words, the problems that pertain to the comparison of Jewish particularism and Christian universalism do not disappear if we replace 'Jewish racial identity' with 'Jewish ethnicity'.

Resituate Paul within Judaism

A second strategy by which we might seek to avoid the problems of reading Paul as transcending Jewish ethnic particularism by creating a universal and open Christianity is represented by the kind of approach that has come to be known as the 'Paul within Judaism' perspective – sometimes also described as the 'radical new perspective'.[30] The diversity of work presented by those loosely grouped under this label is too great to allow any single description of their approach to be adequate, but a central concern is to reject the established conviction that Paul articulates a critique of Judaism, or (more strongly) rejects or breaks with Judaism, from the perspective of his commitment to Christ. On the contrary, as Lloyd Gaston argues in a seminal contribution to this approach: 'Paul is . . . concerned to argue for the full right of Gentiles to be equal members of the people of God', but also assumes 'the right of Israel to remain Israel . . . All of the positive things Paul has to say about the righteousness of God effecting salvation for Gentiles in Christ need not at all imply anything

---

[26] Buell 2005, 13–21.
[27] Buell 2005, 18.
[28] Buell 2005, 14, 20, respectively.
[29] Esler 2016, 183.
[30] See Zetterholm 2009, 127–63; Nanos and Zetterholm 2015.

negative about Israel and the Torah.'[31] As a more recent proponent, Pamela Eisenbaum, puts it: 'whatever Paul says applies specifically to Gentiles . . . Christ has provided an alternative to Torah observance for Gentiles . . . Paul certainly never condemns Jews' observation of Torah, never advocates their abstaining from circumcision.'[32]

In other words, key to this approach is the insistence that Paul remains 'within Judaism', and neither abandons the Jewish way of life (and its Torah observance) himself nor expects other Jews to do so. His message about salvation in Christ is a message specifically for gentiles – who, in Paul's view, need not, and must not be compelled to, become Jewish, or take on themselves the full yoke of the Torah, including circumcision, in order to be saved by Christ. This may bring him into conflict and disagreement with some of his fellow Jews, but his apostolic activity and the assemblies of believers that result from this remain essentially within the framework of first-century Judaism. Anders Runesson and Mark Nanos have thus suggested the label 'apostolic Judaism' to describe what Paul represents and promotes.[33] Situating Paul in this way prevents him being misappropriated as a founder of a universalistic 'Christianity' in contrast to particularistic Judaism, since Paul remains firmly within the latter context.

Space does not permit a detailed consideration of the various versions of this approach to Paul, which is presently gaining significant support. But three issues seem to me worth highlighting as critical difficulties.[34]

First, Paul's emphatically universal language, especially in Romans and Galatians, seems clearly and explicitly to include both Jews and gentiles within the scope of the 'problem' he elucidates and the 'solution' he believes God has provided in Christ. Romans 3, for example, with its emphatic and repeated use of *pas*, is insistent that both 'Jews and Greeks' are under the power of sin (3.9) and can be 'righteoused', without distinction, only through the faithfulness of Christ (3.22) and by sharing in that faith.[35] Likewise, referring to Galatians 3.10–12, Andrew Das insists that Paul is 'grounding his conclusions for *all people* in biblical passages

---

[31] Gaston 1987, 34. Cf. also Gager 2000.

[32] Eisenbaum 2012, 139–40; cf. Eisenbaum 2009, 216–19, 224. Cf. also Nanos 2015, 141.

[33] See, e.g., Runesson 2015, 67; also Nanos 2015, 121.

[34] For a sympathetic but probing assessment, see Donaldson 2015.

[35] For a more extended exegesis along these lines, see Wright 2013, 836–49. Following the objective (rather than subjective) genitive interpretation of the *pistis Christou* phrases, but otherwise sharing the key contours of this exegesis, see Barclay 2015, 454, 462. For a broader argument against restricting the message to gentiles only, see Hays 1996, responding to Stowers 1994, another important landmark in the 'Paul within Judaism' perspective.

that employ *universal* language. At a minimum the Jewish Scriptural passages he provides in support require the *inclusion* of the Jews.'[36]

Second, the insistence among 'Paul within Judaism' advocates that Paul's letters both intend and imply a gentile audience can be overplayed. It is indeed important to do justice both to Paul's self-understanding as apostle to the gentiles (Romans 11.13; Galatians 1.16; 2.2–9) and to the explicit indications that he addresses gentiles at specific points in his letters (Romans 11.13; 1 Corinthians 12.2). The argument of Galatians only makes sense as addressed to those who are considering, for whatever reasons, undergoing circumcision, and cannot therefore apply with equal relevance to already-circumcised Jews. Yet the opening addresses of Paul's letters make clear that his envisaged audience is cast not in these terms, but in other, more encompassing ways: 'to all [*pasin*] God's beloved in Rome, who are called to be saints [*klētois hagiois*]' (Romans 1.7);[37] 'to the assembly of God [*tē ekklēsia tou theou*] that is in Corinth, to those sanctified in Christ, called to be saints [*klētois hagiois*]' (1 Corinthians 1.2; similarly 2 Corinthians 1.1); 'to all the saints in Christ Jesus who are in Philippi' (Philippians 1.1); more briefly, 'to the assemblies of Galatia' (Galatians 1.2; cf. 1 Thessalonians 1.1). In none of these cases is a specifically gentile identity signalled, nor is this restriction suggested by Paul's indications elsewhere as to who is included in the *ekklēsia*, or reckoned as *hagios*. Indeed, 'those who are called' – a designation used at the opening of Romans and 1 Corinthians – explicitly includes both Jews and gentiles (Romans 9.24). In 1 Corinthians, where we may certainly assume a largely gentile group of addressees, given 12.2, Paul declares his 'rule' for all the assemblies, that those circumcised should not remove the marks of circumcision, and those uncircumcised should not undergo circumcision; these differentiating marks are *ouden*, nothing (7.17–19). What matters is the common calling which all the members of these assemblies share.[38] This implies that Paul's sense of an *ekklēsia* – to which he addresses his letters – is precisely of an assembly that includes both Jews and gentiles. This is further borne out by the varying identities of those who are named in Paul's correspondence (e.g. at Corinth, cf. Acts 18.2–28; Romans 16.3, 21; 1 Corinthians 1.1, 14; 3.5–6; 16.19). This point is further strengthened if we accept, despite the widespread scholarly custom of referring to 'Pauline churches', that Paul wrote not to ideologically and

---

36 Das 2003, 99; see 96–106 for a critique of the 'two covenant' approach, a label applied to earlier versions of the 'Paul within Judaism' perspective.

37 Unless otherwise noted, Scripture quotations in this chapter are adapted from the NRSV.

38 On the nature of this 'calling', see Bartchy 1973, 132–55.

socially distinct groups of Pauline believers in Christ, but to local assemblies of Christ-followers.[39] Paul had often (though not always) played a key role in establishing these assemblies, but the evidence of his letters suggests that these same assemblies related to, and received, other early Christian leaders or their representatives: Peter, James, Apollos and so on (1 Corinthians 1.12; Galatians 2.11–12). The arguments Paul engages in might not have emerged were this not to have been the case.

Third, what also seems clear from Paul is that Christ has become definitive for personal and group identity and practice. His own identity is radically reoriented in this way (so Galatians 2.16–21 and Philippians 3.3–9), such that his most concise label for someone such as himself – and for others in these assemblies – is a person 'in-Christ' (*anthrōpos en Christō*: 2 Corinthians 12.2; cf. Romans 16.7; 1 Corinthians 1.2; 3.1; 2 Corinthians 5.17; Galatians 1.22; Philippians 1.1; 4.21, etc.). Paul does not know the term 'Christian' (*Christianos*), and scholars are understandably wary of using a term that can convey anachronistic and misleading implications for the period of Paul's activity.[40] But insofar as Paul's 'in-Christ' language constitutes his chosen way to denote the central identity- and boundary-marker for the assemblies he addresses, the word Christian is functionally equivalent, though one could perhaps avoid the risks of anachronism by using 'in-Christ' as a somewhat clumsy neologism, transliterating Paul's own language: 'Paul writes to the in-Christs at Corinth' and so on. (This might helpfully 'de-familiarize' our sense of the identity of these converts;[41] and perhaps we might avoid anachronistic implications and do justice to Paul's sense that he is engaged in bringing to fruition the hopes and promises of Israel's God if we labelled this movement 'Christic Judaism'.[42]) Allegiance to Christ has become definitive not only for a sense of identity but also for crucial areas of social practice. Marriage is acceptable if contracted with a fellow in-Christ (1 Corinthians 7.39), and the children of in-Christs also share the holiness of their parent(s) (1 Corinthians 7.14).[43] Likewise, meals are regulated and defined in relation to the Lord Christ: the communal meal is defined as the Lord's meal, and embodies a unity in his one body (1 Corinthians 10.16–17; 11.20–33; cf.

---

[39] Cf. Horrell 2008, 186–96.

[40] See, e.g., Runesson 2015.

[41] On the value of such de-familiarization, see Runesson 2015, 55–7.

[42] I think this might be preferable to 'apostolic Judaism', since that label could imply any kind of missionary Judaism focused on sent or commissioned figures, and 'Christic' would do justice to Paul's heavy Christ-focus, while avoiding the ambiguities of the term 'messianic'.

[43] See further Horrell 2016, 446–52.

Galatians 2.12–13); cultic meals focused on sacrificing to 'idols' are to be shunned (1 Corinthians 10.14–22). It seems that for Paul the crucial group-boundary in terms of moral obligation and social interaction is between those who are in Christ and those who are not; distinct group-identities for Jewish and gentile converts seem hardly to be in view.

It is important to be reminded that Paul cannot plausibly be located within an anachronistic category labelled 'Christianity' that stands distinct from another category labelled 'Judaism'; but it is equally important to do justice to the extent to which he forcefully refocuses group-identity on Christ, the focus which would define what later came to be called Christianity. Notwithstanding the important correctives and challenges it brings to bear, then, I am not convinced that locating Paul 'within' Judaism can solve the difficulties associated with the scholarly interpretation of Paul's construction of group-identity in Christ as a universalizing, open, inclusive move, in contrast to an ethnically particular Judaism.

Paul's construction of an ethno-social particularity

A third strategy that might help us to avoid the problems of a contrast between Jewish ethnic particularism and universally inclusive Christianity is to stress how the early Christian movement, and Paul's version of it specifically, is itself 'particular', with its own boundaries and patterns of inclusion and exclusion.[44] Wright moves in precisely this direction in his discussion of Paul's view of the Church as constituting, in effect, a 'third race'.[45] Acknowledging the controversy surrounding this phrase, coined rather later than Paul, Wright nonetheless follows E. P. Sanders in 'seeing Paul himself as advocating, if not the phrase "third race" itself, nevertheless something approaching it'.[46] He follows Love Sechrest in suggesting 'that Pauline theology constructs a change in religious belief and practice as a change in ethno-racial identity'.[47] For Sechrest, Christian identity as Paul depicts it 'is that of an *emergent, newly formed, Jewish-like racial group*'.[48] Where Wright departs from Sechrest's conclusions is with regard to her suggestion 'that for Paul the church is a *"completely new* ethno-social particularity"'.[49] Rather, on Wright's reading of Paul, this 'new particularity

---

[44] For an early challenge to the contrast between Jewish particularism and Christian universalism, see Dahl 1977, 178–91. See also Barclay 1997b.
[45] Wright 2013, 1443–9.
[46] Wright 2013, 1446; cf. also 1448, and Sanders 1983, 171–9.
[47] Wright 2013, 1446; Sechrest 2009, 15.
[48] Sechrest 2009, 206 (italics original).
[49] Wright 2013, 1448, quoting Sechrest 2009, 210, with Wright's italics.

is the very thing God promised to Abraham in the first place.[50] In other words, the new community which incorporates both Jews and gentiles is itself a fulfilment of the hopes and promises of Israel's story, now made possible through the faithfulness of God's Messiah Jesus. Thus, for Wright, there is for gentile converts a greater sense of 'radical discontinuity' with their former life, but for Jews too identification with the Messiah is crucial to their inclusion in this 'essentially Jewish' people-group.[51]

This move to understand early Christian identity as itself constructed in ethnic or racial terms, deploying what Buell has called 'ethnic reasoning' in its own patterns of identity-construction, seems to me both significant and compelling. Just as Jewish identity drew on discourses of ancestry, kinship, shared history and commemoration, religious and cultural practices, so too, *mutatis mutandis*, did Paul's constructions of identity in-Christ – unsurprisingly, since, as Wright stresses, his own understanding and depiction of what God had done in Christ drew so heavily on Jewish Scripture, and on convictions regarding the eschatological fulfilment of scriptural hopes. I have already mentioned Paul's insistence that those 'in Christ' should practise endogamy (1 Corinthians 7.39), and his declaration that the children of a believing parent are themselves holy (1 Corinthians 7.14). As we move on into the second and third generations, we find in the evolving Pauline tradition a more developed and explicit sense of the importance of the Christian household as a social setting in which the faith is passed on from parents to children – who are to be reared *en paideia kai nouthesia kyriou* (Ephesians 6.4).[52] The frequent designation of fellow believers as *adelphoi* – Paul's most frequently used label for insiders, and another indication of the crucial focus for group-definition – further reinforces this quasi-ethnic familial ethos.[53] And the practices of baptismal initiation and sharing of the Lord's Supper (during which Jesus' death and hoped-for return are recalled), probably on Sunday, the first day of the week (1 Corinthians 16.2),[54] all begin to indicate the distinctive and identity-forming customs which Paul presumes as facets of the assemblies' common life.

Since ethnicity and race are constructions, created and maintained through discourse and social practice, it makes little sense to draw a sharp

---

50 Wright 2013, 1449 (italics original).
51 Wright 2013, 1449.
52 Barclay 1997a, 76–7.
53 See further the recent overview of the evidence in Trebilco 2012, 21–38.
54 For a discussion of the early evidence concerning the emergence of Sunday as the distinctive day of Christian worship, see Llewelyn 2001; Alikin 2010, 40–9.

distinction between 'real' ethnic identities and 'fictive' uses of ethnic identifications – as is sometimes done when contrasting Jewish or Judean ethnicity with early Christian group-identity. Moreover, given the close – though varied and fluid – connections between religion and ethnicity (both of which, as we have noted, are modern and not unproblematic constructions), neither category provides a neat alternative into which we can slot either Jewish or early Christian identity. It seems better, therefore, to explore the particular ways in which various facets of discourse and practice, including those associated with ethnic identities, are deployed in both Jewish and early Christian texts, recognizing that in both (inter-woven) traditions, 'belonging' involves a sense of being part of a distinct people-group, expressed *in nuce* in Paul's differentiation of Jews, Greeks and the *ekklēsia tou theou* (1 Corinthians 10.32). As Wright puts it: 'Paul's communities live . . . as the *ekklēsia tou theou*, composed equally of Jews and gentiles but also defining themselves over against both those catego-ries in and as a strange new entity.'[55] Just as Paul does not use the later phrase 'third race', so too he does not explicitly identify the members of the *ekklēsia* as a 'people' – again, this move would be made later (emphati-cally, within the NT, in 1 Peter 2.9–10).[56] But Paul does move further in this direction than is sometimes acknowledged, particularly in applying scriptural language to the members of the Christian assemblies.[57] In Romans 9, citing the same scriptural text quoted in 1 Peter 2.10, and dis-cussing God's calling of people from among both Jews (*ex Ioudaiōn*) and gentiles (*ex ethnōn*), Paul quotes Hosea: 'Those who were not my people I will call my people' (*kalesō ton ou laon mou laon mou*, Romans 9.25). Scriptural quotation is also the source in 2 Corinthians 6.16, where Paul implicitly identifies his readers as the *laos theou* (quoting Leviticus 26.12; Ezekiel 37.27; cf. also Jeremiah 31.33). In this famously disjunctive passage calling for distinction and separation from unbelievers (2 Corinthians 6.14—7.1), Paul describes himself and his readers as the temple of God (cf. 1 Corinthians 3.16), and applies the scriptural declaration 'I will be their God, and they shall be my people' to his Corinthian addressees, whom he elsewhere describes, as we have noted, as former gentiles (1 Corinthians 12.2).

This kind of reading of Paul does not allow the apostle to remain uncritically located 'within Judaism' and will for some no doubt treat him

---

55 Wright 2013, 626; cf. 394–5, 1446–8.
56 On which see further Horrell 2012, 123–43, revised and expanded in Horrell 2013, 133–63.
57 So, e.g., Johnson Hodge 2007, 151: 'Paul does not develop a language of peoplehood for the established communities of Christ followers.'

as if he had made much more of a break with his ancestral tradition than is convincing. But, as Wright has long stressed, it is not so much a break, at least as Paul sees it, but rather a new understanding of his ancestral traditions and their hopes and promises, reconfigured around the one whom Paul sees as the faithful Messiah of God. While this does not then solve the difficulties raised by Paul's reworking of these traditions, nor the wider problems of Christian anti-Judaism and supercessionism, it does, I want to suggest, through its stress on the 'ethno-social particularity' of the early Christian communities, make possible a comparison of Jewish and early Christian traditions that does not juxtapose Jewish ethnic exclusivism with an implicitly superior Christian universalism.

Patterns of inclusion

If both Jewish and early Christian communities constitute – or are constructed as – some kind of ethno-social particularity, then rather than depicting one form of community as exclusive and ethnocentric and the other as inclusive and open, we need to ask in each case about patterns of inclusion, opportunities for joining (and leaving), and about what it meant to be(come) part of this ethno-social group. To recall Wright's language, cited earlier, each group may in some sense 'confine grace to one race', but differ in how that sense of 'race' is constructed.[58] Needless to say, only a brief sketch can be offered here (though I plan a fuller treatment elsewhere).

In a shift from the dominant perspective of older scholarship, recent work has come to a broad agreement that Judaism at the time of Christian origins was not typified by active missionary activity.[59] With one or two possible exceptions, the evidence seems to point rather to a willingness to instruct and welcome outsiders who were attracted to the Jewish way of life. This forms something of a contrast with the early Christian movement, and Paul in particular, whose missionary zeal is explicit (e.g. Romans 15.15–24; 1 Corinthians 9.16–23; Philippians 1.12–18).

---

[58] This proposal therefore shares something in common, structurally, with recent work on the topic of grace: one of E. P. Sanders' lasting achievements in *Paul and Palestinian Judaism* (Sanders 1977) is to show that there was 'grace' in Judaism, as well as in Christianity, while John Barclay's recent work (Barclay 2015) presses beyond this to explore how 'grace' is differently construed in various Jewish texts, and in Paul's letters to the Romans and the Galatians. Likewise, rather than contrast Jewish 'racial' identity and Christian trans-ethnic identity, we might better ask how both Jewish and early Christian sources draw on racial or ethnic categories to construe and construct a sense of group-identity.

[59] See esp. McKnight 1991; Goodman 1994; Will and Orrieux 1992; Riesner 2000; Bird 2010.

Nonetheless, there is evidence for the widespread appeal and popularity of Jewish customs at the time (e.g. Josephus, *C. Ap.* 2.123; 2.282–4; Philo, *Mos.* 2.17; 2.41–3; Seneca, *De Superstitione*),[60] despite stereotypical polemic about Jewish exclusivism (e.g. Tacitus, *Hist.* 5.5, who criticizes the early Christians in a somewhat similar manner, *Ann.* 15.44). Josephus and Philo may well exaggerate when they depict the popular adoption of Jewish customs. But such exaggeration characterizes Paul's own accounts too: 'from Jerusalem and as far around as Illyricum I have fully proclaimed the good news of Christ' (Romans 15.19). However extensive or limited Paul's success in this endeavour, it is clear enough that he and his associates gained converts: those who, in Paul's terms, 'turned to God from idols' (1 Thessalonians 1.9; cf. 1 Corinthians 12.2). Both the imagery and the instruction Paul presents indicate his sense that this 'conversion' – though there is no precise or standard term in Paul's letters to denote a 'convert' as such[61] – entails a sharp break from a former way of life and a radical abandonment of previous customs and allegiances: death, burial and new life (e.g. Romans 6.1–11; cf. Colossians 2.12–13; 3.1–7); stripping off and reclothing (e.g. Romans 13.14; Galatians 3.27; cf. Colossians 3.8–15); living 'not like the gentiles' but in holiness (e.g. 1 Thessalonians 4.1–7). There is no scope allowed for a halfway house, or for partial commitment. By contrast, Jewish communities often allowed people to affiliate and participate to varying degrees, while remaining, in some cases, involved in other socio-religious networks.[62] Earlier debate about the existence of so-called 'godfearers' seems now to have been largely settled in favour of the view that there were indeed such sympathizers and adherents to Judaism, albeit that such people occupied a broad range of possible levels of participation and did not constitute a specific or designated 'class' of participants,

---

[60] Seneca's text is extant only in Augustine, *Civ. Dei.*, 6.11 (see Stern, *GLAJJ* 1.431–2 §186); also in Bird 2010, 171, and (with discussion) Donaldson 2007, 381–2.

[61] Paul uses *aparchē* twice in this sense (Romans 16.5; 1 Corinthians 16.15); 1 Timothy 3.6 uses *neophytos*. Acts 13.43 uses *prosēlytos* of Jewish converts, but the term is not used of converts to Christ.

[62] A notable example is Julia Severa, referred to in various inscriptions, notably *MAMA* 6.264. For translation and commentary, see Trebilco 1991, 58–60; Donaldson 2007, 463–6. Cf. also Fredriksen 2010, 239. It is striking that Brigitte Kahl implicitly criticizes this as an example of 'tacit syncretism', 'a model of acquiescence', 'in glaring contrast to Paul's [laudably radical, anti-imperial] vision for his Galatian communities as he tries to challenge the smooth and prudent arrangement between the Jewish God and the imperial idols proposed by his "opponents"' (Kahl 2010, 241). This is one indication of how work that is strenuously concerned to avoid any anti-Judaism (cf. Kahl 2010, 13–15) can still end up, it seems to me, replicating a sense of Christian superiority.

as the label 'godfearer' might suggest.[63] It was also possible – at least in the eyes of many Jews[64] – to convert fully, to become a proselyte, though again this specific terminology is not standard (Josephus, for example, nowhere uses the term, though clearly discusses and welcomes the possibility, e.g., in *C. Ap.* 2.209–10). For male converts this entailed the step of accepting circumcision, which marked most clearly the boundary between sympathizing and fully joining, as Josephus' account of Izates' 'conversion' indicates (*Ant.* 20.17–96).[65] Evidence suggests that such proselytes were by no means rare, even if they did not generally result from active Jewish missionizing.[66]

Moral judgements concerning these differing patterns of inclusion and exclusion are not the business of historical analysis. But since such judgements have often been a part, if only implicitly, of the discipline of New Testament studies, dominated as it is by Christian scholars, it is worth offering some evaluation, even if only as a provocation to think differently. While the kind of inclusion 'in Christ' so energetically promoted by Paul is often seen as a model of (post)modern tolerance of diversity, compared with the intolerant demands of his opponents,[67] we might view the historical evidence otherwise. Judaism, it seems, tended not to be characterized by the aggressive proselytizing zeal of the earliest Christians, Paul in particular, but many Jewish communities were evidently more than willing to welcome and instruct those interested in the Jewish way of life: the model of mission was more one of 'passive attraction' than active proselytism. Unlike Paul, who demanded a radical abandonment of former customs and allegiances, some Jewish communities allowed people to affiliate and participate to varying degrees, while remaining, in some cases, involved in other socio-religious networks, or to join in fully and become Jewish. My deliberately loaded summary should at least suggest that, from a modern perspective, the Jewish option could appear

---

63 See the extensive discussion of sources in Donaldson 2007, and also, *inter alia*, Levinskaya 1996; Feldman 1993, 342–82; Wander 1998.

64 For some evidence of exceptions to this, see Thiessen 2011, though Thiessen accepts that 'many Jews' accepted and welcomed the possibility of gentile conversion (e.g. 85) and that the evidence for the contrary view is limited (e.g. 87).

65 On which, see Barclay 2018.

66 See further Donaldson 2007, 483–92; Levinskaya 1996, 19–33; Feldman 1993, 288–341 (though Feldman also argues for energetic Jewish missionary activity).

67 For example, in a recent commentary, Peter Oakes writes that 'the aim of Paul's rhetoric [in Galatians 3.28] is to preserve social diversity rather than to eliminate it' whereas 'Paul's opponents . . . are seeking to eliminate diversity. They want gentiles to adopt circumcision, to Judaize, to become Jews, losing their distinction in identity. Paul wants unity between gentiles as gentiles and Jews as Jews, all together in Christ' (Oakes 2015, 128).

much more 'tolerant' and 'inclusive'. It is somewhat puzzling, then, that it is Christianity, and its iconic figures such as Paul, that tends to be credited with welcoming gentiles, modelling inclusion, diversity and tolerance, or offering the possibility to join in the community which regarded itself as God's people. Once we stress, however, that both Jewish and early Christian communities represented their own forms of ethno-social particularity, we may be provoked to enquire how each presented different opportunities and possibilities to join, and required certain commitments and practices of those who did. It is unclear whether, or indeed if, one should judge either set of practices as 'better' or 'worse' than the other, but I hope at least to have hinted that there is no particular historical reason, aside from a prior commitment to Christianity, to regard the Pauline version as superior.

Bibliography

Alikin, Valeriy A. (2010). *The Earliest History of the Christian Gathering: Origin, Development and Content of the Christian Gathering in the First to Third Centuries*. Leiden / Boston, MA: Brill.

Barclay, John M. G. (1997a). 'The Family as the Bearer of Religion in Judaism and Early Christianity'. In *Constructing Early Christian Families: Family as Social Reality and Metaphor*, edited by Halvor Moxnes, 66–80. London / New York, NY: Routledge.

—— (1997b). 'Universalism and Particularism: Twin Components of Both Judaism and Early Christianity'. In *A Vision for the Church: Studies in Early Christian Ecclesiology in Honour of J. P. M. Sweet*, edited by Markus Bockmuehl and Michael B. Thompson, 207–24. Edinburgh: T&T Clark.

—— (2015). *Paul and the Gift*. Grand Rapids, MI: Eerdmans.

—— (2018). Ἰουδαῖος: Ethnicity and Translation'. In *Ethnicity, Race, Religion: Identities and Ideologies in Early Jewish and Christian Texts and in Modern Biblical Interpretation*, edited by David G. Horrell and Katherine M. Hockey, 46–58. London / New York, NY: Bloomsbury/T&T Clark.

Bartchy, Scott S. (1973). *ΜΑΛΛΟΝ ΧΡΗΣΑΙ: First-Century Slavery and the Interpretation of 1 Corinthians 7:21*. Society of Biblical Literature Dissertation Series. Missoula, MT: Society of Biblical Literature.

Baur, Ferdinand Christian (1873–5). *Paul the Apostle of Jesus Christ: His Life and Works, His Epistles and Teachings*. 2 vols. London / Edinburgh: Williams & Norgate.

—— (1878–9). *The Church History of the First Three Centuries*. 2 vols. London / Edinburgh: Williams & Norgate.

Bird, Michael F. (2010). *Crossing Over Sea and Land: Jewish Missionary Activity in the Second Temple Period*. Peabody, MA: Hendrickson.

Brubaker, Rogers (2015). *Grounds for Difference*. Cambridge, MA: Harvard University Press.

Buell, Denise Kimber (2005). *Why This New Race: Ethnic Reasoning in Early Christianity*. New York, NY: Columbia University Press.

Dahl, Nils Alstrup (1977). *Studies in Paul*. Minneapolis, MN: Augsburg.

Das, Andrew A. (2003). *Paul and the Jews*. Peabody, MA: Hendrickson.

Donaldson, Terence L. (2007). *Judaism and the Gentiles: Jewish Patterns of Universalism (to 135 CE)*. Waco, TX: Baylor University Press.

—— (2015). 'Paul within Judaism: A Critical Evaluation from a "New Perspective" Perspective.' In *Paul within Judaism: Restoring the First-Century Context to the Apostle*, edited by Mark Nanos and Magnus Zetterholm, 277–301. Minneapolis, MN: Fortress.

Eisenbaum, Pamela (2009). *Paul Was Not a Christian: The Original Message of a Misunderstood Apostle*. New York, NY: HarperCollins.

—— (2012). 'Jewish Perspectives: A *Jewish* Apostle to the Gentiles.' In *Studying Paul's Letters*, edited by Joseph A. Marchal, 135–53. Minneapolis, MN: Fortress.

Esler, Philip F. (2016). 'Giving the Kingdom to an *Ethnos* That Will Bear Its Fruit: Ethnic and Christ-Movement Identities in Matthew.' In *In the Fullness of Time: Essays on Christology, Creation, and Eschatology in Honor of Richard Bauckham*, edited by Daniel M. Gurtner, Grant Macaskill and Jonathan T. Pennington, 177–96. Grand Rapids, MI: Eerdmans.

Feldman, Louis H. (1993). *Jew and Gentile in the Ancient World: Attitudes and Interactions from Alexander to Justinian*. Princeton, NJ: Princeton University Press.

Fredriksen, Paula (2010). 'Judaizing the Nations: The Ritual Demands of Paul's Gospel.' *New Testament Studies* 56: 232–52.

Gager, John G. (2000). *Reinventing Paul*. Oxford / New York, NY: Oxford University Press.

Gaston, Lloyd (1987). *Paul and the Torah*. Vancouver: University of British Columbia Press.

Gerdmar, Anders (2014). 'Baur and the Creation of the Judaism-Hellenism Dichotomy.' In *Ferdinand Christian Baur und die Geschichte des Urchristentums*, edited by Martin Bauspiess, Christof Landmesser and David Lincicum, 107–28. Tübingen: Mohr Siebeck.

Goodman, Martin (1994). *Mission and Conversion: Proselytizing in the Religious History of the Roman Empire*. Oxford: Clarendon.

Hannaford, Ivan (1996). *Race: The History of an Idea in the West*. Washington: Woodrow Wilson Center / Baltimore, MD: Johns Hopkins University Press.

Harris, Horton (1975). *The Tübingen School*. Oxford: Clarendon.

Hays, Richard B. (1996). '"The Gospel Is the Power of God for Salvation to Gentiles Only?" A Critique of Stanley Stowers' *A Rereading of Romans.' Critical Review of Books in Religion* 9: 27–44.

Hegel, Georg Wilhelm Friedrich (1975 (1830)). *Lectures on the Philosophy of World History. Introduction: Reason in History.* Cambridge: Cambridge University Press.

Horrell, David G. (2008). 'Pauline Churches or Early Christian Churches? Unity,

Disagreement, and the Eucharist.' In *Einheit der Kirche im Neuen Testament*, edited by Anatoly Alexeev et al., 185–203. Tübingen: Mohr Siebeck.

—— (2012). '"Race", "Nation", "People": Ethnic Identity-Construction in 1 Peter 2.9.' *New Testament Studies* 58: 123–43.

—— (2013). *Becoming Christian: Essays on 1 Peter and the Making of Christian Identity*. London / New York, NY: Bloomsbury/T&T Clark.

—— (2015). *Solidarity and Difference: A Contemporary Reading of Paul's Ethics*. Cornerstones. London / New York, NY: Bloomsbury/T&T Clark.

—— (2016). 'Ethnicisation, Marriage, and Early Christian Identity: Critical Reflections on 1 Corinthians 7, 1 Peter 3, and Modern New Testament Scholarship.' *New Testament Studies* 62: 439–60.

Johnson Hodge, Caroline (2007). *If Sons, Then Heirs: A Study of Kinship and Ethnicity in the Letters of Paul*. Oxford / New York, NY: Oxford University Press.

Kahl, Brigitte (2010). *Galatians Re-imagined: Reading with the Eyes of the Vanquished*. Paul in Critical Contexts. Minneapolis, MN: Fortress.

Kelley, Shawn (2002). *Racializing Jesus: Race, Ideology and the Formation of Modern Biblical Scholarship*. London / New York, NY: Routledge.

Kidd, Colin (2006). *The Forging of Races: Race and Scripture in the Protestant Atlantic World, 1600–2000*. Cambridge: Cambridge University Press.

Levinskaya, Irina (1996) (ed.). *The Book of Acts in Its Diaspora Setting*. Grand Rapids, MI: Eerdmans / Carlisle: Paternoster, 1996.

Llewelyn, S. R. (2001). 'The Use of Sunday for Meetings of Believers in the New Testament.' *Novum Testamentum* 43: 205–23.

McKnight, Scot (1991). *A Light among the Gentiles: Jewish Missionary Activity in the Second Temple Period*. Minneapolis, MN: Fortress.

Miller, David M. (2012). 'Ethnicity Comes of Age: An Overview of Twentieth-Century Terms for *Ioudaios*.' *Currents in Biblical Research* 10: 293–311.

Nanos, Mark D. (2015). 'The Question of Conceptualization: Qualifying Paul's Position on Circumcision in Dialogue with Josephus's Advisors to King Izates.' In *Paul within Judaism: Restoring the First-Century Context to the Apostle*, edited by Mark D. Nanos and Magnus Zetterholm, 105–52. Minneapolis, MN: Fortress.

Nanos, Mark D. and Zetterholm, Magnus (2015) (eds). *Paul within Judaism: Restoring the First-Century Context to the Apostle*. Minneapolis, MN: Fortress.

Oakes, Peter (2015). *Galatians*. Paideia: Commentaries on the New Testament. Grand Rapids, MI: Baker Academic.

Riesner, Rainer (2000). 'A Pre-Christian Jewish Mission?' In *The Mission of the Early Church to Jews and Gentiles*, edited by Jostein Ådna and Hans Kvalbein, 211–50. Tübingen: Mohr Siebeck.

Roetzel, Calvin J. (1997). 'No "Race of Israel" in Paul.' In *Putting Body and Soul Together: Essays in Honor of Robin Scroggs*, edited by Virginia Wiles, Alexandra Brown and Graydon F. Snyder, 230–44. Valley Forge, PA: Trinity Press International.

Runesson, Anders (2015). 'The Question of Terminology: The Architecture of

Contemporary Discussions of Paul.' In *Paul within Judaism: Restoring the First-Century Context to the Apostle*, edited by Mark D. Nanos and Magnus Zetterholm, 53–103. Minneapolis, MN: Fortress.

Sanders, E. P. (1977). *Paul and Palestinian Judaism*. London: SCM.

—— (1983). *Paul, the Law and the Jewish People*. London: SCM.

Sechrest, Love L. (2009). *A Former Jew: Paul and the Dialectics of Race*. London / New York, NY: T&T Clark.

Stowers, Stanley K. (1994). *A Rereading of Romans: Justice, Jews and Gentiles*. New Haven, CT / London: Yale University Press.

Thiessen, Matthew (2011). *Contesting Conversion: Genealogy, Circumcision, and Identity in Ancient Judaism and Christianity*. Oxford / New York, NY: Oxford University Press.

Trebilco, Paul (1991). *Jewish Communities in Asia Minor*. Cambridge: Cambridge University Press.

—— (2012). *Self-Designations and Group Identity in the New Testament*. Cambridge: Cambridge University Press.

UNESCO. 'The Race Question. Text of the Statement Issued 18 July 1950.' <http://unesdoc.unesco.org/images/0012/001282/128291eo.pdf> (accessed 16 December 2015).

Wander, Bernd (1998). *Gottesfürchtige und Sympathisanten. Studien zum heidnischen Umfeld von Diasporasynagogen*. Tübingen: Mohr Siebeck.

Will, Edouard and Claude Orrieux (1992). '*Proselytisme Juif?' Histoire d'une erreur*. Paris: Les Belles Lettres.

Wright, N. T. (1991). *The Climax of the Covenant: Christ and the Law in Pauline Theology*. Edinburgh: T&T Clark.

—— (1992). *The New Testament and the People of God*. Christian Origins and the Question of God 1. London: SPCK / Minneapolis, MN: Fortress.

—— (2013). *Paul and the Faithfulness of God*. Christian Origins and the Question of God 4. London: SPCK / Minneapolis, MN: Fortress.

Zetterholm, Magnus (2009). *Approaches to Paul: A Student's Guide to Recent Scholarship*. Minneapolis, MN: Fortress.

Saints re-formed: the extension and expansion of *hagios* in Paul

SCOT McKNIGHT

Introduction

New Testament scholarship across the board, especially since the discovery of the Dead Sea Scrolls and the broadly respected synthesis of Judaism in the works of E. P. Sanders, most especially his pathbreaking *Paul and Palestinian Judaism*, seeks to avoid the faintest whiff of supersessionism. It has become sport to call the other options in Pauline scholarship a grand example of supersessionism. Hence, the New Perspective scholars see supersessionism in the old, or Reformation, perspective while thinking of their own as a grand example of sensitivity. Then along comes the apocalyptic approach to Paul and at times one hears that especially the New Perspective – excluding of course E. P. Sanders – is supersessionistic. New Perspective scholars, and I avoid footnotes in this entire paragraph to protect the innocent and the guilty, in turn think the apocalypticists among us are supersessionists. Then the post-New Perspective comes along and tosses mud on the whole lot and here we stand, all accusing and being accused. Most define supersessionism as 'replacement theology', as in the Church replacing Israel, while what 'replacement' means and how it relates not only to other Jewish sects like the Essenes or to words like 'fulfilment' and 'salvation history' as used by New Testament authors – including Jesus – goes undefined, if not ignored. It is enough for some to gain the upper hand, like progressives and conservatives in some political battle, by all but damning the other with the S-word. I have myself more than one time wondered if the word 'fulfilment' is not inherently supersessionist at some level. Can a confessing Christian claim what he or she claims about Jesus as God's Messiah or even the second person of the Trinity without crossing the threshold?

In Larry Hurtado's new and penetrating *Destroyer of the Gods* we read that gentile converts to Jesus and the Jesus movement did not become Jews but remained gentiles, even if they acquired a new identity.[1] His emphasis

---

[1] Hurtado 2016.

is that the earliest Christians formed a 'translocal and transethnic' kind of 'Christian identity'. In that context, however, 'Jewish believers, among whom he counted himself, remained Jews, and his pagan converts likewise retained their various ethnic identities'. Just what he means by 'retained' could have been teased out, but that's not done nor do I want to press him beyond his own words. These gentile converts, he states, are no longer the same as ordinary pagan gentiles, but they remain gentiles. From the opposite side of the many nuances Hurtado is fond of establishing, he argues that Paul 'portrays his pagan converts as having acquired a radically new religious identity'. Then he summarizes his even bigger conclusions:

> But I repeat that they have not become Jews. Their baptism did not make them members of the Jewish people/nation. They remained Gentiles. In the case of the Thessalonian converts, they remain Greeks. But, in their religious life, they have become a different kind of Gentiles. They have now become obedient to the true God, the biblical/Jewish God and his Son, to whom now they are to give exclusive religious devotion and from whom they are now to derive exclusively their new religious identity. To repeat a point made in chapter 2, this was new territory and an unprecedented status for his pagan converts. To put it in more prosaic terms, early Christians took up a new kind of religious identity that, uniquely, was both exclusive and not related to their ethnicity.[2]

Back and forth he goes, but I walk away unsettled in spite of the careful nuances and sensitivities clearly at work. If it is 'new' it is not the 'same', and if it is the 'same' then it is not a 'new kind of religious identity'. 'Sameness' in the early Church, I shall contend in this paper, is not the portal into which new believers entered.

'Newness' is the right portal, and it makes all the difference to be a new kind of people. There is a resistance today to think of the Church, the congregations Paul was forming in his mission, as a 'third race' as was stated in *The Apology of Aristides*, who famously said there are four races: barbarians, Greeks, Jews and Christians.[3] Or as a 'new race' as in *The Epistle to Diognetus*:

> Since I see, most excellent Diognetus, that you are extremely eager to learn about the religion of the Christians and are making such an exacting and careful inquiry about them, wishing to discover which God they obey and how they worship him, so that they all despise the world and disdain

---

2   Quotations are from Hurtado 2016, 92–3. To speak of 'nation' and 'people' here as if they are nearly the same (hence, 'people/nation') is where I would take a step back.
3   *The Apology of Aristides* 1; 17 (translation from the Syriac in Harris and Robinson 1891).

death, neither giving credence to those thought to be gods by the Greeks nor keeping the superstition of the Jews, and what deep affection they have for one another, and just why *this new race or way of life* came into being now and not before, I welcome this eagerness of yours and ask God – who enables us both to speak and to hear – that I may be allowed to speak in such a way that you derive special benefit by hearing, and that you hear in such a way that the speaker not be put to grief.[4]

But I am wondering aloud if it is possible to be 'new' without being a 'new race' or a 'third race', to use the terms of those early texts. If one is not a gentile as one was, and if one is not a Jew as one was, then what is one if not something else? Perhaps we need a spectrum scale from the 'fully gentile' to the 'barely gentile'.

The words used by the apostles in the New Testament for who they were or what they were or their new identity include these famous expressions from 1 Peter 2.9–10 (all quotations from the Bible in this chapter are from the NRSV unless otherwise noted):

> But you are a chosen race, a royal priesthood, a holy nation, God's own people, in order that you may proclaim the mighty acts of him who called you out of darkness into his marvellous light. Once you were not a people, but now you are God's people; once you had not received mercy, but now you have received mercy.

We have already in the New Testament, then, the usage of *genos*/race for the (apparently mostly if not entirely gentile) Church, and we have in this text, too, the use of 'nation' in 'holy nation', and it is that term 'holy' that I will focus on in this study. The use of 'God's own people' (*laos eis peripoiēsin*, a common Old Testament designation for God's people) presses upon the readers the sense that others are not God's own people.

Take also another exceptional study, this one by Paul Trebilco,[5] who examines the early Church's self-designations brothers and sisters, believers, saints/holy ones, the assembly/church, disciples, the way and Christians. While not always on the top shelf for terms used by Jews or ancient Israelites for themselves, at least some of these terms were self-designations of Jews and most of them more or less Jewish expressions of identity. I want to take one of his self-designations, the term *ekklēsia* or 'church', and rehearse his conclusions. First, the term as used by the earliest Christians derives from the LXX and that is its background, and that Jewish context formed the meaning for the Pauline mission's use of this

---

4 *Epistle to Diognetus* 1.1 (trans. Ehrman 2003). Greek: *kainon touto genos ē epitēdeuma*.
5 Trebilco 2012.

term for the congregations Paul formed throughout the Roman Empire.[6] Second, the term refers to an assembly or a congregation, and in Pauline literature in the canon (Pauline or not), it refers at times to the local congregation but acquires, too, the sense of the Church as a whole scattered from Jerusalem to Rome. Third, in Lucan literature it clearly evokes continuity with Israel (e.g. Acts 7.38). In fact, Trebilco contends it got its start among the Hellenists in Jerusalem in order to connect the 'Church' with Israel of God's covenant. As such the term *ekklēsia* distinguishes the people of Jesus from the synagogue that did not embrace Jesus as Messiah. He furthers this to suggest that over time it moved from being an alternative to the synagogue to opposition to the synagogue. In that sense, the term becomes supersessionist. A further point from Trebilco's study is that this term at times is polemical while at other times shows little suggestion of antagonism with respect to the synagogue. Noticeably, in James the term 'church' and 'synagogue' may refer to the same congregation (James 2.2; 5.14), while the term does not even appear in 1 Peter, and Trebilco is justified in thinking it was not at least a technical term for Peter. Finally, quoting James D. G. Dunn, Trebilco's professor and mine, we read that the term is not used for 'isolated individuals', but was used 'only as a gathering, for worship and for mutual support' and as such its members functioned as the 'assembly of God'.[7]

Holiness

For Paul, at least, the use of the term *ekklēsia* presses upon us the question about self-identity, about relation to Judaism and to the Old Testament, and how he understood the relation of God's covenant with Israel and God's (new) covenant with Jesus and the Church. I find this same tension in the term 'holy' or 'saints'.[8] Before turning to an examination of how Paul re-formed 'saints' through his grid of monotheism (Christology, pneumatology), election and eschatology,[9] a brief sketch of the meaning of holiness/saints will be offered. Paul Trebilco's opening definition, passed over perhaps without noting its profundity or its singular balance, is this:

---

6   Not a few scholars today make much of this term having a Greek, and therefore political, connotation. One does not have to create an either–or: the term has in Greek, both in the Greek world and in the LXX (and Jewish world), a political connotation as well as a religious assembly meaning. For the Greco-Roman context with some important bibliography, see Trebilco 2012, 165–6.
7   Trebilco 2012, 207. He is citing Dunn 1998, 542.
8   On this term, see Barton 2003a; 2003b; Trebilco 2012, 122–63.
9   The framing of Paul's theology along these lines and how they were taken up in the eschatology of Paul is the singular contribution of Wright 2013a.

'The root *q-d-sh* indicates that something belongs exclusively to Yahweh and emphasised that it was set apart from everyday usage.'[10] This is a long leap of improvement over the far more common understanding, repeated in textbooks, lectures and sermons, that 'holy' means (and is reduced to) 'separated'.

The options are well known and sketched by several scholars, but in this essay we can focus on the taxonomy of Philip Jenson, a scholar known for research on the meaning of holiness especially in the Old Testament.[11] He focuses on six approaches to *q-d-sh*:

1 holiness as separation (Leviticus 10.10);
2 holiness as power (Leviticus 10.3);
3 holiness as wholly other (Isaiah 6), with the term evoking the magisterial influence of Rudolf Otto[12] as well as a pervasive history-of-religions-school approach to holiness deriving from experience and the concept of taboo;
4 holiness as character (Exodus; Leviticus 11.44–45; but esp. also Isaiah);
5 holiness as the realm or sphere of God's dwelling (Exodus 3.5; 15.13; 19.23; 26.33–34; 28.29, 35, 43; 29.30; et al.);
6 holiness as the presence of God (Exodus 25.8).

Yes, one might say at each point. I am reminded of something Nancy Mairs, one of the USA's few essayists, said about God: 'Precise terms, no matter how intricate, will never quite catch God in the act.'[13] No term is perhaps less susceptible to precise definition than holiness, and one reason is that it is multifaceted. As another essayist, Brian Doyle, once said, 'Holiness wears different clothes every day.'[14] Still, it is the last idea that precipitates the others: it is the divine presence that transforms sacred space, people and utensils into holiness. Again, holiness is more than separation (see (1) above). Not only is the Hebrew term *p-r-sh* more appropriate to the idea of separation, but the concept of holiness in the Old Testament – and who is there to deny its curves and reshapings over time in the Bible from Exodus to Isaiah to Ezekiel and the scholarly debates about ordering the ideas?[15] – is far more than separation from. The term frequently describes things

---

10 Trebilco 2012, 122.
11 Jenson 1992; 2003. See also Wells 2000.
12 Otto 1958.
13 Mairs 1993, 12.
14 Doyle and Doyle 1996, 149.
15 A particularly innovative and influential study is Knohl 2007. For an approach focusing on holiness in various Old Testament traditions, see Gammie 1989.

made sacred/holy by connection to the God of Israel, who is holiness. Hence, holiness can point us at an item (grain), or a piece of furniture (lampstand), or a person (priest, Levite), or the nation of Israel (Exodus 19.6; Psalms 16.3; 34.9; Daniel 7.18) or the Qumran community (CD 20.2, 5, 7; 1QS 1.1; 2.25)[16] – things which are devoted and given over to God and, because of that donation, are withdrawn from normal usage (eating, lighting, living an ordinary life). But as Jenson reminds us, it is because God is present that presence makes something holy. The deepest category for holiness then is divine presence, and that presence transforms space, people (priests) and utensils into fittedness for the divine presence. In particular, divine presence renders an Israelite into a 'saint'. But our concern now is the New Testament and the mission of Paul.

Paul and the Church as 'saints'

I turn as a starting point to Colossians 1.2, which reads: *tois en Kolossais hagiois kai pistois adelphois en Christō; charis hymin kai eirēnē apo Theou patros hēmōn.*[17] The description of the Christians of the house churches[18] in Colosse is complex, unified and can be translated as the 'holy/saintly-and-faithful brothers[-and-sisters]-in-Christ who are in Colosse'. Our focus is on 'holy' or 'saintly'. C. F. D. Moule, in still one of the most elegant commentaries ever written on any book of the New Testament, accurately assesses what this term means: 'perhaps best rendered "dedicated," "God's own," because it represents the O.T. conception of "the dedicated people" whose members are "the dedicated ones"'.[19] If we turn back to the sketch of Jenson above, the term 'saints' or 'holy ones' describes those in whom God, through the Spirit, is present, and through that divine presence holiness pervades those persons in such a way that they are dedicated to God, withdrawn from common usage in the world, and the impact of such divine presence is that the saints become a sacred place in the Roman Empire. As Tom Wright has observed, we must ever remind ourselves that a 'saint', with all due respect to a growing Roman Catholic classification system, is

---

16 The word is used ubiquitously at Qumran. At 1QS 8.5–6 the community sees itself as 'a Holy of Holies for Aaron'.

17 This section is rooted in my forthcoming commentary; see McKnight 2018. Authorship questions are examined in the Introduction, and I line up with those who think the letter is Pauline. The 'holy' term in the New Testament occurs as a noun (e.g. 1 Corinthians 6.1; 16.1; 2 Corinthians 1.1; Romans 1.7; 8.27; 16.15) and as a verb (e.g. 1 Thessalonians 5.23; 1 Corinthians 1.2; 6.1; Romans 15.16). On the word group, see Silva 2014, 1:124–33.

18 On the house churches, see Gehring 2004. But see now also Adams 2015.

19 Moule 1957, 45. For further discussion along our lines but without an emphasis on Colossians, see Bohlen 2011.

not a special kind of Christian (as in Saint Francis or Saint Clare) but an ordinary Christian rendered holy by divine presence.[20] 'Holy' or 'saint' is not a description of a person's height of moral achievement or miraculous accomplishments but a divine verdict based on the gracious presence of the divine. With the ground now cleared I propose the following four theses for understanding what happens to the term 'saints' in the Pauline mission.[21]

First, *the term 'saints' is an obvious case of adopting and adapting a term used in the Old Testament and Jewish tradition for Israel, a people who are 'saints' not by extraordinary holiness but by God's electing grace to locate them in his presence.*

Especially in the priestly traditions, the Old Testament sense of holiness, holy and saints derives from the holiness of God (Leviticus 10.3; 11.44, 45; Psalm 111.9; Isaiah 45.11; 47.4) and everything connected to that divine presence. As such, the term is used especially for the Temple, its utensils and its priests. Why? Because they are in the Lord's presence and therefore become sacred, saintly and holy (Exodus 29.33; 30.30; Leviticus 21.6–8; Ezekiel 42.13–14; 43.12). A particular case, then, is the holiness of the Nazirites (Numbers 6.8). This largely priestly-shaped concept of holiness is expanded occasionally to include the elect people of Israel. Israel is a 'priestly kingdom and a holy nation' (Exodus 19.5–6)[22] and the people are commended to 'consecrate yourselves, therefore and be holy' (Leviticus 20.7; cf. 20.26). But something special happens to the priestly emphasis on the Temple and priests as holy when we read Deuteronomy and its tradition, and it would not be inadmissible to suggest there is a far greater democratizing of holiness to the whole people: 'For you are a people holy to the Lord your God; the Lord your God has chosen you out of all the peoples on earth to be his people, his treasured possession' (Deuteronomy 7.6; cf. 14.2, 21; 26.19; 28.9; Ezra 9.2 ('holy seed'). Hence, Psalm 31.23 can speak of 'all you his saints' (cf. too Isaiah 4.3; 6.13; 63.18; Jeremiah 2.30) and Daniel speaks of the 'holy ones' on a number of occasions (7.18, 21, 22, 25, 27; 8.24; 12.6). References to the people of God being 'saints' or 'holy ones' could be multiplied by referring to apocalyptic and Qumran texts, but the point has been made: the *saints* are more than the priests, for the term often

---

20 Wright 2008, 50.
21 For parallel and complementary sketches of New Testament uses of holiness, see Barton 2003b; Weima 1996, 98–119.
22 This passage is a focus in Wells 2000, 27–57. Her conclusions are that Israel is unique, belongs to God, must live for God and must relate to others. The presence of God – the theophany at Sinai – runs right through these categories.

now refers to Israel, but noticeably and not surprisingly the term is not used for the gentiles. Israel, and then the New Testament Church, can be called 'holy' because it belongs to God, as Jo Bailey Wells has demonstrated.[23]

When Paul calls the people of his churches 'saints' he has, to give the understatement, courageously incorporated gentiles into the one 'holy' family of Israel. He is re-forming the 'saints' into the 'Church' and, while carrying on the Deuteronomic so-called democratization of holiness to the congregation of Israel, he has expanded that even further to include gentiles in the one people of God (Romans 11.11–24). What was in Paul's past story of Israel in its widest sense an exclusive description for *Israel* has become in his hands a description of an expanded Israel, the Israel of God (Galatians 6.16). The most graphic example is perhaps Ephesians 2.11–22.

Stephen Barton, in his exceptional study of holiness in the New Testament, describes this transformation under the terms of 'dislocating and relocating holiness'.[24] With Jesus as the new temple (Mark 14.58; 15.29; Matthew 12.6; John 2.19–20) and the incarnation of God in Christ (John 1.1–18), divine presence has been dislocated from the Temple as the exclusive location of the divine presence and relocated in Jesus. In addition, it is the apostolic emphasis on pneumatology that also partakes in the themes of dislocating and relocating, not least in the overflow of 1 Corinthians 3.16–17; 6.19; 2 Corinthians 6.16 as well as Ephesians 2.21. These two themes – pneumatology and Christology – will be developed in what follows as the pioneering moments that lead to the re-formation of saints.

Second, *one becomes a 'saint' in Pauline theology by the new covenant and eschatological indwelling Spirit of God through baptism.*

The Spirit of God in the Old Testament is at times called the 'holy spirit', and the apostle Paul's theology is a pneumatology[25] that begins there but has a powerful eschatological vanguard that revamps everything said about the Holy Spirit in the Old Testament. David, in prayer, can ask God 'do not take your holy spirit from me' (Psalm 51.11) while Isaiah can speak of Israel grieving the holy spirit (Isaiah 63.10; cf. too v. 11). I am inclined to see more 'spirit' language in the New Testament to be about the Holy Spirit, just as I am inclined not to divorce the human 'spirit' from the divine 'spirit' because the human spirit partakes in the divine spirit.[26]

---

[23] Wells 2000, 208–40. Wells did not examine the Pauline contribution to the meaning of 'holy'.
[24] Barton 2003b.
[25] Paul has well over a hundred references to the Spirit in the canonical letters.
[26] For an important discussion of this theme, see the exceptional study of Levison 2009. For New Testament studies, Dunn 1970; 1975; Twelftree 2009; Fee 2009; Wallace and Sawyer 2013; Burke and Warrington 2014; Thiselton 2016.

Hence, one should not too cleanly divorce the divine spirit (Holy Spirit) from the human spirit in either Colossians 1.8, where we hear of 'your love in the Spirit [or: spirit]', or 2.5, where we see 'I am with you in spirit'.[27] While pneumatology is often the dominant category when sorting out what Paul is saying, N. T. Wright has often warned against dropping the connection of indwelling to the Temple.[28]

Having said that, however, 'saint' is not connected to the Holy Spirit so explicitly in the Old Testament. Holiness derives from proximity to the Holy One of Israel, to the presence of God, most especially in the Temple. What is novel in early Christian missionary theology is the shift to the Holy Spirit, rather than the glory of God, becoming a primary 'contagion' of holiness. Thus, in Paul's theology what makes a human being – Jew or gentile – a 'saint' or 'holy' is the indwelling presence of God's Holy Spirit, and this presence converts the individual and the Church into the new temple. There was a fairly extensive expectation – not least deriving from especially Ezekiel – that the eschatological age would unleash the Spirit among the people of God. Paul's claim, like Peter's, is that that age has arrived (e.g. Acts 2; 10.34–48). That Spirit now unleashed into the people of the Church turns the people of the Church into 'saints'. This eschatological dimension to 'saint' can afford no more space in this paper, but it should be observed that Paul is first and foremost an eschatologian.[29]

Paul's theology is pervaded by the gift and power of the Spirit at work in the churches. Thus, Paul draws a line in his theological argument over the simple affirmative to his interrogating question to the Galatians with this: 'The only thing I want to learn from you is this: Did you receive the Spirit by doing the works of the law or by believing what you heard?' (3.2), but that gift of the Spirit is clearly the reception of the eschatological anticipation of the Spirit, as seen at 3.14: 'in order that in Christ Jesus the blessing of Abraham might come to the Gentiles, so that we might receive the promise of the Spirit through faith.' The mark of the Christian is the reception of the Spirit, not of the world, but of God (1 Corinthians 2.12). One must see the divine presence in not only theological but also temple categories here.[30] Those in the Church are those who have the Spirit as the 'first instalment', yet another instance of the Spirit as eschatological gift (2

---

27 It is more than noticeable in N. T. Wright's many writings that we read 'spirit' rather than 'Spirit'.
28 E.g. Wright 2013a, 355–8.
29 All major Pauline theologies are eschatologically oriented, and the apocalyptic turn among some is eschatology on steroids: see Ladd 1993; Dunn 1998; Wright 2013a; Campbell 2013.
30 On this, see the development in Wright 2013a, 709–28.

Corinthians 1.22; 5.5). This Spirit liberates in an important sense from the law (Romans 7.6), while those who live in the Spirit do the law (and more) as they are liberated from the flesh (8.1–6),[31] and the Spirit prompts Abba-prayer in the heart of the believer (8.15; cf. Galatians 4.6). Perhaps most important of all the Spirit references in Pauline literature is 1 Corinthians 12.13, which reads, 'For in the one Spirit we were all baptized into one body – Jews or Greeks, slaves or free – and we were all made to drink of one Spirit.' What is said here, then, is why Paul had earlier interrogated the Galatians and rooted his argument in their common and experiential reception of the Spirit (Galatians 3.1–5). 'Anyone', Paul declares categorically, 'who does not have the Spirit of Christ does not belong to him' (Romans 8.9; cf. Ephesians 2.18). As James D. G. Dunn has said:

> Paul does not say: 'If you are Christ's, you have the Spirit; since you are sons of God, you are led by the Spirit.' In both cases, Paul puts it the other way round: 'if you have the Spirit, you are Christ's; if you are being led by the Spirit, you are God's sons.' The fact which was immediately discernible was not whether they were Christ's – attested by baptism or confession – a fact from which their possession of the Spirit could be deduced as a corollary. That which was ascertainable was their possession of the Spirit; that was the primary factor from which their relation to Christ could be deduced. Their Christian status was recognizable from the fact that Christ's agent was in evident control of their lives.[32]

Hence, Paul can speak of the fellowship of one Christian with another through the Spirit and call it the 'communion of the Holy Spirit' (2 Corinthians 13.13). Before we get too far astray from the subject at hand, it is the presence of God in the *Holy* Spirit that renders a person a 'saint'.

In perhaps one of the most stunning claims of the apostle Paul we read that creation is moaning and groaning for the redemption of the children of God (Romans 8.18–25). While it is not as explicit for creation as it is for the redemption of the children of God, the Spirit has been unleashed to effect this redemption, and part of that redemption is the prayer life of the believer where the Spirit is turning wordlessness into clear communication with the Father (8.26–27; cf. 1 Corinthians 2.11–14). Just as stunning is that what is said of Israel's Temple is said of the New Testament believers: they are the temple of the Spirit. Inasmuch as holiness is rooted in God's presence, so now the presence of the eschatological gift of the

---

[31] Dunn sees Romans 8 as the 'high point of Paul's theology of the Spirit'. See Dunn 1998, 423.
[32] Dunn 1998, 430.

presence of God in the Spirit makes the Christian and the Church the new temple (1 Corinthians 3.16; 6.19; 2 Corinthians 6.16; Ephesians 2.21). It is, Paul's letter to Titus tells us, the 'water of rebirth and the renewal by the Holy Spirit' (3.5).

Yet again, 'saints' is re-formed in an eschatological–temple–pneumato-logical mode: the Spirit has arrived, Paul announces, and it is given to all, Jews and gentiles, slave and free, males and females, as well as to barbar-ians and Scythians (Galatians 3.28; Colossians 3.11), and one can find the saints in every church Paul established (cf. Ephesians 2.18, 22). To be a 'saint' then is to be filled with the presence of God, a presence real and experienced through the *Holy* Spirit. To be a saint is to become the temple of God.

Third, *the 'saints' are those who are defined by life under the cosmic Christ of Colossians 1.15–20 as well as by being indwelt by the Christ.*

We back up again to Jenson's typology to remind ourselves that to be holy was a statement about being in God's presence. God is holy; where God is becomes holy; the Temple as the dwelling place of God makes it and everything in it holy. Remarkably, in Ephesians 5.25–27 it is *Christ* who makes church people 'holy':

> Husbands, love your wives, just as Christ loved the church and gave himself up for her, in order to make her holy by cleansing her with the washing of water by the word, so as to present the church to himself in splendour, without a spot or wrinkle or anything of the kind – yes, so that she may be holy and without blemish.

Christ here has become not only the redemptive agent of God but the presence of God who, through his sacrificial death and resurrection, makes what is unholy (humans, especially gentiles) holy. The claim must be seen for what it meant in the world of the apostles and the churches in the Roman Empire: Paul here claims for Christ what was exclusively reserved for God in Israel's story.

How can Paul turn from God as holy and the source of all holiness to Christ as the source of holiness? There is only one Jewish way to do this and Paul does just that:

> yet for us there is one God, the Father, from whom are all things and for whom we exist, and one Lord, Jesus Christ, through whom are all things and through whom we exist.[33]

> (1 Corinthians 8.6)

---

33 I have examined this text in the light of the Shema in McKnight 2016.

He is the image of the invisible God, the firstborn of all creation; for in him all things in heaven and on earth were created, things visible and invisible, whether thrones or dominions or rulers or powers – all things have been created through him and for him. He himself is before all things, and in him all things hold together. He is the head of the body, the church; he is the beginning, the firstborn from the dead, so that he might come to have first place in everything. For in him all the fullness of God was pleased to dwell, and through him God was pleased to reconcile to himself all things, whether on earth or in heaven, by making peace through the blood of his cross.

(Colossians 1.15–20)

For in him [Christ] the whole fullness of deity dwells bodily . . .

(Colossians 2.9)

> [Christ Jesus] who, though he was in the form of God,
>   did not regard equality with God
>   as something to be exploited,
> but emptied himself,
>   taking the form of a slave,
>   being born in human likeness.
> And being found in human form,
>   he humbled himself
>   and became obedient to the point of death –
>   even death on a cross.
> Therefore God also highly exalted him
>   and gave him the name
>   that is above every name,
> so that at the name of Jesus
>   every knee should bend,
>   in heaven and on earth and under the earth,
> and every tongue should confess
>   that Jesus Christ is Lord,
>   to the glory of God the Father.

(Philippians 2.6–11)[34]

Holiness once again spreads from the presence of God to the Temple, to items in the Temple, to the priests and eventually to the covenanted people of God, Israel. In the New Testament, that holiness spreads to the Church of Jewish and gentile believers. But this happens not only because the *Holy*

---

[34] One could include Romans 9.5 and Titus 2.13 as well; on this, see Harris 1992, 143–72, 173–85. For a wider canvassing of deity discussions about Christ, Fee 2007; Hurtado 2003; Bauckham 2008; Tilling 2015. In addition, there are any number of items from N. T. Wright, including now Wright 2013a.

Spirit indwells the believer, but also because Christ indwells each believer and the Christ who indwells is God.

A few observations, which must be far too brief. First, in 1 Corinthians 8.6 Paul has creatively appropriated the Jewish creed, the Shema (Deuteronomy 6.4–9), separated 'God' (*Elohim* as Father) from 'Lord' (YHWH, who is Jesus the Messiah), maintained without blinking the Jewish faith in the one true God, and affirmed that both the Father and the Son are truly divine.[35] Second, Paul's hymn and adaptation of Wisdom in Colossians 1.15–20[36] announces Christ as supreme in all creation (1.15–17), with Christ as the image of God, the firstborn and the creator himself (!), while in the second stanza he announces Christ as supreme in redemption (1.18–20), again as the beginning and firstborn. Noticeably, he is creator and redeemer with a grounded foundation: 'For in him all the fullness of God was pleased to dwell' (1.19). That claim is all but repeated in 2.9 when Paul says that in him 'the whole fullness of deity dwells bodily'. The human being, the incarnate one, is the fullness of God in human flesh. Jesus, then, is that divine presence that can make the Church holy. Third, the hymn of Philippians 2.6–11 has a historical narrative at its core, but where it begins it ends: with Christ in the form of God and equal to God and on the throne of God where he is confessed as the world's true Lord.[37]

With that inadequate sketch in hand I lay on the table now the reason why the saints of the priestly and deuteronomic writings can now be found in the Church of Jesus Christ. How so? Jesus Christ, alongside the *Holy* Spirit, is the *presence* of God who indwells the believer and thus makes such persons *holy* or saints. Put more Pauline-ly, we are 'in Christ' and Christ the new temple is 'in us', and that union with Christ makes us the holy people of God's very presence. Thus, Paul can say believers are 'in Christ' (Colossians 1.2, 4), 'in whom we have redemption' (1.14), 'you have come to fullness in him' (2.9) and 'this mystery . . . is Christ in you' (1.27).[38] The indwelling is mutual, but the one in whom believers dwell and the Christ who indwells the believer is the fullness of God in a human

---

[35] Cf. Wright 2013a, 661–70.

[36] About which the literature is immense; I have sketched my own take in my forthcoming Colossians commentary. See Gordley 2007; 2011. A full Bibliography can be found in Gordley. For a sampling of some representative studies, see Bruce 1984; Wright 1991; Beasley-Murray 1980, 169–83; Hengel 1983, 78–96; Arnold 1996, 246–70; Cox 2007, 161–93.

[37] One still begins with Martin 1983.

[38] See Dunn 1998, 390–401. N. T. Wright's important emphasis for decades has been the theme of Messiah and Israel and incorporation. Thus, Wright 1991; 2013b.

body. The presence of the holy God in Christ, who is in the believer, makes every believer a 'saint'.

Fourth, *the indwelling Spirit and the divine Christ become the trans-formative power of God to make Christian 'saints' a people of love, justice, peace and reconciliation.*

The saints, or the holy ones, of the Pauline churches are not saints merely by contact with the presence of God, because the term 'holy' carries with it an ethical connotation. The folks of Paul's churches have been washed (1 Corinthians 6.11), they know the power of God (2.4; Romans 15.19), the freedom of God (Galatians 5.1, 13; Romans 8.2, 21–23; 2 Corinthians 3.17), the gifts (1 Corinthians 12—14) and fruit of the Spirit (Galatians 5.16–18, 22–23), and they now have hope and eternal life (5.5; 1 Corinthians 15.45; 2 Corinthians 3.6). As such, they are to live in love (Romans 15.30), joy (1 Thessalonians 1.6) and holiness (5.23; 2 Thessalonians 2.13). In sum, they are saints called to worship God (Philippians 3.3). Surely these various angles on Christians as saints is the only way to explain the remarkable claim of the apostle Paul in 2 Corinthians 3.17–18 (cf. Exodus 34.29–35):[39]

> Now the Lord is the Spirit, and where the Spirit of the Lord is, there is freedom. And all of us, with unveiled faces, seeing the glory of the Lord as though reflected in a mirror, are being transformed into the same image from one degree of glory to another; for this comes from the Lord, the Spirit.

So, too, Ephesians 5.18: instead of carousing and bending the knee to Dionysus or Bacchus, as one reads in Petronius's *Satyricon*, they are to be 'filled with the Spirit'. That is, enjoying life in the *Holy* Spirit and living under King Jesus with whom they are in union, they are to become moral agents of saintliness or holiness. As Gordon Fee summarizes this pneu-matological theory of sanctification:

> We have been invaded by the living God himself, in the person of his Spirit, whose goal is to infect us thoroughly with God's own likeness. Paul's phrase for this infection is the fruit of the Spirit. The coming of the Spirit, with the renewing of our minds, gives us a heavenly appetite for this fruit. The growing of this fruit is the long way on the journey of Christian conversion, the 'long obedience in the same direction,' and it is altogether the work of the Spirit in our lives.[40]

Colossians makes this more than abundantly clear, and all that can be done here is a sketch of the major contours of 'saints re-formed' because

---

[39] Another of Wright's favourite texts; cf. e.g. Wright 2013a, 980–4.
[40] Fee 1996, 112.

of the indwelling Spirit and union with Christ, the presence of God.[41] I begin with this: the Colossians are converts and God has qualified them for a place at the table with the saints (Colossians 1.12–14,[42] 21–23). As rescued converts, the saints are continually growing in faith, hope and love (1.4–6), and these cardinal 'virtues' are rooted in a theme vital to Paul in his concerns for the Colossians: knowledge and wisdom (1.9). But all of this is the result of the transformative power of God's grace, the Spirit and the indwelling Christ (1.10–11). To back up to their conversion, Paul says their alienation was based on their 'evil behaviour' (1.21) 'but now' they are reconciled to God so they can be presented before the Father as 'holy' and 'without blemish and free from accusation' (1.22).[43] The presence of God in the Spirit, in the Son and in the Father, then, is a contagion of holiness: nothing in the presence of God remains as it was but becomes what God is – holy.

I skip the several problems associated with discerning the troublesome ideas at work in Colosse[44] to the solutions Paul offers to the saints. They are to live 'in Christ' (2.6–7) and, because in Christ all the solutions (2.8–15) are found, they are to deflect the accusations of the Jewish halakhic mystics (2.16–23) by dying and rising with Christ (2.20; 3.1–4, 5–11). The one in whom the fullness of God dwells is the one who died on the cross and who was raised from the dead,[45] and their co-death and co-resurrection slays the flesh and sin (3.5, 8–9)[46] and gives new life to a 'new self' (3.10) that is nothing less than the Church that includes Greeks and Jews, barbarians and Scythians, as well as slaves and the free (3.11) – saints one and all.

If one may frame this somewhat sacramentally, the presence of the Spirit and Christ in the others draws one into a circle of the holy presence of God. Saints make for saint-ing others. I return to Philip Jenson's six categories, and appeal to his favourite the fifth (holiness as the realm or sphere of God's presence): holiness derives from God's presence, but God's

---

41 For a broader approach to Colossians, I mention these: Yates 1991; Meeks 1993; Knowles 1996; Rosner 1995.

42 The Greek of 1.12 provokes much thought: *eucharistountes tō patri tō hikanōsanti hymas eis tēn merida tou klērou tōn hagiōn en tō phōti.* One might think the 'share in the inheritance' refers to gentile incorporation into the existing people of God. On which, see my Colossians commentary at 1.12.

43 Bible quotations in this sentence are taken from the NIV.

44 A good place to start is Smith 2006.

45 Barton 2003b, 205–8.

46 Great work has been done on the cruciformity theme, which I prefer to call 'Christo-formity', by Gorman 2001; 2009; 2015.

presence occupies space and makes it sacred space (tabernacle, Temple). If Barton's dislocating and relocating expressions can serve us for the moment, we can say that *the sacred space of the Pauline mission extends from the presence of God in Christ and the Spirit to the individual believer as well as to the local church.* In Pauline theology, the gathering of the saints into an *ekklēsia* is the creation of sacred space in this world. The Church, in other words, has become a mobile temple.

The indwelling of all (Colossians 3.11) is where saints re-formed becomes most obvious in Paul's letter to the Colossians. The term 'saint' is not a term for a singular person but a term describing priests and the people of God who are drawn into the presence of God. The saints re-formed of the Pauline mission are a church people, a people surrounded by other saints who are learning how to live out the new creation unleashed by Christ and the Spirit. What does that kind of holy fellowship look like? Once again, holiness as separation will not serve us adequately, for in Paul's mind holiness is the action of love:

> As God's chosen ones, holy and beloved, clothe yourselves with compassion, kindness, humility, meekness, and patience. Bear with one another and, if anyone has a complaint against another, forgive each other; just as the Lord has forgiven you, so you also must forgive. Above all, clothe yourselves with love, which binds everything together in perfect harmony. And let the peace of Christ rule in your hearts, to which indeed you were called in the one body. And be thankful. Let the word of Christ dwell in you richly; teach and admonish one another in all wisdom; and with gratitude in your hearts sing psalms, hymns, and spiritual songs to God. And whatever you do, in word or deed, do everything in the name of the Lord Jesus, giving thanks to God the Father through him.
>
> (Colossians 3.12–17)

A saint becomes in the hands of Paul's mission not a contemplative, but an agent of grace and love in the context of a life lived in the community of other saints. They are 'God's chosen ones' and that means they are both 'holy and beloved [by God in Christ]'. As such, sainthood means the graces of love because love 'binds everything [all the needed practices and actions and attitudes] together in perfect harmony' (3.14). A saint for Paul is not someone 'separated' as was the *yahad* of Qumran's scrolls, but someone in the thick of action in the midst of a fellowship surrounded by the Roman Empire. The virtues Paul must extol, then, while they must surely all form their highest point in love, are the virtues of living with others in close proximity and growing in the graces of courtesy, reconciliation and forgiveness. On forgiveness, a fruit that does not grow easily in most churches, Bonhoeffer has some important words:

> The law of Christ, which must be fulfilled, is to bear the cross. The burden of a sister or brother, which I have to bear, is not only his or her external fate, manner, and temperament; rather, it is in the deepest sense his or her sin. I cannot bear it except by forgiving it, by the power of Christ's cross, which I have come to share. In this way Jesus' call to bear the cross places all who follow him in the community of forgiveness of sins. Forgiving sins is the Christ-suffering required of his disciples. It is required of all Christians.[47]

Such forgiven and forgiving saints of Paul's churches explode into song and praise and worship (3.16), and no matter what happens this is their rule of faith: 'And whatever you do, in word or deed, do everything in the name of the Lord Jesus, giving thanks to God the Father through him' (3.17).

Surely issues arise, and for Paul there is a profound (and far more often ignored or deleted) strategy: 'And let the peace of Christ rule in your hearts, to which indeed you were called in the one body' (3.15). When a quarrel breaks out, the umpire (*brabeuetō*) is Mr and Mrs Peace, or as Wright translates: 'Let the king's peace be the deciding factor in your hearts' (*Kingdom New Testament*). A saint is one who preserves the fellowship and avoids division, and who seeks to embody in a local church the reconciliation the Lord of creation and redemption has accomplished (1.20).

Conclusion

In summary, under the strong vision Paul has for eschatology, his conviction that Jesus is the Messiah and ruling Lord for all, his experience and belief in the radical presence of the *Holy* Spirit and Christ, and the indwelling of the Spirit and Christ, Paul has freshly re-formed a great old word in his Bible – the *q-d-sh* word group – into the one expanded people of God, the Church, where everyone is a saint and working out what sainthood means in bustling little cities like Colosse.

It is a great honour to me to offer this study to Tom Wright, from whom I have learned so much and with whom I have enjoyed much fellowship over the years of our mutual academic life. I first read Tom's *The New Testament and the People of God* in preparation for a lecture that had an energy unlike almost any other lecture I have ever given. His narratival

---

[47] Bonhoeffer 2001, 88.

or storied approach to reading Israel's story in the Bible has become part of my own work – with revisions of course – but it is his person and his routine chatting about family that have endeared Tom to me the most. Once on a Chicago seminary campus Tom and I were walking to a chapel session when Tom said to me, 'Without worship I could not do what I do.' He joins the Colossians in that, and I join him.

Bibliography

Adams, Edward (2015). *The Earliest Christian Meeting Places: Almost Exclusively Houses?* Revised edition. New York, NY: Bloomsbury/T&T Clark, 2015.

Arnold, Clinton E. (1996). *The Colossian Syncretism: The Interface between Christianity and Folk Belief at Colossae.* Grand Rapids, MI: Baker, 1996.

Barton, Stephen (2003a) (ed.). *Holiness Past and Present.* New York, NY: Bloomsbury/T&T Clark.

—— (2003b). 'Dislocating and Relocating Holiness: A New Testament Study.' In *Holiness Past and Present*, edited by Stephen Barton, 193–213. New York, NY: T&T Clark.

Bauckham, Richard (2008). *Jesus and the God of Israel: God Crucified and Other Studies on the New Testament's Christology of Divine Identity.* Grand Rapids, MI: Eerdmans.

Beasley-Murray, Paul (1980). 'Colossians 1:15–20: An Early Christian Hymn Celebrating the Lordship of Christ.' In *Pauline Studies: Essays Presented to Professor F. F. Bruce on His 70th Birthday*, edited by Donald A. Hagner and Murray J. Harris, 169–83. Grand Rapids, MI: Eerdmans.

Bohlen, Maren (2011). *Sanctorum Communio: Die Christen als 'Heilige' bei Paulus.* Beihefte zur Zeitschrift für die neutestamentliche Wissenschaft 183. Berlin: de Gruyter.

Bonhoeffer, Dietrich (2001). *Discipleship.* Dietrich Bonhoeffer Works 4. Minneapolis, MN: Fortress.

Bruce, F. F. (1984). 'Colossian Problems, Pt. 2: The "Christ Hymn" of Colossians 1:15–20.' *Bibliotheca Sacra* 141: 99–111.

Burke, Trevor J., and Keith Warrington (2014) (eds). *A Biblical Theology of the Holy Spirit.* Eugene, OR: Cascade.

Campbell, Douglas A. (2013). *The Deliverance of God: An Apocalyptic Rereading of Justification in Paul.* Grand Rapids, MI: Eerdmans.

Cox, Ronald (2007). *By the Same Word: Creation and Salvation in Hellenistic Judaism and Early Christianity.* Beihefte zur Zeitschrift für die neutestamentliche Wissenschaft 145. Berlin: de Gruyter.

Doyle, Jim, and Brian Doyle (1996). *Two Voices: A Father and Son Discuss Family and Faith.* Liguori, MO: Liguori Publications.

Dunn, James D. G. (1970). *Baptism in the Holy Spirit: A Re-Examination of the New Testament Teaching on the Gift of the Holy Spirit in Relation to Pentecostalism Today.* Philadelphia, PA: Westminster John Knox.

—— (1975). *Jesus and the Spirit: A Study of the Religious and Charismatic*

Experience of Jesus and the First Christians as Reflected in the New Testament. Philadelphia, PA: Westminster John Knox.

—— (1998). *The Theology of Paul the Apostle.* Grand Rapids, MI: Eerdmans.

Ehrman, Bart D. (2003) (ed.). *The Apostolic Fathers, Volume II.* Loeb Classical Library 25. Cambridge, MA: Harvard University Press.

Fee, Gordon D. (1996). *Paul, the Spirit, and the People of God.* Grand Rapids, MI: Baker.

—— (2007). *Pauline Christology: An Exegetical-Theological Study.* Peabody, MA: Hendrickson.

—— (2009). *God's Empowering Presence: The Holy Spirit in the Letters of Paul.* Grand Rapids, MI: Baker.

Gammie, John G. (1989). *Holiness in Israel.* Overtures to Biblical Theology. Minneapolis, MN: Fortress.

Gehring, Roger W. (2004). *House Church and Mission: The Importance of Household Structures in Early Christianity.* Peabody, MA: Hendrickson.

Gordley, Matthew E. (2007). *The Colossian Hymn in Context: An Exegesis in Light of Jewish and Greco-Roman Hymnic and Epistolary Conventions.* Wissenschaftliche Untersuchungen zum Neuen Testament 2/228. Tübingen: Mohr Siebeck.

—— (2011). *Teaching through Song in Antiquity: Didactic Hymnody among Greeks, Romans, Jews, and Christians.* Wissenschaftliche Untersuchungen zum Neuen Testament 2/302. Tübingen: Mohr Siebeck.

Gorman, Michael J. (2001). *Cruciformity: Paul's Narrative Spirituality of the Cross.* Grand Rapids, MI: Eerdmans.

—— (2009). *Inhabiting the Cruciform God: Kenosis, Justification, and Theosis in Paul's Narrative Soteriology.* Grand Rapids, MI: Eerdmans.

—— (2015). *Becoming the Gospel: Paul, Participation, and Mission.* Grand Rapids, MI: Eerdmans.

Harris, J. R., and J. A. Robinson (1891). *Apology of Aristides: Texts and Studies 1.* Cambridge: Cambridge University Press.

Harris, Murray J. (1992). *Jesus as God: The New Testament Use of Theos in Reference to Jesus.* Grand Rapids, MI: Baker.

Hengel, Martin (1983). *Between Jesus and Paul: Studies in the Earliest History of Christianity.* Translated by John Bowden. Minneapolis, MN: Fortress.

Hurtado, Larry W. (2003). *Lord Jesus Christ: Devotion to Jesus in Earliest Christianity.* Grand Rapids, MI: Eerdmans.

—— (2016). *Destroyer of the Gods: Early Christian Distinctiveness in the Roman World.* Waco, TX: Baylor University Press.

Jenson, Philip Peter (1992). *Graded Holiness: A Key to the Priestly Conception of the World.* Library of Hebrew Bible/Old Testament Studies 106. Sheffield: Bloomsbury/T&T Clark, 1992.

—— (2003). 'Holiness in the Priestly Writings of the Old Testament.' In *Holiness Past and Present,* edited by S. C. Barton, 93–121. London: T&T Clark.

Knohl, Israel (2007). *The Sanctuary of Silence: The Priestly Torah and the Holiness School.* Winona Lake, IN: Eisenbrauns.

Knowles, Michael P. (1996). '"Christ in You, the Hope of Glory": Discipleship in Colossians.' In *Patterns of Discipleship in the New Testament*, edited by Richard N. Longenecker, 180–202. Grand Rapids, MI: Eerdmans.

Ladd, George Eldon (1993). *A Theology of the New Testament*. Revised edition. Edited by Donald A. Hagner. Grand Rapids, MI: Eerdmans.

Levison, John R. (2009). *Filled with the Spirit*. Grand Rapids, MI: Eerdmans.

McKnight, Scot (2016). 'Few and Far Between: The Life of a Creed.' In *Earliest Christianity within the Boundaries of Judaism: Essays in Honor of Bruce Chilton*, edited by Alan J. Avery-Peck, Craig A. Evans and J. Neusner, 168–86. Leiden: Brill.

—— (2018). *The Letter to the Colossians*. New International Commentary on the New Testament. Grand Rapids, MI: Eerdmans.

Mairs, Nancy (1993). *Ordinary Time: Cycles in Marriage, Faith, and Renewal*. Boston, MA: Beacon Press.

Martin, Ralph P. (1983). *Carmen Christi: Philippians ii 5–11 in Recent Interpretation and in the Setting of Early Christian Worship*. Revised edition. Grand Rapids, MI: Eerdmans.

Meeks, Wayne A. (1993). '"To Walk Worthily of the Lord": Moral Formation in the Pauline School Exemplified by the Letter to Colossians.' In *Hermes and Athena: Biblical Exegesis and Philosophical Theology*, edited by Eleonore Stump and Thomas P. Flint, 37–58. Notre Dame, IN: University of Notre Dame Press.

Moule, C. F. D. (1957). *The Epistles to the Colossians and to Philemon*. Cambridge Greek Testament Commentaries. Cambridge: Cambridge University Press.

Otto, Rudolf (1958). *The Idea of the Holy*. Translated by John W. Harvey. 2nd edition. New York, NY: Oxford University Press.

Rosner, Brian S. (1995) (ed.). *Understanding Paul's Ethics: Twentieth-Century Approaches*. Grand Rapids, MI: Eerdmans.

Silva, Moisés (2014) (ed.). 'Hagios.' In *New International Dictionary of New Testament Theology and Exegesis*, 1:124–33. 5 vols. 2nd edition. Grand Rapids, MI: Zondervan.

Smith, Ian K. (2006). *Heavenly Perspective: A Study of the Apostle Paul's Response to a Jewish Mystical Movement at Colossae*. Library of New Testament Studies 326. London: T&T Clark.

Thiselton, Anthony C. (2016). *A Shorter Guide to the Holy Spirit: Bible, Doctrine, Experience*. Grand Rapids, MI: Eerdmans.

Tilling, Chris (2015). *Paul's Divine Christology*. Grand Rapids, MI: Eerdmans.

Trebilco, Paul (2012). *Self-Designations and Group Identity in the New Testament*. Cambridge: Cambridge University Press.

Twelftree, Graham H. (2009). *People of the Spirit: Exploring Luke's View of the Church*. Grand Rapids: Baker.

Wallace, Daniel B., and M. James Sawyer (2013) (eds). *Who's Afraid of the Holy Spirit? An Investigation into the Ministry of the Spirit of God Today*. Dallas, TX: Biblical Studies Press.

Weima, Jeffrey A. D. (1996). '"How You Must Walk to Please God": Holiness and Discipleship in 1 Thessalonians.' In *Patterns of Discipleship in the New Testament*, edited by Richard N. Longenecker, 98–119. McMaster New Testament Studies. Grand Rapids, MI: Eerdmans.

Wells, Jo Bailey (2000). *God's Holy People: A Theme in Biblical Theology.* Sheffield: Bloomsbury/T&T Clark.

Wright, N. T. (1991). 'Poetry and Theology in Colossians 1.15–20.' In *The Climax of the Covenant: Christ and the Law in Pauline Theology*, 99–119. Edinburgh: T&T Clark.

—— (2008). *Colossians and Philemon.* Tyndale New Testament Commentaries 12. Downers Grove, IL: IVP.

—— (2012). *The Kingdom New Testament: A Contemporary Translation.* (San Francisco: HarperOne.

—— (2013a). *Paul and the Faithfulness of God.* Christian Origins and the Question of God 4. London: SPCK / Minneapolis, MN: Fortress.

—— (2013b). *Pauline Perspectives: Essays on Paul, 1978–2013.* London: SPCK / Minneapolis, MN: Fortress.

Yates, Roy (1991). 'The Christian Way of Life: The Paraenetic Material in Colossians 3:1–4:6.' *Evangelical Quarterly* 63: 241–51.

The healing of the blind and the lame in the Temple: David, 'Canaanites' and the reconstitution of Israel in Matthew 21.14[1]

GRANT LeMARQUAND

Introduction

By any measure, Jesus' entry into Jerusalem and demonstration in and disruption of the Temple was a climactic event in his life and ministry. Whether one is attempting to reconstruct the life of Jesus, the redactional emphases of the Evangelists, or simply trying to understand the narrative world of the synoptic Gospels, the events of Jesus' arrival in Jerusalem are pivotal for the story.

The synoptic accounts vary in their telling, of course, and only Matthew mentions (very briefly) one episode which is often overlooked by scholars in spite of the massive output of writing on the Temple event. According to Matthew, 'the blind and the lame came to [Jesus] in the temple, and he healed them' (21.14).[2] If, as the majority of scholars believe, Mark was Matthew's primary source, this is an addition either from 'M' or from Matthew's own redaction.[3] Luke does not mention the event. In fact this is the only mention of Jesus healing in the Temple precincts in the synoptic tradition.[4]

One would expect the strangeness of this text to attract the attention of scholarship. After all, a text about a young man losing his robe at the time of Jesus' arrest (Mark 14.51–52) has kept scholars in the writing business for centuries. In spite of some helpful comments from various

---

1   I am grateful to my friend Dr Sylvia Keesmaat for reading and commenting on a draft of this essay. It is better because of her kindness.
2   Unless otherwise noted, Bible quotations in this chapter are taken from the RSV.
3   Gundry (1982, 413) thinks the verse is Matthean redaction based on his assessment that, together with the rest of vv. 14–17, it exhibits 'Matthew's favorite diction and habit of alluding to the OT'.
4   But see, for example, John 5 where Jesus does heal in the vicinity of the Temple. According to Acts (3.1–10), the apostles do not think it inappropriate to heal in the Temple area (following Jesus' example?).

writers, however, the text is largely overlooked.[5] There might be various reasons for the neglect of Matthew 21.14: there are so many other mysterious happenings in the events surrounding Jesus' last week that such a short comment by one Evangelist seems almost trivial; Jesus was, after all, always healing people – comment on yet another example might seem wasted; if one is following traditional historical-critical methodology in looking for bedrock in assessing whether an event goes back to the historical Jesus, this verse does not fare well – single attestation of an event usually (but not always) means it will not be included in the data base of most critics' 'authentic' Jesus material.

And yet the text is intriguing. It is the only synoptic example of Jesus healing in the Temple area. It is a clear example of one of Matthew's favourite things: allusion to an Old Testament passage.

For our purposes, this text fits in with the attention Matthew gives to two recurring themes. One is a theme frequently mentioned by scholars: Jesus as 'Son of David' (albeit in a strange, counter-intuitive way). The second theme is one mentioned only rarely by scholars: the reversal of the command to annihilate the Canaanites. This second theme might be considered a subset of another topic: Matthew's view of gentiles, or perhaps a subset of an even more pervasive theme in all the Gospels: Jesus' care for those who are marginalized. This paper will argue, however, that Matthew 21.14 draws two interlocking themes to a climax: Jesus as a new kind of Son of David, in fact an anti-David, and Jesus as the bringer of mercy to those previously thought to be beyond redemption, the Canaanites, the archetypal enemies of God's people. In bringing these two themes to a

---

5   Beare's commentary (1981, 417) on this verse says only, 'Matthew is alone in reporting miracles of healing in the temple.' John P. Meier's massive second volume of his *A Marginal Jew* is devoted largely to the miracles of Jesus – the title of the volume is *Mentor, Message and Miracles* (1994) – and yet there are references to Matthew 21.14 in only five pages of the more than 1,000-page book, each of those references brief mentions in footnotes. The fine book by Gaiser (2010) has no reference to Matthew 21.14 in the Index. One of the few articles exclusively devoted to our text is Mulloor 1994. Tom Wright's *Jesus and the Victory of God* (*JVG*/1996), as well as in his various other books and articles about Jesus, gives great attention to the Temple event (especially in chapters 9 and 11 of *JVG*). Strangely Matthew 21.14 only appears once in *JVG* (Wright 1996, 192 n. 179). Matthew 21.14 is one of a list of references given attesting that Jesus healed the blind. In fact, if I have one criticism of *JVG* it would be the lack of attention given to the miracle tradition in the Gospels. Although he spends many chapters elucidating the parables of Jesus and showing how they fit into Jesus' aims and vocation, Tom deals with the miracles of Jesus, in an extremely abbreviated fashion, in Chapter 5 ('The Praxis of a Prophet') in a six-page subsection entitled '"Mighty Works": Interpretation'. Could Tom's neglect of this aspect of Jesus' ministry be a part of a post-Enlightenment embarrassment with the subject of the miraculous? Just asking . . .

climax, Matthew reveals Jesus as a new king of a new people of God, newly constituted by God's mercy.

Jesus as 'Son of David'

It is frequently noted that Matthew lays stress on Jesus as 'Son of David'. The comment of Larry Hurtado expresses the consensus well: 'from the opening words in 1:1 onward, Jesus' Davidic sonship is much more frequently echoed in Matthew (e.g. 9:27; 12:23; 15:22; 20:30; 21:9, 14–16), and plays a more prominent role in Matthew's presentation of Jesus.'[6] The theme of Davidic sonship is found throughout the New Testament, of course – Matthew simply gives the subject more emphasis. Mark, for example, mentions the title twice: once in the story of the blind man Bartimaeus (10.47–48, just before the 'triumphal entry') and once when Jesus himself raises the issue in a controversy story (12.35–37, just after the Temple event). Luke uses the title more frequently than Mark (following Mark in 18.38–39 and 20.41–44), noting Jesus' clan affiliation with the house of David, especially in the infancy narrative: Joseph is mentioned as being from 'the house of David' (1.27; 2.4); Mary is told by the angel Gabriel that her son would be 'Son of the Most High' (a probable allusion to Psalm 2 and 2 Samuel 7) who would inherit the 'throne of his father David' (1.32); Jesus is born in the 'city of David' (2.11); in the genealogy David is listed as one of Jesus' ancestors (3.31).

David 'the king' in Matthew's genealogy

Although the Davidic sonship of Jesus is by no means neglected in the rest of the New Testament, it is Matthew's Gospel that most emphasizes this theme. Matthew mentions David in no fewer than 16 passages. These will all require some attention, but we begin with an examination of the genealogy (1.1–17).[7]

There are four mentions of David in the genealogy (1.1; 1.6; 1.17, twice). Matthew divides the genealogy of Jesus ('Jesus Christ, the son of David, the son of Abraham', 1.1) into three equal parts: 14 generations from Abraham to David ('the king', 1.6); 14 generations from David to the exile; and 14 from the exile to Jesus ('who is called Christ', 1.16; 'the

---

6 Hurtado 2003, 326.
7 It is not our purpose to argue here that Jesus himself applied the term 'Son of David' to himself, although there is no reason to suppose that a theme which is an emphasis in Matthew's redactional work could not go back to the historical Jesus. See already Cullmann 1959 (1957), 133.

Christ', 1.17). But why *14* generations in each of the three divisions of the genealogy? It is tempting to think that Matthew may be thinking of the number 14 as a multiple of 7 the 'perfect number', but then why not divide the genealogy into six groups of 7? It is probable that the answer is to be found in the exegetical practice known as gematria. This technique was used by Babylonian and Greek writers as well as Jewish exegetes. The method assigns a numerical value to letters, so that a hidden meaning of a word or a name can be found by deciphering its numerical value: an obvious example of this practice in the New Testament is in Revelation 13.18 where the numerical value of the name *Neron Kaisar* (when it is transliterated into Hebrew script) corresponds to 666.[8] Similarly the Hebrew name for David yields a numerical value thus: 'D' (4) + 'V' (6) + 'D' (4) = 14.[9] Weight is added to this hypothesis when it is noted that not only are there 14 generations in each of Matthew's three genealogical divisions, and not only does David's Hebrew name tally up to 14, but in the genealogy itself David's name is in the fourteenth position. In other words, the list of ancestors of 'Jesus the Christ' is 'Davidic' through and through.

Of course, David does not actually come off well in the genealogy. He may be the 'king', he may be the central figure, along with Jesus himself, in Matthew's list, but he is spoken of negatively, as a kind of anti-hero. Immediately following the note that David is 'David the king' (1.6a). Matthew describes him as 'the father of Solomon by the wife of Uriah' (1.6b). This description is noteworthy not only because the mother of Solomon is one of several gentile women mentioned in the genealogy, but also because her name (Bathsheba, of course) is not mentioned. Matthew is not ignorant of her name but substitutes the designation 'the wife of Uriah'. To have said 'by Bathsheba' would have reminded perceptive readers of the sin of adultery which resulted in Solomon's birth, just as the superscription to Psalm 51 reminds the reader of that same event. But to say 'by the wife of Uriah' draws attention to the fact that David was not merely an adulterer (take note – the mother of Solomon was still, says Matthew, Uriah's wife); more than that – David was a murderer. The cipher 'Uriah' draws attention to David's double guilt. David the king, the one

---

8 See the standard commentaries of Revelation for details: a good summary is found in Caird 1966.

9 A good discussion of this phenomenon in Matthew's genealogy is found in Brown 1979, 74–81. Brown notes (1979, 80 n. 38) an article by P. W. Skehan (Skehan 1967), which argues that the accepted numerical value of David's name appears to have been 14 as early as the time of the composition of the book of Proverbs.

who should have defended justice and righteousness among God's people, as Psalm 72 makes clear is the vocation of the Davidic ruler, failed in his calling.

The genealogy leaves us with a puzzle, then. Jesus is 'the Christ', the rightful descendant of David 'the king'. But what kind of king is this Jesus? Will he follow in David's footsteps, or will he forge a different path?

Other 'kingly' figures in Matthew's Gospel

The meaning of Jesus' kingship takes shape as Matthew begins to narrate the story, although, once again, Matthew chooses to contrast Jesus' royal status with others who claim the royal status. 'David' is mentioned only once in the infancy stories, but a cluster of terms related to royalty appears. The birth of Jesus is introduced by an episode centred on the appearance of an angel to Joseph, in which the angel addresses him as 'Son of David'. In the following episode, the visit of the magi, royal terms are multiplied.

Herod the king

When the magi enquire of Herod the Great concerning the birth of a child, they refer to him as the 'king of the Jews' (2.2), a loaded term since Matthew has already informed us that Herod is 'the king' (2.1). Matthew continues to lay stress on Herod's royal claim: 'when Herod the king heard this, he was troubled' (2.3); 'when [the magi] had heard the king they went their way' (2.9). And the story emphasizes that Jesus is to be born in Bethlehem (2.1, 6, 8), the place where a ruler is to be born (2.6, quoting Micah 5.2).

Herod's claim to be the king of the Jews is well known. Tom Wright has well summarized Herod's lifelong attempt to gain acceptance as Israel's king:

> He made every effort to legitimate himself and his successors as genuine kings: he married Mariamne, who was the granddaughter of Hyrcanus II and thus a Hasmonean princess; above all he set in motion the rebuilding of the Temple, as the true coming king was supposed to do.[10]

Whatever historical judgement we may render about the incident with the magi and the aftermath in the slaughter of the innocents in Bethlehem, it is clear that waving the banner of the birth of a new king in front of a megalomaniac (and few would deny Herod that epithet) is likely to produce horrific results. Whether in history, or simply in the narrative world of

---

[10] Wright 1992, 160. On Herod see Richardson 1999.

Matthew, the result seems inevitable. Tyrants crush opposition – even the rumour of opposition – and they do so violently. For Matthew the kingship of Herod the Great is the illegitimate reign of a threatened puppet ruler, a client-king of the Roman Empire. The contrast between Herod and Jesus could not be more stark. Herod's type of kingship is revealed in the slaughter of children of Bethlehem. Jesus is a king who will save his people from their sins (1.21), who will be 'Emmanuel (which means, God with us)' (1.23).[11]

Solomon in all his glory

The original 'Son of David', David's successor on Israel's throne, was of course Solomon. Solomon, who has already been mentioned (in somewhat negative terms) in Matthew's genealogy, makes two more appearances in Matthew's Gospel. Both of these 'Solomon' texts come from the sayings material common to Matthew and Luke.

In Matthew 6.28–33 (cf. Luke 12.27–31) Jesus continues a discussion begun in 6.25 concerning anxiety. One of Jesus' examples concerns clothing: 'the lilies of the field . . . neither toil nor spin' (6.28). And yet, says Jesus, the flowers are better dressed than Solomon 'in all his glory' ever was. At first sight this appears an innocent figure of speech. Warren Carter, however, noting that 'glory' is something that should belong to God alone (Matthew 4.8; 5.16), discerns a more sinister backdrop:

> Solomon's reign in 1 Kings (cf. lxx 3 Kingdoms) shows that he violates God's will for kings set out in Deut 17:15–17b and 1 Sam 8. He acquires many wives, horses, and great wealth, by military conscription, forced labor, requisitioned property, heavy taxation, and slavery. He gains great wealth not by trusting God but by demonstrating such anxiety about material possessions that he employs the typical unjust and exploitative strategies of imperial powers which God had forbidden. By contrast, the flowers trust God, and God clothes them in a way superior to that of the distrustful anxious Solomon.[12]

Matthew 6.29–35, therefore, has an anti-imperial edge. But what of Jesus' other reference to Solomon? In Matthew 12.42 (cf. Luke 11.31) Jesus compares himself to Solomon, pointing out that Solomon's wisdom was so

---

11 A recent essay (Park 2013) suggests that Matthew sets up a deliberate contrast between the infanticide in Bethlehem under Herod and the parable of separation of the sheep from goats in Matthew 25.31–46. It could be that several texts in Matthew's Gospel (including the healing of the blind and the lame in the Temple in Matthew 21.14) should be understood in contrast to the kind of imperial force exercised by Herod in Bethlehem.

12 Carter 2000, 178.

great that 'the queen of the South' (i.e. the Queen of Sheba, 1 Kings 10; 2 Chronicles 9) came 'from the ends of the earth' to hear Solomon's wisdom. There is no denial here that Solomon possessed wisdom. Jesus' wisdom, however, is greater than that of the wisest king of Israel. 'Something greater than Solomon is here,' says Jesus. The wisdom of Solomon is lacking – perhaps because although Solomon's words were wise, his actions did not match. Ellen Davis points out that:

> The queen of Sheba had her breath taken away, not only by Solomon's ability to tell her anything she wanted to know, but also by the food of his table and the seating of his servants and their attire and his cupbearers . . . (1 Kings 10.25), and the happy result of her breathlessness was a trade agreement.[13]

Solomon not only impressed with his opulence and feasting; he also used his wealth to further his own trade interests, themselves rooted in exploitation and oppression. As Carter emphasizes, his anxious desire for wealth and power, his willingness to exploit and oppress for gain (contrast Psalm 72.14), rather than to defend the poor and the needy (contrast Psalm 72.4, 12–13) renders Solomon's wise words empty.

Caesar

Behind the power of the Herods was another king, Caesar. Caesar is mentioned only once in Matthew's Gospel, in Matthew 22.16–22, the story of the question of whether Jews should pay taxes to Rome. But the Roman Empire is pervasive; it is the unseen malevolent power behind all the events of Matthew 27: behind Pilate, the scarlet robe, the mocking, behind the cross, the crown of thorns, the *titulus*, the guard at the tomb.

The 'kingly' personalities who feature in Matthew's Gospel, Herod, Solomon, Caesar and David himself, do not measure up to the ideal of royalty presented in Deuteronomy 17 where the future king is directed not to acquire many wives or great wealth, but to uphold the law and its statutes. The king should not exalt himself (like 'Solomon in all his glory') but hold to the commandments of God. Likewise, Psalm 72 (with its ironic superscription 'Of Solomon') paints a picture of the ideal king: he upholds justice and righteousness, and defends the poor, the needy, the weak, those who have no other helper; 'from oppression and violence he redeems their life, and precious is their blood in his sight' (Psalm 72.14). The just king is not a king like David who murders the one who stands in the way of his lust, not like Herod who soaks the soil of Bethlehem in the blood of

---

[13] Davis 2001, 113. Thanks to Sylvia Keesmaat for the reminder of Ellen Davis's work at this point.

children, not like Solomon who seeks his own glory in the acquisition of wealth and women, certainly not like Caesar who established the *pax Romana* – making 'peace' by the blood of the cross (Colossians 1.20). For Matthew, something greater than Solomon and these other kings is here.

Jesus as Davidic king in Matthew 20.29—21.18

But before we mention what that 'something greater' might be, there are three issues that we have already mentioned in passing that need a bit more development at this stage, since they are all prominent in Matthew 20.29—21.18. First, one does not necessarily have to use the name 'David' (or Solomon, or Herod, or Caesar) to allude to Davidic kingship: there are other titles which elucidate an understanding of what it means to be 'Son of David'. Second, as well as titles, we must pay attention to symbolic actions which may also be in some way 'Davidic': the most obvious is Jesus' entry into Jerusalem and his action in the Temple. Third, and closely related to our second point, is the theme of David as a conquering king, a military leader (see *Psalms of Solomon* 17, for example) – an expectation which Jesus declines to fulfil. Elucidation of these three motifs in the context of a discussion of Matthew 21 will lead us to highlight a fourth theme, much neglected in discussions of 'Jesus as David', which is the Son of David as a healer.

1 Son of David and other royal titles

It will not be necessary to go into great detail to demonstrate that at least two prominent titles for Jesus in Matthew, and indeed pervasively in early Christianity, are royal titles, closely related to the title 'Son of David'. Many, including Tom Wright, have already argued this case thoroughly. Briefly and by way of reminder, we will highlight two of these titles.

First, we must note that the Old Testament speaks of the 'Son of David' as the 'Son of God'. Two texts make this clear: Psalm 2, widely seen as a royal enthronement psalm, speaks of the kings of the nations setting themselves against both the Lord and his anointed king. The Lord shows his approval of Israel's king by setting 'my king on Zion, my holy hill' (Psalm 2.6) and by asserting his paternity over the king: 'You are my son, today I have begotten you' (Psalm 2.7). The king, therefore, is 'Son of God'. The second text comes from the narrative of David's life. Before he dies, David is assured that his 'son' (Solomon) will reign after him:

> When your days are fulfilled and you lie down with your ancestors, I will
> raise up your offspring after you, who shall come forth from your body, and

I will establish his kingdom . . . I will be a father to him, and he shall be a son to me.

(2 Samuel 7.12, 14, NRSV)

As in Psalm 2, so in 2 Samuel 7, David's son is 'God's son'.

Clearly the primary context in which we should understand the title 'Son of God' in the New Testament is not the context of later Patristic thought in which 'Son of God' means the second person of the Trinity (there are plenty of other titles and texts and early devotional practices which gave the early Church all the material it needed to assert the divinity of Jesus). The primary meaning of the title 'Son of God' in the New Testament is the king of Israel.[14]

The second royal title is closely related: 'Christ' (the Greek translation of the Hebrew 'Messiah'), like 'Son of God', is also a royal title, not a divine epithet. Psalm 2 also points us in this direction since the king is the Lord's 'anointed one' (Psalm 2.2). Centuries of Christian use of the term 'Christ' have deafened our ears to the original connotations, but it is clear that when Jewish people spoke of a coming Messiah, they did not mean that God was coming in the flesh, but that they expected a human deliverer, one chosen by God to save his people from their enemies.

The Passion narrative of Matthew, like the other Gospels, is filled with this royal language of Jesus as the Christ, the Son of God. The clearest expression of the royal connotations of the two titles comes in the 'trial' before the Sanhedrin where Jesus is asked, 'Are you the Christ, the Son of God?' (see 26.63). That Jesus answers by using another title, 'Son of Man' (26.64), should not surprise us, since that title derives from Daniel 7 and describes one who is given kingship and 'dominion and the greatness of the kingdoms under . . . heaven' (Daniel 7.13, 27). Neither should it surprise us when, armed with Jesus' rather enigmatic 'confession', the Sanhedrin turns to Pilate who then questions Jesus concerning its accusation that he is 'King of the Jews' (27.11) and 'Christ' (27.17, 22), and that Pilate believes that this justifies the *titulus* which he causes to be fixed to the cross reading 'This is Jesus the King of the Jews' (27.37). And so, although 'Son of David' is an important pointer to Jesus' identity, especially the way Matthew tells the story, the titles 'Son of God' and 'Christ' also point in the same direction: Jesus is the true king of Israel. But what kind of king? Jesus' healing in the Temple in Matthew 21.14 is not what one expects of the Son of David.

---

14 We must hasten to add that the king is 'Son of God' in a representative way: Israel is God's Son (Exodus 4.23; Hosea 11.1); therefore Israel's head, her representative, is also 'Son of God'.

2 The Son of David and the Temple

The narratives of all three synoptic Gospels draw a close connection between Jesus' entry into Jerusalem and action in the Temple and his subsequent arrest, trial and execution as a royal/messianic figure. Jesus' denunciation of the Temple and/or its leadership, his disruption of Temple activities (which may be a symbolic prophetic enactment of the Temple's destruction) and his prediction of the Temple's demise all seem to raise the question of whether Jesus has the authority to do these things. His hearing before the Sanhedrin, its accusation that Jesus' apparent Temple saying implies his messianic status, the bringing of the charge to Pilate that Jesus claims to be king, and Pilate's placing of the *titulus* on the cross all point to a strong connection between the Temple and the king. In short, Jesus' Temple action leads those who witness it, or hear about it, to assume that Jesus thinks that he is the Davidic Messiah, the king.

Several of Tom Wright's works draw attention to the Jewish connection between the king and the Jerusalem Temple.[15] David, of course, wished to build the Temple, his son Solomon did, and their successors saw rebuilding and dedicating the Temple as signs of their true kingship.[16]

> [T]he Temple was completely bound up with Israel's royal ideology. The somewhat shaky line from David and Solomon, through Jehoash, Josiah and Hezekiah, to Zerubbabel, Judas Maccabaeus, Herod the Great, and finally Bar-Kochba, bears witness to this link, as do passages such as Zechariah 6 and Psalms of Solomon 17. Did Jesus make this link himself? Was his Temple-action not only prophetic, but deliberately (though no doubt paradoxically) messianic? Did the onlookers get the point? I think the answer to all three questions is Yes.[17]

Messianic, yes, but in Matthew 21.14 Jesus acts within the Temple to bring healing to a group previously excluded (by David) from the precincts (2 Samuel 5.6–10, which we will examine more below). If this action points to David, it points to David in order to reverse an ancient Davidic curse, rather than fulfil a Davidic type. The Son of David's healing in the Temple is an anti-type of David. But before we turn to Jesus' healing in the Temple, we must briefly mention the usual Davidic expectation – that the Messiah would be a military leader.

---

15 See, for example, Wright 1992, 224–6, 307–20; 1996, 94, 413–28, 483, 490–3.
16 Wright has drawn attention to the seminal article by Runnalls (1983).
17 Wright 1996, 427–8.

3 The Son of David and military conquest

One of the most common messianic themes in the Second Temple period was that the Messiah would be a military leader like David. Psalm 2 already speaks of the anointed one breaking Israel's enemies with a rod of iron and smashing them like a pot (v. 9). Military movements from Judas Maccabeus and Judas the Galilean through to Bar Kochba had messianic overtones in their rhetoric. Among the several messianic expectations of the Qumran community was the hope of a coming military leader. Perhaps the clearest of these Davidic military expectations is found in the *Psalms of Solomon*, especially *Psalm* 17, where the Son of David would destroy unrighteous rulers and purge Jerusalem from gentiles and sinners. Wright sums up this military dimension of messianic expectation well:

> The king was to be the one who would fight Israel's battles. David had defeated Goliath and the Philistines; the sign that he was going to be king was already clear when the women sang that 'Saul has slain his thousands, and David has slain his tens of thousands' [1 Samuel 18.7–9; 21.11]. His true successor, according to the biblical Psalms, would attain his Lordship by defeating Israel's enemies [Psalm 110].[18]

That Jesus entered David's city with the Temple as his destination, and that he was hailed in Davidic terms by the blind on the road outside Jericho (20.30–31), upon his entry into the city (21.9) and then by the children in the Temple (21.15–16), sets up the expectation that Jesus has come as a messiah, to fight Israel's battle. Of course the expectation that Jesus is a military leader is mitigated by the cry of the blind men to the Son of David to 'have mercy' (20.30–31) and by Jesus' mode of entry (on a donkey, not on a war horse), echoing Zechariah 9.9 and implying that he comes humbly, for peaceful, not warlike, purposes (21.5). The fact that it is children who sing his praises (21.15–16) also confuses the matter – would a messianic military leader not first of all appeal to able-bodied fighters?

It is within this ambiguous context – of clear Davidic expectations being met by strange, humble and apparently peaceful (in spite of the Temple disruption) actions – that we must read Jesus' healing of the blind and the lame in the Temple. Once again, the title Son of David leads us to think of royalty, of Messiah, of authority to rebuild the Temple and, of course, of military conquest. But what does it mean that this 'Son of David' heals in the Temple?

---

18 Wright 1996, 484.

All three of the motifs we have identified in this section – the titles which elucidate what it means to be 'Son of David', the connection between the Temple and Israel's royal ideology seen in Jesus' prophetic action against the Temple, and the military connotations of 'Messiah' – leave us with the clear conclusion that Matthew 20.29—21.17 is saturated with Davidic language and ideas. This should not surprise us, because the narrative of Matthew leading up to this point has prepared us to understand Jesus in Davidic terms. But Jesus' healing of the blind and the lame in the Temple in Matthew 21.14, although it alludes to the story of David, seems to imply that Jesus is, rather than a 'normal' Davidic messiah, an anti-David.

4 Jesus as the healing 'Son of David' in Matthew

Jesus' healing ministry is strongly attested in Matthew's Gospel. In 4.23–25, one of a series of summary statements, we read:

> And he went about all Galilee, teaching in their synagogues and preaching the gospel of the kingdom and healing every disease and every infirmity among the people. So his fame spread throughout all Syria, and they brought him all the sick, those afflicted with various diseases and pains, demoniacs, epileptics, and paralytics, and he healed them. And great crowds followed him from Galilee and the Decapolis and Jerusalem and Judea and from beyond the Jordan.

No doubt a part of the attraction of Jesus was his teaching, and Matthew proceeds for the next three chapters (5—7) to give an extended account of some of that teaching. Matthew's emphasis in this statement, however, is on Jesus as a healer. In this summary Matthew is at pains to describe the variety of illness, twice mentioning that 'every' physical or spiritual problem came under his authority, and listing a wide variety of ailments that Jesus cured.

Following the so-called Sermon on the Mount, a block of teaching material, Matthew places a block of material consisting mostly of healing stories. In the midst of this section Matthew comments on the extensiveness of Jesus' healing ministry:

> That evening they brought to him many who were possessed with demons; and he cast out the spirits with a word, and healed all who were sick. This was to fulfil what was spoken by the prophet Isaiah, 'He took our infirmities and bore our diseases.'
>
> (8.16–17)

Similarly, at the end of this block of healing stories, another summary statement informs the reader that 'Jesus went about all the cities and villages, teaching in their synagogues and preaching the gospel of the kingdom, and healing every disease and every infirmity' (9.35).

When the disciples of the Baptist come to Jesus with a question from their imprisoned teacher: 'Are you he who is to come or shall we look for another?' (11.3), Jesus' answer is that John should be informed about Jesus' ministry of healing (and, yes, preaching): 'the blind receive their sight, and the lame walk, lepers are cleansed and the deaf hear, and the dead are raised up, and the poor have the good news preached to them. And blessed is he who takes no offense at me' (11.5–6). The passage is roughly a paraphrase combining Isaiah 29.18–19 and 35.5–6 concerning the coming age. What is not often noticed is that the preface to the oracle in Isaiah 29 is a warning against Israel in which God compares himself with David when he laid siege to Jerusalem (2 Samuel 5). To the incident in 2 Samuel we must return later. For now it is sufficient to note that Jesus' word to the Baptist is that the day of exile, the day of leaderless chaos, is coming to an end. It will be ended not by one who wields violence, but by one who brings healing.

Further mentions of Jesus' healing the many brought to him are found in 12.15 and 14.35, but special attention should be given to 15.30–31. Here, as in Jesus' words to the Baptist, the blind and the lame are once again mentioned, this time twice:

> And great crowds came to him, bringing with them the lame, the maimed, the blind, the dumb, and many others, and they put them at his feet and he healed them, so that the throng wondered, when they saw the dumb speaking, the maimed whole, the lame walking, and the the blind seeing; and they glorified the God of Israel.

Although those without speech and the maimed are also mentioned, the pairing of 'the blind and the lame' was already found as the first two categories of healed persons in 11.5. These passages, 11.5 and 15.30–31, anticipate Matthew 21.14.

Furthermore, in contrast to other royal figures mentioned in Matthew's Gospel, it is Jesus' healing ministry that repeatedly reveals that he is a different kind of king, a different kind of David.[19] In 9.27 Jesus encounters

---

[19] It is tempting to see an allusion in the healing ministry of Jesus to traditions about Solomon as a healer and exorcist. These traditions may have their origins in the prayer of Solomon in 1 Kings 3 in which he asks for wisdom; his request may have given birth, in later tradition, to an assumption that Solomon had wisdom and knowledge in every area, including the healing arts. The major sources for this understanding of Solomon, however, do not predate the time of Jesus or the writing of the Gospels. The earliest mention we know is by Josephus (*Ant.* 8.2.5.42–9). The other major source for this idea is a Christian document, *Testament of*

two blind men who implore him, 'Have mercy on us, Son of David.' In fact, Matthew records three separate incidents in which the blind are able to 'see' that Jesus is the Davidic king (as well as 9.27 see 20.30–31; 21.14). In chapter 12 Jesus heals a blind and speechless demoniac, leading observers to ask if Jesus could possibly be 'the Son of David' (12.22–23). Clearly, for Matthew, 'Son of David' can have a positive connotation: a connection with healing, with wholeness and restoration.

Another key passage for our purposes is the story of the Canaanite woman in 15.21–28. There the woman asks for 'mercy' from the 'Son of David' (15.22). Before we turn to Matthew 21.14, we will consider this story further. This passage, however, occurs in the larger context of a second and less obvious Matthean theme: Canaanites.

Canaanites in Matthew's Gospel

Matthew's Gospel is the only book of the New Testament that uses the word 'Canaanite'. It has often been noted that Matthew makes important references to gentiles, and even that this most Jewish of Gospels has a 'gentile bias'.[20] The Gospel opens with a genealogy which features several gentile women (1.1–16) and with a story of the pagan 'magi' (2.1–12). Bookending these opening references to non-Jews, the so-called 'Great Commission' of Jesus sends the Eleven to make disciples of 'all nations' (28.16–20). In the midst of the Gospel are two stories in which Jesus marvels at gentile faith: the story of the centurion (8.5–13) and the story of the Canaanite woman (15.21–28).

It is not so often noted, however, that Matthew is aware that not all gentiles are the same. There appear to be three passages in Matthew which mention or allude to Canaanites: the genealogy (1.1–16); the story of the Canaanite woman (15.21–28); and the story of the healing of the blind and the lame in the Temple. As we shall see, all three passages also feature references to David.

1 Canaanites in Matthew's genealogy (1.1–16)

It is rare for women to be mentioned in Jewish genealogies. When references do occur it is because of some unusual event connected to the woman in question. In addition to Mary the mother of Jesus, four women

Solomon, written some time between the first and the third centuries (although it may possibly contain some earlier Jewish traditions).
[20] Clark 1947.

are included in the opening unit of Matthew. Three are certainly gentiles (Tamar, Rahab, Ruth) and one is either a gentile or at least married to a gentile: 'the wife of Uriah' (1.6). Uriah, as we see in 2 Samuel 11.3, was a Hittite. It is probable that two of these gentile women are Canaanites: Rahab and Tamar. The narrator of Genesis 38 tells us that Judah's wife was a Canaanite and implies that Judah, while living in Canaan, also arranged the marriage between Tamar and his son Er, leaving the reader with the impression that Tamar was a Canaanite. The case of Rahab is more obvious: she was a resident of Jericho at the beginning of the Israelite conquest (Joshua 2). Thus we have the odd situation at the head of Matthew's Gospel where we find a genealogy in which foreigners, even Canaanites, the worst of foreigners, are held up as ancestors of the Messiah. No doubt the text is signalling an anticipation of the mission to the gentiles not made explicit until 28.19. But it seems that it is not just 'gentiles' in the abstract, but even gentile enemies, Canaanites, who are considered to be within the scope of those who are redeemable.[21]

It should be noted that the genealogy, which, as we have seen, is Davidic through and through, is also a passage which holds out hope for gentiles – and even for Canaanite gentiles. They already have a place in the ancestral lineage of the Messiah.

2 The healing of the Canaanite woman's daughter (15.21–28)

The only explicit reference to a Canaanite in the New Testament is found in 15.21–28. In this story we find Jesus in gentile territory, in the district of Tyre and Sidon (15.21). Although Mark, Matthew's probable source, refers to the same woman as a Syro-Phoenician (Mark 7.26), Matthew chooses to call her by the archaic term 'Canaanite', which I have argued elsewhere is a bit like calling a modern-day Swede a 'Viking'.[22] The use of this archaic term draws the attentive reader's mind to the place of Canaanites in the larger biblical narrative. They are the quintessential enemies of Israel and of God himself. They were set apart not only for judgement, but also for extinction. In fact, the Deuteronomic command to annihilate them uses telling language: 'show no mercy to them' (Deuteronomy 7.2). In Matthew's story the woman not only implores Jesus to heal her daughter, but asks for the very thing that Canaanites were to be denied: 'Have mercy on me, O Lord, Son of David' (Matthew 15.22).

---

[21] This paragraph is based on my 2005 essay. Cf. Jackson 2002, 61.
[22] LeMarquand and Keesmaat 2007.

Again note should be taken of the fact that Canaanites and Davidic language are found together in this text. This woman looks to Jesus as the kind of David who can act with mercy.

We are left to consider one further text having to do with Canaanites: Matthew 21.14.

3 Jesus' healing in the Temple (Matthew 21.14) in the light of 2 Samuel 5.6–10

As has been noted, the story of Jesus' entry into Jerusalem and disruption of the Temple includes a detail unique in this Gospel. In Matthew's Markan source we hear only that Jesus inspected the Temple and then retreated to Bethany for the night – the Temple demonstration happens the next day. In Matthew we do not have a two-day sequence – the action continues seemingly on the same day:

> Then Jesus entered the temple and drove out all who were selling and buying in the temple, and he overturned the tables of the money-changers and the seats of those who sold doves. He said to them, 'It is written, "My house shall be called a house of prayer"; but you are making it a den of robbers.'
> The blind and the lame came to him in the temple, and he cured them. But when the chief priests and the scribes saw the amazing things that he did, and heard the children crying out in the temple, 'Hosanna to the Son of David', they became angry and said to him, 'Do you hear what these are saying?' Jesus said to them, 'Yes; have you never read, "Out of the mouths of infants and nursing babies you have prepared praise for yourself"?'
> He left them, went out of the city to Bethany, and spent the night there.
>
> (Matthew 21.12–17, NRSV)

It is clear that Matthew 21.4, 'The blind and the lame came to him [Jesus] in the temple and he cured them', contains an allusion to 2 Samuel 5.6–10.[23] What is the significance of this allusion? The brief episode narrated in 2 Samuel 5.6–10 recounts David's conquest of Jerusalem and brings the story of David's rise to power to its climax. As Walter Brueggemann states, these verses form 'the successful ending [to] the long tale beginning in 1 Samuel 16:1'.[24] God has brought David to power, step by step. However, the story now turns from a narrative of God's faithfulness to David and becomes a story of 'ruthless military consolidation and self pre-occupation. The David who was content to receive gifts now becomes

---

23 Wright 2002, 71; Gundry 1982, 413.
24 Brueggemann 1990, 240.

a David who grasps at power.'[25] David's occupation of Jerusalem is both the apex of the David story and the beginning of its decline.

> [6]And the king and his men went to Jerusalem against the Jebusites, the inhabitants of the land, who said to David, 'You will not come in here, but the blind and the lame will ward you off' – thinking, 'David cannot come in here.' [7]Nevertheless, David took the stronghold of Zion, that is, the city of David. [8]And David said on that day, 'Whoever would strike the Jebusites, let him get up the water shaft to attack "the lame and the blind," who are hated by David's soul.' Therefore it is said, 'The blind and the lame shall not come into the house.' [9]And David lived in the stronghold and called it the city of David. And David built the city all round from the Millo inwards. [10]And David became greater and greater, for the LORD, the God of hosts, was with him.
>
> (2 Samuel 5.6–10, ESV)

The story itself paints an ambiguous picture of the king. His defeat of the Jebusites is almost miraculously easy. Although the city appears impregnable (at least to the Jebusites who occupy it, v. 6), David's forces slip in (according to v. 8, through a water shaft[26]) and take the city. No battle is mentioned. It is as if the city simply hands itself over. What the Jebusites had mockingly predicted – an easy defeat of David ('even the blind and the lame could defeat David's army') – is turned on its head as David simply takes the city as his own and renames it as his (vv. 7, 9).

But the story reveals a military leader lacking in mercy. Even after the defeat David is said to hate the blind and the lame (v. 8). David's hatred, according to 2 Samuel, leads to a prohibition of the lame and the blind from access to 'the house', a probable allusion to the Temple which David's son will eventually build, an allusion made more explicit in the LXX: 'into the house of the Lord' (*eis oikon kuriou*). This attitude is strangely at odds with the David who will treat with kindness the surviving member of Saul's family, Mephibosheth, a lame man who, the text is anxious to tell us, 'was crippled in [both] his feet' (2 Samuel 9.3, 13). The tension between the David who 'hates' the blind and the lame in chapter 5 and the one who shows *hesed* to the crippled son of Jonathan is not resolved in the story.

The story has an aetiological character to it – the defeat of Jerusalem is presented as the origin of the prohibition of anyone who is disabled from

---

25 Brueggemann 1990, 241.
26 Driver 1913 argues that the water shaft (the Hebrew term can mean a pipe, spout or water-channel) may refer to 'Warren's shaft' discovered in 1867, although this would involve both an emendation of the Hebrew word and a great deal of courage on the part of some 'adventurous Israelites' (Driver 1913, 259–60).

entering the Temple. Because of this incident, we are told, 'The blind and the lame shall not come into the house [i.e. the Temple]' (2 Samuel 5.8). David's curse excludes at least the blind and the lame from full participation in cultic worship.

Numerous passages in the Hebrew Bible speak of the exclusion of the blind, the lame and others with deformities, 'defects' (*mumim*), from various aspects of Israel's worship life. The Holiness Code excludes 'defective' priests from offering sacrifices, as outlined by the following passage in Leviticus:

> And the LORD spoke to Moses, saying, 'Speak to Aaron, saying, None of your offspring throughout their generations who has a blemish may approach to offer the bread of his God. For no one who has a blemish shall draw near, a man *blind or lame*, or one who has a mutilated face or a limb too long, or a man who has an injured foot or an injured hand, or a hunchback or a dwarf or a man with a defect in his sight or an itching disease or scabs or crushed testicles. No man of the offspring of Aaron the priest who has a blemish shall come near to offer the LORD's food offerings; since he has a blemish, he shall not come near to offer the bread of his God. He may eat the bread of his God, both of the most holy and of the holy things, but he shall not go through the veil or approach the altar, because he has a blemish, that he may not profane my sanctuaries, for I am the LORD who sanctifies them.'
>
> (Leviticus 21.16–23, ESV; italics added)[27]

The Dead Sea Scrolls perpetuate and extend these prohibitions in *The Community Rule*:

> . . . (no) man who is afflicted with the (following) afflictions shall take (his) stand within the Congregation: And any one who is afflicted in his flesh, crippled in the legs, the hands, *lame or blind* or deaf or dumb or if he is stricken with a blemish in his flesh visible to the eyes; or a (tottering) old man who cannot maintain himself within the Congregation; these may not en[ter] to stand firm [wi]thin the Congregation of the m[e]n of the name, for holy angels [(are) in] their [Coun]cil.
>
> (1QSa 2.3–9; italics added)[28]

Other Second Temple Jewish texts are similar. Within the Dead Sea Scrolls, 4QMMT [= 4Q394 8 iii–iv) similarly prohibits various categories of people from entering the sanctuary. 1QM (*The War Scroll*) excludes

---

27 Cf. Leviticus 13.12–17; 24.19–20; Numbers 12.12; Deuteronomy 23.1–2. For a thorough discussion of these texts, see Olyan 2009.

28 The Hebrew text and an English translation of 1QSa may be found in Charlesworth and Stuckenbruck 1994.

'the lame and the blind' and others from taking part in the eschatological battle. The Mishnah (*m. Hag.* 1.1) excludes the disabled from the Temple.

It is unclear how far actual Jewish practice went in excluding those with 'defects' from the Temple grounds in Jesus' day. As Davies and Allison point out, Matthew 21.14 is not the only New Testament text which mentions that some with physical disabilities were found in the Temple area (John 9.1 and Acts 3.1).[29] It could be that the outer court was an acceptable space for those who were imperfect according to the standards of the Torah.

Within the Old Testament purity tradition the kinds of exclusion we have been discussing were justified for symbolic reasons. According to Gordon Wenham, 'The idea emerges clearly that holiness finds physical expression in wholeness and normality.'[30] If God is perfect, those who lead the worship of God's people must reflect that perfection as closely as possible.

It is clear that the majority of Old Testament and Second Temple Jewish texts, including 2 Samuel 5, take it for granted that physical imperfections excluded Israelites from cultic activity in the Temple. Two prophetic texts, however, both from Isaiah, may give us a new perspective on David's cursing and Jesus' healing of the blind and the lame. The first text is from Isaiah 29:

> Ah, Ariel, Ariel, the city where David encamped . . . I will distress Ariel, and there shall be moaning and lamentation, and Jerusalem shall be to me like an Ariel.[31] And like David I will encamp against you; I will besiege you with towers and raise siege-works against you . . . And the multitude of all the nations shall fight against Ariel . . . so shall the multitude of all the nations be that fight against Mount Zion.
>
> (vv. 1–3, 7–8, NRSV)

This passage from Isaiah 29 has a direct bearing on our interpretation of Matthew 21.14. Like Matthew 21.14, Isaiah 29 alludes to the same incident in David's life – his besieging and conquering of Jerusalem. The contrast between Isaiah 29 and Matthew 21.14 is instructive, however. In 2 Samuel 5.6–10 (and 1 Chronicles 11.4–6) David lays siege to a Jerusalem which is inhabited by Jebusites – the last bastion of Canaanites in the land of Israel. In fact, we can read the episode of David's conquest of Jerusalem

---

29 Davies and Allison 1997, 3:140.
30 Wenham 1981, 292; cf. his important 1982 article. The idea of holiness as 'symbolic' is based on the work of the social anthropologist Mary Douglas: Douglas 1984 (1966).
31 An 'ariel' is an 'altar hearth'. The passage seems to mean that Jerusalem, like an altar hearth, will be burned up.

as the climax of the story of the conquest of the land which began in the book of Joshua. The conquering King David completes the work given to Israel when it entered the land: the extermination of the Canaanites. With David's occupation of Jerusalem all of Israel is freed from Canaanite rule and fully in the hands of the people of Israel.

In Isaiah 29, however, God acts as the conquering David, and Israel is the new Canaan. God will now use the nations to defeat Israel and send them into exile. But then suddenly the picture morphs: after describing the devastation of the exile, Isaiah 29.18–20 turns to a message of hope:

> On that day the deaf shall hear . . . the eyes of the blind shall see. The meek shall obtain fresh joy in the LORD, and the neediest people shall exult in the Holy One of Israel. For the tyrant shall be no more . . .
>
> (Isaiah 29.18–20, NRSV)

God in his mercy turns from judgement on his people to become their source of healing and joy: 'the eyes of the blind shall see.'

The context of Isaiah 35.5–6 is similarly suggestive. In Isaiah 34 God promises vengeance on Israel's enemies. The place of battle following the bloody defeat of the nations will be a place of chaos, uncreation: 'They shall name it No Kingdom There, and all its princes shall be nothing' (Isaiah 34.12, NRSV). The land will be a desolate, desert place, with no king, no righteous rule. But then comes the reversal:

> The wilderness and the dry land shall be glad, the desert shall rejoice and blossom . . . They shall see the glory of the LORD, the majesty of our God . . . 'He will come and save you.' Then the eyes of the blind shall be opened, and the ears of the deaf unstopped; then the lame shall leap like a deer, and the tongue of the speechless sing for joy.
>
> (Isaiah 35.1a, 2b, 4b–6, NRSV)

The oracles in Isaiah 29 and in Isaiah 34—35 present visions of different possible models of kingship and kingdom. Isaiah 29 reminds us that the kingship of David is that of a conqueror who attacks and defeats Jerusalem, destroying the last vestiges of the hated Canaanites and making Mount Zion his own, 'The City of David'. In this text God himself takes on this Davidic role, laying siege to Jerusalem and carrying disobedient Israel into exile. The result of exile is the kingdom-less chaos of Isaiah 34, an ecological wasteland, ruled by no one. But Isaiah 29.18–19 and Isaiah 35.5–6 present a new kingdom, a new age, a new day ('on that day', Isaiah 29.18, NRSV). And, it should be noted, both Isaiah passages mention the blind and the lame as beneficiaries of this new kingdom.

Reading Matthew 21.14 as an allusion to 2 Samuel 5.6–10 reveals a stark contrast between the David of 2 Samuel and the son of David in Matthew 21. The first David curses; the second brings healing. The first David defeats the Jebusites, seemingly the last Canaanites, and mocks them as 'blind and lame'. As Gundry notes: 'David was using "the lame and blind" as a figurative epithet for the Jebusites.'[32] Jesus, however, as in the story of the Canaanite woman in Matthew 15, sees 'the blind and the lame' as people in need of healing and mercy. Seeing Matthew 21.14 and 2 Samuel 5.6–10 in the light of Isaiah 29.18–19 and Isaiah 34—35 uncovers a prophetic promise: Jesus is the fulfilment of the Isaianic promise that after the exile, the blind and the lame would be freed from their Davidic curse.

Conclusion and application

In Matthew 21.14, therefore, the story of the healing of the blind and the lame brings to a climax the themes of Jesus as anti-David in Matthew's Gospel. Unlike David, who ruled with military might, and violence, and who excludes the hated Canaanites from the Temple – exemplified in the blind and the lame – Jesus comes in peace, to be a king who brings healing, who reinstates the enemies of God, and welcomes the blind and the lame who have been cursed.

Tom Wright has written much about the 'reconstitution of Israel', the remaking of God's people as a worldwide people no longer divided by ethnicity, but united in the Messiah. Matthew 21.14 shows how deep that reconstitution goes: even the worst of God's enemies, the hated Canaanites, the blind and the lame Jebusites, have a place under God's mercy.

I am not writing this essay from the comfort of a library in the Western world, but from Gambella, Ethiopia, the poorest part of one of the poorest countries in the world. I hope that the editors, the readers and Tom will excuse me if I make just a few comments about how this text can be heard in this particular place.

It is a rare day that I do not encounter the literal 'blind and lame' in this place. They beg on the streets in the major cities. They sit in front of or inside the gates of the Ethiopian Orthodox churches where the faithful are expected to bring them food. They come to our house where my wife attempts with few resources to bring them what medical (and spiritual!) help she can.

---

[32] Gundry 1982, 413.

Matthew 21.14 read in the light of 2 Samuel 5, however, reveals another dimension to this text. 'The blind and the lame' is a 'cipher' for Canaanites, enemies, those excluded from God's care and God's presence. Gambella, Ethiopia, is a place of refugees who have fled war in South Sudan. That war, begun in December 2013, quickly became an ethnic conflict between two of the larger groups in South Sudan, the Jieng (often known as Dinka) and the Nuer. The conflict, as with many such conflicts, is about land and power. In this struggle the local people are encouraged by their leaders to dehumanize their enemies. Revenge for ancient hurts provides the motivation for present atrocities. The Christian message has been widely received, but not always deeply understood. The culture here often says, 'If your neighbour kills your relative, you must act in vengeance.' But the Christian message insists that 'the blood of Jesus speaks a stronger word', a word of forgiveness, 'than the blood of Abel' which cries for vengeance (see Hebrews 12.25). The gospel message proclaims, 'The blind and the lame' – the hated outsiders – must be healed, not exterminated.

One more possible application must be considered. For centuries the imperial house of Ethiopia looked to Solomon, the Son of David, as its model. The emperor was termed the Lion of the Tribe of Judah,[33] the Ethiopian people (and especially the Ethiopian Orthodox Church) were the true Israel, ruled by the Solomonic dynasty and accompanied into battle by the Ark of the Covenant, thought to reside in Axum. Instead of the new people of God being a worldwide people constituted around the healing Messiah, Jesus, the Ethiopian people and Church were directed by their rulers to see themselves as the only true people of God. A new ethnic people of God (now African, rather than Hebrew) was constituted in Ethiopia. Religious and political power (for better and for worse) gave the country unity. But monarchy too often became tyranny, and the legacy of the Ethiopian Solomonic regime includes ethnic division and repression.

Jesus as the anti-Davidic king in Matthew 21.14 provides a different model of kingship, a model of healing and restoration, a model of reconciliation and mercy, rather than one of hatred, vengeance and domination.

---

[33] The Solomonic rule of Ethiopia goes back centuries and found justification in the Kebra Nagast, the codification of Ethiopian tradition concerning the encounter between the Queen of Sheba and Solomon. See the English translation of the Kebra Nagast (The Glory of the Kings) in Budge 1932; cf. LeMarquand 2007. 'Decree No. 3 of 1944' still spoke of the 'Conquering Lion of the Tribe of Judah Haile Selassie I Elect of God Emperor of Ethiopia'. A full text can be found as Appendix B of Trimingham 1950.

Bibliography

Beare, Frank W. (1981). *Matthew*. San Francisco, CA: Harper & Row.

Brown, Raymond (1979). *The Birth of the Messiah: A Commentary on the Infancy Narratives in Matthew and Luke*. New York, NY: Doubleday.

Brueggemann, Walter (1990). *First and Second Samuel*. Louisville, KY: Westminster John Knox.

Budge, E. A. Wallis (1932). *The Queen of Sheba and Her Only Son Menelik*. London: Oxford University Press/Humphrey Milford.

Caird, George (1966). *The Revelation of St John the Divine*. London: Adam & Charles Black.

Carter, Warren (2000). *Matthew and the Margins: A Socio-Political and Religious Reading*. London / New York, NY: T&T Clark.

Charlesworth, James H., and Loren Stuckenbruck (1994). 'Rule of the Congregation (1QSa).' In *The Dead Sea Scrolls: Hebrew, Aramaic, and Greek Texts with English Translations, Volume 1: Rule of the Community and Related Documents*, edited by James H. Charlesworth, 114–17. Tübingen: Mohr Siebeck.

Clark, K. W. (1947). 'The Gentile Bias of Matthew.' *Journal of Biblical Literature* 66: 165–72.

Cullmann, Oscar (1959 (1957)). *The Christology of the New Testament*. London: SCM.

Davies, W. D., and Dale C. Allison (1997). *A Critical and Exegetical Commentary on the Gospel According to Saint Matthew*. 3 vols. International Critical Commentary. Edinburgh: T&T Clark.

Davis, Ellen (2001). *Scripture, Culture, Agriculture: An Agrarian Reading of the Bible*. Cambridge: Cambridge University Press.

Douglas, Mary (1984 (1966)). *Purity and Danger: An Analysis of Concepts of Pollution and Taboo*. London / New York, NY: Routledge.

Driver, S. R. (1913). *Notes on the Hebrew Text and the Topography of the Books of Samuel with an Introduction on Hebrew Palaeography and the Ancient Versions*. 2nd edition. Oxford: Clarendon.

Gaiser, Frederik J. (2010). *Healing in the Bible: Theological Insight for Christian Ministry*. Grand Rapids, MI: Baker.

Gundry, Robert (1982). *Matthew: A Commentary on His Literary and Theological Art*. Grand Rapids, MI: Eerdmans.

Hurtado, Larry (2003). *Lord Jesus Christ: Devotion to Jesus in Earliest Christianity*. Grand Rapids, MI: Eerdmans.

Jackson, Glenna (2002). *'Have Mercy on Me': The Story of the Canaanite Woman in Matthew 15:21–28*. Journal for the Study of New Testament Supplement Series 228; Sheffield: Sheffield Academic Press.

LeMarquand, Grant (2005). 'The Canaanite Conquest of Jesus (Mt 15:21–28).' In *Essays in Honour of Frederik Wisse: Scholar, Churchman, Mentor*. Published as a special edition of the journal *ARC: The Journal of the Faculty of Religious Studies, McGill University* 33: 237–47.

—— (2007). 'The Queen of Sheba and Solomon's Wisdom: A Biblical Story in

Ethiopian Tradition.' In *Human Wisdom and Divine Wisdom in the Bible: Biblical Readings in the Context of the Church as Family of God in Africa. Proceedings of the Twelfth Congress of the Panafrican Association of Catholic Exegetes. / Sagesse humaine et sagesse divine dans la Bible: Lectures bibliques dans le contexte de l'Eglise Famille de Dieu en Afrique: Actes du douzième congrès de l'Association Panafricaine des Exégètes Catholiques. Mélanges offerts à S. E. Mgr Laurent Monsengwo Pasinya à l'occasion de ses 25 ans d'épiscopat. Kinshasa, du 04 au 11 septembre 2005*, edited by Jean-Bosco Matand Bulembat, 263–75. Nairobi: APECA/PACE.

LeMarquand, Grant, and Sylvia C. Keesmaat (2007). 'Genocide or Healing?' *The Banner*: <https://www.thebanner.org/features/2011/01/genocide-or-healing>.

Meier, John P (1994). *A Marginal Jew, Volume 2: Mentor, Message and Miracles*. New York, NY: Doubleday.

Mulloor, Augustine (1994). '"The Blind, the Lame and the Children in the Temple": Mt 21,14–17 as a Model of Action.' *Bible Bhashyam* 20.1: 29–41.

Olyan, Saul M. (2009). *Disability in the Hebrew Bible: Interpreting Mental and Physical Differences*. New York, NY: Cambridge University Press.

Park, Eugene Eung-Chung (2013). 'Rachel's Cry for Her Children: Matthew's Treatment of the Infanticide by Herod.' *Catholic Biblical Quarterly* 75.3: 473–85.

Richardson, Peter (1999). *Herod: King of the Jews and Friend of the Romans*. Minneapolis, MN: Fortress.

Runnalls, Donna (1983). 'The King as Temple-Builder.' In *Spirit within Structure: Essays in Honor of George Johnston on the Occasion of His Seventieth Birthday*, edited by E. J. Furcha, 15–37. Allison Park, PA: Pickwick.

Skehan, P. W. (1967). 'Wisdom's House.' *Catholic Biblical Quarterly* 29: 468–86.

Trimingham, J. Spencer (1950). *The Christian Church and Missions in Ethiopia (Including Eritrea and the Somalilands)*. London: World Dominion Press.

Wenham, Gordon (1981). *The Book of Leviticus*. New International Commentary on the Old Testament. Grand Rapids, MI: Eerdmans.

—— (1982). 'Christ's Ministry of Healing and His Attitude to the Law.' In *Christ the Lord: Studies in Christology Presented to Donald Guthrie*, edited by H. H. Rowdon, 115–26. Leicester: IVP.

Wright, N. T. (1992). *The New Testament and the People of God*. Christian Origins and the Question of God 1. London: SPCK / Minneapolis, MN: Fortress.

—— (1996). *Jesus and the Victory of God*. Christian Origins and the Question of God 2. London: SPCK / Minneapolis, MN: Fortress.

—— (2002). *Matthew for Everyone, Part 2: Chapters 16–28*. London: SPCK.

Tom (aka N. T.) Wright on Galatians

PETER OAKES

Introduction

The trick with Striding Edge is to pick a day when it isn't too windy. (It goes without saying that there also mustn't be snow and ice: under those, Striding Edge, like Crib Goch on Snowdon, really needs ropes.) On a still day it is safe, and really exhilarating. On a windy day there is a bit of danger of being blown off. The exhilaration does, however, require willingness to handle exposure. Standing on an arête, where you can see hundreds of feet down on both sides, requires a willingness to be radically out in the open.

Reading Tom's *Paul for Everyone* commentary on Galatians, I was surprised to learn that he has not actually been along Striding Edge. Professionally, however, he has been doing it throughout his career. The Tom Wright who is constantly aware of the vertigo-inducing needs of speaking to a popular audience, in their thousands of distinct lives and their unsettling willingness to put their trust in (some) scholars, and to act on that trust, is also N. T. Wright, conscious of the different quality of vertigo induced by awareness of the vast landscape of scholarship that you look out across when you try to engage seriously with the text and ideas of the New Testament. Tom is N. T. There is no substituting of a standardized message when Tom writes for a broader audience. What comes across is the same distinct scholarship seen in N. T.'s weighty output.

My most formative encounters were with Tom, not N. T., although the formal distinction in authorial names is not strictly relevant because the encounters were not through written works at all. As an engineering undergraduate in *c.*1980 Cambridge, one of my first acts was to go and hear Tom, then chaplain at Downing College, speak on the topic 'Why Study Theology?' upstairs in the room that acted as a hall to the Round Church. Tom's answer: we all do theology; the question is whether or not we do it well. Soon after that came an electrifying series of Christian Union 'Bible Readings', talks that packed out the Cambridge Union debating hall on Saturday evenings. With 'Here comes the king', and other such titles, Tom expounded his recently completed doctoral thesis on Romans, but as a reading of the last part of Luke. When, after a few years of school-teaching and earning a theology degree, I came to look for a doctoral supervisor, I wanted to study with Tom. I applied to Oxford because he was there, rather than vice versa.

The ease with which Tom applied to Luke his thesis on Romans was indicative both of the power and scope of the core idea in his thesis and of the extent to which he sees each of the biblical books as carrying that idea. The effectiveness with which his talks on Luke gripped a non-theological student audience showed Tom's willingness and ability to teach his scholarly ideas in a popular forum.

Tom Wright's For Everyone series encapsulates all this, as well as giving expression to broader characteristics of his writing, such as a fairly conservative but relatively inclusive theology, put across in a pastorally committed way. The format of the series is of a two-page series introduction (with a tailored final paragraph), then straight into a sequence of studies of sections of the text, which is divided into units suitable for something like devotional daily Bible study. Galatians is split into 22 roughly equal sections, adding up to 83 small-format pages. As a fellow commentator, I was very struck by the tremendous constraint of keeping all the sections the same length: only four pages to deal with 2.15–21! Each section begins with Wright's very accessible translation. There is then an anecdote, an explanation of a few key points from the passage and some thoughts about present-day Christian life in relation to those points.

Two questions spring to mind. To what extent can Tom Wright put across substantial scholarly ideas within such a constrained format and for a popular audience? What kind of mix of ideas does Wright communicate? Competing views? Consensus ones? Those of particular groups of scholars? His own distinctive views? We will consider these questions by working through the commentary on Galatians 1—3.

Galatians 1: Paul as announcer of the messianic king

Wright begins on 1.1–9 with a powerful analogy for Galatians, imagining a project that was building a multiracial community centre in Apartheid South Africa. The project is interrupted, then completed by new builders, but in segregated form.[1] This is frankly brilliant communication of substantive scholarship. At a stroke, Wright turns his church readers away

---

[1] Wright 2002, 3.

from the more general theological discourse that many will have expected as they approached Galatians, to a framing of the letter in ethnic terms. This is a move that would command fairly broad consensus among Pauline scholars.

Wright then narrows the consensus by immediately moving to place the letter under Claudius with the imperial cult as an issue in the region. Jesus 'is the Jewish Messiah, a kind of king-to-end-all-kings (sounds like a challenge to Emperor Claudius)'.[2] Interestingly, the narrowing of consensus here will be mainly some loss of support from the right: objection to Wright's maxim 'Jesus is "Lord", therefore Caesar is not',[3] has been most vocal among some (although not all) fairly conservative writers.[4] In this quote comparing Jesus and Claudius, we are still far from something uniquely 'Wrightian', but the reader is being guided towards a sector of NT scholarship, in this case, the more political sector. Next in the commentary, we do read something very specifically Wrightian: the Messiah would 'have to have just one family'[5] – more of which below. Many other aspects of Wright's initial exposition of the situation that Paul faces in Galatia are fairly mainstream.

On 1.10–17, Wright likens Paul to Elijah, both in zeal and in receipt of revelation at Sinai (in 'Arabia'). Wright puts 'Judaism' in verse 13 in inverted commas but does not elaborate. God's son is revealed 'in' Paul rather than 'to' him. Wright's reading of the rest of chapter 1 is fairly uncontroversial. In verse 22 he translates *tais ekklēsiais* as 'to the messianic assemblies'. These are 'on the way to being what we would call "churches", but at the moment simply synagogues whose members had all become Christians'.[6] The extent to which this diverges from the kind of view held by Mark Nanos, Magnus Zetterholm and others of the 'Paul within Judaism' school becomes evident later.[7]

Galatians 2: two badges of identity

Wright launches into chapter 2 by describing circumcision as an identity marker: a 'badge of identity'.[8] On 2.3–5, he tells his readers of scholarly

2 Wright 2002, 4.
3 For instance, Wright 1990, 11–17 (here 14).
4 See, for instance, most of the contributions in Modica and McKnight 2013.
5 Wright 2002, 4.
6 Wright 2002, 10, 12.
7 See Nanos and Zetterholm 2015.
8 Wright 2002, 14.

options as to whether Titus actually was circumcised. Wright offers Acts 16.3 as evidence in favour of the view that Titus was, then expresses his conclusion that it is unlikely. An interesting translational move in 2.8 is to say that God 'gave Peter the power' to be apostle to the circumcision. Wright's readers could go astray here, hearing this in what would be Greek *exousia* terms. In fact, there may be a Wrightian redactional history to be traced here, because the discussion of the passage offers the quote, 'The one who energized Peter and me . . .'[9] On the chronological issues in 2.1–10, Wright implies some type of conservative line on the relationship to Acts, seeing the Galatians 2 visit as being that of Acts 11.27–30.[10]

The commentary sees the inclusion of the Antioch incident in Galatians as probably being due to Paul's opponents using it in persuading the Galatians, who 'may have heard a version of the story in which Peter had the strongest arguments; and the story, told in this way, was powerful reinforcement for their own case'.[11] This is a point at which my own commentary is in radical disagreement with that of Wright. For me, Paul acts creatively in bringing in the Antioch incident: his key rhetorical move in the letter is to take a presenting issue in Galatia about circumcision and reframe it as an issue about Jews and Gentiles eating together.[12]

As one would expect, Wright packs a great deal into the section on 2.15–21. He departs radically from 'Paul within Judaism' scholars: 'The question Paul and Peter have run into . . . is . . . who is God's true Israel? Who are the true people of God? Is it all who belong to the Messiah? Or is it only Jewish Christians . . . ?'[13] The posing of that either–or question places Wright outside the strand of scholarship running from Krister Stendahl to Zetterholm and others. However, there are large swathes of historic and current Christian scholarship that would go along with something like that formulation. What comes next, however, is definitively Wrightian: 'Paul focuses his answer on the most basic point of all. God's true Israel consists of one person: the Messiah. He is the faithful one. He is the true Israelite. This is the foundation of identity within God's people.'[14] This centre-point of Wright's view – and, in Wright's view, of all of history – is then applied in a very bold attempt to explain to a popular audience a key line of argument of his doctoral thesis:

---

9   Wright 2002, 17, 19.
10   Wright 2002, 19.
11   Wright 2002, 22.
12   Oakes 2015, xi.
13   Wright 2002, 25.
14   Wright 2002, 25.

Those who belong to the Messiah are *in the Messiah*, so that what is true of him is true of them. The roots of this idea are in the Jewish beliefs about the king. The king represents his people (think of David fighting Goliath, *representing* Israel against the Philistines); what is true of him is true of them.[15]

In comparison with these academic fireworks, the fact that Wright takes a view on the *pistis Christou* issue, a 'subjective genitive' one,[16] that will be controversial to many in his audience (this time, mainly the more conservative side) seems relatively tame. Also controversial among many conservative readers is the whole strategy of interpreting Paul's righteousness language here through categories of identity marking,[17] rather than through categories that have been more traditional in much Protestant preaching and theology.

Galatians 3: one seed is one family

On Galatians 3, Wright runs counter to much thought in the Calvinist Reformed tradition by firmly seeing the regulations of Jewish law as not being relevant for Christian life. On 3.2–5 he writes, 'Being a Christian starts and continues as a matter of faith. The Jewish law has nothing to say to it.'[18] He reinforces this on 3.19–22: 'precisely because of the Christian story of God's dealings with his people from Abraham onwards, the regulations designed to keep Israel as it were in quarantine are now set aside.'[19]

Wright's reading of *ek pisteōs* in 3.7 puts him on the side of his friend Richard Hays in allowing *pistis* to be used of Christians as well as of Christ: 'it's people of faith who are children of Abraham.'[20] This flexibility contrasts with Martin de Boer, who reads *pistis* more consistently as primarily a property of Christ, including in 2.7.[21] De Boer's approach has the advantage of fending off James Dunn's argument that *ek pisteōs* here suggests how we should read that phrase in 2.16.[22] Wright's acceptance that *pistis* in Galatians is sometimes a characteristic of people is indicative of his not going along with the most radical 'apocalyptic' end of the group of scholars who favour 'faithfulness of Christ' readings of *pistis Christou*.

---

15 Wright 2002, 25 (his emphasis).
16 Wright 2002, 23, 26.
17 Wright 2002, 26.
18 Wright 2002, 30.
19 Wright 2002, 39.
20 Wright 2002, 27.
21 Except Galatians 5.22; see de Boer 2011, 191.
22 Dunn 2008, 351–66 (here 358–60).

For de Boer and his teacher, J. L. Martyn, God's salvation is firmly cosmic: the cross changes the world; consequently, the question of human πίστις (*pistis*) comes to be much less pertinent than was envisaged in Lutheran theology.[23] Wright, while rejecting several aspects of Lutheran readings of Galatians, still holds on to many of the soteriological structures of Lutheranism. On Galatians 3.10–14, Wright's ideas on Israel come through very forthrightly:

> To appeal to Abraham, as it were over the head of Moses, was simply to ignore the main part of the Jewish story, the heart of Jewish practice, a key element in Jewish theology. But Paul doesn't ignore it. He tells the story differently. He speaks of a gigantic roadblock in the plan of God. God's promise to Abraham wasn't simply about the Jews; it was designed for all the nations. The very opening lines of Genesis 12 said so. That was the road down which the plan was supposed to be going. Abraham's family were to bring God's plan of salvation to the rest of the world. That's why there was such a family in the first place. But what happened to this family? And what, in consequence, had happened to God's plan and promise?
>
> Here and elsewhere, Paul is quite clear on his answer: the physical family of Abraham, the Jewish people, had overturned like a huge truck in the road, and were now blocking the original intention.[24]

Paul then shows how Christ's taking on of the law's curse solves this problem, not only for the world but also for Israel:

> ethnic Israel is not left in the ditch, nor simply shunted to one side. What Israel needed, according to the prophets . . . was for the covenant to be renewed at last: for God to pour out his spirit on Israel and enable it to believe . . .[25]

Wright reads 3.14b as, 'so that we [that is, Jews who believe the gospel] might receive the promise of the spirit through faith'.[26] Implicit in Wright's points above is a very radical reading of 3.16. He translates the text as: 'Well, the promises were made "to Abraham and his seed", that is, his family. It doesn't say "his seeds", as though referring to several families, but indicates a single family by saying, "and to your seed", meaning the Messiah.'[27] Wright defends and explains this interpretation: 'the "seed" is singular, meaning the Messiah – who, for Paul, represents God's people,

---

23 Martyn 1985.
24 Wright 2002, 32–3.
25 Wright 2002, 34.
26 Wright 2002, 34.
27 Wright 2002, 35.

so that the "singular seed" means *the single family, incorporated into the Messiah, that God always intended*.[28]

Although scholars would generally agree that Paul is heading towards his statement at the end of Galatians 3, that all who are 'in Christ' constitute Abraham's single seed, it is an important element of Wright's distinctive reading of Paul that the singleness of the family is to be read into Paul's focus on the singleness of *sperma* in 3.16, rather than Paul's point being Christological in a more limited way. More deeply, the point about the single family lies behind much of Wright's view of Israel. For Wright, Paul saw God's plan as always having been to create a single multi-ethnic family, right back when calling Abraham, and even beyond. Scholars would generally accept that Paul links his conclusion in 3.29 back to the points about Abraham and those 'in' him in 3.8–9. Wright's radical moves are to see this as being directly present in 3.16, and then to see Israel's failure to fulfil this as being central to the problems referred to in 3.10–12.

We must briefly jump to Wright's comments on the phrase 'the Israel of God' in 6.16.

> Those who respond in faith are thus given the title of great honour: they are (verse 16) 'the Israel of God' . . . Of course, we should remember that when Paul was writing, the majority of Christians were Jews by birth. We should not allow our reading of him to suggest, as some have tragically done, that God has turned his back on the Jews and has allowed a Gentile community to take over instead. This is what Paul sets his face against in (for instance) Romans 9—11. But we should not allow our awareness of that problem to prevent us seeing and feeling the force of what he says here. The Galatians – and all who believe in Jesus – are now God's Israel, God's light to the world . . .[29]

Scholars will vary in their evaluation of Wright's warning here against supersessionism.

Popularizing academic ideas in a devotional format

Tom Wright shows that, with sufficient skill, commitment and a suitable market, ideas in academic biblical studies can be popularized, even in the field of devotional literature, which is presumably the primary market for the series. His For Everyone commentaries are far from either being bland

---

[28] Wright 2002, 36 (his emphasis).
[29] Wright 2002, 85.

re-narrations and applications of biblical texts or being predominantly articulations of a particular denominational or similar agenda, as many popular commentaries are. The For Everyone commentaries communicate a range of ideas that have come about specifically through work carried out in academia, including a considerable amount from the last 40 years – to pick an obvious point marked by the publication of E. P. Sanders' *Paul and Palestinian Judaism*.

Many of the ideas that Wright communicates would command a wide consensus within current Pauline scholarship. Others of his ideas would command a consensus among broadly New Perspective scholars. Some ideas would be shared by scholars who follow what is now often called an Empire Criticism approach.[30] Others would be shared by scholars who read *pistis Christou* as 'faithfulness of Christ'. Many of the ideas would be shared by scholars towards the orthodox, conservative end of the theological spectrum. They would be particularly shared by those whose orthodoxy is of a relatively ecumenical and inclusive type. Others of Wright's ideas are specific to his own academic work, so would be shared by scholars who are persuaded by the central lines of argument of his doctoral thesis and subsequent work based on that.

Popularization requires, *ipso facto*, a market. Wright can popularize because not only does he have the necessary writing skills, but he delivers work that non-academics in churches find valuable. His work provides a fresh and serious approach to NT texts that enables devotion and action in churches right across the English-speaking world and in many denominations.

Part of the reason for this undoubtedly lies in Wright's reputation as a defender of traditional Christian beliefs, for instance on the resurrection. Part of the reason probably also stems from the relative inclusivity of Wright's work. Church ministers, especially because of their academic training, often hold somewhat more inclusive views than would be most common among the members of their congregations. Wright is a writer who can be recommended to congregants as reasonably conservative (albeit in ways that may be seen as trickily idiosyncratic) but who is, for instance, fairly ecumenical rather than parochially sectarian.

All this adds up to Wright having found an extensive forum for communicating academic ideas: consensus ones, those of various scholarly groups, and his own distinctive ideas. Wright has then had the skills and commitment to do the communicating.

---

30 For the term, see Modica and McKnight 2013.

The space in the commentary given to competing views is extremely limited. Wright has taken part in a large number of face-to-face or written debates with scholars whose views compete with his. However, my impression is that the debates that have the type of audience who would use the For Everyone commentaries have generally been on topics such as justification: they have been debates with more conservative scholars, for audiences concerned about whether Wright is too problematically idiosyncratic to be read by conservative Christians. Wright's debates on subjects that academics might see as more pertinent, such as his SBL debate with John Barclay on NT and empire, have nowhere near such a wide reach among Wright's popular audience. The kinds of debate that biblical scholars would be most interested in, between, say, Wright and Pamela Eisenbaum on Paul and Israel, either do not happen or, if they do take place, do not find a wide audience among the readership of the For Everyone series.

As well as the issue of popularity, there is that of writing for use in personal devotion or preaching preparation. Many biblical scholars would not have beliefs that led them to do that anyway. Among those that would attempt it, there would be an acknowledgement that there is a limit to the amount of academic debate that can usefully be included in such literature. However, some would see the teaching of uncertainty as having significant value, even in this format. Wright does not go down this line although, as noted above, there is a degree of ecumenical inclusiveness in his writing that works against some sectarian dogmatism. However, Wright is sufficiently confident of his own line of thought to see it as offering something of devotional value to a wide audience. Actually, we should maybe turn that round. A wide audience, and publishers who provide books to them, have found Wright's ideas devotionally valuable. Of how many other current biblical scholars can this be said to be the case?

Bibliography

de Boer, Martinus C. (2011). *Galatians: A Commentary*. New Testament Library. Louisville, KY: Westminster John Knox.

Dunn, James D. G. (2008). 'ΕΚ ΠΙΣΤΕΩΣ: A Key to the Meaning of ΠΙΣΤΙΣ ΧΡΙΣΤΟΥ'. In *The Word Leaps the Gap: Essays on Scripture and Theology in Honor of Richard B. Hays*, edited by J. Ross Wagner, C. Kavin Rowe and A. Katherine Grieb, 351–66. Grand Rapids, MI: Eerdmans.

Martyn, J. Louis. (1985). 'Apocalyptic Antinomies in Paul's Letter to the Galatians.' *New Testament Studies* 31.3: 410–24.

Modica, Joseph, and Scot McKnight (2013) (eds). *Jesus Is Lord, Caesar Is Not: Evaluating Empire in New Testament Studies*. Downers Grove, IL: IVP.

Nanos, Mark D., and Magnus Zetterholm (2015) (eds). *Paul within Judaism: Restoring the First-Century Context to the Apostle*. Minneapolis, MN: Fortress.

Oakes, Peter (2015). *Galatians*. Paideia: Commentaries on the New Testament. Grand Rapids: Baker.

Wright, N. T. (1990). 'The New Testament and the "State"'. *Themelios* 16.1: 11–17.

—— (2002). *Paul for Everyone: Galatians and Thessalonians*. London: SPCK.

The source of the problem: source arguments and the role of women in the world and in the Church

BEN WITHERINGTON III

Introduction

Sometimes the only way to deal with a problem is to deal with the source of the problem.[1] And in the case of the role of women in the Church, a major source of the problem is the profound misreading of what the Bible actually says about the creation and the nature of men and women. Words like 'complementarian' or 'egalitarian' are frankly inadequate and inaccurate when it comes to getting at the nuances of what the Genesis story actually says and what the later uses of the story by Jesus, Paul and others actually mean. How so?

The term 'complementarian' emphasizes the differences between man and woman, whereas the term 'egalitarian' emphasizes not merely their equality, but their *sameness*. What then do you do with a situation where both difference and sameness are involved because the whole issue of human beings and their interrelatedness is a complex matter? In regard to sameness, the assumption is all too often that the only basis of equality must be sameness of some sort in regard to all roles. The Bible by contrast doesn't agree with that sort of assumption.

While men and women are both equally created in God's image, equally of sacred worth, equally endowed with some tasks such as filling the earth and subduing it, they are also said to not be the same when it comes to *some* of the roles they play. And herein lies the rub. As much as I might have desired to take one for the team and be pregnant with one of our children, alas I didn't have the right equipment to do so. I was not equally

---

[1] I am very pleased to provide this essay for the Festschrift for my old friend Tom Wright, who, I trust, will find some congenial arguments here about narrative, biblical theology and the role of women in the Church. A form of this essay was delivered orally on 22 July 2017 at the Christians for Biblical Equality annual meeting in Orlando, Florida, on which occasion I was presented with a lifetime achievement award for supporting women in ministry.

able to perform this task, and I never could be 'the mother of the living', to borrow a familiar phrase.

In an age where it is even assumed that gender identity determines nothing, and one can therefore choose one's gender orientation, or even have surgery so one can change one's gender identity, it is no surprise to learn that we are confused about these issues. Ontological equality is one thing; 'sameness' in the sense of women and men being equally able to perform any and all roles in life is another. And the failure to realize this causes nothing but mischief and misunderstanding.

It is this unvariegated approach to the matter in the Bible that has led to assumptions such as that a woman's role in the physical family should limit, or even dictate, what roles women can play in the Church. This kind of reasoning, however, doesn't work because the physical family and its physical roles are one thing, and roles in the family of faith are another. The former is to some extent dictated by gender; the latter is determined by who is gifted and who is graced by God's Spirit to fill what role in the Church. And what gets in the way of women doing the latter is assumptions about the subordination of women to men in general, and wives to husbands in particular. But the very basis of the subordinationist argument (if we are *not* talking about the mutual subordination referred to in Ephesians 5.21) involves a profound misreading of Genesis 2—3, a misreading that does not recognize that the subordination of women to men is a result of the Fall, indeed a result of the curse on women due to sin: 'your desire will be for your husband and *he will lord it over you.*'[2] To love and to cherish becomes to desire and to dominate. This was not the original creation plan, or the original blessing. It was the original curse, and it led to patriarchy according to Genesis. It is no accident that the patriarchs, Abraham, Isaac and Jacob, do not show up until after Genesis 3. The conditions for patriarchy were not created by creation itself; they were created by the Fall.

But herein lies another problem – in the twenty-first century many Christians, even some Evangelical ones, no longer believe in the historical Fall of humanity. *They have a doctrine of creation without a doctrine of fallenness*, and so they assume that 'whatever is' is the way God made us, and is good. This is the very basis of the arguments about homosexuality being something God gifted some persons with. Again, a profound misunderstanding about source arguments is involved. That being the case,

---

2 All quotations from Scripture in this chapter are my own translations, or else they are taken from the NIV.

we need to revisit the story of Creation and Fall once more, and the use of those stories in the NT as well.

I shall not be dealing with the household codes in Colossians 3—4 and Ephesians 5—6; one can consult my commentary on those passages.[3] Those passages are examples of Paul the pastor dealing with his people where they are, not where he would like them to be, and where they are is enmeshed in a profoundly patriarchal household structure, which Paul is trying to ameliorate the harsher effects of, in an effort to change and make more Christian an existing fallen situation from the inside out, giving wives, children and slaves and their roles a chance to be viewed differently.[4] So – it is time to go *ad fontes*!

The genesis of the problem

From the start, we note that the Genesis narrative appears to be presented as a historical account by the author, hence a saga or legend from hoary antiquity, not a creation myth. Thus, Eden is perhaps seen as a country, though the word means 'delight' or 'paradise' (the English term comes from the LXX translation of 'parkland'). Here Eden is located in the East, and from what follows about the rivers, we are to think of a place either in the Armenian mountains or north of the Persian Gulf in the area of the fertile crescent, according to some scholars.[5] The mention of the Tigris and Euphrates clearly locates this place in space and time. Eden is usually thought of as a garden. *Gan*, however, can mean a park or orchard with trees and is originally a Persian word referring to a nobleman's park. The implication is that humanity is getting the royal treatment by God.

God forms *adam* from the ground and gives him the 'kiss of life', breathing into his nostrils, as the text says. Humanity is living dust, a true miracle. There is no body–soul dualism in this creation, but body–life dualism.[6] Humanity is not distinguished from animals in being a living

---

[3]   Witherington 2007.
[4]   In fact, where Paul's argument is going is shown in Philemon. He thinks that when someone is 'in Christ' he should be treated no longer as a slave, but more and other than a slave: as a brother in Christ. What we see in Colossians 3—4 and then in Ephesians 5—6 is preliminary remarks on the way to the declaration in Philemon. There is some Christianizing of the household structure in Colossians, even more in Ephesians with its call for mutual submission, and then even more in Philemon as we have examples of different levels of moral discourse, ranging from the opening salvos spoken to people Paul has not met in Colossae, to taking further steps in Ephesians, and finally remarks to a co-worker and intimate.
[5]   Kidner 1982, 64.
[6]   Arnold 2008, 58, stresses that *nephesh hayah* refers to the totality of the person. The problem

being (*nephesh hayah*, cf. Genesis 1.21, 24, 30), but by being a creature who can relate to God freely and freely choose to respond to his will and word. The capacity of special relationship and the power of moral choice set humanity apart, as the story makes clear by what follows.

Two trees are planted in the middle of the garden: one which could lead to everlasting life, the other to death (whether physical or spiritual or both is not made clear). It seems to be implied that Adam was *not* immortal by nature, but that this gift was available to him for the taking. God said he *could* even eat of the tree of life, but not of the tree of the knowledge of good and evil. It is possible as well that Adam and Eve, while vulnerable to being killed, were not *inherently, due to their very nature*, mortal. In any case, knowledge (*yada*) here probably implies not merely intellectual knowledge, but the experience of the gamut of good and evil; that is what the serpent offers. Clearly, God has already defined what is wrong for humankind. Not knowledge itself, but presuming to be the captain of one's own fate, doing what is right in one's own eyes, is at issue here. God's word has defined one thing that is wrong: eating of the tree which leads to death. The experience of all evil or even the knowledge of it (the wages of sin) leads only to death. Note that God did not make evil; it is not a tangible thing. God, of course, knows all that is good and evil, yet God is not tempted or tainted thereby.

God has provided everything humankind needs: a supportive environment, readily available food, a meaningful job of tilling the soil and tending the garden, and a relationship with God. All *adam* lacks is a mate. The naming of the animals story indicates that humankind is given power and authority over them. In Hebrew culture to name is to define, to order, to organize, and not merely to label. Biblical names normally connote something about the nature of the one named. Verse 20b appears to imply that in this process of examining the animal world, *adam* was also looking for a mate. It indicates how close *adam* is to the animals that he would look among them. But, though animals are living beings, they are not to be one with humankind. Only woman is bone of his bone and flesh of his flesh; no animal bears that intimacy and kinship with humanity. God formed them separately.

We must also go on to add that there is no idea of an androgynous Adam in *this* creation story either. Woman is not taken out of man. Rather,

---

with this explanation is there was already a body formed by God the potter, a body which was not a *nephesh hayah* and it is only when God breathed into that form that a living being existed. I agree, however, that the author is not referring here to the later concept of the 'soul'.

she is built up out of a part of him. Adam was looking for his female companion, and she was not simply the other half of his own nature. If man is *ish* in Hebrew, woman is *ishah*, the one who comes out of man. However, as we shall see, calling the woman *ishah* is not giving her a personal name, like later in 3.20 after the Fall, when man tries to take control. Here is not a naming ritual and so an asserting of authority over the woman, but a cry of joy, on finally finding the one for whom you are looking. The key phrase is important here: 'it is not good for *man* to be alone', something not said of the woman.

Adam was made for relationship with God, but also with fellow humans. He is made to be a social, not a solitary creature. Indeed, only so can he survive. The phrase goes on: 'I will make a helper or companion suitable for [corresponding to] him.' Here we should not translate 'helpmate'. The old King James translation 'helpmeet' does not mean a helpmate but rather a helper who is 'meet', i.e. suitable for the task. Woman is not man's maid, nor merely his assistant, but a 'suitable companion', corresponding to him. She is the crown of creation, God's last act which makes it all very good.

Woman is just like man in that she shares the same nature (bone of my bone) and the same capacity for relationship with God. She is also different, a complement that completes human creation, not a duplicate that is redundant. The Hebrew phrase *kenegedo* implies both similarity (correspondence) and supplementariness. Woman is the mirror in which man recognizes himself for who he truly is, a special creature made for special relating. It should be stressed that the Hebrew here for 'helper' or 'companion' is also used of Yahweh himself in the OT as a helper of God's people, so subordination is *not* implied in the use of that term here.[7] As Arnold notes, Adam's 'at last' suggests he has been looking among the animals for a mate, and not finding one until Eve appears on the scene.[8]

Various commentators see here the celebration of the first marriage. God brings the woman to the man. Verse 24 suggests this and also indicates that marriage should lead to the one-flesh union, not be preceded by it. Intercourse was the joyous climax of marital sharing, not a result of the Fall, and certainly not the content of the knowledge of good and evil. It was something that would be shared without shame. Adam and Eve were able to engage in this total sharing without shame or self-consciousness or loss of identity, unlike fallen creatures. All seems well, until we turn the page and learn of human infidelity.

---

7   See Arnold 2008, 60.
8   Arnold 2008, 60.

Let us be very clear about chapter 3. The problem of theodicy, the problem of where evil came from, is *not given any full answer here*. This chapter is not about the origin of evil, but about the original sin, its nature and circumstances. We are not told that the snake is Satan; that notion first occurs in later Jewish literature (cf. Wisdom of Solomon 2.23–24; Sirach 21.2; *4 Maccabees* 18.8; cf. Revelation 1.9; 20.2). The connection is a conclusion one draws in the light of later and developing revelation. The snake is called crafty or shrewd (*arum*), surely a wordplay on the description of humans as naked in the immediately preceding verse (*arrumim*). The nudes have been duped by the shrewd, and in their desire to be shrewd they discovered the naked facts about themselves and become prudes, hence the need for clothing.[9] The first question the snake asks the woman, appearing to seek information but trying to plant a seed of doubt, is: 'Did God really say you cannot eat of any tree of the garden?' Of course, the answer to this is no, with one exception. The woman's first reply is a case of stretching the truth or exaggerating it. She adds to the divine prohibition about the fruit that '*we must not touch it or we will die*'. Problems are already brewing here. We are not told that the fruit in question is an apple.[10] Next, we have the frontal attack on God's word.

The serpent pretends to know better than the woman or even than God. This is typical arrogance from the powers of darkness. The serpent insinuates that God is jealously guarding his position as deity. The snake is suggesting that there is no metaphysical difference between God and humanity; it is just that God knows more. The text may perhaps be translated, 'will be like gods', since the word for god is the plural *elohim* here. In the context of Genesis, however, *elohim* is normally used of the one true God, so it should be taken to mean this here. The woman must choose whether to base her decisions about what is best and true on her own judgement or on God's revealed will.

This is still humanity's dilemma. It is clear that the woman is free to choose to resist the temptation and obey God. But her eyes are already opened to the possibilities of sin, taking the fruit. It offers physical satisfaction as food; it has aesthetic appeal, being pleasing to the eye. But the best

---

9 This modifies the playful way Arnold (2008, 63) renders the storyline here, following Wenham 2014, 72.

10 Here is where basing a translation on the Latin text got various English translators into trouble. One of the Latin words for apple is *malum*, which not incidentally is also the word for bad, or even evil. If this is about a fruit that conveys the knowledge of good and evil, by rendering the original Hebrew or Greek as *malum* it was possible to conclude that the author was not merely talking about just any bad or enticing fruit, but was talking about a bad apple.

part is that it is desirable for wisdom. Some scholars have suggested that this event is being alluded to in 1 John 2.16 where we hear that 'everything in the world – the lust of the flesh, the lust of the eyes, and the pride of life – comes not from the Father but from the world' (NIV). More pertinent are the references to Eve in the NT (in 2 Corinthians and 1 Timothy) where she is said to have been deceived. Deception is what happens to someone who is not properly instructed or knowledgeable in the first place, and a close reading of Genesis shows that it was Adam alone who was given the single commandment, and apparently the responsibility to correctly inform Eve. This perhaps explains why later commentators, such as Paul in Romans 5.12–21 and Romans 7.7–13, put the blame for the Fall clearly on the shoulders of Adam rather than Eve. This is not mere patriarchal thinking; it comes from a close reading of Genesis. And indeed, the whole argument in 1 Timothy 2.8–15 depends on the assumption that Eve was not properly instructed, like the high-status women in Ephesus, and was prone to deception. The story goes on to show how the curse was reversed in Mary through 'the childbearing', which could only happen because of her willing acceptance – 'be it unto me as you have said; I am the hand-maiden of the Lord.' The story of Creation and Fall is what helps one make sense of these later uses of the story in the NT.

Adam is the silent partner to Eve's sin. First, he commits a sin of omission. If he was with her, why did he not do something to prevent this? Second, he commits a sin of commission, for he too eats. Their eyes were indeed opened, but what they saw was not their divinity, but the bare facts about their very frail humanity. The fig leaves are a pathetic attempt to hide their most obvious and vulnerable parts that indicate their full humanity. The issue here is not mere nudity, but rather shameful naked-ness, a combination of desire, self-knowledge, disobedience. Our attempt to cover up our nakedness, never mind our sins, is always inadequate and pathetic. Next, we are told that the couple heard the sound of God coming after them (not the sound of his voice, as some have translated). Their response is fright and flight. Such is always the response of sinful human beings fearful of judgement, not wishing to be revealed or seen for what they are. God does not at this point take a confrontational approach. He simply says, 'Where are you?' The creatures God has made personally and specially and given special treatment to are now running from their Maker. It is only sinful humankind who has something to fear from God. Shame is the proper response to sin, but sin also leads to rationalizing.

When humanity is confronted with its sin, rebel humans blame God or other humans. The man blames God and the woman ('this woman whom *you* gave me'), and the woman blames the snake. The human art of passing the buck has been inaugurated. God judges these three in reverse order, starting with the source of the trouble, the snake, then the first perpetrator of the sin, and finally the accomplice. Genesis 3.15 suggests that world history will be an ongoing enmity and battle between humanity and the powers of darkness.

Notice, however, that even in judgement there is mercy, because the seed of the woman will crush the head of evil and its source. This is poetic language and conjures up the image of evil snapping at our heels. Some have seen here the first proclamation of the gospel remedy for sin.

Notice also the mercy of God: he does not curse the man or the woman, but gives them 'labour pains' in their primary life-tasks – the man in working the ground, the woman in childbearing. The woman's punishment is not her desire for her husband, which is not bad, but rather it is that her sinful man will try to take advantage of her and dominate her. The Greek OT has the sense of it right here: 'your desire will be for your man and he will lord it over/dominate you.'

Interestingly, what we have here is a case of poetic justice, literally, for the sentence here is in poetic form.[11] For the man, his work becomes toilsome: the ground will produce not just good fruit, but also thorns and thistles. Thus, work indeed becomes wearying, contributing to the shortening of the life span. In any event, implied is the ongoing of human life. Though humans will die, they will not completely die out. Also, probably implied in God's judgement is that *adam* is dirt (*adamah*) and will return to dust (die), but we are not told whether this involves more than physical death. Painful death, spiritual decay and deterioration, or eternal death may be implied. And then there is the matter of ongoing struggle – there is wordplay in the verdict on the snake as well – 'you will snap [*tensuppenu*] at his heel; he will crush [*yesupeka*] your head.' Advantage humans. While Judaism saw in 3.15 messianic hope for victory over Satan, the later Church Fathers Justin and Irenaeus, taking *zera* (seed) to refer to an individual and therefore not a collective noun, saw this verse as a sort of *protoevangelium* – a foreshadowing of the victory of Christ over Satan (cf. Romans 16.20). *It should be clear that the curse on Eve is descriptive of the effects of sin, not prescriptive of how God intends male–female relationships to be.*

---

11 Westermann (1994, 257) notes how verdicts were expected to be in poetry.

The exegesis of Jesus and Paul

The discussion of Jesus' views on marriage and singleness is always fraught with peril these days, not least because large segments of the Western world, and certain segments of the Church, are busily trying to redefine what marriage means, or at least who are the proper persons who should be allowed to get married. But first we should say something about Jesus' hermeneutics if we are to understand his approach to the Genesis material, bearing in mind that no one in early Judaism before Jesus seems to be taking the position he does – namely no divorce of those whom God has joined together.

In his discussion of the issue of marriage in Mark 10 and Matthew 19 Jesus interjects a remark as to 'why' exactly Moses gave the teaching he did, allowing divorce. He calls it '*sklerokardia*', the spiritual hardening of the arteries, or as we more conventionally call it, 'hardness of heart'. Now the importance of this is not just that God is aware of our spiritual condition, but that God gave his instructions with this condition in mind. And Jesus is saying that *now that the kingdom is breaking into the human situation those rules don't apply any more.* He is suggesting that there was an original creation-order intention of God when it comes to marriage. But apparently, Jesus thinks that the coming of the kingdom involves all kinds of other new arrangements as well – for example, arrangements in which disciples foreswear violence altogether, and promise to love enemies and pray for those who persecute them.

And this leads to the following point. If God, in his graciousness, condescends to teach us in ways and at the level where we can receive his teaching, and if there is a major difference between what is the case once Jesus and the Spirit have come and what was the case before those two things happened, when it comes to the human ability to receive, believe and live by God's always-intended highest and best for his people, then this changes entirely how we should view ever so many things in the OT, including marriage, divorce and singleness.

Take for example the famous *lex talionis* – 'an eye for an eye, a hand for a hand . . . a life for a life'. This was God's attempt to limit, not *license*, revenge taking. *God knew we would be doing it anyway, and so what he is saying is 'Only an eye for an eye, only a hand for a hand . . . ' and so on.* In other words, there are all sorts of teachings in the OT that take into account not only the lack of the indwelling Spirit which changes the human heart, but the presence of hardness of heart in God's people. Now once this basic principle – announced by Jesus, and then implemented by Paul and James

274

and Peter – is understood, it really will revolutionize the way one reads so many things in the OT. Take for example Levitical law, including laws about stoning children, and other harsh decrees. We should never take such statements as a clear revelation of either God's divine character or his highest and best will for his people. We should take them as God's attempt to limit the harm and sin and missteps his people may take. That's the way the Ten Commandments functioned by and large as well. And this is all the more the case when we are dealing with the *harem* or holy war in Joshua and Judges. This is hardly God's preferred course of action for his people to take. Think about it for a minute. Do we really believe that God couldn't have just got all of the strangers out of the land by various means other than through the *harem* or human warfare? Of course he could have done so.

What we see throughout much of the early part of the Old Testament is God's attempt to deal with his fallen and sinful people, who behave very much like other Ancient Near Eastern peoples, sometimes quite barbarically. The point is that God is trying to limit their vengeance, limit their propensity to divorce, limit their bad behaviour in general – hence the Mosaic laws of various sorts. But when Messiah comes, and the kingdom with him, new occasions teach new duties. This is not to say that there is not a recapitulation of some essential Old Testament teaching by Jesus and the early Christians, which we find in the New Testament. There is. It is the positive teaching God gave that was not merely an attempt to restrain ancient sin. Teaching like 'Love the Lord your God with all your heart, and neighbour as self . . .' and so on.

I could say a good deal more on this subject, but here will simply draw three conclusions: (1) the only safe and appropriate way for Christians to read the Old Testament and draw conclusions about God's will and character is to read it the way that Jesus and his followers did – with the eyes of Christ, and in the light of the coming of the kingdom and the Spirit; (2) only those teachings in the Old Testament that are reiterated and reaffirmed in the New Testament or are a legitimate extension of something said in the new covenant are binding on Christians; (3) one should never mistake God's attempts to deal with God's people where they are in their spiritual progress in the Old Testament as the clearest revelation of the character and will of God for any of his peoples since Jesus and the Spirit have come. A Christian reading of the Old Testament must be normed and guided by the sort of principles we find in the New Testament on the lips of Jesus and others. So what about marriage and divorce, and singleness in the teaching of Jesus?

Mark 10: the appeal to the beginning

It is often overlooked in an age where it is assumed that the newest is the truest and the latest is the greatest, that ancient societies, including that of early Judaism, thought the opposite was the case. For example, unless a religion or a law or a custom had ancient roots it was considered suspect. This is why, for instance, Josephus not only named one of his works *Antiquities* but went out of his way to show just how ancient the Jewish religion really was, even suggesting that Greek philosophy and key ideas were indebted to Moses! In that sort of context, an appeal to antiquity, or even the 'beginning' of human civilization, was considered a strong appeal indeed, and quite persuasive from a rhetorical point of view. This helps us understand the discussion of Jesus with his fellow Jews in Mark 10, and it is in order to quote the text here.

> Some Pharisees came, and to test him they asked, 'Is it lawful for a man to divorce his wife?' He answered them, 'What did Moses command you?' They said, 'Moses allowed a man to write a certificate of dismissal and to divorce her.' But Jesus said to them, 'Because of your hardness of heart he wrote this commandment for you. But from the beginning of creation, "God made them male and female." For this reason a man shall leave his father and mother and be joined to his wife, and the two shall become one flesh. So they are no longer two, but one flesh. Therefore what God has joined together, let no one separate.'
>
> Then in the house the disciples asked him again about this matter. He said to them, 'Whoever divorces his wife and marries another commits adultery against her; and if she divorces her husband and marries another, she commits adultery.'
>
> (Mark 10.2–12)

The essence of this teaching is reiterated by Paul in 1 Corinthians 7.10–11 when Paul affirms that Jesus said, 'No divorce.' Clearly, the Markan form of this discussion seems likely to be closer to the original than that found in Matthew 19. The prohibition of divorce seems to be unprecedented in early Judaism before Jesus offers it. Our interest, however, lies primarily in Jesus' use of the Genesis tradition. There is some justice in E. Schüssler Fiorenza's remark that

> divorce is necessary because of the male's hardness of heart [i.e. in this setting only men could divorce], that is because of men's patriarchal mind-set and reality. However, Jesus insists, God did not intend patriarchy, but created persons as male and female human beings. It is not woman who is given into the power of man in order to continue 'his' house and family line,

but it is man who shall sever connections with his own patriarchal family and 'the two shall become one *sarx*.'[12]

She is on the right track here, but there is more to say.

Jesus is raising the question of what force laws should have, now that the kingdom/divine saving activity is breaking into their midst, laws that were originally written due to the hardness of human hearts, that is as a concession to human fallenness which has affected everything since the time of Adam and Eve. Jesus seems prepared to appeal to God's original creation intentions and design for marriage over against the later rulings of Deuteronomy 24.1–4 which reflect the sinful human condition. Jesus is paraphrasing several verses here, including Genesis 1.27, 5.2 and 2.24 in Mark 10.6–7. It is probably correct to say that the form of the Genesis text here is closest to the LXX; in fact Evans claims that the LXX of Genesis 1.27 is followed verbatim here.[13] For example, the quote from Genesis 2.24 follows the LXX which has the phrase 'the two' as the subject of the end of 2.24 in Mark 10.8a. The MT lacks any designation for 'the two' here.[14]

Mark's Jesus says that God made the human race male and female, and because of this duality, a man will *leave* his mother and father and *cleave* to his wife. In that context, the two will become 'one flesh' or share a 'one flesh' union (v. 8). The implication seems to be that the one-flesh union is more constitutive of their being than their uniqueness. Jesus takes the following for granted: (1) there was a beginning to the human race, and it involved God making human beings male and female; (2) part of the intent and purpose of that was so that marriage and the fulfilment of the creation command 'Be fruitful and multiply' could be accomplished; (3) the appeal to something more ancient, near the beginning, has a higher and prior authority than something later like Deuteronomy 24, and in particular the appeal to God's pre-fallen design and plan trumps later laws given due to the fallen condition of humanity, which involves hardness

---

12 Schüssler Fiorenza 1985, 143.
13 Evans 2012, 472.
14 See Ahearne-Kroll 2012, 30, and the discussion in Evans 2012, 472–3. Evans goes on to discuss the fact that the Hebrew of the Genesis text does not explicitly affirm monogamy, and in fact polygamy was practised by Jews right through the whole biblical era, when it could be afforded. Jesus' teaching, then, would have been at odds with the ancestral traditions on this, as well as on the divorce issue. If marrying a second woman while the first one is alive amounts to adultery and a violation of the one-flesh union with the first wife, then it is a combination of Jesus' ideas that leads to the affirmation of monogamy. Contrast Josephus who says that polygamy, not monogamy, was the ancestral custom (*Ant.* 17.14), and he does not condemn it. In fact it was not until the eleventh century that polygamy was banned by Jewish authorities. See Instone-Brewer 2000.

of heart, in particular that of the men who had the power of divorce in a patriarchal society, as Deuteronomy 24 suggests. Stephen Ahearne-Kroll comments:

> Mark's Jesus uses the double quotation of Genesis 1.27 and 2.24 to express the divine intention for male and female, thus he argues for the principle of monogamy as in line with the divine intention. This principle allows Jesus not only to forbid divorce but to equate it with adultery when his disciples ask him in private to elaborate on his teaching about divorce (Mark 10.10–12).[15]

Notice that the use of Genesis 2.24 in Ephesians 5.31 quotes the portion in regard to the 'one flesh union' between a man and woman, in the context of making an argument about marriage, but in 1 Corinthians 6.16 surprisingly Paul quotes this verse and applies it to the sexual relationship a man might have with a prostitute, an inappropriate relationship which conflicts with and is contrasted with being 'one spirit' with the Lord. Clearly, Paul knows Genesis 2.24 is about marriage, but equally clearly, he thinks that other kinds of one-flesh unions are possible and should be avoided if one is a Christian.

What, then, are the exception clauses about in Matthew 5.32 and 19.9? They have to do with *porneia*, not *moixeia*, which is to say they have to do with something other than adultery or marital unfaithfulness. The latter Greek word is the term for this and it is used in the phrase where Jesus reiterates and intensifies the Mosaic commandment against adultery. But that is not the subject in the exception clauses; their subject is *porneia*, which has three possible meanings.

1 Its root meaning is prostitution, as a *porne* is a prostitute in the ancient world, and it is of course where we got the word 'pornography' from.
2 It can also refer to an especially heinous sin, namely incest, and probably this is exactly what it refers to in the exception clauses in Matthew 5.32 and 19.9. It will be remembered that Jesus' cousin John lost his head for criticizing the incestuous marriage between Herod Antipas and Herodias, his brother's wife. If Jesus is likewise criticizing this sort of 'alternative' approach to marriage, then what is being said is that marriage in God's eyes only involves those whom God can and does bring together – namely a man and a woman who are previously unrelated. An incestuous relationship is not a proper marriage to start with. Period. It should not be called a marriage, and it should be ended promptly.

[15] Ahearne-Kroll 2012, 34.

3 *Porneia* can also refer to a panoply of different sexual sins when used
   in a general sense, but this sense makes no sense of Matthew 19, for
   the reaction of the disciples to Jesus' teaching is 'If that's the way it is
   between a man and a woman, better not to marry.' There is no way
   they would have reacted in this manner if Jesus had been much more
   tolerant than Moses on the issue of divorce. It will be remembered
   that Deuteronomy 24 said divorce was allowed on grounds of *erwat
   dabar*, 'some unseemly thing' the wife had done. The rabbis interpreted
   this variously to mean anything ranging from adultery to burning the
   mazot.

Marriage was a male privilege in that world, and it was arranged in
advance. It was not about modern Western notions of romance and
courtship. Women in most settings could not divorce, though they could
precipitate a divorce in some cases. In other words, Jesus is stricter in
regard to both marriage and divorce than Moses, hence the question of his
interlocutors: 'Why did Moses permit/command divorce?'

Jesus' ruling not only provides more security for women in marriage
by ruling out divorce and so taking away a male privilege, but also shows
that now, as the kingdom comes, the original creation-order design
is being reinstituted. Moses only 'permitted' divorce due to the hardness of men's hearts; he did not command it. Jesus is assuming that the
'no divorce' ruling applies to believing couples 'whom God has joined
together'. He is not commenting on what we would call secular marriage
or on relationships that violate other commandments of God (such as
the incestuous marriage between Herod Antipas and Herodias, his own
brother's (former) wife).[16]

The undergirding assumption of Jesus, based on his reflection on
Genesis 1—2, is that God in creation made two distinct but complementary or compatible human genders. God then also brought them together
in marriage. Anyone who seeks to divide such a couple is attacking both
the one-flesh union of the couple and also the Creator. The Creator and
the creation order undergird marriage. There can be little doubt that Jesus
believed in an original couple, Adam and Eve, 'in the beginning', and not
surprisingly, Paul is in complete agreement with this, and knows of Jesus'

---

16 My former doctoral student Dr Susann Liubinskas rightly reminded me that God also guides
   non-Christian people to get married in various cases, for instance devout Jews, and others as
   well. Obviously, the case of Adam and Eve, as a paradigm, does not involve two Christians
   being joined together in Christ.

teaching on marriage and divorce. We will turn to his use of the Genesis tradition shortly.[17]

I stress that Jesus speaks of 'those whom God joins together'. He does not speak of those who join themselves together, or who have been joined together by benefit of clergy or the Church. Ancient marriage in his day didn't involve ceremonies in a church with the aid of clergy, nor did it involve a certification by the state. None of that makes a marriage a marriage in Jesus' eyes. God joining two people together, as he did with Adam and Eve, on the other hand, does create a marital bond, leading to a one-flesh union, the creation of a God-blessed couple. Let me be clear that not all persons married in a church with benefit of clergy would be seen as married in the eyes of the Lord by Jesus. And furthermore, the dissolving of such marriages that are not God-initiated would not qualify as divorce in Jesus' teaching. Nowadays people are all the time coupling and joining themselves together, even in the Church, quite apart from God's will or leading. The Church should never have become a hatching, matching and dispatching bureau for the general public. Holy matrimony requires not only genuinely Christian participants if it is to be a Christian marriage; it also requires God's leading and more.

Jesus also provides in Matthew 19 an alternative which he himself chose – remaining single, a eunuch, for the sake of the kingdom. The word 'eunuch' had a quite clear meaning in those days – a person not sexually active, indeed in the literal sense not sexually capable. The setting up of singleness for the kingdom was a revolutionary teaching in a Jewish world where it was assumed that every able-bodied man and woman should fulfil the creation-order mandate to 'be fruitful and multiply'. 'Not so,' says Jesus, and 'Not so,' says Paul as well. Marriage is an earthly institution for our earthly good, and the bond is dissolved in death as Romans 7 says – the wife is free from the law of the husband when he dies. She can remarry or she can, preferably, says Paul, remain single.[18] For women following Jesus, being single meant they did not have to perform wifely or many other domestic duties. They could be free to serve the Lord without distraction, without family responsibilities. This is not to say any of those duties are in any way bad. It is to say that Jesus offered the possibilities of some new roles for women who were not gifted and graced for marriage.

Paul, in reflecting on all this, says that marriage, like singleness in the Lord, requires a *charisma*. A specific grace gift. In the kingdom, marriage

---

17 For much more on all this see Witherington 2001, 274–8, and also Witherington 1984.
18 See my commentaries on 1 Corinthians, Matthew, Mark.

is no longer viewed as the normal course of life; it is viewed as 'for those to whom it is given' by God. Everything falls under the aegis of God's eschatological will, as revealed by Jesus and his later followers like Paul. Marriage becomes a blessed option for God's people, not an obligation.

It is a travesty and a tragedy that the Church, including the conservative Protestant Church, still hasn't got the memo. I once attended a church that had an Adult Sunday School class named 'Pairs and Spares' – as if single people were like spare tyres that needed at some point to be hitched to another one. Jesus and Paul would have been very upset with this view of Christian singleness. What would happen if the Church today taught that either being married or being single in the Lord is an equally good calling of God, and requires equal grace and aid from God? What would happen if we stopped pressuring our children into marriage, some of whom are not cut out for marriage? One thing that would happen is we would not continue to have as high a divorce rate within the Church as in the culture in general. But I digress. Let us look more closely at Paul's source argument in 1 Corinthians 11.

1 Corinthians 11: the appeal to the beginning

Paul's discussion of why women should wear head-coverings includes an argument from the creation of humanity. The clearest allusion is of course to Genesis 2.22–23 in 1 Corinthians 11.8.[19] Paul stresses that the first woman was taken out of the first man (*gynē ex andros*) and he also says she was created *dia ton andra*; while some have translated this 'for the sake of the man', or better 'because of the man', and taken this to mean that that implies the subordination of the woman to the man, since nothing is said about subordination in the Genesis 2 account it is far more likely that Paul means that since 'it was not good for the man to be alone' the woman was created to compensate for the man's need to have a companion, and the term translated 'companion' does not mean a subordinate. It means a suitable companion.[20] Nothing is said in Genesis 2 about a woman's need for a companion. Indeed, she is depicted as the crown of creation, after which God stopped creating and declared it all 'very good'.

David Lincicum suggests that Paul's reading of Genesis 2 controls the way he reads Genesis 1 in 1 Corinthians 11.7 where he speaks of the man being the image and glory of God, while the woman is said to be

---

[19] See Lincicum 2012, 102.
[20] It is right to note the difference of meaning between *dia* with the genitive and *dia* with the accusative. The meaning in one case is 'on account of' and in the other case is instrumental, meaning 'through'. Paul uses it both ways in this passage.

the glory of man. Lincicum assumes that Paul has read Genesis 1 retrospectively when it speaks of humankind being created in God's image, meaning that Adam was created that way, *not Eve*. This, however, is hardly plausible since not only does the Genesis 1.27 passage say that the image involves both male and female, but elsewhere Paul himself uses that very phrase, *arsen kai thēly*, from Genesis 1.27 LXX, to speak of what is now different in the context of Christ (Galatians 3.28). Furthermore, 1 Corinthians 11 goes on to state in verse 12 that ever since the first creation of woman out of man, the process has been reversed such that *ho anēr dia tēs gynaikos*, and here the *dia* must surely mean 'through', not 'because of'.

In any case, the real function of the argument here is to establish several key points: (1) women so long as they wear the head-covering may pray and prophesy in worship; (2) since in worship only God's glory should be evident, and since a woman's hair is her glory and she is the glory of man, *that* human 'glory' should be hidden under a head-covering, which head-covering can also double as (3) a sign of her authority to speak in worship, and finally (4) 'because of the angels' indicates that they are the guardians of the proper order of creation and of worship, and the head-covering preserves the affirmation of the male–female distinction while at the same time affirming a woman's right to speak in worship. It is 'authority' down from or on her head, which all can see, rather like a clergy person wearing a collar today.[21]

Interestingly the NA[27] but *not* the NA[28] suggests an allusion to Genesis 3.16 in 1 Corinthians 11.3, which would mean that Paul was arguing for hierarchy based on the Fall and the curse on Eve, but this is unlikely on several grounds: (1) the argument about the *kephalē* ('head') is a positive one, not a negative one, including a statement about God being the *kephalē* of Christ, and (2) probably the argument here is about source, not hierarchy, which is the other meaning of *kephalē*. There is a play on several meanings of this word in this passage, including the literal anatomical meaning of it.[22] But let's probe a little further and deeper. We should quote the context at this juncture:

> For a man ought not to have his head covered, since he is the image and reflection of God; but woman is the reflection of man. Indeed, man was not made from woman, but woman from man. Neither was man created for the sake of woman, but woman for the sake of man. For this reason a

---

21 On other aspects of this argument, see Witherington 2017, 361–70.
22 Witherington 2017, 361–70.

woman ought to have a symbol of authority on her head, because of the angels. Nevertheless, in the Lord woman is not independent of man or man independent of woman. For just as woman came from man, so man comes through woman; but all things come from God.

(1 Corinthians 11.7–12)

This is in the first instance a discussion about source, not headship – the Father is the source of the Son; the Son, the co-creator with God, depicted as fulfilling the role of personified Wisdom in 1 Corinthians 10—11, is the source of man; and Adam is the source of the woman, Eve.[23] For Paul human duality, maleness and femaleness, is good and to be celebrated, just as the interdependence of male and female is to be appreciated. Maleness and femaleness are part of the good order of creation, and that order is reaffirmed in the new creation.[24]

It is a mistake in interpretation to simply concentrate on verses 8–10 and ignore the '*nevertheless*' which introduces verse 11. So, Paul affirms that woman comes from man (again Genesis 2.4ff.) and that she was created for the man because 'it was not good for the man to be alone'. Man had a need that only the woman could meet if there was to be a 'one-flesh union' that fulfils the creation-order mandate about multiplying. Verse 10 could be taken as a reason for what is said in verse 9, but more likely the 'for this reason' phrase is completed by the phrase at the end of that sense unit, 'because of the angels'.

In between, Paul says woman should have a sign of authority/power on her head, a sign of authorization from above, so she may pray and prophesy in worship. This seems to be especially because there were some Jewish men in the worship service who might expect women to simply be silent during worship. Verse 11 then introduces how things are 'in the Lord'; namely men and women are interdependent, not least because though Eve came from Adam, ever since then the reverse has been the case: all men have come forth from women, and in any case, since this is a source argument, the thing that really matters is that all things come from God. Human beings are not the ultimate source of their own exist-ence, identity, or authority and power. In short, from start to finish the argument's appeal is based on an *ad fontes* or source assumption, the kind of argument apt to carry weight in a culture where the earlier or older something was, the more likely it was assumed to be true, time-tested and reliable, especially when it came to matters of religion and philosophy. The

---

23 Witherington 2017, 361–70.
24 See Witherington 1996, 232–7.

argument requires that the hearer or reader go back to the source texts, to understand the source arguments, in this case Genesis 1—3.

What one sees in the argument in 1 Corinthians 11 is Paul at both his principial and pragmatic best. He, as a good pastor, must start with his people where he finds them. On the one hand his audience is enmeshed in a patriarchal world and social situation, a world in which women's roles in worship, especially in a Jewish but also to some extent in a Greco-Roman context, were limited in comparison to men's roles. Paul knows this, and knows he must provide an *extra rationale* for women praying and prophesying in a mixed congregation of men and women, Jews and Gentiles. Women needed extra authorization, which he is providing here, with a playful argument based on the various meanings of the term *kephalē*, including its literal meaning. Women need to wear a head-covering, says Paul, as a sign of authority to speak, but also because of the angels. Why a head-covering and not something else, say a veil? Paul believes all authority in the Church comes from above, and so a head-covering is a symbol of authority *from above*, not unlike a clerical collar today, but that is not all. Paul is concerned that only God's glory be manifested in Christian worship, and since he has said a woman's hair is her glory, that glory should not be evidenced in worship. But there is a practical side to Paul's argument as well, not just a theological rationale.

One needs to remember that especially high-status women often wore elaborate hairdos in public, even including putting gems and other reflective materials in their hair to draw attention to themselves. This is probably what Paul is objecting to in 1 Timothy 2, but that is a story for another time. Think practically for a moment. If a woman came into the evening worship service with such a coiffure, and we are talking about a room in a villa with lots of lamps lit, she would appear to be a walking disco ball, a distraction. So Paul says, 'Cover it up.' Only God's glory, not human glory, should be evident in worship; but again, what about those angels? While it is not impossible this is a reference to lustful angels, as in Genesis 6.1–4, more likely Paul is thinking along the lines of the fact that angels in early Judaism were seen as the guardians and protectors of worship, because they were the guardians both of the creation order and of God's people. If only God's glory should be evident in true worship, and worship is where the creation order should be obvious and manifested – all creatures great and small bowing down and glorifying the one true God – then head-coverings are necessary to preserve the creation order, and this brings us to the last point.

The argument in 1 Corinthians 11 which does indeed empower women to speak inspired speech in worship is also an argument that says the goodness of the differences between men and women should be manifest in worship, hence the head-covering as well. Woman is the crown of creation according to Genesis, but in worship we cast down our crowns before the throne of God. Rather than being a crown, the apex and climax of creation, submission to God, and his creation order, which does not mean submission to men, is required. Here then is an argument for equality of roles in Christ, and at the very same time gender differences are being celebrated, even in worship. Only in a modern or postmodern context would we see Paul as simply repristinizing patriarchy here, when in fact he was celebrating the goodness of creational differences, and also our sameness in being in the image of God, and equally able to serve our God. These things must be held in tension, not set at odds with one another.

Conclusion

Creation, Fall and Redemption are three crucial Christian doctrines well grounded in the biblical text. They affect the way we view the roles of men and women, as they should do, both their roles in the physical family and in the family of faith. Part of our problem of course is that as biblical illiteracy increases, we adopt alternative, indeed unbiblical, models about the equality of men and women, about the nature of marriage, about who should get married and what counts as divorce. And much of the problem comes from a profound misreading of Genesis 2—3, the texts about sources and the consequences of the Fall. Jesus tells us that we should go back to the creation narrative, behind the later Mosaic allowances of divorce, and re-envisage the roles of men and women as God originally intended them, including their roles in both the physical family and the Church.

If we were to properly do so, we would realize that maleness and femaleness is a good thing, that it is an inherent part of who we are by creation. We would also realize that in the new creation we do not cease to be males and females, but what is the case is that in Christ there is no longer the necessity of females being joined to males in order to be full participants in God's perfect will for their lives. This is what no 'male *and* female' means in Galatians 3.28. The Genesis mandate to be fruitful and multiply becomes in Christ a good and godly option, but one no longer required by God of his people. Were it still a mandate, Jesus and Paul violated it. The new creation is, after all, a genuinely new creation, in which creation is redeemed and restored to its original purpose, not supplanted or left behind by new creation and resurrection.

The source of our problems is in large measure our problems with our sources, including texts like Genesis 2—3, 1 Corinthians 11 and Matthew 19 / Mark 10. But it need not be so. Better exegesis and hermeneutics, not the jettisoning of certain texts which give us problems (notice I did not call them 'problem texts'), is the way forward.

Bibliography

Ahearne-Kroll, S. P. (2012). 'Genesis in Mark's Gospel.' In *Genesis in the New Testament*, edited by Maartin J. J. Menken and Steve Moyise, 27–41. London: Bloomsbury/T&T Clark, 2012.

Arnold, B. T. (2008). *Genesis*. New Cambridge Bible Commentary. Cambridge: Cambridge University Press.

Evans, Craig A. (2012). 'Genesis in the New Testament.' In *The Book of Genesis: Composition, Reception, and Interpretation*, edited by Craig A. Evans, Joel N. Lohr and David L. Petersen, 469–94. Leiden: Brill.

Instone-Brewer, D. (2000). 'Jesus' Old Testament Basis for Monogamy.' In *The Old Testament in the New Testament: Essays in Honour of J. L. North*, edited by S. Moyise, 75–104. Sheffield: Sheffield Academic Press.

Kidner, Derek (1982). *Genesis*. Tyndale Old Testament Commentaries. Downers Grove, IL: IVP.

Lincicum, David (2012). 'Genesis in Paul.' In *Genesis in the New Testament*, edited by Maartin J. J. Menken and Steve Moyise, 99–116. London: Bloomsbury/T&T Clark.

Schüssler Fiorenza, Elisabeth (1985). *In Memory of Her: A Feminist Theological Reconstruction of Christian Origins*. New York, NY: Crossroad, 1985.

Wenham, G. (2014). *Genesis 1–15*. Word Biblical Commentary. Reprint. Grand Rapids, MI: Zondervan.

Westermann, Claus (1994). *Genesis 1–11: A Continental Commentary*. Minneapolis, MN: Augsburg.

Witherington III, Ben (1984). *Women in the Ministry of Jesus*. Cambridge: Cambridge University Press.

—— (1996). *Conflict and Community in Corinth: A Socio-Rhetorical Commentary on 1 and 2 Corinthians*. Grand Rapids, MI: Eerdmans.

—— (2001). *The Gospel of Mark: A Socio-Rhetorical Commentary*. Grand Rapids, MI: Eerdmans.

—— (2006). *Matthew*. Smyth & Helwys Bible Commentary. Macon, GA: Smyth & Helwys Pub.

—— (2007). *The Letters to Philemon, the Colossians and the Ephesians: A Socio-Rhetorical Commentary on the Captivity Epistles*. Grand Rapids, MI: Eerdmans.

—— (2017). *Isaiah Old and New: Exegesis, Intertextuality, and Hermeneutics*. Minneapolis, MN: Fortress.

Sex, Scripture and improvisation

BRIAN J. WALSH

Introduction

The conversation would sometimes go like this.

'Have you ever heard of N. T. Wright?' a student would ask.

'Why yes,' I would reply, 'I've heard of him', not letting on that Tom has been one of my closest friends for more than three decades.

'Well, N. T. Wright saved my faith.'

When I would enquire about how Wright's work had had such an impact on this young adult, the response would have something to do with being released from Evangelical individualism, and liberated from an otherworldly piety. Then, somewhere in the conversation, my new young friend would invariably say something about being 'given back' the Bible. Not only had the Bible been set free from the shackles of pietist dualism, but Wright's model of the Bible as an unfinished drama had made the Scriptures alive, dynamic and relevant in this person's life in radically new ways.

After such a conversation, there would be an email from me to Tom. I would want to share with my friend how his work had saved someone's faith. This was the pastoral and evangelistic heart of his whole project. This young person's life outweighed by an infinite degree all of the accolades, awards and honorary degrees that Tom had been receiving. I would try to write a message to my friend that rejoiced in the rich fruit that his work was bearing in real people's lives, while reminding him that *this* is what it was really all about. All of Tom's publishing and academic success is for the sake of real people making life-and-death decisions to follow Jesus, or not.

Jeremy Begbie has also noted that Wright's model of biblical authority, and specifically the proposal that the Church is called to faithful improvisation within an unfinished drama, has had a deep resonance within what has been called the 'emergent church' movement. Wright's Shakespearean analogy is so well known that it hardly bears rehearsing, but I do so briefly. Wright suggests that biblical authority is like an unfinished five-act drama.

Creation is Act 1. The 'Fall' is Act 2 wherein the most fundamental plot tension is introduced. Act 3 recounts the tortuous path to plot resolution in the story of Israel. And in Act 4 plot resolution is at hand in the life, death, resurrection and Ascension of Jesus. And while Act 5 begins with the birth of the Church at Pentecost and unfolds with the writing of the New Testament, including a profound indication of where the whole drama is going, the Church remains in Act 5, without a script to perform. This is where improvisation comes into the model. The drama is unfinished and the Church is called into an improvisatory performance that carries the story forward to its narrative goal in a way that is faithful to the preceding acts, as well as the earlier scenes of Act 5, and yet engages the changing realities in which the actors find themselves in time and place throughout history with innovation and creativity.[1]

'It is not hard to see', writes Begbie, 'how such an understanding resonates with the concerns of many in the emerging church networks, especially those keen to retain a strong sense of the authority of the scriptural text while also being aware of the need to be light-footed, engage nimbly with the social and cultural particularities in which they find themselves, and avoid imposing fixed schemes and importing grand plans.'[2] Here is where we find the student at the beginning of this paper, and so many other young adults struggling to find or sustain a vibrant Christian faith in the twenty-first century. Suspicious of fixed schemes (read: totality claims) and incredulous when faced with grand plans (read: metanarratives), there is a longing for a biblical faith that is light-footed where so much Christian faith has come across as heavy-handed, and

---

[1] Wright's model was first articulated in his 1991 article, and was then developed further in Wright 1992, 139–43; Wright, 2011. The 2011 publication is an extended version of *The Last Word*, confusingly titled *Scripture and the Authority of God* in its original UK edition. All references to *Scripture and the Authority of God* in this essay are to the 2011 US edition, which includes two chapters that were not in the earlier versions of the book. While many authors have picked up on Wright's model there have been two significant proposals to amend the schema. J. Richard Middleton and I (1995) suggested that there needed to be a clearer distinction between the Church and the eschatological resolution of the narrative, so we abandoned the Shakespearean five-act model by adding a sixth act, namely the consummation. Sylvia C. Keesmaat and I (Walsh and Keesmaat, 2004, 133–6) followed that six-act model. The second modification comes from Wells 2004. He too wanted to establish a stronger distinction between the Church and the eschaton, but managed to maintain the five-act conceit by including the 'fall' in Act 1. This also nicely places the story of Jesus at the very heart of the drama, so that the acts are 1. Creation/Fall, 2. Israel, 3. Jesus, 4. the Church, and 5. Eschaton. In this model, Act 4 takes the place of Wright's Act 5, and remains a place of faithful improvisation (Wells 2004, 51–5). There is much to recommend Wells' revision, but for our present purposes I will maintain Wright's five-act model throughout this essay.

[2] Begbie 2011, 197.

nimbly engaged where so much of their experience of the Church is disconnected at best and violently ideological at worst. It is not surprising, then, that Wright's improvisatory hermeneutic was received with great enthusiasm and hope by so many.

Of course, such a hermeneutic raises all sorts of questions. If the Church's Act 5 improvisations are to be faithful, then there needs to be some clarity about the story that is told in the first four acts and the opening scenes of Act 5 of this unfinished drama. And it is fair to say that the bulk of Wright's work has been precisely on discerning the shape of that story from creation, through the fall into sin, the covenantal story of Israel, and its climax in the story of Jesus. What is this story? How does the New Testament, especially Paul, tell this story of Jesus and, in so doing, reinterpret the story of Israel?

Further, just as our improvisations need to be faithful to these prior acts of the drama, they will also need to anticipate and direct the lived narrative of the Church (and the world) to its proper *telos* and fulfilment. But what is that? Where is this story going? While Wright suggested that we had a rather clear understanding of what the eschatological end looked like, he has, in fact, had to spend considerable energy disabusing the Church of a false, neo-Platonic eschatological vision of a heavenly destiny. Whether the story is going towards an eternal life in a heavenly realm or towards the resurrection of the dead in the new creation will have profound implications for what is considered to be faithful or unfaithful improvisations.[3] And again, Wright's understanding of resurrection and new creation have resonated deeply with the very same people who want to 'engage nimbly with the social and cultural particularities in which they find themselves'.[4] Why else would one want to engage with such social and cultural particularities if this world, this creation, has no eternal significance?

But then we need to address the question of those particularities. How do we interpret our cultural context with its own unique challenges and struggles? If we are in an unfinished drama, though accompanied and led by the Spirit of God, how do we discern where the Spirit is at work in our times, and in our neighbourhoods? And, of course, we need to acknowledge that how we read these particularities will depend upon how we understand both the broader biblical story in which we live, and our own social, economic, ecclesiastical and cultural context. Wright is a

---

3   I refer, of course, to the incredible impact of Wright 2008. A powerful companion volume to this book, which has decidedly called the Church to repent of its debilitating and unbiblical theology of heaven, is Middleton 2014.
4   Begbie 2011, 197.

white, affluent, culturally privileged, heterosexual bishop of the Church of England. None of this is said to dismiss his significant contribution, but only to situate that contribution and, yes, to provide some relativization of it as well. As Wright notes, we need to always be attuned to our own contextuality and the way it 'predisposes us to highlight some things in the Bible and quietly ignore others'.[5] The same thing needs to be said of what we see or don't see in the particularities of our contemporary socio-economic, cultural and sexual-ethical context.

So now we come to the crux of my essay. While I deeply, deeply rejoice with someone like the young adult whose testimony I recounted above, and while I think that Wright's improvisatory hermeneutic is one of his most fruitful gifts to the Church, I grieve with those who have found Wright's position on homosexuality to be heavy-handed, rather than light-footed. Rather than nimbly negotiating the liberating and redemptive force of the biblical story in relation to the particularities of following Jesus as people who identify themselves within the LGBTQ+ spectrum, his comments on homosexuality have been criticized as un-nuanced, harmful and un-pastoral.[6] You see, while there are so many in my ministry who have found a deep renewal of Christian discipleship in reading Wright, sometimes it seems that there are just as many who have felt betrayed. I have repeatedly heard the question, 'Where, in Tom Wright, is the good news for LGBTQ+ people?' And let me be clear that this too is a matter of life and death, often literally. While the student at the beginning of this essay found new life by reading Wright, everyone in the Christian LGBTQ+ community knows someone who has taken his or her own life in the struggle due to shame and condemnation that each person has experienced from within the Evangelical Church. My friend, Tom, is not responsible for these deaths. And I know that his pastoral heart grieves before such tragedy. But his published theology has not helped, nor has it brought good news and pastoral care to my LGBTQ+ friends.

Is it appropriate to address such a painful subject, such a profound disagreement, in a Festschrift? I can imagine that many would think that this is no way to celebrate such an esteemed career. I'm wagering that Tom

---

5 Wright 2011, 128. In a similar vein, Wright acknowledges that there is no such thing as a neutral, objective observer (Wright 1992, 36). I should perhaps add that I am also a white, culturally privileged, heterosexual male.

6 I will use the acronym LGBTQ+ throughout this essay while acknowledging that even these terms – lesbian, gay, bisexual, transgender, queer – are themselves in flux and debated within the queer community itself. The '+' is to leave the categorization open. From my reading, Wright has only addressed 'homosexuality' in his occasional comments on the subject.

would disagree. I write as a friend for a friend, as a pastor to a pastor. Indeed, I offer this essay as a testimony to the creative and redemptive potential of Tom's own improvisatory hermeneutic. People of faith, struggling to be faithful innovators and improvisers, prayerfully discerning the way of the Spirit at a different place in the unfinished drama, do not always agree on what faithful innovation looks like. There is nothing new about such disagreement. The New Testament is full of it. And it is part of the genius of Wright's model that it can result in very different conclusions.[7] So we begin with some reflection on the model itself and the hermeneutical implications it poses for our subject, before proceeding to more exegetical and pastoral considerations.

Improvisation revisited

Consider Wright's description of the parameters of improvisation:

> As all musicians know, improvisation does not at all mean a free-for-all where 'anything goes', but precisely a disciplined and careful listening to all the other voices around us, and a constant attention to the themes, rhythms and harmonies of the complete performance so far, the performance which we are now called to continue. At the same time, of course, it invites us, while being fully obedient to the music so far, and fully attentive to the voices around us, to explore fresh expressions, provided that will eventually lead to that ultimate resolution which appears in the New Testament as the goal, the full and complete new creation which was gloriously anticipated in Jesus' resurrection. The music so far, the voices around us, and the ultimate multi-part harmony of God's new world: these, taken together, form the parameters for appropriate improvisation in the reading of scripture and the announcement and living out of the gospel it contains.[8]

Carefully balancing the creative innovation that must characterize all improvisation with maintaining a fidelity to the story, performance or drama that has come before, Wright refers no fewer than three times to an attentive listening to the 'voices' around us while also making a threefold appeal to an attention and obedience to the performance that precedes us, together with its ultimate goal of the new creation. Appropriate improvisation is faithful to the story while being attentive and listening closely to the voices of those who are in this improvisatory moment with us.

---

7 As he notes, such an improvisatory hermeneutic 'offers quite a range of possibilities' (Wright 1992, 140). This essay is testing just how wide the range might be.
8 Wright 2011, 127.

Improvisation fails if it loses track of where the story is going and where it has come from. When that happens, the improvisors hijack the story, lose the plot and replace the story they are in with another one.[9] That's why it is so important that improvisation is not a matter of 'anything goes'. And yet improvisation also fails when the performers revert to cliché or mere repetition. Faithfulness is not a matter of repeating the lines, themes and insights of the earlier acts of the drama, but in living out of that previous story in ways that are appropriate to its unfolding at this moment and in this place. Wright makes this point forcibly when he argues that the task of the actors invited to improvise the final act of an unfinished drama 'will be to immerse themselves with full sympathy in the first four acts, but not so as merely to parrot what has already been said. *They cannot go and look up the right answers*.'[10] Faithfulness, not repetition. This is a crucial point and will be part of my critique below of Wright's position on homosexuality. Contrary to his own improvisatory hermeneutic, has Wright in fact gone to the text to 'look up the right answers', thereby reverting to *repeating* lines from the drama?

Wright sums up this hermeneutic as being 'ferociously loyal to what has gone before and cheerfully open about what must come next'.[11] This brings us back to the question of voices. It is impossible to be open to what comes next, that is, to be open to how this performance is unfolding in real time, without a careful and intense listening to the voices of those with whom we are improvising this fifth act, this redemptive jazz performance.

I suspect that Wright would agree with me that if we want to think deeply about musical improvisation then the theological authority on the subject is none other than the previously cited Jeremy Begbie. Like Wright, Begbie is also adamant that improvisation is not an undisciplined free-for-all, but a performance subject to certain constraints. The time and place of the performance, the disposition of the improvisor, and, of course, the other participants in the improvisation are all constraints. So also are musical dimensions such as melody and idioms. Begbie describes the improvisatory relationship as 'giving space' to the other through alert attentiveness, listening in patient silence, contributing to the growth of others by '"making the best" of what is received from them such that they are encouraged to continue participating'.[12] Note that this giving space to

---

9   Given the nature of the subject, the mixing of theatrical, literary and musical metaphors seems inevitable.

10   Wright 1992, 140 (italics added). Cf. Wright 2010, 186.

11   Wright 2011, 123.

12   Begbie 2000, 206.

the other is a necessary 'constraint' of improvisation. Without such giving of space, there is no improvisatory movement at all because the performance devolves into a monologue, a monopoly of one authoritative voice that need not listen to others. In such a situation the other actors walk away, or the other musicians abandon the stage and go for a drink. They haven't been listened to, their voice hasn't been welcomed and encouraged, they have been ruled out, and the improvisation has no further need for their voice.

In improvisatory theatre an actor makes an offer, whether it be a gesture, a line, a movement, and that offer is then accepted or blocked. When offers are consistently blocked the improvisation dies. Begbie notes that vibrant improvisation engages in an over-acceptance of all offers wherein each offer is received as a gift, 'something from which fruit can come'. The offer of the other is 'an inherently valuable constraint . . . from which a novelty (a counter-gift) can be generated which is consistent with the "story" of the drama, and which in turn provides further novelty'.[13]

Indeed, Begbie argues that this dynamic of accepting or blocking gift is at the very heart of the biblical story, the drama of creation:

> Humankind finds its true being in improvising on the givenness of the created world with the others who are given to us, never treating givens as something to be owned or enclosed in finality, but 'over-accepting' them in such a way that they are regarded as intrinsically interesting, and rendered more fully felicitous for a potentially enormous number of fresh melodies, harmonies and metres.[14]

For many LGBTQ+ Christians, the Church is experienced as a place that blocks their gifts and closes down space for them. Rather than graciously accepting what they have to offer, rather than making space for the improvisatory melodies that they bring, the Church has met them with censure and monologue. Quite literally, for LGBTQ+ voices are seldom allowed to participate in the study processes and synodical discussions that have shaped ecclesiastical decisions in many denominations. What if, on the other hand, using this model, we imagined the LGBTQ+ community to bring the fresh melodies and harmonies that Begbie describes? When Begbie went on to say that we are invited in the Spirit 'to be implicated in a continuing and endless "giving back" to God in joyful, ecstatic gratitude, an improvisational process which always involves giving and receiving, which can never be finished, and which is endlessly different

---

13 Begbie 2000, 251.
14 Begbie 2000, 252.

and continually unpredictable',[15] I wonder if he imagined that such redemptive improvisation could include the full-embodied participation of those in the Christian LGBTQ+ community?

In contrast to an ecstatic improvisation in the Spirit that is never finished, endlessly different and continually unpredictable, Wright's various comments on homosexuality tend to be rather predictable, no different from what the traditionalist position has been, and seemingly final. There is no improvisation going on at all. And this is because while Wright's method insists on the interplay of faithfulness and creativity, of fidelity to the story and attentive listening to the voices of others, his interpretative practice will always privilege faithfulness to the story over the creativity and listening that is required of fruitful improvisation. It is hard to discern such careful listening in Wright's views on homosexuality. Now it may be that there is no listening necessary because the voices of the LGBTQ+ community and their allies are, in Wright's estimation, simply outside the story. These are not voices to be attended to in the fifth act because they have lost the plot of the first four acts. These are not voices to be listened to in the jazz improvisation because they have no legitimate place in the band. These are voices that are received more as threat than gift, and therefore they must be blocked and not over-accepted.[16] Before arguing that these are necessary and indispensable voices in the Church's improvisation of creative fidelity at this time, however, there is another matter of hermeneutical method that needs to be addressed.

Consider these two comments. First on the matter of experience as an authority in theology:

> 'Experience' is far too slippery for the concept to stand any chance of providing a stable basis sufficient to serve as an 'authority,' unless what is meant is that, as the book of Judges wryly puts it, everyone should simply do that which is right in their own eyes. And that, of course, means that there is no authority at all.[17]

Adopting the classic Anglican view of authority as the threefold cord of Scripture, tradition and reason, experience can be given no standing

---

15 Begbie 2000, 254.

16 I simply note here that I am more concerned about the lack of any evidence that Wright's position is informed by deep and ongoing friendships with LGBTQ+ people than the fact that there is no evidence of Wright engaging with the vast array of biblical and theological scholarship on the subject. Perhaps the latter is a result of the former. Indeed, the only sources that Wright ever seems to appeal to are Hays' chapter on homosexuality (Hays 1996) and Gagnon 2001. This is not exactly a representative sample.

17 Wright 2011, 102.

as an authority for theological reflection.[18] Now compare that with this comment in defence of male–female monogamous marriage:

> There is, it seems, something very powerful about the unique bonding of a man and a woman, however much other pressures can then come to break it up. It is as though most humans know in their bones that this is, indeed, one of the foundations of wise and healthy human living. In fact, 'in their bones' may be literal fact (once we include blood, nerves, and so on as well): this may be a knowledge that literally resides in the body itself, rather than simply an idea which some people have in their heads.[19]

While this second quote is in tension with Wright's own critique of an 'essentialist' argument for something like a homosexual orientation earlier in the same book,[20] I am more struck by the language of knowing something 'in our bones' alongside Wright's insistence that experience has no authority in matters of theology and ethics. What would it mean to know something 'in our bones' if not to appeal to some sort of deep experience that is then assumed to have anthropological universality? Never mind that countless people experience serious gender dysphoria and do not know 'in their bones' the gender binary that Wright takes to be final and self-evident. Make no doubt, this is an appeal to experience, and it is contradicted by the experiences of transgender and non-binary people. Wright's binary essentialism is proclaimed with neither argument nor sensitivity to those who experience gender very differently. I can't imagine making such a statement if one ever had a close friend who was transgender or non-binary.

Now it needs to be acknowledged that if our debate about the Church and its LGBTQ+ members is to proceed only on the basis of the Anglican threefold authority of Scripture, tradition and reason, ruling out experience as an authoritative voice, then there is no resolution available. While we may debate the meaning of biblical texts, the currents of tradition and what a so-called rational analysis of all of this might look like, there will be no possibility of change without accounting for, attending to and

---

18 In Wright 2013, 262–3, we find this appraisal of experience in theological method. 'In order to have any serious discussion about ethical issues, we need to remind ourselves the whole time of the importance of Reason (along with, and obedient to Scripture and Tradition) as one strand of the classic threefold Anglican cord. The current fashion for substituting "experience," which all too easily means "feeling," or "reported feeling," is simply not the same sort of thing. Experience matters, but it doesn't belong in an account of authority; put it there, and the whole notion of "authority" itself deconstructs before your very eyes.'

19 Wright 2011, 192. The same point is made in Wright 2010, 33–5.

20 Wright 2011, 15.

being hospitable towards the lived experience of our Christian LGBTQ+ siblings.[21] If that experience is ruled out of order and dismissed as having no theological or ethical significance, then we really have nothing to talk about.[22] We also end up with a theology with suspiciously clean hands.

But this is also in tension with Wright's own epistemology. While Wright's critical realism has always been more inclined to err on the side of naive realism than to ever be tempted by postmodern constructivism, his own epistemology of love offers a more excellent way forward.[23] This is a relational epistemology.

> To know is to be in a relation with the known, which means that the 'knower' needs to be open to the possibility of the 'known' being other than had been expected or even desired, and must be prepared to respond accordingly, not merely to observe from a distance.[24]

One wonders what would be the result if Wright applied such an openness to the other, and such an epistemological intimacy, to the LGBTQ+ community. If this is a hermeneutic of love, a practice of interpretation in which 'the lover affirms the reality and otherness of the beloved', then what happens if the beloved is a gay man, a lesbian woman, a transgender person? Wright describes such an epistemology of love beautifully when he writes, 'Love does not seek to collapse the beloved in terms of itself.' In such an epistemology, '"love" will mean "attention": the readiness to let the other *be* the other, the willingness to grow and change in oneself in relation to the other'.[25] This is a rich, evocative and deeply biblical epistemology.

---

21 'Christians have no reason to think they understand how the Holy Spirit weighs in on the issue of homosexuality until they welcome homosexuals into their homes and sit down and eat with them.' See Fowl 1998, 122.

22 It is also curious that the apologetic argument of *Simply Christian* does, in the end, affirm an attention to experience as central. Wright's argument is that if you look closely at the human longing for justice, spirituality, relationships and beauty then you will hear echoes of a voice – the voice of God. What kind of an apologetic is this if not an attending to profound human experiences? With regard to relationality, Wright (2010, 38) evocatively suggests, 'One of the central elements of the Christian story is the claim that the paradoxes of laughter and tears, woven as it is deep into the heart of all human experience, is woven deep into the heart of God.' Yes, such laughter and tears speak volumes of both the human experience and the heart of God. What happens if the laughter and tears of the LGBTQ+ experience are also woven into the heart of God? Does that change our theology?

23 Middleton and I (1995, 167–8) offered a critique of Wright's critical realism while affirming the richness of his notion of epistemological love.

24 Wright 1992, 45.

25 Wright 1992, 64. Reflecting on Wittgenstein's dictum, 'It is *love* that believes the resurrection', Wright says that if we are to glimpse this new world of resurrection 'we will need a different kind of knowing, a knowing that involves us in new ways, an epistemology that draws out

It is also an epistemology that has no grounding without hospitable and loving attention to *experience*. What theological, pastoral and ethical results would come from such an attentive knowing? What does it mean to let the LGBTQ+ other *be* the other and to grant a level of epistemological (and hermeneutical) authority to that person's experience?[26] And in what ways will the Church and its traditions be challenged to grow and change in relation to the otherness of LGBTQ+ Christians?

In musical improvisation, writes Begbie,

> there is a vivid sense that we are in the realm not of a tight, closed and necessarily unfolding temporality but of a flexible responsiveness. The music's past engages with the particularities of the present occasion in such a way that the music is intuited as strongly undetermined . . . And, moreover, the music's past, by being particularised in the present, opens up new futures for both cultural and occasional restraints: a range of unforeseen and inherently unpredictable possibilities can burst forth.[27]

If this is improvisation, then it is hard to see an improvisatory dynamic at work in Wright's views on homosexuality. If the 'logic of improvisation is the logic of *surplus*, non-equilibrium, propelled by contingency and constraints in interplay',[28] then it is difficult to discern any surplus in Wright's engagement with the issue of LGBTQ+ Christians and the Church. On this issue it would appear that Wright refuses to allow any contingencies, any voices, to disturb the equilibrium of his traditionalist position.

---

from us not just the cool appraisal of detached quasi-scientific research but also that whole-person engagement and involvement for which the best shorthand is "love," in the Johannine sense of *agapē*.' Further, 'Love is the deepest mode of knowing because it is love that, while completely engaging with reality other than itself, affirms and celebrates that other-than-self reality.' See Wright 2008, 73. While it would be unfair to push this to mean that all 'other-than-self' realities are to be celebrated, it is fair to say that Wright's views on homosexuality seem to be characterized more by detachment than 'whole-person engagement'.

26 There is no space to pursue this matter further, but I would also argue that insofar as the LGBTQ+ experience is intimate with suffering and lament, it should be given an epistemological priority. The voice of lament invariably cuts through the comfortable visions of the status quo. It is in lament that the story is tested against lived experience, and no responsible theology can proceed in our day without hearing and responding to the lament that arises from LGBTQ+ Christians to the throne of God. Just as I would affirm that the 'preferential option for the poor' is deeply biblical, so I would argue that the corollary of this preferential option is the epistemological privileging of suffering. Following Gustavo Gutiérrez, it seems to me that theological language cut off from experience, especially the experience of suffering, is more likely to function as an ideological cover-up than a disclosure of truth. Gutiérrez (1987, 30) rightly insists that 'the one directional movement from theological principles to life really goes nowhere'. See also, Ellington 2008.

27 Begbie 2000, 215.

28 Begbie 2000, 216.

Improvisation is suffused with risk. The whole performance could devolve into a screeching cacophony. The story could grind to a halt. Our improvisation could fail. However, Begbie notes that 'space to fail is *necessary* for a superlative performance'.[29] Playing it safe is the enemy of improvisation.

> In other words, to 'clutch reflexively' at safety so that nothing is 'thrown up,' to withdraw from risk by a panic retreat into cliché means that nothing new is learned. The music lapses into lifeless monotony. First rate improvisation is marked by a restful restlessness.[30]

Restful restlessness. What a wonderful description of Christian discipleship. Indeed, what a wonderful description of the discipleship of my friend Tom Wright. Resting secure in a deep, deep faith, there has been a restlessness about Tom's contribution over the years. Restless with dualistic Evangelicalism. Restless with a church sold out to global capitalism. Restless with the reigning paradigms in biblical studies. Restless with the imposed separation of biblical scholarship from the ministry and calling of the Church. But when it comes to homosexuality, Wright rests in a position that takes no risks. Dare I say that on this issue he has clutched reflexively at safety and withdrawn from risk by a panic retreat into cliché? 'No,' he will reply. He will insist that he has recognized a grave danger in the improvisatory life of the Church and has determined that the voices of those who are advocating for wider inclusion and hospitality to LGBTQ+ Christians are discordant with the melody of the Scriptures, and unfaithful to the story found in the previous acts of this unfinished drama. While faithfulness without creativity is the orthodoxy of a dead tradition, creativity without faithfulness becomes preoccupied with a relevance that loses all Christian identity and biblical depth.[31] And so we must now turn to the question of biblical depth, and explore whether fidelity to the story demands the exclusion of LGBTQ+ voices.

Scripture revisited

Commenting on Richard Hooker's debate with the Puritans, Wright observes:

> Human society develops and changes ... and the church, itself at one level a human society, has an organic rather than a static life, and must grow

---

[29] Begbie 2000, 243.
[30] Begbie 2000, 244.
[31] Cf. Walsh and Keesmaat 2004, 134–5.

and change appropriately. As it does so, it will inevitably *go beyond what scripture explicitly teaches*, as for example, the great creeds undeniably do.[32]

There is something wonderfully refreshing about this perspective, and it is perhaps surprising that the example Bishop Wright employs is nothing less than the creeds themselves. Consequently, the affirmation of the authority of the Scriptures 'is always a way of saying that the church in each generation must make fresh and rejuvenated efforts to understand scripture more fully and live by it more thoroughly, even if that means cutting across cherished traditions'.[33] This, of course, raises two important questions: *when* should faithful improvisation legitimately go beyond the Scriptures and *which* cherished traditions do we need to cut across in order to do so? When it comes to homosexuality, Wright's answer is clear. We should never go beyond the Scriptures on this matter, nor should we ever cut across cherished traditions of heterosexual essentialism and total abstinence from all homoerotic expression.

For Wright the New Testament teaching on sexuality is 'stark and brisk'.[34] The biblical model of marriage is limited to the fidelity of a monogamous heterosexual union. From the creation of the first humans in gendered complementarity through to the image of the eschatological marriage of Christ with his bride, the Church, the alpha and omega of biblical faith is clear. Heterosexuality is where the story begins and where it ends. Anything that will deviate from heteronormativity will be a disobedient innovation, an improvisatory move that must be blocked. In the light of my argument above, it seems justified to suggest that this is a hermeneutics of repetition, not improvisation.

Since the focus of this essay is on Wright's hermeneutic, there will not be enough space to engage in a full critique of Wright's exegesis of the relatively few texts that he takes as foundational to a Christian engagement with homosexuality. But there are three issues that should be addressed: the improvisatory practice of the Church in Acts 10—15; Romans 1 and the character of God; and the question of new creation and heteronormativity.

The argument that the contemporary Church, struggling with the question of the inclusion of LGBTQ+ believers, would do well to learn from the experience of the early Church and the way it came to accept the inclusion

---

32 Wright 2011, 80 (italics added). To go beyond what Scripture explicitly teaches is a necessary implication of the unfinished nature of the biblical drama. As Wells (2004, 63) puts it, 'There is more to the Christian story than the pages of the Bible disclose.'
33 Wright 2011, 92.
34 Wright 2010, 230.

of the Gentiles is well known. While Luke T. Johnson and Stephen Fowl have offered such a reading, Sylvia Keesmaat does so with explicit reference to the improvisatory hermeneutic of an unfinished drama.[35] Significant in this line of interpretation is that it does not resort to the repetition of a few fragmentary texts as finally authoritative, but follows the improvisatory practice of the early Church addressing a decidedly analogous situation. In Acts 10—15 we have a stunning account of how the early Church engaged in fifth-act improvisation. Rather than rehearsing the whole argument here, I will simply offer some hermeneutical observations regarding the relation of Scripture, tradition and experience.

Those who argued, 'with no small dissension and debate' (Acts 15.2),[36] that Gentile converts must submit to the requirements of Torah, including circumcision, were on solid biblical grounds. For them there was no debate necessary, no improvisation and certainly no innovation. Just as Wright insists that heteronormativity and homoerotic abstinence have clear biblical support, so also 'those who proposed circumcision and Torah-observance for Gentile believers in Jesus had a strong case'.[37] Scripture and tradition were on their side. But the Spirit wasn't. As with all improvisation, two things needed to happen if the Church was to live out its faith with fidelity and creativity, faithfulness and innovation. The early believers could only discern where the Spirit was leading the Church if they first listened to the testimonies of the outpouring of the Spirit on the Gentiles and if they could then interpret this surprising and unpredictable development as consistent with the promises of God in the narrative that had preceded them.

We come back to improvisation and listening. How does the Church hear these voices that bring new cadences, melodies and rhythms to the ongoing performance of redemption? The testimonies in the days of the apostles could not be denied. They came with credible witnesses and they were, make no mistake of it, narratives of the experience of the Spirit in the midst of the Gentiles. If the Jerusalem Council had held to a Wrightian–Anglican three-cord view of authority residing in Scripture, reason and tradition, without any authoritative standing for experience,

---

[35] Johnson 1996, 60–108; Fowl 1998, 101–27; Keesmaat 2004a. Keesmaat's article is also available online at: <http://empireremixed.com/media/welcoming-the-gentiles.pdf>. While not appealing to Acts 10—15, Wells (2016, 99–115) also applies such an improvisatory hermeneutic to the question of LGBTQ+ inclusion in the Church.

[36] Unless otherwise noted, Bible quotations in this chapter are taken from the NRSV.

[37] Fowl 1998, 110.

then the results would have been very, very different for the history of the Church.

If the Holy Spirit experience of the Gentiles is true, and if by such an outpouring God has cleansed their hearts and erased the distinction between them and Jews, then, Peter asks of the traditionalists, 'why are you putting God to the test by placing on the neck of the [Gentile] disciples a yoke that neither our ancestors nor we have been able to bear?' (Acts 15.10). Of course, the response could have been, 'Because the Bible says so.' The response could have been a repetition of orthodoxy. But Peter has already discerned not only that the testimonies are true, but also that they mean that the promises of cleansed hearts are being fulfilled in the strangest places and that imposing the full restrictions of Torah on these believers is not only an unduly harsh yoke to bear, but is nothing less than putting God to the test. This is, if you will, a blasphemy against the Holy Spirit.

When James then cites Amos's vision of the return from exile and the rebuilding of the booth of David 'so that all other peoples may seek the Lord – even all the Gentiles over whom my name has been called' (15.16–18; quoting Amos 9.11–12), the debate is deemed finished. Never mind that Amos says nothing about whether Gentiles need to be circumcised. Never mind that James is disregarding clear Torah stipulations. Lived experience here shapes the reading of Scripture, as Scripture provides a lens to interpret that experience. Keesmaat comments:

> Only after the stories had been told of God's work in the present did James appeal to a biblical text. Note, however, the unusual introduction he gives to the citation: 'The words of the prophets agree with this' (Acts 15.15), *not* 'this agrees with the prophets.' Scripture is seen to agree with the contemporary working of the Spirit, not the other way around.[40]

In this identity-shaping moment experience precedes exegesis. Of course, the experience itself is interpreted through a Scripture-soaked imagination, but the traditionalist interlocutors would have argued that Scripture required a blocking of that experience, disregarding the testimonies of the Gentiles because they contradicted the stark authority of the tradition.

Fowl sums up the story of the Jerusalem Council this way:

> Without requiring circumcision and Torah observance, God has poured out the Spirit on the Gentiles. Hence, the fact that the Gentiles have received the

---

40 Keesmaat 2004a, 38. Keesmaat is arguing that the NRSV has a mistaken translation of the Greek text.

same Spirit as the Jewish believers apart from circumcision indicates that circumcision should not now be required of them.[39]

Now what happens if we imagine (and there is no creative or faithful improvisation without imagination) that the issue isn't Gentiles in the first century, but the outpouring of the Holy Spirit on LGBTQ+ Christians in the twenty-first? What would happen if we listened to the testimonies of these siblings in Christ? Might we be able to rewrite Fowl's summary as follows?

> Without requiring celibacy or an imposed conformity to the male–female binary of Genesis, God has poured out the Spirit on LGBTQ+ believers. Hence, the fact that these siblings in Christ have received the same Spirit as heterosexual Christians, apart from either celibacy or some sort of reparative therapy, indicates that celibacy should not now be required of them.

Might this be a faithful conclusion to draw if we engaged in careful and respectful listening to the testimonies of our LGBTQ+ siblings in Christ? Might this be a faithful improvisation in the life of the Church in the twenty-first century?[40]

Wright doesn't think so. Such an improvisatory offer must be blocked because it is in such deep disharmony with the stark and brisk perspective on homosexuality found in the biblical witness, not least in Romans 1. And so to Romans 1 we now turn.[41]

I agree with Wright when he argues that 'it will not do, within serious debate, simply to appeal . . . to Romans 1 to forbid homosexual practice'.[42] Nonetheless, Romans 1.26–27 is at the heart of the debate. Whether Paul's critique of certain kinds of erotic practices in these two verses (the only full sentence on such matters in the whole New Testament!) speaks to the contemporary debate as clearly as is sometimes argued remains a matter of some disagreement. Richard Hays is right: 'neither Paul nor anyone else in antiquity had a conception of "sexual orientation."'[43] How does this affect

---

[39] Fowl 1998, 110.

[40] A full interpretation of Acts 15 would also require a discussion of the parameters set upon Gentile inclusion. This is not an 'anything goes' improvisatory move. I refer the reader to Keesmaat (2004a, 40–2) for further discussion.

[41] The interpretative debates around Genesis 19.1–11, Judges 19.22–26, Leviticus 18.22 and 20.13, 1 Corinthians 6.9–10 and 1 Timothy 1.9–10 have become irrelevant to the issues before us in this paper. Indeed, in this ever-evolving conversation, Genesis 1 and Romans 1 have increasingly become the focus of the discussion.

[42] Wright 2011, 16. Sandra Boehringer (2015, 150) argues that we should not 'look back to the ancient world for a category that has existed for scarcely more than one hundred and twenty years'.

[43] Hays 1996, 388.

how we hear Paul speaking into the contemporary conversation? There is also an historical debate to be had about whether 'homosexual marriage' was known and condoned in the first century. Wright says it was; other classical historians disagree.[44] These are important points of debate that we will not have time to rehearse in this essay. But if we are seeking to discern what fidelity to the biblical narrative requires of us in this improvisatory moment, then we need to ask what such fidelity meant to Paul when addressing the sexual practices of the Roman Empire.

Reading Romans 1.26–27 in the context of what Paul has said about creation and idolatry, Wright assumes that the subtext here is Genesis 1—3. 'Humans are commanded to be fruitful: they are to celebrate, in their male-plus-female complementarity, the abundant life-generating capacity of God's good world.'[45] What is wrong with homosexuality is that it is a mode of sexual relationality that goes against the grain of the order of creation, distorting the image of God in humankind through idolatry. But is this what Paul is really saying? How strong is the intertextual echo of Genesis 1—3 in Romans 1.18–26?

Paul is describing the wrath of God that is revealed against all injustice by those who 'by their injustice suppress the truth' (1.18, author's translation).

> For what can be known about God is plain to them, because God has shown it to them. Ever since the creation of the world his eternal power and divine nature, invisible though they are, have been understood and seen through the things he has made.
>
> (Romans 1.19–20)

Note that the truth that is being suppressed here is not a truth about creation, or even a truth about humanity, and certainly not a truth about

---

44 Thomas Hubbard (2015, 128–9) makes no reference to homosexual marriage in either Greek or Roman culture. Indeed, every reference to marriage in this important collection of essays assumes a heterosexual union in which procreation is crucial. Wright's (2004, 22) appeal to the homosexual 'marriages' of Nero is also problematic. In the first instance it is probably the case that these unions happened after Paul had written Romans. But more importantly, neither Nero's 'marriage' to Doryphorus nor that to Sporus Sabina can be seen as anything other than a deliberate and farcical reversal of cultural norms. Far from what we would call a homosexual relationship between two people of the same gender, in each of these relationships there was gender role reversal. With Doryphorus Nero took on the female role. With the boy chosen to replace Nero's deceased wife, Sabina, there was castration involved (the irony of naming the lad 'Sporus' is cruel) and the partner took on a female persona. Not only is there nothing in these relationships that is analogous to the contemporary debate about same-sex marriage; they were also universally condemned by ancient writers. See Champlin 2005, 145–50, 164–71.
45 Wright 2004, 21. See also Wright 2002, 433–4; 2013, 266–7.

male–female complementarity. The truth is the truth about *God* that has been revealed *through* creation. The emphasis here is on God, not on creation order or the creation narratives.[46] And the apostle keeps the emphasis on God as he continues: 'though they knew God they did not honour him as God' (1.21); 'they exchanged the glory of the immortal God for images' (1.23); 'they exchanged the truth about God for a lie and worshipped and served the creature rather than the Creator' (1.25). Idolatry is what happens when humans who are created in the image of God refuse to image that Creator, and idolatry bears the bad fruit that Paul is about to describe, beginning with human sexual life but then proceeding to address vices that tear apart the fabric of social and economic life through their promotion of injustice (Romans 1.28–32).

None of this makes sense, however, if we don't understand what it is about God that is revealed through creation and suppressed in idolatry. Paul's focus is clear: God's 'eternal power and divine nature, invisible though they are, have been understood and seen through the things he has made' (Romans 1.20). What does Paul mean by God's eternal power and divine nature? What does God's power and nature look like? If we were to seek an intertext for what Paul is getting at, we would find more fruitful literary allusions in the Psalms than in Genesis 1—3.[47] Doesn't Psalm 19.1–4 employ the very same oxymoron as Romans 1.20 of that which is invisible being seen?[48] And doesn't the psalmist confess that creation is eloquent, proclaiming the very glory of God that Paul says is exchanged in idolatry (Romans 1.23)?[49] And what is that glory? What does creation reveal about the divine nature? Consider Psalm 33.4–5:

> For the word of the LORD is upright,
>   and all his work is done in faithfulness.
> He loves righteousness and justice;
>   the earth is full of the steadfast love of the LORD.
>   (Psalm 33.4–5)[50]

---

[46] Commenting on Romans 1.18–32, Fitzmyer (1992, 274) argues, 'The alleged echoes of the Adam stories in Genesis are simply nonexistent.'

[47] Wright (2002, 424, 433) notes that Paul evokes Psalm 71 in Romans 1.16 and that 1.24–27 clearly echoes Psalm 81.12.

[48] Fitzmyer 1992, 280. Cf. Wisdom of Solomon 13.1–9; Job 12.7–12. The revelatory power of creation is, of course, also a central theme in wisdom literature. 'For the wise, God is known most basically in and through the experience of creation. That is, wisdom is so built into the infrastructure of the creation that God's character and purposes for the world can be reasonably, if not fully discernible to human probing and reflection.' See Fretheim 2005, 219.

[49] And note that Paul cites this very psalm in Romans 10.18.

[50] Cf. Psalms 119.64; 136.4–9. Concomitant with the revelatory character of creation is

The earth is full of the covenantal love of the Creator. Creation is saturated by and overflows in that love. The very 'word' through which 'the heavens were made' (Psalm 33.6), through which 'all the earth . . . came to be . . . and stood firm' (Psalm 33.8, 9), is an upright word, and the creation that it has wrought bears witness to the Creator's righteousness and justice. Indeed, the very justice of God that is revealed in the gospel (Romans 1.16) is an echo of the justice to which all of creation is an eloquent witness. Moreover, Psalm 98, which Paul echoes in Romans 1.16–17, describes not only the salvation, justice and truthfulness of God (Psalm 98.2–3) but also the way in which the seas and the sea creatures, the earth and the creatures who live there, the floods and the hills rejoice in God's justice and salvation (Psalm 98.7–8).[51] No wonder Paul says that such a creationally revealed truth about God is repressed through injustice.

In Psalm 145 we meet one of the most common refrains in Hebrew scriptures that describe God:

> The LORD is gracious and merciful,
>> slow to anger and abounding in steadfast love.
>> (Psalm 145.8)

This is the divine nature: showing grace and mercy, and overflowing in steadfast love. Moreover, in the imagination of the psalmist, this steadfast love permeates all of creation:

> The LORD is good to all,
>> and his compassion is over all that he has made.
> All your works shall give thanks to you, O LORD,
>> and all your faithful shall bless you.
>> (Psalm 145.9–10)

Notice the repetition of 'all'. The Lord is good to *all*, his compassion is over *all that he has made*, *all your works* give thanks, and *all your faithful* shall bless you. Not only is all of creation saturated with the love of God, but also the psalmist confesses that compassion goes all the way down. As all creatures look to God for 'their food in due season' (Psalm 145.15), God opens his hands, 'satisfying the desire of *every living thing*' (Psalm 145.16), and that is why the psalmist sings:

> The LORD is just in all his ways,
>> and kind in all his doings.

---

creation's praise, bearing witness and in response to God's justice, righteousness and truth. Cf. Psalms 96 and 98.

51 Keesmaat 2004b, 142–3. Keesmaat also notes that Psalm 106.20 is echoed in Romans 1.23.

> The LORD is near to all who call on him,
>   to all who call on him in truth.
>   (Psalm 145.17–18)

'Ever since the creation of the world', wrote Paul, God's 'eternal power and divine nature . . . have been understood and seen through the things he has made' (1.20). And it is clear from the poetry of Israel that the creation reveals the divine nature to be characterized by faithfulness, justice and covenantal love. And this, it would seem, is what humanity is blind to in its idolatry. By rooting his critique of idolatry in the context of what creation reveals about God, Paul is not making a point about the creational normativity of heterosexuality. Rather, he is alluding to the most foundational criteria by which imperial sexuality will be judged in Romans 1.26–27. Paul is attacking erotic practices that transgress what is known about God from the very creation of the world, not what is known about human gender identity and reproduction. Sexual lives that are steeped in infidelity, injustice and insatiable consumption are brought under judgement because they fall so short of our calling to image God in faithfulness, justice and love.

If this reading has merit, then we can reopen the question of whether Paul's strong dismissal of certain kinds of homoerotic practices excludes an improvisatory move promoting same-sex marriage in the Church today. If the fundamental criteria are faithfulness, justice and covenant love, and not heteronormativity, then I propose that we can responsibly affirm and encourage monogamous same-sex marriage as an appropriate improvisation precisely because it is faithful not just to the covenantal story in which we live, but more deeply, it is faithful to the very character of God as revealed for all to see in creation. It is this Creator God whom we are called to image in all of our lives, not least in the stewardship of our sexuality.[52]

Faithful improvisation is always seeking to discern a way of life in Act 5 that reflects the joyful heritage of the four acts that preceded it, while anticipating the breathtaking climax of this story.[53] Wright puts it this way: 'Learning to live as a Christian is learning to live as a renewed human

---

[52] There is, of course, much more going on in Romans 1 than can be discussed in this essay. Engaging the moral argument of 1.24–27 vis-à-vis lust and desire, purity and impurity, honour and shame, and what is and is not 'against nature', Brownson (2013; cf. Part III) offers a nuanced and carefully constructed argument that this text cannot be used to rule out of order the promotion of same-sex marriage.

[53] I am paraphrasing Wells (2016, 104) here because, as we have seen, he employs a different drama schema than Wright. But the point still stands.

being, anticipating the eventual new creation in and with a world which is still longing and groaning for that final redemption.'[54] The problem is that since 'it is by no means clear what to renounce and what to rediscover', the improvising community will

> have to work out which styles of life and behavior belong with the corrupting evil which must be rejected if new creation is to emerge, and which styles of life and behavior belong with the new creation which must be embraced, struggled for, and celebrated.[55]

We now come to the eschatological crux of the matter. Just as character and virtue are always shaped through the anticipation of the *telos* of life, so also are all ethics eschatological. So the question becomes: what does sexuality and marriage look like in the new creation? Interestingly, the New Testament is almost totally silent on this issue. The one exception would be that when Jesus was questioned by the Sadducees about marriage and the resurrection he clearly relegated marriage to the present age, 'but those who are considered worthy of a place in . . . the resurrection from the dead neither marry nor are given in marriage' (Luke 20.35). We meet here a significant discontinuity between the present time we inhabit in the unfinished drama and its final resolution in the eschaton. Wright's comment on this text concludes that Jesus is teaching that sexual relations become irrelevant in the new creation.[56] If that is the case then we need to ask: how does a marriage-less, indeed sexless, *telos* shape the life of sexual relations in the present age? How do we live in a way that faithfully anticipates such an eschatological vision?

Wright provides the following answer:

> The point about new creation is that it is a new *creation*. And, though we are told that procreation won't be necessary in God's new world (because people won't die), the very imagery which the Bible uses to describe that new world – imagery about the marriage of the Lamb (Revelation), or about the new world being born from the womb of the old (Romans) – indicates that the male/female relationship, woven so centrally into the story of creation in Genesis 1 and 2, is not an accidental or a temporary phenomenon, but is, rather, symbolic of the fact that creation itself carries God-given life and procreative possibility within it.[57]

---

54 Wright 2010, 223.

55 Wright 2010, 224.

56 'Death will have been abolished, and so sexual relations, and especially the need to continue a particular family line, will be irrelevant.' See Wright 2001, 245.

57 Wright 2010, 232 (italics in original). In what follows, I will limit my comments to Wright's appeal to the marriage of the Lamb and leave discussion of Romans 8 to another time.

There may not be marriage in the new creation, and perhaps not even sexual relations, Wright argues, but because the eschatological metaphor is of a male-plus-female wedding, this *telos* serves both to affirm the original creational intent of the heterosexual binary in marriage and to inscribe such marriage as a singularly normative anticipation of the age to come.

Indeed, Wright will speculate that Genesis binaries such as heaven and earth, sea and dry land, and ultimately, male and female, are foundational to creation and will meet their complementary union in the eschaton.[58] To affirm anything other than heterosexual marriage, then, is to stand radically outside both the creational origin of the narrative and its eschatological fulfilment.

There are two problems with this argument. The first is that if we move from the marriage of the Lamb in Revelation 19 to the vision of the New Jerusalem adorned as a bride for her husband in Revelation 21, we will see that creational binaries are falling like flies. Indeed, with little more than a parenthetical remark, 'and the sea was no more' (Revelation 21.1), the vision begins with overthrowing the distinction between sea and dry land of the third day of creation (Genesis 1.9–14). And then, just a few verses later, the vision proceeds to totally undermine the binary between day and night established on the fourth day of creation (Genesis 1.14–19). Revelation 21.23–25 has no difficulty imagining a world with neither sun nor moon, but rather eternal day. Here are two binaries that are not brought to harmonious complementarity, but are simply eradicated. Of course, it could be argued that this is a much too simplistic and literalistic reading of these texts. The point isn't to overthrow a creational distinction between sea and dry land, but to imagine a world without that primordial symbol of chaos, the sea. And rather than erasing the sun and the moon, isn't the point of the vision precisely to evoke an incredibly beautiful image of the glory of God as the light of the New Jerusalem and the Lamb as the lamp? Don't we need to pay careful attention to what the metaphors are meant to accomplish in this apocalyptic vision?

This brings us to the second problem with Wright's argument. Just as it is saying too much to argue that this apocalyptic vision overthrows the binaries of the third and fourth days of creation, so also is it over-reading the metaphor of the Lamb and the Bride to make a point that is not in the purview of the text. This vision has nothing to do with re-inscribing creational binaries. There is nothing surprising about this employment of the metaphor of heterosexual marriage, but the point is covenantal

---

58 See his interview in Schmitz 2014.

faithfulness, not gender binaries.[59] Of course the vision evokes marriage. What richer metaphor of covenant is there? But the eschatological focus is the homecoming of God and humanity in the new creation wherein God will dwell with humankind in the radical healing of all things, the wiping away of tears, and the end of all mourning. To push this metaphor, in the face of how other binaries are metaphorically falling all around it, as an eschatological justification for ruling out the possibility of same-sex marriage is a case of special pleading.

So what *do* we draw from this eschatological vision? If virtue is 'anticipating-the-life-of-the-age-to-come' then how does this vision of the marriage of the Lamb shape our lives in this improvisatory moment?[60] Biblically insisting that 'the ultimate goal is neither a disembodied heaven nor a mere rearrangement of life on the present earth, but the redemption of the whole creation', Wright argues that

> our calling is to live in our bodies *now* in a way which anticipates the life we shall live *then*. Marital fidelity echoes and anticipates God's fidelity to the whole creation. Other kinds of sexual activity symbolize and embody distortions and corruptions of the present world.[61]

Yes. The goal is not a mere rearrangement of life on the present earth, not even a rearrangement of the first act of the drama, or of patriarchal or even heterosexual marriage. Rather, we are looking for marital fidelity. Anything less is a distortion and a corruption that does not image God's covenantal fidelity in the story from alpha to omega.

If there is no procreation in the new earth, and if there is no marriage, then what does this mean for our sexual lives now? Well, we certainly need to abandon the biological (and anatomical) reductionism of gender and sexuality to procreation. Not even Genesis 2.18–24 sees gender complementarity in terms of procreation! The primary issue is the deep intimacy of communion.[62] But more importantly, we need to lovingly insist that relationships of sexual intimacy live and flourish under the canopy of marriage. If we are to live our lives in anticipation of being the 'bride' in the marriage of the Lamb, then Christian marriage needs to be subject to the covenantal criteria of faithfulness, justice and steadfast love that we

---

[59] Indeed, in the metaphor all humankind is female!
[60] Wright 2012, 68.
[61] Wright 2010, 232–3.
[62] I also note that nowhere in the New Testament is marriage explicitly connected to procreation. Indeed, Rowan Williams (1996, 67) suggests that sexuality without reproduction is one of the foremost biblical metaphors for the God–humanity relationship in Scripture. The issue isn't procreation, but attraction and desire. Cf. Brownson 2013, 110–26.

have seen in Romans 1.[63] Marriage needs to be a place of homecoming, of deep dwelling in intimacy together. Faithful marriage, rooted in the story that has gone before and anticipating this eschatological end, is a covenant in which tears are wiped from our eyes. If the eschatological vision is of a marriage where 'mourning and crying and pain will be no more' (Revelation 21.4), then faithful improvisation at this time in the history of the Church calls us to end the mourning, crying and pain we have inflicted upon the LGBTQ+ community and offer the full support, encouragement and blessing of same-sex marriage. This, I suggest, is a style of life and behaviour that belongs with the new creation and should, therefore, 'be embraced, struggled for, and celebrated'.[64] This is how we can anticipate the making of all things new that is our eschatological hope.

Sex and embodied fidelity

Let us return to Wright's model of fifth-act improvisation. 'A good fifth act', he has written,

> will show a proper final development, not merely a repetition, of what went before. Nevertheless, there will be a rightness, a fittingness about certain actions and speeches, about certain final moves in the drama, which will in one sense be self-authenticating, and in another gain authentication from their coherence with, their making sense of, the 'authoritative' previous text.[65]

I've made the argument that when it comes to the LGBTQ+ community, Wright's own improvisatory moves do not go beyond repetition. Nor, I have argued, do they gain quite the authentication from the previous text that he suggests. But now we need to conclude this essay by asking, again, how we would discern the fittingness of certain improvisatory moves in the unfinished drama that is biblical faith. Yes, they are, in one sense, self-authenticating. But we know that there is no such thing as unambiguous self-authentication. What might seem totally right and fitting to some

---

63 The linen of this bride's gown will be woven from the justice and righteousness of the saints (Revelation 19.8).

64 Wright 2010, 224. And so I agree with Wright that the image of marriage at the end of the book of Revelation is a profound symbol of the *telos* of human existence. 'Virtue grasps that goal by faith and learns the lessons of living in the present in such a way as genuinely to anticipate that future, by fidelity within marriage and abstinence outside of it.' See Wright 2012, 252. The significant difference is that I think such marriage is the call for committed same-sex relationships as well.

65 Wright 1992, 141.

people will be abhorrent and repulsive to others. And I don't know what we can do about this apart from testimony.

So I close by bearing witness. I bear witness to the fruit of the Spirit in the lives of so many of my LGBTQ+ friends. I bear witness to lives of rich love, joy, peace and patience. Patience. My goodness, what patience they have had in the life of the Church, still waiting to be fully welcomed. The Spirit has been poured out in my friends' lives with an incredible kindness and generosity to me, my family, my ministry and my church community. And they have been faithful. In fact, on those days when I am depressed, disappointed, hurt and angry, those days when I am seriously considering abandoning the Church altogether, I remember my LGBTQ+ siblings in Christ. They are still in the story. They hold on to Jesus even when the traditions and practices of the Church keep telling them that Jesus doesn't hold on to them! And they do so with gentleness and self-control. There is a gentleness with each other when my Christian LGBTQ+ friends gather together. There is a quiet holding of each other in their pain, their rejection. And there is, contrary to the traditionalist stereotypes, a self-control in this community. These are not people driven by out-of-control lust. They are not looking for sexual relationships as commodities of gratification. They are looking for the same thing that any of us are looking for in the depths of our hearts. Communion. Intimacy. Love. Commitment.[66]

I so long for my friend Tom Wright to meet these siblings in Christ, to hear their stories, experience their deep discipleship and discern the Spirit of God being outpoured in their lives. The degree to which their lives, and their voices, are blocked in the improvisatory movement of the Spirit in our midst is the degree to which our improvisations will fail and we will be found unfaithful.

I will conclude with some more testimonies, bearing witness to the discipleship of my LGBTQ+ friends. And I will name names.

Marj is a nurse who retired early to spend her days gently binding up the wounds of the many homeless people who come through her church doors each day. Daniel was a widely respected crown attorney who wisely

---

[66] My experiences are rooted in many years of worship with LGBTQ+ siblings in Christ at the Church of the Redeemer in Toronto; my local parish of St James, Fenelon Falls and Christ Church, Coboconk; and the Wine Before Breakfast community that I have pastored for the last 18 years at the University of Toronto. But I need to also bear witness to the Generous Space communities across Canada. This amazing ministry of support for LGBTQ+ Christians and their allies bears all the fruit of the Spirit that Paul identifies in Galatians 5.22–23. Once a year Sylvia Keesmaat and I host a camp-out with these friends at our farm. I refer the reader to the fine book by the founder of this ministry, Vander Wall-Gritter 2014.

nurtured the members of our church youth group as they navigated what it meant to be faithful Christians in the difficult terrain of urban adolescence. Cynthia left a successful career in engineering to start up a bike shop that trains street-involved men and women in bicycle repair and customer service. Phyliss has created a dynamic and joyful arts ministry for street-involved young adults. Billy has the gift of healing and an amazingly generous spirit. Amy's prayers during worship invariably bring together the deepest longings of the community. Danice puts her musical skill and pastoral gentleness to work in her care for LGBTQ+ youth. Beth is a woman of deep resources of love and one of the finest preachers I know. Karen and Heather are a stunningly beautiful example of what committed love looks like through decades of faithfulness. There is an air of peace to our friend Chris who has quietly held many fractious children through many a Eucharist. John's choices of songs that are theologically rich and biblically faithful rival the best sermon on a Sunday morning. Susan cares for the sick, comforts the broken, buries the dead and advocates for the vulnerable. I could go on and on. Most of these siblings in Christ are in deeply committed, monogamous relationships. Some of them are married. In all of their lives there is a self-authenticating ring of truth.

As I write this, I am astounded by the stories, overwhelmed by the blessing, and deeply humbled that these people are in my life and community. Is this experience unusual? For some yes, for others no. It all depends, I suspect, on what kind of people are welcomed around the table of the Lord. It all depends on how we discern the Spirit and improvise faithfully in the midst of this unfinished drama of Christian faith.

So here's the question. What happens if we listen closely to the stories of these and countless other LGBTQ+ Christians?[67] What happens if, like the Jerusalem Council, we put aside the theological debate just long enough to respectfully and humbly hear these stories and get to know these siblings in Christ? Might it be that we would begin to see, in the daily lives of these friends, nothing less than the Spirit of God doing a beautiful work in our midst? Might we even see in their committed relationships nothing less than a sexuality that has profoundly rejected the idolatrous, predatory and consumptive eroticism of our age, and embraced the faithfulness, justice and love that creation tells us is the very nature of God? And if we received the testimony of the Holy Spirit through the lives of these friends, might

---

[67] There are too many books that bear witness to such stories to be able to list here. But I do refer the reader to the essays in the previously mentioned collections, along with Dunn and Ambidge 2004. Another important book that has been deeply formative for many Evangelicals is Lee 2012.

that also open to us new readings of Scripture, new paths of fidelity, as we discern the path forward? Might we see committed Christian same-sex relationships not as a threat to marriage but as its restoration?

It is only in the telling of such stories in our communities that we as a people will be able to live out the unfinished drama of our faith in ways that are both faithful to the witness of Scripture and attentive to the new working of the Spirit in our midst. And when we live lives of such creative fidelity, then we will be a people for whom the Bible is not merely a book of rules, but a living and authoritative word. That, I believe, is at the heart of my friend Tom Wright's vast theological project. I have so rejoiced over the years in the testimonies of those who found faith anew through reading the work of this great teacher of the Church. I can only imagine the range of pastoral good and evangelistic outreach that would be let loose if my friend reconsidered his outright rejection of the LGBTQ+ community and offered a more nuanced, sensitive and life-giving word.

Bibliography

Begbie, Jeremy (2000). *Theology, Music and Time*. Cambridge: Cambridge University Press.

——(2011). 'The Shape of Things to Come? Wright amidst Emerging Ecclesiologies.' In *Jesus, Paul and the People of God: A Theological Dialogue with N. T. Wright*, edited by Nicholas Perrin and Richard B. Hays, 183–208. Downers Grove, IL: IVP.

Boehringer, Sandra (2015). 'Female Homoeroticism.' In *A Companion to Greek and Roman Sexualities*, edited by Thomas K. Hubbard, 150–63. Oxford: Blackwell.

Brownson, James V. (2013). *Bible, Gender, Sexuality: Reframing the Church's Debate on Same-Sex Relationships*. Grand Rapids, MI: Eerdmans.

Champlin, Edward (2005). *Nero*. Cambridge, MA: Harvard University Press.

Dunn, Greig, and Chris Ambidge (2004) (eds). *Living Together in the Church: Including Our Differences*. Toronto: Anglican Book Centre.

Ellington, Scott A. (2008). *Risking Truth: Reshaping the World through Prayers of Lament*. Princeton Theological Monograph Series. Eugene, OR: Pickwick.

Fitzmyer, Joseph A. (1992). *Romans*. Anchor Bible. New York, NY: Doubleday.

Fowl, Stephen E. (1998). *Engaging Scripture: A Model for Theological Interpretation*. Oxford: Blackwell.

Fretheim, Terence E. (2005). *God and the World in the Old Testament: A Relational Theology of Creation*. Nashville, TN: Abingdon.

Gagnon, Robert A. (2001). *The Bible and Homosexual Practice: Texts and Hermeneutics*. Nashville, TN: Abingdon.

Gutiérrez, Gustavo (1987). *On Job: God-talk and the Suffering of the Innocent*. Translated by Matthew J. O'Connell. Maryknoll, NY: Orbis.

Hays, Richard B. (1996). *The Moral Vision of the New Testament: A Contemporary Introduction to New Testament Ethics*. New York, NY: HarperCollins.

Hubbard, Thomas K. (2015). 'Peer Homosexuality.' In *A Companion to Greek and Roman Sexualities*, edited by Thomas K. Hubbard, 128–49. Oxford: Blackwell.

Johnson, Luke T. (1996). *Scripture and Discernment: Decision Making in the Church*. Nashville, TN: Abingdon.

Keesmaat, Sylvia C. (2004a). 'Welcoming in the Gentiles: A Biblical Model for Decision Making.' In *Living Together in the Church: Including Our Differences*, edited by Greig Dunn and Chris Ambidge, 30–49. Toronto: Anglican Book Centre.

—— (2004b). 'The Psalms in Romans and Galatians.' In *The Psalms in the New Testament*, edited by Steve Moyise and Maarten J. Menken, 139–61. London / New York, NY: T&T Clark International.

Lee, Justin (2012). *Torn: Rescuing the Gospel from the Gays-vs-Christians Debate*. New York, NY: Jericho Books.

Middleton, J. Richard (2014). *A New Heaven and a New Earth: Reclaiming Biblical Eschatology*. Grand Rapids, MI: Brazos.

Middleton, J. Richard, and Brian J. Walsh (1995). *Truth Is Stranger Than It Used to Be: Biblical Faith in a Postmodern Age*. Downers Grove, IL: IVP.

Schmitz, Matthew (2014). 'N. T. Wright on Gay Marriage: Nature and Narrative Point to Complementarity.' *First Things*: <https://www.firstthings.com/blogs/firstthoughts/2014/06/n-t-wrights-argument-against-same-sex-marriage>.

Vander Wall-Gritter, Wendy (2014). *Generous Spaciousness: Responding to Gay Christians in the Church*. Grand Rapids, MI: Brazos.

Walsh, Brian J., and Sylvia C. Keesmaat (2004). *Colossians Remixed: Subverting the Empire*. Downers Grove, IL: IVP.

Wells, Samuel (2004). *Improvisation: The Drama of Christian Ethics*. Grand Rapids, MI: Brazos.

—— (2016). *How Then Shall We Live? Christian Engagement with Contemporary Issues*. London: Canterbury Press.

Williams, Rowan (1996). 'The Body's Grace.' In *Our Selves, Our Souls and Bodies*, edited by Charles Hefling, 58–68. Boston, MA: Cowley Publications.

Wright, N. T. (1991). 'How Can the Bible Be Authoritative?' *Vox Evangelica* 21: 7–32.

—— (1992). *The New Testament and the People of God*. Christian Origins and the Question of God 1. London: SPCK / Minneapolis, MN: Fortress.

—— (2001). *Luke for Everyone*. London: SPCK.

—— (2002). 'The Letter to the Romans.' In *The New Interpreter's Bible*, Volume X, edited by Leander Keck, 393–770. Nashville, TN: Abingdon.

—— (2004). *Paul for Everyone: Romans, Part 1*. London: SPCK / Louisville, KY: Westminster John Knox.

—— (2005a). *The Last Word*. New York, NY: HarperCollins.

—— (2005b). *Scripture and the Authority of God*. London: SPCK.

—— (2008). *Surprised by Hope: Rethinking Heaven, the Resurrection, and the Mission of the Church*. New York, NY: HarperCollins.

—— (2010). *Simply Christian: Why Christianity Makes Sense.* New York, NY: HarperCollins.

—— (2011). *Scripture and the Authority of God: How to Read the Bible Today.* New York, NY: HarperCollins.

—— (2012). *After You Believe: Why Christian Character Matters.* New York, NY: HarperOne. Originally published as *Virtue Reborn.* London: SPCK, 2010.

—— (2013). 'Communion and Koinonia: Pauline Reflections on Tolerance and Boundaries.' In *Pauline Perspectives: Essays on Paul, 1978–2013*, 255–69. London: SPCK / Minneapolis, MN: Fortress.

Paul and obedience

ANDREW J. GODDARD

1 Introduction

Tom Wright's 1978 Tyndale Lecture, his first major articulation of his reading of Paul, drew attention to the importance of the subject of obedience in Pauline theology and ethics: Jesus' 'real historical obedience to God' was 'at the heart of Paul's theology *and as the object of faith*'. Indeed, Paul's 'doctrine of the obedience of Jesus Christ' (that 'not only did Jesus offer God the obedience which Adam had failed to offer: he offered God the obedience which Israel should have offered and had likewise failed in, obedience to the vocation of redemptive vicarious suffering for the sins of the world') is 'the theology which, in Romans 5, ties together all the other strands of the epistle'.[1] In the same year, his popular book *Small Faith, Great God* also addressed (though discussing Hebrews, not Paul) the question of the importance of our own obedience and rejected a common crude opposition between faith and obedience:

> Faith means totally relying on God, and committing ourselves to God, for time and for eternity, trusting his promises, *obeying his commands* . . . Faith may sometimes seem like a leap in the dark: but it is always a leap *made in obedience to a voice coming out of the darkness* . . .[2]

Wright's later work also, as we shall see, often draws attention to the subject of obedience in Paul,[3] but as here it does so *en passant*, and he has never addressed obedience in a focused or systematic manner nor made it as central in his account of Paul's theology and ethics as some of his statements might imply it should be.[4]

---

1 Wright 2013b, 12: 'The Paul of History and the Apostle of Faith' (1978), 3–20; originally published in *Tyndale Bulletin* 29 (1978): 61–88.
2 Wright 1978, 27 (italics added).
3 For example, in relation to Christ's obedience, a similar statement to that from 1975 quoted above appears in Wright 2013a, 889ff., and in his commentary on Romans 1.5 he notes the significance of our obedience and rejects concerns in relation to justification by faith (Wright 2002, 420).
4 The occasional and relatively marginal nature of the subject is illustrated by the fact that the

This paucity of discussion reflects the peripheral place of obedience within Pauline scholarship more widely.[5] Various reasons could be given for this neglect in both popular and academic engagement with Paul: our culture's focus on autonomy (freedom simply as negative 'freedom from') which makes the language of obedience unwelcome to many and even seemingly opposed to Paul's emphasis on freedom; an assumption that obedience is to be understood only in relation to commands and so is to be subsumed within the broader subject of Paul's attitude to the law;[6] and a belief that obedience is tied to human works and so contrasts with faith and is at best in tension with, perhaps even in contradiction to, central Pauline teaching on justification and grace.

Whatever the reasons, there has been a failure to give a due place to the significance of obedience within Paul's account of the purposes of the one God for his one people through his Messiah. By focusing particularly on those passages explicitly using language of obedience, what follows argues, in contrast, for its importance in Paul's missiology, Christology and ethics. Section 2 shows, especially from Romans and 2 Corinthians, that obedience – closely tied to faith – is a fundamental defining goal of Paul's mission to the Gentiles. His fresh perspective on it both builds on and reframes the Old Testament emphasis on the obedience of Israel (now extended to the nations) and presents a pattern of obedience showing both continuities with, and also radical differences from, that demanded of the nations by imperial Rome (section 2). This new form of obedience is understood and defined (section 3) by relating it to the person and work of Christ. His life and death is presented, in Philippians 2 and Romans 5, in terms of obedience, and this is best correlated with Paul's references to the 'faith of Christ' and understood not in relation to his obeying the law but his obedience to the call and will of God. Finally, in section 4, it is argued that, as is most evident in Romans 6, Paul's Christological reworking of

---

Index of *Pauline Perspectives* (Wright 2013b) does not have an entry for obedience and *Paul and the Faithfulness of God* (Wright 2013a) only has an entry of 'Obedience, of Messiah' with just two references (although the theme of obedience appears more frequently in both books than these figures imply). The few major authors focusing on obedience in Paul are not cited or included in the Bibliographies (e.g. Garlington 1987; Miller 2000). A larger number of page references appear in the Index of Wright 1991 under 'Christ, obedience unto death of'.

5 For a helpful recent study on obedience in the New Testament, with reference to the Old Testament background, see Green 2014.

6 Obedience is often reduced to concepts of law and an ethic of divine command. See, e.g., Barton 2014, 127; Green et al. 2012, 558. In contrast, as noted below, Paul has a much richer, more expansive understanding of obedience, writing of obeying the gospel and the truth, even obeying obedience.

obedience to God's will in terms of total self-offering in response to God's grace lies at the heart of his account of the moral calling of the new-covenant, 'return-from-exile' people of God united to the obedient Messiah.

2 Obedience among the nations: the goal of Paul's global mission

The significance of obedience in Paul's own understanding of his calling and mission is highlighted by the phrase unique to Paul in ancient literature which connects faith and obedience at the start (1.5) and end (16.26) of Romans: *hypakoē pisteōs*.[7] Why has he received grace and apostleship through God's Son, Jesus Christ? In order to call people from among all the Gentiles to the obedience of faith.[8]

The obedience of faith

As reflected in different translations, there continues to be debate as to how best to understand the genitive in this key phrase, and hence the relationship between obedience and faith.[9] It is most likely to refer to (a) the obedience which arises from faith (genitive of source or subjective genitive) or (b) believing obedience (adjectival genitive) or (c) the obedience which consists in faith (genitive of apposition). In the last option when the focus shifts to *pistis* as the form of obedience there is the danger of reducing obedience to faith and then narrowing faith's definition solely to assent or trust without any reference to patterns of faithful behaviour. This would fail to do justice to the phrase as a whole in which, in Oliver O'Donovan's words countering any view which would separate hearing from doing, 'is contained the whole of our response to God, from hearing, understanding and assenting, to willing and acting'.[10] Further, such reductionism distorts the meaning of *pistis*, which must be related to obedience

---

7 Debate continues as to whether Romans 16.26 is a later addition; see Wright 2002, 768, for a defence of its authenticity.

8 In his doctoral thesis, Wright argued that Romans 1.5 was a programmatic statement of Paul's gospel. Scholars with varied understandings of the phrase and Paul's theology note its significance. Garlington 1990, 201, claims it 'gives voice to the design of the apostle's missionary gospel'. Dunn 1988, 1:17, describes it as 'a crucial and central theme, structurally important in understanding the thrust of the letter'. Nanos 1996, 219–20, presenting a distinctive understanding, says this 'fascinating programmatic phrase . . . actually knits together and succinctly defines the various strands' of the letter.

9 See Garlington 1990, 205ff.; Longenecker 2016, 79–82.

10 O'Donovan 1986, 110.

more generally. As Teresa Morgan, professor of Greco-Roman history, argues in her important recent study of the language of faith:

> *Pistis* . . . is often associated with obedience and the language of service, and 'the obedience of *pistis*' is best read as a genitive of apposition, referring to Paul's sense that the *pistis* into which he brings gentiles is, like his own, a relationship of slavish obedience to Christ.[11]

This insistence that faith cannot be separated from obedience is supported by numerous New Testament and Pauline scholars such as Michael F. Bird,[12] Don Garlington,[13] Douglas Moo[14] and Douglas Campbell,[15] and has been extensively argued for recently by Matthew W. Bates.[16]

However we read the phrase, and syntax alone cannot decide this, *obedience* (whatever its relationship to faith and how we then fill out its details) is what Paul's calling and mission seeks to bring about among all the nations. In the words of Miller, '[t]he interpretive debate over this expression should not cause one to lose sight of the fact that Paul is emphasizing the first term in this phrase, "obedience."'[17] This global vision for obedience, overcoming the various patterns of disobedience, is integral to Paul's vocation and identity, as he himself is obedient, as an apostle, to God's call. It should therefore not be a surprise that at the end of the letter he again highlights the fruit of his mission precisely in terms of obedience. He does so not only in the highly significant (but textually disputed) *inclusio* of *hypakoē pisteōs* in 16.26 (the gospel now revealed and made known 'for the obedience of faith among all the nations'). In 15.18, in his peroration, Paul writes, perhaps echoing Genesis 49.10,[18] 'far be it from me, you see, to speak about anything except what the Messiah has accomplished through me for the obedience of the nations',[19] and in 16.19

---

11 Morgan 2015, 282–3.
12 Bird 2016, 31.
13 Garlington 1990, 208.
14 Moo 1996, 52.
15 Campbell 2005, 187.
16 Bates 2017.
17 Miller 2000, 46.
18 In Genesis 49.10 Jacob/Israel blesses Judah with the words 'The sceptre will not depart from Judah, nor the ruler's staff from between his feet, until he to whom it belongs shall come and the obedience of the nations shall be his.' (Unless otherwise noted, Bible quotations in this chapter are taken from the NIV.) Although *eis hypakoēn ethnōn* does not appear in the LXX, this is one of only two verses in the Hebrew Bible to use *yiqhah* (the Hebrew word for obedience).
19 I have taken the translation from Wright 2004b, 120. Wright does not comment on the language of obedience in his commentary (see 2002, 754) though Dunn 1988, 2:856, notes that 'the thematic [*hypakoē*] (v 18) provides a thread which unites missionary impulse,

he tells the members of the Roman church that it is their obedience (cf. 1.8 on their *pistis*) that is well known to all.

God's mercy overcoming human disobedience and lack of *pistis*

Obedience is, then, a fundamental category for Paul when it comes to understanding the appropriate response to his mission and the gospel he proclaims. It is why Paul and Titus celebrate the obedience of the Corinthians (2 Corinthians 7.15). It is why from his early letters his concern is when there is a failure to obey the truth (Galatians 5.7). It is why he can warn of punishment for those whom he describes not simply as unbelievers but as those who do not obey the gospel (2 Thessalonians 1.8; cf. Romans 2.8).

Just as obedience is correlated with *pistis*, so disobedience is connected with the lack of *pistis* as most vividly captured at Romans 10.16. Having described the need for missionary preachers, Paul acknowledges that not all *obeyed* the gospel, a response Isaiah spoke of when he asked who *believed* his report. Whether this is a reference to Israelite or Gentile (as Wright argues) unbelief, it is also clear that Israel's problem with which Paul wrestles, particularly in Romans 9—11, is that, faced with the good news of the Messiah, they have not been obedient, failing to submit to God's righteousness (10.3) revealed in Christ (3.21ff.). Paul therefore reminds the Gentile Christians in Rome of the universal nature of human disobedience and how this dynamic is evident among both Jews and Gentiles:

> Just as you who were at one time disobedient to God [*ēpeithēsate tō theō*] have now received mercy as a result of their disobedience [*tē toutōn apeitheia*], so they too have now become disobedient [*nyn ēpeithēsan*] in order that they too may now receive mercy as a result of God's mercy to you. For God has bound everyone over to disobedience [*eis apeitheian*] so that he may have mercy on them all.
>
> (Romans 11.30–32)

Paul's mission extending Israel's call to obey to the nations – reaffirming but reshaping Israel's ethic of obedience

Obedience being central to the response Paul seeks among the Gentiles should not be a surprise given its centrality within Judaism. John Barton notes that 'obedience to the declared will of God is probably the strongest model for ethical obligation in most books of the Hebrew Scriptures',[20] and

---

theological rationale, and paraenesis (1:5; 5:19; 6:16)'. Later, Dunn adds: 'The use of the thematic [*hypakoē*] is no accident: it was part of Paul's most basic conviction regarding his mission' (862).

[20] Barton 2003, 47. See also Barton 2014, 127–56.

Joseph Ryan Kelly, while critiquing aspects of this view, acknowledges that 'the predominance of Obedience as an ethical basis in the Hebrew Bible remains largely unquestioned in biblical scholarship'.[21] Don Garlington, in his thesis examining 'the obedience of faith' in the context of pre-Pauline Jewish usage, is clear that although the phrase is lacking, 'the idea is clearly present':

> The obedience of God's people, consisting in their fidelity to his covenant with them, is the product of prior belief in his person and trust in his word . . . faith's obedience is the appropriate response of Israel, the covenant partner, to the election, grace and mercy of God . . . there is every reason to believe that when he [Paul] formulates the phrase in Rom 1.5, he does so cognizant of its roots in Jewish tradition.[22]

Indeed, in his famous treatment of 'covenantal nomism', E. P. Sanders argues that 'in all the literature surveyed, *obedience maintains one's position in the covenant, but it does not earn God's grace as such*'.[23]

There are, however, two important shifts in Paul. First, Paul's particular concern is with the obedience *of the Gentiles*. This universal call to obedience post-Christ is not for Paul the pattern of obedience in the Mosaic covenant where obedience was both defined in relation to the law and also tied to Jewish identity. Indeed, for Paul, it was in part the Jewish (mis)understanding of what it meant to obey the law that led the Jews to disobey the gospel (Romans 9.30–33). So Garlington refers to Jewish obedience as being faithful to the covenant embodied in the law of Moses but concludes in relation to Romans 1.5: 'Paul's declaration is tantamount to a manifesto that faith's obedience and, therefore, Israel's identity, privileges and responsibilities were a possibility apart from the assumption of Jewish ethnico-theological distinctives.'[24]

Second, and related, the obedience sought is the obedience *of faith*. This is to be understood not primarily in relation to obeying a set of commands but in relation to obeying the gospel of the lordship of Jesus the Messiah by responding with *pistis* in the pattern of Christ's own obedience (see below).[25] In Wright's words:

---

21 Kelly 2013, 6.
22 Garlington 1987, 329.
23 Sanders 1977, 420 (italics original).
24 Garlington 1987, 357.
25 Clearly this does not mean that the Old Testament has no relevance to Christian living but 'believers in Christ . . . are not obliged to obey the law . . . What counts is not the law, but faith expressing itself through love, the new creation, keeping the commandments of God, and righteousness, peace and joy in the Holy Spirit' (Rosner 2013, 221–2).

When Paul thinks of Jesus as Lord, he thinks of himself as a slave and of the world as being called to obedience to Jesus' lordship. His apostolic commission is not to offer people a new religious option, but to summon them to allegiance to Jesus, which will mean abandoning other loyalties. The gospel issues a command, an imperial summons; the appropriate response is obedience.[26]

Paul's missionary call for the nations to obey and be captive to Christ – the context of Rome's imperial mission

Wright's language of 'imperial summons' points to the other context in which Paul's language of obedience generally, and 'the obedience of faith' more specifically, needs to be set: that of the Roman Empire. As Jason Myers has recently demonstrated through examination of various Greek and Latin and non-literary (such as Augustus' *Res Gestae*) sources, the idea and language of the nations' obedience would have been very familiar from its function in Roman imperial rhetoric.[27] Obedience is exactly what was demanded of those Rome conquered and embraced within the Empire and it provided the means for those nations to experience peace rather than war. So, Virgil in the *Aeneid* speaks of Rome making 'the world obey'.[28] Similarly, Polybius notes that 'The Roman conquest . . . was not partial. Nearly the whole inhabited world was reduced by them to obedience.'[29] For Polybius, this obedience is a consequence of entering into the 'faith of the Romans'.[30] Myers concludes in relation to Greek sources that

> it is explicitly clear from Polybius to Plutarch that the adjective *hypēkoos* is the preferred term for describing those territories and peoples that are subordinate to Rome. Such use of a term highlights the central role of obedience in Rome's process of describing and identifying those within its Empire.[31]

Similarly he comments: 'throughout the Latin sources, obedience is connected with the nations and is the evidence of faith and is the key to securing peace.'[32]

---

26 Wright 2002, 420.
27 I am grateful to Jason Myers for providing me with a copy of his doctoral thesis (Myers 2015), which will soon be published by de Gruyter.
28 Virgil, *Aeneid*, 6.852, cited in Myers 2015, 3.
29 Polybius, *Histories*, 1.2.3, cited in Myers 2015, 3, and discussed more fully at pp. 53–65.
30 On 'The Faith of the Romans' in Polybius see Myers 2015, 58–64.
31 Myers 2015, 94.
32 Myers 2015, 130.

Thus, in making obedience central, Paul is showing continuity with his Jewish heritage and world and also offering an alternative narrative to the dominant one of the Roman Empire.[33] The fundamental difference from both is that at the centre of his account of obedience is the Messiah: Paul's task is 'to bring the world, all the nations, into loyal allegiance – *hypakoē pisteos*, the obedience of faith – to this universal Lord'.[34]

The passage which most fully captures this and also has the strongest echoes of, and contrast with, the pattern of obedience sought by Rome through imperial conquest and weapons of war is Paul's description of his mission in 2 Corinthians 10.3–6:

> Yes, we are mere humans, but we don't fight the war in a merely human way. The weapons we use for the fight, you see, are not merely human; they carry a power from God that can tear down fortresses! We tear down clever arguments, and every proud notion that sets itself up against the knowledge of God. We take every thought prisoner and make it obey the Messiah (*kai aichmalōtizontes pan noēma eis tēn hypakoēn tou Christou*). We are holding ourselves in readiness to punish every disobedience, when your obedience is complete.[35]

Understood, as here in Wright's translation and almost universally, as an objective genitive – obeying the Messiah – the use of *tēn hypakoēn tou Christou* combined with the language of completing one's obedience (*hotan plērōthē hymōn hē hypakoē*) in verse 6 confirms the centrality of obedience as a goal of Paul's mission.[36]

That obedience here is also very explicitly tied to the Messiah. Christ is generally understood as the one to be obeyed, but it should not be ruled out that the phrase is a subjective genitive – the Messiah's obedience – as has recently been argued by Kibbe, building on Stegman.[37] As these authors note, there are contextual arguments for Paul speaking here of Christ's obedience such as the subjective genitive in 2 Corinthians

---

33 As Myers 2015, 131–59 demonstrates, the language of obedience connects Paul not only to Jewish and imperial worlds but also to another major concern of Wright in *PFG*: Greek and Roman philosophy.

34 Wright 2013b, 240: 'Paul and Caesar: A New Reading of Romans' (2002), 237–54; originally published in *A Royal Priesthood: The Use of the Bible Ethically and Politically* (ed. C. Bartholomew; Carlisle: Paternoster, 2002), 173–93.

35 Translation taken from Wright 2003, 104.

36 The reference to one's thoughts as an integral part of this process suggests possible connections with Romans 12.2 (see section 3 below).

37 Kibbe 2012, 41–56, extending the argument of Stegman 2005, 121–37. Campbell 2005, 187, comments: 'Christ is explicitly described as obedient to God in certain important texts (Rom. 5.19; Phil 2.8; and 2 Cor 10.5?!).'

10.1 where Paul writes of the humility and gentleness of the Messiah (*tēs prautētos kai epieikeias tou Christou*) and the letter's wider concern to relate Paul's ministry to the pattern of Christ in terms of suffering and power-through-weakness in sharp contrast with his opponents' form of ministry and account of Christ. These verses not only connect the language of obedience to that used by Rome, but also open up the two other central elements in any account of obedience in Paul: the subjective-genitive reading links this passage in 2 Corinthians to the two undisputed 'obedience of Christ' passages (section 3), while on either reading the significance of obedience in the Christian life and the connection between obedience and slavery is clearly stated (section 4).[38]

Conclusion: obeying the gospel

Matthew's Gospel famously ends with Jesus' call to the apostles to go and make disciples by securing the obedience of all the nations. Accounts of Paul's missionary goals rarely give obedience so prominent a place, and such an emphasis might appear paradoxical to many, given his law-free gospel. It is, however, the obedience of the nations which frames his great epistle to the Romans, and obedience is the response he seeks to the gospel. This is because, in Wright's words, 'the gospel . . . is a royal summons to submission, to obedience, to allegiance; and the form that this submission and obedient allegiance takes is of course faith. That is what Paul means by "the obedience of faith."'[39] The substance of that faithful obedience or obedient faith is neither the Torah nor the pattern of obedience sought by Rome, but rather the obedience that lies at the heart of the gospel which is obeyed: the Messiah's obedience.

3 The obedience of Christ: a crucial element in Paul's theology

The obedience of Christ is only explicitly referred to in two passages of Paul (apart from its possible appearance in 2 Corinthians 10) but the significance of those passages and the central and decisive role played by

---

[38] If *tēn hypakoēn tou Christou* refers to Christ's own obedience the language of 'taking prisoner' or 'taking captive' still clearly implies the convert's own obedience (also referred to explicitly in v. 6) and portrays the Christian as a slave not simply to Christ but to Christ's own obedience (cf. Romans 6.16 discussed below).

[39] Wright 2013b, 278: 'New Perspectives on Paul' (2003), 273–91; originally published in *Justification in Perspective: Historical Developments and Contemporary Challenges* (ed. Bruce L. McCormack; Grand Rapids, MI: Baker Academic, 2006), 243–64.

Christ's obedience within them warns against minimizing the importance of this theme in his theology on the basis of the paucity and brevity of direct references to it.[40]

Philippians 2: Christ the obedient slave and Christian obedience

In Philippians 2 Paul calls on Christians to have the same mindset as (or the mindset that they have in) Christ Jesus (2.5). He then proceeds to describe that mindset in the famous Christ-hymn: Christ took the form of a servant or slave (v. 7) and humbled himself (v. 8). How? By becoming obedient (*genomenos hypēkoos*, v. 8), obedient through to death on a cross.

Here we see again the importance of being obedient in Paul's understanding of the form of the Christian life as confirmed by the verses that immediately follow the hymn whose terminology of obedience is often overlooked: 'as you have always obeyed [*kathōs pantote hypēkousate*] . . . continue to work out your salvation with fear and trembling' (2.12). But we also see that the basis for making obedience central in the Christian life, and the shape and pattern of this obedience, is now defined by the obedience of Christ.

> The obedience of the Philippians (*hypekousate*) recalls the obedience of Christ (*hypekoos*) . . . Paul is urging his readers again to follow the pattern of Christ, who, by his humble obedience, attained his vindication from God. Christians are to follow suit and attain *their soteria*, vindication by God, by their obedience with fear and trembling.[41]

Although the focus in Philippians 2 is particularly on Christ's death, this is presented as the climax and culmination of his whole life which is here characterized as one of obedience. That characterization and summation of Christ's life as one of obedience is even more explicit in the other Pauline passage: Romans 5. There Christ is contrasted with Adam who is seen by many, including Wright, as also present, albeit hiding, in Philippians 2.[42]

Romans 5: Christ's redemptive obedience

Within the argument of Romans Paul has already argued that all human beings – both Jews and Gentiles – are sinners and has described their patterns of life in various ways, including disobeying the truth (2.8), which

---

[40] So, rightly, Gorman 2001, 107: 'Only two times in his letters does Paul refer to the obedience of Christ, but the significance of these two occurrences is weighty.' On the issue more broadly in the New Testament, see Longenecker 1974, 142–52.

[41] Anderson 2016, 305. Cf. Bockmuehl 1997, 150.

[42] See Wright 1991, 90ff.; 2013a, 686.

will lead to God's future wrath. He has also announced how God has acted to redeem this situation by demonstrating his righteousness *dia pisteōs Iēsou Christou* (3.21ff.). In Romans 5.12–21, which Wright describes as '*both* . . . the place where the "poetic sequence" of the letter is summed up *and* . . . the place where the underlying "narrative sequence" of Paul's theology finds its most fundamental statement', Paul relates these two stories again, comparing and contrasting Adam with the gracious gift of Christ in various ways.[43]

In relation to the language of obedience, the key verse is verse 19:

> For just as through the disobedience of one person [*dia tēs parakoēs tou henos anthrōpou*] many received the status of 'sinner', so through the obedience of one person [*dia tēs hypakoēs tou henos*] many will receive the status of 'in the right'.[44]

This grounds verse 18, which picks up the argument begun in verse 12 containing a similar contrast:

> So, then, just as, through the trespass of one person [*di' henos paraptōmatos*], the result was condemnation for all people, even so, through the upright act of one person [*di' henos dikaiōmatos*], the result is justification – life for all people.[45]

The structure of both verses is the same: a contrast between the actions of the two representative figures and the results of their actions for others. What Christ brings into human history is here summed up simply as 'obedience' (paralleled with 'one upright act'). The consequence here is not that he himself is exalted by God following his obedience (as in Philippians 2) but that many are rendered righteous (*dikaioi*, paralleled with justification and life).[46]

Obedience is, it seems, what God was seeking but humanity – *in toto*, both Jew and Gentile – was lacking following the disobedience of Adam. Just as in Philippians 2, obedience is what is embodied in Christ's life and supremely his death, here also described as God's gracious gift. As Campbell notes, 'It seems especially significant, then, that *hypakoē* is used

---

[43] Wright 2013b, 107: 'Romans and the Theology of Paul' (1995), 93–125; originally published in *Pauline Theology*, III (ed. David M. Hay and E. Elizabeth Johnson; Minneapolis: Fortress, 1995), 30–67.

[44] I have taken the translation from Wright 2004a, 93.

[45] Wright 2004a, 93.

[46] For discussion of similarities and differences between obedience in Philippians 2 and Romans 5, see Fowl 2005, 114–17.

as a strategic summary of Christ's saving activity,[47] or, in Wright's words, '*the obedience of the Messiah* is the means by which the purpose of election, the rescuing and restoration of the human race, is accomplished.'[48]

Christ as obeying the law?

As in Philippians 2, there is no statement in Romans 5 concerning what or whom Christ obeys. This has led to developments in later Christian dogmatics, particularly in strands of Reformed covenantal and federal theology. Appealing to Paul, and in particular to Romans 5, these have given obedience, including Christ's obedience, the sort of prominence in theology and ethics argued for here as genuinely Pauline, but they have set this within a theological framework less faithful to Paul's lines of thought.[49] This tradition has, from the late sixteenth century, used the language of Christ's active obedience and his passive obedience, a distinction which is variously understood.[50] For some, these refer, broadly, to his sinless life (active) and his atoning death (passive), whereas for the majority 'the distinction between the active and passive obedience is not a distinction of periods' but rather 'the recognition that the law of God has both penal sanctions and positive demands. It demands not only the full discharge of its precepts but also the infliction of penalty for all infractions and shortcomings.'[51] Here Christ's active obedience is his complete obedience to the demands of God's law,[52] either the law of the Mosaic covenant or, in some strands, a pre-lapsarian law which was part of an Adamic covenant of works.[53] Within this systematic theology, this active legal obedience of

---

[47] Campbell 2009a, 611–12.
[48] Wright 2013a, 890 (italics original). Cf. Moo 1996, 315.
[49] Wright's familiarity and youthful sympathies with this tradition are evident from his co-authorship of *The Grace of God in the Gospel* (Cheeseman et al. 1972). His rejection of it as 'almost certainly not what Paul has in mind here' is clear in Wright 2002, 529, and his fuller discussion of it as 'something of a parody' in Wright 2013b, 372: 'Reading Paul, Thinking Scripture: "Atonement" as a Special Study' (2007), 356–78; originally published in *Scripture's Doctrine and Theology's Bible: How the New Testament Shapes Christian Dogmatics* (ed. Markus Bockmuehl and Alan J. Torrance; Grand Rapids, MI: Baker Academic, 2008), 59–71. See also Anderson 2016, 133.
[50] See Venema 2009. See also his earlier critique of Wright from this perspective in Venema 2005.
[51] Murray 1961, 21.
[52] This contrasts with Adamic humanity because 'God requires of men that they should be holy as he is holy, and that they should obey the Law, failure to do which is precisely the sin of mankind' (Cheeseman et al. 1972, 24).
[53] The latter view is summed up in the Westminster Confession of Faith, VII (where Romans 5.12–19 is cited as a scriptural proof) and VIII.5.

Christ is then an essential element of his righteousness, and the imputation of this to us is the basis for our justification.[54]

Despite its proper emphasis on the importance of obedience, in terms of Paul's argument in Romans 5 (and his theology more widely), the problem with this is that Paul never speaks of an Adamic covenant of works requiring obedience and never appeals to the law as what Christ obeyed. Rather than working with law as a general moral category, his use of *nomos* is overwhelmingly focused specifically on the Torah, as in the next verse (5.20) after he speaks of Christ's obedience. It there has a quite different purpose from that of being the expression of God's will which Christ obeyed: the law comes in to increase Adam's original trespass, which is exactly what occurred within Israel: 'All day long I have held out my hands to a disobedient and obstinate people' (Isaiah 65.2 quoted in Romans 10.21).

Rather than importing the category of law (which makes even less sense of the language of obeying in Philippians 2), it is much better to read Paul in both these passages as viewing Jesus simply as obedient to God, an appropriate relationship and pattern of life for one who is God's Son. So Fowl, noting that in the slave language of Philippians 2.8 'no master is explicitly named', nevertheless says: 'it becomes clear that in his obedience, even to the point of death, Christ was being obedient to God . . . This systematic obedience to God is the way in which Christ manifests the appearance of a slave.'[55]

Paul frequently emphasizes God's will[56] and God's call,[57] both categories to which the appropriate response is obedience and, unlike an appeal to

---

[54] So the Westminster Confession on justification speaks of God 'imputing the obedience and satisfaction of Christ unto them' (XI.1, again citing Romans 5.17–19 as proof). Toplady's hymn 'A Debtor to Mercy Alone' sums up the tradition: 'The terrors of law and of God with me can have nothing to do; My Saviour's obedience and blood hide all my transgressions from view' (quoted in Cheeseman et al. 1972, 82). On this Reformed tradition, see VanDrunen 2006.

[55] Fowl 2005, 97–8.

[56] In Galatians 1.4 (NIV), though the language of obedience is not present, Paul writes of Christ acting according to God's will when he 'gave himself for our sins to rescue us from the present evil age, according to the will of our God and Father'. The will of God is the basis of Paul's own apostleship (1 Corinthians 1.1; 2 Corinthians 1.1; Ephesians 1.1; Colossians 1.1); it is what the law instructs Israel in (Romans 2.18), what is made known in Christ (Ephesians 1.5, 9), what Christians are to discern (Romans 12.2), understand (Ephesians 5.17) and do (Ephesians 6.6), and what Paul prays they will know (Colossians 1.9). It is a will for holiness or sanctification (1 Thessalonians 4.3).

[57] Language of God's call clearly overlaps in Paul with that of God's will, for example in relation to Paul's apostleship (Romans 1.1; 1 Corinthians 1.1; Galatians 1.15) and the call to be holy (Romans 1.7; 1 Thessalonians 4.7). In Galatians 5.7–8 the Galatians' failure to obey the truth is described as incompatible with the work of 'the one who calls you'.

God's law, these make sense of all his uses of obedience, including Christ's obedience. If we ask what call in particular Christ is obedient to in Romans 5 there may be a clue in the description of obedience's consequence as 'many will be made righteous', an echo which points the attentive reader back to the obedient Suffering Servant of Isaiah 53.[58] This should already have been heard in Romans 4.25 (where 'He was delivered over to death for our sins and was raised to life for our justification' echoes Isaiah 53.5, 12) and resonates afresh in the conclusion of 5.19, given the witness of Isaiah 53.11 that 'my righteous servant will justify many'.[59]

Christ's obedience, the obedience of faith, and *pistis Christou*

Understanding the obedience of Romans 5 and Philippians 2 in terms of Christ's response to the call and will of God, rather than obeying the law, also enables an important connection to be made with where we began this study of obedience and the argument of both Romans 1—3 and Philippians 2—3. What is the pattern or form of Christ's obedience? It is one not of comprehensive compliance with legal obligations but one of *pistis* understood as faithfulness or allegiance in response to God's will and call. As such, this obedience answers not only the disobedience of Adam but also the faithlessness of Israel (Romans 3.2, 3) and it surpasses any pattern of obedience which might be thought to establish an Israel-based righteousness from the law (Philippians 3.9, summing up Philippians 3.3–6). As Wright[60] and a growing number of scholars including Luke Timothy Johnson,[61] Michael J. Gorman,[62] and Douglas A. Campbell[63] have argued, this gives a strong basis for connecting the language of

58 Bauckham 2008, 42–4, sees this passage as well as Isaiah 52.12 behind Paul's mention of obedience in Philippians 2. See also Wright 2013a, 682ff.
59 Wright 2002, 529; 2013a, 999. There may be a further echo of Isaiah 53.12 in Romans 8.34 in relation to intercession, perhaps a witness to the ascended Christ's ongoing obedience.
60 Wright connects Christ's obedience and *pistis* in various places, e.g. his popular commentary on Romans 5.19 says, 'Jesus acted as the embodiment both of God's covenant faithfulness and of the faithful obedience which Israel (3.2) should have offered to God but failed to do. Here Paul is summing up what he said about the Messiah's faithfulness in 3.22' (2004a, 94). See also Wright 2002, 529.
61 Johnson 1982, reads Romans 5.12–21 as expounding 'the faith of Jesus Christ' (see especially 87–9).
62 Gorman 2001, 82, describes Christ's death as 'an act of obedience, righteousness, and faith(fulness)'. He goes on to present 'the thesis that Christ's obedient death is also his act of faith' (Gorman 2001, 95–121). See also Gorman 2009, 57–8: 'Paul also interprets Christ's death as an act of *obedience* (to God the Father) and similarly as an act of "*faith*", in the sense of "*covenantal faithfulness*" or "faithful obedience"' (58).
63 Campbell 2009b.

obedience to the phrase *pistis Christou* understood as referring to Christ's own *pistis*. What is described as obedience in Romans 5.19 (and one righteous act in 5.18) and Philippians 2.8 is effectively synonymous with the 'faithfulness of [Jesus] Christ' in Romans 3.22 and Philippians 3.9.

It is, however, important to recognize that although this connection between Christ's obedience and *pistis Christou* is significant and opens up further avenues for exegetical, theological and ethical exploration, the significance of Christ's obedience within Paul's theology and ethics is not dependent on it. As James Dunn, who is not persuaded by the 'faith of Christ' case,[64] writes:

> The Pauline emphasis on Christ's mission as a Jew and his obedience to his commission is not dependent on the 'faith of Christ' rendering of [*pistis Christou*]. That emphasis is quite clear and should be given appropriate attention in modern restatements of Paul's theology, regardless of what decision is made about [*pistis Christou*]. Let us not make the mistake of suggesting that without 'the faith of Christ' interpretation of *pistis Christou* we have lost sight of that important emphasis which Paul (and other NT writings) place on Christ as the pattern for the 'obedience of faith'.[65]

The obedience of Christ is, then, not to be defined as his obedience to the law as it has been in those parts of the Christian tradition which have retained an important place for it in their theology. This would entail a theology in which the pattern of obedience is not defined by Christ but rather Christ is subordinate to the law rather than being its *telos* (10.4). Or, rather, if we are to speak of Christ's obedience in relation to law we need to do so in the light of the form of his own obedience or faithfulness and of Romans 3.27 (*dia poiou nomou; tōn ergōn; ouchi, alla dia nomou pisteōs*): Christ obeys the law of *pistis*. His obedience is thus the paradigmatic embodiment of the obedience of faith which Paul seeks to secure from Gentiles because 'Christ proved his trustworthiness by trusting God in complete obedience to the divine will.'[66]

---

[64] Writing at an earlier stage in the *pistis Christou* debate Dunn commented (1998, 383 n. 200), 'the Adam parallel is made by emphasising Christ's *obedience*, not his faith (Rom 5.19, Phil. 2.8)'.
[65] Dunn 2009, xvii.
[66] Williams 1980, 275. Cf. Romans 5.18–19.

4 The obedience of the Christian: the pattern of faithful new covenant life in Christ

What, then, does this obedience of Christ have to do with Paul's understanding of the nature and place of obedience in the Christian life? As we have already seen in Philippians 2, the obedience of Christ appears in the context of references to the Philippians' own obedience – they are to have the same mind (Philippians 2.5), and have obeyed and need to continue doing so (2.12). The same pattern appears in Romans, as Bockmuehl comments on Philippians 3.9:

> And just as in Romans the believers' *hupakoé pisteôs* ('obedience of faith': 1.5; cf. 10.16; 15.18; 16.19, 26) could be said to derive from Christ's own *pistis* (3.22, 26) and *hupakoé* (5.19), it is not unreasonable in Philippians to link Christ's *pistis* (3.9) and being *hupékoos* (2.8) with those same qualities in the believers (1.25, 27, 29; 2.12, 17; 3.9). (Cf. the comparable logic in Heb 5.7–9).[67]

The importance of the Christian's obedience

Following the obedience of Christ in Romans 5.19, there is the strongest concentration of obedience language in the Pauline corpus in Roman 6.12ff. These verses, in developing the Adam–Christ theme, reveal how Paul conceptualizes obedience and its importance for those in Christ.[68] Cranfield comments that Paul 'wanted at this point specially to emphasize the thought of obedience'.[69]

In Romans 6.1–14 Paul explains why, even though grace increased even more where sin increased (5.20), we should not remain in sin (6.1). This is because in baptism we are united with Christ in his death (6.2–10) and so have died to sin and should reckon ourselves dead to sin but alive to God in Christ (6.11).[70] Paul then refers again to Christian obedience, in relation not to Christ but to obeying the power of sin: Christians are

---

67 Bockmuehl 1997, 211.
68 Similarly, if 2 Corinthians 10.4 refers to Christ's obedience it is in the context of an appeal to the pattern of Christ's life (10.1) and a reference to Christian obedience (10.5).
69 Cranfield 1975, 323. Cf. Barrett 1971, 131, on the importance of showing 'that obedience has a place in the system of grace and faith'.
70 Although not explicitly stated, the language of being baptized into Christ's death (6.3), united with him into a death like his (6.5) and dying with Christ (6.8) all point, given the importance of his death at the heart of his pattern of obedience, to us thereby participating through union with Christ in his obedience. So Gorman (2009, 74–5) notes: 'what is described in Romans 6:1—7:6 is a participatory death-and-resurrection experience that . . . is implicitly grounded (in context) in the faith/obedience and love of Christ (5:19; 8:34–35).'

not to let sin reign in their mortal bodies, if they do then they will obey sin's desires. Here obedience is set in a wider context in which desires are what are obeyed.[71] Our obedience, which Paul significantly proceeds to describe in terms of an offering of our members (6.13), signals who or what is reigning in our life.

Obedience and slavery to the obedient Christ

In 6.16 Paul picks up that language in order to expound its connection with obedience and to connect it to another central image, that of slavery. He does so with an analogy from his social world: 'Don't you know that when you offer yourselves to someone as obedient slaves, you are slaves of the one you obey . . .?' In short, to obey is to be a slave and to be a slave is to obey.[72] After this general point about obedience, Paul returns specific- ally to the Adam–Christ typology of the previous chapter. He describes the two contrasting forms of offering, slavery and obedience, with which we are faced: obedience in some form is, it seems, simply unavoidable as part of being human.[73] Reworking the earlier discussion in chapter 6 of the life we are to leave behind, and recalling the effect of Adam, someone can be a slave who obeys sin, and this leads to death. This picks up the connection between sin and death made back in 5.12 ('just as sin entered the world through one man, and death through sin, and in this way death came to all people, because all sinned').

What is noteworthy is how Paul then expresses the contrasting pattern: a slave who offers himself or herself and obeys *obedience*, leading to right- eousness. First, there is the 'surprising and striking'[74] language of obeying, offering oneself and being a slave to 'obedience', rather than to God or Christ. Dodd, describing it as 'probably little more than an inadvertence in dictating', writes that 'Paul has confused the matter . . . it is certainly not felicitous to suggest that the master who is obeyed is Obedience!'[75] But he

---

[71] In Romans 1.24 God gave people over in the desires of their hearts, and in Romans 7.7, 8 the commandment quoted is that relating to desire. In Romans 13.14, Galatians 5.16, 24 and Ephesians 2.3 Paul speaks of the desires of the flesh. A life of desire is what marks out the Gentiles who do not know God (1 Thessalonians 4.5) but whom Paul is calling to the obedi- ence of faith.

[72] There is the danger that linking obedience to slavery may suggest simply a sense of duty and obligation or even coercion whereas Paul stresses obedience from the heart and *pistis*. Byrne, 1981, 564, describes 6.16–23 as 'employing the rather unattractive "slavery image"' but acknowledges 'a skilful vindication of the necessity of obedience in an epoch of grace'.

[73] 'Paul's concern is to rule out the possibility of neutrality' (Käsemann 1980, 180). Or, as Bob Dylan memorably put it, 'You're gonna have to serve somebody.'

[74] Dunn 1988, 1:342.

[75] Dodd 1932, 97. Similarly Wright 2004a, 113: 'strange to think of being obedient to obedience,

also acknowledges, without exploring further, a better explanation – 'the fact that the righteousness of Christ has been described as obedience'.[76] In fact, the best reading is that Paul is indeed highlighting this aspect in the earlier account of Christ. 'Obedience' here should be understood as 'synecdoche for Christ's obedience (5:19) and hence Christ himself',[77] just as 'sin' – the other possible master – represents Adam. What we are to obey is Christ's own pattern of obedient life. This is confirmed, second, by the description in 6.16 of obedience leading to righteousness. In contrast to obeying sin leading to death, one might have expected obedience here to lead to 'life'. Alternatively, given the outcome is righteousness, one might expect the language of 'faith' rather than 'obedience' to mark the contrast with sin (cf. Romans 1.17, 14.23). However, just as sin/death picks up Adam in 5.12, so obedience/righteous(ness) picks up the connection made in relation to Christ back in 5.19 that 'through the obedience of the one man the many will be made righteous.'

In summary, future righteousness is through the obedience of Christ (5.19). Being united with Christ in his obedience (supremely in his death) entails being obedient to him after the pattern of his own obedience which is the path to righteousness (6.16).[78] The language of being a *slave to obedience* in 6.16 clearly alludes to the social reality of slave labour and obedience in Paul's world[79] and probably also to slaves and slavery in Jewish tradition,[80] but it goes much deeper and sheds further light on the nature of obedience in Paul. The calling of Christians here is to be slaves of Christ[81] who, although confessed as Lord, was himself marked out by his obedience. That is why they are described as slaves to obedience. And Christ's obedience was that of one who, as Philippians 2 makes clear,

---

but he needs something to contrast with "sin" and this will do for the moment.'
[76] Dodd 1932, 97.
[77] Gorman 2009, 76 n. 99. Similarly, Wright 2002, 544: 'The "obedience" to which one offers obedience is, of course, a periphrasis (or circumlocution); behind it stands the obedience of Christ in 5:19 . . . This explains, though it hardly excuses, the unclarity.'
[78] This opens up the issue of how a focus on Paul's teaching on obedience might also help shed light on the debate about connecting present justification by faith to future judgement by deeds.
[79] Paul uses the language of obedience in ethical teaching concerning social relations of children to parents (Ephesians 6.1; Colossians 3.20), ruled to rulers (Romans 13.1; Titus 3.1) and slaves to masters (Ephesians 6.5; Colossians 3.22).
[80] See Goodrich 2013.
[81] Paul regularly introduces himself as a slave of Christ (Romans 1.1; Galatians 1.10; Philippians 1.1) and calls on Christians to be, or describes them as, slaves of Christ or those serving him as a slave (Romans 12.11; 14.18; 16.18; 1 Corinthians 7.22; Ephesians 6.6–7; 2 Timothy 2.24; Colossians 1.7; 4.7; 4.12). See Harris 1999.

himself took the form of a slave. Slavery, and obedience which is so intrinsically connected with it,[82] are thus Christologically reconfigured in Paul's account of the Christian life. As Geoffrey Turner comments:

> Righteousness, faithfulness, obedience and slavery are all tied together in these chapters . . . Paul has introduced the metaphor of slavery into this context, not because it is any kind of aberration, but for the positive reason – odd as it might seem to us in our social situation – that a slave is an exemplar of what it is to be faithful and obedient, which Paul has chosen as the highest of virtues before God. Being obedient, then, is as ineluctable a dimension of being human as is being a slave. The fundamental issue is: who shall we obey, to whom shall we be enslaved, to whom shall we be faithful? Sin or God? And in place of God we can speak of his emissary Jesus Christ, the prototype of obedience, faithfulness and the slave.[83]

The Roman Christians' obedience from the heart: God's new-covenant, return-from-exile people (Romans 6.17)

Having introduced these two contrasting forms of slavery and obedience in 6.16, Paul explores them further in 6.18–23 (though without explicitly using language of obedience). He does so in terms of being either enslaved to sin/impurity which leads to increasing lawlessness/death or enslaved to righteousness[84]/God which leads to holiness/eternal life. But before he does this he gives thanks to God for obedience already exhibited by the Roman believers (even though they used to be slaves of sin). Again he does so using terms which are unexpected: 'you have become obedient from the heart to the pattern of teaching to which you were committed' (*hypēkousate de ek kardias eis hon paredothēte typon didachēs*).[85] Before exploring what is obeyed, three key points need to be noted.

First, this is a real, past obedience. This may refer to the Roman believers' conversion, which we've seen Paul can speak of in terms of obeying the gospel (Romans 10.16; 2 Thessalonians 1.8),[86] or to the fact they have already, perhaps in baptism, moved their allegiance and pattern

---

[82] 'Obedience is a necessary correlate to slavery (*douloi este hō hypakouete*, v16), so that those who present themselves to God/righteousness to serve him as slaves must obey him, rather than obey sin, if in fact they truly are God's slaves (6:16–19)' (Goodrich 2013, 529).

[83] Turner 2013, 10.

[84] Space prevents further discussion here, but the extent to which 'righteousness' in Paul, at least here, overlaps with 'obedience' is an important one as is how, in different language, these contrasts are picked up again in Romans 8 in reference to both *nomos* and the contrast of the flesh and the Spirit.

[85] Wright 2004a, 111.

[86] For example, Moo 1996, 400–1.

of obedience away from sin/Adam/impurity so as to obey obedience/ Christ/righteousness.

Second, that obedience is related to having been handed over. This highlights that whatever the Roman Christians obey has a directive role and is different from the more common description of Paul handing over teaching to Christians. The passive language of 'handing over' prob- ably points to a divine handing over, emphasizing that obedience is a response to a decisive and transformative divine initiative. This is a gra- cious contrast to, even reversal of, God's wrathful handing over described in Romans 1.24, 26 and 28 (in part a handing over to the desires of their hearts whereas here the handing over has produced obedience from the heart). In what is perhaps (particularly given the earlier argument in Romans 6) an allusion to baptismal practice, being handed over also signals the transfer of lordship and has further echoes of slavery.

Third, this pattern of Christian obedience is, very significantly, further explained as being 'from the heart', the only use of *ek kardias* in Paul outside the Pastoral Epistles. Already in Romans the heart has been revealed as part of the human problem (1.21, 24; 2.5) but also where, in fulfilment of the promised new covenant, God will be at work – writing the work of the law on the heart (2.15, a reference to willing and delighted obedience, cf. Psalm 40.8), effecting circumcision (2.29) and pouring out the love of God by the Holy Spirit (5.5). It is from such a divinely trans- formed heart that this form of obedience flows. Later (10.6–10), the heart is, according to the righteousness of faith, a heart in which is to be found the word of faith which Paul preaches.[87] This is evident in the confession of Jesus as Lord (with all its implications in terms of obedience[88]) and the heart believing that God raised Jesus from the dead unto justification (*eis dikaiosynēn*, 10.10; see also 6.16). The words of the righteousness of faith quoted here in Romans 10, which speak of this heart, are taken from Deuteronomy 30.14, and the word is in the heart so that it may be done, but this doing is reinterpreted by Paul, as Dunn explains:

> The implication is that when Deut 30:14 speaks of the word in the heart Paul understands it to be speaking of the law written in the heart (Jer 31:33), understands the obedience called for to be the 'obedience of faith' and not merely the obedience of works . . . He can take Deut 30:11–14 as

---

87 Hays, 1989, 163, comments: 'Paul can read Deut. 30:11–14 to mean that the presence of God's word in the community of God's people empowers the obedience of faith.'
88 On Romans 10.8, Wright 2002, 664, comments on Paul's 'own announcing of Jesus as the risen Lord, summoning people to "the obedience of faith" (1.5)'.

characterizing 'righteousness from faith', not only because it speaks of a deeper level of obedience, of the level of obedience which the law properly understood really looked for, of the level of obedience which his gospel in continuity with the law of righteousness now proclaims; but also because its wording invites a reference to the cosmic lordship of Christ proclaimed by the same gospel.[89]

Indeed, that whole climactic chapter of Deuteronomy 30, related to the return from exile, is saturated with obedience language alongside many of the other themes from Romans noted above in relation to the heart.[90] It is when, having been dispersed among the nations, the people of Israel obey God's voice from their whole heart (*kai hypakousē tēs phōnēs autou . . . ex holēs tēs kardias sou kai ex holēs tēs psychēs sou*, LXX 30.2, with echoes of the Shema), that the Lord will bring them back from exile (30.3–5) and circumcise their hearts so that they will love him (30.6) and obey him, turning to the Lord with all their heart (30.8, 10). In Wright's words, 'Paul's basic claim about Deuteronomy 30 is that the great change in Israel's fortunes which that chapter describes . . . is precisely what has come about through Jesus the Messiah.'[91]

We can now see how all this relates to obedience: it is Christ's whole-hearted obedience, even to death, which has led (through his resurrection) to the return from exile: 'Paul infuses Deut 30:12–14 with a Christological *pro nobis*. Within Deut 30, these verses function as an exhortation to the obedience requisite to restoration, but Paul suggests that God has fulfilled the condition for restoration in Christ.'[92] God's work of restoration now extends even to the Gentiles, including those in Rome, whose hearts are circumcised so that they are no longer slaves to sin but rather they obey, with the obedience of faith, from the heart. In the words of Ciampa:

> Moses looks forward to a future day when God's presence and word would be restored to his people and they would love him and obey him again. That would come about after they had returned to God and seen the end of their exile. Paul seems to understand that God himself has turned his chosen

---

[89] Dunn 1988, 2:614–15.

[90] On the heart and obedience in Paul, see Wells 2010.

[91] Wright 2013a, 1172.

[92] Lincicum 2009, 171. Wright 2013b, 352, captures the narrative, though without reference to obedience: 'The fundamental issue is Paul's eschatological claim that Israel's God has now acted in Jesus, demonstrating him through the resurrection to be Israel's Messiah (Romans 1.4), and so declaring that the new age has been inaugurated, the age promised in Deuteronomy 30'. This is from the essay 'Romans and the Theology of Paul' (1995), 93–125, originally published in *Pauline Theology*, III (ed. David M. Hay and E. Elizabeth Johnson; Minneapolis: Fortress, 1995), 30–67.

people's heart back to him through the death and resurrection of Christ (that one, world-transforming, act of obedience) and the proclamation of the same.[93]

We therefore find, once again, here in the language of Romans 6.17 the importance of obedience for Paul, but who or what is it that the Roman Christians have already obeyed in this way? This is unclear. What Paul says we obey is, as in 6.16, unexpected and confusing. Rather than repeating any of the terms already used to describe what is to be obeyed, Paul writes of obeying 'the *typos* of teaching' to which they were handed over. Longenecker notes that Paul's phrase here 'has been notoriously difficult to translate and understand' so that scholars 'have often been at a loss as to how to interpret it'.[94] Some even argue it is a later interpolation.[95] Two points need to be emphasized. First, all that has been said above about the nature of this obedience stands, however we interpret this phrase, and may help in assessing different translations and interpretations. Second, Paul quite clearly does not talk of obedience to the law or commandments or any of the other Deuteronomic language of what is to be obeyed. This is, as we have seen, one of the crucial moves in his thinking: he is maintaining the importance, even centrality, of obedience as in the Old Testament, particularly Deuteronomy, but reshaping its character and redefining its object by detaching it from the Torah, as traditionally understood, in the light of Christ and the Spirit.

In considering what is obeyed, one solution is to emphasize that what is obeyed is simply teaching. Here appeal can be made to Romans 16.19 ('Everyone has heard about your obedience', speaking again of a past obedience) in the light of 16.17 ('the teaching [*didachē*] you have learned').[96] But this gives no sense as to the content of the teaching. Nor does it explain why Paul does not write just 'teaching' but inserts *typos*. The use of *typos* has led to various options, four of which connect in different ways with what has already been said about obedience in Paul.

First, some have translated this as a genitive of source and see Paul referring simply to ethical instruction – the 'model' or 'rule' or 'pattern' of conduct provided by teaching. So Dodd, showing his disdain for what

---

[93] Ciampa 2007, 109.
[94] Longenecker 2016, 623. The fullest discussion remains Gagnon 1993.
[95] Bultmann, 1967, 283, dismisses the phrase as a stupid insertion ('stupiden Zwischensatz'), and Furnish (1968, 198) views it as reflecting 'a completely un-Pauline view of obedience'.
[96] This is the only other use of *didachē* in Romans; the word occurs elsewhere in the Pauline corpus only at 1 Corinthians 14.6, 26 (as an example of what might be offered in worship), 2 Timothy 4.2 and Titus 1.9.

he views as Paul's substandard argument in this section, refers to a 'lower level' of thought which 'speaks as though conversion were simply the acceptance of the ethical teachings of a rule of faith'.[97] Some have then tied this teaching to baptismal catechesis, given the 'handed over' language.

Second, a number of significant commentators have taken this further and drawn on the idea of *typos* as a mould or stamp. They speak of this teaching itself shaping the Christian who is handed over to it. So Nygren speaks of the Christian teaching as

> the pattern or type in keeping with which the whole life of the Christian is to be shaped . . . The life of the Christian is not something independent in relation to the work which God has effected in him through Christ. This is rather the pattern which must set its stamp on the life of the Christian . . . This is the 'obedience to the faith' about which Paul spoke earlier (1:5).[98]

Third, because *typos* usually has a personal reference in Paul's usage and/or is something which is a model to imitate,[99] Paul has been read as referring here specifically to Christ as such a model or pattern. So Dunn translates it as, 'you gave your obedience from the heart to the one to whom you were handed over as a pattern of teaching' and comments:

> Paul is probably still thinking here of Christ in Adamic terms with Christ as the archetypal new man, Christ as the pattern of obedience . . . there is now a different norm and model of obedience – no longer the law, but Christ.[100]

Fourth, Gagnon has drawn on the use of *typos* in Jewish writers contemporary with Paul to refer to an impression or imprint made on someone or something. He translates the verse as 'you obeyed from the heart the imprint stamped by teaching, to which (imprint) you were handed over.'[101] He argues that 'the "imprint of teaching" in Rom 6:17b is of one piece with the eschatological promise of a heart engraved with the law (Jer 31:33), of a new heart (Ezek 11:19–20; 36:26–27), and of a circumcised heart (Deut 30:6; *Jub.* 1:23) made possible by the gift of the Spirit' and also relates this to the law of the Spirit of life in Romans 8.2.[102]

---

[97] Dodd 1932, 98.
[98] Nygren 1980, 296, 297.
[99] So, Romans 5.14; 1 Corinthians 10.6; 1 Thessalonians 1.7; 2 Thessalonians 3.9; Philippians 3.17; 1 Timothy 4.12; Titus 2.7.
[100] Dunn 1988, 1:353–4.
[101] Gagnon 1993, 687.
[102] Gagnon 1993, 685. This internal impact/imprint of the teaching on the Christians handed over to it might also be related to the word in the heart (Romans 10.8), 'Christ . . . in you' (Romans 8.10) and the law 'written on their hearts' (Romans 2.15).

There is probably no satisfactory answer to be given here. The phrase is one we do not understand but have to assume Paul thought his original readers would. If we gain clarity by offering a strong argument that it refers to something else we do understand (ethical teaching, Christ etc.) then we are left unclear as to why, if that was what Paul really meant, he didn't simply refer to that. Each of the four options sketched here has its problems, but each also shows how the phrase may be related to the wider account of Paul's understanding of obedience which has been developed. Gagnon's connections with both the new-covenant prophecies of Jeremiah 31 and Ezekiel 36 and how these connect to Paul's argument elsewhere in Romans are particularly helpful and have been further developed by Wells who concludes:

> Thus if Paul can trace obedience back to heart-circumcision (2:25–29/ Deut 30:6), he can also attribute it to an internal divine inscription (6:17b/ Jer 31:33) or to God's Spirit-gift (5:5/ Ezek 36:26–27) . . . If Paul is alluding to restoration narratives to describe the Christ event, then the peculiar language is explicable by the scriptural reverberations, which serve to speak of something far more profound than Christians remembering commands and obeying them because of doctrinal instruction. As an interjection of thanksgiving to God, Paul celebrates God's gospel initiative to established obedient agents through Christ and Spirit. Even if the scriptural language appears peculiar because it gets subsumed by Paul's Gospel explication, buried beneath the surface of 6:17 lies a reading of Deuteronomy, Jeremiah and Ezekiel.[103]

The shape of Christian obedience: Christlike total self-offering in response to God's grace

How, finally, might we describe Christian obedience in Paul's understanding? This opens up the enormous subject of Paul's ethical teaching on a range of specific issues which cannot be explored here. Our concern is simply to demonstrate the significance and shape of obedience in Paul's theology and ethic: a new-covenant, return-from-exile obedience of *pistis* from the heart which is defined by Christ's own obedience, to which we have been united by baptism. However, the language of self-offering in Romans 6.13, picked up in the connection to slavery in 6.16 and amplified further in 6.19, signals what lies close to the heart of obedience for Paul: offer yourselves to God as those who have been brought from death to life; and offer every part of yourself to him as an instrument of righteousness

---

[103] Wells 2010, 217–18.

(*parastēsate heautous tō theō hōsei ek nekrōn zōntas kai ta melē hymōn hopla dikaiosynēs tō theō.*)

The importance of this as the pattern of Christian obedience is then confirmed when Paul reverts to very similar language at the crucial transition of Romans 12.1 as he begins to describe the way of life to which the Roman believers are called: 'Therefore, I urge you, brothers and sisters, in view of God's mercy, to offer your bodies [*parastēsai ta sōmata hymōn*] as a living sacrifice, holy and pleasing to God – this is your true and proper worship.' Although the language of obedience is not explicitly used here, Cranfield entitles his discussion of 12.1—15.13 'the obedience to which those who are righteous by faith are called', Barrett remarks that 'obedience well summarizes' these words, and Wright speaks of faith leading to '"obedience" in terms of 12.1'.[104] Here we have encapsulated the heart of Christian obedience: a total trusting self-offering, patterned on Christ's pattern of self-emptying obedience as described in Philippians 2. This is the pattern of the 'obedience of faith' in Christ which Paul seeks among the Gentiles handed over to obey the type of teaching they have received. It is, in turn, a mirror image and reversal of their life in Adam, the faithless disobedience described in the opening chapter as a result of God's wrathful handing over, because 'the thesis for the redeemed existence in Romans 12:1–2 is composed as an antidote to the fallen Adamic existence described in Romans 1:18–32'.[105]

Romans 12.1 also makes clear in both its location and content – 'Therefore . . . in view of God's mercy . . .' – that we need not fear that such obedience stands opposed to the priority and unmerited nature of grace. As John Barclay's recent work has argued, there are different facets of grace which have been perfected or radicalized by different parts of the Christian tradition. One reason for failing to do justice to obedience in Paul has undoubtedly been a concern that to do so would in some sense diminish the grace of God in the gospel. But, as Barclay has argued, an unconditioned gift which is given without reference to the worth or merit of the recipient – which is what God gives us in Christ and the Spirit – does not mean the gift is also unconditional in the sense of not expecting, even demanding, something in return. So Barclay concludes his discussion of Romans 1.1—5.11 with words which return us to where we began with the centrality of obedience in Paul's mission:

---

[104] Cranfield 1975, 592; Barrett 1971, 231; Wright 2013b, 123: 'Romans and the Theology of Paul' (1995), 93–125; originally published in *Pauline Theology*, III (ed. David M. Hay and E. Elizabeth Johnson; Minneapolis: Fortress, 1995), 30–67.
[105] Kim 2011, 119.

The incongruous and unconditioned gift in Christ is not also unconditional, in the sense of expecting no alteration in the recipients of the
gift. God's grace is designed to produce obedience, lives that perform, by
heart-inscription, the intent of the Law . . . As apostle to the Gentiles, Paul
is perpetually conscious of the incongruity of grace as gift to the ungodly
and disobedient; but his goal is not their continuing disobedience, but 'the
obedience of faith' (1.5). Deriving from *faith*, this obedience is the product
of a life created through God's incongruous gift; as *obedience*, it is committed to patterns of behaviour that befit its new allegiance.[106]

5 Conclusion

As Tom Wright has argued, the scarcity of explicit covenant terminology
in the Pauline letters should not prevent us from seeing how central a
theology of covenant is to his theology. Similarly, the scarcity of explicit
language of obedience (although we have seen it is more common than
is often recognized) should not prevent us from seeing how central
obedience is to Paul's missiology and Christology, his anthropology and
ethics.

The one people of God are to be marked out as a people obedient to the
one God whose people they are. The good news Paul brings to both Jew
and Gentile is that, despite the nations living under God's wrath in slavery
to sin and despite Israel's repeated disobedience and unfaithfulness, which
demonstrate we are all in Adam, God has demonstrated his righteousness
in the obedience, even to death on the cross, of his Son, the Messiah, Jesus.
God has raised and exalted the obedient Jesus as Lord and so rescued his
people from exile in fulfilment of his promise of a new covenant. Paul's
mission, in obedience to, and as a slave of, his Lord, is now to declare this
good news and call the nations, in response, to obey the gospel. That obedience, a contrast to that sought by Rome, is in continuity with the obedience
of Israel but is not now defined as obedience to the law. It is the obedience of faith, defined by the obedience of the Christ to whom the people of
God are united and who is the *telos* of the law: a total, trusting self-giving
to God and his will from the heart. God's gift of grace in his obedient
Messiah is intended to lead to this free response of obedience to God's will
among those who are in Christ. As Barclay concludes, following discussion of both Romans 5.12—8.39 and 12.1—15.13, this denies neither grace
nor freedom properly understood:

---

[106] Barclay 2015, 492.

Plenty of statements can be made regarding believers as responsible agents who are required to present their bodies in one direction rather than another. Christian obedience is thus vital, but only ever in a responsive mode: it arises in conjunction with faith and gratitude as the answer to a prior gift. The gift is entirely undeserved but strongly obliging: it creates agents who are newly alive, required to live the life they have been given. This obedience is not instrumental (it does not acquire the gift of Christ, nor any additional gift from God), but it is integral to the gift itself, as God wills newly competent agents who express in practice their freedom from sin and slavery to righteousness. God's grace does not exclude, deny, or displace believing agents; they are not reduced to passivity or pure receptivity. Rather, it generates and grounds an active, willed conformity to the Christ-life, in which believers become, like Christ, truly human, as obedient agents (5:19). Without this obedience, grace is ineffective and unfulfilled.[107]

For Paul, the wholly undeserved grace of God in the gospel calls all peoples into the freedom for which Christ, by his own free obedience, has set us free and that, far from meaning autonomy, means a call into a 'free human engagement in the ordered reality which God has made and restored . . . described by Saint Paul in a single Greek word, *hypakoē*'.[108]

Bibliography

Anderson, Garwood P. (2016). *Paul's New Perspective: Charting a Soteriological Journey*. Downers Grove, IL: IVP.

Barclay, John M. G. (2015). *Paul and the Gift*. Grand Rapids, MI: Eerdmans.

Barrett, C. K. (1971). *The Epistle to the Romans*. Black's New Testament Commentary. London: A. & C. Black.

Barton, John (2003). *Understanding Old Testament Ethics: Approaches and Explorations*. Louisville, KY: Westminster John Knox.

—— (2014). *Ethics in Ancient Israel*. Oxford: Oxford University Press.

Bates, Matthew (2017). *Salvation by Allegiance Alone: Rethinking Faith, Works, and the Gospel of Jesus the King*. Grand Rapids, MI: Baker.

Bauckham, Richard (2008). *Jesus and the God of Israel*. Milton Keynes: Paternoster.

Bird, Michael F. (2016). *Romans*. The Story of God Bible Commentary. Grand Rapids, MI: Zondervan.

Bockmuehl, Markus (1997). *The Epistle to the Philippians*. Black's New Testament Commentary. London: A. & C. Black.

Bultmann, Rudolf (1967). 'Glossen im Römerbrief.' In *Exegetica: Aufsätze zur Erforschung des Neuen Testaments*, 278–84. Tübingen: Mohr Siebeck.

Byrne, Brendan (1981). 'Living Out the Righteousness of God: The Contribution

---

[107] Barclay 2015, 519.
[108] O'Donovan 1986, 109–10.

of Rom 6:1–8:13 to an Understanding of Paul's Ethical Presuppositions.' *Catholic Biblical Quarterly* 43: 557–81.

Campbell, Douglas A. (2005). *The Quest for Paul's Gospel: A Suggested Strategy.* London: T&T Clark.

—— (2009a). *The Deliverance of God: An Apocalyptic Rereading of Justification in Paul.* Grand Rapids, MI: Eerdmans.

—— (2009b). 'The Faithfulness of Jesus Christ in Romans 3:22.' In *The Faith of Jesus Christ: Exegetical, Biblical, and Theological Studies*, edited by Michael F. Bird and Preston M. Sprinkle, 57–71. Milton Keynes: Paternoster.

Cheeseman, John, Philip Gardner, Michael Sadgrove and Tom Wright (1972). *The Grace of God in the Gospel.* London: The Banner of Truth Trust.

Ciampa, Roy E. (2007). 'Deuteronomy in Galatians and Romans.' In *Deuteronomy in the New Testament*, edited by Steve Moyise and Maarten J. J. Menken, 99–117. London: T&T Clark.

Cranfield, C. E. B. (1975). *A Critical and Exegetical Commentary on the Epistle to the Romans.* International Critical Commentary. Edinburgh: T&T Clark.

Dodd, C. H. (1932). *The Epistle to the Romans.* The Moffat New Testament Commentary. London: Hodder & Stoughton.

Dunn, James D. G. (1988). *Romans.* 2 vols. Word Biblical Commentary. Dallas, TX: Word.

—— (1998). *The Theology of Paul the Apostle.* Grand Rapids, MI: Eerdmans.

—— (2009). 'Foreword.' In *The Faith of Jesus Christ: Exegetical, Biblical, and Theological Studies*, edited by Michael F. Bird and Preston M. Sprinkle, xv–xix. Milton Keynes: Paternoster.

Fowl, Stephen E. (2005). *Philippians.* Two Horizons New Testament Commentary. Grand Rapids, MI: Eerdmans.

Furnish, V. P. (1968). *Theology and Ethics in Paul.* Nashville, TN: Abingdon.

Gagnon, Robert (1993). 'Heart of Wax and a Teaching that Stamps: τύπος διδαχῆς (Rom 6:17b) Once More.' *Journal of Biblical Literature* 112: 667–87.

Garlington, Don B. (1987). '"The Obedience of Faith": A Pauline Phrase in Historical Context.' PhD Diss., Durham University.

—— (1990). 'The Obedience of Faith in the Letter to the Romans, Part 1: The Meaning of *hupakoe pisteos* (Rom. 1:5; 16:26).' *Westminster Theological Journal* 52: 201–24.

Goodrich, John K. (2013). 'From Slaves of Sin to Slaves of God: Reconsidering the Origin of Paul's Slavery Metaphor in Romans 6.' *Bulletin for Biblical Research* 23: 509–30.

Gorman, Michael (2001). *Cruciformity: Paul's Narrative Spirituality of the Cross.* Grand Rapids, MI: Eerdmans.

—— (2009). *Inhabiting the Cruciform God: Kenosis, Justification and Theosis in Paul's Narrative Soteriology.* Grand Rapids, MI: Eerdmans.

Green, Bradley G. (2014). *Covenant and Commandment: Works, Obedience and Faithfulness in the Christian Life.* New Studies in Biblical Theology. Downers Grove, IL: IVP.

Green, Joel B., Rebekah Miles, Jacqueline E. Lapsley and Allen Verhey (2012) (eds). *Dictionary of Scripture and Ethics*. Grand Rapids, MI: Baker.

Harris, Murray J. (1999). *Slave of Christ: A New Testament Metaphor for Total Devotion to Christ*. New Studies in Biblical Theology. Leicester: Apollos.

Hays, Richard B. (1989). *Echoes of Scripture in the Letters of Paul*. New Haven, CT: Yale University Press.

Johnson, Luke T. (1982). 'Romans 3.21–26 and the Faith of Jesus.' *Catholic Biblical Quarterly* 44: 77–90.

Käsemann, Ernst (1980). *Commentary on Romans*. London: SCM.

Kelly, Joseph Ryan (2013). 'Orders of Discourse and the Function of Obedience in the Hebrew Bible.' *Journal of Theological Studies* 64: 1–24.

Kibbe, Michael (2012). '"The Obedience of Christ": A Reassessment of τὴν ὑπακοὴν τοῦ Χριστοῦ in 2 Corinthians 10:5.' *Journal for the Study of Paul and His Letters* 2: 41–56.

Kim, Seyoon (2011). 'Paul's Common Paraenesis (1 Thess 4—5; Phil 2—4; and Rom 12—13): The Correspondence between Romans 1:18–32 and 12:1–2, and the Unity of Romans 12—13.' *Tyndale Bulletin* 62: 109–39.

Lincicum, David (2009). 'St. Paul's Deuteronomy: The End of the Pentateuch and the Apostle to the Gentiles in Second Temple Jewish Context.' DPhil Diss., Oxford University.

Longenecker, Richard N. (1974). 'The Obedience of Christ in the Theology of the Early Church.' In *Reconciliation and Hope: New Testament Essays on Atonement and Eschatology Presented to L. L. Morris on His 60th Birthday*, edited by Robert Banks, 142–52. Grand Rapids, MI: Eerdmans.

—— (2016). *The Epistle to the Romans: A Commentary on the Greek Text*. Grand Rapids, MI: Eerdmans.

Miller, James C. (2000). *The Obedience of Faith, the Eschatological People of God, and the Purpose of Romans*. Society of Biblical Literature Dissertation Series 177. Atlanta, GA: Society of Biblical Literature.

Moo, Douglas J. (1996). *The Epistle to the Romans*. New International Commentary on the New Testament. Grand Rapids, MI: Eerdmans.

Morgan, Teresa (2015). *Roman Faith and Christian Faith: Pistis and Fides in the Early Roman Empire*. Oxford: Oxford University Press.

Murray, John (1961). *Redemption: Accomplished and Applied*. London: The Banner of Truth Trust.

Myers, Jason (2015). 'Obedience Across Romans: Tracing a Book Wide Theme and Illustrating Obedience with Greco-Roman Literature.' PhD Diss., Asbury Theological Seminary.

Nanos, Mark D. (1996). *The Mystery of Romans*. Minneapolis, MN: Fortress.

Nygren, Anders (1980). *Commentary on Romans*. Philadelphia, PA: Fortress.

O'Donovan, Oliver (1986). *Resurrection and Moral Order*. Downers Grove, IL: IVP.

Rosner, Brian S. (2013). *Paul and the Law: Keeping the Commandments of God*. New Studies in Biblical Theology. Downers Grove, IL: IVP.

Sanders, E. P. (1977). *Paul and Palestinian Judaism*. Philadelphia, PA: Fortress.

Stegman, Thomas (2005). *The Character of Jesus: The Linchpin to Paul's Argument in 2 Corinthians.* Roma: Editrice Pontifico Istituto Biblico.

Turner, Geoffrey (2013). 'The Christian Life as Slavery: Paul's Subversive Metaphor.' *Heythrop Journal* 54: 1–12.

VanDrunen, David (2006). 'To Obey Is Better Than Sacrifice: A Defense of the Active Obedience of Christ in the Light of Recent Criticism.' In *By Faith Alone: Answering the Challenges to the Doctrine of Justification,* edited by Gary L. W. Johnson and Guy Prentiss Waters, 127–46. Wheaton, IL: Crossway.

Venema, Cornelis P. (2005). 'N. T. Wright on Romans 5:12–21 and Justification: A Case Study in Exegesis, Theological Method and the "New Perspective on Paul."' *Mid-America Journal of Theology* 16: 29–81.

—— (2009). 'Calvin's Doctrine of the Imputation of Christ's Righteousness: Another Example of "Calvin Against the Calvinists?"' *Mid-America Journal of Theology* 20: 15–47.

Wells, Kyle B. (2010). 'Grace, Obedience, and the Hermeneutics of Agency: Paul and his Jewish Contemporaries on the Transformation of the Heart.' PhD Diss., Durham University.

Williams, Sam K. (1980). 'The "Righteousness of God" in Romans.' *Journal of Biblical Literature* 99: 241–90.

Wright, N. T. (1978). *Small Faith, Great God.* Eastbourne: Kingsway / New Jersey, NJ: Revell.

—— (1991). *The Climax of the Covenant: Christ and the Law in Pauline Theology.* Edinburgh: T&T Clark.

—— (2002). 'The Letter to the Romans.' In *The New Interpreter's Bible,* Volume X, edited by Leander E. Keck, 393–770. Nashville, TN: Abingdon.

—— (2003). *Paul for Everyone: 2 Corinthians.* London: SPCK.

—— (2004a). *Paul for Everyone: Romans, Part 1: Chapters 1—8.* London: SPCK.

—— (2004b). *Paul for Everyone: Romans, Part 2: Chapters 9—16.* London: SPCK.

—— (2013a). *Paul and the Faithfulness of God.* London: SPCK / Minneapolis, MN: Fortress.

—— (2013b). *Pauline Perspectives: Essays on Paul, 1978–2013.* London: SPCK / Minneapolis, MN: Fortress.

Neither sober nor of sound mind: Timothy's spirit of *sōphronismos*

OLIVER O'DONOVAN

Introduction

At the opening of the second letter to Timothy, the bishop of Ephesus is told of a spirit of cowardice that God has not given, neither to him nor to anyone else, and also of the Spirit that God has in fact given, which is 'of power, love and *sōphronismou*'. The uncertainty provoked by this last word has left its mark on the history of English translation, and doubtless on translation in other modern languages, too. The earliest versions followed the Vulgate (not the work of Jerome at this point) which had *sobrietatis*: 'sobernesse' (Wyclif, Tyndale, Cranmer) or 'sobrietie' (Rheims Bible).[1] The humanists behind the Geneva Bible, who consulted patristic sources, went back to the earliest Latin version, used by Tertullian, which had *sanae mentis*, which appeared as 'sounde mynde', adopted with appropriate spelling-changes by King James's translators. The nineteenth-century revisers also looked for patristic guidance, and sensibly consulted Chrysostom, who offered them two proposals for *sōphronismou*: the first was 'health of mind and soul' (not far from the Tertullian–Geneva tradition) and the second, which he preferred, was explained as follows:

> Or else *sōphronismou* stands for *our being made* sound of mind [*sōphronizesthai hēmas*], if something terrible should occur to make us so and to cut back our excesses. Let us not, then, resent such terrible experiences when they occur, for this is a *sōphronismos*.[2]

This guided the Revised Version (RV) of 1880–4, which wrapped it up in the single word 'discipline'.[3]

---

1 On this point the Vulgate followed earlier Latin translations, known to Ambrose and Augustine. Historical English versions are from the 1891 edition of *The English Hexapla*. All quotations from Scripture are translated on my own responsibility.

2 Chrysostom, *Homiliae in Secundam Epistolam ad Timotheum* 1.2 (PG 62.604).

3 With a footnote to represent the literal sense of *sōphronismos* as 'sobering', not making it quite clear that this form was intended as an English noun.

Chrysostom's ambivalence presents its own interesting questions, to which we shall return shortly. First, however, we follow the strange course of English Bible-translation. On the face of it Chrysostom and the RV have won the day; 'discipline' and its synonyms crop up throughout the twentieth-century English versions, *Besonnenheit* in German versions. A small minority of English translators, including N. T. Wright, prefers variations on judgement, discretion, sense, prudence, and so on, an option favoured in major Romance-language translations (*sagesse, sagezza,* etc.), while the KJV lookalikes cling to soundness of mind (especially popular with versions advertising themselves as 'literal'!). On close inspection, however, it is clear that Chrysostom has not influenced the development at all. His *sōphronismos* was a sobering experience befalling us unexpectedly, an affliction sent from heaven for our good, but the preponderance of recent translations understand it as a discipline to be imposed upon ourselves: 'self-control' (RSV, Jerusalem Bible) and 'self-discipline' (New English Bible, NIV and NRSV), spawning a multitude of imitators. But this lies much nearer to the sense of the Vulgate than to Chrysostom's intentions. So we have, in effect, a solid post-Latin translation tradition going straight back to the Old Latin versions, which understands this Greek noun as a virtuous habit of mind, a synonym of *sōphrosynē*, and disagrees only on the question of whether it is primarily intellectual or voluntative. Let us put on record at this point that the early Syriac translators are reported to have taken the word quite differently, to mean 'moral instruction'.[4] Not many in the West have looked favourably on that interpretation. Robert A. Wild in 1989 and Luke Timothy Johnson in 1996 were exceptions; it will be the implication of what follows that they were right to be such.[5]

To support the established renderings there are, of course, arguments regularly adduced. Commentators observe that the moderation of passion is a major emphasis throughout the Pastoral Epistles.[6] They argue that words deriving from the stem *sōphron-* always have this range of sense.[7] Alternatively, they argue that, even though the word *sōphronismos* sometimes, or even often, has a different sense, the context in 2 Timothy 'clearly suggests' the conventional interpretation.[8] And they proceed to plead that

4 Bauer, Arndt, Gingrich 1957, ad loc.
5 See Wild 1989, ad loc., and Johnson 1996 ad loc. The latter indicated that he found the Syriac translation 'tempting'. In his later Anchor Bible commentary, Johnson continued to confess to temptation, but was determined to resist it (Johnson 2001, ad loc.).
6 E.g. Saarinen 2008, ad loc.
7 E.g. Mounce 2000, ad loc.
8 Moulton and Milligan 1952, ad loc. It is worth mentioning in passing that no use in papyri

a reference to self-discipline is just what one would look for in a characterization of the exercise of ecclesiastical authority.[9] We may postpone the arguments from context until later, and the argument from the theme of moderation may be left to fend for itself, since, whatever may justifiably be said along these lines about the Pastorals, it cannot claim support from the word *sōphronismos* without some prior linguistic assumptions, and it is these that are now in question. The single important argument at this juncture, then, is the philological one.

It is a question of how we understand a Greek word, and the arbiters will have to be those who themselves spoke and wrote the Greek language in the ancient world. They will settle it, if it can be settled, in two ways: first by commenting on the meaning of this text; second by employing the word *sōphronismos* for themselves. Their comments on the text are accessible to us today essentially on the same terms as they were to the translators of the Renaissance; access to their usage, however, has been revolutionized in recent years by database-searching, so that fools may now rush in where experts once feared to tread. With the aid of the invaluable database of *Thesaurus Linguae Graecae* I have compiled 140 uses of *sōphronismos* (hereafter, *s.*) in pagan and Christian texts from the half-millennium separating the end of the first century BC from an arbitrarily chosen point at the end of the fifth century AD. Though not even contemporary search-engines allow us the certainty of being exhaustive, this sample, larger than anything available to older lexicographers, is enough to permit some general conclusions.

Before exploring the results, however, we need to make some familiar points about the word-stem and the word-form. The adjective *sōphrōn*, the verb *sōphroneō* and the noun *sōphrosynē* all have the idea of self-control centrally within their generous semantic range (though translations such as 'good sense', 'judiciousness' and 'even temper' also lie well within its bounds). But does *s.* command the same range as *sōphrosynē*? We have Chrysostom's assertion that it can mean 'health of mind and soul', and Chrysostom cannot be wrong about this.[10] Yet three things must be borne in mind: his Greek is the Greek of the fourth century, not of the era of the Pastoral Epistles; he was personally uncertain as to how the word should be taken in the biblical text; he adopted a different interpretation. And it is not

---

or non-literary sources is offered by the authors for this word.

[9] E.g. Spicq 1947, ad loc.

[10] That this remained a possible interpretation in later Greek is indicated by the commentary on the text in the Pseudo-Oecumenian *catena* (PG 119.204), which glosses *s.* simply: *peri bion orthon.*

hard to see why. *S.* bears on its face the character of a noun of action formed from the verb *sōphronizō* (like *oneidismos,* 'reproach', from *oneidizō,* to reproach; or *kataklysmos,* 'flood', from *kataklyzō,* to flood). Like many verbs formed in zeta, *sōphronizō* has a *factitive* sense (e.g. *kakizō,* 'to make look bad' or 'criticize', *potizō,* 'to cause to drink', 'to water'). It is not an equivalent of *sōphroneō,* 'to *be* sensible', but means 'to make sensible', 'to instruct' or (of emotions) 'to bring to order'. In a lost play of Euripides a character observes, in a line worthy of a drawing-room comedy, 'I have learned never to give advice [*ou sōphronizein emathon*]; one may make a habit of it, and find it irritates people'. Simply on formal grounds we would anticipate that *s.* will refer to an *act or event* of instructing, calming, advising, making sensible, and so on. Formal grounds are not conclusive, and factitive senses can become eroded with use. (I heard an educated English-speaker the other day use 'soporific' to mean 'sleepy'.) Yet they create a presumption for interpretation, and we ought not to discount their influence upon speakers too quickly as we read and interpret actual examples of how a word is used.

The verb *sōphronizō* is of greater antiquity than the noun *s.* and much more frequently used. In the high classical period the noun *s.* did not exist, though the verb was already in common use, surrounded by a cluster of derivatives which interest us as shedding light on how *s.,* when it came to be coined, was understood. Among these was the noun *sōphronisma,* an 'instructive saying': in Aeschylus' *Suppliant Women* the prosy Danaos is so full of these that he advises the chorus to write them down, including such pearls of wisdom as 'You never know what a crowd will do next', and 'Everyone is quick to abuse a foreigner.'[11] Among them, too, was the *sōphronistēs,* who was something like a youth-counsellor, and since youth-counsellors, then as now, were only intermittently effective in counselling youth, there was the *sōphronistērion,* a term coined by Plato for a prison with a remedial purpose, a 'correctional institution', as we would say. For a noun of action Plato employs an odd formation, *sōphronistys,* which nobody later thought worthy of imitation.

The first appearance of *s.* is in the late first century BC in the geographer Strabo, suggesting that the word was of comparatively fresh coinage when we meet it in 2 Timothy.[12] But Philo of Jerusalem had used it 8 times by then, and Josephus 4 times, two authors who, as contemporary Hellenistic

---

11 Aeschylus, *Supplices* 991–3.

12 This needs defending against (1) two 'fragments' of the Pythagorean Aristoxenus (s. iv BC) which, however well they may report his views, are phrased in the language of Strabo and Plutarch, and (2) the *Peri Politeias* ascribed by Stobaeus to Hippodamus of Miletus (s. v BC), an ascription generally considered spurious.

Oliver O'Donovan

Jews, are of special interest for New Testament use.[13] In the same century Plutarch used it 6 times. Yet it remained comparatively rare, with only 3 second-century and 5 third-century occurrences showing up, until a sudden explosion of fashion in fourth-century sources produces 81 instances, to which Chrysostom himself contributes a hefty 32.[14]

The semantic field of *s.* forms a spectrum from non-coercive to coercive senses, from moral instruction at one end to punishment at the other. It is convenient to organize it under five headings, while being mindful of the difficulty of counting colours in a rainbow.

1 We find *s.* meaning *moral instruction*, as given (in Philo) by Moses or by the Divine Word for the benefit of those who are capable of receiving it. Methodius Olympius has the plural with the sense of *sōphronismata*, *moral maxims*.[15] Plutarch uses *s.* for the moral education of the young, which is also the context of its use in Strabo, alluding to the Pythagorean educational system that required the teaching not only of philosophy but of music, the one to produce conviction, the other *s.*, a harmonious *formation*.[16] The young need *moral training*, Pseudo-Hippodamus declares, and Plutarch (followed by Porphyry) is ready to include kicks administered to dogs or horses as *s.*, since they are meant to train their dispositions.[17]

2 Commonly *s.* means *warning*. A tale of Aesop has the moral that our neighbour's misfortunes serve us as *s.* In Philo *s.* is often a synonym for *nouthesia*, while Josephus views the history of the Herods as a useful *s.* for the human race. The historian Appian writes of the survival of Carthage as a *sobering warning* for Rome.[18] In Old Testament commentary severe judgements are seen as *s.* for observers and later generations, while prophetic threats are *s.* for contemporaries.

3 An important cluster of senses gathers around the notions of *restraint* and *amendment*. Sumptuary *s.*, a policy pursued by the elder Cato in Rome, was to be attained in Christian moral teaching by fasting.[19] The regime of a *paidagogos* is a *s.* The true function of law is *restraint*, not

---

13 Borgen, Fuglseth and Skarsten 2000.
14 This tally excludes eight occurrences which quote, or allude directly to, 2 Timothy 1.7; it includes one from a *catena* on Psalm 7, ascribed both to Chrysostom and to the fifth-century Cyril of Alexandria.
15 Methodius, *Symposium* 1.1 (PG 18.37).
16 Strabo, *Geographicon* 1.2.3.
17 Plutarch, *Moralia* 961d; Porphyry, *De abstinentia* 3.22.
18 Appian, *Lybica* 65.
19 Basil, *De ieiunio* 2 (PG 31.193): *nēsteia . . . ho tou biou sōphronismos.*

threatening as an end in itself. The control of rational reflection over
the passions is a *s.*, and so, even, is fear, in that it restrains tendencies
to irresponsibility. Both Josephus and Iamblichus use the term to mean
dissuasion from disorderly conduct.[20]

4 Directed immediately at a wrongdoer, *s.* is *reproof.* Prophetic pronouncements of sword, famine and disease upon Israel were meant as
s. of Israel's sins. Eusebius of Caesarea sees the cause for which Israel
was given over to the Assyrian rod as *s.* and conversion.[21] Isidore
of Pelusium thinks the birth of handicapped children is a *s.* of their
parents, whose poor diet and lifestyle are responsible.[22] Hierokles the
Platonist philosopher thinks that a suitable balance between indulgence
and rigour in society can be maintained by mutual *s.*, *criticism* of one
another's lifestyles.[23] *S.* is often distinguished in this context from punishment, *timōria.*

5 But in other contexts the two ideas are associated, so that *s.* means
chastisement, that is, punishment with a remedial purpose, sometimes
distinguished from pure retribution. According to Hierokles, all *dikē*
aims at *s.*[24] Fathers who punish sons are a typical case, often referred
to. Sometimes with an apparently technical sense it means *ecclesiastical
penance.* Punishment lighter than might be expected can be called *s.*, as
often in discussion of the punishment of Cain. The sack of a city may
be referred to as a *s.* euphemistically, perhaps a *pacification.* And so the
term reaches the other extreme of its range, meaning a well-deserved
downfall or *overthrow*, such as defeat in battle or the collapse of a regime.

Two observations about this semantic spectrum will carry our enquiry
forward. First, it is very clear that in most of its occurrences *s.* is an *event*,
something said, something done, something experienced, which makes,
or is intended to make, a moral difference to the one who perceives or
experiences it. Sometimes the event is entirely beyond the scale of human
control: 'Once flourishing communities made desolate, cities left empty
of populations', 'cities wiped off the face of the earth, earthquakes, floods,
armies annihilated, fleets sunk, mass destruction of human life . . .'[25] Uses

---

20 Josephus, *Bellum Judaicum* 2.1.3; *Antiquitates Judaicae* 17.9.2; Iamblichus, *Vita Pythagori*
  30.174.
21 Eusebius, *Commentarius in Isaiam* 1.61 (PG 24.168).
22 Isidore, *Epistle* 1251 (IV.140) (PG 78.1221).
23 Hierokles, *In aureum carmen* 11.20.
24 Hierokles, *In aureum carmen* 11.15.
25 Philo, *De Praemiis et Poenis* 133; Basil of Caesarea, *Quod Deus non auctor malorum* 5 (PG
  31.337).

in which it refers to a *moral state* or *habitual practice* are very few indeed. We have one from Pseudo-Macarius, speaking of God as 'bringing [*sc.* the sanctified] to *s.* of virtue and purity of heart', while Epiphanius tells of a converted thief who comes 'to a state of understanding and *s.*'.[26] These two instances support Chrysostom's first interpretation, but it cannot escape our notice that they are few, and both are from the fourth century. Arndt and Gingrich thought they could find two examples in Plutarch, but were certainly wrong. Perhaps with diligence a couple more examples might be argued for where the texts are not explicit. But in the end we have to yield to the overwhelming preponderance of the literary evidence. Rendering *s.* in 2 Timothy as a virtue of 'self-discipline', 'sound mind', or any other equivalent to *sōphrosynē*, requires a contextual case so strong that it can bear the weight of supporting a rare exception. The context of 2 Timothy 1.7, as we shall argue, points formidably in the opposite direction.

Second, the semantic spectrum we have traced from cognitive to coercive senses of *s.* broadly corresponds to a historical development. The suddenly expanded use of the word in the fourth century coincided with a new interest – there will doubtless be those who call it 'Constantinian' – in the practice of punishment and the rationale of law and force. Virtually all uses in the first two centuries fall under the first three of our headings, and speak of moral direction, warning and restraint. Which raises an important question about Chrysostom's *second* interpretation of 2 Timothy 1.7. Chrysostom confronted *s.* as a familiar word, one that he himself regularly used with a set of resonances and contexts different from those surrounding the new coinage of the first century. Could he even have misunderstood?

Sōphronismos from the first to the fourth century

To pursue this question further, we must introduce another way of analysing the semantic range of *s.*, which is in terms of its verbal voice. The verbal noun, like the verb it represents, can be in the active or the passive voice: *s.* may be an event of *giving* information, warning or correction, reproof or punishment; or an event of *receiving* information or warning, *suffering* reproof, correction or punishment. And in between the two, it may be impersonal, drawing attention neither to the action nor to the

---

26 Pseudo-Macarius, *Sermones l* 4.25.411 (PG 34.492); Epiphanius, *Panarion* 1–2.30.10 (PG 41.421).

suffering, but simply to the occurrence of the event as such, the concrete and particular instance of an instruction, a warning, a correction, reproof or punishment that is given. To illustrate, let us produce a paradigm of each.

Philo, allegorizing the story of Tamar, imagines her asking,

> Whose is the ring, the pledge of faith, the seal of the universal, the archetypal idea by which all things without form or quality before were stamped and shaped? Whose is the cord, that is, the world-order, the chain of destiny, the correspondence and sequence of all things with their never-broken chain? Whose is the staff, that is, the firmly planted, the unshaken, the unbending? [T]he admonition [*nouthesia*], the instruction [s.], the discipline [*paideia*], the sceptre, the kingship? Whose are they?[27]

And since the answer is, 'Are they not God's alone?', it is evident that the genitive used with the three nouns of action – admonition, instruction and discipline – represents the agent: it is *God* who admonishes, instructs, disciplines, and so on. *S.* is one of the actions God performs.

The recurrent proverbial thought that one person's disaster is another's *s.* illustrates the impersonal voice. We may notice a passage from Chrysostom's fifteenth sermon *De statuis*, finding in Zechariah 5.4 an illustration of what has transpired in Antioch. 'What purpose does it serve to pull down the stones and the beams [of the house] of one who takes an oath? That his calamity may be a warning [s.] to others.'[28] *S.* is the sobering warning conveyed by the particular calamity of some other or others. A recurrent phrase, *hypothesis sōphronismou*, means an '*occasion of warning*'.[29]

For the passive voice Chrysostom again supplies an example. In his forty-first sermon on Acts he speaks of how the affliction of demon-possession may, in the providence of God, make the victim 'more sober' (*sōphronesteron*), and then imagines someone in his congregation calling out, 'God forbid that I should ever have such a *sōphronismos*!'[30] What the one who calls out wishes not to have is the *experience* of being made sober by such a drastic affliction.

With these two spectra spread before us, then, we compare the usages of the first century with those of Chrysostom himself. The period from

---

27 Philo, *De Mutatione Nominum* 135 (Colson and Whitaker, Loeb). I have changed their translation of *s.* from 'chastisement' to 'instruction' for reasons that will be clear from what has just been said.

28 Chrysostom, *Ad populum Antiochenum homiliae de statuis* 15.5.13 (PG 49.160).

29 Lampe, 'ὑπόθεσις', *PGL*, 1d.

30 Chrysostom, *In Acta Apostolorum homilia* 41.4 (PG 60.293).

the end of the first century BC to the end of the first century AD yields us eighteen uses (excluding 2 Timothy 1.7 itself).[31] These contain on a reasonable impression ten examples of sense (1), 'moral instruction', three of sense (2), 'warning', and five of sense (3), 'correction'. There are no probable examples of senses (4) or (5), 'reproof' and 'punishment'. Furthermore, there are, again on a reasonable impression, fifteen examples of the active voice, three of the impersonal and none of the passive voice. Of Chrysostom's thirty-two examples, on the other hand, I identify three with sense (1), eleven with sense (2), thirteen with sense (3), three with sense (4) and two with sense (5), which suggests a noticeable but undramatic shift away from the instructional senses towards the coercive. In respect of the voice the shift is more marked: ten active uses, twelve impersonal and ten passive. There can, of course, be nothing decisive about such head-counts. Words are not always used with precision, and even where they are, differences of interpretation are possible. The value of such a survey lies in the generalizations, which are best illustrated by a review of some typical instances that allow the patterns of common usage to emerge into view. Such a review by no means suggests that Chrysostom need have been baffled by the use of the *s.* in a first-century text, but it does point to a new range of applications that the word had acquired by his time, some of which, in pursuit of an interpretative interest, he could have read into the text.

In Philo *s.* is constantly paired with *nouthesia* ('warning and instruction'), and so are the corresponding verbs *noutheteō* and *sōphronizō*, and the agential nouns *nouthetētēs* and *sōphronistēs*. The active sense of the noun is often stressed: giving of counsel and instruction is the work of Moses ('very ready to give warning and instruction to those capable of receiving them'), of Scripture, of the law, of the *logos*.[32] Jacob, the wise, gives counsel and instruction to Enoch, expelling ignorance and indiscipline from his soul.[33] Pedagogues, teachers, parents, elders, laws and poets are *sōphronistai*.[34] While the suggestion of constraint and correction is often present, the distinction between them is clear: counsel and instruction may depend upon discipline (*paideia*) and punishment, but they follow them, as beneficial consequences.[35] That is how when Scripture says that Sara 'afflicted' Hagar, it means only that she gave her counsel

[31] The authors are Strabo, Philo, Josephus and Plutarch.
[32] Philo, *De Migratione Abrahami* 14.
[33] Philo, *Legum Allegoriae* 3.193.
[34] Philo, *De Migratione* 116; *Quod Omnis Probus Liber* 143.
[35] Philo, *De Posteritate Caini* 97; *De Virtutibus* 115.

and instruction.[36] Reproofs (*elenchoi*) refer to the past, encouragements (*paraineseis*) to the future, but counsels and instructions refer to the present, the present point of action.[37]

In passing, the construction *epi sōphronismō* should be remarked on, as it remained very common. The force of the preposition is purposive, indicating an active sense of the noun: Moses criticized the tribes who settled in Moab 'not to humiliate them, but to instruct them' (*ouk ep' oneidei sōphronismō de*).[38] The divine word gives particular guidance 'to counsel, to instruct and to correct the way of life'.[39] We find the same phrase in both of Josephus' major works, used in the same story of how Archelaus unsuccessfully dealt with rioters by sending a general in 'to talk sense into them (s.) and to dissuade them'.[40] His own narrative of the Herods Josephus thinks of as a *s.*, or 'warning', especially to those who think their good fortune will last for ever.[41] Plutarch turns to the word in his lives of the two Catos to name the policies of 'sumptuary restraint' that they urged.[42] S. serves Plutarch's educative interest with the meanings 'instilling good sense' and 'counselling'; there is an interesting impersonal use in the plural for the excellent 'moral maxims' found in Menander's comedies, which compensate for their improper plots.[43]

In Chrysostom the impersonal voice is used in conjunction with the sense 'warning' in multiple variations on the proverbial wisdom that one person's calamity is another's *s.* From the fall of the Tower of Babel to the demolition of the oath-takers' houses in Zechariah, from Cain to Ananias and Sapphira, there is no shortage of suggestive disasters for later generations to treat as warnings. The most consistent application of the active voice is with sense (3), which speaks of bringing to bear restraint and order, sometimes spilling over indeterminately into (4) or (5). God used fear of reprisals for the disorder at Antioch to instil a sense of responsibility.[44] In the prophetic warnings of exile and their fulfilment God acted *epi s.*, to bring Israel to its senses.[45] He did similarly in punishing Cain, mixing *philanthrōpia* with *timōria*, while Noah, in punishing Canaan,

---

[36] Philo, *De Congressu* 158, 161, 172, 179.
[37] Philo, *De Virtutibus* 75.
[38] Philo, *De Vita Mosis* 1.328.
[39] Philo, *Quod Deus Sit Immutabilis* 182.
[40] Josephus, *Bellum Judaicum* 2.1.3; *Antiquitates* 17.9.2.
[41] Josephus, *Antiquitates* 18.5.3, 19.16.2.
[42] Plutarch, *Cato Maior* 5.1; *Cato Minor* 19.8.
[43] Plutarch, *Moralia* 14b, 653c, 712c.
[44] Chrysostom, *Ad populum Antiochenum homiliae de statuis* 15.1.3 (PG 49.154).
[45] Chrysostom, *Fragmenta in Jeremiam* 3.33 (PG 64.784, 989); *In Psalmum* 124.2 (PG 55.358).

acted as any father would, to correct him.[46] S. is, indeed, the purpose of law as a whole, which does not issue threats merely for the sake of it.[47] It is also 'restraint' of wealth and extravagance.[48] As for the passive voice, the distinctive new fourth-century departure, we often read in Chrysostom of those who receive s. for better or worse. The well-to-do receive it from texts of Scripture which offer nothing but encouragement to those who are struggling.[49] Saints gain much s. from the trials God visits them with, though when he executes judgement it is the wicked that receive the s.[50] In great undertakings s., roughly administered, is what our nature needs, though unwelcome.[51] The suffering of reproof can be the occasion of s., as can fear; but fear may also serve in place of it, producing restraint where the experience of moral awakening is lacking.[52] The restraint imposed on the righteous by the dominion of the wicked is a s.[53] But a train of thought, too, can be a s., sufficient to deflect us from rash speech, while a reference in Scripture to the greatness of some sin, without explicit mention of a punishment, can be enough to make the intelligent reader careful, and that is a s.[54] The new departure, that of a passive sense of s., governs the way Chrysostom interprets 2 Timothy 1.7, and so to that text, finally, we turn.

Commentary on 2 Timothy 1.7

We should, perhaps, find it strange that Chrysostom's first and less favoured interpretation of s. has been so widely followed at the expense of the second. But in addition to the unbroken Latin tradition pointing in that direction, there are puzzling features in the second of Chrysostom's readings that have, perhaps understandably, turned interpreters away

---

[46] Chrysostom, *Homiliae in Genesim* 26.2 (PG 53.231); 29.7 (PG 53.271).

[47] Chrysostom, *In Psalmum 110*.6 (PG 55.288).

[48] Chrysostom, *In epistulam i ad Corinthios homilia* (PG 61.225); *In Acta Apostolorum homilia* 7.1 (PG 60.65).

[49] Chrysostom, *Homiliae ad populum Antiochenum de statuis* 16.5.12 (PG 49.169); *Expositio in Psalmum* 9.10 (PG 55.138).

[50] Chrysostom, *In Matthaeum homiliae* 10.7 (PG 57.192); *Expositio in Psalmum* 7.14 (PG 55.103).

[51] Chrysostom, *In Heliam et viduam* 10 (PG 51.346); *In Acta Apostolorum homilia* 41.4 (PG 60.293).

[52] Chrysostom, *Ad populum Antiochenum homiliae de statuis* 15.1.3 (PG 49.154); *Homiliae in Genesim* 21.4, 29.6 (PG 53.161, 270).

[53] Chrysostom, *In Psalmum 124*.2 (PG 55.358).

[54] Chrysostom, *In Joannem homiliae* 47.4 (PG 59.262); *In Matthaeum homiliae* 18.7 (PG 57.272).

from it. If we look at the whole paragraph of his commentary on the verse, we begin to see the problem.[55] After quoting the text he continues:

> That is to say, we did not receive this spirit in order to cower, but to be bold. The spirit of cowardice is given to many, as we see in war. We are told in the Book of Kings that 'a spirit of cowardice fell upon them,' which means, he instilled fear in them.[56] To you, though, he has given the opposite spirit, of power and of love to himself. This is of grace, but not simply of grace; it requires that we should first perform our part. For the Spirit that makes us cry 'Abba! Father!' instils love to him and to our neighbour, so that, as the text says, 'we may love one another.' Love arises from power and from overcoming cowardice. Nothing is so prone to dissolve friendship as is cowardice and the slightest rumour of betrayal. *For God did not give us a spirit of cowardice, but of power, love and s.* Either he speaks of *s.* as health of mind and soul, or *s.* stands for our being made sound of mind [*sōphronizesthai hēmas*], if something terrible should occur to make us so and to cut back our excesses. Let us not, then, resent such terrible experiences when they occur, for this is a *s.*[57]

Almost all the comment is devoted to the first two members of the triad, power and love. It is not difficult to feel that Chrysostom has lost sight of the third member, and that when he turns to explain it he takes his eyes off the text, and forgets the context of Paul's exhortation to Timothy in talking of terrible experiences. What follows may reinforce that impression. All Chrysostom's exegetical works are homilies, and the pattern they follow is invariable: half the homily devoted to verse-by-verse running commentary, the other half to an exhortation on a theme arising, sometimes loosely, out of it. The exhortation in this first homily begins with the words, 'Let us not, then, resent . . .'[58] and continues with a catalogue of sorrows inseparable from this mortal life, before concluding with a very characteristic exhortation to generosity in the relief of suffering. It is tempting to suppose that the second meaning of *s.* was introduced, regardless of the bent of the text, merely to create a transition to an exhortation he wanted to give, for which the text offered too little opportunity.

---

55 Chrysostom, *Homiliae in Secundam Epistolam ad Timotheum* 1.2 (PG 62.604).
56 A misquotation, possibly remembering Exodus 15.16.
57 'This' (*touto*) referring loosely to the terrible experiences (*tois deinois tois sumpiptousi*), not, as Philip Schaff took it, to not resenting them (see *NPNF*[1] 13:477). Schaff, assuming that *s.* meant 'sobriety of mind', could not make much sense of Chrysostom's observation. To bear with terrible experiences is not sobriety, but patience; sobriety is a response to joys and excitements.
58 Thus Schaff, correctly.

But this would be to underestimate Chrysostom. He has a consistent reading of the second letter to Timothy, which focuses on the dangers and afflictions that beset the Christian life. Timothy is the type of the life of faith, the faith that he learned from his mother and grandmother (1.5), while the mention of his ordained 'charisma' (1.6) is brushed over with the briefest of remarks. The verb 'rekindle' is made the occasion for a more extended reflection on grace in general, not the grace of ordination. Augustine would hardly have approved of it: 'as fire requires fuel, so grace requires our enthusiasm.'[59] Timothy's relationship with Paul is that of each member of the flock to its pastor. As Paul has suffered, so must the flock be ready to suffer after him. To set the tone of the letter, Chrysostom quotes 4.6, 16 within a few lines of the opening of the first homily: 'I am already on the point of being sacrificed', and 'At my first defence no one took my part.' 'God did not make us apostles merely to encounter danger,' he imagines Paul as saying, 'but to die, and so to have the total experience of suffering.'[60] Other Christians are to expect no better. The exhortations of 1.6–7, then, are prompted by Timothy's state of prostration with grief: 'See how he portrays him as in extreme dejection and gloom!'[61] And such is the state of every member of Chrysostom's congregation: there are domestic griefs, the sorrows of emperors, the *ennuis* of the wealthy, the sufferings of illness, the general discontents that all experience in their callings, the frustrations of youth and age, and it is on these, rather than the persecution of the gospel or the harassment of preachers, that the second letter to Timothy will shed light. To carry through his reading, Chrysostom needs a handhold; the noun *s.*, explained with the passive infinitive (*sōphronizesthai hēmas*), provides him with what he needs. In the second homily, which takes up at the words 'Do not therefore be ashamed' (1.8), Chrysostom treats the question of 'shame' as relating to suffering and death, beginning with a brief reflection on Galatians 6.14.

> That is to say, do not be ashamed of proclaiming the crucified one, but take pride in it. Death and imprisonment and chains are matters for shame and reproach in themselves, but when the cause is supplied and the mystery seen plain, one will find each of them a matter for great boasting and solemn celebration.

Extending the text to the words, 'take your share of suffering', he immediately makes a connection back to 1.7. 'He had already hinted at this,

---

[59] 1.2 (PG 62.603).
[60] 1.1 (PG 62.601).
[61] 1.2 (PG 62.603).

and made it plain in what he said before. In saying *God gave us a spirit of power, love and s.*, he anticipated what is said subsequently, namely, *take your share of suffering*.[62] It is an interpretation that focuses constantly on Timothy's emotional experience, not his service to the life of the Church. Chrysostom therefore had a strong interpretative interest in understanding *s.* in the passive voice.

What other courses of interpretation were open? The reader who has followed the argument to this point is unlikely to be in much doubt as to what I suppose to have been intended by the words of 2 Timothy 1.7. The Syriac translators were right. The spirit given to the Church (not to Timothy as a private Christian!) is one of power, love and *moral instruction*. Timothy, urged to stir up the gift conferred by ordination, is encouraged to be active in a ministry that displays the Church's character, confronting hostility (power), reconciling differences (love) and sustaining the teaching of the Christian way of life that has been received from the apostles.

Chrysostom was not the only figure in the Greek patristic Church to undertake the exposition of the Pastoral Epistles, though it is striking how little attention was devoted to them as compared with the Psalms, the Gospels and the major Pauline Epistles. We know that they were read, for we find seven other quotations of 2 Timothy 1.7 in the literature, all without exegetical comment.[63] We know of one lost commentary by Severianus of Gabala.[64] But there also survive two other Greek commentaries by fellow Antiochenes of Chrysostom, showing his influence to a degree, though without his homiletic aspirations. His contemporary and friend Theodore of Mopsuestia wrote one, and in the next generation Theodoret of Cyrus, prominent as a critic of Cyril and of the Council of Ephesus, wrote another. Neither had a great deal to say about 2 Timothy 1.7, but what they did say is revealing.

Theodore's comment reads:

> It is unfitting to show a cowardly face before evils brought to bear on us from outside. Why? Because within us we have the grace of the Spirit, a grace sufficient to empower us, to bind us tightly to the love of God and to make us consistently more ordered [*sōphronesterous poiein*] in our private deliberations.[65]

---

[62] 2.1 (PG 62.607).

[63] For the record: in Clement of Alexandria, Origen (two), Ephraem, Pseudo-Didymus, *De Trinitate* (three), Chrysostom, Callinicus.

[64] *Clavis* 1974, 2:477 n. 4219. Fragments survive in *catenae*, but nothing relating to our text.

[65] Theodore of Mopsuestia, *Commentarii in Epistolas Pauli minores* (PG 66.945).

Theodoret's runs:

> God gave us the grace of his All-holy Spirit, not that we should be cowardly
> before the perils entailed in the pursuit of religion, but that we should be
> sustained by divine power, should be warm in our love for him, and should
> bring to order [*sōphronisōmen*] the chaos of passions that reside within us.[66]

These interpretations are no less personalizing than Chrysostom's was.
Neither is interested in the ecclesial functions of Timothy: no comment on
verse 6 survives from Theodore, while that of Theodoret, barely alluding
to ordination, sees it as an opportunity to echo Chrysostom's views on
grace in more frankly Pelagian language: 'as oil makes the flame in the
lamp burn brighter, so the soul's enthusiasm attracts the grace of the All-
holy Spirit.' What is telling, however, is that they agree in paraphrasing the
noun *s.* with a verbal phrase in the active voice. The Spirit of power and of
love is a Spirit of *ordering*. For Theodore, ordering is what the Spirit does;
for Theodoret it is what we do. That they both conceive this activity in
terms of the Christian's individual moral life and thought, not in terms of
the ministry of the Church, is disappointing. But it gives us the clue as to
how two intelligent followers thought Chrysostom's second interpretation
needed adjustment to bring it into harmony with the natural sense of the
word *s.*

We are free to draw out the social and ecclesial aspects of the context
for ourselves, even if they did not. Timothy does not need more discretion,
self-control, *Besonnenheit* or even *sagesse*. He needs to be more forthright
and outspoken. The exhortation has to do with Timothy's charism, the
special ministry committed to him by ordination (v. 6). His friendship
towards Paul (the 'tears', v. 4), and the faith he learned from his mother
and grandmother (v. 5), are all presupposed; it is not about them that
he needs exhortation, but about his charism, which must be 'rekindled'.
As an ordained minister of the gospel he is required 'not to be ashamed'
of bearing witness to the Lord (v. 8), not to be reticent about his association with the imprisoned Paul, but to 'take a share of the abuse' to which
the gospel, as God's public disclosure of his saving power in Christ, is
exposed. As a minister he must expect to suffer what Paul, the 'herald,
apostle and teacher', has endured (v. 11); the style in which he teaches must
be modelled on the style in which Paul taught (v. 13). To emerge from
his low-profile stance and assume a more exposed position, he needs to
understand the nature of God's gift – the Spirit 'of power, love and moral

---

[66] Theodoret, *Interpretatio in xii epistulas sancti Pauli*, ad loc. (PG 82.833).

instruction', a gift given not privately to Timothy, but 'to us', that is, the whole Church, just as it is 'in us' that the Spirit has made his dwelling (v. 14). But having the charism of ministry means to minister within the provisions of this gift, to be free with administering the *s.* which the Church needs. The Spirit guards the deposit of the apostolic gospel (v. 12); it is the Spirit, therefore, who will enable Timothy, too, to guard it (v. 14). The Spirit which empowers the community to withstand the pressure of opposition, and which draws the community together in a tighter bond of mutual identification and love, also confers the linguistic communication by which its life and action may be given order and authenticity. Timothy is to draw upon that.

The text is, one might say, a charter for the work of a theologian bishop, never reticent, even from his academic chair, in giving the Church the instruction the Spirit has provided for it, ministering to the power and unity of the Church with pointed and effective guidance about its faith and life. One who has been privileged to count Tom Wright a friend since shared student days may be permitted, perhaps, to recall through this text what has been of irreplaceable value in his ministry as a church leader in our generation, and to indulge with him once again an old shared enthusiasm for the service of classical philology to the reading of the sacred text. *Kai tōnd' homoion ei ti mē peithō. Ti gar?*

Bibliography

Bauer, W., W. F. Arndt and F. W. Gingrich (1957) (eds). *A Greek-English Lexicon of the New Testament and Other Early Christian Literature.* Chicago, IL: University of Chicago Press.

Borgen, Peder, Kåre Fuglseth and Roald Skarsten (2000). *The Philo Index.* Grand Rapids, MI: Eerdmans.

Chrysostom (1886–9). *Homilies on the First Epistle to Timothy.* In vol. 13 of *The Nicene and Post-Nicene Fathers*, Series 1. Edited and translated by Philip Schaff. 14 vols. Repr. Peabody, MA: Hendrickson, 1994.

Clavis Patrum Graecorum (1974–87). Edited by Maurice Geerard. 5 vols. Turnhout: Brepols.

Johnson, Luke Timothy (1996). *Letters to Paul's Delegates.* Valley Forge, PA: Trinity Press International.

—— (2001). *The First and Second Letter to Timothy.* New York, NY: Doubleday.

Lampe, G. W. H. (1961). *A Patristic Greek Lexicon.* Oxford: Clarendon.

Migne, J.-P. (1857–86) (ed.). *Patrologia Graeca.* 162 vols. Paris: Imprimerie Catholique.

Moulton, J. H., and G. Milligan (1952). *The Vocabulary of the Greek Testament Illustrated from the Papyri and Other Non-literary Sources.* London: Hodder & Stoughton.

Mounce, William D. (2000). *Pastoral Epistles*. Word Biblical Commentary. Nashville, TN: Nelson.

Philo (1934). *De Mutatione Nominum*. In *Philo*, translated by F. H. Colson and G. H. Whitaker. Loeb Classical Library 275. Cambridge, MA: Harvard University Press.

Saarinen, Risto (2008). *The Pastoral Epistles with Philemon and Jude*. Brazos Theological Commentary on the Bible. Grand Rapids, MI: Brazos.

Spicq, Ceslas (1947). *Les Épitres Pastorales*. Paris: Lacoffre.

Wild, Robert A. (1989). 'Pastoral Letters.' In *New Jerome Biblical Commentary*, edited by Raymond F. Brown et al., 891–902. London: Chapman.

Paul, poverty and the powers: the eschatological body of Christ in the present evil age

BRUCE W. LONGENECKER

Introduction

Over 100 years ago, August Mau, one of the premier archaeologists of Pompeii and Herculaneum, stated that '[t]he people with whom we should most eagerly desire to come into contact' when excavating those first-century sites are 'the cultivated men and women of the ancient city'.[1] To Mau, evidently, the tedious life of the poor was relatively uninteresting.

In the field of Pauline scholarship, Paul has sometimes been characterized as having a view much like Mau's – uninterested in the everyday lives of the ordinary poor who were all around him in the urban contexts of the Greco-Roman world. Of course, Paul would probably have been very interested in them as potential joiners in his 'good news' communities, but within those communities and beyond, the conditions in which the poor found themselves were left largely untouched by Paul's theological discourse. His gospel shot straight towards a target that had nothing to do with the poverty that coursed its way through the Greco-Roman world. Or so this line of thinking often goes.

A lot of early twenty-first-century scholarship, including some of my own, has tried to chip away at this long-standing monolith, so that things are notably different today than they were a generation ago, perhaps even a decade ago.[2] But there is more to be done, and further conversations to be had. One of those conversations involves the relationship between poverty and Paul's conception of the cosmic powers. In Paul's world, poverty was an urban reality; in Paul's symbolic world, malignant forces

---

[1] Mau 1902, 481–2.
[2] If debates about these matters were happening in earlier generations of scholarship, they must have been happening in peripheral backwaters of the discipline, without influencing the mainstream scholarship of the twentieth century. For my own contribution, see especially Longenecker 2010.

were ever-present realities; and in Paul's convictional world, the body of Christ was an eschatologically charged reality. How do these facets converge, and how are we to conceive of Paul's discourse concerning the poor and the transformation of identity in Christ? This essay explores some of the interplay between these facets as they converge within Paul's theological discourse.[3]

Paul's analysis of social Darwinism

A discussion of poverty and the powers has any number of starting points. I will foreground here Paul's analysis of what is sometimes called 'the human condition'.

Starting from what he knows about God's salvation in Christ, Paul's anthropological discourse is usually quite dark. There are multiple texts to illustrate the point, and often those texts assess that condition from different angles. One angle is evident in Romans 7. Regardless of how the 'I' of Romans 7 is to be interpreted, it is clear that the speaker of that chapter experiences his struggle with sin (and ultimately the power of Sin) in the form of covetousness (*epithymia*). When the 'I' of Romans 7 cries out that he is infected with 'every kind of coveting' (7.8, NIV),[4] he is confessing that covetousness has invaded the whole of his moral character.

The term 'covet' can be unpacked using terms such as: brute self-interestedness, sordid self-centredness, unabashed self-promotion.[5]

---

3   It is a privilege to present this essay in honour of N. T. Wright. We can trace our friendship back to at least 1990 – although in my memory it goes back even into the late 1980s. It was then that I sent him a little note about how I had found an essay of his to be especially stimulating, and was utterly surprised to find a handwritten letter in the post a few days later expressing encouragement for my PhD studies (these were the days before email). Since those days, I have benefited from Tom's generous friendship and from many of his ideas that have stimulated my own on a number of fronts. With regard to the issue under consideration here, Tom has gone on record as recognizing that he has not been able to engage with it within his larger research projects (e.g. see his comments in Heilig, Hewitt and Bird 2016, 757). Knowing that he will soon rectify that deficit (see now his frequent incorporation of the issue in Wright 2018), and developing one of my own research areas beyond earlier publications, I offer this essay with respect and gratitude.

4   Unless otherwise noted, Scripture quotations in this chapter are the author's own translation.

5   The term 'covet' (*epithymia*) tips easily into a semantic field in which economic relationships are at play. Clearly, this is not the only semantic field in which it might operate, however. It can be used at times to indicate simple eagerness, as in Jesus' statement that he has 'greatly desired [epithymia epethymēsa] to eat this Passover' with his disciples (Luke 22.15). But when the term is used in the context of moral formation, it highlights a deficiency in the character of the agent who strongly desires to acquire something that does not belong to him or her. (See, for instance, Louw and Nida 1988–9, 25.20.) This might be the desire for sexual

Covetousness is, ultimately, the all-pervasive *libido dominandi*, or 'the will to power', writ small in the life story of the speaker of Romans 7. Its semantic spectrum here gravitates towards the character of acquiring gain at the expense of others. The covetousness that is foregrounded in that chapter, then, is the theological equivalent of social Darwinism, the notion of 'the survival of the fittest' played out within human relationships, in which regard for 'the other' is virtually vacuous, except as a prop to increase one's own power. It would not be surprising if Paul imagined this moral cancer to pervade the needy human condition. If even the admirable 'I' of Romans 7, who so desperately wishes his situation were different, cannot escape this configuration of his character, that same condition must be something like an anthropological constant. If human beings are always relational, Paul identifies a filter through which human relationships pass (apart from Christ), and that filter is encapsulated in the word 'covetousness'.

This form of competitive covetousness is on display elsewhere in Paul's letters, not least in Galatians. Paul imagines that conformity to his 'good news' will prevent Galatian Jesus-followers from 'biting and devouring each other' and being 'destroyed by each other' (see 5.15, NIV). It might sound a bit extreme to analyse the Galatians' situation in these terms, but it is a natural outworking of Paul's theologically informed view of what is on offer beyond a Christian community that is properly formed by, *in*formed by, and in *con*formity with, the good news.

Paul seems to have imagined that when the good news has no foothold, interpersonal relationships become precarious, the spawning ground of chaos. So, while Paul includes in his Galatian list of 'works of the flesh' things like sexual immorality, drunkenness and idolatry, his list includes far more entries that target violent attitudes and activities between people and people-groups. Eight entries from Galatians 5.20–21 demonstrate the point, with six of them being listed in the plural, as if to speak not simply of attitudes (for example, 'hatred') but of actions undergirded by those attitudes (that is, acts of hatred):

1 acts that induce hatred between people;
2 competitive strife between people;
3 envious jealousy between people;
4 acts that are motivated by and incite anger between people;
5 acts that promote rivalry between people;

---

acquisition or 'lust' (as in Matthew 5.28; probably 2 Timothy 2.22), but equally it can refer to acquiring the economic commodities of others (as in Acts 20.33).

6 acts that promote division between people;
7 acts that induce schisms between people;
8 acts of selfish envy.[6]

These entries articulate a moral ethos that Paul will later identify in Romans 7 as 'covetousness', not unlike what he says in Galatians 5.26, where human 'conceit' is amplified in terms of 'provoking and envying each other' (NIV). For Paul, if human covetousness were left unchecked, social destruction would be the end result, being the natural *telos* of this moral world beyond the Christian community.[7] Here Paul seems to imagine that the gospel is being promulgated in a world dominated by a destructive moral ethos. It is not hard to see how an economic component might well be included within this broad analysis of capricious human relationality – an issue considered in more depth below. Initially, however, it will serve us well to consider Paul's discourse regarding the moral ethos of in-Christ communities.

Envisaging the moral ethos of Jesus-groups

Paul's view of (what would later be called) social Darwinism provides us with the clearest picture of the moral configuration that is (to be) transcended within communities of Jesus-followers animated by the Spirit. For Paul, the moral opposite of covetousness seems to be 'faith working practically [*energoumenē*] through love' (Galatians 5.6) – that is, a faith that is configured in relation to 'the Son of God, who loved me and gave himself for me' (Galatians 2.20). Paul defines 'love' in the light of the story of the self-giving Son of God. This is why Paul begins his letter to Galatian Jesus-followers referring to Jesus as the one who 'gave himself' (1.4) and later exhorts the Galatians to 'become slaves to one another through love' (5.13) – a charge amplified a few verses later in the instruction to 'bear one another's burdens' (6.2). Burden-bearing among Christians is, in essence, a reflection of and participation in the saving event of Jesus' self-giving in death and his resurrection to life and lordship by God the Father.

---

6 These entries are translated in a way that diverges from common translations in order to bring out the sense of the plurals that Paul uses, which correspond to the word 'acts' in this translation.
7 Evidently Paul knew this destructive moral world well, or so he suggests in one of his autobiographical reflections (Galatians 1—2), in which he depicts himself as having been a man of violence prior to the coming alive of the self-giving Jesus Christ within him (Galatians 1.13).

There are, of course, various forms of burden-bearing, but we would be tone deaf if we could not hear an economic harmonic within the Pauline voice. This is true across a spectrum of Pauline texts, whether with undisputed or disputed authorship. In undisputed texts, Paul encouraged Thessalonian Jesus-followers to 'comfort the discouraged' and to 'help the weak', making sure to 'always pursue what is good for one another and for all' (1 Thessalonians 5.14–15). He exhorted Galatian Jesus-followers not to be slow in doing good to others (Galatians 6.9–10) – something that the Corinthians were commended for, as they exhibited 'generosity . . . with all' (2 Corinthians 9.13).[8] And Jesus-followers in Rome were exhorted to offset the needs of others as an expression of Christian love (Romans 12.13) – part of what it means to 'let love be genuine' (12.9).

These (and other) charges from Paul are matched by similar instructions in the disputed letters. The author of Ephesians charged those with selfish histories to 'do good with their own hands, so that they may have something to share with those in need' (Ephesians 4.28, my translation). The author of 1 Timothy exhorted his audience 'to do good, to be rich in good deeds, to be generous givers, sharing with others' (6.18). The author of Titus proposed that Jesus-followers should 'devote themselves to good works in order to meet urgent needs' (Titus 3.14). The Pauline voice, both within and beyond the undisputed letters, is consistent. In contrast to the covetousness that is completely out of sync with the good news, a Christian lifestyle does not shrink from economic need but engages those needs directly to find creative solutions for relieving them.

For Paul, then, 'the gospel train' is not a non-stop express that bypasses the landscape of poverty. In fact, when he discusses in 2 Corinthians 8—9 what he calls elsewhere the collection for 'the poor among the saints at Jerusalem' (Romans 15.26), Paul cloaks his rhetoric in markedly theological terms. Caring for others in need is depicted as a demonstration of Christian 'obedience to the confession of the gospel of Christ' (2 Corinthians 9.13), is spoken of with reference to divine 'grace' (8.1, 6–7, 9, 19; 9.8, 14), to Christian 'service' (8.4; 9.1, 12, 13) and to 'righteousness' (9.9–10) – both the righteousness of God himself and of those who would be obedient to him. Here, economic self-giving by Jesus-followers is depicted as an intrinsic component of the content of the gospel that Paul

---

8 As noted above, that generous disposition had not infiltrated the whole of the Corinthians' practices. When economic differentiation among Jesus-followers started to creep into the Corinthian observance of the Lord's Supper, Paul chastised them fiercely, claiming that they had undermined the essence of the meal itself and the community's embodied proclamation of the good news (1 Corinthians 11.17–34).

proclaimed – with a Christological model at the heart of it all (8.9). This was because the gospel, itself 'the power of God for salvation' in which 'the righteousness of God' is revealed (Romans 1.16–17), shows God to be setting the world to right and to be doing so in the first instance in communities of self-giving love, animated by the Spirit who replicates Jesus Christ in the eschatological living of Jesus-followers.[9]

The powers and economic imbalance

If the Spirit animates the forging of solutions to economic need within Jesus-groups, does Paul's assessment of social Darwinism go beyond the covetous character of the human heart? Are cosmic powers part of the mix – the so-called 'cosmos grabbers of this present darkness' spoken of in Ephesians 6.12 (*tous kosmokratoras tou skotous toutou*)? We cannot get far in Paul's discourse without coming across them in some form or another – those suprahuman powers that seem to have their own intentionality and perpetuate situations that run contrary to the will of God.[10] Does Paul involve them in matters of economic imbalance?

Unsurprisingly, he does. In Romans 1 Paul registers an economic dimension within his portrait of the world out of joint. He speaks in 1.29 of *pleonexia*, a different word from the one used in Romans 7 (*epithymia*) but one that also highlights acquisitiveness, and, for this reason, is also usually translated 'covetousness'. Our lexicons inform us that this word references 'a strong desire to acquire more and more material possessions or to possess more things than other people have, all irrespective of need' (Louw and Nida, who offer the synonyms 'greed, avarice, covetousness'); or that it references 'greediness, grasping, or gain' with a view to one's own advantage over someone else (Liddell and Scott).[11]

Evidently Paul included economic injustice in his depiction of the world

---

9 For much more on this issue, see especially my arguments in Longenecker 2010, 135–56.

10 Although some strands of Pauline scholarship underplay the importance of these malignant powers within Paul's theologizing, others rightly place them front and centre in Paul's symbolic world. One of my personal favourites in this regard (and for a number of other reasons) is Beker 1980. Beker situates Paul's 'apocalyptic' discourse firmly in relation to God's covenant faithfulness to Israel (not unlike the honorand of this volume). I regret that Beker's work is not more to the fore of Pauline studies today (as evidenced in its complete absence from John Barclay's impressive new book: Barclay 2015). Among the most important contributions to Pauline theology in the past generation is Beker 1986, 10–16.

11 When the author of Colossians uses this word, he qualifies it as a form of idolatry (Colossians 3.5), just as the author of 2 Peter includes being 'experts in greed' within his own depiction of social Darwinism (2 Peter 2.14, NIV; see the animalistic Darwinism in his portrait at 2.12).

out of joint in Romans 1 – a world that provokes the wrath of a deity of justice. This, then, becomes a key resource for our interests, especially when Paul goes on to claim in Romans 3.9 that his case has already contended (earlier in the letter, I take it) that all of humanity, without distinction, is under the power of Sin.[12] Here, we are in the realm of the cosmic powers. The lordship of the cosmos grabbers has, as one of its manifestations, the covetousness that fosters self-enhancement at the expense of others. Paul will go on to tease this out further in Romans 7, as we have seen, where the cosmic power of Sin takes the initiative, actively seizing the opportunity (*aphomēn labousa*, 7.8, 11) in order to produce covetousness (*kateirgasato en emoi pasan epithymian*, 7.8) within the speaker.

Of course, in neither Romans 1—3 nor in Romans 7 does Paul give us a developed analysis of the relationship of human avarice and the cosmos grabbers. Nor does he tease out the relationship between avarice and poverty in an explicit fashion. Is there reason to believe that a Pauline assessment of covetousness could include within its purview the poverty that was all around him? Did it dawn on him, for instance, that structural poverty itself might derive from and testify to the covetous impulse of the human condition? And beyond that, did it dawn on him that poverty might result from the chaos-inducing effects of the cosmos grabbers? How far was Paul able to connect these dots in his theological discourse?

Perhaps the connections between avarice, poverty and the powers are things to be probed in theologically informed socio-economic analysis among those who are interested in 'thinking through Paul' – that is, attempting to think Paul's thoughts after and beyond him. For instance, Paul does not seem to foreground structural poverty when assessing the grip of the cosmos grabbers upon this world. In Romans 1, he outlines phenomena against which 'the wrath of God' is directed, foregrounding idolatry and sexual immorality and other things; in that outline, poverty itself seems not to make an appearance. If we expect to find Paul saying something like 'God gave them over to an unbalanced economic society, in which structural poverty became entrenched in every culture due to the influence of suprahuman powers', we are disappointed. But if Paul had been asked whether the powers had orchestrated a world in which some inevitably went hungry while others thrived, if he did not see the point immediately, or if he did not say 'Yes, that's exactly what I was saying in

---

12 Of course, Paul has not made this charge explicitly. Evidently he imagined that charge to be self-evident in his depiction of human sinfulness in Romans 1—2.

Romans 1—3 and Romans 7', then I imagine he would at least scratch his head, think for a minute and then say something like 'Well, yeah, that makes good sense.' And it makes good sense, precisely because Paul saw the world as animated by spiritual forces of one kind or another. If beneficial relationships among those in Christ are empowered by the Spirit of God's Son, Darwinian relationships driven by acquisitive greed and covetousness are empowered by spiritual forces of an altogether different kind. Or at least Paul (would have) thought so.

Fine-tuning the discussion

I want, in both this section and the next, to move beyond what seems to me to be the relatively straightforward aspects of this terrain to its less straightforward regions, since it is there that intriguing contours emerge in Paul's discourse about poverty and the powers. This is not easy terrain, however, nor is it uncontroversial. But in my view this terrain captures something of Paul's theological vision in both its ancient genius and, in some ways perhaps, its contemporary contestability.

Let me head in this direction by citing Ephesians 3.10 (regardless of its authorship): 'so that through the church the wisdom of God in its rich variety might now be made known to the rulers and authorities in the heavenly places'. This statement captures something that lies deep in the heart of Paul's theological discourse, that is, relational configurations within the body of Christ are tell-tale signs to the cosmic powers that they are not ultimately sovereign. Instead, sovereignty rests with the one who reconfigures relational practices in communities of Jesus-followers.

To amplify the point, it seems legitimate to consider what it might mean if the phrase 'neither rich nor poor' could magically be inserted into Galatians 3.28, which of course reads: 'There is no longer Jew or Greek, there is no longer slave or free, there is no longer male and female; for all of you are one in Christ Jesus.'[13] What might a non-canonical inclusion of 'neither rich nor poor' entail? What would the inclusion of that phrase look like in small groups of Jesus-followers?

At this point, our investigation would benefit by briefly revisiting Steve Friesen's seven-point 'poverty scale' or, as I have renamed it elsewhere,

---

[13] Note that the pairing of 'slave' and 'free' is not an economic pairing; some better-placed slaves had economic resources that enabled them to loan money to freemen, for instance. The issue is complicated and would take us beyond the confines of this discussion. For a discussion of concrete situations, see Longenecker 2016b, 268–78.

'economy scale' of the Greco-Roman world.[14] Plugging different economy-scale identifiers into our discussion will help us to identify the contours of the issue more clearly by delineating varieties of need and, in turn, different forms of economic involvement.

The bottom of the economy scale, labelled ES7 ('economy scale level 7'), includes those who were economically destitute, unsupported by household structures and in dire straits; without assistance from others or a change in their situation, these people were fast moving towards the inevitable grip of 'the last enemy' (1 Corinthians 15.26) – the power of Death. Slightly higher up the economy scale, at ES6, were those who, while poor in the sense of not having many excess resources, were nonetheless in a stable economic situation. They worked with their hands and provided for their own basic needs, with perhaps only a meagre surplus. They were more vulnerable to dipping into destitution by way of a downward 'change in fortune' than those more securely placed on the economy scale, but unless that dip occurred, their lives were not economically threatened. Life might have been extremely hard at times and they might not have had much but, unlike those at ES7, their lives were not calamitously desperate. Economy-scale levels move through the ES5 level, in which resources are more noticeable and secure than in the relatively insecure ES6 situations, the middling groups of ES4, where differences with ES6 situations become quite evident, and up to the elite at various levels of wealth (ES3 to ES1), who shunned 'working with their hands' and whose enormous reserves were opulently displayed as frequently and effectively as possible.

Even with these very basic descriptors, the economy-scale signifiers can add clarity to our conceptualization of issues. For instance, it seems to me that Paul entertained the hope that Christian groups would be able to extend generosity towards those in ES7, but probably he did not see the same urgency with regard to those in ES6. This can get tricky, of course, since those in ES6 might simply say, 'I might as well stop working and let the community care for me as I drop into ES7.' In fact, an attitude along these lines seems actually to have taken root among some Thessalonian Jesus-followers (although perhaps with greater theological finesse than I have depicted it here), suggesting that our proposal might be on the right track.[15] In writing to Thessalonian Jesus-followers caught in that unhelpful mindset, Paul differentiates between those who were truly

---

14 Friesen 2004, 323–61; Longenecker 2010, 36–59.
15 On the Thessalonian situation, see Longenecker 2010, 146–8.

deserving of community support and those who were not – a pragmatic differentiation intended to preserve the limited reserves of Jesus-groups (2 Thessalonians 3.6–12).[16]

It was not Paul's intention to place generosity central in theory but vacuous in practice. For instance, at the very first ecclesiastical council of the Christian Church (described in Galatians 2.1–10), Paul and the leaders of the Jerusalem community (James, John and Cephas/Peter) agreed that only two things are to define Jesus-followers in their various indigenous settings: (1) devotion to Jesus (implied) and (2) care for those entrenched in ES7 situations. Their words, of course, were 'remember the poor' (*tōn ptōchōn hina mnēmoneuōmen*, Galatians 2.10), which we might dare to fine-tune as 'remember the destitute' (a phrase that, contrary to popular belief, was not referencing the Jerusalem community exclusively).[17] Paul's account in Galatians 2.1–10 highlights the apostolic agreement that, wherever Jesus-groups were to be established by apostolic initiatives, and regardless of whether those groups were composed of predominantly Jewish or gentile constituents, Jesus-groups were to exhibit generosity towards those in ES7. Generosity of this kind was deeply embedded within Jewish practice, tradition and Scripture, and it (rather than the practice of circumcision) was to characterize all forms of Jesus-devotion, regardless of all other variations in the indigenous character of local communities.[18] The apostles of the first ecclesiastical council of the Christian Church determined that disparate Jesus-groups were not to be constrained by certain forms of identity (such as circumcision), but would nonetheless be united in a posture of economic generosity – an outworking of their devotion to the resurrected Lord.[19]

It occasionally gets proposed that virtually all Jesus-followers 'shared fully the bleak material existence which was the lot of more than 99% of the

---

[16] The author of 1 Timothy adopts a similar differentiation when giving instructions regarding care for widows, with care being necessary only if the widows are in exposed situations where their vulnerability cannot be resolved in other ways (1 Timothy 5.3–16). That author's concern to use corporate funds prudently only for those in desperate need (i.e. those in ES7) seems to me to be a natural application of Paul's own attitude.

[17] For my argument that 'remember the poor' did not refer to Jerusalem Jesus-followers, see Longenecker 2010, 157–206. Paul's collection effort was a specific application of a more general principle about remembering the poor in general, with Jesus-groups being charged in Galatians 2.10 to care for the indigenous needy – not unlike the Nazarene whom they proclaimed as Lord. For a poorly executed interpretation of the phrase 'remember the poor' in Galatians 2.10 improperly thought to reference Jerusalem Jesus-followers, see Orlando 2014.

[18] In this way, remembering the poor might be said to be, in a sense, a form of identification with the cultural life of the Judean homeland, no matter how far afield the Christian good news was spread.

[19] These claims require the much fuller elaboration that I offer in Longenecker 2010, 157–206.

inhabitants of the Empire'.[20] And it is against this kind of a backdrop that some have suggested that what we see in early Jesus-groups is the practice of corporate mutuality among the destitute. I remain unconvinced, since such views (1) flatten out the economic levels of early Jesus-followers and (2) constrain the economic relationality among early Jesus-followers. Early Jesus-followers sometimes, perhaps often, rose above the lower levels of poverty. A key passage in this regard is 1 Corinthians 1.26. There, Paul's comment that not many Corinthian Jesus-followers had been 'powerful' or 'well-born' prior to adopting devotion to Jesus Christ suggests (as has long been noted) that at least a few Corinthian Jesus-followers had been well-born – at least, relatively speaking (perhaps ES4). Of course this might simply have been a Corinthian aberration from the norm, but other glimpses suggest that this was not the case. The author of the first Johannine epistle, for instance, addressed some Jesus-followers whom he thought commanded economic resources beyond destitution when he asked, 'How does God's love abide in anyone who has the world's goods and sees a brother or sister in need and yet refuses help?' (1 John 3.17). The author of the epistle of James expected Christian communities to be composed of various economic levels (James 2.1–17), asking:

> If a brother or sister is naked and lacks daily food, and one of you says to them, 'Go in peace; keep warm and eat your fill', and yet you do not supply their bodily needs, what is the good of that?
>
> (James 2.15–16)

In each of these instances, those above ES7 levels are expected to help those at ES7. Similarly, the author of 1 Peter thought that some Christian women were 'wearing gold ornaments or fine clothing' (1 Peter 3.3, something he discourages); the author of Hebrews knew of Christians who had experienced 'the plundering of [their] possessions' (Hebrews 10.34); and the author of Revelation depicted some Jesus-followers in Laodicea as proclaiming 'I am rich, I have prospered, and I need nothing' (Revelation 3.17). Even if we add a degree of rhetorical flourish to all of these pronouncements, they (and others) nonetheless suggest that some Jesus-followers were at economic levels above utter destitution.

It is unlikely, then, that gallant mutuality among the utterly impoverished lay at the heart of the Christian vision for remembering the poor. The declaration that God 'sent his son, born of a woman . . . in order that we might receive adoption as sons and daughters' (Galatians 4.4–5) has

---

[20] Meggitt 1998, 99.

within it an incarnational narrative that Paul metaphorically articulated in economic terms: 'although he was rich, yet for your sakes he became poor, so that by his poverty you might be enriched' (2 Corinthians 8.9; translation mine). And that economic metaphor was useful when Paul sought to form a consciousness of economic relationality among Jesus-followers. So he expected those in 'present abundance' to offset the 'need' of others – and by so doing, they would be in alignment with the scriptural pronouncement that 'the one who had much did not have too much, and the one who had little did not have too little' (2 Corinthians 8.15).[21]

It is little wonder, then, that Paul offered harsh words regarding the way 'the Lord's supper' was being practised among some Corinthian Jesus-followers (1 Corinthians 11.17–34). In Paul's view of their unbalanced practice, some Corinthians 'with houses' (*oikias*) were ultimately showing 'contempt for the church of God' and 'humiliat[ing] those who have nothing' (*kataischynete tous mē echontas*, 1 Corinthians 11.22). Like the authors of 1 John and James, Paul did not expect those who have nothing to take the initiative to offset each other's needs (i.e. hunger, 11.21) through economic mutuality of some kind. The failure of those 'with houses' to recognize the needs of 'those who have nothing' (a phenomenon captured perfectly in narrative terms in the parable of the rich man and Lazarus in Luke 16.19–31) is actually a failure of their theological imagination, a failure to recognize new patterns of relationality within the body of Christ (*mē diakrinōn to sōma*, 11.29). There is nothing here to suggest that it is good simply for the destitute to eke out forms of basic mutuality among themselves, despite the utterly dire and desperate situation that engulfed them, leaving the economically advantaged out of that loop altogether. Such scenarios are to be lauded, should they be achievable. But what Paul has in his sights is the callous failure of those with resources to care for 'those who have nothing', since that failure is itself drawing the judgement of God upon the community (11.29–32).

Against this backdrop, it is easy to see why Paul was so keen to take the collection of money from his communities to the Jesus-followers in Jerusalem. It was not to illustrate that destitute Jesus-followers were involved in reciprocal sharing out of their economic insufficiencies – insufficiencies that left them on the cusp of death. That would not have

---

21 Paul goes so far as to suggest that Jesus-followers in Macedonia have participated in his collection efforts despite 'their extreme poverty . . . even beyond their means' (2 Corinthians 8.2–3). He is probably referring here especially to Jesus-followers in Thessalonica, who appear elsewhere in his letters to include ES5 members at best. Philippian Jesus-groups may well have included ES4 members. For more on this, see Longenecker 2010, 253–8.

impressed anyone, being simultaneously a romanticized and insensitive view of the destitute. Instead, the collection was to demonstrate that gentile Jesus-followers situated above destitution (i.e. from ES6 on up) were reaching into their reserves for the benefit of impoverished Jewish Jesus-followers in Jerusalem. The fact that this was being done by gentiles for 'all' (2 Corinthians 9.13) was noticeable enough; that it was being done by gentiles for Jews in particular (through the collection effort) was more than noticeable. The contribution of gentile Jesus-followers for 'the poor' among Jesus-followers in Jerusalem was simply a further extension of what Paul expected Jesus-groups to be doing more indigenously (as in Galatians 2.10), with those in supra-destitute situations offsetting the economic needs of the destitute, whose end was otherwise inevitable.

It would seem reasonable to suggest that in Paul's frame of reference, such initiatives for offsetting the economic needs of the destitute were testimonies to and against the powers – an embodied demonstration to 'the rulers and authorities in the heavenly places' of 'the wisdom of God in its rich variety' that is now being 'made known' to those authorities 'through the church'. In Paul's terms, economic initiatives of this kind illustrate that some who have been gifted by God with economic resources (Romans 12.8; 1 Corinthians 12.28; cf. 1 Corinthians 1.26) are not victims of the covetousness sponsored by the powers; instead, they are animated by the power of the Spirit, through whom their faith is put into practical service in terms of bearing the economic burdens of others within the body of Christ.

This does not mean, of course, that the destitute are otherwise of little worth, except for the initiatives undertaken on their behalf by those better off. Such a supposition runs directly counter to Paul's view of the body of Christ, in which each member contributes different resources to nourish the interdependent membership. If the destitute benefit from the initiatives of those gifted with economic resources, those with economic resources benefit from the gifts essential for the body of Christ that are introduced by those who would otherwise be destitute.

This point cannot be overemphasized, but too often has been underemphasized. Participating in the death of Jesus Christ, the destitute transfer from the realm overseen by the power of Death and are freed from economic fragility through their immersion in the realm of Spirit-empowered self-giving and Spirit-enhanced corporate-gifting. In the process, their full potential as human beings gifted by God in relation to others is nurtured. But this process is no different from that for any other Jesus-follower, except in the specifics of the Spirit's gifting. Every member, regardless of his or her multidimensional status matrix, is gifted with a contribution to the body of Christ. If ES4 members contribute financially, for instance, that would be of no greater significance than members without financial resources contributing a non-financial gift to the body – perhaps encouragement, or prophecy, or compassion, or wisdom, or discernment (all of these from Romans 12.6–8), or some skill gifted to them by the Spirit. It is extremely important to note that when Paul affirmed his support for 'remembering' those in economic need (i.e. at ES7), he was not naively sponsoring some destructively synergistic loop that promoted the interests of the powerful, with charity going to the impoverished of ES7 in order simply to promote the reputation and status of the wealthy.[22] To imagine things along those lines is to lose the threads of Paul's theological discourse. Those who are unable to gift the community through their economic reserves are to be seen as gifting the community through whatever non-economic resources the Spirit inevitably brings alive in them. To imagine that non-economic gifts are lesser gifts, or that the gifting of those with economic reserves amounts to nothing other than charity, is to follow a route similar to the Corinthian Jesus-followers whom Paul chastised for their insufficient view of spiritual gifting (1 Corinthians 12—14) – with certain gifts acquiring more status than others.[23] To interpret relationality among Jesus-followers through solely economic frames of reference is one of the things that Paul sought so hard to deconstruct among Jesus-groups wherever he went. We tie ourselves in unnecessary knots of theologically ill-formed perceptions when we imagine it demeaning to the destitute if economically secure Jesus-followers were expected to extend Spirit-enhanced economic resources on their behalf. By analogy, we would have to say that it is demeaning to extend encouragement to those who would benefit from it. Something is wrong in the house of Pauline studies when

---

[22] Recent studies show that people explain their motivations for 'charitable giving' in one of three ways: (1) the 'purely altruistic', in which the donor values the social good that is done as a result of giving; (2) the 'impurely altruistic', in which the donor derives positive self-worth from contributing to the social good; and (3) the 'not-at-all altruistic', in which the donor seeks to demonstrate his/her abundance of resources to others in his/her peer group. See <https://www.theguardian.com/voluntary-sector-network/2015/mar/23/the-science-behind-why-people-give-money-to-charity>.

[23] In his discussion of the gifting of the Spirit, Paul first articulates a rather 'egalitarian' view (1 Corinthians 12.4–26) and then moves to a hierarchical view (12.27–31) – with both strategies intended to offset the Corinthian prioritization of the gift of tongues over other giftings. I take it that Paul is more comfortable with the former strategy than the latter, since it is the 'egalitarian' depiction that Paul adopts when rearticulating the matter in Romans 12.3–8, without any trace of hierarchical relationality.

we arrive at this point, precisely because we have lost sight of the theological moorings of Paul's understanding of the body of Christ.[24]

Transforming hostility between relational differences

As a consequence of the preceding discussion, we can better see that, if we are permitted to expand the 'rich variety' of identities in Christ beyond the three pairs listed in Galatians 3.28, an economic pairing 'neither rich nor poor' would not imply that Jesus-groups should be devoid of those with few economic resources. Paul did not expect those in Christ to have the same income or reserves, and all in the middling level, or above, or below. Instead, he expected Jesus-groups, as part of their essential identity, to take initiatives to bolster the most economically disadvantaged against the cosmic power of Death in instances when the power of Death could get a foothold through the absence of life-sustaining resources. Perhaps what Paul calls 'fair balance' (*isotēs*) when referring to the relationality between participants in his collection would be just as applicable to healthy forms of Christian economic relationality in general. Paul expected Jesus-followers to offset the financial needs of others, but the end goal is not economic sameness (even if the extremes at each end of things are to be avoided). Fair balance involves the recognition that one's own self and one's community always stand in relation to the needs of the destitute and the undertaking of initiatives within the orb of one's relational identity to benefit those in desperate economic need – and, moreover, to see this process as rooted in the transforming power of God's Spirit.[25]

This becomes clearer if we tease out the significance of the phrase 'neither free nor slave' embedded within Galatians 3.28. This task requires us to recognize two tendencies within Paul's theological discourse. On the one hand, Paul seems not to have decried the enslaving cosmic powers when he saw a slave. It seems unlikely that Paul ever denounced the powers embedded in the ancient structures of slavery. Paul's discourse simply does not move along those lines – whether we focus on Philemon,

---

[24] The preceding paragraphs are intended to address the view (occasionally articulated at academic meetings) that it is morally deficient to expect the economically advantaged to initiate economic benefits for the destitute of ES7. It is understandable what such a view is seeking to avoid, but nonetheless, this way of assessing things has little foothold in Paul's discourse of the body of Christ. Nor does it seem to have been the view of any other New Testament author.

[25] We might distinguish between 'numerical equality' and 'proportional equality', recognizing Paul as adopting the latter but not the former. See Welborn 2013, 73–90; Ogereau 2012, 360–78.

1 Corinthians 7, the *Haustafeln* of Colossians and Ephesians (Colossians 3.22; Ephesians 6.5–6), or the Pastoral Epistles (1 Timothy 6.2; Titus 2.9).[26] Paul's discourse does not depict slavery as an evil to be eliminated.[27] The elimination of slavery within Christian circles and beyond is, arguably, a legitimate expansion of Paul's theological vision, even if it seems not to have been a component of Paul's explicit theological discourse.

On the other hand, it also needs to be noted that, although Paul may not have gone as far along the road as our twenty-first-century sensitivities might want, Paul's discourse could at times move 'in the right direction'. We might recognize hefty components in his theological discourse that, when teased out and developed along certain lines, can be deployed to dismantle oppressive systems, even linking those systems to 'the Domination System' animated by the cosmic powers.[28] At the very least, relationships among Jesus-followers were being redefined in corporate gatherings in ways that have some transformational distinctives when judged against the backdrop of general practices and attitudes of the first century. To varying degrees, the Pauline discourse on slavery suggests that relationships between slaves and masters were to be informed in new ways by the good news. In particular, during the weekly meetings of Jesus-followers, relationships between masters and slaves were to be experiments in relational novelty and the infusion of eschatological invigoration.[29]

---

[26] I need to amplify my claim with regard to 1 Corinthians 7. Throughout 7.17–24, Paul states on three occasions that Jesus-followers are to stay in the condition in which they were initially called (7.17, 20, 24). This instruction animates his instruction concerning circumcision (7.17–20), which overspills into his instruction concerning slaves (7.21–24). He clearly does not want free(d) men and women to become enslaved to human owners (7.23), and the reason for this is probably that their missional freedom would be severely impeded as a consequence. On the other hand, Paul also has a fairly cavalier attitude to slaves earning their freedom, regardless of how we are to read his frustratingly ambiguous words in the second half of 7.21. Here again, a missional interest trumps concerns for the freeing of Christian slaves; that is, Paul seems to think it good that Christians are embedded within as many situations as possible, in order to bring a Christian influence within those situations. This explains why he encourages them not to be too concerned about their freedom (7.21), and why his overarching vision is for Jesus-followers to stay in the situations in which God called them.

[27] In this, he was like almost all of his contemporaries who 'took slavery for granted as part of the social and economic fabric of the society in which they lived' – a characteristic of Philo, Josephus and the rabbis, as well as Greco-Roman authors in general; so Hezser 2006, 380, 384–9.

[28] My use of the term 'Domination System' derives from the stimulating work of Wink 1992, esp. 13–32, 65–104.

[29] For a narrative depiction of this, see Longenecker 2016a. On the relevance of Philemon, see Longenecker 2016b.

If these two tendencies help us to interpret the phrase 'neither slave nor free' in Galatians 3.28 (NIV), they also provide interpretative guidelines for the verse as a whole. Paul is not implying that distinct identities are to be collapsed and folded in on each other into some indistinct goo. Instead, he is asserting that, within Christian communities, new relationships (are to) transpire between distinct identities of all kinds. The transformative character of Paul's theological vision lies not in some magical *removal* of distinct identities *from* Jesus-groups but in the pragmatic *restoration* of healthy relationships *between* distinct identities *within* Jesus-groups. Those distinct identities themselves are to be kept in play. Gentiles do not become Jews in Jesus-groups, but so too, Jews do not become gentiles.[30] Nor was Paul saying that God sent God's Son, born of a woman, in order that sexual differentiation might be transcended among Jesus-followers.[31] In the same way, Paul was not saying that slaves in Christ are set free from their situation as slaves to earthly masters.

This is again where the cosmos grabbers enter the scene. While Paul imagines that these distinct identities are preserved in Christ, he envisages a scenario in which relationships between those distinct identities are transformed. He goes some way in re-conceptualizing how people with these distinct identities are to conceive of themselves in relation to each other.[32] Fundamentally, the patterns of engagement between distinct identities are no longer to be characterized by the covetous hostility induced by the cosmic powers (or in the case of Galatians, the *stoicheia*, as in 4.3, 9); instead, covetousness is replaced by relational 'other-concern' as the Spirit brings Jesus Christ alive among Jesus-followers. These distinct identities (and presumably others that Paul would deem legitimate before God) are not to be removed from the picture of relationships in Christ; instead, they become the focus of the cruciform picture itself. In this

---

30 Contra Tertullian (*Against the Jews*, 3.8), who claims that God had revealed that 'the first circumcision would cease' and be replaced by 'the new law'. Barclay 2016, 13, makes the point well: '[Paul's] strong relativizing statements (Galatians 3.28) do not eradicate ethnic identities, but they place them within a new orientation where inherited ethnicity is variously valorized and no longer determinative of practice.'

31 The expectation that women could shake off their womanhood in Christ seems to be what Paul is trying to argue against in his discourse of 1 Corinthians 11.1–16. Compare the *Gospel of Thomas* 22 and, differently, 114.

32 For instance, slaves find freedom in Christ, and the free find that they are slaves to Christ (1 Corinthians 7.22). Further, gentiles find themselves to be a part of the 'true circumcision' (Romans 2.25–29; Philippians 3.3), while Jews recognize that their cultural distinctives are non-essentials for others (Romans 14.1—15.6). Further still, males find that they are free to depict themselves in roles usually preserved for women (e.g. 1 Thessalonians 2.7; Galatians 4.19).

way, eschatologically configured Jesus-groups testify to the defeat of the powers and the eradication of the moral chaos of social Darwinism that those powers induce.[33] In Christ, each form of identity is affirmed even while it is transformed in its relationality to other forms of identity. In Christ, each identity is secure, is secured and (to use an economic term) is 'securitized'. In cruciform transformation, each is released from having to compete with, or assert itself against, the other. In Christ, the vulnerability of identities is removed, with the anxious and destructive competitiveness of social Darwinism left at the door of a worshipping Jesus-group. Complemented by other identities and complementing them in turn, each member of the body of Christ contributes to a harmony that reflects God's creative intention over against the cosmos grabbers.[34]

Case studies

Paul's letters offer further resources for conceptualizing how people with distinct economic identities might conceive of themselves in relation to each other – that is, how 'neither rich nor poor' might be teased out within a cruciform community animated by Spirit-gifting.

In the first instance, members of such communities would probably need to be weaned off their attachment to the game of status-capture that was deeply ingrained in Greco-Roman culture. If a few Jesus-groups in Corinth met in houses of middling-group members (i.e. ES4), those members might well have been the primary (but not the exclusive) financial sponsors of the community's gatherings. In normal social codes, financial sponsors of that kind would be regarded as deserving recipients of special esteem and repute. A simple look at a typical list of members of Greco-Roman associations makes the point in a moment's reflection: in those membership lists, the association's financial sponsors are given

---

[33] The *stoicheia* are not defeated, for instance, by some process of unravelling the identity of the ethnic people whom God chose in covenant election (a covenant relationship that has a foothold even within Galatians; e.g. 3.13; 4.4; probably also 6.16). That would hand a significant victory to the *stoicheia*, in their attempts to have God's world chaotically devour itself and its ordering (cf. 5.15). And not giving the *stoicheia* a victory in this regard may have contributed to Paul's affirmation of 'the Israel of God' in Galatians 6.16, and why he affirms that 'all Israel will be saved' in Romans 11.26 – both of which probably reference the ethnic people of Israel (the latter especially). There is more going on in each of these last two instances, but certainly not less.

[34] Compare Johnson 1996, 131: 'The differences are not removed, but they are relativized. Their only importance is that they reveal the church as a place of reconciliation; distinctions that in the world always lead to separation, here are perceived as the possibility of gift-giving in peace (see Ephesians 2:11–21).'

prominence.[35] If a membership list of Corinthian Jesus-followers were to be drawn up, Paul would insist, I think, that the list not be configured in accordance with societal expectations about economic status. 'Ownership' of Jesus-groups was not devised in those terms in Paul's theological discourse.[36]

In support of this claim, I would refer us to two passages as case studies. First, Paul's 'letter of thankless thanks' – otherwise known as Philippians. Having sent money to support Paul, the Philippian Jesus-followers hear about Paul's reception of that money only in the final paragraphs of the four-chapter letter. Comments about the reception of money would normally have been expected to appear much sooner in a letter's structure, and would normally have included notable expressions of gratitude for the generosity of the giver/givers. Paul goes a different route. He rejoices in the generosity of the Philippians, not because he himself has been helped (Paul says he is satisfied in whatever situation he faces) but because their generosity both demonstrates the goodness of God in their lives and enhances their heavenly account before God (Philippians 4.12–20). Here we have an example of 'value inversion'. Those who supported others financially were expected to receive rich praise. Paul offers nothing of the kind in this letter. Instead, he lets it be known that he himself is not indebted to the generous givers, nor are the generous givers to imagine themselves as deserving praise; God alone is worthy of praise. All this would have been rather extraordinary to most first-century ears. Consequently, we can see how codes of honour are being redrawn among Jesus-followers in a situation where an economic relationship is to the fore.

A second passage of note is 1 Corinthians 16.1–4 – precisely because in one respect it offers the converse of what we see in Philippians. This text is extraordinary in its implications, although this is rarely noticed. The text gives the appearance of offering a simple instruction about how Corinthian Jesus-followers should store up resources for the collection for the poor among Jesus-followers in Jerusalem. What is significant about

---

[35] See, for instance, the first-century BCE dining association from Sparta (*IG* 5.1, 209) that revolved around the two sons of a man named Pratolas, in which five family members (including one woman) sponsored 29 others; translation and discussion appear in Ascough, Harland and Kloppenborg 2012, 35. This example illustrates the general pattern of associational ethos. For examples of inscriptions in which members honour their financial benefactors, see Ascough, Harland and Kloppenborg 2012, inscriptions/graffiti numbers 2, 12, 14–17, 24, *passim*. For discussion of inscriptions listing people in order of status, see examples Harland 2009, 33; Wallace-Hadrill 2011, 138–44.

[36] Paul's own preference for sitting light to financial sponsors comes into clear focus here as well. See further Briones 2013.

this simple instruction is the economic level that it assumes: 'each of you is to put aside and save whatever extra you earn, so that collections need not be taken when I come' (16.2). Evidently at this point in his expectations for the collection, Paul did not want the collection to be seen as an initiative sponsored by middling-group Jesus-followers. It would have been fairly easy for a few Corinthian Jesus-followers at the ES4 economic level (say, Gaius, Erastus, Phoebe; perhaps also Crispus and/or Stephanas) to put together, in relatively quick timing, a sizable bundle of denarii when Paul passed through to collect the Corinthians' contribution. The same could easily have been replicated among ES4 members of Jesus-groups in Philippi, Ephesus and elsewhere. In this way, the collection could have been fairly easy to orchestrate, and would inevitably have been quite sizable. But Paul preferred a different way of going about things. Evidently he did not want the hoped-for success of the collection being attributable to the generosity of the economically well-endowed, who did such things inevitably within the status-conscious culture of benefaction and patronage. Instead, those whom he enlisted for his collection in particular are those at ES6 and, perhaps, ES5. The impression is that they are to put a few small coins under their straw mattress every week, in order that, together and over time, their small contributions could amount to a sizeable donation. This is not to imply that Paul would have refused contributions from ES4 members. Probably assuming that ES4 members would contribute anyway, Paul placed the spotlight on ES6 members, not to place a burden on them but, evidently, to allow them to be seen (by themselves and by others) in a new light – that is, as valuable contributors to the health and well-being of the Jesus-movement.

There are two sides to this coin. On the one side, Paul is giving ownership of a theologically significant financial initiative to those who were never seen as privileged enough to be in that role. But this bold move also has dangers, as the other side of the coin demonstrates. That is, Paul's discourse bypasses those who, in any other context, would have expected to be praised for taking on this task as part of their role as benefactors of the association. As the material remains of the ancient world repeatedly illustrate, those in the middling group of society were fiercely concerned with their reputation as upwardly mobile members of society. They expected to be recognized as such, and they reinforced their increasing status at each and every opportunity.[37] In most contexts beyond Jesus-groups, then, Paul

---

[37] Regarding benefactors (not patrons), Philo wrote the following (*Cher.* 122–3): 'Those who are said to bestow benefits sell rather than give; and those who seem to us to receive them in

would be seen to be playing with fire, intentionally failing to recognize those for whom such an initiative would have provided a further opportunity to reinforce their status. In communities of Jesus-followers, however, Paul sees the opportunity to redefine relationships of status.[38] Tasks are being reassigned in Christ, as both 'rich' and poor find themselves in new structures of relationship to each other. These reconfigured relationships between 'rich' and poor in Christian communities are part of the display of the wisdom of God that, according to the author of Ephesians, is revealed 'to the rulers and authorities in the heavenly places' (3.10).[39]

Divine triumph over the powers lies at the heart of all this. Paul wanted Jesus-followers to offset the needs of the destitute as a sign of God's triumph – the overthrow of the powers that oversee and promote the chaotic self-interestedness that runs rampant throughout God's good creation. This seems to have involved financial 'self-giving' of various kinds within Jesus-groups. This includes even the self-giving of the relatively poor themselves (ES6), sometimes in financial configurations, sometimes in non-financial initiatives. Paul did not expect there to be no ES6 members within Christian communities. Nor did he sense that there could be an end to poverty in its ES7 form. He is not much of a role model for the 'End Poverty' campaign of today. And there may have been times when Paul himself did not model the best of his theological tendencies, or when other priorities complicated his strategies (thinking here of his privileging of a middling-group household in 1 Corinthians 16.15–18).[40] But at key moments Paul seems to have imagined the

---

truth buy. The givers are seeking commendation or honor as their return and look for their benefits to be repaid, and so under the false name of a gift, they in truth carry out a sale.'

[38] Some of the tough times that lay ahead of Paul in his relationship with the Corinthians may even be attributable to Paul's words in 1 Corinthians 16.1–4, with some middling-group Jesus-followers in Corinth feeling slighted by his daring discourse. In return, they seem to have snubbed Paul, depicting him as a charlatan who preyed on the poor in order to relieve them of whatever small reserves they might have had (2 Corinthians 11.7–11; 12.16–17). The transition from Paul's words at the end of 1 Corinthians (16.1–4) to these accusations in Paul's next letter to the Corinthians (i.e. the 'tearful letter') makes perfect sense. On 2 Corinthians 10—13 as the 'tearful letter', see Longenecker and Still 2014, 139–62.

[39] Second Corinthians illustrates that Paul was not able to retain this approach in his theological discourse about the collection. Some within Corinthian Jesus-groups went on to accuse Paul of being a charlatan (as noted above). Accordingly, the next time he addresses the issue of the collection (2 Corinthians 8—9), his discourse is much broader in scope, including those higher up the economy scale than simply ES6–ES5. Even then, however, Paul makes it clear that what they are giving to others comes from God's abundant resources; those who give, then, do not receive the glory, but only God does, since it is his 'indescribable gift' (9.15), not theirs.

[40] Johnson 1996, 132, suggests that Paul fails to maintain his subversive theology at this point. My own view is that Paul is not attempting to prioritize middling-group gifting over

vitalization of the relatively poor (at ES6 and ES5) as valued players in the life of the generous association of Jesus-groups, sometimes even in financial involvements. Presumably they could take initiatives of that sort because they belonged to a community wherein members 'had each other's backs', no matter in what form their need arose (financial or otherwise). When placed within Paul's robust theology of the gifting of the body, there is nothing here about charity, but neither is there much about ending structural poverty within society in general.[41] Instead, Paul's vision is all about the transformation of relationships between diverse identities in the body of Christ. The task of remembering the destitute is linked in Paul's theological discourse to the gifting of the eschatological body of Christ, testifying to and enacting the in-breaking of right relationships that transpires as a result of the Spirit's transforming power over against the relational hostility induced by the powers.

In brief

One of the most entrenched myths of the Greco-Roman world was that only the elite and the upwardly mobile were capable of making meaningful contributions to those in embedded relationships with others. At key moments, Paul's theological discourse ran along completely contrary lines. His theological reconfigurations of economic relationality are part of 'the good news' that he preached, and they testify to the transforming power of the Spirit of God for the body and for the world – all as part of the eschatological defeat of the powers and their programme of social Darwinism.

At times in our readings of Paul, poverty and the powers, we need to filter out both right-wing Fox News on the one hand and left-wing MSNBC on the other. Paul did not imagine that his gospel would make everyone rich, nor would it make everyone's income the same, at some middle-class level or below. Instead, the Christian message is about the value of all people, working practically together as members of the body

---

poverty-group gifting but, instead, is prioritizing one middling-group assembly that is favourable to him over other middling-group assemblies that might seem less favourable to him (and perhaps take the lead in stirring up the trouble that is soon to come his way from among the Corinthians). Even if this takes some of the sting out of the issue, the passage nonetheless illustrates how standard patterns of thinking were replicated at times even by Paul.

41 If it is true that Paul's vision is neither about charity nor about structural resolution, his theological discourse offers theological resources that might be used across the spectrum from immediate relief of needs to long-term structural development.

of Christ, sharing their giftings in indigenous settings that overspill in various ways from member to member and, potentially, beyond the body of Christ, for the benefit of others. This has some semblance to what some today are calling ABCD – asset-based community development.[42] That is, in his best moments, Paul imagined the body of Christ to be the epitome of the abundant community (whose resources were supplied by an abundant Spirit), where all needy members had important contributions to make, regardless of their prosopographic profile, and where each incarnation of the body built its identity and mission around the indigenous resources (gifts) brought to it by its Spirit-endowed members. And, if Paul's discourse usually makes it appear as if the sharing of economic giftings is applicable only within intramural boundaries of Jesus-groups, at times Paul surprises us; even those boundaries are porous (Galatians 6.10; 1 Thessalonians 5.15; cf. 2 Corinthians 9.13).

The valuing of identities in Christ (and beyond) foregrounds the valuing of those who held minimal forms of social value and who were minimized by those in control of society's cultural stories. It is not simply having 'something to share with those in need' that testifies to and against the powers (Ephesians 4.28, NIV) – although even that plays some role. The testimony to and against the powers of 'this present evil age' (Galatians 1.4) involves cherishing those who are most vulnerable on the scale of socio-economic status – those whose stories are usually drowned out through infatuation with the socio-economically elite. Moreover, it involves recognizing that those least advantageously placed on the socio-economic scale (i.e. ES7s) have resources of their own to contribute – resources as essential as economic resources for the operation of a healthy cruciform community.

This valuing of the small things is, in the words of a Christian hymn, an 'old, old story'. It is embedded deeply within the Jewish Scriptures about little things that make a difference, about the importance of the whisper rather than the wind, fire or earthquake. It is a story that a Jewish sage from Nazareth elaborated when he spoke about the importance of the small mustard seed, or about the widow who gave more relevantly in her tiny offering than the givers of large donations. It is embedded within the story of the little boy who gave his loaves and fish in a gesture that has fed the souls of many for two millennia. These are the stories that strip away the satanic myth that only the powerful make worthy contributions and

---

[42] See the Asset Based Community Development website at abcdinstitute.org. See also McKnight and Block 2012; Corbett and Fikkert 2014.

that the poor have unimpressive stories because their initiatives could only be, as August Mau seems to have thought, uninteresting and insignificant.

It was the power of this inspiring 'old, old story' that many early Jesus-followers found to be so attractive, and so transforming. In Paul's 'good news', they were to learn about a resurrected Lord who benevolently empowers his followers with giftings that flow along novel configurations that bypassed the status configurations of the first-century world. Beyond this 'good news', the story of the day, perpetuated by the elite and masked by their overwhelmingly generous benefactions to society, perpetuated the view that only the powerful are significant, and the rest shall rejoice and be glad in them. The story that Paul told, in its purest form, unmasked and opposed the story stage-managed by the elite, showing it to be a satanic lie, perpetuated by the powers in this present evil age of social Darwinism.

Bibliography

Ascough, Richard S., Philip A. Harland and John S. Kloppenborg (2012). *Associations in the Greco-Roman World: A Sourcebook.* Waco, TX: Baylor University Press.

Barclay, John (2015). *Paul and the Gift.* Grand Rapids, MI: Eerdmans.

—— (2016). 'Pauline Churches, Jewish Communities and the Roman Empire: Introducing the Issues.' In his *Pauline Churches and Diaspora Jews*, 3–36. Grand Rapids, MI: Eerdmans.

Beker, J. Christiaan (1980). *Paul the Apostle: The Triumph of God in Life and Thought.* Minneapolis, MN: Fortress.

—— (1986). 'The Faithfulness of God and the Priority of Israel in Paul's Letter to the Romans.' In *Christians among Jews and Gentiles*, edited by G. W. E. Nickelsburg and G. W. MacRae, 10–16. Minneapolis, MN: Fortress.

Briones, David E. (2013). *Paul's Financial Policy: A Socio-Theological Approach.* Library of New Testament Studies. New York, NY: Bloomsbury/T&T Clark.

Corbett, Steve, and Brian Fikkert (2014). *When Helping Hurts: How to Alleviate Poverty without Hurting the Poor . . . and Yourself.* Chicago, IL: Moody.

Friesen, Steven J. (2004). 'Poverty in Pauline Studies: Beyond the So-called New Consensus.' *Journal for the Study of the New Testament* 26.3: 323–61.

Harland, Philip A. (2009). *Dynamics of Identity in the World of the Early Christians.* New York, NY: Continuum.

Hezser, P. Catherine (2006). *Jewish Slavery in Antiquity.* Oxford: Oxford University Press.

Johnson, Luke Timothy (1996). *Scripture and Discernment: Decision Making in the Church.* Nashville, TN: Abingdon.

Liddell, Henry George, and Robert Scott (1889). *An Intermediate Greek-English Lexicon Founded upon the Seventh Edition of Liddell and Scott's Greek-English Lexicon.* Oxford: Clarendon.

Longenecker, Bruce W. (2010). *Remember the Poor: Paul, Power, and the Greco-Roman World*. Grand Rapids, MI: Eerdmans.

—— (2016a). *Lost Letters of Pergamum: A Story from the New Testament World*. 2nd edition. Grand Rapids, MI: Baker Academic.

—— (2016b). *The Crosses of Pompeii: Jesus-Devotion in a Vesuvian Town*. Minneapolis, MN: Fortress.

Longenecker, Bruce W., and Todd D. Still (2014). *Thinking Through Paul: A Survey of His Life, Letters, and Theology*. Grand Rapids, MI: Zondervan.

Louw, Johannes P., and Eugene A. Nida (1988–9) (eds). *Greek-English Lexicon of the New Testament Based on Semantic Domains*. 2 vols. New York, NY: The United Bible Societies.

McKnight, John, and Peter Block (2012). *The Abundant Community: Awakening the Power of Families and Neighborhoods*. San Francisco, CA: Berrett-Koehler Publishers.

Mau, August (1902). *Pompeii: Its Life and Art*. Translated by F. W. Kelsey. New York, NY: Macmillan.

Meggitt, Justin J. (1998). *Paul, Poverty and Survival*. Edinburgh: T&T Clark.

Ogereau, Julien (2012). 'The Jerusalem Collection as Κοινωνία: Paul's Global Politics of Socio-Economic Equality and Solidarity.' *New Testament Studies* 58.3: 360–78.

Orlando, Robert (2014). *The Apostle Paul: A Polite Bribe*. Eugene, OR: Cascade.

Thompson, James W., and Bruce W. Longenecker (2016). *Philippians and Philemon*. Paideia: Commentaries on the New Testament. Grand Rapids, MI: Baker.

Wallace-Hadrill, Andrew (2011). *Herculaneum Past and Future*. London: Frances Lincoln.

Welborn, Lawrence (2013). '"That There May Be Equality": The Contexts and Consequences of a Pauline Ideal.' *New Testament Studies* 59.1: 73–90.

Wink, Walter (1992). *Engaging the Powers: Discernment and Resistance in a World of Domination*. Minneapolis, MN: Fortress.

Wright, N. T. (2016). 'The Challenge of Dialogue: A Partial and Preliminary Response.' In *God and the Faithfulness of Paul: A Critical Examination of the Pauline Theology of N. T. Wright*, edited by Christoph Heilig, J. Thomas Hewitt and Michael F. Bird, 711–68. Wissenschaftliche Untersuchungen zum Neuen Testament 2/413. Tübingen: Mohr Siebeck.

Wright, N. T. (2018). *Paul: A Biography*. San Francisco: HarperOne.

Walking with the oppressed: lament and new-creational hope

SYLVIA C. KEESMAAT

Introduction

When I first began reflecting on the theme of new creation in Romans many years ago, it should have been no surprise that I began with a wandering journey into the exodus tradition. For, in a world in thrall to death (to use Paul's metaphor from Romans 5), it is impossible to envisage the new creation unless we resist the deathly grip of empire, following God through the uncertainty of wilderness to the new place of hope and promise. It should not have surprised me this time either, when I sat down to revisit the new creation theme, to discover that lament became the guiding framework for my reflections. Throughout the biblical story, and especially in the prophets, the cry of lament in the face of injustice is what galvanizes God to act for justice in new creational hope.[1] In the exodus story, the crying out of the Israelites moved God to hear and respond in salvation; lament became the basis for hope.[2] So I once again find myself writing about new creation by way of more foundational themes. My first exploration into this topic was as a doctoral student working with Tom. This time I write not only as a student for a teacher, but also with deep gratitude to my teacher and friend. In so doing, I hope not only to affirm much of Tom's work, but also to challenge, deepen and push some of his conclusions in new and fruitful directions.

Central to Wright's understanding of Paul is a larger biblical narrative of God's vision and intent for the renewal of all creation. This new-creational horizon informs all of Paul's thought, Wright argues: his rootedness in *monotheism*, understood as the affirmation of God as the creator; *election*, defined as God's intention for Israel to be the ones through whom the new creation would be accomplished; and *eschatology*, when the new

---

[1] Ellington 2008, 70.
[2] On the groaning of the Israelites as central in the exodus tradition, and also on the new exodus in Romans 8, see Keesmaat 1999.

creation would not be merely inaugurated, but also established in the new heavens and the new earth.[3] This framing of the biblical story is a radical one: when new creation is the goal and *telos* of God's story for the world, the implications are far-reaching and transformative. Rather than the creation-denying hope for disembodied escape from the earth that has shaped many strands of Christian theology and faith, human beings are affirmed in their creational calling as earth creatures, *adam* from *adamah*. The reverberations for embodied creational life are deep and tangible.

It is precisely on the implications of this vision for our creaturely existence in the present that I would like to focus this chapter. For, as Wright argues, this new creation is not merely a future hope: 'Paul envisages a renewed humanity in terms of *new creation*, a new world in which the creator's original intention would at last be fulfilled; and this new world is to be seen in advance in the Messiah's people.'[4] If the community of those who follow Jesus is a new-creational community, what does this look like both in Paul's time and in our own? This is the 'so what' question, a question that Wright has addressed again and again in his work, particularly in his popular writings.[5] Although in these works Wright has outlined very clear implications of the new-creational shape of the Christian community, these are limited, I suggest, by a reluctance to describe the early Christian community in any way which would have deeply challenged the worldview of the first century. (I am aware that Wright would be shocked at this assertion; however, there is ample textual evidence in support of this viewpoint.[6]) In addition, his description of the practical outworking of Paul's thought are primarily restricted to the themes of unity and holiness, the latter invariably interpreted as sexual purity. Of course, Wright himself would assert that the implications of Paul's thought are much wider than this narrow emphasis. And yet his reading of Paul seems far removed from the world where a craftsman worried about whether there would be enough food for a meal that day; where a slave wondered how many of her master's guests would require her sexual services that

---

3   These themes are unpacked at length in chapters 9–11 of Wright 2013, 609–1265. For the purposes of this essay I will interact primarily with this work as the most recent and comprehensive treatment of Paul in Wright's writings.

4   Wright 2013, 1117; see also pp. 706, 1072; 2002, 604–6.

5   Particularly in Wright 2008; 2010; 2012.

6   Witness the places where Wright emphasizes the way in which Christian ethics affirm what he calls 'basic moral norms' (Wright 2013, 1108), and the necessity of continuing to work 'within the system' like Daniel (1274–5), not to mention being 'good citizens' (1298). Wright also argues that there are all kinds of parallels between Paul's ethics and those of his contemporaries (1371). I shall address this in depth below.

evening; a world where a householder contemplated which city officials should be invited to the next banquet – and which, perhaps, would enjoy his new slave; a world where a farmer knew that the troops stationed in the nearby town would soon requisition all of his grain, leaving none for food or planting the next year; a world where the elite landowner was contemplating how much interest to demand from that same farmer so that next year he could claim his land in payment. These are all common issues in the ancient world – hunger, sexual abuse, loss of land.[7]

Most of those to whom Paul's letter to the Romans was addressed lived on or below subsistence levels in contexts shaped by both economic and physical suffering. Their interest in Paul's letter would have been shaped by such suffering. But their concerns were not unique. In the Scriptures, the hope for a new creation also begins in a deeply rooted specific context of suffering and pain. There is pain over how the story has gone awry, pain in the heart of God, and pain at the heart of humanity and creation. Such pain is found in the mourning of both God and creation, and in the cry of lament that is found woven through the story from Genesis to Revelation.[8] Throughout the Scriptures, the new-creational horizon – from Torah to the prophets to the end of the story – was deeply rooted in grief and sorrow over the distortion, violence and infidelity that was causing the suffering of the earth, humanity and God.

As Walter Brueggemann has indicated, a prophetic imagination that intends to bring transformation with new symbols of hope needs to begin by articulating the depths of the darkness. It is impossible to imagine newness without acknowledging the pain and grief that are the result of violence and sin.[9] Does Paul also begin where the prophets, and indeed the whole biblical story, begins? Does he also begin with the pain and grief of the communities to whom he is writing? And, if so, what are the implications of this starting point for the new creation that these communities mirror?

It is my argument in this chapter that Paul's letter to the Romans was deeply rooted in the pathos and grief of both God and those who followed Jesus in Rome. As a result, this letter is shaped by both the laments of Israel's past, and the cries of those who experienced oppression, injustice

---

7   On these contexts as background for Paul's letters see Oakes 2004; 2009; Friesen 2004; Longenecker 2009; 2010; MacDonald 2007.

8   For an excellent overview of this theme in the biblical story as a whole, see Ellington 2008. Terence Fretheim (1984, 112) describes how 'God's grieving goes back to the morning of the world.'

9   Brueggemann 1978. See also Brueggemann 1986.

and violence in their daily lives at the heart of the empire. Moreover, I will argue that this context calls us to be a people of lament, who mourn with those who mourn, and who walk with the oppressed (Romans 12.15–16). In so doing, we will not only bear the image of God and the crucified Son, but we will also be a truth-telling people who name the pain of sin and embody the hope of a new creation, where the Spirit also groans along with our laments. In addition, I will argue that such a calling to cruciform suffering love is the dominant marker of the covenantally faithful community, more important than any other ethic because it is a sign, paradoxically, of the new creation in our midst. In making this argument I hope to deepen and build upon the work of Wright, with whom I first began to explore these themes.

The pain and grief of the community in Rome

We begin, then, with the community of those who were known to be followers of Jesus in Rome. It is the perennial temptation of biblical scholars to construct an ideal reader as we interpret the biblical text.[10] In reality, those who first heard the letter to the Romans read by Phoebe were an assortment of Judeans and gentiles as far removed from an academic seated at his or her comfortable desk as we can imagine. As Peter Oakes has convincingly demonstrated, the community to which Paul wrote in Romans would have consisted of a cross-section of people: householders (who were probably craftworkers of some sort) and their slaves, children, families and one or two other dependants; members of households whose head was not part of a house church, both free people, slaves, and free or freed dependants; people who were homeless; migrant workers and others who rented space in shared rooms.[11] Oakes points out that those involved in the house churches would have had various relationships with each other: they would have been family members, slaves, friends, neighbours, relatives, customers, suppliers, casual employees and (informal) clients.[12] For many in this list, life at the centre of the empire would have been tenuous and anxious, with no assurance of adequate food from day to day. Those who were slaves had some level of security, although their lives were

---

10 Wright describes a similar dynamic: 'We have done so much of our scholarship under the shadow of the Enlightenment that we have reduced historiography to the tracing of lines of ideas, of who *thought* what, who *was influenced by* what, who *read* which texts in what way.' Wright 1998, 285.
11 Oakes 2009, 96.
12 This list is directly from Oakes 2009, 93.

governed by fear, violence (often sexual) and control. How would Paul's letter have been heard by these people?

Perhaps one way into this text is to engage in an act of historical imagination.[13] What if we looked at this letter through the eyes of two of its hearers, possible members of the community in Rome, each of whom would have heard the letter in very different ways. Since we know from Romans 16.11 that there were members of the household of Narcissus among the recipients of the letter, and since there are also a high number of slave names in Romans 16, let us posit a member of Narcissus' household, a slave, who would have been among those who heard this letter. We will call her Iris, a slave name found in Pompeii.[14] Iris, as I am imagining her, is a slave woman who looks after her master's children and, until recently, two children that she herself had given birth to, offspring of either her master or one of his friends. In addition to and while tending the children, she helps her mistress with various tasks such as dressing, shopping, and general fetching and carrying, and, since she is fairly young and attractive, she is also used sexually both by her master and by his friends on a regular basis. Since such use had resulted in children, Iris had also functioned as the wet-nurse for her master's sons. When her own son was six, and her daughter was three, they had been taken by her master to the marketplace, and sold. Since then, another slave in her household had told her about Jesus, and along with a few other slaves of the household of Narcissus, she had become a follower of the Way.

Iris had not always been a slave. She had been captured, along with her mother, in Mauretania, when she was 12, and had memories of a previous life of freedom and family.[15] Trauma and grief shaped Iris's life: grief over the loss of her mother, and of her native land; the shame and grief of sexual abuse; and, most recently, the grief of the loss of her children. This was a loss she could not even acknowledge, since, in the eyes of her master, she didn't have children. She had borne him two bodies, property to dispose of as he wished. Iris's story is typical. Her life was the life of over half the slaves in Rome, and typical of many members of the house churches in

---

13 Such a method is, indeed, suggested by Wright himself: 'Serious historiography proceeds by the disciplined and controlled use of historical imagination, the reconstrual of a world other than our own, and the testing of that, as a hypothesis, by a fresh and further reading of all the evidence.' Wright 1998, 284.

14 On the incidence of slave names in Romans, see Jewett 2007, 955–72. Oakes (2009, 33–7) describes graffiti with the name Iris. In that case, the graffiti suggests that Iris was sold to men for sex. That is not the persona of Iris in this story.

15 Bradley 2004, 301–4. Rome was fighting to subdue Mauretania from 40 to 44 CE (p. 302). Ancient Mauretania was located in what today is western Algeria and northern Morocco.

Rome – it had been shaped by the trauma of loss of family and home, and by ongoing grief and physical suffering. How might Iris have heard Paul's letter to the Romans?

And how might Iris's hearing of this letter have differed from that of a freedperson and a Judean?[16] We know from Romans 16 that there were also a number of Judeans in the community in Rome. Some of these would have been descendants of Judeans captured by Pompey in 63 BCE and taken to Rome as slaves.[17] Many lived across the Tiber in the slums. One of those mentioned in Romans 16, Nereus, could well have come from such a background. The son of Judean slaves, freed after a generation in Rome, Nereus could easily have been someone who worked in one of the pottery workshops, making mass-produced clay lamps, living in one of the tiny slum apartments in Transtiberium, trying to be both a faithful Judean and a follower of Jesus. He would have lived a precarious existence, with not quite enough to eat, and very little free time outside working hours. But he, along with his sister, would have belonged to a network of others with a similar background, some of whom were also followers of Messiah Jesus.

Iris and Nereus lived very different lives and, as we shall see, heard Paul's letter to the Romans in very different ways, but there were some similarities between them. Both of them were, in a sense, homeless. Alienated by Roman imperial forces from their ancestral lands, they both found themselves in exile in Rome, living among those who were not their people. They both lived in a society structured around honour and shame, and both of them, for different reasons, were not worthy of honour. Nereus, as a Judean, the descendant of a slave, and a common labourer, was considered both shameful and of no account. Iris, as a woman and as a slave, was considered beyond the boundaries of honour. Her sexual use would be considered shameful, if she were considered a person. Which she wasn't. Both Iris and Nereus lived in a world of generational trauma, grief and longing: the Roman imperial story had delivered suffering and sorrow for both of them. They longed for a different world, a world where, at the very least, they would be in their own land, among their own people. A world where they would be at home.[18]

---

16 I use the term Judean rather than Jew to better reflect the Greek (*Ioudaios*) and to capture the overtones of the connection that Nereus would have felt to Judea, the land of his ancestors.

17 On slaves brought to Rome as a result of conquest, see Bradley 2004, 298–318. On the descendants of Jewish slaves in Rome see Bradley 2004, 309 n. 17; Beard, North and Price 1998, 272.

18 The material on Iris and Nereus on this and the following pages is based on much longer

Although these two people are constructs with very specific character-istics, they would have been representative, I suggest, of a cross-section of those in the house churches of Rome: slaves and descendants of slaves born free but of very low status, Judeans and gentiles, men and women. Many of those who lived in Rome were immigrants: descendants of slaves, farmers whose lands had been lost to taxes or bad crop years, immigrants whose lands had been conquered by Rome: those who are the collateral damage of the policies of empire. This isn't just what the historians tell us. As we shall see, Paul's letter assumes such a background as well.

Paul names the pathos of the community: Nereus

When we try to imagine both Iris and Nereus listening to the letter to the Romans, we are struck first by the fact that they would have listened very differently. Nereus was probably used to hearing readings when he met together with other Judeans. As a result, he was used to following an argu-ment. For him, listening to such a letter would not be unusual. It is entirely possible that he would have described the letter using language like this:

> It was a surprising letter from someone who had never been to Rome. Paul clearly knows the suffering we have gone through here. In fact, he named the idolatry that is found everywhere around us.[19] The idolatry of my patron shapes not only his worship, but also the work that he expects me to do. He is a hard man, and Paul described him perfectly at the start of his letter. He is sexu-ally violent, using his boy slaves to satisfy his desires. He is greedy and arrogant, telling tales about fellow merchants and the quality of their work to harm their businesses, and he is devious in his dealings. He really is heartless and ruthless. It was as if Paul had my patron in mind when he wrote those words.[20]
>
> The letter was also full of comfort. When Paul described how famine and nakedness and persecution couldn't separate us from the love of the Messiah, I felt as though he was talking directly to me and the way my sister and I have struggled. I've known famine, and persecution, and in the winter my clothing is never quite enough.[21]
>
> Oddly enough Paul's letter felt like a lament to me. When he began to talk about how idolatry has led to violence, it sounded like he was echoing God's grief over such violent idolatry in the history of my people.[22] And he

---

reconstructions of their first-century context found in Keesmaat and Walsh, forthcoming, chs 2–4.

[19] Romans 1.23.
[20] Romans 1.24–32.
[21] Romans 8.35. Tamez (1993, 53) indicates that when Paul lists his own hunger, nakedness and homelessness, he is describing the lives of most working people.
[22] Jeremiah 2.11, Hosea 4.7 and Psalm 106 are all echoed in Romans 1.23. On Paul's echo of these texts, see Keesmaat 2015, 93–4.

kept returning to the psalms of lament. These psalms were prayed by my ancestors who cried out to God day and night. In them, I hear the voices of the poor who are taken advantage of by the rich, the unwary who are caught in the traps of the unjust, the innocent who are surrounded by enemies, and the people of God who are at the mercy of the violent assaults of other nations.[23] In some cases the psalmist knows that suffering is the result of sin; but more often the psalmist is crying out in the face of injustice, just as I cry out, questioning God's absence in the face of suffering.[24] Again and again I have cried out to God, asking 'How long, O Lord?' and sometimes even, 'Why have you abandoned me?' And there has been no answer.[25]

So when Paul echoed Psalms 71 and 44 at the beginning of his letter, I heard my questions behind his words.[26] Just like the psalmist, I have asked God for a sign of his justice, I have asked him to act in faithfulness to his covenant, I have insisted that he no longer put his people to shame.[27] At one point Paul quoted from five or six psalms, all of which overwhelmingly identify the wicked with the other nations, whom God will punish when he delivers his people.[28] This hope of punishment for the wicked nation that captured and continues to enslave my people has been my hope and prayer for many years. These psalms also make clear that the just, those who hope in God,[29] the poor and the oppressed,[30] people like me are the ones for whom God will act.[31] These are psalms that comfort me. But Paul also seems to be in anguish in this letter over our people who do not know the way of the Messiah.[32] Just like the prophets who struggled with my disobedient ancestors, Paul twists these psalms of lament so that the judgement that was originally levelled against the nations is now levelled against my people Israel. And the anguish of God is also raised in Paul's struggle, a struggle I

---

23 The psalms of lament that Paul quotes, echoes or alludes to in Romans are: Psalms 5; 10; 14; 18—19; 32; 35—36; 44; 53; 59; 62—63; 69; 71; 94; 110; 117—118; 140; 143. It should be noted that lament psalms make up a full third of the book of Psalms (with additional laments found in Jeremiah and Lamentations). Many of these psalms are treated in Crisler 2016. Crisler's approach is quite different from my own with fundamentally different theological assumptions at play.

24 Cf. Bauckham 2008, 257.

25 Ellington (2008, 2) points out that 'it is anguish and not theological curiosity that energizes the cries of "How long oh Lord?" and "Why have you abandoned me?"'

26 Psalms 71.1–2 and 44.10 are echoed in Romans 1.16. See Keesmaat 2004, 141; Hays 1989, 38.

27 Cf. Psalm 44.15; 71.13.

28 Psalms 9.6, 12, 20–21; 10.16; 14. The psalms echoed in these verses are: Romans 3.12 = Psalm 14.1; 53.3–4; Romans 3.13 = Psalm 5.10 and Psalm 140.4; Romans 3.14 = Psalm 10.7; Romans 3.15 = Isaiah 59.7; Proverbs 1.16; Romans 3.18 = Psalm 36.2.

29 Psalms 5.13; 140.14.

30 Psalms 9.9, 12, 18; 10.12, 14, 18; 14.6; 140.12.

31 Keesmaat 2004, 146.

32 Romans 9.2.

also know from the prophets: is God still faithful to my people in spite of our unfaithfulness?[33]

This tension between God's faithfulness and our unfaithfulness runs throughout Paul's letter. I could feel it in my bones. In spite of the insistence on God's justice, the question is an open one through much of Paul's anguished argument. And I could understand why. It is a source of anguish in my own heart as well.

This anguish is familiar to me from the prophets, who ask 'Where is God if the story is ending this way?'[34] Like me, Paul is struggling with precisely this question. If this is the end of the story, if gentiles are now grafted in, recipients of the blessing and salvation, joyful heirs of the promise, where is God in relation to Israel according to the flesh? These are questions of deep sorrow and turmoil for me: can God still be trusted if God appears to be absent for Israel? In his retelling of the story of my people, Paul reveals the deep struggles of Jeremiah, Hosea and Isaiah, and also of the prophet Elijah.[35] This is always a hard story for me to hear. Will God continue to be absent and remain in judgement? Or will God act in compassion, once again, for my people?

It was no surprise that this struggle over Israel's story came after Paul talked about the groans of creation, and the cries of believers, especially since he had tied our groaning to the groaning of the Holy Spirit.[36] Just like our God lamented our faithlessness in the prophets, so Paul, a prophet for our time, laments that faithlessness, joining with the lament of the Spirit of God.

Nereus is able to hear the whole letter. He catches the allusions to his Scriptures, the echoes of the psalms of lament, the narrative arc of Romans within the whole story of Israel, a story both of covenantal brokenness and covenantal faithfulness. As a result, he is able to situate his own suffering, described by Paul, in the larger context of the suffering of both his people throughout the story and the suffering of God as God longs for that people to be faithful.

Paul names the pathos of the community: Iris

For Iris, however, the whole experience would be different. First of all, she was unused to listening to anything like this kind of letter. And while Nereus would also have heard the letter in cramped quarters, Iris was

---

[33] Romans 3, 9–11. I treat these psalms and the themes they evoke in much more depth in Keesmaat 2004.

[34] Ellington 2008, 87–8.

[35] Romans 11.2–4. Hays 1989, 64, also suggests that Romans 9—11 has the fundamental shape of lament.

[36] Romans 8.18–26.

probably meeting in secret in the kitchen or another extremely crowded, smelly and poorly lit room in her master's house.[37] She would have puzzled over all of the references to the Jews, and wondered at the references to Abraham and the long history of Israel described later in the letter.[38] In addition, she had been up part of the night satisfying her master's needs, and so she was sleepy. It is possible that during the long description of Israel's relationship with God she either lost track of the argument or fell asleep altogether.[39] Even so, there would have been parts of the letter that spoke to her. She may have described the letter in this way:

> After we had quietly sung a hymn and had passed around some barley cakes that the cook had made and saved for us, Phoebe began to read Paul's letter. From the very first sentence it was not what I expected. Paul began by calling himself a slave of Jesus the Messiah – he identified himself not with the honourable, not with the freeborn, but as the slave of another Master, Jesus, whom his followers called the Messiah, a Jewish name for a king. I found this startling. Why would a free person call himself a slave, even of someone who was such a good Master as Jesus? To be a slave means you are shameful. To be a slave means that no one ever shows you honour. To be a slave means that you can be beaten at will, even tortured, and no one will defend you. To be a slave means you have no place, no father to belong to, no son to care for you, no homeland, no home.[40] Why would Paul say that he is a slave? How can he even understand what the life of a slave is like? How can he even imagine knowing what it is like to be a slave?
>
> I was almost unable to listen any further, but immediately another phrase caught my attention: 'the triumphant good news of God, concerning his son'.[41] Usually the triumphant good news is what Caesar offers after a fresh victory – and we know what that good news means.[42] More captured people will be brought as slaves to Rome, just as my mother and I were brought from Mauretania 12 years ago. Caesar's good news is always bad news for most of us. But Paul said that this good news was the good news of salvation. I wondered what this salvation would look like for me.

---

37 On the way in which the architecture of the parts of homes which were frequented by slaves were small, dark and cramped, see Joshel and Peterson 2014, 40–58. Even the doorways used by slaves were significantly lower than those used by the rest of the household. Latrines were often located in kitchens where slaves slept.

38 Romans 9—11.

39 We know from Acts 20.9 that sleep occasionally overcame those who listened to Paul in person. It is entirely possible that this letter would have had the same effect on some people.

40 On natal alienation and slavery, see Glancy 2002, 25–6.

41 Romans 1.3, my translation.

42 The Greek word *euangelion* can be translated as 'gospel' or 'good news'. In the Roman Empire the terms were used for the good news of a military victory. See Elliott 2000, 24; Georgi 1991, 83; Wright 1994, 226–8.

Other parts of the letter were much easier to understand. When Paul condemned all the sexual violence of the imperial house – and the violence of my own master, too! – I knew what he was talking about.[43] And Paul also seemed to understand at least something of what it means to be a slave when he said that with his mind he is a slave to the law of God, but that with his flesh he is a slave to the law of sin.[44] That's exactly what it is like – wanting to live a life of virtue and piety but forced to do things my master demands even when they are shameful.[45] That's why Paul talked about our groaning as we wait for our bodies to be redeemed.[46] We cry out until we are fully free; the freedom of the children of God, he said. When that freedom comes we will no longer be in bondage, our bodies forced to be slaves to sin. I have always known that groaning deep within me and it seems to have only become more intense since I've started following Jesus.

In Iris's ears, Paul's letter spoke to the deep suffering that she experienced in her life, particularly as a slave. But even though she and Nereus, as gentile and Judean, slave and free, would have heard different things, some parts of the letter would have spoken to both of them. If they had in some later meeting discussed their responses to this letter, they might have come to this conclusion:

We could both see our own suffering in Paul's words, particularly when he referred to the distress, hardship, persecution, famine, nakedness, peril and even the imperial sword that hangs over our heads.[47] When Paul talked about the imperial rule of death, as opposed to the imperial rule of justice that comes through Messiah Jesus, well, that made so much sense.[48] We could both see how the imperial rule of Caesar has brought death for so many: death to those who have been conquered, death for those who work in the fields and build the roads, death for those who work in the mines, death to slaves who are beaten by their masters, death to the children starving on the streets while one more temple is built to honour Rome, and yes, death to so many Judeans in their homeland.

For these two very different followers of Jesus in Rome, Paul's letter evokes not only the oppressive praxis of those who have control over them (Iris's master and Nereus's patron), but also the oppressive praxis of the imperial rule of death that keeps them in exile far from home. Both overtly and by

---

43 Romans 1.26–27.
44 Romans 7.14–20.
45 So also Oakes 2009, 147.
46 Romans 8.23.
47 Romans 8.35.
48 Romans 5.13–21. 'Imperial rule of death' and 'imperial rule of justice' are my translations of *ebasileusen ho thanatos / ho thanatos ebasileusen* (vv. 13 and 17) and *basileusē dikaiosyn ēs* (v. 21).

use of contrast, Paul's letter also alludes to the violent nature of the story that gives meaning to this praxis (the imperial 'gospel', the 'peace' that comes from Rome, and the sword that is wielded by the state).[49] In addition, the letter describes the symbols that reinforce this story in the minds of the people: the images that result in both sexual and economic violence, the sword that sums up the violence of Roman power, and the honour–shame dynamic that keeps the whole system in balance.[50] It is no wonder that Iris and Nereus could hear Paul speaking a word of comfort into the midst of suffering and grief. Rather than a theological treatise, they hear a letter that speaks into their daily struggles and sorrow.

Paul describes the pathos of creation

The climax of Paul's description of the suffering of the community is Romans 8.35–39 where he ties together the laments of the followers of Jesus (those 'who have the first fruits of the Spirit', v. 23, NRSV), with the laments of creation. I have argued elsewhere that rather than making a general theological statement about the fallenness of creation, Paul is here referring to the environmental destruction that was evident to many in the ancient world.[51] Just as the psalms of lament that Paul echoes are rooted in concrete situations in the lives of individuals and the community, and just as the references to suffering in the letter to the Romans (8.35–39; 12.14–15) would have mirrored the suffering that actual community members experienced, so Paul's reference to creation described the suffering of creation in the ancient world.

Oddly enough, both Nereus and Iris, in their own contexts, would have known of traditions where the suffering of creation made sense. For Nereus, the prophets graphically describe the mourning and grief of creation as a result of both Israel's sin and God's punishment of that sin.[52] And God's return would result not only in salvation for God's people, but also fertility, blessing and new relationships for creation.[53] In the meantime, extinction of creatures, infertility of the soil, drought and famine were signs of the broken relationship between God and humanity.[54]

---

49 Gospel: Romans 1.1, 3, 9, 16; sword: 8.35; 13.4–7; peace: 1.7; 5.1; 12.1–21; 14.7; 15.13; 33. Some of these allusions are only evident as a result of Paul's more explicit descriptions of imperial violence in 1.23–32; 8.35 and 13.4–7. On peace see Wright 2002, 515–16.
50 Romans 1.23–32; 12.3–16; 13.4.
51 See Keesmaat 2015, 90–103.
52 Isaiah 24.4–13; Jeremiah 4.23–28; Hosea 4.1–3.
53 E.g. Isaiah 35; 55; 65; Ezekiel 34; 36.
54 Extinction: Jeremiah 4.23–28; Hosea 4.1–3; infertility, drought and famine: Leviticus 26.19–20; Deuteronomy 32.22–24; Isaiah 24.4–13; Jeremiah 4.23–28; Hosea 4.1–3.

Iris, too, would have understood Paul's language regarding the laments of creation. Because she was the one who took her master's sons to the Forum, she would have seen the *Ara Pacis* and the images of abundance and fertility that accompanied Roman military rule and conquest.[55] But she had also seen in her own land how conquest devastated the earth. Iris would have known those who had come to Rome as a result of losing their land to drought and increasing infertility. Just as she knew that the story of Roman 'peace' was really a story of violence, Iris had heard how Roman 'abundance' was really a story of environmental degradation.[56] Both Iris and Nereus knew that their own suffering was mirrored in the suffering of the earth.

Paul echoes and describes the pathos of God

The lamenting groans of both creation and believers are gathered up in Romans 8.26 in the groans of the very Spirit of God. This is not the first time, however, that the pathos of God is described by Paul. At the very outset of the letter, where Paul describes God's wrath as revealed against the unjust and the ungodly, we find ourselves in a storyline that describes the tension between, on the one hand, God's judgement on the people of Israel and, on the other hand, God's compassion for God's people. This storyline is revisited again and again in Romans where Paul repeatedly contrasts God's judgement with God's compassion and love. The wrath of Romans 1 gives way in Romans 2.4–5 to the kindness, patience and forbearance of God. In Romans 3.3–4 and 21–26 the unfaithfulness of the people is met with the faithfulness, grace, justice and forbearance of God. God's passing over of sins is emphasized in 3.25 and the grace of the promise is outlined in 4.16–25. Romans 5 describes God's love for sinners and enemies (5.8–10) and the free gift of grace and eternal life (5.15–21). Romans 7 and 8 describe how even slaves to sin are not condemned but set free (8.1–2), ending with the assertion that nothing can thwart God's love (8.35–39). In these first eight chapters, Paul constantly moves back and forth between judgement and forgiveness, humankind's sin and God's love. In so doing he is moving in the world of the prophets, who described the pathos of God

---

55 Zanker 1988, 172–5, argues that the altar was meant to be viewed as a continuous story: the military weapons depicted on the one side made possible the creational abundance and harmony depicted on the other, which in turn was dependent on the military weapons on the other side.

56 Tacitus (*Agricola*, 30.3—31.2) has Calgacus describe the Romans in this way: 'To plunder, butcher, steal these things they misname empire: they make a desolation and call it peace.' Quoted in Wengst 1987, 52.

in just this way: in the midst of grieving the loss of a faithful partner, God continues to wrestle with the possibility of a new thing. Ellington puts it this way, 'Yahweh is finally a reluctant spouse who, despite extreme provocation, cannot bring himself to sign the divorce papers.'[57] The result of such reluctance, such a desire to maintain the relationship, is that God bears the pain of the relationship, God mourns and weeps the loss of the relationship, God endures and lingers in the anguish of this relationship.[58] Even though God might respond in silence or anger initially, God's compassion and love are too great to let anger ever be the last word.[59]

Furthermore, just as the prophets bear the turmoil and pain of God's struggle, so Paul begins Romans 9 by talking about his great sorrow and unceasing anguish (9.2), echoing the anguish of both Jeremiah and Hosea (prophets whom he has echoed in Romans 1.23, 9.25–26 and 11.27). Throughout Romans 9—11 he highlights God's love, compassion, patience, desire for salvation, grace, kindness, and desire to welcome back those who have been cut off.[60]

In the prophets it is this desire to stay within the bonds of the covenant that enables God to envisage a different ending to the story. In the same way it is the deep desire of God to act out of compassion and salvation that enables the new vision of Romans where all the people of Israel will be shown mercy and be saved (11.26, 31), where there will be a new covenant when God takes away their sins because they are beloved.[61]

Paul's telling of this story portrays exactly the same struggle, passion and hope that is found in the prophets upon whom he draws. And, in so doing, he reveals the deep pathos at the heart of God, the deep desire to be in right relationship with his people, and through them with the world.

A community in the image of the suffering God

So why does this all matter? What does it matter if the letter to the Romans describes the pathos of God, the language of God's grief and God's lament

---

57 Ellington 2008, 135.
58 Jeremiah 8.18—9.3. Also Ellington 2008, 47–52, 133–43; O'Connor 2012, 61–4.
59 Hosea 11.5–9. On the dynamic of God's suffering over Israel's infidelity, and God's constant desire for salvation in the midst of such suffering, see Ellington 2008, 44–52, 136–41; Fretheim 1984, 109–48; Heschel 1962, 263–5. Fretheim (1984, 112) puts it this way: 'Grief is always what the Godward side of judgement looks like.'
60 Love: 9.13, 9.25; compassion: 9.15, 16; 11.30–32; patience: 9.22; desire for salvation: 10.1, 9–10, 13; 11.11, 14, 26; grace: 11.5–6; kindness: 11.22; desire to welcome back those who have been cut off: 11.23–32.
61 Romans 11.27; cf. Isaiah 27.9; Jeremiah 31.31; Romans 11.28; cf. Hosea 2.23.

over the people? What does this have to do with the laments of the community to whom Paul writes his letter? Why does the pathos of God, or even of creation, matter to the recipients of this letter?

A central question for the community in Rome, I suggest, is 'What kind of a God do we follow, anyway?' For someone like Nereus the question of God's abandonment of God's covenant people is a live one, as it clearly was for Paul in Romans 9—11. When Nereus prays the psalms of lament, when he cries out to God to rise up because God's people are being shamed, the nations are mocking and the unjust are plotting ways to take advantage of the innocent, he is asking for something specific: for God to come and overthrow the pagan nation that has enslaved him and restore justice and wholeness to creation. This is the expectation of the psalms of lament, that God is on the side of justice, on the side of the poor, partial to those who are taken advantage of by the powerful. This God is the one who can bring salvation.

If only God will answer. For the other side of the psalms of lament – and of Nereus's experience – is that God is absent. The cry 'My God, my God, why have you forsaken me?' (Psalm 22.1, NRSV) asks why God has allowed this to happen and done nothing to help.[62] Is God truly the God of justice? Or is this a God who has abandoned God's people to suffering, a God who doesn't hear, a God who is impotent?

The act of lament itself anticipates the answer. For lament is the insistence that God not remain silent.[63] In crying out to God, the suffering one reveals the character of the one to whom he or she prays. 'The prayers of lament rage against a God who pretends to be impassive and immutable, knowing intuitively that these are the qualities of idols, and therefore wholly alien to the God of Israel.'[64]

In Romans, as we have seen, Paul insists again and again that God is *not* silent, that God is a God of justice, and a God of compassion.[65] But Paul also insists (and here he is following Deutero-Isaiah) that God is seen most clearly in the suffering and death of Jesus.[66] If we have exchanged the image-bearing glory of the immortal God for images (Romans 1.23), in Jesus we are able to bear that glory once more as children of God, who are conformed to the image of the suffering Messiah (Romans 8.17, 21, 29–30). That is to say, we now image God in our identification with God's

---

[62] Bauckham 2008, 257.
[63] Ellington 2008, 128.
[64] Ellington 2008, 58.
[65] Romans 9.15–16; 11.30–32.
[66] See Bauckham 2008, 33–46.

suffering Son. However, Paul makes it clear that the Spirit bears this suffering as well – for the Spirit intercedes with the very wordless groans that creation and believers send up to God (8.26). It is noteworthy that the groans of lament that creation and humanity voice are not translated into well-articulated petitions by the Spirit. No, the turmoil and grief of creation and believers is the same turmoil and grief at the heart of the Spirit, resulting in the wordless groans of distress at the very heart of God. For those familiar with prophetic lament this is nothing new.

It is difficult to know how Nereus would have responded to this identification of the Spirit of God with the suffering grief of his own life. For the psalms of lament that are woven through Romans demonstrate the expectation that God will act to end injustice and suffering. They are part of a trajectory in Nereus's Scriptures that fully expects that when God comes, pagan oppressors will be the ones who suffer and God's people will be vindicated (Isaiah 34; 59.15–20; 63.1–6; Ezekiel 25—32). However, as a follower of Jesus, Nereus has heard a different ending to the story, an ending where God has been revealed in the crucified Messiah. In Jesus the gracious and compassionate God of Nereus's Scriptures has engaged in an act of ultimate self-giving love, showing finally and completely who he is: the servant, the one who is not only *with* but identifies *as* the lowest of the low.[67]

Even if Nereus had not been able to hear the echoes of Isaiah 40—55 here, Paul, at least, is providing an answer to the cry of lament, an answer not expected by those who prayed the psalms. Romans 5 sums up most clearly the identity of the God who offers God's self for us:

> For while we were still weak, at the right time Christ died for the ungodly. Indeed, rarely will anyone die for a righteous person – though perhaps for a good person someone might actually dare to die. But God proves his love for us in that while were still sinners Christ died for us. Much more surely then, now that we have been justified by his blood, will we be saved through him from the wrath. For if while we were enemies, we were reconciled to God through the death of his Son, much more surely, having been reconciled, will we be saved by his life.
>
> (Romans 5.6–10, NRSV, variant reading)

The love of God, evident throughout the Scriptures, and the desire of God for reconciliation in the face of persistent rejection and injustice (for

---

67 The phrasing is Bauckham's (2008, 55; see also 51). My argument here is based on Bauckham's entire piece which connects the pattern of Isaiah 40—55 with Philippians 2, and argues that the pattern of humiliation and exaltation in these passages reveals the unique divine identity. This is also the pattern, I would argue, of Romans 8.17–34.

how else can the 'ungodly' of v. 6 and the 'enemies' of v. 10 be described than those who have rejected God and practise injustice?), is shown in the death of his Son. This is God's love. This is who God is. This is God's answer to the prayer of lament. All this to say, the cross doesn't just show God's love; it *is* God's love in action.[68]

For Nereus, crying out to God in the face of suffering, these verses, along with Romans 8.17–39, provide the answer to the question of God's absence. Rather than suffering being evidence that God has *not* answered the cry of lament, the suffering of the community demonstrates that they truly *are* the children of God, heirs to the promise (8.17), image-bearers of God and conformed to the image of the suffering Son (8.29). In fact, the suffering of the members of this community demonstrates that they are more than conquerors (8.37); that they have transcended the categories of victory so beloved by Rome and that God's love is relentlessly present for them in their suffering (8.35–39). Bauckham helpfully articulates this: 'God redeems and renews humanity in this way, by entering humanity at the deepest level of human plight: the absence of God.'[69] In Romans 8 Paul is speaking to precisely this point, the question of God's absence in the face of suffering. And his reassurance for someone like Nereus is precisely the point that Bauckham is making about the Gospel of Mark: God is most truly revealed in God's identification with those like Nereus who are suffering deeply at the heart and hands of the empire.

What kind of a God is this, then? A God who enters into the darkness in relentless solidarity with God's people; a God who does not shrink from suffering; a God who is willing to risk abandonment for the sake of new life; a God who was tortured and brutally killed at the hands of imperial injustice.

Moreover, this is a God who reveals that such suffering is not merely punishment or discipline but rather vocation, a 'way to live into the future'.[70] If, as we saw, God's pathos is central not only in the prophets, but in Romans as well, then what kind of a community are we called to be? If we truly see who God is, the depths of God's love in God's suffering for and with us, then our calling is clear. We are to be a community of such suffering love. This is our primary calling, for this vocation is at the heart of the God we worship.[71] At the centre of this calling, as Paul indicates in Romans 8.22–26, is the practice of lament. To that we now turn.

---

[68] Bauckham 2008, 267.
[69] Bauckham 2008, 269.
[70] Brueggemann 1984, 97.
[71] The work of both Heschel 1962 and Fretheim 1984 has been instrumental in my coming to this reading of not only the prophets but also Romans.

Lament and truth-telling: evoking the new creation

The importance of a God who engages in lament with the people cannot be overestimated. For, at bottom, the practice of lament is the practice of *truth-telling*, the practice of naming the injustice, naming the pain, naming the horror that violence and lies create.[72] God is unremittingly the God of truth-telling; that is why God is in such pain, as a witness to the terror that human beings continually inflict on one another and the world. And it is because God is committed to naming the suffering that God is able to envisage a future beyond such suffering. God's very self desires reconciliation, healing, forgiveness. The overwhelming confessions of God's compassion and forgiveness mean that God needs to name the sorrow, so that it can be dealt with, healed, borne, forgiven. This is what creates both the pain of death at the heart of God, and the possibility of resurrection.

As those who image this God, such truth-telling is our calling as well. That is why I began with a description of the pathos of the community in Rome, with a description of what life was like for a slave and a subsistence labourer. Unless we are willing to name the injustice of sexual abuse, economic oppression, human trafficking, an honour system that brings shame to slaves and Judeans, and the exclusion of the stranger, we have no way of understanding either the word of hope that the gospel brought into these situations of pain, or the radical nature of Paul's language in Romans. When Paul condemns violent sexual abuse of boys and temple prostitutes in Romans 1.26–27, and the injustice, arrogance, greed, death-dealing, lies and ruthlessness of the Roman economic system in 1.29–32 – and the death that they lead to – he is talking about something specific. When Paul describes those who are self-seeking and ignore the truth for injustice in 2.8; when he describes the deceivers, whose mouths deliver death, and who bring bloodshed, ruin and misery because they do not know the way of peace in 3.13–17; when he talks about the imperial rule of death and sin that works for injustice in 5.17 and 6.12, those to whom he wrote heard Paul naming the sexual abuse they experienced, the economic violence that made them hungry, homeless and enslaved, the lies that made such a system possible, and the misery and ruin that Roman colonialism visited upon other peoples. Paul wasn't talking about sin or injustice in general. He was naming the experience of those to whom he wrote, those who lived in Rome in the middle of the first century CE.

---

72 Rah 2015, 44–59, discusses the importance of lament and truth-telling in relation to the realities of racial injustice in the USA. See also Beckett 2016, 209.

Walter Brueggemann calls this the *critique of ideology* that enables *the public expression of pain*.[73] Without such a critique, the depths of the suffering of the community is not acknowledged, and the need for far-reaching healing is never envisaged. Because Paul was naming the pain and violence that shaped the lives of so many in this community, and because their suffering shaped his writing, his vision for what this community was called to be in the image of the Son was truly radical and healing. In Romans 12—15 Paul describes a community that overturns the social structures that make possible the honour–shame system. It is hard to maintain the boundaries of honour when you are practising love and mutual affection and trying to show more honour than you receive (12.10). It is hard to practise an economics of ruthless greed and lying arrogance if you are not thinking of yourself more highly than you ought (12.3), contributing to the needs of others in the community, extending hospitality to strangers (12.13), avoiding haughtiness and walking with the oppressed (12.16). It is hard to sexually abuse your slaves if you are acting in genuine love and mutual affection, hating evil, and holding fast to what is good (12.9). It is hard to inflict violence on your neighbour when you are blessing those who persecute you (12.14), weeping with those who weep (12.14), and providing food and drink to your enemy (12.20). It is hard to continue to treat others with arrogance and injustice when you are welcoming the powerless to your table and doing so because Christ welcomed you (15.1–7).

The neglect of the suffering of the community, and the lament that such suffering occasioned, results in what can only be described as a quiescent reading of Paul's ethics, a result that does not do justice to the brilliance of Wright's reading of Paul. Although Wright does in various places emphasize the importance of a community drawn together around the crucified Messiah, and the importance of sharing in the death of the Messiah with the suffering that entails, he generally fails to draw out the ethical implications of such a suffering discipleship, almost always moving on to other points rather quickly.[74] When he indicates that for Paul suffering was a basic and non-negotiable part of 'being in the Messiah', the only example he gives of Paul's suffering is that he 'agonizes over communities, or individuals, or people who need discipline', and even there he is emphasizing how Paul differs from the Stoics.[75] Paul's actual list of powerlessness, beatings,

---

[73] Brueggemann 1984, 97.
[74] Wright 2013, 393, 431, 435, 856, 906, 931, 1023–5; 1127, 1373, 1425, 1490, 1507, 1510.
[75] Wright 2013, 452.

stonings, hunger, thirst, inadequate clothing, nakedness, homelessness and persecution (1 Corinthians 4.10–13; 2 Corinthians 11.23–29), all suffering that he would have shared with people like Nereus and Iris, is not mentioned. Wright asserts that the ethic of unity and holiness which shapes this community arises out of the self-emptying and crucified Messiah, but then moves on quickly to discuss unity and holiness in abstraction from the suffering of the community.[76] As a result, the radical implications of Paul's new-creational vision are not explored.

For instance, throughout *Paul and the Faithfulness of God*, Wright emphasizes the need to be good citizens and good neighbours.[77] He bases this call not only on Pauline texts themselves (including Romans 13.1–6), but also on two texts from Paul's scriptures: Jeremiah 29.4–7 and Daniel 1–6, neither of which quite supports his point. Surely the Daniel narratives suggest a higher level of imperial resistance than Wright implies. Within a context that can only be described as cultural genocide (Daniel 1.3–7), we meet a narrative of resistance in which the death penalty is freely and repeatedly applied. This is a complex story about imperial violence and control over captive people, and not as straightforward as Wright suggests.

Nor is Jeremiah's counsel to the exiles to 'seek the welfare of the city' a call to good and quiet citizenship. Rather, this is an audacious call to live as a community that not only undermines the empire's own ethic of violence, control and servile obedience, but also prefigures that other radical theme from Jesus and Paul, the call to love the enemy, even the enemy who has taken you into exile. This pattern of loving the enemy is not new to Jeremiah, for it is also found in the Elisha tradition with regard to the healing of Naaman and the feeding by Elisha of the army that had come to kill him (2 Kings 5; 6.1–23). Paul, of course, picks up on this theme in Romans 12.20–21 (NRSV): 'If your enemies are hungry, feed them' is a call to such a profoundly counter-imperial practice that it will be received as if 'burning coals' were being heaped on imperial heads. Paul continues with this theme in Romans 13.1–8 where he concludes that all that is really owed to the state is love – the one thing that not only undermines every aspect of what is perceived to be good citizenship in the empire, but also leads to healing service and identification with those the empire has most seriously oppressed.[78]

---

76 Wright 2013, 687. I will address these two ethical emphases below.
77 In addition to the references in n. 6 above, see Wright 2013, 1311, 1375–7, 1381.
78 On these passages and the echo of 2 Kings 6, see Keesmaat 2007, 146–8.

Given Wright's emphasis on good citizenship, it is not surprising that he also ends up blurring the distinction between Pauline and pagan ethics. In his discussion of ancient philosophy he is at some pains to emphasize the 'overlap between what Paul saw as living in accordance with the new creation and what his contemporaries saw as living in accordance with the world as they knew it'.[79] To be sure, Wright emphasizes the differences between Paul and the philosophers – although even there he states that Paul has 'reworked' the virtue ethic of Plato, Aristotle, Cicero and beyond.[80] But in the end the Roman Christians are called to be 'basically good neighbours'.[81] The basis for this line of argument seems to be twofold. One the one hand, Wright argues that Paul wants to guard against charges that followers of Jesus are 'socially, culturally and politically subversive in ways which were not in fact a reflection of the gospel'.[82] On the other, he wants to argue that 'the gospel is not meant to make people odd or less than fully human; it is meant to renew them in their genuine, image-bearing humanness'.[83] What these two points seem to beg is the question of whether the empire demands that people be less than human. There is a tension between Wright's assertions about the dehumanizing power of idolatry and his affirmation that pagan society has achieved a surprising degree of wisdom.[84] In order to function in her daily life, Iris is not considered human; as a slave she is something less. Similarly Nereus, as a Judean and a workman, is not considered worthy of the same treatment as those with status and honour who are more fully human. In this context, to believe that Nereus and Iris are renewed to their genuine image-bearing humanity in Jesus is in fact socially, culturally and politically subversive in ways which *do* reflect the gospel.

Suggesting that Paul was calling this community to be 'good citizens' overlooks the violence towards women, slaves and the poor upon which Roman society depended, along with the economic violence and ecological destruction that shaped the praxis of imperial life. To be a good citizen in ancient Rome would have meant participating in the demeaning practices that made the patronage system possible. To be a good citizen in Rome meant maintaining the boundaries of social status between men

---

[79] Wright 2013, 1372.
[80] Wright 2013, 1373–4.
[81] Wright 2013, 1375.
[82] Wright 2013, 1375.
[83] Wright 2013, 1376. See also, Rah 2015, 153–5.
[84] On the dehumanizing power of idolatry: Wright 2013, 743, 745; 2002, 434–5. Affirming the wisdom of pagan society, see Wright 2013, 1376.

and women, slave and free, Roman and barbarian. To be a good citizen in ancient Rome meant participating in an economic system founded upon and sustained by slavery, death and violent colonization. To be a good citizen in Rome meant lauding the stories of Rome, stories that vilified the enemy, excluded the stranger, and extolled sexual dominance and consumption. None of these things is possible if one is a follower of Jesus. All of these are challenged by Romans 12—15. Only by ignoring what life was like on the ground for the average hearer of Paul's letter, only by ignoring the laments of the suffering ones, could 'good citizenship' be embraced as the ethic of the early Christian community.

Instead, Paul calls out the violence and destruction which undergird Roman society. As a result he is able to envisage a community that practises a radically different ethic: a truth-telling community led by those who mourn.

A community led by those who mourn

It is no accident that I chose a gentile slave woman and a Judean labourer to help us find our way into the letter to the Romans. In both Romans 5 and 8 Paul emphasizes the importance of suffering for both the nurturing of hope and the possibility of glory. When Paul emphasizes so strongly in 8.23 that those who have the first-fruits of the Spirit groan with the same birth pangs as creation, he is saying something deeply resonant about our calling. This chapter is the linchpin of the whole book: the descriptions of the suffering of the community and of God's pathos in relation to the community come to their crescendo in these great words about suffering. And they become the springboard for Paul's anguished and prophetic description of God's ongoing grief over the people of Israel that follows in Romans 9—11.

The letter finds its centre here, with the assertion that those who bear the image of the Son are those who suffer with him. These are the ones who lament the brokenness and violence of the world, who long for resurrection life and the new creation, and who cry out 'How long?' along with the saints from the psalms. When Paul tells us to 'walk with the oppressed' therefore, in Romans 12.16, he is doing so partly because it is precisely the oppressed, those who mourn, who can teach us what the Christian walk looks like.[85] It is they who can help us to name the pain and the grief

---

85 *Tois tapeinois sunapagomenoi*, which I have translated 'walk with the oppressed', is usually translated 'associate with the lowly'. The latter loses some of the force of the Greek. In relation

that is required for the 'normal' functioning of a violent culture. In my country, Canada, it is indigenous communities who still bear the trauma of the residential schools who show us the violent outcomes of the colonialism that shapes Western culture.[86] In many countries, it is those who are unable to find homes or living-wage jobs who show us how our economic system grinds down those who don't start ahead of the game in middle-class families. It is those who have had their housing destroyed to make way for a more gentrified neighbourhood who show us the hopelessness and homelessness that our genteel ideas of class breed for the poor. It is those who have been jailed without bail – or even shot to death – for a traffic violation who show us the injustice that white privilege makes possible. It is those who have had their lands contaminated by the mines that produce mobile-phone components who show us the violence that our lives inflict on the earth. It is those who have been displaced by famine and war who show us the environmental toll that our constant consumption places on the livelihoods of the poor. It is those who are gay and trans who show us how the exclusion practised by our churches is nothing less than a covenant with death. It is only when we share in the suffering of these people that we truly understand the need for repentance, that we truly understand the sins for which we must ask forgiveness.[87] Only those who have suffered from the dominion of death can show us how life-giving the dominion of justice really is (Romans 5.21). Without the leadership of those who mourn, how can we possibly understand the suffering of those for whom the promise of new creation is truly gospel, good news? Without the leadership of those who mourn, how can we possibly understand the pathos of a crucified God?

---

to Jeremiah 31.8–9, O'Connor 2012 describes how in the prophets 'the feeble and vulnerable, the lowly and the wounded – will become the center of new life' (105). Similarly, 'Although they [the forgotten, the disabled and the vulnerable] are the lowest in the society, they will be the beating heart of the new community' (106).

[86] For most of the twentieth century, indigenous children in Canada were removed from their families and forced to attend residential boarding schools run by the churches where they were not allowed to speak their own languages, eat their own food or use their own names. The majority of the children suffered sexual, physical and emotional abuse at the hands of those who ran the schools. The findings of Canada's Truth and Reconciliation Commission on this era of cultural genocide can be found on the Truth and Reconciliation Commission website at <www.trc.ca>.

[87] Further on this see Rah 2015, 89–97; Moloney 2016, 320.

A new creation born out of the longing of sorrow

So what does this mean for the ethic of this community, this community that Wright describes as the Messiah's people, in whom this new world, the new creation, can be seen in advance? Wright describes this new community as shaped by two main ethical practices: unity and holiness. I'll provide a brief word on each. While unity is indeed important for Paul, to emphasize unity without qualification misses the point. Even the empire emphasizes unity – particularly the unity evident when everyone participated appropriately according to rank and status. Paul's emphasis, rather, is on unity in suffering love.

But more concerning is Wright's description of holiness. Throughout *Paul and the Faithfulness of God*, Wright suggests that such holiness looks primarily like sexual chastity.[88] In some places his translations even privilege this reading. For instance, he translates '*epithymia*' as deceitful lusts in contexts where 'covetousness' makes just as much or more sense.[89] Here a word with economic overtones is reduced to a matter of sexual purity. In one case, in the middle of a larger translation of Colossians 3.1–10, Wright skips a few verses, indicating in parenthesis: 'there follows a double list, of sexual sins on the one hand and sins of the tongue on the other'. This is a reductionistic way to describe a list that includes *epithymia* (covetousness) and *pleoneksian* (greed), which, Paul goes on to say, is idolatry.[90] His emphasis can be best seen in this key passage concerning what the new creation looks like, which emphasizes both unity and sexual behaviour:

> Paul envisages a renewed humanity in terms of *new creation*, a new world in which the creator's original intention would at last be fulfilled; and this new world is to be seen in advance in the Messiah's people. Angry speech and behaviour destroys that vision within the church, whose unity we saw in Part II was for Paul the central symbol of the Christian worldview. Sexual immorality destroys the vision of new creation in which the purpose begun in Genesis 1 and 2 can at last find fulfilment. Genesis 1, 2 and 3 stand, after all, rather obviously behind his great eschatological passages, Romans 8 and 1 Corinthians 15. The new creation is the renewal of creation the way it was meant to be. It is not the scrapping of the present world and the launching of something quite different. This is why his sexual ethic focuses so clearly on

---

88 E.g. 445–6; 1114; 1117; 1125; 1372; 1435; 1508.
89 *Epithymia* is used to indicate covetousness in both Exodus 20 and Deuteronomy 5 LXX, and is the word translated as 'covetousness' in Romans 7.8.
90 Wright 2013, 1373, is here referring to Colossians 3.5–9. Brian Walsh and I (2004, 160–8) have offered a reading of this text that attends to its imperial and economic overtones.

marriage as the norm for sexual behaviour. [1 Cor. 5.1–13; 6.9–21; 7.1–40; Gal. 5.13–21; Phil. 3.17–19; Col. 3.1–11; 1 Thess. 4.3–8].[91]

Of the references given, 1 Corinthians 5.9–13 and 6.9–21, Galatians 5.13–21 and Colossians 3.5–11 contain lists of sins that include sexual immorality, along with sins that tear apart community, *as well as* sins of injustice such as greed, robbery, thievery and idolatry. Wright does not address the latter group of sins. Not one of these passages indicates that marriage is the norm for sexual behaviour in Paul. Marriage is, rather, a *guard* against sexual immorality (1 Corinthians 7.2, 9). For Paul, celibacy is the preferred norm for sexual behaviour (1 Corinthians 7.1–40).

My point here is not so much to say that Wright has left out a few key economic references (although that is true). Rather, it is important to note that in using the language of holiness, Paul was using the *covenantal language* of Torah. Israel was to be a community where holiness was practised in a way that permeated every area of life. So the great chapter on holiness in Leviticus 19, not surprisingly, covers a wide range of things: laws concerning offerings; leaving the edges of the harvest for the poor and the stranger; not stealing; not defrauding your neighbour; not lying in order to cheat your neighbour; rendering just judgements; not taking vengeance; how to breed your animals and sow your fields; what your clothes are made of; sanctions against someone who rapes a slave promised to another man; how you cut your hair and prune your trees; loving the stranger; and having honest weights and balances. To say that holiness is mainly seen in sexual chastity doesn't even come close to the depth of faithful living that the Torah envisages. This is a holiness evident in a certain kind of generous economics, in the eschewing of violence, in care for the land, its people and its creatures. This isn't that different from the sort of community that Paul describes, a community where the hope of God was evident in economic sharing, forgiveness and the welcome of enemies, and the counter-intuitive bearing of the burden of slaves and women and the poor in its midst (Romans 12.9–21).

Throughout Romans, when Paul describes the new life in the Messiah, he consistently uses the Greek word *dikaiosynē*. Although *dikaiosynē* is usually translated into English as 'righteousness' in the New Testament, in the Septuagint it is used to translate two Hebrew words, *tzedeqah* (usually translated as 'righteousness') and *mispat* (usually translated as 'justice'). The Greek word *dikaiosynē*, therefore, has both of these meanings. It is inconceivable that Paul, who quotes Isaiah, Jeremiah and the psalms of

---

91 Wright 2013, 1117–18.

lament so extensively, would not have intended the overtones of justice in this term. When we realize that Paul is talking about justice when he uses *dikaoisynē*, and alter our translations accordingly, we not only see the positive aspects of new life in terms of justice (i.e. by talking about justice as the gift of faith), but we also notice that Paul uses the word *adikia* (literally 'injustice'; often translated as 'wickedness') to describe life under the dominion of death.[92]

For instance, in Romans 1.18, God's wrath is poured out on all injustice (*adikia*) and ungodliness. The list of vices in Romans 1.29 begins: 'They are filled with every kind of injustice [*adikia*] . . . ' (my translation). In 2.8 Paul contrasts those who obey the truth with those who obey injustice (*adikia*), and in 3.5 he contrasts the injustice of humanity (*adikia*) with God's justice (*dikaiosynē*). Furthermore, in the crucial contrast in Romans 6.13, Paul calls us to 'no longer present your members to sin as weapons of injustice [*adikia*]' which he contrasts with the call to 'present your members to God as weapons of justice [*dikaiosynē*]' (my translations). Interestingly, when Wright quotes Romans 6.12–13 in order to describe the new life in the Messiah, he not only leaves out the contrast between justice and injustice in these verses, but also leaves out the reference to covetousness.[93] This may be a small matter, but when such references are regularly excised in quotations, the cumulative effect is to silence Paul's emphasis on justice.

Walter Brueggemann emphasizes that the *critique of ideology* (which we discussed above as *truth-telling*) and *the embrace of pain* makes possible the *embrace of newness* and *the release of social imagination*.[94] This dynamic roots the possibility of imagining a new creation in the critique of ideology. That is to say, unless injustice is named, unless sin is described on the ground in Paul's context and our own, there is no possibility of acknowledging the suffering and the pain it has created. And unless that suffering is embraced, and lamented, no vision of hope for the future can even be imagined. This is the dynamic I have outlined above as truth-telling and being led by a community that mourns. It is the dynamic not just of the prophets, but also of Romans. Perhaps it would even be accurate to say that *because* it is the dynamic of the prophets it is the dynamic of Romans, written by an apostle who was deeply steeped in the prophetic

---

92 In translating *dikaiosynē* as 'justice' we are following Tamez, 1993. Wright (2002, 432, 439) emphasizes the importance of translating *adikia* as 'injustice' in Romans 1.18 and 2.8, noting that injustice is 'the crucial symptom of the world's out-of-jointness' (432).

93 Wright 2013, 1103; see also Wright 2002, 542–3.

94 Brueggemann 1984, 89–107.

tradition. In Romans Paul begins with the critique of ideology (Romans 1—7), moves to the embrace of pain (Romans 8—11), and then outlines visions of an alternative future that challenge the ruling ideology and worldview (Romans 12—16).

In making this argument, I am not arguing for anything that Wright would not agree with. It is clear that Wright knows the importance of being a cruciform community, and, in places, he even emphasizes the importance of lament.[95] But because he does not allow the sorrows of either Paul's world or our own to shape his reading of Romans, in the end the far-reaching and earth-renewing character of Paul's new-creational vision is muted and tamed. For the community that follows Jesus, our unity will be an expression of our solidarity in suffering, and our holiness will be as wide-ranging as the laws for justice that shape the covenant.

We heard at the outset of this chapter of the deep sorrow of Iris, of the shame she bears over her sexual abuse, her grief over the loss of her children, the pain she carries as an exile and a piece of property to be used by her master and his household. We heard of the deep sorrow of Nereus, alienated from his land, a labourer, hungry and cold, living in the crowded, stench-filled and violent streets of the slums. They were not unique in the first century and not unique in our world of refugees, increasing urban poverty and crowding, and extraction-fuelled wars that create starvation and dislocation.

We heard of the sorrow of the earth, groaning in the first century and today under the extraction economy necessary to maintain and increase our comfort levels. And we heard of the suffering and pain of God; committed to both this world and the people and creatures who inhabit it, yet suffering because of and along with creation.

Does any of this give us a glimpse of what new creation could possibly look like? Paul, in Romans 12, seems to think so. In a world where status and honour insisted on the shaming and denigration of the poor and slaves, Paul called this community not only to welcome all, but also to offer dignity and respect to those who had never experienced it (Romans 12.10, 16). Can we also envisage communities where the homeless, those with mental illness and those with intellectual disabilities are treated with dignity and respect? In a world where economic divisions were clearly maintained and households were in competition with one another, Paul called this community not only to practise a sharing economy in their communities, but also to welcome the stranger (Romans 12.13). Can we

---

95 Wright 2013, 1127.

envisage a world where we ensure that no one has too much, all have enough and where no one is attacked on the streets or deported because of his or her skin colour, accent, gender identity or sexual orientation? In a world where the enemy is vilified, Paul calls for generous blessing and hospitality for those who have wronged us (Romans 12.14, 20). Can we imagine a world where we offer political aid rather than aggressive attacks, where our churches preach forgiveness rather than militancy? In a world where the pain of the suffering was denied and ignored because it was considered collateral damage in the good ordering of society, Paul called this community to weep with those who weep and walk with the oppressed (12.15–16). Can we envisage a world where the voices of the suffering are allowed to subvert the ideology of militarism and consumption that dominate our imagination? Can we imagine a world where those of us with privilege sacrifice that privilege in order to enter into the suffering of others, of creation, of God? It is clear that Paul could envisage such a world. And Wright's rich reading of Paul lays the basis for imagining such a world. If we truly walk with the oppressed and allow ourselves to be led by those who mourn, perhaps we will find ourselves, with Iris and Nereus, not only imagining the new creation, but living in such a way that others, too, will recognize it when it arrives.

Bibliography

Bauckham, Richard (2008). 'God's Self-Identification with the Godforsaken: Exegesis and Theology.' In *Jesus and the God of Israel: God Crucified and Other Studies on the New Testament's Christology of Divine Identity*, 254–68. Grand Rapids, MI: Eerdmans.

Beard, Mary, John North and Simon Price (1998). *Religions of Rome, Volume 1: A History*. Cambridge: Cambridge University Press.

Beckett, Joshua (2016). 'Lament in Three Movements: The Implications of Psalm 13 for Justice and Reconciliation.' *Journal of Spiritual Formation and Soul Care* 9.2: 207–18.

Bradley, Keith R. (2004). 'On Captives under the Principate.' *Phoenix* 58.3/4: 298–318; plates: 374–90.

Brueggemann, Walter (1978). *Prophetic Imagination*. Minneapolis, MN: Fortress.

—— (1984). 'Unity and Dynamic in the Isaiah Tradition.' *Journal for the Study of the Old Testament* 29: 89–107.

—— (1986). 'The Costly Loss of Lament.' *Journal for the Study of the Old Testament* 36: 57–71.

Crisler, Channing L. (2016). *Reading Romans as Lament: Paul's Use of the Old Testament Lament in His Most Famous Letter*. Eugene, OR: Wipf & Stock.

Ellington, Scott A. (2008). *Risking Truth: Reshaping the World through Prayers of Lament*. Princeton Theological Monograph Series. Eugene, OR: Pickwick.

Elliott, Neil (2000). 'Paul and the Politics of Empire: Problems and Prospects.' In *Paul and Politics: Ekklesia, Israel, Imperium, Interpretation: Essays in Honor of Krister Stendahl*, edited by Richard Horsely, 17–39. Harrisburg, PA: Trinity Press International.

Fretheim, Terence (1984). *The Suffering of God: An Old Testament Perspective.* Philadephia, PA: Fortress.

Friesen, Steven (2004). 'Poverty in Pauline Studies: Beyond the So-called New Consensus.' *Journal for the Study of the New Testament* 26.3: 323–61.

Georgi, Dieter (1991). *Theocracy in Paul's Praxis and Theology.* Translated by David E. Green. Minneapolis, MN: Fortress.

Glancy, Jennifer A. (2002). *Slavery in Early Christianity.* Oxford: Oxford University Press.

Hays, Richard (1989). *Echoes of Scripture in the Letters of Paul.* New Haven, CT: Yale University Press.

Heschel, Abraham (1962). *The Prophets, Volume II.* New York, NY: Harper & Row.

Jewett, Robert (2007). *Romans: A Commentary.* Hermeneia. Minneapolis, MN: Fortress.

Joshel, Sandra R., and Lauren Hackworth Peterson (2014). *The Material Life of Roman Slaves.* Cambridge: Cambridge University Press.

Keesmaat, Sylvia C. (1999). *Paul and His Story: (Re)Interpreting the Exodus Tradition.* Journal for the Study of the New Testament Supplement Series 181. Sheffield: Sheffield Academic Press.

—— (2004). 'The Psalms in Romans and Galatians.' In *The Psalms in the New Testament*, edited by Steve Moyise and Maarten J. J. Menken, 139–61. London / New York, NY: T&T Clark.

—— (2007). 'If Your Enemy Is Hungry: Love and Subversive Politics in Romans 12–13.' In *Character Ethics and the New Testament*, edited by Robert Brawley, 141–58. Louisville, KY: Westminster John Knox.

—— (2015). 'Land, Idolatry and Justice in Romans.' In *Conception, Reception and the Spirit: Essays in Honour of Andrew T. Lincoln*, edited by J. Gordon McConville and Lloyd J. Pietersen, 90–103. Eugene, OR: Cascade.

Keesmaat, Sylvia C., and Brian J. Walsh (forthcoming). *Romans Disarmed: Resisting Empire, Demanding Justice.* Grand Rapids, MI: Brazos.

Longenecker, Bruce W. (2009). 'Exposing the Economic Middle: A Revised Economy of Scale for the Study of Early Urban Christianity.' *Journal for the Study of the New Testament* 31.3: 243–78.

—— (2010). *Remember the Poor: Paul, Poverty and the Greco-Roman World.* Grand Rapids, MI: Eerdmans.

MacDonald, Margaret Y. (2007). 'Slavery, Sexuality and House Churches: A Reassessment of Colossians 3.18–4.1 in Light of New Research on the Roman Family.' *New Testament Studies* 53: 94–113.

Middleton, Richard J. (2005). *The Liberating Image: The Imago Dei in Genesis 1.* Grand Rapids, MI: Brazos.

Moloney, Katherine (2016). 'Weeping, Warning and Woe in Revelation 18: The

Role of the Lament in Establishing Collective Responsibility and Enabling Collective Repentance.' *Expository Times* 127.7: 313–28.

Oakes, Peter (2004). 'Constructing Poverty Scales for Greco-Roman Society: A Response to Steven Friesen's "Poverty in Pauline Studies."' *Journal for the Study of the New Testament* 26.3: 367–71.

—— (2009). *Reading Romans in Pompeii: Paul's Letter at Ground Level*. London: SPCK.

O'Connor, Kathleen M. (2012). *Jeremiah: Pain and Promise*. Minneapolis, MN: Fortress.

Rah, Soong-Chan (2015). *Prophetic Lament: A Call for Justice in Troubled Times*. Downers Grove, IL: IVP.

Tamez, Elsa (1993). *The Amnesty of Grace: Justification by Faith from a Latin American Perspective*. Translated by Sharon H. Ringe. Nashville, TN: Abingdon.

Walsh, Brian J., and Sylvia C. Keesmaat (2004). *Colossians Remixed: Subverting the Empire*. Downers Grove, IL: IVP.

Wengst, Klaus (1987). *The Pax Romana and the Peace of Jesus Christ*. Translated by John Bowden. London: SCM.

Wright, N. T. (1994). 'Gospel and Theology in Galatians.' In *Studies in Corinthians, Galatians and Romans for Richard W. Longenecker*, edited by L. Ann Jervis and Peter Richardson, 222–39. Sheffield: Sheffield Academic Press.

—— (1998). 'The Servant and Jesus: The Relevance of the Colloquy.' In *Jesus and the Suffering Servant: Isaiah 53 and Christian Origins*, edited by William H. Bellinger Jr and William R. Farmer, 281–97. Harrisburg, PA: Trinity Press International.

—— (2002). 'The Letter to the Romans.' In *The New Interpreter's Bible Commentary*, Volume X, edited by Leander Keck, 393–770. Nashville, TN: Abingdon.

—— (2008). *Surprised by Hope: Rethinking Heaven, the Resurrection, and the Mission of the Church*. New York, NY: HarperOne.

—— (2010). *Simply Christian: Why Christianity Makes Sense*. New York, NY: HarperOne.

—— (2012). *After You Believe: Why Christian Character Matters*. New York, NY: HarperOne.

—— (2013). *Paul and the Faithfulness of God*. Christian Origins and the Question of God 4. London: SPCK / Minneapolis, MN: Fortress.

Zanker, Paul (1988). *The Power of Images in the Age of Augustus*. Translated by Al Shapiro. Ann Arbor, MI: University of Michigan Press.

ONE FUTURE

Reclaiming all Paul's Rs: apostolic atonement by way of some Eastern Fathers

EDITH M. HUMPHREY

Introduction

During Lent, I am delighted to join in a liturgy ascribed to St Basil of Caesarea, a Church Father of the fourth century.[1] At the Anaphora, we 'lift up' our hearts as the celebrant prays:

> For, since through man sin came into the world and through sin death, it pleased Your only begotten Son, who is in Your bosom, God and Father, born of a woman, the holy Theotokos and ever-virgin Mary, born under the law, to condemn sin in His flesh, so that those who died in Adam may be brought to life in Him, Your Christ . . .

This prayer bears a family likeness to passages in St Paul's letters, and in the Church Fathers – the knitting together of themes and of soteriological moments. In one sentence are integrated echoes of the Gospel and at least five passages from the Epistles. We also glimpse the glory of creation, God's call of Israel, the Incarnation, the crucifixion and the resurrection – all of these connected with the atonement made for our sake. This way of integration, however, is not as frequently followed by contemporary scholars. It seems that one unfortunate effect of Aulén's celebrated *Christus Victor* was to harden what seem to some to be irreconcilable constructs: human frailty rather than sinfulness eliciting God's anger; the conquest of death over against reparation for sin; the 'Eastern' metaphor of rescue against 'Western' images of sacrifice and law court.

In this paper, I will sketch some reactive 'paths not taken' by me, and then examine how key Church Fathers from the Christological period of the fourth and fifth centuries read pertinent passages from Colossians,

---

[1] The first version of this paper was originally given as the keynote address for the Institute of Biblical Research, San Antonio, 2016. All the Scripture quotations here cited are my own translation.

Galatians and 2 Corinthians.[2] We find in these a fertile field for various pictures of how the Son acted *pro nobis* and discover how the ancient theologians negotiated the mystery that we can, with some neutrality, call 'atonement' – the making 'at one' of God and humankind. To cleave to the Scriptures, and to inhabit the same tradition as our older siblings in the faith, means that we will want to reclaim *all* the 'Pauline Rs' – redemption, reparation, representation, righteousness, rescue (i.e. Christus Victor), recapitulation and reconciliation. (And now, with the advent of Tom Wright's latest book,[3] we are tempted to add a *double* R: revolutionary recreation!) With my friend Michael Gorman, I want to demonstrate how St Paul himself moved 'seamlessly'[4] from one metaphorical cluster to another in illumining this mystery, as did many Fathers. Similarly, we will take account of how they called upon the entire action of the God-Man, from Incarnation to Ascension, in describing all that he has done for us. To these ends, we will close with St John Chrysostom's neglected sermon 'On the Ascension of Our Lord'.

Paths not taken

Aulén's strength was that he alerted some Western scholars to their myopia. Those who had long felt uneasy about the playing off of Father against Son, mechanical penal substitution, and Western overemphasis on escape from

---

2 I will refer particularly to Colossians 1.13–23, Galatians 3.13–14, 23—4.6 and 2 Corinthians 5.14–21. Certainly, other passages could have been chosen from these epistles in order to demonstrate the apostle's wide use of metaphorical language to explain the atonement. One thinks particularly of the thematic treatment of these and other passages, especially Romans 3, in Fee 2005, or the masterful treatments of Romans 8 and Colossians 2 (the latter particularly in terms of Christus Victor over the powers) in Wright 2016a. My passages are selected because they densely combine the metaphors, and because the patristic commentators treat them in interesting ways. To fill out carefully the *meaning* and *interrelationships* of the various metaphors would require a concentration upon other passages, both in Paul's letters and in the patristic reception of them.

3 I refer to *The Day the Revolution Began*, which provides yet another example of our friend N. T. Wright's bracing and faithful readings of the New Testament. My own steady attention to the 'multi-coloured' wisdom of God as seen in the apostle Paul's letters was first nurtured by my perceptive mentor, Tom Wright, who during my graduate days opened up the riches that I had missed in my formative Salvation Army context. I offer these reflections, some of which may well go in different directions from his own, with profound gratitude, and in the hope of further discussion of how God has acted for us in Christ Jesus.

4 Gorman 2011 details the epistle of Romans, but includes (on p. 15) a brief comment on 2 Corinthians 5.21, where he notes the 'seamlessly interwoven' themes of transformation and justification. I will, in this paper, make a friendly amendment that in this passage the *dikaiosynē theou* is not confined to the idea of justification.

the final judgement, now rallied to 'the East'.[5] However, in their reaction, some seem to have constructed a caricature of the Eastern Fathers that downplays their awareness of sin and sacrifice. Recently Benjamin Myers gave an absorbing lecture[6] in which he draws out not only what he sees as the patristic theory of atonement, but also the 'mechanism' by which it works. His goal is laudable: not to give in too quickly to the hegemony of 'mystery' that many (wrongly) assume to have taken Orthodox theology captive. Instead, he works assiduously through saints Athanasius, John Chrysostom, Cyril of Alexandria, Gregory of Nyssa and Gregory Nazianzus. His argument traces 12 steps and discloses three patristic assumptions: that there is a universal human nature, that death is a privation of reality and that the divine nature is impassible. He concludes: 'Human mortality is reversed when the life-giving divine nature makes contact with human nature at the point of its slide into non-being.'[7] This is the 'mechanism', the hinge, upon which the 'patristic model' works. What happens to Christ happens to human nature as a whole, and so humans are free from the power of death and restored. Moreover, humans, now united with God, receive benefits far beyond rescue from death.

Myers' presentation recoups much of the scope of patristic teaching on atonement, and is friendly to *theōsis*. It makes sense of St Athanasius' argument that the Incarnation was necessary, St Cyril of Alexandria's teaching of the *communicatio idiomatum*, St Gregory Nyssa's insistence that God can touch death without suffering harm, and St Gregory Nazianzus' dictum: 'We needed a God made flesh and made dead that we might live.' It is, however, selective, since it has little to say about that other enemy, sin, or about the sacrificial language abundantly present in the traditional Divine Liturgies and dominating patristic commentaries on Paul. Certainly the apostle and the Fathers match human death to Christ's resolving Incarnation – but not so as to dismiss the human problem of sin or to ignore the cross.

But it is not only the West that is overreactive: I must be a fair and equal-opportunity offender! Though some Orthodox have made eirenic

---

5 Mosser 2005 makes a compelling corrective case, showing how the concept of divinization has not been limited to Eastern theologians, in either the distant or more immediate past.
6 'Atonement and the Image of God', Third Annual Los Angeles Theology Conference on Atonement. The entire argument can be heard in his lecture, available at the site below (accessed February 2017), and was subsequently published in a proceedings volume from the conference (Myers 2015). I have presented only a brief summary that does not do justice to his argument. See <https://www.youtube.com/watch?v=DzdgDdZkSOY&feature=youtube>.
7 'Atonement and the Image of God'.

moves – for example, the rehabilitation of Anselm by David Bentley Hart[8] – we regularly find polarizing polemics among them. The most balanced writers feel it necessary to specify Orthodox views of atonement by virtue of what they are *not*. Father John Meyendorff, for example, writes:

> Communion in the risen body of Christ; participation in divine life; sanctification through the energy of God, which penetrates true humanity and restores it to its 'natural' state, *rather than justification, or remission of inherited guilt* – these are at the center of the Byzantine understanding of the Christian gospel.[9]

Father John Breck explains that in 'the Greek patristic tradition, the Pauline notion of *dikaiosynē* [is seen as] "righteousness," rather than as "justice" in the forensic sense'.[10] In response to these restrictive, if nuanced, Eastern descriptions of atonement, Fr Matthew Baker (of blessed memory!) recommends the trajectory traced by the great Fr Georges Florovsky, who at the end of his career more easily embraced some Western construals. Fr Matthew suggests: 'A more honest study of the language of substitution, debt-satisfaction, ransom, and law in general within patristic literature is . . . in order.'[11] I agree: and a closer reading of what some of the Fathers say as they deal with St Paul is a good start.

Before we proceed in our analysis of Scripture, however, we note another contemporary method that says, in effect, 'A pox on both your houses!' – or, more politely, it seeks a *tertium quid*. This would be the style of our beloved N. T. Wright, whose latest brilliant book *The Day the Revolution Began* seeks to 'reimagine' redemption. Jesus, as the NT *hilastērion*,[12] is to be understood neither in terms of expiation, nor of pagan propitiation, but as the *place* where God and humanity meet. He is the new-covenant archetype

---

8 Hart 1998.
9 Meyendorff 1974, 146.
10 Breck 2006.
11 Baker 2016, 125.
12 See Wright 2016a, 302, 327–34. It is important to clarify that Wright does not deny the importance of substitutionary sacrifice as a facet of the atonement. His argument about the meaning of *hilastērion* in Romans 3.24–26 is more fully explicated in Wright 2016b. Using a pincer movement in moving forwards from Romans 2 and backwards from Romans 4, he contends (2016b, 153) that it is mistaken to take *hilastērion* in Romans 3 according to the 'distantly possible sense of "a means of propitiation"', though substitutionary sacrifice (always to be balanced with representation) is to be found elsewhere in the New Testament. My friend and I may disagree about the nuances of Romans 3.24, but we are in accord concerning the person of Jesus as the place where God and humanity meet, about the importance of his death as both substitutionary and representative, and about the prominence of Jesus as Victor in the New Testament.

who replaces the cover to the ark, where blood is spilled, and cleansing and reconciliation procured. Here Wright sends us to LXX Leviticus, which uses the word *hilastērion* for the cover to the ark. He reminds us that the animal was not slaughtered on this holy place, but in the outer precincts of the Temple, argues that the slaughtering was merely the prelude to the cleansing sprinkling of blood, and sidelines the concept of penal sacrifice associated with the death of the seven Maccabean youths, because these stories are 'not in the biblical literature'. (To all this I would remark that *hilastērion* is employed in LXX Ezekiel and Amos to gesture at the *altar*,[13] that slaughtering took place, significantly, in the sight of the people and 'before the Lord', that 2 Maccabees is 'canonical' for some of us, and that even *4 Maccabees*, though extra-canonical,[14] offers contextual explanations!)

In Wright's depiction, neither any Eastern view that might allow the resurrection to overshadow the cross, nor any Western fixation upon a punishing sacrifice that puts away God's wrath, adequately represents the apostle's soteriology. There is a third way, by which we are to avoid platonizing, moralizing and paganizing results. He insists: we must 'forget the false either/or that plays different theories of atonement against one another'.[15] I agree entirely on this point! However, I am not as confident as my friend that we should *reimagine* in order to 'enter this powerful, sprawling, many-sided, richly revelatory narrative'.[16] Instead, I want to acknowledge the many vistas the Fathers have spied in St Paul's writings, seeing where they form a single horizon, and where they stand in stark contrast to one another. This will mean, I am afraid, allowing the old language of 'punishment', 'atoning sacrifice' and even 'propitiation' to jostle against more palatable views. (The Gospels have their Johannine bolt from

---

[13] Amos is a complex situation, where the Hebrew refers to 'knobs', but the LXX has rendered this *hilastērion*. In Ezekiel, the reference is to the steps of the altar. In *4 Maccabees* the Greek word is more obviously connected with death, blood and sacrifice.

[14] It is accepted, however, by the Georgian Orthodox community. In *4 Maccabees*, the narrator comments that the martyrdom was undertaken by those 'consecrated for God . . . having become, so to speak, a life-exchange [*antipsychon*] for the sin of our nation . . . and an atoning sacrifice [*tou hilastēriou*] through their blood . . . and death' (17.21–22). Even here, where there are no qualms in describing martyrdom as ritual slaughter, this element is advanced with the qualifier *hōsper* ('so to speak'). After all, the holy martyr is not simply a holocaust to avert God's wrath, but a participant who 'dies for the sake of God' and 'lives in God'. Even where the vicarious aspect of martyrdom is fully registered, God is not finally depicted as a punishing exactor, but as the creating and resurrecting One in whom martyrs retain hope as they engage in a 'divine' contest (17.11–16), showing the character of God, by consecrated deaths.

[15] Wright 2016a, 416.

[16] Wright 2016a, 415–16.

the blue, and Chrysostom has his discomfiting moments of penal sacrifice!) It is not reimagining, but retrieval that I have in mind.

Recapitulation and the other Rs (Colossians 1.13–23)

We begin with Colossians 1.13–23, unpromising because of its disputed authorship, but helpful as a departure point. The passage is marked by poetic nimbleness.

> [13]He has **rescued** us from the dominion of darkness and transplanted us to the kingdom of his beloved Son, [14]in whom we have **redemption**, the forgiveness of sins.
>
>> [15]He is the image of the invisible God,
>> the firstborn over all creation;
>> [16]Since in him all things were created,
>> in heaven and on earth, seen and unseen
>> (whether Thrones or Dominions or Archōns or Powers).
>> All things were created through him and for him.
>> [17]He is before all things, and in him all things cohere.
>>
>> [18]And he is the head of the body, the Church;
>> He is the beginning, the firstborn from the dead,
>> that he in everything might be the First.
>> [19]For in him all the fullness of God was pleased to dwell,
>> [20]and through him to **reconcile** to himself all things,
>> whether on earth or in heaven,
>> peacemaking through the blood of his cross.
>
> [21]And you, who once were alienated and at enmity in mind, as you did evil deeds, [22]now he has **reconciled** in the **body of his flesh through his death**, so as to present you **holy and without blemish** and **blameless before his face** – [23]so long as you remain established upon the faith, both steadfast and not changing your position away from the hope of the gospel which you heard, which has been preached to every creature under heaven, and of which I, Paul, became a minister.[17]

In these 11 verses, many given over more to the praise of Christ than to the question of soteriology, we are impressed with the theme of Recapitulation, where Christ is seen to sum up, or head up, all things. But the shades of the palette also include:

---

[17] The translation is my own: I have left in the verse numbers for reference, and put in bold the terms or phrases that indicate underlying stories or pictures of atonement.

- rescue from imprisonment and death (v. 13);
- redemption from slavery (v. 14);
- reconciliation with God and others (v. 20);
- reparatory sacrifice ('the body of his flesh through his death', v. 22);
- righteousness in the context of judgement ('blameless before his face', v. 22).

As far as reparation is concerned, we meet a twist in the anticipated language: it is *we* who are detailed as enemies, not God. If propitiation is implied in the sacrificial language, it is thereby also qualified. In this complex picture, Christ is bound up with us – both in creation and in the new creation – so that we are presented as a holy and perfect sacrifice to the Father. Christ's sacrifice, then, is both substitutionary and representative. Again, this Christ-hymn suggests more than a mere restoration of the creation, but a remaking – dare we say a revolution? The firstborn from the dead, the Head over the Church, forges a previously unthinkable unity between heaven and earth. Given the absolute language concerning the scope of Christ's recapitulation and service *pro nobis*, we may be surprised to see that the apostle ends with a qualification: 'so long as you remain . . .' The atonement is accomplished, but not automatic. Even while Christ's victory is declared, the apostle calls for apostolic action and the steadfast response of those who have been so securely established.

Redemption and the other Rs (Galatians 3.13–14; 3.23—4.6)

These same themes present themselves in our passage from Galatians, in different combinations and concentrations. *Dikaiosynē* is frequently connected with Galatians, but here, other ideas dominate:

> [13]Christ **redeemed** us from the curse of the Law, when **he became a curse for us** (for it is written, 'Cursed be everyone who hangs upon wood') [14]so that the blessing of Abraham might come upon the Gentiles in Christ Jesus, that we might receive the promise of the Spirit through faith [or faithfulness] . . .
>
> [23]But before the coming of Faith, we were hedged around by Law, kept **under restraint** until the time that Faith was unveiled. [24]For this reason, the Law was our custodian until Christ came, that we might be **'righteoused'** because of Faith. [25]But now that Faith has come, we are no longer under a custodian; [26] for in Christ Jesus you are all sons of God, through Faith.
>
> [27]For as many of you as were baptized into Christ have **put on Christ**. [28]There is neither Jew nor Greek, there is neither slave nor free, neither is

there male and female; for you are all one in Christ Jesus. [29]And if you are Christ's, then you are Abraham's seed, heirs according to the promise.

[4.1]I am saying that the heir, as long as he is a child, is **no better than a slave**, though he is the master of everything; [2]but he is under guardians and trustees until the time appointed by his father. [3]So also it is with us; when we were children, we were **enslaved** to the elemental spirits of the cosmos. [4]But when the fullness of time had come, God sent forth his Son, **born of woman, born under the Law** – [5]so that he might **redeem** those who were under the Law, so that we might receive **adoption as sons**. [6]But because you are sons, God has sent the Spirit of his Son into our hearts, crying, 'Abba! Father'.[18]

(Galatians 3.23—4.6)

In this passage, we have, cheek by jowl, the language of

- redemption (v. 13a, implied in the slavery metaphor of 4.1, and reiterated at 4.5);
- reparatory sacrifice as Christ becomes accursed (v. 13b);
- rescue from imprisonment (implied by the phrase 'under restraint' in v. 23);
- righteousness (v. 24);
- recapitulation (of both humanity and Israel, 4.4);
- 'revolution' (vv. 27–28 radically qualify the categories of the original creation).

Redemption is the controlling category here. The apostle begins and ends with slave-language: 'Christ redeemed us' (3.13); 'so that he might redeem those who were under the Law' (4.5). For the sake of his argument, the apostle applies this language of bondage and being bought back to Israel, though the nation's members possessed, as children, the promise of inheritance. A minor child is no more an autonomous agent than a slave: Paul does not have to clarify, when he casts the Torah in the role of custodian, that he also has in mind the more hostile elemental spirits under whom the Gentiles were suppressed before their rescue.

Intertwined with redemption is rescue from imprisonment. The Jewish people, consigned to a Rapunzel-like existence, need a liberator as much as the Gentiles who are imprisoned by their idolatrous ignorance. In this

---

[18] Again, the translation is my own, and the pertinent words and phrases are in bold. For the sake of simplicity, I have elided verses 15–22. These omitted verses are utterly important in showing St Paul's understanding of the law and its relation to Christ, but are not necessary in demonstrating the dominance of redemption language here, coupled with the variety of ways in which he has pictured atonement.

dual situation, there *is* neither slave nor free – for those who are enslaved will be freed, and those who think they are free are in fact enslaved until the time has fully come. Indeed, the very liberation of the minor children is bound up with the enfranchisement of the Gentiles, promised to Abraham. So the apostle speaks both of the establishment of the Jewish believers in sonship, and the inclusion of Gentile believers. Together, the unified community cries, 'Abba! Father!' As the blessed Augustine reminds us, '[W]e see that [Paul] has elegantly, and not without reason, put together words from two languages signifying the same thing because of the whole people, which has been called from Jews and Gentiles into the unity of the faith' (Augustine, *Galatians* 31; 1B.4.6; Migne, PL 35.2127). Redemption and rescue issue in adoption and a previously unimagined unity within a single 'Christly' family.

Embedded within this series of metaphors is the language of reparatory and substitutionary sacrifice: redemption *from the curse* . . . that we might receive the blessing (3.13–14). 'He became a curse for us' (see 3.13) deftly recalls the plight of all humankind (the curse upon the ground and childbearing), 'the curse and oath written in the Law of Moses' (Daniel 9.11; cf. Deuteronomy 11.26), and the duo of sacrificial animal and banished scapegoat, who together assume the curse of death and sin. The colourful word *katara* ('curse'), the participle *genomenos* ('becoming') and the little phrase *hyper hymōn* ('for us') speak poignantly of 'curse' being exchanged for 'blessing'. Telling is the interplay between the beneficiaries in verses 13 and 14: 'Christ redeemed *us* from the curse of the Law, when he became a curse for *us* . . . so that the blessing of Abraham might come upon *the Gentiles* in Christ Jesus, that *we* might receive the promise of the Spirit'. It seems that the first 'us' denotes Jewish believers under Torah, the second reference is to the Gentiles, and the third 'us' implies the entire community.

By rephrasing Romans 3.23, St John Chrysostom explains the universal aspect of blessing and curse in our passage: 'All have sinned and are *under a curse*.' He explains that in Galatians, St Paul does not immediately articulate this assumption, 'in case he should seem to be running ahead of his own demonstration' (*Comm. Gal.* 3.11),[19] which is to stress the curse of the *law*. 'Ambrosiaster', that elusive fourth-century Latin commentator, stresses penal substitution:

> [A]ll were convicted by the curse of the law, so that it was right to punish them. But Christ, born as a man and offered for us by his Father, redeemed

---

[19] Here and elsewhere when citing St John Chrystostom, I offer my own translation, using Migne's PG. Bold and italics are mine.

us from the devil. He was offered for those who were liable to the curse of the law. Jesus was made a curse in the way that under the law a victim offered for sin is said to be sin . . . Thus [St Paul] did not say 'cursed for us' but *made a curse*.

(Ep. to Galatians 3.13.1–2; CSEL 81.3.34–35)

Lest we think that this is wholly a Western view, we return to Chrysostom, who takes his cue from Deuteronomy 27.26 to explain the curse that attends the non-fulfilment of Torah. He is, however, more circumspect than Ambrosiaster in his explanation, using the language of exchange, and coupling sin with the problem of death:

For the people were liable, since they had not fulfilled the whole Law, but Christ took upon himself a different curse, '*Cursed is everyone that hangs on a tree.*' Since both the one who is hanged and the one who transgresses the Law are accursed, Christ, who was going to lift that curse, could not *properly* be made liable to it yet had to receive a curse in its place. He received the curse instead of being liable to it and through this lifted the curse. Just as, when someone is condemned to death, another innocent person who chooses to die for him releases him from that **retribution**, so Christ also did. For he did no sin . . . Even as by dying he rescued from death those who were going to die, so also when he received the curse he freed them from the curse.

(Hom. Gal. 3.13)

(By the way, those of you who are using that helpful florilegia, the *Ancient Christian Commentary*, should be aware that its translation of this passage attributes much more 'penal' language to Chrysostom than he actually uses. In a stricter translation such as I have offered, the motif is found *once* in the word for 'penalty' or 'retribution.') The cumulative effect of St John's commentary is to move us to awe concerning Christ's exchange. St Gregory the Theologian registers the same amazement, and speaks of the Suffering Servant 'taking up our transgressions and bearing our sicknesses' (*Letter* 101.61).

We return to our passage in Galatians. We may be surprised, given the context of this particular letter, which combats the Judaizers, to see that here the themes of righteousness and recapitulation are only briefly registered. Verse 24 declares: 'For this reason, the Law was our custodian until Christ came, that we might be "righteoused" because of Faith.' Hedging my bets, I adopt Sanders' neologism: does the apostle mean 'declared' or 'rendered' righteous? Is this merely a law-court metaphor, acquitting those under the curse? Or is there a clue to the new character of the one in Christ as well, since in verse 11 we have heard (via Deuteronomy) of the *righteous* (not merely those who are *declared righteous*) who live by faith? I want to leave both paths open to us, as I think the apostle does. (Mike Bird's term, 'incorporated righteousness', is helpful.[20]) Surely, the full meaning of *dikaiosynē* takes its colour here from the ideas that surround it – adoption, inheritance and participation as sons who, in Christ, become like their Father. The immersion of the Son into our world as a recapitulation is suggested by 4.4: 'But when the fullness of time had come, God sent forth his Son, born of woman, born under the Law'. Jesus is both the new Adam, born of a woman, and the new Israel, born under the Torah. Indeed, he is the One who has long been promised, 'as the apostle has shown at great length', comments Chrysostom, by mentioning Abraham and his seed (4.4–5). This One comes when the time is right, becoming at home in human time and space, to redeem it. St Ambrose comments: 'He was made from a woman by assuming flesh and made under the law by observing the law' (*On the Faith* 1.14). Theodoret remarks, '[St Paul] has linked the sending of the eternal Son with the Incarnation' (*Epistle to the Galatians* 4.4–5). And St John the Golden-Mouthed marvels: 'Here [the apostle] states two . . . effects of the Incarnation: deliverance from the curse of the Law, and promotion to sonship' (*Comm. Gal.* 4.4–5).

St John's joy leads us to the final R, revolutionary recreation. Throughout his commentary on these verses, the Golden-Mouthed turns his wide eyes upon the new state in which believers find themselves. He notes that the apostle must use two different ways of explaining this overturning of things – we have both 'put on Christ' and 'been made sons' (4.4–5). The sign of the revolution is that we now *together*, having been freed, clothed and adopted, can call God 'Father'. The division between Jew and Gentile has been reversed, the separation between humanity and God has been repaired, and the relation between the faithful and God has been rendered surprisingly intimate. St John expostulates:

> Oh my! How mighty is the power of Faith, and the way that, when He makes his procession, he reveals this power . . . See what an insatiable soul [the apostle has]! . . . He does not stop [with the picture of adoption], but tries to find something greater, which may serve to express an even closer oneness with Christ . . . 'You are all One in Christ Jesus', that is, you have all one form and one mould – that of Christ. What could give us chills of wonder more than these words? The one who yesterday was a Greek, or a Jew, or a slave,

---

[20] As in, for example, Bird 2004.

goes around, possessing the form not of an angel or archangel, but of the Lord of all, and in his [or her] very being shows forth Christ!

(*Comm. Gal.* 3.24–8)

To St John's wonder, we add that of Marius Victorinus, whose neo-Platonic tendencies do not blind him to the concerted effort of the Godhead: 'For . . . the Father sent his own Son, who himself . . . sent the Spirit' (*Ep. Gal.* 2.4.6). The remarks of these ancients disclose how this passage, though concentrating upon the idea of redemption from slavery, flows between various metaphorical systems, and assumes the integrity of the crucifixion, the Incarnation and future glory.

Reconciliation, the other Rs and the righteousness of God (2 Corinthians 5.14–21)

We finish with the controverted text of 2 Corinthians 5.14–21. So much has been written on this, as I have noted elsewhere,[21] that it is perhaps imprudent to co-opt it only briefly for our purposes. Here I cannot enter into all the fraught issues, but will show its special contribution to our study of Pauline atonement, and how the ancient commentators construed its mysteries. The apostle's larger argument, which begins with thanksgiving at 2.14 and ends in joy at 7.4, runs the gamut of human expression and emotion, while it builds on a foundation of theological, Christological, pneumatological, soteriological and ecclesial concepts. More proximate to our smaller passage are the themes of resurrection (5.1–9), judgement (5.10–11) and cooperation with God's grace (*passim* ch. 5). St Paul's focus in verses 14–21 is upon the primary and ongoing reconciling actions of God in Christ, the apostles, and in his body, the Church:

> [14]For the love of Christ constrains us, because we have decided this: that One died **on behalf of all**, therefore all have died. [15]And he died on behalf of all, so that those who are living would live not only for themselves, but for him who died and was raised on their behalf. [16]Therefore, we no longer know anyone 'according to the flesh'. And if once we also knew Christ according to the flesh, now we no longer know him in that way. [17]For if anyone is in Christ – new creation! **The old has gone its way, and behold, all is new!** [18]But all these things are from God who in Christ **reconciled** us to himself, giving us the ministry of reconciliation. [19]That is to say, God was in Christ **reconciling** the cosmos to himself, **not accounting their trespasses** against them, and establishing among us the word of reconciliation. [20]Therefore,

[21] Humphrey 2017.

on behalf of Christ, we act as ambassadors, as though God were making an entreaty through us: We beg you, on Christ's behalf, be reconciled to God! [21]For the One who did not know sin, on our behalf he made **to be sin**, so that we might become the righteousness of God in him.[22]

This passage is a prime example of the call for Christians to become, as Michael Gorman puts it, 'cruciform': we, who have died in Christ, are to live no longer for ourselves! Similarly, the representative nature of Jesus' death is stressed, as Ben Blackwell points out, in the statement of verse 14, 'therefore all have died'[23] – though he thinks it may suggest substitution as well. I would myself go further: substitution is *required* by the detail supplied by the apostle, that Jesus knew no sin. His death is deliberate, and far deeper than ours! As with our earlier passages, however, the substitution does not imply a *pagan* notion of propitiation: it is *we* who must be reconciled, for God is not reluctantly moved to mercy, but entreats us. If the dominant metaphor of the passage in Colossians is Recapitulation, and that of Galatians 3 is Redemption, the dominant idea here is Reconciliation. But all the other pictures, with the exception of Redemption from slavery, are gathered up under that major theme: Rescue from death, Reparation for sin, Righteous status (or character) in exchange for guilt, Recapitulation and Revolution (a new creation).

The most evocative verse is 5.21, about which Ben Blackwell ruefully remarks that 'virtually every aspect . . . is debated'.[24] Commentators, past and present, expound this verse in parallel with Romans 8.3 ('in the likeness of the flesh of sin') and Galatians 3.13 ('becoming a curse for our sake'). Ancient debates centred around the shock of calling Jesus 'sin'; contemporary debates have revolved around 'the righteousness of God'. Many Eastern Fathers join the idea of 'becoming sin' with Christ's taking on of humanity, including our death; St Cyril of Alexandria, however, resorts to the sacrificial offerings of twin goats and birds of Leviticus 14 and 16 in order to expound the passage![25] I would remark that the idea of sacrifice and assumption of humanity need not be mutually exclusive:

---

22 Again, the translation is my own, and the pertinent words and phrases are in bold.

23 Blackwell 2010, 203. I am pleased to have endorsed the recent publication of this very helpful thesis as a book, and documented it in the works cited at the end of this paper.

24 Blackwell 2010, 207.

25 See especially sections 10–15 of his *Letter 41 to Acacius of Meliteni* (FC 76:168–82). His purpose is to expound on the dual natures of Christ, but he does not shy away from a sacrificial analogy in doing so. This, presumably, he considers to be the literal meaning of the text – that Christ, in being 'named sin', was made an atoning sacrifice, and that this shows his semblance to the sacrificed animals, who are shown to us in pairs.

indeed, the Christ-hymn of Philippians and many Church Fathers depict the Incarnation as a sacrifice which finds its nadir (or apex!) in the cross (and the descent to Hades). As for our 'becoming righteousness', it connotes something deeper than a forensic situation, though it seems unlikely that the phrase is wholly divorced from the spectre of judgement. St Paul has already invoked the judgement seat (5.10) and a God who has not [yet] 'accounted sin' (5.19). But the apostle goes beyond envisaging us as 'righteoused' – whether this is a status or a state. St John Chrysostom rejoices in a patristic parallel to the Passover cry, *Dayenu!* – 'it would have been enough':

> Had He achieved nothing else but only done this, think what great a thing it would have been to give His Son . . . But [the apostle] mentioned that which is far greater than this . . . Reflect therefore how great the things are that He bestowed on you . . . 'For the righteous,' he says, 'He made a sinner; that He might make the sinners righteous.' But he doesn't say it that way. Indeed he says something far greater . . . He does not say 'made [Him] a sinner,' but 'sin'; and not only 'He who had not sinned,' but 'He who had not even known sin,' that we also 'might become' (he does not say 'righteous,' but) 'righteousness,' and 'the righteousness of God.'
>
> (*Hom. 2 Cor.* 11.5)

We hear of the depth of the exchange, and also the unforeseen results – not only that the condemned might be 'saved' and 'cleared' but that they might be 'subsequently promoted to great dignity' and 'advanced . . . to that glory unspeakable' (*Hom. 2 Cor.* 11.5).

At stake in interpretation is the identity of the 'we'; is it exclusively apostolic, or does it at some points embrace the entire believing community? On analogy with the flexibility that we have seen in Colossians, I would argue the latter. The apostle has been speaking of trespasses and future resurrection, common to humanity. Moreover, he glosses verse 18 by verse 19: 'giving us the ministry of reconciliation' means 'establishing among us the word of reconciliation'. The 'word' is established among believers as a whole (not simply among the apostles), and its effect is cosmic in scope! It is unlikely, then, that 'becoming the righteousness of God' is the prerogative only of the apostles. Further, with the Golden-Mouthed, we must note how the apostle's language is so extravagant, the exchange so stark: the passage cannot simply be about forensic justification. It is about the revolution that has taken place, and how God accomplished it. Christ was not made sin that we could be cleared from sin; Christ was not made sin that we might be considered or made righteous human beings; Christ was not made sin that the apostles might have a cruciform ministry. No, at 5.21, we glimpse the glory of what human beings are meant to 'become'. This exception proves the well-taken rule of Wright. God's righteousness *is* his very own – unless He invites human beings into glory through the Son. All the other things 'would have been enough' to show God's justice and mercy – but there is more. We are to *become* the righteousness of *God*!

Gathering the threads

This conjunction of recapitulation with substitution, redemption with adoption, reconciliation with sacrifice, death with life, humiliation with divine glory, is surprisingly summed up for us in one of St John Chrysostom's meaty (and, alas, untranslated!) sermons. In his exposition of the Ascension of the Lord, he ties together all the episodes in Christ's actions for us, showing that a revolution – the *theōsis* of the faithful – has begun. Though he would no doubt agree with Tom Wright that something wonderful had been accomplished by six o'clock on Good Friday,[26] the entire God-directed action, up to the Ascension, is in view. So, too, are the many scriptures that he enlists in encouraging us to offer our thanksgiving: our three passages, but also texts from Romans, Hebrews, Luke–Acts, Genesis, the Psalms and Isaiah:

> So that you may learn that [God] did not hate our nature, but that he was turning away evil . . . [remember that] we who appeared to be unworthy of the earth, were this day [through his Ascension] brought up to the heavens. For we, who from the beginning were not even worthy of what was below, have come up to the kingdom on high; we have gone beyond the heavens; we have grasped hold of the royal throne.
>
> Even that very [human] nature, on account of which the Cherubim had to guard Paradise, this day is seated above the Cherubim! But how has this great wonder happened? How did we who were stricken – who appeared unworthy of the earth and were banished below from the earliest ages – how did we come up to such a height? How was the battle destroyed and how was the wrath lifted? How?
>
> For this is the wonderful thing: that it wasn't we who had grown unjustly angry with God who made the appeal, but that One who was justly vexed, who called us to his side, who entreated us, so that there was peace. '*For on Christ's behalf we are ambassadors, as though God were entreating you through us.*'

---

[26] Wright 2016a, *passim*.

What is this? Is the One who is himself abused the very same One who encourages? Indeed, yes! For he is God and, because of this, our philanthropic Father entreats us. And look what happened! The Son of the One who is making the appeal is the mediator – not a human, nor an angel, nor an archangel, nor anyone of the household slaves.

And what did this mediator do? The work of a mediator! For it is as if two had been turned away from each other and since they were not willing to talk together, another one comes, and, placing himself in the middle, loosens the hostility of each of the two. And this is also what Christ did. God was angry with us, for we were turning away from God, our human-loving Master. Christ, by putting himself in the middle, exchanged and reconciled each nature to the other. And how did he put himself in the middle? He himself took on the punishment that was due to us from the Father and endured both the punishment from there and the reproaches from here.

Do you want to know how he welcomed each? Christ, Paul says, *'redeemed us from the curse of the law, having become a curse for us'*. You have seen how he received from on high the punishment that had to be borne! Look how also from below he received the insults that had to be borne: 'The reproaches of those who reproached you,' Scripture says, 'have fallen upon me.' Haven't you seen how he dissolved the enmity, *how he did not depart before doing all, both suffering and completing the whole business, until he brought up the one who was both hostile and at war – brought that one up to God himself, and he made him a friend?*

And of these good things, this very day is the foundation. Receiving, as it were, the first-fruits of our nature, he bore it up in this way to the Master. And indeed just as it happens in the case of plains that bear ears of corn, it happens here. Somebody takes a few ears, and making a little handful, offers it to God, so that because of the little amount, he blesses the whole land. Christ also did this: through that one flesh and 'first-fruits' he made to be blessed our [whole] race . . . Therefore he offered up the first-fruits of our nature to the Father, and the Father was so amazed with the offering, both because of the worthiness of the One who offered and because of the blamelessness of the offering, that he received the gift with his hands that belonged, as it were, to the same household as the Son. And he placed the Offering close to himself, saying, 'Sit at my right hand!'

(*In Ascensionem D.N.J.C.*, Migne, PG 50, 444–6)[27]

This splendid sermon, like our chosen passages from the apostle Paul, lends no support to those who drive a wedge between Christus Victor and sacrificial or forensic notions of the atonement. Here, the ideas of

---

[27] The translation is original. I gratefully acknowledge the help of my colleague Robert Gagnon in dealing with the translational subtleties of this difficult passage, which is nowhere, so far as I have been able to discover, available in English.

reconciliation and renewed friendship are the controlling ones, since the Golden-Mouthed has evidently taken his point of departure in describing atonement from 2 Corinthians 5.20: God entreats us. But this generous and active God enfolds us by all the other Rs in St John's explanation of *how* the reconciliation has taken place – except for Redemption, which he amply expounds in other sermons.

In this passage, we begin with our unworthiness of Christ's ascended glory, hear the Father's appeal, gaze upon the God-Man in the middle as he receives punishment and scorn on the cross, and rejoice in his triumph, where he presents us to the Father as a blameless thank-offering. All this both fulfils the Old Testament sacrifices, and confirms their inadequacy to deal with God's anger over sin. 'God was angry with us, the human-loving Lord' so that an 'exchange' of natures was necessary – something only the God-Man could accomplish. We need not follow that influential French theologian, who (unfortunately) reads Chrysostom's sermon by way of Leo's Latin translation, which emphasizes 'appeasing the Father'[28] by sacrifice. This crude view of propitiation is enjoined neither by St John Chrysostom nor the apostle Paul, his source. Instead, Jesus' priestly nature is connected by the Golden-Mouthed without embarrassment to the creation, fall, crucifixion, resurrection and Ascension, and promises divine glory, or *theōsis*, to those who are in him. Sacrificial death is the necessary shape that his divine priestly service takes in a fallen world: but his service is not something super-added. Instead it is indicative of the very nature of the Son, who eternally defers to the Father and who willingly 'will also be subjected to' the Father at the end (1 Corinthians 15.28). All this is so that God may be present in everything to everyone. We hope for nothing less than a *total* atonement, by means of redemption, reparation for sin, representative substitution, righteousness, rescue, recapitulation, reconciliation and revolutionary recreation, or *theōsis*!

Bibliography

Ambrose of Milan (1962). *On the Faith*. In Corpus Scriptorum Ecclesiasticorum Latinorum 78. Edited by O. Faller. Vienna: Tempsky.

Ambrosiaster (1966). *Epistle to the Galatians*. In Corpus Scriptorum Ecclesiasticorum Latinorum 81. Edited by H. J. Vogels. Vienna: Tempsky.

Baker, Matthew (2016). '*In Ligno Crucis:* Atonement in the Theology of Fr. Georges Florovsky.' In *On the Tree of the Cross*, edited by Matthew Baker, Seraphim Danckaert and Nicholas Marinides, 101–26. Jordanville, NY: Holy Trinity Seminary Press.

---

[28] Migne PL 54, 1183, is followed by de La Taille 1940, 1:254.

Bird, Michael (2004). 'Incorporated Righteousness: A Response to Recent Evangelical Discussion Concerning the Imputation of Christ's Righteousness in Justification.' *Journal of the Evangelical Theological Society* 47.2: 253–75.

Blackwell, Ben (2016). 'Christosis: Pauline Soteriology in Light of Deification in Irenaeus and Cyril of Alexandria.' PhD Diss., Durham University, 2010. Recently published as *Christosis: Engaging Paul's Soteriology with His Patristic Interpreters*. Grand Rapids, MI: Eerdmans.

Breck, John (2006). 'God's "Righteousness".' *Orthodox Church in America*. <https://oca.org/reflections/fr.-john-breck/gods-righteousness> (1 September). Accessed February 2017.

Cyril of Alexandria (1987). *Letter 41 to Acacius of Melitene*. In *St. Cyril of Alexandria Letters 1–50*, translated by John I. McEnerney, 168–72. Fathers of the Church 76. Washington, DC: Catholic University of America Press.

Fee, Gordon D. (2005). 'Paul and the Metaphors for Salvation: Some Reflections on Pauline Soteriology.' In *The Redemption: An Interdisciplinary Symposium on Christ as Redeemer*, edited by Steven T. Davis, Daniel Kendall and Gerald O'Collins, 43–67. Oxford: Oxford University Press.

Gorman, Michael J. (2011). 'Romans: The First Christian Treatise on Theosis.' *Journal of Theological Interpretation* 5.1: 13–34.

Gregory of Nazianzus (1954). *Epistle 101 to Cledonius against Apollinaris*. Translated by Charles G. Browne and James D. Swallow. In *Christology of the Later Fathers*, edited by Edward R. Harvey, 215–24. Loeb Classical Library 3. Philadelphia, PA: Westminster.

Hart, David Bentley (1998). 'A Gift Exceeding Every Debt: An Eastern Orthodox Appreciation of Anselm's *Cur Deus Homo*.' *Pro Ecclesia* 7.3 (1998): 333–49.

Humphrey, Edith (2017). 'Becoming the Righteousness of God: The Potency of the New Creation in the World.' In *Participation, Justification and Conversion: Eastern Orthodox Interpretation of Paul and the Debate between Old and New Perspectives on Paul*, edited by Athanasios Despotis, 125–57. Wissenschaftliche Untersuchungen zum Neuen Testament 2/442. Tübingen: Mohr Siebeck.

La Taille, Maurice de (1940). *The Mystery of Faith: Regarding the Most August Sacrament and Sacrifice of the Body and Blood of Christ*. 2 vols. New York, NY / London: Sheed & Ward.

Marius Victorinus (1972). *Epistle to the Galatians*. In *Bibliotheca Scriptorum Graecorum et Romanorum Teubneriana*. Volume 44. Edited by A. Locher. Leipzig: Teubner.

Meyendorff, John (1974). *Byzantine Theology*. New York, NY: Fordham University Press.

Migne, J.-P. (1857–86) (ed.). Patrologia Graeca. 162 vols. Paris: Imprimerie Catholique.

—— (1844–64). *Patrologia Latina*. 217 vols. Paris: Imprimerie Catholique.

Mosser, Carl (2005). 'Deification: A Truly Ecumenical Concept.' *Perspectives 08* (July/August): 8–14.

Myers, Benjamin (2015). 'The Patristic Atonement Model.' In *Locating Atonement:*

Explorations in Constructive Dogmatics, edited by Oliver D. Crisp and Fred Sanders, 71–88. Grand Rapids, MI: Zondervan.

—— 'Atonement and the Image of God.' Conference lecture delivered in January 2015: <https://www.youtube.com/watch?v=DzdgDdZkSOY&feature=youtube>.

Schaff, Philip (1886–9) (ed.). *The Nicene and Post-Nicene Fathers*. Series 1. 14 vols. Reprinted edition. Peabody, MA: Hendrickson, 1994.

Schaff, Philip, and Henry Wace (1890–1900) (eds). *The Nicene and Post-Nicene Fathers*. Series 2. 14 vols. Reprinted edition. Peabody, MA: Hendrickson, 1994.

Theodoret of Cyrus (2001). *Commentary on the Letters of St. Paul*. Translated by Robert C. Hill. Volume 1. Brookline, MA: Holy Cross Orthodox Press.

Wright, N. T. (2016a). *The Day the Revolution Began*. New York, NY: HarperOne.

—— (2016b). 'God Put Jesus Forth: Reflections on Romans 3:24–26.' In *In the Fullness of Time: Essays on Christology, Creation and Eschatology in Honor of Richard Bauckham*, edited by Daniel M. Gurtner, Grant Macaskill and Jonathan T. Pennington, 135–61. Grand Rapids, MI: Eerdmans.

N. T. Wright and justification revisited: a contrarian perspective

J. ANDREW COWAN

On cheeky rabbis, Kanye West and precise lexicography: an introduction to a conversation with my theological father

When I was first invited to contribute an essay to this Festschrift in honour of my esteemed *Doktorvater*, N. T. Wright, I hesitated. Not, of course, because of any lack of desire on my part to honour one whom I hold in such high regard, but rather because I was invited to contribute an essay on a topic about which Professor Wright and I are not in full agreement. Nevertheless, upon further reflection, it occurred to me that complaints from American Evangelicals about one aspect or another of Wright's proposals about justification have been a hallmark of his career, so perhaps an essay like the present offering is a fitting tribute.

In addition to his many public debates on the subject with Evangelicals and others, justification is a topic about which Wright and I have been in private dialogue for many years. The first time that I spoke with Wright in person came during a conference in 2004 at a panel discussing his work on the resurrection. During the intermission, I eagerly approached Wright to quiz him on justification, and, although he might have preferred to spend his time thinking about the points that he wanted to make in the following discussion with John Dominic Crossan, he graciously took a few moments to address my questions and clarify his views. This dialogue continued throughout my time as a student at the University of St Andrews, and I hope that he will not mind if I take this occasion to make my side of our discussion public.

Unfortunately, the majority of Wright's engagement with the Evangelical world regarding justification has continued in the same mode as my first encounter: clarification of his views. This is because Wright feels that many of his Evangelical critics simply do not understand what he means.[1] As we shall see, although there are a few exceptions, Wright is correct that

---

[1] Cf. the expression of his frustration at this phenomenon in Wright 2009, 4–6.

he has frequently been misunderstood. Nevertheless, this does not mean that his views are entirely correct.

When I reflect on my own engagement with Wright on the issue of justification, a story from the Talmud comes to mind:

> Rabbi Eliezer said to the Sages, 'If the *halakha* agrees with me, may a proof come from Heaven.' Then a heavenly voice went forth and said, 'Why do you dispute with Rabbi Eliezer? The *halakha* agrees with him in every place.' Then Rabbi Joshua rose up on his feet, and said, 'It is not in the heavens' [quoting Deuteronomy 30.12]. What did he mean by quoting this? Rabbi Jeremiah said, 'He meant that since the Torah has been given already on Mount Sinai, we do not pay attention to a heavenly voice, for You have written in Your Torah, "Decide according to the majority"' [Exodus 23.2]. Rabbi Nathan met the prophet Elijah. He asked him, 'What was the Holy One, blessed be He, doing in that hour?' Elijah said, 'He was laughing and saying, "My children have defeated me, my children have defeated me."'[2]

Now, rest assured, I have never mistaken Wright for God, nor, to my knowledge, has he ever felt defeated or even persuaded by any of my arguments (although I have on occasion caused him to laugh). Nevertheless, this story reflects two important aspects of my perspective on Wright and justification. First, I disagree with some of Wright's conclusions about justification, but, much like the rabbis in the story, I do so because I think that I am following his own hermeneutical cues more closely than he does. Second, despite our differences in this area, I genuinely consider myself to be one of Wright's theological children. I have thought of Wright as a theological father for many years, and none of the disagreements that I have with his conclusions about justification diminish in the least the appreciation and affection that I feel for him. After reading my essay, he may very well want to ask for a paternity test, but, in my own mind, I am simply having a conversation with a theological father about applying the hermeneutical rules that he taught me.

There is, of course, much to like about Wright's exposition of justification. In my estimation, the six most admirable features are: (1) he insists that all of the relevant evidence belongs on the table; (2) he emphasizes that justification is, for Paul, a matter of inaugurated eschatology; (3) he recognizes the central place that incorporation into Christ plays in Paul's view of justification; (4) he insists that justification is forensic and not transformative; (5) he highlights how justification language is often integrated into

---

2 *b. Bava Metzia* 59b; translation adapted from Maccoby 1978.

discussions of the relationship between Jews and Gentiles; (6) he points out that Paul brings up Abraham not merely as an example but also because justification brings about the fulfilment of God's covenantal promise to Abraham of a multinational family. I find all of these emphases immensely helpful, and there is much that I could say about each one, but points of disagreements are always far more interesting, and like Kanye West, 'I'm so gifted at finding what I don't like the most.'[3] Consequently, this essay will focus on the aspects of Wright's proposals that I find less convincing.

Nevertheless, one may ask, if I am in agreement with Wright on all of the points listed above, where then is the disagreement? Wright states in *Paul and the Faithfulness of God* (*PFG*): 'Part of the question before us has to do with *balance* between different elements and with the *precise meanings* of Paul's own key terms.'[4] Yes, that is the question. And on this score, I'm not persuaded that Wright's proposals strike the proper balance or locate the meanings of key terms with precision. As we shall see, Wright proposes a developmental scheme for Paul's understanding of justification that depends on the view that the key terms refer primarily to the issue of covenant membership. This view of the primary meaning of the key terms, however, is problematic.

Justification, righteousness and covenant: Wright's developmental proposal

According to Wright, scholars have discerned seven main emphases in Paul's writings: justification, anthropology, being in Christ, salvation history, apocalyptic, transformation and covenant. Among these, he asserts, covenant provides the 'unifying perspective' within which all of the others, including justification, find their proper place.[5] As in every other area of Paul's thought, Wright claims that Paul's understanding of justification is a reworking of traditional Jewish views in the light of God's work through Christ and the Spirit. Wright presents what he describes as a 'tentative hypothesis' about the development of Paul's theology of justification:

> In Galatians and Philippians one can read the 'justification' language almost entirely in terms of 'covenant' and its redefinition, whereas in Romans that

---

3 Kanye West, 'Runaway'. Perhaps I should clarify that, unlike Kanye, I have also never mistaken myself for God.
4 Wright 2013, 782 (emphasis original).
5 Wright 2013, 781–2.

meaning is interwoven with the 'law court' imagery. My developmental proposal, then, is that since the only sort of 'justification' of which we are aware
in second-Temple Judaism had to do with the redefinition of covenant
membership, there is a possibility that Paul, having used the language in that
primary sense in Galatians, went on from there to explore and develop its
potential forensic meanings as a second layer.[6]

Thus, Wright suggests three stages of development: (1) the Jewish tradition used the language of justification with reference to 'the redefinition
of covenant membership'; (2) Paul initially spoke of justification in
Galatians and Philippians with precisely these covenantal connotations;
(3) Paul then developed his mature view in Romans by exploiting the
potential forensic significance of justification language as a subsidiary
level of meaning within the primary covenantal frame of reference. As
Wright puts it earlier in *PFG*:

> the explicitly 'forensic' nature of justification is unique to Romans. If we
> only had Galatians and Philippians, the only reason for supposing that the
> language of 'righteousness' and 'justification' was 'forensic' would have to
> lie in the meaning of the words themselves, which would be problematic.[7]

To my knowledge, the proposal of development within Paul's conception
of justification is new to *PFG*, but the claim that justification primarily has
to do with the redefinition of covenant membership has been central to
Wright's views for many years. Wright has frequently argued that the direct
question under consideration in the divine courtroom is not one's moral
acceptability before God, but rather whether or not one is a member of
God's covenant people. In fact, Wright claims that for first-century Jewish
thinkers the central concept evoked by the relevant Greek and Hebrew
terms for righteousness is covenant: 'for Paul *dikaiosyne*, like its Hebrew background *tsedaqah*, is easily flexible enough to mean, if you
like, "covenant-ness," with the different nuances appropriate for different
contexts flowing from this.'[8] Consequently, Wright understands justification to mean 'the declaration that one is a covenant member' and
righteousness to mean 'the status of covenant membership'. Wright is
quick to add that this does not mean that justification is unrelated to
the issues of sin and forgiveness. According to Wright, the covenant was

---

6   Wright 2013, 965.
7   Wright 2013, 777.
8   Wright 2011, 56. He makes this statement in the context of distinguishing his understanding
    of what righteousness means when applied to humans ('covenant membership') from what it
    means when applied to God ('covenant faithfulness').

given to deal with the problem of human sin and so being forgiven is a part of being a covenant member, but the thing that is *directly* declared in justification is covenant membership, not one's moral status.[9]

This argument has been noted but often underappreciated by many of Wright's Evangelical critics. For example, in his book-length critique of Wright on justification, John Piper carefully lays out Wright's interpretation of righteousness as covenant membership,[10] but he then goes on to place the brunt of his theological critique on Wright's claim that final justification will be rendered 'on the basis of the whole life lived'.[11] Piper tentatively suggests that Wright's use of the word 'basis' in such claims means that, in the final judgement, God declares people to be righteous because they have, by the power of the Holy Spirit, actually lived righteous lives. According to Piper, the result is that the obedience of believers plays the same role in Wright's view that Christ's obedience plays in traditional Reformed views. Because Wright describes the final verdict as being 'based' on and not merely 'in accordance with' believers' lives, Piper worries that Wright's exposition of Paul means that, in the end, the lives of believers stand as their righteousness before God. Piper admits that this reading of Wright's work may be incorrect, and he very politely asks for clarification from Wright, but this construal of Wright's views has persisted in some quarters, and scholars from the Evangelical world have continued to raise questions about Wright's use of the term 'basis' for the function of believers' works at the final judgement.[12]

This construal, however, is incorrect. The problem is that Piper ultimately filters Wright's views back through a definition of the word 'righteousness' to which Wright does not subscribe. For Wright, righteousness is the status of membership within God's covenant people, not a moral record that establishes one's standing before God. Consequently, for Wright to say that one's obedient life is the 'basis' for the final verdict means that one's life serves as the definitive evidence that one is a member of God's covenant people, nothing more and nothing less. It is the 'basis' for the final verdict in the same way that a paternity test can stand as the 'basis' for a verdict in a case about the identity of a child's father. A Christian's obedient life is definitive proof that one is a covenant member, but it is not

---

[9] Cf. Wright 1997, 96–9, 117–33; 2005, 121–2, 147–8; 2013, 184–7, 928–9, 965.

[10] Piper 2007, 39–55.

[11] Piper 2007, 117–32.

[12] Cf. the similar concern with Wright's use of the term 'basis' in Moo 2013; Schreiner 2011, 20–1; 2014, 24–5.

in and of itself covenant membership (what Wright takes 'righteousness' to mean) nor the thing that makes one a covenant member.[13]

Thus, much of the Evangelical discussion of Wright's views has started off on the wrong foot. It has focused on his use of the word 'basis' instead of the broader frame within which Wright uses this word. That frame, however, significantly resituates the issue and renders the distinction between final justification 'on the basis of' or 'in accordance with' believers' lives a moot point. The central issue is not Wright's use of the word 'basis', but rather his proposal that the primary issue in view when Paul speaks of justification is the redefinition of covenant membership. Consequently, the remainder of the present essay will examine the evidence that Wright presents in support of this particular proposal, beginning with the meaning of 'justification' and 'righteousness' in Second Temple Judaism.

Righteousness as 'covenant membership' in Judaism: re-examining the evidence

In *PFG*, Wright claims that justification is a topic about which Paul's Jewish contemporaries had very little to say. Nevertheless, he attempts to reconstruct what they probably would have said about it if they had been interested. He writes:

> Many [Jews], then, might have put the question like this: (a) Israel's God will bring about his new world, raising his people from the dead to share in it; (b) clearly, not all Jews will have a share in this new world; so (c) how can we tell, *in the present time*, who will be among that newly constituted, resurrected and reigning eschatological people? That is the precise context in which questions about 'works' might arise – though, since 'justification' is not a major topic in second-Temple Judaism, this is rare, with Qumran providing (in 4QMMT) the only solid example . . .[14]

Thus, Wright claims that justification language in Judaism referred to 'how we can tell, *in the present time*, who will be among [the] newly constituted, resurrected and reigning eschatological people', or, in short, who is a covenant member, and he admits that this claim primarily rests upon a single text, 4QMMT.

---

13 Cf. Wright's own discussions of his use of the word 'basis' in Wright 2011, 60–2; 2014, 100–1; for further reflections on this issue, see my guest post on Justin Taylor's blog regarding Wright's 2010 appearance at the Evangelical Theological Society (Cowan 2010).

14 Wright 2013, 929 (emphasis original); cf. 184–5, 187.

We will examine 4QMMT in a moment, but a few general points should also be borne in mind. First, regarding the verb 'justify', Hebrew verbs built on the stem *tsadaq* and the Greek verb *dikaioō* occur numerous times in the Hebrew Bible and the Septuagint, but they never mean 'declare to be a covenant member'. In fact, Wright does not point to any texts outside the writings of Paul in order to provide examples of the use of the verb 'justify' with this meaning. The same is true of the Hebrew and Greek adjectives meaning 'righteous': *tsaddiq* and *dikaios*. Although Wright claims that being righteous means being a covenant member, he presents no examples outside Paul's writings in which he argues that this is the clear meaning of *tsaddiq* or *dikaios*. His case instead depends primarily on the claim that the noun 'righteousness' (*tsedaqah* in Hebrew and *dikaiosynē* in Greek) at times bears the meaning 'covenant membership'.

Nevertheless, despite reading every biblical verse that contains the words *tsedaqah* and *dikaiosynē* multiple times, I cannot find one instance where either of these words directly means 'covenant membership'. Although these terms are not univocal, when they are used in conjunction with humans they usually mean something along the lines of 'justice', 'right behaviour' or 'the status of having done what is right'.[15] Consequently, as most lexical studies recognize, when the 'righteousness' word group is used in a covenantal context, it typically refers either to the right behaviour that fulfils one's covenantal obligations or the positive status that results from having fulfilled one's covenantal obligations. It does not refer to the bare fact of one's membership within the covenant.[16] The meaning 'right behaviour' is illustrated by the frequent use of the nouns *tsedaqah* and *dikaiosynē* as the direct object of the verbs *'asah* and *poieō*, 'to do', in the Jewish Scriptures. For example, consider Psalm 106.3 (105.3 LXX): 'Blessed are those who keep justice and do righteousness [*'ōśēh tsedaqah / poiountes dikaiosynē*] at all times!'[17]

---

[15] Wright pays lip service to the meaning 'right behaviour' in Wright 2013, 796–7, but this meaning quickly fades from view when Wright turns to the actual exposition of justification in Paul.

[16] Cf. Schrenk 1964, 196: '[*dikaiosynē*] is the observance of the will of God which is well-pleasing to Him'; Seebass 1978, 3.355: 'Righteousness in the OT is not a matter of actions conforming to a given set of absolute legal standards, but of behaviour which is in keeping with the two-way relationship between God and man'; Ziesler 1972, 38–9: 'The act of grace required a continuing response, and that response was to a large extent righteousness, the behaviour proper to the covenant.'

[17] Cf. Genesis 18.19; 20.13; 21.23; 24.49; 32.10 (32.11 LXX); Deuteronomy 33.21; 1 Samuel 2.10; 12.7; 2 Samuel 8.15; 1 Chronicles 18.14; 2 Chronicles 9.8; Psalms 99.4 (98.4 LXX); 119.121 (118.121 LXX); Isaiah 56.1; 58.2; Jeremiah 9.24 (9.23 LXX); 22.3; 22.15; 23.5; Ezekiel 3.20; 18.5,

The ethical or behavioural significance of righteousness language is also central when this term is used in a forensic context. Contrary to Wright's claim that, in the Hebrew law court, 'righteousness' is often used as a term for the status that one possesses when the court finds in one's favour, there are no actual examples of *tsedaqah* or *dikaiosynē* being used in this way. Instead, every actual occurrence of *tsedaqah* or *dikaiosynē* with reference to one of the parties before a judge in the context of a courtroom scene in the Jewish Scriptures refers to the right behaviour that should result in a positive verdict from the judge. For example, 1 Kings 8.32 states:

> Hear from heaven and act and judge your servants, to condemn the wicked by bringing his way upon his head and to justify the righteous [*lehatsddiq tsaddiq / dikaiōsai dikaion*] by giving to him in accordance with his right-eousness [*ketsidqatô / kata tēn dikaiosynēn autou*].[18]

Although Wright is correct to insist that in legal contexts the word 'right-eousness' often does not refer to one's *general* moral character, its meaning is still always tied to the conduct of the person to whom it is applied; it simply refers to the rightness of their behaviour in relation to the specific issue under consideration before the judge.[19]

As the work of several scholars critical of Wright's views suggests, when used with reference to humans, the 'righteousness' word groups bear an ethical or behavioural meaning so frequently that one would probably only want to suggest an alternative meaning if one could not make sense of a text with an ethical or behavioural interpretation.[20] Nevertheless, there are two main passages in the Jewish Scriptures in which Wright thinks that there are strong contextual factors that suggest the interpretation of

---

17, 19, 21, 22, 24, 27; 33.14, 16, 19; 45.9. Translations from the Bible are my own throughout this essay.

18 Cf. 2 Chronicles 6.23; for other occurrences of these terms in conjunction with the concept of judgement or a courtroom scene, see 1 Samuel 26.23; 2 Samuel 22.21, 25; Psalms 7.9; 18.20 (17.21 LXX); 18.24 (17.25 LXX); Job 33.26. Chris Thomson (2015, 9) similarly notes regarding the adjective *tsaddiq*: 'the word *never* denotes a person with the status of one whom a court has found in favour of. Not once, in any of its 200-odd occurrences in the Hebrew Bible, nor in the 100 others in the non-biblical Qumran scrolls and Ben Sira, nor, so far as I can see in rabbinic literature.'

19 Starling (2014, 42 n. 12) sharply observes that, in *PFG*, Wright initially suggests that in the Hebrew courtroom righteousness can refer to either the status that results from a verdict or the moral character of one of the parties in relation to the lawsuit under consideration (cf. Wright 2013, 797), but within a few pages Wright argues as if the latter is the only legal meaning for the term. This latter meaning, however, lacks compelling evidence.

20 Cf. Gathercole 2006, 236–7; Seifrid 2001, 434–40; Starling 2014, 39–42; Westerholm 2004, 286–91; 2013, 58–65; and esp. Thomson 2015.

the words *tsedaqah* and *dikaiosynē* in terms of 'covenant membership': Genesis 15.6 and Psalm 106.31 (105.31 LXX).

Psalm 106.28–31 recounts the story from Numbers 25 of Israel's worship of Baal of Peor and the intervention of Phinehas, which turned back God's wrath from the people. Psalm 106.31 (105.31 LXX) concludes this account by stating, 'And it was reckoned to him [Phinehas] for righteousness [*tsedaqah* / *dikaiosynēn*] from generation to generation, forever.' According to Wright, this verse demonstrates that the term 'righteousness' means 'covenant membership' because the story in Numbers concludes with God granting Phinehas a covenant of eternal priesthood (Numbers 25.13), and the psalmist concludes his account by describing an eternal 'reckoning of righteousness'.[21] One can easily see the logic by which Wright has reached this conclusion, but the Achilles' heel of the argument is the other use of the term 'righteousness' within the psalm itself. As we have seen, Psalm 106.3 (105.3 LXX) sets up the rest of the psalm by proclaiming, 'Blessed are those who keep justice and do righteousness [*'ōśēh tsedaqah* / *poiountes dikaiosynēn*] at all times!' When read in the light of this opening, it becomes apparent that the psalmist's purpose in speaking of righteousness being reckoned to Phinehas is not to refer directly to the covenant that God granted to him (although an allusion to that result of his righteous behaviour may be present by way of synecdoche), but rather to present him as an example of one whose actions fulfilled the ideal commended at the start of the psalm.[22]

This reading of Psalm 106.31 (105.31 LXX) is supported by *Jubilees'* rewriting of Genesis' account of the slaughter of the Shechemites. Scholars have long noted that the author of *Jubilees* rewrites this story with echoes of the biblical accounts of Phinehas.[23] The purpose of this rewriting is in part to suggest a causative relation between Levi's participation in the slaughter and the priesthood granted to the Levitical tribe, but what is interesting for our study is the manner in which this passage appropriates the formulation from Psalm 106.31 (105.31 LXX). The author writes:

> they slew them under tortures, and it was reckoned unto them for righteousness, and it is written down to them for righteousness . . . And we remember the righteousness which the man [Levi] fulfilled during his life, at all periods of the year; until a thousand generations they will record it, and

---

21 Wright 2013, 849 n. 215; cf. Wright 2011, 56.
22 Cf. the expositions of this passage in Bethune 1986, 129–33; Moberly 1990, 125–6; Schliesser 2007, 152–71; Watson 2004, 174–82.
23 Cf. Endres 1987, 150–1; Hengel 1989, 178–9.

it will come to him to his descendants after him, and he has been recorded in the heavenly tablets as a friend and a righteous man.[24]

Thus, the author of *Jubilees* reuses the formulation of Psalm 106.31 (105.31 LXX) in order to describe the slaughter of the Shechemites as a righteous act that will be remembered for generations to come. This righteous act is depicted as the reason for God's selection of the Levites for priesthood, but the phrase 'reckoned for righteousness' clearly refers not to the establishment of a Levitical priestly covenant but rather to the moral evaluation of the slaughter. This deployment of the phraseology from Psalm 106.31 (105.31 LXX) significantly weakens Wright's argument.

The second main text in Wright's case is Genesis 15.6, and here also I think that his argument is unpersuasive. After an account of God's reassurance that he will fulfil his promise to provide Abraham (technically 'Abram' at this point) with an heir, Genesis 15.6 states, 'And he believed in YHWH, and he reckoned it to him as righteousness [*tsedaqah / dikaiosynēn*].' Wright highlights that in the immediate aftermath of this proclamation, Genesis 15 goes on to narrate God's establishment of a covenant with Abraham, and he suggests that the phrase 'he reckoned it to him as righteousness' thus stands as a heading over this subsequent covenant ceremony.[25] This reading, however, is doubtful.

The book of Genesis consistently uses righteousness terminology in the typical ethical or behavioural sense. Noah is referred to as 'righteous' by way of contrast to the evil conduct of his contemporaries,[26] Abraham is commanded to teach his household to 'do righteousness',[27] Abraham attempts to negotiate with God over whether there are enough 'righteous' (as opposed to 'wicked') people in Sodom in order to warrant the sparing of the city,[28] and Judah declares that Tamar is more 'righteous' than he because he had wronged her by failing to give her his son Shelah in marriage.[29] Because of both this specific evidence from Genesis and the general lack of evidence for the view that the Hebrew and Greek words for 'righteousness' ever mean 'covenant membership', I find unlikely the suggestion that the temporal coincidence between this statement and the following covenant ceremony indicates that 'righteousness' here means 'covenant membership'.

---

24 *Jubilees* 30.17–20. Translation adapted from Charles 1913.
25 Wright 2013, 788–90.
26 Genesis 6.9; 7.1.
27 Genesis 18.19.
28 Genesis 18.23–28.
29 Genesis 38.26.

Apparently, so did Paul's near-contemporaries. The first book of Maccabees 2.52 interprets the word 'righteousness' in Genesis 15.6 as a reference to Abraham's subsequent righteous behaviour, particularly his willingness to sacrifice Isaac. Philo explains that faith in God is the most difficult and praiseworthy action possible, and he thus concludes that faith is reckoned to Abraham as righteousness because faith actually is the most righteous act that one can perform (*Her.* 90–5). Later, the Rabbis appealed to this verse in order to prove that Abraham practised righteousness (e.g. *Midr. Prov.* 16.31). In all of these texts, it is clear that the interpreters thought that the word 'righteousness' in Genesis 15.6 means something like the typical meaning for this term in the Jewish Scriptures – doing what is right or the status of having done what is right, not covenant membership.[30] Thus, it seems likely that the reckoning of righteousness to Abraham is meant to be viewed as distinct from his covenant with God, just as the evaluation of Noah as 'righteous' is distinct from and prior to the covenant that God initiates with him.

What then should we make of 4QMMT, the one key text in Wright's case regarding the meaning of 'righteousness' in Second Temple Judaism?[31] The passage in question reads:

> Then you will rejoice at the end of time, in that you find some of our words true, and it will be reckoned to you for righteousness [*tsedaqah*], in that you have done what is right and good before him, for your good and for Israel.
>
> (C 30–2)

In his most extensive exposition of this passage, Wright suggests that 4QMMT shares with Paul a perspective of inaugurated eschatology. In both 4QMMT and Paul, Wright claims, Israel's history is mapped on to the covenantal sequence of exile and restoration described in Deuteronomy 30, and recent events are presented as the initial fulfilment of the promised restoration and blessing. Within this framework, Wright claims, 4QMMT C 30–2 addresses the issue of how one may know which people are the true covenant people who are participating in this restoration and will be vindicated at the end of time.[32]

Wright is doubtless correct that Deuteronomy 30 plays a significant role in this text, and his proposal that 4QMMT is working within the framework of a covenantal narrative is very plausible. Nevertheless, his

---

[30] Cf. the surveys of Jewish interpretations of Genesis 15.6 in Bethune 1986, 128–86; Schliesser 2007, 152–220.

[31] Cf. Wright 2013, 146–8; 184–5; 929–30.

[32] Wright 2006, 104–32.

interpretation of the statement regarding 'righteousness' (*tsedaqah*) within C 30–2 is doubtful. Several features of the text suggest that it should be taken to mean that those who follow the advice of this letter will receive 'the status of having done what is right' at the final judgement. First, the close connection between the line about rejoicing at the end of time and the line about the reckoning of righteousness suggests that the latter refers to one's status in the final judgement, not a present anticipation of this status.[33] Second, the qualifying phrase 'in that you have done what is right and good before him' appears to define either the content or the basis of 'righteousness' in precisely the manner that one would expect based on the most common meaning for this term in the Jewish Scriptures; it explicitly states that the 'righteousness' of those addressed in the passage will consist in or be based on their right actions in fulfilment of their covenantal obligations, not their membership within the covenant.[34] Third, as John Strugnell suggested in the initial publication of 4QMMT, two phrases from C 30–2 probably echo Deuteronomy 6.24–25, which clearly has in view righteousness as right standing on the basis of obedience to the law:

> YHWH commanded us to do all these statutes, to fear YHWH our God for our good at all times, to preserve us, as it is at this day. And it will be righteousness [*tsedaqah*] for us, if we are careful to do all this commandment before YHWH our God according to what he commanded us.[35]

The echoes of this passage in the phrases 'for your good and for Israel' and 'before him' in 4QMMT suggest that the author of the latter work had Deuteronomy 6.24–25 in mind. In Deuteronomy 6.24–25, however, the term 'righteousness' clearly refers to the status of having done what is right.

Each of these features suggests that 4QMMT C 30–2 describes how, at the end of time, having done what is right and good will be reckoned as righteousness. On the basis of their obedience to the law (their 'works of the law' as 4QMMT says three lines back), those who take the advice of 4QMMT will be approved by God as having done what is right, just as Phinehas was approved according to Psalm 106. At one point in *PFG*, Wright himself even appears to endorse this interpretation of 4QMMT.

---

33 Cf. Gathercole 2002, 93–5; Schliesser 2007, 199–200.

34 Cf. Doering 2014, 75–6; Gathercole 2002, 93–5; Schliesser 2007, 198–200; Sprinkle 2013, 163–4.

35 Deuteronomy 6.25. Cf. Qimron and Strugnell 1994, 63; this proposal is followed by Schliesser 2007, 197–200; Sprinkle 2013, 164. For suggestions of further passages from Deuteronomy that may have influenced the wording of this passage, see Weissenberg 2009, 216–18.

After suggesting that this text is proclaiming the time of renewal promised in Deuteronomy 30, he writes, 'the whole point of the text is to say: *this is happening at last; you can be a part of it; and here is what you must do for that to happen.*'[36] Unfortunately, Wright quickly loses this emphasis on the text addressing '*what you must do*' and lapses back into his standard paradigm in which the issue is 'how you can tell' who will be a part of God's renewed people. Despite his helpful insights on the covenantal framework within which 4QMMT works, however, this latter view of the function of 4QMMT's righteousness terminology fails to persuade.

Thus, when Wright says, 'There is, however, not much evidence that pre-Christian Jews spoke of that kind of "advance marking out" in terms of "justification"',[37] I am inclined to agree. I just think that this lack of evidence should be explained by the very simple solution to which it points: justification language doesn't mean the advance marking out of those who will be declared covenant members at the end of the age, and the Greek and Hebrew words for 'righteousness' do not mean 'covenant membership'. The weight of historical evidence is against this proposal in every text.

The trial of justification and Leviticus 18.5: a matter of life and death

As illustrated by my reading of 4QMMT, the question that I think justification language addresses, both in Judaism and in Paul, is not *how can you tell* who will be among the resurrected and reigning eschatological people on the last day, but rather the more direct question, *how can you be* one of the people who receives a positive verdict from God on the last day. This latter issue was not simply an assumed part of the mental furniture in first-century Judaism; it was an important and disputed question. Each of the Synoptic Gospels reports that a man came to Jesus to ask, 'What must I do to inherit eternal life?'[38] Additionally, Acts 15.2 describes people responding to Paul's ministry by saying: 'Unless you are circumcised according to the custom of Moses, you cannot be saved.' Now, of course, one should not merge salvation and justification language completely (each makes its own distinct contribution), but the text in Acts demonstrates that the question of circumcision and observance of the law was

---

[36] Wright 2013, 147 (emphasis original); cf. 186–7, where he makes a similar statement about the views of the Pharisees.
[37] Wright 2013, 930; cf. 184.
[38] Mark 10.17, par.

raised in response to Paul's ministry not in terms of how you can tell if one will receive eternal life but rather in terms of what one must do in order to receive eternal life.[39] In fact, I think that you can see that this is the question that Paul is addressing in his discussions of justification if you pay attention to the particular passages from the Jewish Scriptures to which Paul refers and also look at the treatment of those same passages among his Jewish contemporaries, a practice I have often seen commended by Wright himself.

A text of obvious importance for Paul in discussions of justification is Leviticus 18.5: 'And you will keep all my ordinances and all my judgments, and you will do these things which, having done them, a person will live by them.' This passage is quoted in both Galatians 3.12 and Romans 10.5. But Leviticus 18.5 was related to the language of 'righteousness' long before Paul. Consider the reworking of Leviticus 18.5 in Ezekiel 33.19: 'And when the sinner turns from his lawlessness and does justice and righteousness he will live by them.' In this verse (and many others within Ezekiel 18 and 33), Ezekiel rewrites Leviticus 18.5 in order to make explicit that the life promised in the latter is contingent upon doing 'justice and righteousness'. The way Ezekiel lines up the language, doing righteousness is the requirement and basis for receiving the life that Leviticus promises.[40]

In a monograph on Paul's use of Leviticus 18.5, Preston Sprinkle goes so far as to call Leviticus 18.5 the 'John 3:16 of Early Judaism'.[41] As Sprinkle goes on to demonstrate, Leviticus 18.5 was understood in different ways within early Jewish literature, but it was often interpreted as offering eternal life upon the condition of obedience to the law. This interpretation indisputably occurs in CD (the *Damascus Document* of Qumran) 3.12–16, *Psalms of Solomon* 14.2–3, *Targum Pseudo-Jonathan* Leviticus 18.5 and *Targum Onqelos* Leviticus 18.5. For each of these texts, Leviticus 18.5 describes what one must do in order to attain a positive verdict from God in the final judgement and thereby receive the life of the age to come.[42]

This appears to be the kind of interpretation with which Paul is interacting when he quotes Leviticus 18.5 in Galatians 3.11–12. Paul writes, 'Now it is evident that no one is justified before God by the law, for "The

---

[39] Cf. Gathercole's emphasis on the prevalence of the concept of attaining eschatological life in early Jewish and Christian literature (Gathercole 2002, *passim*).

[40] Cf. Lyons 2009, 127–31; Sprinkle 2008, 36–7.

[41] Sprinkle 2008, vii.

[42] Cf. the expositions of the early Jewish texts in Sprinkle 2008, and the rabbinic texts in Avemarie 1996.

righteous shall live by faith." But the law is not of faith, rather "The one who does them shall live by them."' Paul thus contrasts the promise of life in Leviticus 18.5 with the alternative promise of life in Habakkuk 2.4, and it appears that he lines up the correspondence between righteousness language and life in precisely the same way as Ezekiel. Receiving life on the basis of obedience to the law is described as being 'justified before God by the law'. In my estimation, the implicit logic behind this connection is again that righteousness is the basis for receiving life.[43] Justification by faith is presented as the answer to the question, 'How can a person attain a positive verdict at the final judgement and thereby receive life?'

Wright, however, presents an alternative explanation for the connection between righteousness and life. In his view, the link is that life is the ultimate covenant blessing, and justification is therefore the declaration of those who will receive life because it is the declaration of covenant membership.[44] I suppose that if all we had were Galatians 3.11–12, that might be arguable. But consider Romans 10.5–8, the other passage where Paul quotes Leviticus 18.5:

> For Moses writes about the righteousness from the law, 'The one who does them shall live by them.' But the righteousness from faith says, 'Do not say in your heart, "Who will ascend into heaven?"' (that is, to bring Christ down) 'or "Who will descend into the abyss?"' (that is, to bring Christ up from the dead). But what does it say? 'The word is near you, in your mouth and in your heart' (that is, the word of faith that we proclaim).

As in Galatians, Paul is again drawing a contrast regarding righteousness, placing Leviticus 18.5 on one side and faith on the other.[45]

In describing the righteousness from faith, the main text to which Paul alludes is Deuteronomy 30. Wright, of course, seizes on this and suggests that this clearly indicates the covenantal meaning of 'righteousness' in this text because Deuteronomy 30 is God's promise of a post-exile covenant renewal.[46] But this argument underestimates the significance of the first words that Paul puts on the lips of the righteousness from faith: 'Do not say in your heart . . .' It is widely recognized that these words are an allusion to Deuteronomy 8.17 and 9.4.[47] Upon turning to Deuteronomy 9.4,

---

[43] Cf. Romans 8.10; Galatians 3.21.

[44] Wright 2013, 936.

[45] He is probably also drawing on the implicit allusions to Leviticus 18.5 in Romans 7 where he explains that the law promises life but cannot deliver because sin takes advantage of the good commandment and brings death.

[46] Wright 2013, 1167.

[47] Cf. Hays 1989, 78–9; Watson 2004, 338–9.

one discovers that the continuation of this prohibition fits like a glove with what Paul is saying in Romans 10. Deuteronomy 9.4–5 states:

> Do not say in your heart . . . 'It is because of my righteousness that the LORD has brought me in to possess this land' . . . Not because of your righteousness or the uprightness of your heart are you going in to possess their land, but because of the wickedness of these nations the LORD your God is driving them out from before you, and that he may confirm the word that the LORD swore to your fathers, to Abraham, to Isaac, and to Jacob.

There are many connections that could be drawn here, but the point that I want to highlight is that the word 'righteousness' in Deuteronomy 9.4 does not and cannot mean 'covenant membership'. The Israelites are commanded to believe that God's covenant is the very reason why God *is* bringing them into the land. The thing that they are prohibited from thinking is that God is bringing them into the land because they have done what is right.[48] That is what the words 'my righteousness' mean in Deuteronomy 9, and I would suggest that this is the echo that Paul intends to reverberate between Deuteronomy 9 and his contrast between the righteousness from the law (represented by Leviticus 18.5) and the righteousness from faith, which comes through the death and resurrection of Christ. As in Ezekiel, this echo implies that the way in which 'righteousness' vocabulary fits into the picture is that 'righteousness from the law' would consist in the right behaviour that fulfils the condition for receiving life set forth in Leviticus 18.5. Of course, this does not mean that Paul is here contrasting righteousness by faith with some sort of crass moralism; Leviticus 18.5 is a promise given in the context of God's covenantal relationship with Israel. What it does mean is that 'righteousness' is a status that relates to behaviour, not membership.

When Wright himself addresses the allusion to Deuteronomy 9, he appears to come to a similar conclusion; he suggests that Israel was trying to invoke a status 'based it seems on an imagined success in keeping God's law, which will make Israel automatically superior to the other nations'.[49] Thus, even he sees that in Deuteronomy 9 'righteousness' is a matter of doing what is right. But, alas, although his good exegetical sense here gets the better of his theological system, he never fully realizes the significance of this observation for the meaning of 'righteousness' in Romans 10.

---

[48] This same point about Deuteronomy 9.4–5 is made in Thomson 2015, 13; Westerholm 2004, 288. Neither Thomson nor Westerholm, however, notes that this is a text to which Paul makes a significant allusion.

[49] Wright 2013, 1171–2.

The trial of justification and Psalm 143.2: a matter of moral reckoning[50]

Let us approach things from another angle. As Wright correctly insists, the verb 'justify' (*dikaioō*) signifies for Paul a verdict given in a trial. For such forensic uses of the verb 'justify', however, the content of what it means to be justified depends on the nature of the trial in which the verdict is rendered. For example, if a person is on trial for assassination and the court finds in his or her favour, for that person to be 'justified' means that he or she is declared innocent of the assassination. Such a verdict may *imply* that the person on trial is not a member of a revolutionary group, but that is not what the verdict itself *means*. The actual meaning of a verdict always relates directly to the charges under consideration in the courtroom.

So, what trial does Paul have in mind when he speaks of justification? Again, it is important to pay attention to Paul's use of the Jewish Scriptures. In discussions of justification, Paul utilizes two texts from the Septuagint that actually contain the verb *dikaioō*, Psalm 143.2 (142.2 LXX) and Isaiah 50.8. Although similar observations apply to both, we only have space to look at one, so let us consider Psalm 143.2.[51] This verse reads, 'Do not enter into judgment with your servant because no living person will be justified before you.' In context, these words are an appeal for mercy from God. In this type of psalm, one usually finds the accused or persecuted invoking their innocence as a reason for God's deliverance, but Psalm 143 contains a plea for mercy instead. This difference probably results from the fact that Psalm 143 considers the author's position before God as a whole rather than the author's righteousness relative to specific individual accusations or opponents.[52] The main point to take from this is that the trial in view in Psalm 143.2 is not a trial asking whether or not one is a covenant member, but rather a trial evaluating the behaviour of humans by the absolute standards of God's justice.

This understanding of the trial, of course, fits very well with Paul's extensive description of the charges against all humanity in Romans 1.18—3.20, the prelude to his most extensive exposition of justification by faith.

---

[50] Perhaps I should clarify that, by the term 'moral', I do not intend to imply the kind of moralizing account of humanity's problem criticized in Wright 2016. I only mean to suggest that justification entails the evaluation of behaviour. As Wright insists, the behaviour that is expected of humans is not conformity to a bare set of moral rules but rather the fulfilment of a meaningful vocation within God's world.

[51] For a helpful exposition of Paul's allusion to Isaiah 50.8 in Romans 8.33 that explores the meaning of *dikaioō* in these texts, see Beale 2011, 501–4.

[52] Kraus 1989, 536; Mays 1994, 432; cf. Psalms 7.8; 26.1; 35.24.

Indeed, when Romans 3.10 states, 'None is righteous, no, not one', what Paul has in mind is not that there are no covenant members, but rather that all people fail to live up to the standard of divine justice. As Richard B. Hays puts it, the catena of quotations from the Jewish Scriptures in Romans 3.10–18 is an 'unremitting attack on the moral integrity of human beings',[53] and this is all then summarized by Paul's allusion to Psalm 143.2 in Romans 3.20: 'For by works of the law *no human being will be justified before him*, since through the law comes knowledge of sin.'[54]

Now, Wright may protest that he fully admits that Paul develops the latent forensic meanings of justification language in Romans, and that is fair enough, but I see no reason to take this language in a different sense in Galatians and Philippians. Paul also alludes to Psalm 143.2 at the conclusion of Galatians 2.16, the first verse in which he mentions justification in any of his letters. He writes:

> We know that a person is not justified by works of the law but through faith in Jesus Christ, so we also have believed in Christ Jesus, in order to be justified by faith in Christ and not by works of the law, because by works of the law *no flesh will be justified*.[55]

When I see this allusion and think about what the term 'justification' means in the original context of Psalm 143, I feel tempted to say, 'Physician, heal thyself. What you do with allusions everywhere else in the New Testament, do here in your home turf of Paul as well.' The implication of this allusion is that the trial Paul has in mind is God's judgement of humanity with respect to sin and right behaviour, not covenant membership.

The proof of the pudding

Wright has often suggested that his critics need to supply their own readings of extended passages from Paul's letters in order to demonstrate the coherence of their views. Unfortunately, there is not space for such an exercise in this short essay. Although I would have loved to engage text by text with Wright through long stretches of Galatians, Corinthians, Philippians and Romans, I have had to attempt a more strategic outflanking. Nevertheless, in this final section, I will briefly comment on three key texts before I conclude.[56]

---

53 Hays 1989, 50.
54 Cf. the discussions of this allusion in Hays 1989, 51–2; Watson 2004, 67–9.
55 Cf. the discussion of Paul's use of Psalm 143.2 in Galatians 2.16 in Westerholm 2013, 77.
56 Unfortunately, there is also insufficient space to engage with the masses of secondary

First, one of the central verses from Paul's letters to which Wright appeals in support of his view is Romans 4.11. Wright goes so far as to state that this verse 'gives the lie to those who say that the *dikaiosynē* language ought not to be interpreted in "covenantal" terms'.[57] According to Wright, Romans 4.11 demonstrates the covenantal significance of *dikaiosynē* for Paul because Paul here takes a passage from the Jewish Scriptures and directly substitutes the word *dikaiosynē* in place of the word 'covenant'. The passage to which Paul alludes in Romans 4.11 is Genesis 17.11, which speaks of circumcision as a 'sign of the covenant'. Wright translates Romans 4.11 as saying, 'He [Abraham] received circumcision as a sign and seal of the righteousness of faith.'[58]

At first glance, this argument sounds impressive; Genesis 17.11 proclaims circumcision to be a 'sign of the covenant' and Paul states that circumcision is a 'sign and seal of righteousness'. The only problem is that this is not actually what Paul says. Contrary to Wright's translation, the genitive form of *dikaiosynē* in Romans 4.11 does not modify both 'sign' and 'seal'. Instead, Paul states that Abraham 'received the sign of circumcision [*sēmeion . . . peritomēs*] as a seal of the righteousness [*sphragida tēs dikaiosynēs*] of faith'. The genitive *peritomēs*, 'circumcision', modifies the word 'sign', and *dikaiosynēs*, 'righteousness', modifies 'seal'. Thus Paul does not actually say that circumcision is a 'sign of righteousness', placing *dikaiosynē* directly where one finds the word 'covenant' in Genesis 17.11. The direct parallelism that Wright sets forth as proof for his interpretation simply is not there in the Greek of Romans 4.11, despite his creative gloss.

A second key passage for Wright is Galatians 2.11–21. Wright correctly insists that Paul's appeal to 'justification' language in Galatians 2.16 comes in the context of the Antioch incident, in which the central problem was Peter's withdrawal from eating with Gentiles. After highlighting Paul's reference to the Jew–Gentile divide in Galatians 2.15, Wright asserts:

> [The phrase] 'so that we might be justified' in Galatians 2.16 does not simply mean 'so that we might attain a righteous standing before God', though that is obviously part of the core meaning of the term. Rather, it *must* mean, in order for the sentence to work in its context, 'so that we might be declared to be *members of God's single family*' . . . Without this, the passage makes no sense.[59]

literature on these passages.
57 Wright 2013, 848.
58 Wright 2013, 848.
59 Wright 2013, 968 (emphasis original).

The problem with Wright's claim here is that, although he has rightly discerned that Paul's rhetorical point is to address the issue of table fellowship, he assumes that the only way in which it makes sense for Paul to appeal to justification in this context is if justification speaks about this issue directly. In my estimation, however, the function of Paul's appeal to justification is more nuanced, and Wright's attempt to read the table-fellowship issue into the definition of justification itself proves to be a shortcut that misses the most brilliant turns within Paul's speech to Peter. Let us review the beginning of the argument in brief.

In verse 14, Paul starts by describing Peter's hypocrisy: 'If you, being a Jew, live like a Gentile and not like a Jew [in other words, don't keep Torah strictly], how can you force the Gentiles to live like Jews [in other words, to keep Torah]?' Paul thus points out that Peter's separation from the Gentiles implies that the latter group should be keeping Torah. Paul then sets up his introduction of the issue of justification by highlighting that both he and Peter actually are Jews in verse 15: 'We are Jews by nature, not sinners from among the Gentiles.' Paul then builds on this confession of common ethnic heritage in Galatians 2.16:

> But knowing that a person is not justified by the works of the law but through faith in Christ Jesus, even we have believed in Christ Jesus, so that we may be justified by faith in Christ, and not by the works of the law; because by the works of the law shall no flesh be justified.

The point is that even Paul and Peter, men born of the people to whom God gave the Torah, know that right standing with God does not come through obeying the Torah but through trusting in Christ. Having laid out this common confession of justification by faith, Paul then turns to a *reductio ad absurdum* in verse 17: 'But if, while seeking to be justified in Christ, we too were found to be sinners, is Christ then a servant of sin? By no means!' The point here is that those who would conclude that Paul and Peter are sinners because they do not keep Torah strictly but instead trust in Christ for their justification are clearly wrong because this line of thinking would lead to the ridiculous conclusion that Christ is a servant of sin. This is where Paul's line of thought begins to address Peter's separation from the Gentiles directly. What Paul shows is that by implying that Gentiles need to live like Jews (obey the Torah), Peter has inadvertently agreed with their critics and implied that those who seek justification in Christ instead of through the Torah are sinners and that Christ himself is therefore a servant of sin.

We could continue through to the end of the speech, but space is limited and the point should already be clear. Contrary to Wright's claim, it is not

difficult to make sense of this paragraph in relation to the Antioch incident while letting the justification language mean what it clearly means in
Romans and what the allusion to Psalm 143.2 in Galatians 2.16 implies
that it means here. In fact, I think that reading the paragraph in this way
helps one to see that Paul raises the stakes of Peter's separation from the
Gentiles by forcing him to come to terms with what his actions imply
about essential Christian soteriology (how one attains right standing with
God). Paul's argument is that Peter's actions are a betrayal of the central
Christian message.

Finally, let us consider Philippians 3.2–11 for just a moment. Speaking
about this passage, Wright claims, 'Here . . . it is easier than in Galatians
to see that Paul's argument is *solely* about "covenant membership" and its
redefinition through *pistis*.'[60]

Paul writes in Philippians 3.4–6:

> If anyone else thinks he has reason for confidence in the flesh, I have
> more: circumcised on the eighth day, of the people of Israel, of the tribe of
> Benjamin, a Hebrew of Hebrews; as to the law, a Pharisee; as to zeal, a perse-
> cutor of the church; as to righteousness [*dikaiosynēn*] in the law, blameless.

Wright comments about this list:

> Together they strongly suggest that his claim to have been 'blameless' in
> relation to 'righteousness under the law' was not about 'amassing merits
> and achievements' . . . It was a matter of *demonstrating*, through Torah-
> practice, one's covenant membership as per the previous six categories . . .
> All this was a matter of *covenant status*, possessed already in virtue of birth
> and exemplified in terms of Torah-keeping. That is the meaning of the
> *dikaiosynē*, 'righteousness', of which he speaks in verse 6. The whole point
> is to highlight Paul's supreme status as a member of the covenant people in
> excellent standing.[61]

I find it interesting that, in his gloss of this text, Wright has switched from
'covenant membership' to 'covenant status' (perhaps because 'with respect
to covenant membership in the law, blameless' sounds so odd), but I do not
think that either of these options is an accurate description of what Paul
means. When a person says that he or she is 'blameless' with respect to
'righteousness in the law', any first-century reader familiar with the Jewish
Scriptures would have understood this to mean that the person is claiming
to have been blameless in doing what is right according to what the law

---

[60] Wright 2013, 984.
[61] Wright 2013, 988–9 (emphasis original).

commands. I would not want to describe this with the phrase 'amassing merits and achievements' any more than Wright himself would, but trying to push 'covenant membership' into the definition of *dikaiosynē* here is again unnecessary and distracting. The text makes much better sense if one sticks with the typical meaning of the term from the Jewish Scriptures. Being blameless with respect to righteousness in the law is not a claim about membership; it is a claim about behaviour.

In Philippians 3.8–11, Paul concludes this discussion by saying:

> For his sake, I have suffered the loss of all things and count them as rubbish, in order that I may gain Christ and be found in him, not having my right-eousness be that which comes from the law, but that which comes through faith in Christ, the righteousness from God that depends on faith – that I may know him and the power of his resurrection, and may share his suf-ferings, becoming like him in his death, that by any means possible I may attain the resurrection from the dead.

Note two things. First, the phrase that Paul uses to describe the righteous-ness that he does not have is 'righteousness from the law'. This is the exact same phrase that he uses in Romans 10.5 for the kind of righteousness represented by Leviticus 18.5. Second, this passage concludes by focusing on attaining the life of the age to come. These two clues seem to indicate that the righteousness language in this passage is used in precisely the same sense as it is in the fully developed forensic theology of Romans; what Paul has in mind is how one can attain a positive verdict in the divine courtroom and thereby be granted resurrection life in the age to come.

On black hats, angry men and good historical hypotheses: concluding reflections on the continuing conversation

N. T. Wright's view of justification is one aspect of a remarkably creative rereading of Paul's letters. In one of our seminars together, I noted with some amusement that, in *PFG*, Wright has written a long chapter about election that is almost entirely about justification, and this is followed by a long chapter about eschatology that is almost entirely about Romans 9—11. In my estimation, he has the content of these chapters backwards, but this categorization is representative of how radically Wright has re-arranged the pieces on the board of Pauline theology.[62] Nevertheless, as

---

62 This is not to say that Wright does not think that justification is eschatological; he emphati-cally does. But the distinctive thing about his view is that he thinks that the matter with which justification deals directly is the redefinition of the people of God.

we have seen, his solution to the puzzle has not always been understood accurately by his critics.

In addition to misinterpreting his proposals, many Evangelicals who have critiqued Wright have also failed to understand the broader conversations in which he is participating. *PFG* reads as a very different book if one reads it immediately after reading Wright's account of the last century of Pauline scholarship in *Paul and His Recent Interpreters* (2015). For those with the time to digest yet another 1,000-page book, *PFG* also reads very differently after Douglas Campbell's *The Deliverance of God* (2009). Understanding these conversations can lead one to a much greater appreciation of what Wright is trying to do.

Nevertheless, the most unfortunate thing about all of this is that Wright is pushing in the right direction in calling for a covenantal reading of Paul, but his interpretations of righteousness as 'covenant membership' and justification as 'the declaration of who is a covenant member' have proved to be an insuperable stumbling block to many who could benefit from his insights. This is terribly unfortunate because no other point within his grand theological construction requires or depends on interpreting 'righteousness' language in this way, and his persistence in insisting on it leads some to the absurd conclusion that he always wears a black hat. I suspect that if this aspect of his interpretation could be adjusted, he would face far fewer internet mobs singing the song of angry men, and his reading of Paul would prove to be even more attractive in future years.

The proposal that justification language in Paul refers to the declaration that one is a covenant member is almost entirely lacking in solid evidence, it has a great deal of evidence against it, and, most importantly, it does not have the kind of simplicity that is the hallmark of a good historical hypothesis.[63] More evidence is explained more simply by reading justification language in terms of judgement before the bar of divine justice with respect to sin and right behaviour. That is what Paul's explicit statements about the trial imply, that is what the passages from the Jewish Scriptures to which he refers imply, that is what the treatments of these same passages in the literature of Second Temple Judaism imply, and, although there is no space to demonstrate this here, this rendering provides the most satisfying and illuminating reading of Paul's letters as a whole.

What then shall we say to these things? If Paul is for us, who can be against us? He who did not spare the Jewish Scriptures, but gave

---

[63] Cf. the excellent methodological reflections in Wright 1992, 1–144.

quotations and allusions to us all, how shall he not by these clues point us to what he means? Who can bring any objection against Paul's own text? It is historical evidence that justifies exegesis; who is to disagree? For I am persuaded that neither revered confessions nor pastoral concerns, nor book contracts nor tenure boards, nor old perspectives nor new perspectives, nor apocalyptic interpretations, nor high theological aims nor low motives, nor any other pressure in all the world of biblical studies should separate us from the meaning of Paul in his historical context.

Bibliography

Avemarie, Friederick (1996). *Torah und Leben: Untersuchungen zur Heilsbedeutung der Tora in der frühen rabbinischen Literatur.* Texts and Studies in Ancient Judaism 55. Tübingen: Mohr Siebeck.

Beale, G. K. (2011). *A New Testament Biblical Theology: The Unfolding of the Old Testament in the New.* Grand Rapids, MI: Baker.

Bethune, Larry Lynn (1986). 'Abraham, Father of Faith: The Interpretation of Genesis 15:6 from Genesis to Paul.' PhD Diss., Princeton Theological Seminary.

Campbell, Douglas (2009). *The Deliverance of God: An Apocalyptic Rereading of Justification in Paul.* Grand Rapids, MI: Eerdmans.

Charles, R. H. (1913). *The Apocrypha and Pseudepigrapha of the Old Testament.* Oxford: Clarendon.

Cowan, J. Andrew (2010). 'What N. T. Wright Really Said.' *The Gospel Coalition.* 26 November: <https://blogs.thegospelcoalition.org/justintaylor/2010/11/26/what-n-t-wright-really-said/>.

Doering, Lutz (2014). '4QMMT and the Letters of Paul.' In *The Dead Sea Scrolls and Pauline Literature*, edited by Jean-Sébastien Rey, 69–87. Leiden: Brill.

Endres, John C. (1987). *Biblical Interpretation in the Book of Jubilees.* Catholic Biblical Quarterly Monograph Series 18. Washington, DC: Catholic Biblical Association of America.

Gathercole, Simon J. (2002). *Where Is Boasting? Early Jewish Soteriology and Paul's Response in Romans 1–5.* Grand Rapids, MI: Eerdmans.

—— (2006). 'The Doctrine of Justification in Paul and Beyond: Some Proposals.' In *Justification in Perspective: Historical Developments and Contemporary Challenges*, edited by Bruce L. McCormack, 219–41. Grand Rapids, MI: Baker.

Hays, Richard B. (1989). *Echoes of Scripture in the Letters of Paul.* New Haven, CT: Yale University Press.

Hengel, Martin (1989). *The Zealots: Investigations into the Jewish Freedom Movement in the Period from Herod I until 70 A.D.* Translated by David Smith. Edinburgh: T&T Clark.

Kraus, Hans-Joachim (1989). *Psalms 60–150.* Continental Commentary. Minneapolis, MN: Fortress.

Lyons, Michael A. (2009). *From Law to Prophecy: Ezekiel's Use of the Holiness Code.* Library of Hebrew Bible/Old Testament Studies 507. London: T&T Clark.

Maccoby, Hyam (1978). *The Day God Laughed: Sayings, Fables and Entertainment of the Jewish Sages*. London: Robson.

Mays, James L. (1994). *Psalms*. Interpretation. Louisville, KY: John Knox.

Moberly, R. W. L. (1990). 'Abraham's Righteousness (Genesis XV 6).' In *Studies in the Pentateuch*, edited by J. A. Emerton, 103–30. Leiden: Brill.

Moo, Douglas J. (2013). 'Review of N. T. Wright, *Paul and the Faithfulness of God*.' *The Gospel Coalition*. 6 November: <https://www.thegospelcoalition.org/reviews/paul_and_the_faithfulness_of_god/> (accessed 15 January 2017).

Piper, John (2007). *The Future of Justification: A Response to N. T. Wright*. Wheaton, IL: Crossway.

Qimron, Elisha, and John Strugnell (1994). *Qumran Cave 4, Volume 5: Maʿáse Ha-Torah*. Discoveries in the Judean Desert 10. Oxford: Clarendon.

Schliesser, Benjamin (2007). *Abraham's Faith in Romans 4*. Wissenschaftliche Untersuchungen zum Neuen Testament 2/224. Tübingen: Mohr Siebeck.

Schreiner, Thomas R. (2011). 'Justification: The Saving Righteousness of God in Christ.' *Journal of the Evangelical Theological Society* 54.1: 19–34.

—— (2014). 'Paul's Place in the Story: N. T. Wright's Vision of Paul.' *Journal for the Study of Paul and His Letters* 4.1: 1–26.

Schrenk, G. (1964). 'δίκη, δίκαιος κτλ.' In *Theological Dictionary of the New Testament*, edited by Gerhard Kittel and Gerhard Friedrich, edited and translated by Geoffrey W. Bromiley, 2:178–225. Grand Rapids, MI: Eerdmans.

Seebass, H. (1978). 'Righteousness.' In *New International Dictionary of New Testament Theology*, edited by Colin Brown, 3:352–77. Grand Rapids, MI: Zondervan.

Seifrid, Mark A. (2001). 'Righteousness Language in the Hebrew Scriptures and Early Judaism.' In *Justification and Variegated Nomism, Volume 1: The Complexities of Second Temple Judaism*, edited by D. A. Carson, Peter T. O'Brien and Mark A. Seifrid, 415–42. Grand Rapids, MI: Baker.

Sprinkle, Preston M. (2008). *Law and Life: The Interpretation of Leviticus 18:5 in Early Judaism and in Paul*. Wissenschaftliche Untersuchungen zum Neuen Testament 2/241. Tübingen: Mohr Siebeck.

—— (2013). *Paul and Judaism Revisited: A Study of Divine and Human Agency in Salvation*. Downers Grove, IL: IVP.

Starling, David I. (2014). 'Covenants and Courtrooms, Imputation and Imitation: Righteousness and Justification in *Paul and the Faithfulness of God*.' *Journal for the Study of Paul and His Letters* 4.1: 37–48.

Thomson, Chris (2015). 'Righteousness in the Hebrew Bible and Misconceptions in New Testament Scholarship.' Paper presented at the Cambridge New Testament Senior Seminar, Cambridge, 19 May.

Watson, Francis (2004). *Paul and the Hermeneutics of Faith*. London: T&T Clark.

Weissenberg, Hanne von (2009). *4QMMT: Reevaluating the Text, the Function, and the Meaning of the Epilogue*. Leiden: Brill.

West, Kanye (2010). 'Runaway.' *My Beautiful Dark Twisted Fantasy*. Roc-A-Fella/Def Jam.

464

Westerholm, Stephen (2004). *Perspectives Old and New on Paul: The 'Lutheran' Paul and His Critics.* Grand Rapids, MI: Eerdmans.

—— (2013). *Justification Reconsidered: Rethinking a Pauline Theme.* Grand Rapids, MI: Eerdmans.

Wright, N. T. (1992). *The New Testament and the People of God.* Christian Origins and the Question of God 1. London: SPCK / Minneapolis, MN: Fortress.

—— (1997). *What Saint Paul Really Said: Was Paul of Tarsus the Real Founder of Christianity?* Grand Rapids, MI: Eerdmans.

—— (2005). *Paul: In Fresh Perspective.* Minneapolis, MN: Fortress.

—— (2006). '4QMMT and Paul: Justification, "Works," and Eschatology.' In *History and Exegesis: New Testament Essays in Honor of Dr. E. Earle Ellis for His 80th Birthday,* edited by Sang-Won (Aaron) Son, 104–32. New York, NY: T&T Clark.

—— (2009). *Justification: God's Plan and Paul's Vision.* London: SPCK / Downers Grove, IL: IVP.

—— (2011). 'Justification: Yesterday, Today, and Forever.' *Journal of the Evangelical Theological Society* 54.1: 49–63.

—— (2013). *Paul and the Faithfulness of God.* Christian Origins and the Question of God 4. London: SPCK / Minneapolis, MN: Fortress.

—— (2014). 'Right Standing, Right Understanding, and Wright Misunderstanding: A Response.' *Journal for the Study of Paul and His Letters* 4.1: 89–106.

—— (2015). *Paul and His Recent Interpreters.* London: SPCK / Minneapolis, MN: Fortress.

—— (2016). *The Day the Revolution Began: Reconsidering the Meaning of Jesus' Crucifixion.* New York, NY: HarperOne.

Ziesler, J. A. (1972). *The Meaning of Righteousness in Paul: A Linguistic and Theological Enquiry.* Society of New Testament Studies Monograph Series 20. Cambridge: Cambridge University Press.

Newness of life: gospel, Church and the common good in Romans 12—13

S. A. CUMMINS

Introduction

The significant contribution of N. T. (Tom) Wright to biblical and theological studies, and to the life and mission of the Church in the contemporary world, is evident throughout his extensive and influential scholarly and popular publications.[1] His engagement with Pauline theology and especially Romans has played a long-standing and prominent role in this regard, including ongoing interaction with the letter's challenging and contested chapters 12—13. This passage is often portrayed as a series of largely diverse and even disparate segments – for example, on spiritual gifts, the characteristics of the genuine Christian, obeying the governing authorities and loving one's neighbour – which broadly exhort the Church, then and now, to live in an exemplary fashion in the world. While in a general sense this may be said to be so, this essay offers a select exegetical and theological interaction with aspects of this important section, drawing on and developing Wright's own insightful analyses – principally in his *Paul and the Faithfulness of God* (Wright 2013a) and 'The Letter to the Romans' (Wright 2002) – seeking an all the more cohesive and expansive account of its powerful and wide-ranging exhortations.

It does so along the following lines. First, it reviews and considers Wright's understanding of Paul's theological vision regarding new creation and related themes, especially as represented in Romans and particularly chapters 12—13. Second, it outlines the passage's eschatological framework (Romans 12.1–2 and 13.11–14) and its understanding of the renewed people of God and their transformed lives and vocation in the world. Third, this new way of life is then delineated in terms of what

---

[1] This essay is offered in deep appreciation for Tom's gracious contribution to my own life and work.

together it means to be 'one body in Christ' (Romans 12.3–8),[2] loving one another and living peaceably with all (Romans 12.9–21), including concern for governance and the common good (Romans 13.1–7), as this operates within the all-embracing love of God (Romans 13.8–10).

It will be evident throughout that Paul's holistic vision encompasses and extends key Old Testament themes and expectations regarding the outworking of God's love, justice and wisdom for Israel and the world; as this is taken up and realized in Jesus' life, death and resurrection, and the resultant new creation; and thence in Paul's own apostolic and priestly call and vision-casting for the Spirit-shaped church in Rome and beyond. In view of God's mercy and righteousness, explicated at length throughout Romans 1—11, Paul urges the believers (Romans 13.11) to embody and enact their renewed way of life – to 'walk in newness of life' (Romans 6.4) – which, in Jesus and the Spirit, is actualized and operative as they participate in the unfolding economy (plan and providence) of God. It is this that generates, governs and unites Paul's richly textured exhortations, and their compelling vision of God's gospel, the Church and the common good.

Paul's theological vision: N. T. Wright on new creation and Romans

Attempting to delineate Paul's theological vision is a complex and challenging undertaking. This is abundantly evident in the ever-increasing scholarly literature on Paul's theology and related matters, currently much of it constructively tackling the topic under a number of integral and overlapping categories: for example, juristic, salvation-historical, participationist, apocalyptic, theopolitical, sociocultural, and so on.[3] Wright has provided his own massive and multifaceted historical, narrative and especially covenantal account in *Paul and the Faithfulness of God* (Wright 2013a), offering 'a more compelling, if inevitably more complex, single picture'.[4] As is already widely known, this initially entails an outline of Paul's first-century world in relation to the story of Israel, Greek philosophy, the role of religion and culture, and the Roman Empire. He then delineates Paul's worldview and mindset in terms of its key symbols, practices, stories and questions. Underlying and sustaining Paul's worldview

---

2 Throughout this chapter, Scripture translations normally follow the NRSV, here from Romans 12.5.
3 See Wright 2015 for his own extended engagement with certain significant strands of current Pauline scholarship.
4 Wright 2013a; quotation at p. 44; see the concise overview in Wright 2016.

is the development of his theology, encompassing Jewish monotheism, election and eschatology, redefined – refreshed, rethought – in the light of Jesus the Messiah and the Spirit. Wright finally considers how this plays out in Paul's own historical context, again with respect to empire, religion, philosophy and his Jewish setting. Paul's gospel engenders true humanity, spirituality, fellowship and kingdom-life under the lordship of Jesus; and herein one may locate and understand Paul's vocation, mission, churches and letters.[5]

A significant role in all of this is played by Wright's threefold story of Scripture regarding God's relationship with the world, humanity and Israel.[6] This story comprises a 'framing plot of creator and creation' and three subplots: first, that of 'the human creatures through whom the creator intended to bring order to his world'; second, in response to humanity's disobedience, 'the story of Israel as the people called to be the light of the world'; and, third, with Israel's unfaithfulness, the culmination of its story in the death and resurrection of Messiah Jesus, who embodies and enacts the return of YHWH to Zion, defeats evil, ends the exile, brings about a new exodus and covenant life, and inaugurates the new age, including justice to all nations.[7] With this comes the sending of the Spirit, which issues in 'the newly symbolic world of the people of God . . . living under the rule of the one God, as free citizens of his kingdom'.[8]

Wright's illuminating account of the inaugurated new age may be delineated further and with particular reference to Romans and its chapters 12—13.[9] God's righteousness (covenant faithfulness, Romans 1.16–17) has been dramatically disclosed, and Israel's story and hope for 'the life of the age to come' fulfilled, in the climactic death and resurrection of Messiah Jesus, which is 'the eschatological turning-point, the launching of God's new world'.[10] And this new reality (cf. Romans 12.1–2; 2 Corinthians

---

5   See, for example, Wright 2013a, 611–18. Among early responses to *Paul and the Faithfulness of God*, most substantial is the collection of essays edited by Heilig, Hewitt and Bird, 2017.

6   Wright 2013a, 519. On the following comments, see further Cummins 2017, 220–4.

7   Wright 2013a, citations at pp. 484–5 (cf. 518), with the wider discussion at pp. 456–537.

8   Citation from Wright 2017, 63. See Wright 2013a, 528–36, on the threefold story of God and creation, humanity and Israel, especially in relation to the argument of Romans, and its 'single summary story from Adam to the Messiah, and on to "the life of the age to come"'; Paul 'can then draw on this messianic narrative as the framework and context "in which" Messiah-people find their identity' (Wright 2013a, 531).

9   Additional comments on Wright's approach to Romans 13.1–7 in particular will follow below.

10   Wright 2013a, 524. In references to Wright 2013a, here and throughout, I aim to be representative but not exhaustive. All italics are original. Among extended discussions bearing on new creation and related considerations, cf. pp. 438–50, 538–69 (esp. 550–62), 879–902,

5.17; Galatians 6.14–16) 'determines the destiny of the whole creation'.[11] Paul's theology, vocation and mission are 'rooted in and defined by this *christologically inaugurated eschatology*'.[12] Indeed, for Paul a double-reality is involved: 'the unique *achievement* of the Messiah and its *implementation* in the work of the gospel', by the Spirit.[13] Responding to the gospel in the power of the Spirit, believers die and rise with Jesus ('through the Messiah's body', Romans 7.4; cf. 6.2–11, 14), leave the 'present evil age' and enter the risen life of the 'age to come' – a life 'to God' (cf. Romans 6.11; Galatians 1.4; 2.19) – and can now faithfully obey and serve God 'in the newness of the spirit' (Romans 7.6).[14] No longer captive to sin they now may operate 'with a new quality of life' (Romans 6.4),[15] presenting themselves for God's righteous purposes (cf. Romans 6.2–4, 12–14; 12.2; 13.11–14). They must be especially aware of 'what time it is' (Romans 13.11) and taught to be 'daytime people'[16] – a key image here being 'the new day which is dawning' (Romans 13.11–14)[17] – living in the light of God, willingly subject to public scrutiny.[18]

However, while 'decisively launched', with Jesus already exalted in power,[19] the corrupting effects of sin and death remain, and the 'age to come' is not yet complete,[20] with a share in God's glorious final rule still to be fully realized (Romans 8.17–25).[21] This situation is, though, in accord with God's purposes,[22] including his mercy deferring judgement. And it allows an interval, an overlap between the ages, with a now new ethics (behaviour and action) operative,[23] which provides time and space for people to mature as God's image-bearers 'fitted to be [his] partners,

---

1043–128 and much of Part IV, not least ch. 16. References to Paul's letters are likewise selective, focusing on Romans.

[11] Wright 2013a, 478.

[12] Wright 2013a, 1411.

[13] Wright 2013a, 880.

[14] Wright 2013a, 531–2; the Scripture translations in this paragraph are his.

[15] Wright 2013a, 1102; his rendering of *en kainotēti zōēs* at Romans 6.4, following Wright 2011, 320.

[16] Wright 2013a, 1101–2.

[17] Wright 2013a, 1101.

[18] Wright 2013a, 1374–6. Related to being 'daytime people' is the call to 'put on the Lord Jesus Christ' (Romans 13.14; cf. Colossians 3.1–11, on which see Wright 2013a, 1103–4).

[19] Cf. Ephesians 1.20–21; Philippians 2.10–11; 3.20–21; Colossians 1.16–18.

[20] Wright 2013a, 1072.

[21] See Wright 2013a, 1078–95.

[22] Wright 2013a, 1048.

[23] And also 'ethnics', on which see Wright 2013a, 1043–265, including the pressing question of Israel's future and Romans 9—11 at Wright 2013a, 1156–258.

stewards, in the ruling of the creator's new world' (Romans 5.17; 8.17–30).[24] The Messiah's people indwelt by the Spirit thus stand in the gap, and at the intersection of heaven and earth, experiencing the eschatological tension of embodying new life even as they share in the present pain of an as yet unfulfilled creation. Moreover, while their new identity and calling clearly differentiates believers, Paul recognizes that they can also share with others a common outlook on living in the world. This can include, for example, upholding what is true, honourable and just (Philippians 4.8), and widely held convictions on what is 'good' or 'evil', and living 'peaceably with all' (cf. Romans 12.9, 15–18), thereby making a positive impression upon society at large.[25]

Paul's worldview and theology were designed with this new creation in view. And his apostolic mission as a pastor and teacher was to establish covenantal communities belonging to a church he viewed as 'a *microcosmos*, a little world . . . the prototype of what was to come'.[26] Integral to each community and its relation to society as a whole (Romans 12.14—13.10) is a Christian transformation of the ancient virtues – with four particularly in view: 'patience, humility, chastity and above all *agapē*, "love"'.[27] Self-sacrificial love is central to Paul's moral vision: among other things, it fulfils the law, binds together the Messiah's body and is crucial in addressing any disunity.[28] Also central to Christian character development is the 'mind of the Messiah', needed to 'think through' the new-creation life.[29] Believers have 'the mind [set] on the Spirit' which is life and peace (Romans 8.6); its renewal is on display in their transformed lives that discern the will of God (Romans 12.2); and this is to be wisely worked out in various practical ways (cf. Romans 14.5). In love and discernment the community comprises a holy and united people. Indeed, in their 'worship, they believed, heaven and earth came together, God's time and human time were fused and matter itself was transfigured to become heavy with meaning and possibility'.[30] And in and through their life and witness, the reconciliation brought about by Messiah Jesus was

---

[24] Wright 2013a, 1116; wider discussion at pp. 1095–128.
[25] Wright 2013a, 1374–5. In these respects the gospel is embodied in an authentic 'image-bearing humanness' which affirms yet transforms 'the best that the rest of the human race had seen' (Wright 2013a, 1376 and 1378).
[26] Wright 2013a, 1492.
[27] Wright 2013a, 1116. See also Wright 2010; particularly pertinent with respect to Romans 12 is ch. 5.
[28] Wright 2013a, 1118; cf. Romans 14.1—15.13.
[29] Wright 2013a, 1114, 1120–1. Cf. also Wright 2016, 1–20.
[30] Wright 2013a, 1491–2.

implemented in the power of the Spirit throughout all the nations of the world to the worship and glory of the creator and covenant God (Romans 15.7–13).[31]

This is indeed a remarkably illuminating 'thick description' of new-creation life as evident in Romans. Consonant with Wright's overall account of Paul's theology, it is commendably attentive to its historical, narrative, covenantal and creation-wide configuration; rightly centred in its Israel-specific and Messiah Jesus-focused outworking; and explicates its various interrelated eschatological, ecclesial and ethical dimensions. Though not absent from Wright's approach, perhaps in constructing and contemplating new-creation life in Paul and Romans, additional recourse might be made to the rich resources and conceptual categories of the Christian theological tradition. Here, for example, one might reflect even further on an overarching triune divine life and economy; the complex and significant Christological considerations entailed in a pre-existent, incarnate, crucified and risen, and eternally exalted Jesus; and the Spirit-shaped operation of divine and human agency. Such considerations bear on how we envisage and explicate the nature, scope and vastness of all that is in view. This includes, for example, all that is envisaged and entailed in new creation actualized and encompassing transformed time and space and matter, this 'on earth as it is in heaven' (cf. Ephesians 1.20–21; Philippians 2.10–11; 3.20–21; Colossians 1.16–20; 3.1–4; also Matthew 6.10); that which is seen and is as yet unseen (Romans 8.24–25); and the unfolding and ultimate resolution of 'all things'/'all in all' (cf. Romans 8.37–38; 1 Corinthians 15.28; 2 Corinthians 3.18).

Indeed, at a climactic and critical point in Romans Paul extols the ultimately unfathomable magnitude of God's eternal grace, glory and wisdom, manifest in Israel and to all creation (Romans 11.33–36; cf. Isaiah 43.13; Job 15.8; Jeremiah 23.18). This affirms what is evident throughout the letter, that all things are contingent upon and are unfolding according to God's disclosure, action and ultimate ends. And integral to this is God's definitive self-expression in Jesus Christ, accomplishing his once hidden but now manifest purposes and providence (Romans 16.25–27). The people of God, including those in Rome, have been taken up into all of this, even now living out an ever-transforming 'newness of life' (Romans 6.4).[32] This is enacted in their worship-centred lives together and

---

31 Wright 2013a, 1494–5.
32 Moo 1996, 366, observes: '"Newness of life" is a life empowered by the realities of the new age – including especially God's Spirit (Rom. 7:6) – and a life that should reflect the values of that new age.' Barclay 2015, 501, notes that 'newness of life' is 'the believers' new mode

society at large, participating with love and discernment in the renewal and reconciliation of humanity and all creation (Romans 8.18–30). Such a theological vision is assumed and articulated as Paul addresses the believers in Romans 12—13.

New-creation life: transformation, renewal and the will of God (Romans 12.1–2; 13.11–14)

Paul, operating within God's purposes, occupying a leading apostolic role, and having outlined at length the gospel of God's righteousness regarding Israel, the Church and the world in chapters 1—11, now initiates an extended appeal in chapters 12—15.[33] Here he urges the church in Rome to live out its newness of life, addressing various aspects of what this entails, only the first section of which – chapters 12—13 – is considered in some detail here.[34] His exhortations are framed by a programmatic opening appeal at 12.1–2 and telling eschatological remarks at 13.11–14.

Taking his overarching eschatological outlook first (Romans 13.11–14), the believers in Rome must live as those knowing 'what time it is [*ton kairon*]' (Romans 13.11). That is, the new age has been inaugurated and actualized, and they are even now caught up in God's transforming work in their lives and the wider world, which will assuredly and ultimately be realized with the ever-approaching 'day' of the Lord (Romans 13.13; cf. 1

---

of existence – their new allegiances, dispositions, emotions, and actions – [and] is attributable to the miraculous life of Christ himself'. And 'it is experienced by human beings only inasmuch as they share in, and draw from, a life whose source lies outside of themselves, the life of the risen Christ'; thus 'it is an "eccentric phenomenon."' He adds that it 'is established, sustained, and governed not by believers themselves, but by God' (pp. 502–3).

[33] See Longenecker 2011, 55–166, which is recent among various studies related to the addressees, situation and purpose of Romans, within which Romans 12—15 figures prominently (as does Romans 16), especially issues regarding 'the weak' and 'the strong' (Romans 14.1—15.13); on the latter, with respect to Torah-observance, note especially Barclay 2016, 37–59; cf. also the relevant sections of the many commentaries.

[34] Wright 2002, 702, views chs 12—13 as more general and 14—15 as more context specific, the former a foundation for, and with an eye towards, the latter more particular situation. He divides 12—13 as follows: '12:1–2 (introduction and foundation); 12:3–13 (unity in the church through each exercising their gifts); 12:14–21 (the church's life, particularly facing those outside); 13:1–7 (responsibility toward authorities); 13:8–10 (the overriding responsibility of love); and 13:11–14 (living in the light of God's dawning day).' He notes that the most difficult structural decision is whether 12.9–13 belongs with 12.3–8 (his preference), is separate or introduces 12.14–21. On a chiastic structure for chs 12—13, see Horrell 2003, 86–7. This essay sees a trajectory in which the various integral elements entail a dynamic interplay, encompassing new-creation life in relation to God's people and the world at large.

Thessalonians 5.2). The sense of imminence and urgency here – indicated, for example, by the accompanying language of 'hour', 'already', 'now' and 'nearer'[35] – is appropriately understood in terms of the all-embracing comprehensiveness of what God is accomplishing. It need not invite an over-realized eschatology, diminishing or curtailing the importance of the everyday workings of the world; rather, it affirms God's good creation, redeemed and being renewed, with a view to its final completion.[36] Moreover, they are to live in the light, an evocative image invoking God's disclosure, illumination, vision and glory.[37] That is, leaving behind the ever-receding darkness of the night and its related behaviour – and awake and alert, and also properly attired with 'the armour of light' (Romans 13.12), having 'put on the Lord Jesus Christ' (Romans 13.14) – they are to continue walking in the light of the new day.[38] Hence, as evident throughout these chapters, Paul's concern is that the people of God live in the light and love of new-creation life in relation to one another, their neighbours, enemies, governing authorities, and so on, thereby participating in God's reconciling work in the world.

The opening programmatic remarks at Romans 12.1–2 arise out of ('therefore', Romans 12.1) the antecedent overview of God's gracious, righteous and redeeming gospel (Romans 1—11). They are issued as a powerful divine word through Paul, an apostle and a priest in the service of God's mission (cf. Romans 1.1; 11.13; 15.16). And they succinctly set forth, indeed envisage, the essential nature and scope of what is then delineated in some detail. The exhortations are directed at the 'brothers and sisters [*adelphoi*]' (Romans 12.1), the believers in Rome, probably comprising a collection of house churches (Romans 16.5),[39] who are strategically located at the centre of the empire and invited to be involved in Paul's prospective mission in the western Mediterranean (Romans

---

35 Romans 13.11, author's translation.
36 Cf. esp. Romans 8.18–39; see also Romans 11.33–36; 1 Corinthians 15.20–28; Philippians 3.20–21; Ephesians 1.3–14 (cf. Romans 16.25–27); 3.14–21.
37 In the Pauline letters, cf. esp. 2 Corinthians 4.6; Ephesians 5.8–9, 13; Colossians 1.12; 1 Thessalonians 5.5; 1 Timothy 6.16.
38 This includes a pattern of life no longer characterized by the works of the flesh (Romans 13.13–14; cf. Galatians 5.19–21) but, it may be inferred, by the fruit of the Spirit (cf. Galatians 5.22–24). Two pertinent Pauline passages, arguably sharing a comparable theological outlook, and many similar motifs and themes, but which cannot be explored and correlated here, are Ephesians 5.6–20 and 1 Thessalonians 5.1–11.
39 Cf. Romans 16.1, 4, 16, 23. On the originality and integrity of chapters 15—16, see Longenecker 2011, 19–30. See Oakes 2009 for an informative and imaginative archaeological reconstruction of period house churches and an illuminating reading of Romans 12 in relation thereto at 98–126.

1.8–15; 15.14–33). They also belong to the 'one body in Christ' (Romans 12.5), the Church universal participating in the creation-wide purposes of God.

Paul first urges them 'to present your bodies as a living sacrifice, holy and acceptable to God, which is your spiritual [rational] worship' (Romans 12.1). Wright has noted that this evocative temple-related language, especially if related to Genesis 1 seen as a '"temple"-vision', intimates their role as God's 'heaven-and-earth house', those called to be 'his image-bearers, his royal priesthood, summing up the worship of creation and reflecting his wise order into his world'.[40] Indeed, the imagery evokes a rich collocation of Old Testament antecedents: for example, Levitical instructions urging offerings that truly represent faithful worship, obedient hearts, covenant life, and order in the nation (Leviticus 1.1—2.16); and psalms extolling the Creator God and his rule over the world, bidding Israel to worship and glorify his salvation.[41] Moreover, out of this worship will issue 'a new song' (Psalms 40.3; 96.1; cf. Isaiah 42.10),[42] declaring God's glory throughout heaven and the earth, with a new state of affairs signalled, exemplified in faithful worship, care for the needy, and hearts on which are written God's law.[43] All this is a function of God's unfolding purposes and wise governance in and through Israel in the world. For Paul and the church in Rome, what is urged here entails the whole person and indeed the entire community ('bodies'), on an ongoing and self-sacrificial basis, together engaged in the wider world.[44] And, as Paul will indicate, it entails a complex of relationships including one another, neighbours, enemies and governing authorities.

The scope and vastness of all this suggests that the believers' 'spiritual/rational worship [*logikēn latreian*]' (Romans 12.1), and the related matter of their renewed minds (Romans 12.2), should be understood broadly and dynamically. It is 'rational' in that the renewed mind now recognizes, reflects upon and directs an embodied and enacted newness of life

---

[40] So Wright 2013a, 1509.

[41] Cf., for example, Psalms 27.6; 50.5, 14, 16, 23; 96.8; 107.22. Among many studies on the Old Testament in Romans, see Seifrid 2007; regarding Romans 12—13, at 679–84.

[42] See also Psalms 107.22; 117.1 (Romans 15.11).

[43] Cf. Psalm 40.6–8; see also Jeremiah 31.33; Ezekiel 36.26–27.

[44] Although not Pauline, significant here is the illuminating and instructive citation from Psalm 40.6–8 (LXX 39.7–9) in Hebrews 10.5–10, reading it as Jesus addressing God – 'Sacrifices and offerings you have not desired, but a body you have prepared for me . . . I have come to do your will, O God' – in reference to his incarnation and self-sacrificial death (cf. Romans 3.25; 5.9; 8.3).

(Romans 6.4), which is offered in worship and service to God.[45] For Paul 'mind [*nous*]', not least together with the 'body', resonates expansively and evocatively. It can function as a metonym for the person, and the term can be applied collectively to the human condition as a whole, with Romans providing the fullest exposition of this.[46] Here it may also evoke the Shema (cf. Deuteronomy 6.5; and *dianoia* at Mark 12.30 et par.; Colossians 1.21–22), now enabled by the Spirit (Romans 5.5), further suggesting that the entire (renewed) person and community is involved in what he envisages, and that the ensuing exhortations are governed above all by love of God and neighbour, even extending to enemies and presumably everyone in between (cf. Romans 12.9, 21; 13.8–10). Moreover, this 'spiritual/ rational' worship is possible because they are no longer 'conformed to this age',[47] but rather are shaped by the all-searching Spirit who empowers the spiritual person with gifts such as discernment, understanding and right judgement; indeed, as Paul tells the Corinthian believers, 'we have the mind of Christ' (1 Corinthians 2.16).

Thus the members of the church in Rome 'may discern what is the will of God – what is good and acceptable and perfect' (Romans 12.2),[48] a discernment which arises out of and contributes to their newness of life in Christ and the Spirit. While this does not mean 'they will always know what God will do',[49] nonetheless they are participants in the entire work of God. This includes even now being 'transformed . . . from one degree of glory to another' (2 Corinthians 3.18).[50] So while being 'good', for example, importantly includes their moral transformation,[51] it encompasses the totality of the life lived together under God. Paul's programmatic

---

45 Cf. Keener 2009, 143–4; and also Keener 2016, 143–72, for a developed discussion of the renewed mind in Romans 12.1–3.

46 Cf. for example, Romans 1.21; 7.1—8.11. All this even while acknowledging that the 'mind of the Lord' (Romans 11.34; cf. Isaiah 40.13) – who above all is merciful, gracious and glorious – is ultimately unfathomable.

47 See Wright 2002, 705. Among various key correlative texts concerning 'this age', with particular reference to its rulers, cf. 1 Corinthians 2.6–16; 3.18–23; note also Galatians 1.4.

48 Here again drawing upon Old Testament sacrificial imagery. Keener 2009, 143, notes offerings described as 'holy' to God (e.g. Leviticus 6.17, 25; 7.1; 10.12) and Israel's service seen as an offering 'acceptable' or 'pleasing' to God (Ezra 6.10; Psalm 20.3; Isaiah 56.7; Jeremiah 6.20; Malachi 3.4).

49 Rightly Keener 2009, 144 n. 9, noting Romans 1.10; 15.32.

50 Cf. Philippians 3.10, 21; and 2 Corinthians 4.16; also Jesus' Transfiguration (Matthew 17.2; Mark 9.2).

51 J. Thompson 2011 rightly stresses that Paul is concerned with the moral and countercultural transformation of his churches; on Romans, for example, cf. pp. 53–62, 119–33, 144–55, 166–80. See also Wright 2010, with its interest in the virtues, moral life and faithful Christian living, especially pp. 135–79.

remarks, functioning within his overall theological standpoint, are broad and vibrant in all that they envisage. Seeing them as such, and, together with 13.11–14, as functioning within Paul's new-creation outlook, allows the ensuing wide-ranging remarks in chapters 12—13 to be read in more comprehensive, cohesive and compelling ways.

Gospel, Church and the common good

Functioning within Paul's overall theological vision of new-creation life, framed by his programmatic and eschatological remarks at Romans 12.1–2 and 13.11–14, and shaped throughout by continued use of Old Testament and Jesus traditions, Paul's ensuing exhortations in Romans 12—13 (and 14—15) encompass a series of wide-ranging yet still inter-related elements giving expression to all that God is accomplishing. Here, in turn, they are considered as follows: (1) in relation to being one body in Christ (Romans 12.3–8); (2) loving one another and living peaceably with all (Romans 12.9–21); (3) including concern for God's governance and the common good (Romans 13.1–7); (4) as all of this operates in living together in the love of God (Romans 13.8–10). The aim is to offer a cohesive and expansive account of the nature, scope and outworking of the newness of life actualized in the gospel, Church and common good, all a function of the creation-wide economy of God.[52]

1 One body in Christ (Romans 12.3–8)

On the strength of God's grace given to him in the form of his apostolic vocation and authority (Romans 1.5; 15.15),[53] Paul addresses 'everyone among you' (Romans 12.3) who comprise the church at Rome. The phrase may convey something of Paul's broad and inclusive conception of the believers, and their varied and vibrant relationships as the people of God. Paul's initial instruction calls for a common understanding and outlook that is a function of the same faith allocated by (and operative under) God for the benefit of all,[54] exercising sober judgement and eschewing

---

52 Throughout, 'common good' is used broadly in relation to living well together for the good of all, both in the Church and society at large. On the common good in relation to Paul, see especially Furnish 2005 (on Romans 12—13, see pp. 75–83), with which this essay is in some alignment; with respect to pertinent Old Testament antecedents, see Brueggemann 2010.
53 Cf. 1 Corinthians 3.10; 15.10; Galatians 2.9; Ephesians 3.2, 7–8; Colossians 1.25.
54 By 'measure of faith' (12.3), Paul probably means not the (different) 'amount of faith' but rather the same faith for all (cf. 3.27–30), a common standard and 'measuring rod', as variously at work in the spiritual gifts given by God to each member for the benefit of the body as a whole (12.6–8); following Wright 2002, 709.

any sense of superiority.[55] While Paul's use of *phroneō* language ('think, consider, be disposed')[56] conveys the importance of clear-headed and sober thinking, elsewhere in Romans it is also employed in relation to integral, interrelated and expansive considerations such as walking according to the Spirit (Romans 8.5), ever in awe of God's redemptive purposes through elect Israel for the wider world (Romans 11.20), and being spiritually attuned to the relationship between the 'weak' and the 'strong' within the community of faith (Romans 14.6; 15.5; cf. 12.16). Further, if Paul's remarks to the church in Philippi are any indication, it is a Christlike loving and selfless way of life constitutive of the entire community (Philippians 2.2, 5; 3.15) whose members, in all of their relationships (Philippians 1.7; 4.2, 10), function as citizens within the creation-wide rule of God (Philippians 3.20; cf. Colossians 3.2–4).[57] Manifest in all such ways it is 'the mind of Christ' operative in the 'one body in Christ' (Romans 12.5; cf. 1 Corinthians 2.16): broad and inclusive; varied and vibrant; with a common understanding and outlook; walking together in the newness of life.

Wright has variously noted that the Church as 'one body in Christ' – 'the Messiah's body' – is a central symbol for Paul, as the united and holy community caught up in the renewal of the covenant and new creation brought about by the God of Israel revealed in Messiah Jesus and the Spirit.[58] Thus the body metaphor is appropriate on several levels: for example, to denote those who through Christ have died to the 'body of sin/death' (cf. Romans 6.4–6; 7.24; 8.10, 13) and risen to newness of life; to indicate that Christ himself (the head) governs his people (the body); and to stress that the Church (the body) must exhibit unity in diversity (cf. 1 Corinthians 12.12–27), not least in sharing diverse spiritual gifts. Paul may also be mindful of the image's use by pagan writers in reference to 'the body politic'.[59] Yet such elements and associations also show that the metaphor points to the believers' transformed existence and an

---

55 Perhaps the scenario at 14.1—15.13 is already in view; cf. the use of *phroneō* at 14.6; 15.5.
56 See BDAG, 1065–6.
57 See further Fowl 2005, esp. 28–9, 82–4, 89–90 and 164–5, and related wider discussions.
58 Wright 2013a, 1260. On 'the Messiah's body', see, for example, Wright 2013a, 396–404, 825–35 ('Jesus as Israel's *Incorporative* Messiah'), 892–902 ('Romans 7.1—8.11'). Moreover, 'The one God, spoken of . . . in three different ways, shares in the common life of this new community, and the community shares in the life of the divine: the same spirit, the same lord, the same God, operating all these things in everyone' (Wright 2013a, 1333).
59 Wright 2002, 710, cites Plato, *Republic* 462c–d; Livy 2.32; Plutarch, *Aratus* 24.5; *Marcius Coriolanus* 6.2–4. On the Church as a new kind of polis, see Wright 2013a, 1332, 1339–42 and 1492.

all-encompassing new state of affairs – God's grace, presence and power operative in Messiah Jesus and the Spirit to reconcile all things – and being gifted and equipped to participate in this. As such each of the many members are not merely to be numerically aggregated or even combined as complementary parts, but inextricably belong together, both differentiated and dynamically interrelated within the creation-wide purposes of God.

Perhaps then a little caution may be required in recognizing that Paul's use of the reciprocal pronoun 'one another' here indicates a primary focus on looking after family members rather than others outside the community.[60] Without denying the identity and integrity of the community, these elements are taken up in service of God's mission to redeem, renew and realize his purposes for all people, the whole of humanity. Paul recognizes the need to attend to tensions and challenges within the community itself, as seen in the scenario in view at Romans 14.1—15.13. Yet this is with a view to a hospitality which is inclusive and outward-looking, a function of participation in all that God is accomplishing, which is not served by any self-centred concerns which constrict and constrain. The varied and dynamic particularity of the church in Rome, including its anticipated strategic role in Paul's westward mission, is itself an integral part of the emerging and expanding people of God, in relation to the Mediterranean world and beyond, all within the divine life and economy.

Integral to this, and again a function of God's grace and the body's faith and practice, is the allocation, reception and operation of various spiritual gifts (Romans 12.6–8). In a representative but not exhaustive list Paul mentions prophecy, service, teaching, exhortation, generosity, leadership and compassion. Such gifts are to be spiritually discerned, developed, operative and valued, not simply for their own sake, but for the life of the Church, local and universal, and its mission in the wider world. So, by way of example only, prophecy in the Old Testament has an enormously influential and wide-ranging role, addressing society at large and even geopolitical affairs, with respect to God's purposes for

---

[60] Cf. J. Thompson 2011, 57–9. Admittedly the related matter of 'insider' and 'outsider' language is challenging, and not fully reflected upon here. See now the recent work by Trebilco, who in considering Romans 12.14—13.10 contends that 'throughout this passage the actual language he [Paul] uses to refer to outsiders encourages harmonious relations' (Trebilco 2017, 225), and wants his readers to think of 'a larger degree of integration into the wider society' (232). Cf. also Horrell 2003, 91–4, who also addresses the related matter of solidarity and difference within the Christian community, and more extensively so in Horrell 2016 (2005) (on which see Wright 2015, 285–304, interacting with the 2005 edition), also beyond the scope of this essay.

Israel and the nations.[61] Teaching within the Christian community draws on the Old Testament, the life and ministry of Jesus, and his continuing presence by the Spirit among his people, including instruction in the faith (cf. Romans 6.17; 15.4; 16.17), now being expressed in the emerging new-covenant documentation, including Romans itself. Similarly, exhortation, integral to God's admonitions to Israel, and to the often startling words and works of Jesus, is employed throughout Paul's remarks in Romans 12—16. Generosity is tangibly expressed with both ecclesial and eschatological significance in Paul's collection from the Gentile churches for the needy saints in Jerusalem (Romans 15.25–29; 2 Corinthians 8.2; 9.11, 13). Leading or managing might be correlated with those in leadership in house churches in Rome, with all of the wide-ranging spiritual and social issues in play there; and compassion or mercy, evoking Paul's antecedent remarks regarding the redemptive mercy of God for Israel and all people (Romans 11.30–32), indicates actively assisting others, including alms-giving (cf. also Romans 12.13; 2 Corinthians 9.7). Spiritual gifts given to believers are thus exercised in all areas of their lives and vocation, encompassing the Church, local community and society at large; just as the 'one body in Christ' serves the purposes of God for the whole of humanity and all of creation.

2 Loving one another and living peaceably with all (Romans 12.9–21)

Paul's ensuing remarks at Romans 12.9–21 are bracketed by an overarching and crucial call for genuine love that hates evil and holds fast to the good (Romans 12.9, 21). This is explicated in a series of wise sayings, intrinsically wide-ranging in nature and scope, including a prominent appeal to 'live peaceably with all' (Romans 12.18). This is not simply a matter of general commands, the marks of the true Christian, or even moral formation, as important as such are. Again it is to be recognized that in play throughout is Paul's overarching theological vision – shaped and sustained by the Old Testament witness to God's relationship with Israel and the nations, and the kingdom of God realized in the life and teachings, death and resurrection, of Jesus[62] – in relation to the Spirit-empowered new-creation life and mission of the Church. This encompasses the believers

---

61 Prophecy being 'in proportion to faith' (12.6) probably implies it is to be exercised 'to the full extent of that faith' and perhaps also according to the Church's standard of faith, its beliefs; so Wright 2002, 711.

62 On Jesus' teachings in Romans 12.9–21, see the detailed analysis in M. Thompson 1991, 90–110.

in Rome, who are among the 'one body in Christ', their neighbours, the governing authorities, and beyond.

The initial and programmatic 'Let love be genuine; hate what is evil, hold fast to what is good' (Romans 12.9) bears comparison to Old Testament injunctions having similar notable thematic elements (cf. Psalms 37.27; 97.10; Amos 5.14–15). If such associations are any indication, in view and about to be explicated is love that eschews evil and embraces the good; doing so by serving God's continuing commitment to renew all of creation, not least Israel and the nations; and whose key features include righteousness, wisdom and justice. Hence the ensuing exhortations, which begin with a series of admonitions at Romans 12.10–13 involving various virtues and actions, address the believers with a view to their lives together as taken up in the work of God in the world. Included is a deep-seated mutual affection,[63] and esteeming one another, an honouring that is also to extend beyond the community (cf. Romans 12.10; 13.7; 1 Peter 2.17). Also entailed is an eagerness and fervent spirit, in serving the Lord (Romans 12.11). The costly nature yet ultimately glorious outworking of this service is intimated in the immediately ensuing call to 'Rejoice in hope, be patient in suffering, persevere in prayer' (Romans 12.12; cf. 5.1–5; 8.12–30). Also essential is sharing in 'the needs of the saints' – whether in Rome, Jerusalem (cf. Romans 15.26), or wherever God's people are found – and pursuing hospitality (Romans 12.13). The latter, a powerful expression of God's grace, is intrinsic to the vocation of Israel, the welcoming example of Jesus, and the life and mission of the early Church, particularly in providing for those who are vulnerable and needy.[64] Such is new-creation participation together in the economy of God.

Central to this are the teachings of Jesus, evoked in Paul's ensuing imperative to 'Bless those who persecute you; bless and do not curse them' (Romans 12.14; cf. Matthew 5.44; Luke 6.28).[65] Jesus adds to the Shema, the first and greatest commandment, a second commandment to love

---

[63] Cf. 1 Thessalonians 4.9–12, where loving and supporting one another will have a positive impact on those outside the still fledgling Thessalonian community.

[64] Paul may have in immediate view the need for the 'weak' and the 'strong' in Rome to welcome each other (Romans 14.1—15.13), and even his own intended visit (Romans 15.24, 28).

[65] See M. Thompson 1991, 96–105. Wright 2002, 713, is among those who see at Romans 12.14 a shift from members of 'the Christian community taking care of one another . . . to those who would attack and harm them'. Yet certain shared and/or somewhat open-ended language in both Romans 12.9–13 and 12.14–17 – 'one another' (Romans 12.10, 16) and 'suffering' (Romans 12.12) / 'persecution' (Romans 12.14) – itself might suggest more than a pivoting of perspective, and that there is a dynamic and complex interplay involved, both conceptually and experientially.

one's neighbour (Matthew 22.35–40; Mark 12.28–34; cf. Deuteronomy 6.4–5; Leviticus 19.18), and extends the latter to loving enemies and praying for persecutors (Matthew 5.43–44; cf. Luke 6.27, 'do good to those who hate you'). Thus, while one might postulate a particular local scenario involving persecution,[66] Paul's remarks are broad in background and orientation, and related to the challenges always attending God's gospel and the Church's mission. Likewise the following injunction to 'Rejoice with those who rejoice, weep with those who weep' (Romans 12.15; cf. Sirach 7.34–35; 1 Corinthians 12.26) envisages these ongoing aspects of participation in the kingdom of God.[67]

Paul's further use of *phroneō* language – 'Live in harmony with one another' (Romans 12.16) – which operates expansively, and entails a shared mind of Christ at work in the one body of Christ, may also evoke Jesus' example. Further depth and breadth may be given to this by viewing his accompanying admonition 'do not be haughty . . . do not claim to be wiser than you are' (Romans 12.16), with notable Old Testament antecedents which underscore key thematic elements, including the need to turn away from evil (e.g. Proverbs 3.7; cf. 26.12, 16; Isaiah 5.20–21). Similarly the subsequent injunction not to repay evil with evil,[68] but rather have regard 'for what is noble in the sight of all' (Romans 12.17), may also evoke the similar set of sayings in Proverbs (see Proverbs 3.4; 20.22), and again attests to Paul's concern that the Church's character and conduct contribute to society at large, bringing new-creation life to bear not least in the face of ongoing evil in the world.

While the believers in Rome must faithfully and honourably live out their vocation in the world, a matter Paul includes in his ensuing remarks on the governing authorities (cf. 'honour' at Romans 13.7), he knows that this is not an easy task. His next statement is preceded by a twofold qualification – 'If it is possible, so far as it depends on you' (Romans 12.18) – which anticipates the demands of what is being invoked. The immediately ensuing call to 'live peaceably with all' might evince Jesus' sayings (Mark 9.50; cf. Matthew 5.9). It can, though, be read in relation to the

---

66 Keener 2009, 148–9, considers the possibility of 'a local issue', perhaps related to conflicts associated with Emperor Claudius's edict.

67 Wright 2002, 714, suggests that Romans 12.15–16 is best seen 'not as commands about the internal life of the church', but rather as advice to believers on living 'alongside their pagan neighbors' and seeking 'to establish common ground and to find ways of making friends'.

68 This is akin to Paul's statement at 1 Thessalonians 5.15, in a concluding appeal with a similar collocation of elements and themes (1 Thessalonians 5.12–22), whose content is clearly focused on the believers and whose immediate context also entails wider eschatological matters.

significant and wide-ranging references to peace in Romans, collectively attesting that the 'God of peace' (Romans 15.33; 16.20; cf. 1.7) is at work to effect 'glory and honour and peace for everyone who does good, the Jew first and also the Greek' (Romans 2.10; cf. 5.1; 8.6, 'life and peace').[69] In short, to 'live peaceably with all' is an integral aspect of all that God is accomplishing for the common good in all the world.[70]

At this point Paul uses the intimate and evocative term 'beloved' (Romans 12.19; cf. 1.7; 11.28; 16.5, 8–9).[71] The designation may invite association with 'Beloved' as applied to Jesus at his baptism (Matthew 3.17; Mark 1.11; Luke 3.22) and Transfiguration (Matthew 17.5; Mark 9.7; Luke 9.35), key moments in the divine disclosure and affirmation of his identity and mission. For the beloved who belong to the Beloved, living peaceably with all includes never avenging themselves (Romans 12.19),[72] probably evoking the Levitical instruction and its counterpart 'you shall love your neighbour as yourself' (Leviticus 19.18; cf. Matthew 5.39), including 'the poor and the alien' (Leviticus 19.9–10, 33–34) and proper treatment of others.[73] Wright notes that the root of the verb *ekdikeō* conveys 'the doing of justice, which Paul is not forbidding . . . [but only] doing it freelance, in one's own favor'; namely, 'vengeance'. Rather, they are to 'give place to wrath', most likely meaning 'allow God to do justice', perhaps with Romans 13.4 in view, that is, by means of the governing authorities.[74]

This is immediately underscored by explicit citation of the Old Testament in 12.19–20. The initial 'Vengeance is mine, I will repay' (Romans 12.19; cf. Deuteronomy 32.35) is from the Song of Moses (Deuteronomy 31.30—32.43), which brings to view various pertinent interrelated elements: God's lawsuit and judgement issued through his authorized agent Moses, before all heaven and earth, against an unfaithful and idolatrous Israel (Deuteronomy 32.1–25), yet mindful that God will vindicate his faithful people even as he judges their enemies, resulting in the praise

---

69 Cf. Romans 3.17; 15.13, 33. Again, included may be an anticipation of Paul's concern for the 'weak' and 'strong' at Romans 14.1—15.13 (see 14.17, 19).
70 Cf. Wright 2013a, 1375; Furnish 2005, 77–8; also Swartley 2006, on Paul at pp. 189–253.
71 Paul elsewhere also refers to his churches and co-workers as 'beloved'; for example, in Corinth (1 Corinthians 4.14; 10.14; 15.58; 2 Corinthians 7.1; 12.19) and in relation to Timothy (1 Corinthians 4.17).
72 Wright 2002, 714, notes that this is the third in a sequence: 'Do not curse . . . do not repay anyone . . . never avenge' (at Romans 12.14, 17, 19 respectively), which may support his view of 12.14–21 as something of a broad shift from the community to those beyond, though such wide-ranging injunctions could also apply to any and all.
73 For example: not to defraud, rob, withhold wages, show partiality, slander, profit from, etc. (Leviticus 19.13–18).
74 So Wright 2002, 714.

of all (Deuteronomy 32.26–43). As Moses urges Israel to take to heart these covenantal and life-giving words (Deuteronomy 32.44–47), so Paul has exhorted the believers in Rome to heed a gracious God's gospel and righteousness, entailing salvation and judgement (e.g. Romans 1.16—3.31; 9—11; 14.1—15.13). Judgement is God's prerogative, issued in a manner consonant with his mercy and love. Paul, citing Proverbs 25.21–22, indicates that God's people are to exemplify love by caring for their enemies, attending even to their most basic needs for food and drink.[75] Such loving and mindful action will work its way out according to the will of God (cf. Romans 12.2) in one of at least two ways in relation to one's enemies: (a) their judgement (if grace is rejected) or (b) their shame, precipitating remorse and repentance (if grace is received).[76] Paul closes his comments by reinforcing his initial programmatic statement by insisting on overcoming evil with good (cf. Romans 12.9, 21).

Paul, like Moses before him, issues a divine and authoritative exhortation to the people of God in Rome and beyond, those who are the beneficiaries of God's mercy. They are heirs of faithful Israel, members of the 'one body in Christ', constituted, empowered and gifted by the Spirit. They are to be living sacrifices who, transformed and having the mind of Christ, participate in God's work and will in the world, and are to live faithful and fruitful lives. This is manifest above all in a genuine love that hates evil and upholds the good. It encompasses their discerning, developing, dynamic and peaceable relationships with the faithful, neighbours, even enemies and persecutors and, as we now see, the governing authorities; in short, all people. And in all this God discloses and directs, takes up and transforms, ever-actualizing the newness of life that is intrinsic to the gospel, the Church and the common good.

3 God's governance and the common good (Romans 13.1–7)

Wright's wide-ranging account of Paul's theopolitical vision – and not least its eschatological, ecclesial, ethical and socio-political aspects in relation to the Roman Empire – can only be briefly outlined here, and largely with

---

[75] Notably the wider context of Proverbs 25 instructs discernment in word and deed in relation to a wide range of people; for example, kings (Proverbs 25.1–7) and neighbours (Proverbs 25.8–10, 17–18). Cf. also fools (Proverbs 26.1–11); those wise in their own eyes (26.12, 16; cf. 3.7). For a powerful and political reading of Romans 12—13, with the subversive love of enemies at its centre, see Keesmaat 2007.

[76] Commentators have been divided over (a) and (b). Wright 2002, 715, prefers (b). This reading keeps both options open.

Romans 13 in view.[77] For Paul the death and resurrection of Messiah Jesus had now rescued and renewed a sinful humanity, and also 'radically re-defined the very notions of power, empire, kingdom and lordship',[78] in the form of his remarkable self-giving love, the 'mode' of Jesus' sovereignty.[79] Paul thus modifies Jewish creational monotheism, with its affirmation of good order under divine rule while awaiting the coming age, in two respects. First, it is true that God's people are to embody the gospel by living peaceably with all as good citizens, seeking the public welfare and obeying the divinely ordained governing authorities, and so on, *but* Paul 'balances' this with the all-important reminder that the exile was over and the new day was dawning (Romans 13.12).[80] Second, Paul insists that the overreaching human 'rulers of this [present, evil] age' (cf. 1 Corinthians 2.6–8; Galatians 1.4), themselves bound up with an array of 'powers' and their role thus relativized, had *already* been defeated and judged (cf. Colossians 2.14–15; Romans 13.1–7). Hence, whatever the ruling powers might do in the interim, Jesus already reigns as Lord, as implemented and evident in the holiness, unity and above all love of his people.[81] This itself confronts the rulers and civic life in the ancient world,[82] with the resulting conflict and suffering being a sign both of the final destruction of all pre-tentious rule and of a new world being born.[83]

Viewed from this standpoint Romans 13.1–7 is not a broad affirmation of all human governance or Roman rule in particular, but rather concerns living 'wisely under alien rule',[84] at once supporting a stable and lawful society, while ever mindful that rulers themselves stand under divine judgement.[85] For further particulars at this point we may note Wright's commentary on this passage. He helpfully lists and considers four among

---

[77] Cf. especially Wright 2013a, 279–327; 381–4; 1271–319; and previous essays in Wright 2013b, chs 12, 16 and 27. A recent leading dialogue partner is Barclay 2016, chs 18 and 19, on which see Wright 2013a, 1307–19. Again, references to Wright 2013a aim only to be reasonably representative.

[78] Wright 2013a, 1040; cf. 'the very notion of empire, of "world domination", had itself been deconstructed by the cross and remade, in a quite different form, in the resurrection' (Wright 2013a, 1282).

[79] Cf. Wright 2013a, 1282, 1306.

[80] Wright 2013a, 1298.

[81] Wright 2013a, 1283.

[82] Wright 2013a, 1279, 1283.

[83] Wright 2013a, 1298–9. Paul's position is thus 'much more subtle than either a "pro-Roman" or an "anti-Roman" stance' (Wright 2013a, 1298).

[84] Wright 2013a, 1303.

[85] See the discussion at Wright 2013a, 1302–4. Cf. Horrell 2005, 88, on Romans 13.1–7 as both legitimating and limiting and relativizing the authority of the state; cf. Horrell 2016, 277–83.

many theories as to why this passage is here, what it is saying and implications arising therefrom.[86] In turn: (1) it is 'a general statement about ruling authorities. . . . based on a general belief in the desire of the creator God for order within all societies'; (2) it is a statement on the Roman Empire as (a) 'in some sense God-given', (b) guarding Paul from persecution, and (c) seeking the safety of the Jews and/or Christians in Rome; (3) it signals a belief that newly installed Emperor Nero offers a hopeful time for the early Church; and (4) it states 'something that is now true' resulting from Jesus' death and resurrection and his victory 'over the powers of the world'.[87] Wright regards (4) as mistaken inasmuch as Paul here evidently provides no supporting Christological or gospel-based argument; he notes possible variations of (1) to (3); and delineates his preference for (1): namely, Paul affirms that God wants order and justice in the present world.[88] This fits with similar Old Testament affirmations variously evident in Isaiah, Jeremiah, Daniel and elsewhere;[89] and it shows that Romans 12.14–21 and 13.1–7 dovetail: the former urges love within the Christian community while prohibiting private vengeance, while the latter concerns the Church's life in relation to the wider world which involves allowing God-appointed authorities their proper role in justice and due punishment, even as it also subverts pretentious rule and the emperor's claims to divine honours (cf. Romans 1.16–17; Philippians 2.5–11; 3.19–21).[90] But this does not permit anarchy, or an over-realized eschatology that would set aside all earthly government and public order.

Indeed, 'precisely because Paul is holding out' for the day when creation is fully and finally renewed (Romans 8.1–27) and Jesus' lordship is universally acknowledged (Philippians 2.10–11), it is important that excitable believers must not take matters into their own hands.[91] While the Christians in Rome serve Jesus, Messiah and rightful Lord, 'government qua government is intended by God and should in principle command submission from Christian and non-Christian alike'.[92] Thus Paul, who

---

86 Here it may be acknowledged that in later history Romans 13.1–7 has unfortunately been deployed in support of policies and programmes which it clearly does not endorse.

87 Wright 2002, 716–17, with discussion over pp. 716–20, noting representatives of each position.

88 Wright 2002, 717; at n. 514 referencing Towner 1999.

89 Wright 2002, 718, with references listed including Isaiah 10.5–11; 44.28—45.5; 46.11; Jeremiah 29.4–9; 27.6–11; Daniel 1.2; 2.21, 37–49; 4.25, 32; 5.18.

90 Cf. Wright 2013a, 1303–4.

91 Wright 2013a, 719.

92 Wright 2002, 719. On the pressing issue, not taken up in Romans 13.1–7, regarding what is to be done when 'the governing authorities' and the 'persecutors' (Romans 12.14) are one and the same, Wright 2002, 719–20, usefully considers Paul's engagement with the authorities as

views the present in the light of the future, is not presenting a new situation brought about 'by the eschatological events concerning Jesus' – option (4) above – but insisting that believers obey earthly authorities who themselves stand under ultimate judgement. This does not mean remaining socio-politically inactive until all is renewed. Rather the Church must adopt 'the methods of the Messiah' (cf. Romans 12.14–21) and in the present world which is passing away be a sign of the future full coming of Jesus' kingdom.[93]

Wright's broad theopolitical account and related evaluation of Romans 13.1–7 are very instructive. Perhaps, though, one might allow further room for an even more expansive, dynamic/fluid and constructive approach in relation to the role of the governing authorities. Thus (a) insofar as they participate in the arrogant and oppressive misrule of the present evil age and its pretentious powers, they are being held accountable and divine judgement is their end; (b) yet insofar as they are receptive to God's purposes in Jesus and the Spirit, and the faithful people of God, then in particular times, places and ways, they could have a more positive role to play, extending beyond prohibiting private vengeance and avoiding anarchy by maintaining stability to include various additional constructive contributions to the common life and welfare of society at large. The latter – (b) – would stop short of claiming that in the cross the governing authorities simply as such are redeemed and reconciled; but it allows some space for a potentially responsible role consonant with, even taken up within, the going forth of the gospel in the world. If so, then the 'challenge' of the gospel operates in more a wide-ranging complex of ways than a straight line – a 'collision course' – to conflict and subversion.[94]

Further, the gospel's implementation is not only a matter of 'holding out' and supporting stability. The Church and its mission in the wider world encompasses an ultimate allegiance and the collective embodiment of new-creation life by means of various cruciform and Spirit-shaped gifts and vocations. This entails (a) holding the governing authorities to account, countering even at cost all misrule with self-sacrificial love; yet also, with respect to (b), encouraging and even participating in public life and its governance in ways that recognize that new creation can be

---

depicted in Acts, wherein 'he will submit to their authority, but he will also remind them of their duty (see Acts 16:19–40; 22:22–29; 25.6–12)'.

[93] Wright 2002, 720.

[94] Citation Wright 2013a, 1279. Again, though, insofar as (a) is in view, the subversive impact of the gospel is also in play; Keesmaat, 2007 and 2012, effectively presses this matter in relation to the first-century Roman Empire.

variously represented throughout the whole of reality.[95] This would be mindful of the dangers of an over-realized eschatology, while seeking an appropriately substantive inaugurated eschatology. Such would entail God's future world – a matter of transformed time and also space, a new heaven and earth – inaugurated and operative even now in the Church and society for the common good. Included here is the capacity in Jesus and the Spirit to be the 'one body in Christ' who 'have the mind of Christ'; to participate in newness of life in relation to all believers, neighbours and governing authorities in Spirit-shaped qualitatively different ways; and to be a sign of the kingdom which truly and transformatively mediates God's grace and glory in life-giving and far-reaching ways.

In turning to a brief analysis of Romans 13.1–7, it is a challenge to reconstruct with any precision and assurance the specific historical circumstances which may in part have precipitated Paul's remarks here on believers and the governing authorities.[96] But Paul has just indicated the importance of living honourably and peaceably 'in the sight of all' (Romans 12.17–18; cf. 14.16, 18). And what is clearly evident is that his remarks – directed to 'every person [*pasa psychē*]', suggesting the entirety of each person and of all concerned – continue to arise out of and further develop his theological vision for the new-creation people of God. Indeed, God-grounded and wide-ranging statements are prominent throughout 13.1–7: God has brought into existence, instituted, appointed and operates through governing authorities.[97] This frames and sustains Paul's particular remarks. Taken together they suggest that Paul here has in immediate view the role and responsibilities of the representatives of the governing authorities, operating within the economy of God, who ought to act mindfully as his accountable servants with a view to the good of all, and be afforded respect and honour insofar as this is the case.[98]

---

[95] Cf. Furnish 2005, 83–7; among his conclusions: Paul was mindful of the responsibilities (and risks) entailed in an open, constructive and critical engagement with society, what might be termed an '"interactive" model' (Furnish 2005, 86). Note also Towner 1999, concluding that Romans 13.1–7 and Paul's view of the state functions within the wider missiological outlook of Romans, and involves 'a critical engagement in the existing *politeia*' (Towner 1999, 169).

[96] The strategic location of the church in Rome and/or the origins and ongoing effect of the emperor Claudius's edict might be among various contributing factors. Cf. further Keesmaat 2007; 2012.

[97] Furnish 2005, 81, notes that the underlying theological warrant for Paul's argument in Romans 13.1–7 is that the 'authorities are *God's servants* . . . appointed by God to support the public good', and being subject thereto 'is not incompatible with serving God' to the extent they discharge this responsibility – though provisional in that 'it takes place in the "meanwhile" of this present age'.

[98] Thus the injunction that every person 'be subject' is not a call to submission no matter what.

In this way they should engender no fear in relation 'to good conduct, but to bad' (13.3), with earlier programmatic and thematic instances of the key contrasting terms (cf. Romans 12.9, 17, 21), indicating that Paul has in view the good which conforms to God's will and love, is able to overcome evil, is offered in sacrificial service, and so 'will receive its approval'. Conversely, misconduct contravening God-appointed and duly aligned government will feel the force of its offices, for an aspect of its properly discharged role is to address wrongdoing (Romans 13.4). Thus, as Wright notes, while members of the Christian community must not seek vengeance (12.19), the government should act to uphold order, including punishment of wrongdoers. The stark language and imagery at Romans 13.4–5 – for example 'bear the sword' (cf. Romans 8.35); 'avenger [*ekdikos*]' (cf. *ekdikeō* and *ekdikēsis* at Romans 12.19; LXX Deuteronomy 32.43); and 'wrath' (cf. Romans 12.19)[99] – underscores the fact that citizens, including Christians, are not exempt from properly authorized and discharged law-keeping, justice and punishment. Yet, understood within the wider theological context, this again ought to function according to God's justice, and (only) insofar as this is so, the governing authority is 'God's servant for your good' (Romans 13.4; cf. 13.5).

Being subject to God-appointed authorities is also a function of 'conscience' (Romans 13.5). If Paul's use of this word elsewhere is indicative, positively put it most likely means that which is divinely affirmed in a person's heart, and conformed to and confirmed by the Holy Spirit (Romans 9.1).[100] It can attest to oneself and to others that one's service is well known to God; is characterized by his grace, love and wisdom (2 Corinthians 1.12; 5.11); and so is indicative of new-creation life, including God's reconciliation of the world (2 Corinthians 5.16–21). As such it may afford discernment as to the proper role of the governing authorities as 'God's servants'.[101] A particular and practical instance of this is payment of taxes, an aspect of the authorities' administration (Romans 13.6). And Paul quickly broadens the scope by reference to a series of elements – 'taxes . . . revenue . . . respect . . . honour' (Romans 13.7) – to indicate that believers are to be exemplary citizens in contributing to society at large, giving to

---

[99] Cf. instructive earlier instances regarding 'wrath' at Romans 1.18; 2.5, 8; 3.5; 4.15; 5.9; 9.22 (2x).

[100] Compare those within the Christian community deemed to have weak consciences – e.g. on the matter of eating idol meat (1 Corinthians 8.1–12; 10.23–30; cf. Romans 14.1—15.6) – who are seen as still growing in faith.

[101] Cf. Paul as God's servant (Romans 15.16, 27).

all whatever is due.[102] In this, as in all things, believers are to exercise spiritual discernment, as they affirm and participate in the transforming will and work of God in the world, including governance and the rule of law, the operation and outworking of which is not always or yet fully seen. While the members of Paul's small communities currently may have limited prospect of impact, as the socio-politically charged situation with Philemon and Onesimus illustrates (Philemon), they are called to implement the gospel in all areas of life, mindful of its power to rescue, restore and reconcile.

4 Living together in the love of God (Romans 13.8–10)

Paul's injunction 'Pay to all what is due to them' (at Romans 13.7) is immediately extended and elevated to 'Owe no one anything, except to love one another' (in Romans 13.8). On a basic level, this somewhat ambiguous remark exhorts fulfilment of obligations by ensuring that one is not in arrears in taxes, honour and indeed all that is due. Yet, without excluding such, the ensuing 'except' takes this up into the all-embracing commitment to love one another. Properly understood, such love is only possible insofar as it arises from and is enabled by God's love – and, indeed, his unrepayable grace and mercy (Romans 12.1, 3, 6; cf. 3.24 etc.). In loving one another believers fulfil the law (Romans 13.8, 10). Notably the selective citations of the Ten Commandments – on adultery, murder, stealing and coveting (13.9) – concern Israel's role and relationships in society at large (Exodus 20.13–17; cf. Deuteronomy 5.17–21), and are summed up in the command to love one's neighbour (Romans 13.9; Leviticus 19.18).[103] This love 'does not work evil [*kakon*]';[104] rather it overcomes evil with good, and as such ('therefore') fulfils all that is envisaged in the law, itself fulfilled in a Messiah-Jesus-centred and Spirit-constituted faithful way of life (cf. Romans 3.31; 8.1–11; 10.4; also Galatians 5.7; 6.2). In loving God

---

[102] Again, that this does not mean unequivocal concurrence with every aspect of the governing authorities' policies and procedures may be inferred by correlating Jesus' equivocal and expansive responses to his interlocutors on the matter of 'taxes' (e.g. Luke 20.20–26; cf. Matthew 22.15–22; Mark 12.13–17). In view here are the interrelated issues of image-bearing, authority and allegiance: to whom does the world belong? Similarly, the matter of the Roman-imposed Jerusalem Temple 'tribute' (Matthew 17.24–27).

[103] Cf. Romans 2.17–29, including references to the commandments on stealing and adultery (2.21–22). Note also 'sum up' (*anakephalaioō*) at Ephesians 1.10, regarding the Lord Jesus Christ who disclosed God's will 'as a plan for the fullness of time, to gather up all things in him, things in heaven and things on earth'.

[104] Romans 13.10, author's translation; again, see *kakos* at Romans 12.17, 21; 13.3, 4 (2x), 10; cf. 14.20 and 16.19.

and neighbour the believers are irrevocably committed to his will and work in the world (Romans 12.2), which entails the rescue and renewal of all things.

Conclusion

This essay has engaged and developed, in certain modest respects, aspects of Tom Wright's wide-ranging and significant work on Paul's view of new creation, in relation to a select exegetical and theological reading of Romans 12—13. In this rich and resonant part of Paul's most expansive letter, drawing deeply on the Old Testament and the life and teachings of Jesus, the apostle exhorts the believers in Rome and beyond regarding the outworking of the gospel which has revealed God's righteousness to all. Israel's hope for a new age of mercy and justice has been fulfilled in the death and resurrection of Messiah Jesus and the eschatological outpouring of the Spirit. Indeed thereby newness of life has been actualized and is powerfully at work in the Church and the world. The nature, scope and comprehensiveness of its outworking is yet to be fully seen; but the renewal and transformation – of time, space and matter; on earth as in heaven; of all things under God – is under way. This is even now to be enacted in the 'one body in Christ' in ways that embrace neighbours, enemies, governing authorities and more, all for the common good. Indeed, this entails upholding all that is good – within the community, society and the world at large – thereby overcoming evil. This is to participate in faith, hope and above all love in the new creation.

Bibliography

Barclay, John M. G. (2015). *Paul and the Gift*. Grand Rapids, MI: Eerdmans.
—— (2016). *Pauline Churches and Diaspora Jews*. Grand Rapids, MI: Eerdmans. (Originally published Wissenschaftliche Untersuchungen zum Neuen Testament 275. Tübingen: Mohr Siebeck, 2011.)
Brueggemann, Walter (2010). *Journey to the Common Good*. Louisville, KY: Westminster John Knox.
Cummins, S. A. (2017). 'Paul, Exile, and the Economy of God.' In *Exile: A Conversation with N. T. Wright*, edited by James M. Scott, 217–36. Downers Grove, IL: IVP Academic.
Fowl, Stephen E. (2005). *Philippians*. Two Horizons New Testament Commentary. Grand Rapids, MI: Eerdmans.
Furnish, Victor Paul (2005). 'Uncommon Love and the Common Good: Christians as Citizens in the Letters of Paul.' In *In Search of the Common Good*, edited by Dennis P. McCann and Patrick D. Miller, 58–87. London: T&T Clark.

Heilig, Christoph, J. Thomas Hewitt and Michael F. Bird (2017) (eds). *God and the Faithfulness of Paul: A Critical Examination of the Pauline Theology of N. T. Wright*. Minneapolis, MN: Fortress. (Originally published Wissenschaftliche Untersuchungen zum Neuen Testament 2/413. Tübingen: Mohr Siebeck, 2016.)

Horrell, David G. (2003). 'The Peaceable, Tolerant Community and the Legitimate Role of the State: Ethics and Ethical Dilemmas in Romans 12:1–15:13.' *Review and Expositor* 100: 81–99.

—— (2016 (2005)). *Solidarity and Difference: A Contemporary Reading of Paul's Ethics*. 2nd edition. London: T&T Clark.

Keener, Craig S. (2009). *Romans*. New Covenant Commentary Series. Eugene, OR: Cascade.

—— (2016). *The Mind of the Spirit: Paul's Approach to Transformed Thinking*. Grand Rapids, MI: Baker Academic.

Keesmaat, Sylvia C. (2007). 'If Your Enemy Is Hungry: Love and Subversive Politics in Romans 12–13.' In *Character Ethics and the New Testament: Moral Dimensions of Scripture*, edited by Robert L. Brawley, 141–58. Louisville, KY: Westminster John Knox.

—— (2012). 'Reading Romans in the Capital of the Empire.' In *Reading Paul's Letter to the Romans*, edited by Jerry L. Sumney, 47–64. Atlanta: Society of Biblical Literature.

Longenecker, Richard N. (2011). *Introducing Romans: Critical Issues in Paul's Most Famous Letter*. Grand Rapids, MI: Eerdmans.

Moo, Douglas J. (1996). *The Epistle to the Romans*. New International Commentary on the New Testament. Grand Rapids, MI: Eerdmans.

Oakes, Peter (2009). *Reading Romans in Pompeii: Paul's Letter at Ground Level*. Minneapolis, MN: Fortress.

Seifrid, Mark A. (2007). 'Romans.' In *Commentary on the New Testament Use of the Old Testament*, edited by G. K. Beale and D. A. Carson, 607–94. Grand Rapids, MI: Baker Academic.

Swartley, Willard M. (2006). *Covenant of Peace: The Missing Peace in New Testament Theology and Ethics*. Grand Rapids, MI: Eerdmans.

Thompson, James W. (2011). *Moral Formation according to Paul: The Context and Coherence of Pauline Ethics*. Grand Rapids, MI: Baker Academic.

Thompson, Michael B. (1991). *Clothed with Christ: The Example and Teaching of Jesus in Romans 12.1–15.13*. Journal for the Study of the New Testament Supplement Series 59. Sheffield: Sheffield Academic Press.

Towner, Philip H. (1999). 'Romans 13:1–7 and Paul's Missiological Perspective: A Call to Political Quietism or Transformation?' In *Romans and the People of God: Essays in Honor of Gordon D. Fee on the Occasion of His 65th Birthday*, edited by Sven K. Soderland and N. T. Wright, 149–69. Grand Rapids, MI: Eerdmans.

Trebilco, Paul R. (2017). *Outsider Designations and Boundary Construction in the New Testament: Early Christian Communities and the Formation of Group Identity*. Cambridge: Cambridge University Press.

Wright, N. T. (2002). 'The Letter to the Romans.' In *The New Interpreter's Bible*, Volume X, edited by Leander E. Keck, 393–770. Nashville, TN: Abingdon.

—— (2010). *After You Believe: Why Christian Character Matters* (UK title *Virtue Reborn*). San Francisco, CA: HarperOne / London: SPCK.

—— (2011). *The Kingdom New Testament: A Contemporary Translation*. San Francisco, CA: HarperOne.

—— (2013a). *Paul and the Faithfulness of God*. Christian Origins and the Question of God 4. London: SPCK / Minneapolis, MN: Fortress.

—— (2013b). *Pauline Perspectives: Essays on Paul, 1978–2013*. London: SPCK / Minneapolis, MN: Fortress.

—— (2015). *Paul and His Recent Interpreters: Some Contemporary Debates*. London: SPCK / Minneapolis, MN: Fortress.

—— (2016). *The Paul Debate: Critical Questions for Understanding the Apostle Paul*. London: SPCK. (Originally published Waco, TX: Baylor University Press, 2015.)

—— (2017). 'Yet the Sun Will Rise Again: Reflections on the Exile and Restoration in Second Temple Judaism, Jesus, Paul, and the Church Today.' In *Exile: A Conversation with N. T. Wright*, edited by James M. Scott, 19–80. Downers Grove, IL: IVP Academic.

Narrative cross, apocalyptic resurrection: Ephesians and reading Paul[1]

CAREY C. NEWMAN

Introduction

For the last three decades, N. T. Wright has argued that behind the historical Jesus, the rise of Christianity and the New Testament there stands a singular, coherent and historically pervasive narrative. This singular story, abducted from both biblical and non-biblical texts alike, provides a historical context and a literary lens, both of which work to explain Jesus, Christianity and the New Testament. Already implied by the essays that comprised *Climax of the Covenant*,[2] Wright's hypothesis about Christian origins burst on to the scene in *The New Testament and the People of God*[3] and was subsequently worked out, with exegetical detail, in massive studies of Jesus,[4] the resurrection[5] and more recently Paul.[6] From the first inklings that something was afoot to his latest Schweitzer-like recasting of the history of Pauline scholarship,[7] Wright has remained remarkably consistent.[8]

---

1 Earlier (and quite different) versions of this present article were presented in 2015 at the British New Testament Conference (Edinburgh) and in 2016 at the Society for New Testament Studies (Montreal) – and subsequently published in *Perspectives in Religious Studies*. I want to thank those present on both occasions for their critical interaction. I also wish to thank my Baylor colleagues Mikeal Parsons and Beverly Gaventa as well as my New Testament colleagues Rob Wall and Stephen Fowl, all of whom read and commented upon various iterations of this present article. I also must thank the editors of both *Perspectives in Religious Studies* and SPCK for allowing different versions of this article to appear almost simultaneously. Lastly, I wish to thank, publicly, Tom Wright – for his scholarship, yes; his love of the Church, indeed; but mainly for his abiding friendship over the years. While I do disagree with him here and there, I do so knowing that I am but one good conversation with him (and single malt) away from being proved wrong.
2 Wright 1991, esp. 18–40.
3 Wright 1992.
4 Wright 1996.
5 Wright 2003.
6 Wright 2003.
7 Wright 2015.
8 For my take on Wright's work along the way, see Newman 1998, 121–44; 1999, 281–8; 2005, 228–33.

Wright argues that the historical Jesus and rise of Christianity are both best understood within – even as a revision of – God's covenant with Israel. Wright insists that this one story, cobbled together out of key texts, about one people, and their one God, finds resolution in the deeds of the one person, Jesus. Jesus, as prophet, calls Israel to be true Israel. Jesus, as Messiah, lives out Israel's true destiny for, and in the place of, Israel. Jesus, as Lord, is God's own return from exile to Zion to establish the kingdom for ever. Paul, as well as all of early Christianity, in the light of the death and resurrection of Jesus, redefines election, covenant and the Spirit, but always inside the narrative constraints provided by God's story with Israel. In the end, the surprising way that God worked his purposes for Israel in and through Jesus is expanded to reimagine God, God's people and God's purposes for the world.

Wright's reading places a premium on continuity – narrative continuity, covenantal continuity, cosmic continuity – and necessarily opposes any construal that privileges discontinuity. Apocalyptic, in any of its myriad forms, is the great enemy.[9] Apocalyptic hinges on disruption. Apocalyptic emphasizes God's unexpected and surprising invasion of the world in the death and resurrection of Jesus. Apocalyptic places Jesus on a cosmic stage to craft a different set of fundamental claims, claims about how God wages war with the powers in and through Jesus Christ. Wright must tame this wild apocalyptic. Indeed, for Wright, apocalyptic is and must only be just a way to say that God's long covenantal story with Israel has reached its zenith. Narrative must make Jesus as Israel's Messiah the prime meridian against which all else is measured. Narrative reads new creation as new exodus – Jesus' death and resurrection are the climactic events within Israel's pre-existing story. Apocalyptic is binary, slicing time and cosmos in half. Apocalyptic reads new creation as new creation, a completely new state of affairs ushered in by the cross, a sure sign of destruction of all that has come before. Revelation is not just new information (however surprising) about a key moment in an ongoing story; apocalyptic underscores revelation as new information about brand-new events – God's invasion of the human world and God's consequent engagement with the eschatological, cosmic powers. Narrative isolates Israel's failed vocation as the central problem, whereas the apocalyptic identifies the cosmic powers to which humans, and the cosmos, are enslaved. Narrative stresses incarnation (how Israel's God was present and acting in Jesus), while apocalyptic

---

9 Wright's consistent rejection of apocalyptic is everywhere. But, above all, see Wright 1992, 280–338; 2015, 135–220.

features the resurrection as the decisive moment (how God defeats the powers through the Lord). Narrative explains Jesus inside God's covenant with Israel, while apocalyptic does so inside the cosmos. Narrative preaches good news about a God who has brought Israel's covenant to its culmination, while apocalyptic preaches good news about a God who has brought the world to a dramatic new beginning.

Romans and Galatians have been the chief textual battlegrounds for establishing narrative and apocalyptic readings. A narrative reading turns to Romans, with its vast epic expanse and its detailed discussions of Israel, to gain a bit of narrative leverage on Galatians.[10] An apocalyptic reading begins with Galatians to highlight the sharp, apocalyptic features of Romans.[11] By sidestepping the Romans–Galatians tug of war, the question of exactly how Paul might have been heard in the earliest decades of Christianity – and which Paul was received, the apocalyptic or the narrative – is an equally important question. And here, a letter like Ephesians proves fruitful.[12] Reading the letter of Ephesians as the first chapter in the reception history of Paul – particularly how the covenant and cosmic, how narrative and apocalyptic, might figure and fund the theological world of Ephesians – not only aids in understanding Ephesians *qua* Ephesians, but may well, inadvertently, cast some much-needed light on Paul and how to read him. The door of using Ephesians to read Paul – and thus Romans and Galatians – is one Wright himself opened, as he not only views Ephesians as authentically Paul, but also claims that Ephesians is quintessentially Paul.[13]

Apocalyptic Ephesians

Ephesians depicts a wild, unseen, untamed – and decidedly unsafe – world. Chaos reigns supreme. A host of demonic beings, a rogues' gallery of 'rulers', 'authorities', 'powers', 'lords', 'names', 'cosmic lords' and 'spirits',

---

10 Wright began his academic work with an Oxford thesis under G. B. Caird on Romans. One might argue that Wright has never left Romans, nor Caird's view of language, which Wright has baptized for his own use. See Caird 1980.

11 Above all, Wright contests the reading of J. Louis Martyn, which the latter laid out programmatically in Martyn 1997.

12 A point made by Bockmuehl 2014, 59–70.

13 Wright 2013, 1514–15. Wright's only extended reading of Ephesians occurs within a discussion of Paul's theology (Wright 2013, 728–33) and uses Romans 8 to gain leverage on the cosmic, temporal and mystical arc of Ephesians. Wright can thus say Ephesians is uber-Paul only by reading Ephesians via Romans.

roam the heavens (1.21; 2.2; 3.10; 6.11).[14] These are dark lords,[15] wholly ethereal, occupying the space between earth and heaven (2.2, 6.12), and should be clearly distinguished from political potentates and planetary spheres.[16] The powers are not, Ephesians emphatically declares (6.12, ESV), 'flesh and blood'.[17] The powers rule from the four corners of the universe,[18] controlling both time and space (1.10, 21; 2.2, 7; 3.10–11, 21; 4.8; 6.12) – *this* is their world; *this* is their age.[19] In the absence of any rival, the powers command the skies above, the earth and the foul underworld.[20] A single Aeon sits atop the pyramid of archons (2.2).[21] Evil has a name and evil has a face, the devil (4.27; 6.11).

Evil has concocted a diabolical master plan (4.14; 6.11). Through secret teaching and privileged teachers, Evil's methodical calculus holds humanity transfixed.[22] If they be sovereigns of the skies, then the powers equally govern the human heart, twisting it upon itself (3.2). They bend the arc of human life towards their own corrupt ends (2.2). The powers count upon debased human character and then prey upon that very weakness for their own pleasure (2.3). The powers corrupt humans from the inside out (4.18), alter human behaviour (4.17) and blind human judgement (4.18). The downward plunge in a corrosive and inevitable regress results in an inability to respond: humans are in full surrender to the powers and deformation (4.19). Utterly trapped and unable to respond (2.1, 5), humans suffer a final fate determined by the powers: they are, by nature, children of wrath (2.3). Ephesians soberly portrays human inadequacy and human corruption as both stemming from human captivity, and the abductors as determining an ominous human destiny.

---

[14] Cf. Colossians 1.16; 2.10, 15; Romans 8.38–39; 1 Corinthians 3.22; 15.24–25. Ephesians emphasizes 'all' rule and 'every' name. The *tais archais kai tais exousiais* should be read as shorthand for a complete listing.

[15] Cf. Carr 1981.

[16] Cf. Wink 1984.

[17] So Arnold 1989. Arnold effectively relates the power language of Ephesians to Asia Minor's pervasive practice of magic. Cf. Fowl 2012, 61, who does not limit the referent to spiritual beings. (Unless otherwise noted, Bible quotations in this chapter are taken from the RSV.)

[18] I.e. see Schnackenburg 1991, 78.

[19] The strategic use of the near demonstrative in the genitive is telling.

[20] Philippians 2.10; Revelation 5.3. Ephesians, like Paul and the Apocalypse, envisages a three-level cosmos.

[21] Schnackenburg 1991, 91; Fowl 2012, 69; cf. 2 Corinthians 4.4. On *ton aiōna tou kosmou toutou* as a reference to a deity, and not one to time, see the careful weighing of the evidence by Lincoln 1990, 94.

[22] Cf. 2 Corinthians 11.3. See Lincoln 1990, 258–9.

Ephesians marries its sombre cosmological and anthropological assessment to a deep yearning (1.16) for its readers to know the supremacy of God's raw power (1.19). This power, underwritten by God's own relentless capacity (1.19), invades the world in the resurrection of Jesus, confronting and vanquishing any and all that have dared to oppose God (1.20). Might against might. Might over might. Jesus' exaltation places him above all rule, authority, power and lords, and each and every name being called upon, not only in this age but also in the age to come (1.21).

The Ascension of Jesus throws open wide heaven's doors, providing liberation and spiritual empowerment for the humans Evil has held hostage (4.7–11). Jesus' Ascension also turns the tables on humanity's demonic oppressors, who find themselves now the ones forcibly plundered (4.8). These heavenly events link to earthly ones – and even to affairs of the abyss. The death of Jesus equally opens a door to the underworld, through which he himself passes in his *descensus ad Inferos.*[23]

The effects of descent and ascent then ripple outwards; they form the first link in a larger chain of cosmic events. In his despoiling of Evil and his empowering of humanity, Jesus fills the universe (4.10).[24] In Jesus, God gains a purchase on the entire cosmos. Evil's opposition mandated the ultimate subjection of the 'all things'. Everything – the entire cosmos,

---

23 Romans 10.6; 1 Peter 3.18–20; 4.6 (cf. 1 Corinthians 15.6); Ign. *Magn.* 9.2–3; Pol. *Phil.* 1.2; Melito, *Pasch.* 102; Irenaeus, *Haer.* 1.27.2; 4.27.2; 5.31.1; 5.33.1; Tertullian, *An.* 55.2; *Ep. Apos.* 27; *Odes of Solomon* 17.9; 24.5; 42.10–15; Justin, *Dial.* 72.4; Chrysostom, *Hom. Eph.* 11; Jerome, *Comm. Eph.* 2. Christ's descent into hell first appears in a creedal formula in 359 CE. However, its presence there should be viewed as the endpoint, not the beginning, of the Church's teaching about Christ's descent into hell. Decisive is: (1) the Church's early near-univocal interpretation of 1 Peter 3 and 4 and Ephesians 4 as descent into hell – on the assumption that the history of reception of a text has something to say about the text's meaning – as is witnessed by the addition of *prōton* in the ms. tradition (ℵᶜ B C* Dᶜ K P ψ 81 104 181 326 330 426); (2) the prevalence of ancient fascination about descents into the underworld (see Bauckham 1998, 1–48) as well as Jewish fascination (see Himmelfarb 1983) and that *katabasis* is best understood as movement from earth to the underworld (and not from heaven to earth); (3) the fact there was on the ground (!) evidence for the ritual practice of descending into the earth in the very region in which Ephesians probably first circulated (see Kreitzer 1998, 381–93). The interpretation of Psalm 68 was guided by the memory of the actual events of Jesus – life, death and resurrection. The 'on the third day' portion of the earliest confessions gave rise to understanding death as descent. Paul himself seems to indicate some intermediate status for some in the netherworld. If there is no resurrection (1 Corinthians 15.18) then there would be no need to baptize on behalf of the dead (1 Corinthians 15.29). On the history of interpretation of Ephesians 4, see Harris 1996; Bales 2010, 84–100; Ehorn 2013, 96–120.

24 Schnackenburg 1991, 179, links filling with both ascending and taking captive and thus another reference to subjugation, though he notes the connections to 4.11. Cf. 1 Corinthians 15.28.

inclusive of the powers, be they in heaven or on the earth[25] – stands in need of cosmic reconciliation, and thus the entire cosmos faces a final answer before God and in Christ (1.10). Cosmic scores demand settlement, and a Christological accounting will be rendered.[26]

Jesus' resurrection and exaltation splits time in half. The invasion of God in Jesus divides the present age from the one coming. The incursion of God's power in the resurrection correspondingly halves the biography of the faithful as those who 'once' belonged to evil but are 'now' in the possession of Jesus (2.3, 11, 13; 5.8). The resurrection equally bifurcates knowledge of God and God's purposes into a dramatic before and after. Revelation – previously concealed from others, a mystery safely tucked away – has now been decisively and purposefully disclosed (3.5, 9–10).

Apprehension of the hidden-but-now-revealed mystery of God constitutes salvation. Special knowledge, singularly revealed, results in unique comprehension. The possibility of abundant wisdom has now overflowed heaven's borders (1.9). The mystery of God's will has finally been made known (1.10). These gospel events have left nothing to chance or conjecture. God has revealed the comprehensive plan for this anarchic world (1.10; 3.9). God has also gifted humanity with a spiritual aptitude for understanding this deep mystery (1.17). The riddle of human vocation thus finds resolution in human perception of God's plan (1.18), and the initial experiences of salvation launch humans into an ever-deepening process of perception (1.19; 3.19). The faithful disciples are urged onwards towards a full comprehension of the foursquare cosmic power of God (3.18) – a comprehension that, ironically, mirrors the powers that have held tight their grip on the four corners of the universe.[27]

The repetition of intense mystical experiences triggers the process of growth in apprehension. Ephesians flagrantly mixes metaphors to describe what happens when humans achieve progress in their knowledge of God in Christ. The threefold comprehension of God's mystery (3.18–19) occurs through the transformation of the human heart (3.18).[28] Symbols of mystical experience – changes from blindness to sightedness, from darkness to

---

[25] On the use of Psalms 8 and 110 in early Christology, see Hengel 1995, 119–226. Because Psalms 8 and 110 were both royal and cosmic they were eminently attractive for unpacking the apocalyptic implications of Jesus' resurrection.

[26] Philippians 2.10–11.

[27] The four powers mentioned in 3.18 parallel those of 1.21. See Dahl 2000c, who concludes that the rhetorical form of 3.18 works to confirm that all readers/followers were able to understand the revealed mystery in Christ (and that it was not an elitist knowledge, only for the privileged few).

[28] Cf. 2 Corinthians 4.4.

light[29] – interweave with compacted and fused biomorphic symbols (eyes and heart) in a valiant attempt to describe the indescribable.[30] Christian mystical progress is also measured by the anamnesis of the Jesus-story's key moments of cosmic reversal (1.20–22). But memory elides to experience in anamnesis: believers are said to be joined to, and with, and to participate in, mystically, the central biography of Jesus (2.5–6). God and Jesus are not the only ones who wage war on the powers. Believers, too, must enter the fray. The Christian march to maturity occurs when, again in the language of mystical transformation, believers are commanded to clothe themselves in the full armour of God. The elaborate and detailed instructions of preparation bespeak the required mystical praxis for engagement (6.13–17).

As opposed to sociomorphic root metaphors – language exclusively used to mark the initial change in a relationship (e.g. enemy to friend, slave to free, guilty to justified, estranged to reconciled) – Ephesians deploys a panoply of physiomorphic symbols to describe the ongoing life of the believer.[31] In Ephesians the physiomorphic register (see Table 1) includes: changes in *appearance* (in which development in the believer's life is described as taking off old clothes and putting on new ones; as changes in colour from darkness to light; as washing that removes dirt and makes the believer clean; and as growing or becoming stronger); *incorporative* transformations (in which believers are said to belong to and become a part of Christ); changes in *physical position* (in which Christian progress is measured by standing up from sitting or lying down); and inner, *biomorphic* transformations (in which the disciple's forward march is marked by Christ's securing and filling).

Ephesians invokes an apocalyptic world, one in which God has dramatically and decisively invaded via Christ, split time into two and actively engaged in war with the powers. The powers' previously uncontested rule led to human entrapment, deformation and judgement. God's rending of the powers rescues and transforms humans, launches them on a journey of renewal, and effects cosmic reconciliation. Humans experience salvation through an initial apprehension of a mystery and through repeated

---

29 See Segal 1990, 58–71, for a discussion of the early Christian appropriation of Second Temple Jewish mystical vocabulary.
30 In this sense, all mystical experience resorts to a language of approximation to give voice to the unutterable. See Tabor 1986.
31 Theissen 1974, 282–404; see also the discussions of Theissen in Beker 1980, 256–60; Meeks 1983, 183–9; Newman 1991, 213–16.

Table 1 Physiomorphic metaphors used in Ephesians to represent changes in a believer's life

put off/put on	4.22, 24, 25; 6.13
darkness/light	1.8; 5.1, 8, 14
dirty/clean	5.26
isolated/unified	2.5–6; 3.17; 5.7, 11
weakness/strength	3.16; 4.23; 6.10
decay/growth	2.10; 3.17; 4.15
asleep/awake	5.14
sitting/standing	5.14; 6.13
empty/full	3.19; 5.18
loose/secure	1.13; 4.30

mystical transformations that lead humans into a deeper understanding of God's purposes.[32]

Ephesians is *explicitly* apocalyptic – by any measure, by any definition.[33] Apocalyptic infuses Ephesians, and Ephesians channels apocalyptic. Ephesians unfolds its apocalyptic drama on a cosmic stage.

Covenant Ephesians

No figure proves more central to the long arc of Israel's story than does Abraham, and no text more central than Genesis 12.1–3. There, Abraham answers Adam and prefigures Israel.[34] The Janus-like pivot of Genesis 12 – looking backward to the commands given to Adam, looking forward

---

[32] See Fowl 2012, 23–4, for a similar summary.

[33] Ephesians as apocalyptic is grounded in the actual text of Ephesians and is not simply 'arm waving' or an 'untethered balloon', a free-floating phantasm or some knee-jerk reaction to nineteenth-century ideology, as Wright complains is so often the case (see, e.g., Wright 2015, 137–44). Indeed, the determined efforts to define apocalyptic only as, and thus by, a literary genre, a genre defined and governed by just one sterling and pristine exemplar (like *4 Ezra* or *2 Baruch*) misses the mark. Apocalyptic is a literary genre (apocalypse), but it is also a social movement with its own thought-world (apocalypticism), as well as a kind of eschatology (apocalyptic eschatology). See, above all, Hanson 1976, 28–34. Ephesians is certainly not an apocalypse. But Ephesians does perform an apocalyptic eschatology. Up for debate is whether Ephesians belongs to and reflects an apocalyptic community. The profile of Ephesians rehearsed above does lend support to a coherent, distinct apocalyptic ideology, one featuring a dense and calculated use of cosmic, binary, mystical, transformative and spatial language to describe the disruptive and non-iterative power of the death and resurrection of Jesus.

[34] Wright 1991, 18–40.

to Israel's chequered history as God's people – shapes the plot of a grand narrative.[35] It is not insignificant, then, that Ephesians 1.3 echoes Genesis 12.1–3. This literary echo of Genesis 12.1–3 at Ephesians 1.3, in turn, reveals an *implicit* narrative grammar in play in Ephesians – one, quite possibly, in mortal conflict with apocalyptic. Ephesians 1.3 pounds out its own distinctive, lyrical rhetoric amid considerable sub- and meta-textual clatter:[36]

> Blessed [be] the God and Father of our Lord Jesus Christ,
> > Who has blessed us
> > > with all spiritual blessings
> > > in the heavens
> > > in Christ.

Even a translation successfully (re)captures the rhythm and energy of this calculated bit of Hellenistic rhetoric. The strategic use of three cognate forms in the same sentence (*paronomasia*), each with a slightly different shade of meaning (*antanaclasis*), creates freighted semantic tension.

The most powerful rhetorical evocations, though, are reserved for those who have scriptural ears. The elevated diction of 1.3 beckons to a canonical mate (Genesis 12.1–3 LXX):

> And I will make you a great nation
> and I will bless you
> and I will make your name great
> and you shall be a blessing
> and I will bless those that bless you
> and who curse you shall be cursed
> and all the peoples of the earth shall be blessed in you.

Nowhere else in the Greek Bible do the cognates of 'bless' occur in such close proximity, let alone in a singular construction, as they do in Genesis

---

35 Rad 1962, 161–5. Westermann 1985, 146, notes the links and the 'rhythmic' character of Genesis 12, both of which are mirrored in Ephesians 1.3.

36 Dahl 2000b. Ironically, this *short* verse, a construction fraught with internal semantic ambiguity largely due to its overly economical syntax, begins one notoriously *long* Greek sentence – a near-monstrous composition that lumbers along for some 11 verses and nearly 200 words. While similar in *form* and *content* to the openings of Jewish 'benedictions', Ephesians 1.3 *functions* far more like a Pauline 'thanksgiving'. That is, verse 3 saliently previews the contents of vv. 4–14, of chs 1—3, and even of all Ephesians. Whether or not a formal hymn or a baptismal catechesis underlies 1.3–14 – as is deeply suspected – Ephesians 1.3 clearly points backward to Jewish liturgical forms, sideways to the *Hodayot* of Qumran, and forward to the rabbinical 18 Benedictions and the prayers of Merkavah mysticism. When decrypted, Ephesians 1.3 unfolds a virtual chorus of traditions.

12. Just this bit of lexical rhetoric fuses together Genesis 12 and Ephesians 1.3 in the creation of a new figure.

An *inclusio* to Ephesians 1.3, equally echoing Genesis 12, occurs at the end of the passage (1.13–14) and also ties text to text. The identification of the Spirit as the one of 'promise' and as the down payment of the inheritance not only creates narrative time (from promise to inauguration to consummation) but specifically defines the Spirit as the blessing of Abraham now realized in Christ. A second *inclusio* occurs at the end of the section (3.15). The God to whom believers now liturgically bow is none other than the canonical *pater familias* of the entire earth. Ephesians 3.15 links to Ephesians 1.3 and to Genesis 12.3, creating a web of intertextuality and narrative.

Ephesians 1 capitalizes upon the narrative theology unleashed by Genesis 12.[37] Verse 3 confidently identifies God as the one who has blessed us. This declaration divulges a theological grammar that bears a deep structural affinity to the story as conceived by Genesis 12: God promised to bless the world through Abraham; God *has* blessed the world through Christ.

Ephesians finesses the LXX's future passive 'shall be blessed' into the aorist active 'has blessed'. The shift in verb tense suggests that the blessings promised to Abraham (and his descendants) have been decisively realized in and through Jesus Christ. The promise to Abraham becomes historicized and concrete in Christian experience, a process of historicizing that had already begun in Genesis 12.[38] The echo does far more than just whisper that *a new and critical moment has been reached in the long arc of God's purposes.*

In distinction from Genesis 12, the verb's object is in the first person (rather than the third). The readers (and author/s) of Ephesians, whoever they are, are identified as the people of God. While the pronoun only hints at the fact that the boundary lines of the faithful community have been redrawn, it does openly revel in a very charismatic voice – *we* (the author and readers) are the chosen people of promise, the ones through whom God's purposes will be accomplished. Thus, *the echo effect plots the readers into a larger scriptural narrative of Israel.*

Most scandalously, Jesus replaces Abraham as God's chief protagonist. Jesus is arrayed in the narrative horizon stretching from Adam to Israel

---

[37] On the abiding theological influence of Genesis 12, see Wolff 1982, 41–66.

[38] Westermann 1982, 105, notes how the process of historicizing the blessing was begun by Genesis 12.1–3 itself. That is, already in Genesis 12 there is a particularizing of the transcendent discovered in Genesis 1—11. Ephesians 1.3, likewise, begins the process of wrestling between the particular and the universal, the covenantal and the cosmic.

through Abraham. The echo positions Jesus as *the* agent through whom God has, at long last, fashioned a people destined to do God's bidding. In short, *the blending of Genesis 12 and Ephesians 1 identifies Jesus as the true heir of Abraham and the progenitor of God's people.* Corroboration of this echo, and the echo's specific metaleptic effects, can be gauged in the letter itself. Hearing the implicit echo of Genesis 12 at Ephesians 1 explains the repeated use of covenantal language. The very first bit of exegesis Ephesians places on offer (1.4) defines blessing (1.3) as election. There is no more signal way to invoke the covenant God forged with Israel than the language of choosing, as Deuteronomy 7 makes abundantly clear (7.6–8, 13, 14 LXX). Ephesians, analogously to the way Deuteronomy 7 unpacks the blessing of Abraham in Genesis 12,[39] selects the choicest of Israel's covenantal imagery for its expansive commentary on the blessing of 1.3 in 4.4–14 – 'election', 'choice', 'love', 'prospering', 'redemption' and 'purpose'. The echo effect of Ephesians 1.4 telescopes the complex, even tragic, narrative of God's election of Israel as covenant partner, as promised to Abraham (Genesis 12.1–3) and his progeny, right on to Jesus – and in doing so, as Deuteronomy 7 foreshadows, the least has become the greatest, the one has gained a mighty influence over the many.

Hearing the echo of Genesis 12.1–3 at Ephesians 1.3 also explains what has long been a syntactic curiosity. The precise nuance of 'in Christ'/'in him' in 1.3–14 (in specific), and in Ephesians (in general), has been suspected of departing from Paul. However, once it is recognized that Ephesians 1.3 is in the narrative grip of Genesis 12.3, the instrumental shades of 'in Christ' in Ephesians become understandable, even mandatory: Ephesians is simply playing out the narrative implications inherent in Genesis 12.3.[40] It was *by* Abraham, and now *by* Jesus, that God chose to bless. *'In Christ' demonstrates that Jesus, like Abraham before him, is God's chief protagonist.* But no passage bathes in the covenant arc of Genesis 12 like Ephesians 2.11–22. What was implicit in Ephesians 1.3, and 1.4–14, now bubbles up explicitly. Readers are there commanded to remember (2.11) – not only to recall Christian catechesis about the apocalyptic incursion of God in Christ, but, specifically, to array that incursion within Israel's storied covenantal relationship with God.

Ephesians pushes its readers to reject an imposed biography of contested social existence as the uncircumcised (2.11). For Ephesians this

---

39 Fowl 2012, 39.
40 See Macaskill 2014, though his insistence on eradicating all mystical aspects of Ephesians in favour of collapsing all incorporative language into covenant misses completely the apocalyptic character of the letter and, thus, the way 'in Christ' signals mystical transformation.

kind of law observance, and the social labelling and demarcations that it entails, cannot hold. Instead, Ephesians offers a narrative identity. Christian remembrance is the specific recollection that the readers lived lives that were deprived of a messianic future, alienated from the body politic of Israel, estranged from the covenants, hopeless and godless. Encoded symbols that recall the full sweep of Israel's story – monotheism, election, law, covenant, kingship and promise – these monikers effect a 'nationification' of the readers. The readers' past has become the past of the nations of Genesis 12 – a scriptural past, a covenantal past.[41]

But, equally, Israel's future has become their future. Conversion means the readers are no longer strangers. The death of Jesus has closed the fissure between the nations and God's people. The readers are now compatriots. The readers are now the household of God.

Ephesians does not push its Gentile readers to first be circumcised, law-observant Jews in order to become Christians. Instead, Ephesians requires that its readers learn to narrate their past and their future as part of God's covenant with Israel[42] – they were once the nations, standing outside the commonwealth of God's covenant partner, Israel; but now, the readers are covenant partners with God – they *are* Israel. The readers' biography – past and future, from 'nationification' to 'Israelification' – retraces the arc first laid down by Genesis 12.1–3 and its successor texts.

The *many* covenants[43] are thus realized in, and as, the *one* promise (2.12). Israel's single covenant narrative inevitably works towards Christ.

One body and one Spirit
      Just as also you were called by one hope of your calling
One Lord, one faith, one baptism
One God and Father of us all
      The one above all, through all, and in all.[44]

Monotheism and election coalesce in Christology.[45] One Lord means

---

[41] It is highly ironic that what is denied with respect to covenant in 2.11–22 is often embraced at 1.3 (i.e. the Christological shape of election – Christ's past has become the believer's past, and Christ's future has become the believer's future). Ephesians 2 makes exactly the same incorporative move made in Ephesians 1.

[42] See, especially, Fowl 2008, 22–40.

[43] Cf. Romans 9.4. The oscillation between the one and the many, in particular the plural covenants, should not be construed as evidence that Paul was not a covenantal theologian.

[44] Ephesians 4.4–6 (author's translation).

[45] For Wright, the 'Israelification' of Jesus as seen in the Gospels is followed by the 'Messiahification' of the Lord in Paul. Apocalyptic for Wright, then, turns (and must turn!) into just the heightened (even ultimate) way of saying that the covenantal story had reached

one God, and one God means one people. If the Christian gospel is anything for Ephesians it is the *one* story of how the *one* God achieved *one*
people through the *one* Lord – in fulfilment of God's covenant promise
to Abraham. Equally scandalous is the fact that there is just one faith.
Though commonly shared, the faith is decidedly specific.[46] Ephesians here
privileges just one particular telling of the covenant story and, in so doing,
is practising far more than mere scriptural exegesis.[47] The covenant story
Ephesians tells is not just one story among many rivals. It is *the* single
covenant story of Abraham and Israel. Radical Christological monotheism
insists upon a singular faith. One God, One Lord means one, and only
one, faith.

Apocalyptic, alone, is not enough. Ephesians folds God's surprising
incursion into the cosmos in Christ into God's dealings with Israel, a
rewriting that could not have been articulated prior to Christ but one
which must be articulated after Christ.[48] Ephesians mixes apocalyptic
and narrative, and narrative and apocalyptic. What is missed in this
jumble of narrative and apocalyptic is the way that Ephesians privileges
apocalyptic. Ephesians, as the first reader of Paul, hears both narrative and
apocalyptic, but also accords apocalyptic a special power.

Apocalypticizing covenant

Ephesians' penchant for apocalypticizing covenant comes early. It is not
just election; it is election 'before the foundation of the world' (1.4). The
historical, the particular, the covenantal – Ephesians quickly sweeps these
away to the cosmic. That which works inclusion as God's covenant people
is none other than the very power which causes the cosmic 'all things'
to bend to God's will (1.11). The particular again yields to the cosmic.
Ephesians thus hints at its apocalyptic preference. But it is at the very
moment when Ephesians most explicitly employs a covenant theology

---

its denouement. As I will indicate below, while Messiah does assign significance to the cross,
it is the resurrection that transforms that (i.e. the cross and Jesus as a crucified messiah) into
gospel. Or, put differently, Messiah does not figure Lord; Lord transforms Messiah.

46 Harnack 1962, 364–90, esp. 366–9.
47 Cf. Watson 2013, 102–18. While Watson's insistence that Paul was a scriptural theologian,
and not a covenantal one, is a toss-up for interpreting the apostle, his assertion will hardly
hold for Ephesians. Ephesians is indeed covenantal (as is Paul). On this point, I side with
Wright against Watson.
48 I owe this sentence to Stephen Fowl.

(2.11–13, 19–22) that Ephesians engages in a strategic reframing of covenant with apocalyptic (2.14–18).[49]

The body, blood and cross of Christ (1.13, 14, 16) performed apocalyptic work by annihilating (1.14, 15, 16) all that kept humanity apart from each other and God. The body, blood and cross of Christ also did the apocalyptic work of forging a new people (1.14, 16). This is not mere social mediation. Ephesians declares that in Christ God has created, out of the two, Jews and Gentiles, the one new human. This *anthrōpos* is a brand-new creation.[50]

Remarkably absent is any direct *analogy* between this one new *anthrōpos* and Adam that emphasizes similarity. Nor is there a typological *contrast* drawn in Ephesians between this new *anthrōpos* and Adam. Neither is there any reflection in Ephesians on how this new *anthrōpos* is the *restitution* of what was lost in Adam. Neither does Ephesians claim that this second *anthrōpos surpasses* Adam, or is a *transformation* of Adam. Most importantly Ephesians does not claim that this *anthrōpos* is somehow the narrative *culmination* of Adam.[51] Indeed, Ephesians, in direct contrast to Paul in Romans 5 and 1 Corinthians 15, is absolutely mum on the *anthrōpos*–Adam relationship. For Ephesians, Sin and Death as the problems and the powers, introduced by Adam, are replaced by mystery and unity: humanity was lacking the revelation of mystery, and the revelation of mystery is how God is making a new creation in and out of the cosmos.[52] What Ephesians does claim is that there is a decisive, new act of God – one unanticipated and disjunctive with what has come before – that creates the new human. In Christ, Jews and Gentiles have become something entirely new, a third people.[53]

---

[49] Sanders 1965, 214–32, especially 216–18, points out that the composition of 2.14–18 probably preceded that of Ephesians.

[50] Käsemann 1958, 518; Schlier 1957, 134–6, esp. 36. One need not resort to some pre-Christian Gnostic myth to see that the *anthrōpos* here is independent of an Adam–Christ parallel.

[51] I here depend on the typology of possible relationships among protology, history and eschatology as outlined by Dahl 1956, 422–43.

[52] Keck (2015, 1–18) adroitly observes that Christology is a kind of grammar which 'permits a variety of things to be expressed concerning Jesus' identity and significance' and that 'Christological correlations tend to obey the law of parsimony. That is, generally speaking, Christology and soteriology/anthropology are not wasted on each other, because the understanding of Jesus' identity and significance should not exceed what is required to resolve the human dilemma' (4–5). I think that Ephesians (on the one hand) and Romans and Galatians (on the other) share the same Christological grammar but that this grammar has been put to different ends, attempting to solve different problems (unity for Ephesians, Sin and Death for Paul).

[53] Bousset 2013 (1913), 367–8.

Covenant has disappeared in the description of Christ as the *anthrōpos*. Nor can a covenant theology account for the peculiar cosmic description of the Church in 1.23 as Christ's body, which is 'the fullness of [the] all things' (author's translation). If Ephesians 1.10 reveals the universal mystery of the summing up of all cosmic things in Christ, then Ephesians 3.10 assigns the new *anthrōpos*, the community of Jews and Gentiles unified in Christ, an equally new vocation. Were Ephesians slavishly following the script of covenant narrative, then the Church would enjoy the task of preaching the good news of resurrection to the *nations*. Instead, the Church's task is to make God's wisdom known to the powers and authorities in the heavenly places. The Church, as the embodied cosmic *anthrōpos*, is tasked with apocalyptic work.

Ephesians reframes the narrative teleology of an Abrahamic covenant with cosmic apocalyptic. Ephesians does not rest its vision of the future upon the images of a return of Yahweh to Zion, Israel's return from exile, or the ingathering of the nations to Jerusalem. The apocalyptic of Ephesians pushes beyond a covenant theology. In Ephesians, God seeks a universal and cosmic reconciliation – not just a human, national and ethnic one. This universal reconciliation, the gathering together of the cosmos, the 'all things', transcends the temporal markers of Israel's particular history. Creation (Adam) and covenant (Abraham and Israel) yield to the *anthrōpos* and apocalyptic's new creation and the summing up of all things.

In doing so Ephesians practises an epistemology at the end of the ages. Ephesians works from God's decisive interruption in Christ to the future and to the past. Ephesians does not proclaim *Endzeit als Urzeit*; Ephesians embraces *Endzeit als Geschichte*. What has happened in the creation of a new community, now, leads to what can be said about the end and the past. The work of God in Jesus reveals Jesus as the cosmic *anthrōpos*, in whom all humanity and the entire cosmos finds plenitude and unity. What God has done, now, *in Christ* prefigures and (pre)formatively structures the end – what God will do *with all*. For Ephesians it is 'all things' *als* 'in Christ'. Ephesians places covenant narrative on a cosmic apocalyptic stage.

Narrative cross, apocalyptic resurrection

The choice for Ephesians is thus not between narrative *or* apocalyptic, and not even narrative *and* apocalyptic, but narrative apocalyptic or apocalyptic narrative. Like the Jews and Gentiles in Christ, Ephesians fuses narrative and apocalyptic, covenant and cosmos, to create a brand-new theological figure.

At the epicentre of Ephesians' use of narrative and apocalyptic lives the cross and the resurrection. The cross becomes the endpoint of narrative, and the resurrection the beginning of apocalyptic. It is covenant cross and apocalyptic resurrection. Without resurrection's apocalyptic intrusion, the death of Jesus would be trivial – if not an outright empty black hole of tragic history. Resurrection redeemed the cross, rescuing it, Jesus and God's purposes from the hellish clutches of insignificance, from the netherworld of meaninglessness. Without the 'yes' provided by the resurrection, the cross's 'no' would be hollow. But, equally true, without the heavy narrative burden laid upon the cross, without the weight of the submerged long story of Israel and God's promises of covenant faithfulness laid on the shoulders of Jesus, there would have been nothing of significance pinned to the cross. The full meaning of the resurrection's 'yes' depends entirely on the character of the cross's 'no'. If all of Israel's history marched, inevitably, towards the cross, then all cosmic fate hung in the balance as God invaded the world in resurrection, defeating the powers and making life possible.

Covenant narrative thus lives in *correlative tension* with cosmic apocalyptic.[54] The two are in tension precisely because they are incommensurate – there is fundamental structural disagreement between the serial continuity established by narrative and the unique discontinuity imposed by apocalyptic.[55]

But ironically – no less ironic than the gospel itself – gospel narrative needs gospel apocalyptic, and gospel apocalyptic begs for gospel narrative. Alone, narrative runs the risk of covenant domestication, a gospel that dissolves into mere behavioural rules and imposed communal hierarchy. Absent the radical invasion of God there's no transforming power that makes a life of obedience possible. But apocalyptic needs narrative. Alone, apocalyptic runs the risk of rootless, mythic claims for absolute truth and authority, a kind of charismatic and community self-indulgence. Absent the way that God's radical invasion of God's transforming power is anticipated, framed and grounded in the particular and historical, apocalyptic skates dangerously close to Gnosticism. Narrative needs apocalyptic, and apocalyptic needs narrative – just as the cross needs the resurrection, and the resurrection needs the cross.[56]

---

[54] I owe this observation and phrase to Stephen Fowl.

[55] The two, narrative and apocalyptic, appear incommensurate, as incommensurate as cross is with resurrection – no more, no less.

[56] Similarly, Dahl (2000a, 462–3) outlines the two trajectories of Ephesians, one Catholic and one Gnostic. Dahl also notes how Romans and Galatians have funded the Western Church and Ephesians the Eastern.

Ephesians' juxtaposition of cross and resurrection – one an encoded sign of narrative, the other of apocalyptic – sends the two hurtling towards each other as in a theological supercollider. Their collision produces a new message, a good news, and Ephesians is but one possible literary performance of their collision, as is Romans, even if Romans spends most of its time working backwards (reconciling the collision with its narrative origins) while Ephesians looks upwards (unpacking how the future impinges into the present). The cross and resurrection living at the very heart of Ephesians means that gospel is, finally, irreducible, for every performance of the gospel underdetermines that which both constitutes and gave rise to the gospel.[57]

The reason for this underdetermination is that each and every attempt to recover the genesis of Ephesians, and Paul, and even the gospel itself, is made impossible by the very nature of the search. Retracing Ephesians gets us tantalizingly close to the moment of what happens when God raises the dead, the moment when resurrection acts on cross, apocalyptic on narrative, myth on history, universal on particular, and the cosmic on covenant.

Bibliography

Arnold, Clinton E. (1989). *Ephesians: Power and Magic: The Concept of Power in Ephesians in Light of Its Historical Setting.* Society of New Testament Monograph Series 63. Cambridge: Cambridge University Press.

Bales, William (2010). 'The Descent of Christ in Ephesians 4:9.' *Catholic Biblical Quarterly* 72: 84–100.

Bauckham, Richard (1998). *The Fate of the Dead: Studies in Jewish and Christian Apocalypses.* Novum Testamentum Supplement Series 93. Leiden: Brill.

Beker, J. Christiaan (1980). *Paul the Apostle: The Triumph of God in Life and Thought.* Philadelphia, PA: Fortress.

Bockmuehl, Markus (2014). 'Wright's Paul and the Cloud of (Other) Witnesses.' *Journal for the Study of Paul and His Letters* 4: 59–70.

Bousset, Wilhelm (2013 (1913)). *Kyrios Christos: A History of Belief in Christ from the Beginnings of Christianity to Irenaeus.* Waco, TX: Baylor University Press.

Caird, G. B. (1980). *The Language and Imagery of the Bible.* London: Duckworth.

Carr, Wesley (1981). *Angels and Principalities: The Background, Meaning, and Development of the Pauline Phrase hai archai kai hai exousiai.* Society of New Testament Monograph Series 42. Cambridge: Cambridge University Press.

Dahl, Nils Alstrup (1956). 'Christ, Creation and the Church.' In *The Background of the New Testament and Its Eschatology*, edited by W. D. Davies and D. Daube, 422–43. Cambridge: Cambridge University Press.

---

57 See Beker 1980, 352: 'The coherent center of the gospel is only coherent in its particularity.'

—— (2000a). *Studies in Ephesians*. Edited by David Hellhom, Vemund Blomkvist and Tord Fornberg. Wissenschaftliche Untersuchungen zum Neuen Testament 131. Tübingen: Mohr Siebeck.

—— (2000b). 'Das Proömium des Epheserbriefes.' In *Studies in Ephesians*, edited by David Hellhom, Vemund Blomkvist and Tord Fornberg, 315–34. Wissenschaftliche Untersuchungen zum Neuen Testament 131. Tübingen: Mohr Siebeck.

—— (2000c). 'The Cosmic Dimensions of Religious Knowledge (Eph. 3:18).' In *Studies in Ephesians*, edited by David Hellhom, Vemund Blomkvist and Tord Fornberg, 365–88. Wissenschaftliche Untersuchungen zum Neuen Testament 131. Tübingen: Mohr Siebeck.

Ehorn, Seth (2013). 'The Use of Psalm 68(67).19 in Ephesians 4.8: A History of Research.' *Currents in Biblical Research* 12: 96–120.

Fowl, Stephen (2008). 'Learning to be a Gentile: Christ's Transformation and Redemption of Our Past.' In *Christology and Scripture: Interdisciplinary Perspectives*, edited by Andrew Lincoln and Angus Paddison, 22–40. London: Bloomsbury.

—— (2012). *Ephesians: A Commentary*. New Testament Library. Louisville, KY: Westminster John Knox.

Hanson, Paul (1976). 'Apocalypticism.' In *The Interpreter's Dictionary of the Bible, Supplementary Volume*, edited by Keith Crim, 28–34. Nashville, TN: Abingdon.

Harnack, Adolf von (1962). 'Anhang: Materalien zur Geschichte und Erklärung des alten römischen Symbols aus der christlichen Litteratur der zwei ersten Jahrhunderte.' In *Bibliothek der Symbole und Glaubensregeln der alten Kirche*, edited by A. Hahn and G. L. Hahn, 364–90. Hildesheim: Georg Olms.

Harris, W. Hall (1996). *The Descent of Christ: Ephesians 4:7–11 and Traditional Hebrew Imagery*. Arbeiten zur Geschichte des antiken Judentums und des Urchristentums 32. Leiden: Brill.

Hengel, Martin (1995). '"Sit at My Right Hand."' In *Studies in Early Christology*, 119–226. Edinburgh: T&T Clark.

Himmelfarb, Martha (1983). *Tours of Hell: An Apocalyptic Form in Jewish and Christian Literature*. Philadelphia, PA: University of Pennsylvania Press.

Käsemann, Ernst (1958). 'Epheserbrief.' In *Die Religion in Geschichte und Gegenwart: Handwörterbuch für Theologie und Religionswissenschaft*, Volume 2, edited by Hans von Campenhausen, 517–20. 7 vols. Tübingen: Mohr Siebeck.

Keck, Leander (2015). *Why Christ Matters Most: Toward a New Testament Christology*. Waco, TX: Baylor University Press.

Kreitzer, Larry (1998). 'The Plutonium of Hierapolis and the Descent of Christ into the "Lowermost Parts of the Earth" (Ephesians 4:9).' *Biblica* 79 (1998): 381–93.

Lincoln, Andrew T. (1990). *Ephesians*. Word Biblical Commentary 42. Dallas, TX: Word.

Macaskill, Grant (2014). *Union with Christ in the New Testament*. Oxford: Oxford University Press.

Martyn, J. Louis (1997). *Galatians: A New Translation with Introduction and Commentary*. Anchor Bible 33A. New York, NY: Doubleday.

Meeks, Wayne A. (1983). *The First Urban Christians: The Social World of the Apostle Paul.* New Haven, CT: Yale University Press.

Newman, Carey C. (1991). *Paul's Glory-Christology: Tradition and Rhetoric.* Novum Testamentum Supplement Series 69. Leiden: Brill.

—— (1998). '(W)righting the Story of Jesus – A Review Essay of N. T. Wright's *Jesus and the Victory of God.*' In *Critical Review of Books in Religion,* edited by L. Hurtado, 121–44. Atlanta, GA: American Academy of Religion and Society of Biblical Literature.

—— (1999). 'From (Wright's) Jesus to (the Church's) Christ: Can We Get There From Here?' In *Jesus and the Restoration of Israel,* edited by Carey C. Newman, 281–8. Downers Grove, IL: IVP.

—— (2005). 'Resurrection as Re-Embodiment.' *Expository Times* 116: 228–33.

Rad, Gerhard von (1962). *Theology of the Old Testament.* San Francisco, CA: HarperSanFrancisco.

Sanders, Jack T. (1965). 'Hymnic Elements in Eph 1—3.' *Zeitschrift für die neutestamentliche Wissenschaft und die Kunde der älteren Kirche* 6: 214–32.

Schlier, Heinrich (1957). *Der Brief an die Epheser: Ein Kommentar.* Düsseldorf: Patmos-Verlag.

Schnackenburg, Rudolf (1991). *Ephesians: A Commentary.* Translated by Helen Heron. Edinburgh: T&T Clark.

Segal, Alan F. (1990). *Paul the Convert: The Apostolate Apostasy of Saul the Pharisee.* New Haven, CT: Yale University Press.

Tabor, James D. (1986). *Things Unutterable: Paul's Ascent to Paradise in Its Greco-Roman, Judaic, and Early Christian Contexts.* Lanham, MD: University Press of America.

Theissen, Gerd (1974). 'Soteriologische Symbolik in den paulinischen Schriften: Ein strukturalistischer Beitrag.' *Kerygma und Dogma* 20: 282–404.

Watson, Francis (2013). 'Is Paul a Covenantal Theologian?' In *The Unrelenting God: God's Action in Scripture. Essays in Honour of Beverly Roberts Gaventa,* edited by David J. Downs and Matthew L. Skinner, 102–18. Grand Rapids, MI: Eerdmans.

Westermann, Claus (1982). *Elements of Old Testament Theology.* Atlanta, GA: John Knox.

—— (1985). *Genesis 12–36: A Commentary.* Minneapolis, MN: Augsburg.

Wink, Walter (1984). *Naming the Powers: The Language of Power in the New Testament.* Philadelphia, PA: Fortress.

Wolff, Hans Walter (1982). 'The Kerygma of the Yahwist.' In *The Vitality of Old Testament Traditions,* edited by Walter Brueggemann and H. W. Wolff, 41–66. Atlanta, GA: John Knox.

Wright, N. T. (1991). *The Climax of the Covenant: Christ and the Law in Pauline Theology.* Edinburgh: T&T Clark.

—— (1992). *The New Testament and the People of God.* Christian Origins and the Question of God 1. London: SPCK / Minneapolis, MN: Fortress.

—— (1996). *Jesus and the Victory of God.* Christian Origins and the Question of God 2. London: SPCK / Minneapolis, MN: Fortress.

—— (2003). *The Resurrection of the Son of God.* Christian Origins and the Question of God 3. London: SPCK / Minneapolis, MN: Fortress.

—— (2013). *Paul and the Faithfulness of God.* Christian Origins and the Question of God 4. London: SPCK / Minneapolis, MN: Fortress.

—— (2015). *Paul and His Recent Interpreters.* London: SPCK / Minneapolis, MN: Fortress.

Apocalyptic and the history of God: possibilities from Mark's epistemological *inclusio*

J. P. DAVIES

[Apocalyptic] is a useless word which no one can define and which produces nothing but confusion and acres of verbiage.[1]

Introduction

Defining the word 'apocalyptic' has, for a long time, been notoriously troublesome, and has even led some to abandon its use completely.[2] This question of definition forms part of the complex of issues involved in recent discussion about 'apocalyptic' theology in the letters of Paul.[3] N. T. Wright, an important contributor to that recent discussion, has himself suggested that 'this term has proved so slippery and many-sided in scholarly discourse that one is often tempted to declare a moratorium on it altogether'.[4] Nevertheless, he and others have persisted in its use, and the debate about its meaning and employment as a shorthand for some aspects of New Testament theology, particularly in Paul, shows no sign of abating.

This debate over 'apocalyptic' is important not least because it crystallizes a deeper issue in the study of the New Testament, which is the relationship between 'history' and 'theology' (we might say between 'Christian Origins' and the 'Question of God'). Both Wright and his critics have recognized this, though at present there is a sense that there is still much work to do if the debate is to bear fruit, not least on finding

---

1   Glasson 1980, 105.
2   See, e.g., Glasson's bleak assessment, in addition to the epigraph above, that 'the current use of the noun Apocalyptic is so vague and confusing that years ago I came to the conclusion that it was best to drop the term' (Glasson 1980, 99).
3   For an excellent introduction to the debate and a collection of essays by many of the key voices involved, see Blackwell, Goodrich and Maston 2016.
4   Wright 2005, 41.

agreement on the employment of words like 'apocalyptic' and 'history'. While long-running lines of discussion continue, fresh voices are also joining in. One such recent contribution to the debate is that of Samuel V. Adams, in a doctoral dissertation written at St Andrews and published under the inverted-Wrightian title, *The Reality of God and Historical Method*.[5] Adams has sought to bring the 'apocalyptic theologians'' into constructive, though critical, conversation with Wright, particularly in regard to his critical-realist historical method. At one point, however, he suggests that a rapprochement might be possible precisely on the question of Pauline *epistemology*.[6] The present essay is offered as a contribution to that question, though here the focus is not on Paul.

Wright has lamented, in person and in print, the present 'siloing' of the theological sub-disciplines, in particular the separation of Pauline studies from other areas of biblical and theological enquiry.[7] It is one of his great services to the field that his work has attempted to push against the tendency to overspecialization and engage intentionally in the synthetic task. Within my own area of specialism, I am convinced that the recent vibrant discussions on the 'apocalyptic Paul' have much to gain by careful engagement with scholarship on the wider canon of Second Temple Jewish and early Christian apocalyptic texts, the book of Revelation in particular,[8] and on apocalyptic thought in the Gospels. With that in mind, this essay will approach the question of apocalyptic thought in the New Testament through the lens not of Paul but of Mark, and in particular his 'apocalyptic epistemology'.

Eschatology is important, but it's not the end of the world: the epistemological 'essence of apocalyptic'

For those involved in the discussion of apocalyptic thought in the New Testament today, there are two commentaries that fall into the category of essential reading. For the Pauline discussion, it is J. Louis Martyn's

---

5   See Adams 2015. Conversations with Sam at St Andrews were also instrumental in shaping my own thesis, though we soon found ourselves on opposite 'sides' of the debate. For an appreciative, though not uncritical, review, see Tilling 2016, 168–77.

6   Adams 2015, 237.

7   'New Testament scholarship has had a dangerous though perhaps inevitable tendency to operate in silos, inside each of which some things are assumed which are elsewhere controversial, and other things elsewhere taken for granted seem to make no sense' (Wright 2013, 513).

8   This was the premise of my own contribution to the debate, Davies 2016a.

seminal Anchor Bible commentary on Galatians.[9] For the Gospels, Joel Marcus' two-volume commentary on Mark, in the same series, must be engaged.[10] A distinctive feature of Marcus' work on the second Gospel is undoubtedly his view that Mark is characterized by an 'apocalyptic' mode of thinking, a line of Christian apocalyptic thought that can be traced back to the apostle Paul and to Jesus himself.[11] Specifically, Marcus argues that Mark's affinity with Jewish apocalyptic thought is signalled by the two themes of *cosmic warfare* and *imminent eschatology*. 'His outlook can be termed "apocalyptic,"' Marcus argues, 'because his narrative is from start to finish set within the context of the approaching end of the world.'[12] In support of this eschatological definition, Marcus directs the reader to the work of Paul Hanson, John Collins and Martinus de Boer, for whom eschatology lies at the heart of apocalyptic thought. In this way, Marcus allies himself with one influential stream of discussion in the study that considers a particular kind of eschatology the *sine qua non* of apocalyptic thought. This view, exemplified by Hanson and Collins, but also advanced by Philipp Vielhauer, D. S. Russell and Ernst Käsemann,[13] has been influential to the degree that the words 'apocalyptic' and 'eschatological' seem sometimes to be practically synonymous.

An important dissenting voice to this position, however, is that of Christopher Rowland. For Rowland, the heart of apocalyptic is not eschatology but epistemology. While not wishing to sideline discussion of eschatological themes in apocalyptic thought, Rowland argues that this 'concentration on the future orientation of the apocalypses has at times given a rather distorted view of the essence of apocalyptic.'[14] Speaking of the apocalyptic writings, he argues that eschatology is 'not their most distinctive feature, nor does it deserve to become the focus of attention in the study of apocalyptic to the exclusion of the other secrets which the apocalypses claim to reveal.'[15] Rowland is by no means alone in his assessment. Martin Hengel has drawn our attention to the importance of 'higher wisdom through revelation' and has argued for the 'epistemological basis

---

9 Martyn 1997.

10 Marcus 1999.

11 See Marcus 1999, 73. On the connection with Paul, see Marcus 2000, 473–87. The language of 'modes of thinking' is Marcus' own, but I made use of the same term in Davies 2016a, building on the work of the literary critic Alastair Fowler. See also Davies 2016b, 339–59.

12 Marcus 1999, 71.

13 E.g. Vielhauer 1964a, 588–9. For further discussion of this deployment of eschatology as a 'litmus test' for apocalyptic, see Davies 2016b, 343–6.

14 Rowland 1982, 2.

15 Rowland 1982, 26.

of apocalyptic'. This epistemological basis, for Hengel, is 'the notion of the "revelation" of special divine "wisdom" about the mysteries of history, the cosmos, the heavenly world and the fate of the individual at the eschaton, hidden from human reason'.[16] In this view, the structuring theme of apocalyptic thought is not the *imminent parousia* but the *open heaven*.[17]

Thus, while mindful of Marcus' caution that 'neither the apocalypticists nor Mark possessed a systematically worked out, philosophical "theory of knowledge"',[18] we may still enquire as to what Mark's use of the apocalyptic 'open heaven' motif tells us about his epistemology, understood in this non-technical sense. In this essay, I will offer a discussion of two 'architectonic'[19] Markan texts, forming a cosmic and epistemological *inclusio* to the Gospel, each of which demonstrates an apocalyptic epistemology in its employment of the 'open heaven' motif. In each case, as we shall see, this motif is placed in close proximity to a redemptive-historical statement about the long-awaited 'kingdom of God'.[20] Exploring the significance of this epistemological juxtaposition is my central concern.

The 'open heaven' and Mark's apocalyptic epistemology

The baptism of Jesus and the open heaven (Mark 1.9–11)

The first occurrence of the 'open heaven' motif in Mark is the baptism scene in 1.9–11. Jesus comes up out of the water and sees the heavens torn open, a clear echo of Isaiah 64.1 (63.19 LXX), which Marcus is not alone in recognizing and which he identifies as 'an apocalyptic theophany'.[21] Mark's Gospel is unique among the synoptics in its use of the verb *schizō* here, rather than the tamer *anoigō* of Matthew, Luke and the LXX.[22] Just as Jesus is not simply 'led (up) by the Spirit' (*anagō*, Matthew 4.1 / *agō*, Luke 4.1) into the wilderness but is '*driven out*' (*ekballō*, Mark 1.12), so Mark describes the heavens as not merely 'opened', but '*rent asunder*' (my translation).[23] The cosmic violence of the Markan phrasing is not just

---

16 Hengel 1974, 250. Hengel goes on to argue, importantly, that 'the apocalyptic picture of the world and history . . . fundamentally still rests on an Old Testament conception of salvation history' (251).

17 Käsemann 1969, 109 n. 1. Cf. Rowland 1982, 455 n. 7.

18 Marcus 1984, 558 n. 4.

19 Marcus 2004, 201.

20 As noted by Marcus 2004, 67.

21 Marcus 2004, 56–7. See also Watts 2001, 102.

22 Perhaps this reflects a reliance on the Hebrew text tradition in his citation, or perhaps it is evidence of Markan redaction and a preference for more dramatic language.

23 Unless otherwise stated, translations from the Bible are from the NRSV throughout this essay.

a matter of style but is another tell-tale sign of a Gospel written in the apocalyptic mode.[24]

At this point commentators usually draw out the eschatological implications of the baptism scene. A good example is Adela Yarbro Collins' Hermeneia commentary.[25] In her discussion, Collins notes that the 'open heaven' motif is more often deployed for 'theophanic, epiphanic, or revelatory purposes'[26] but nevertheless does not draw out the epistemological importance of the motif in Mark's baptism account, whereas the eschatology of the scene is given much more importance.[27] To the extent that the temporal dimension is a distinctive feature of Mark, Collins' characterization of the second Gospel as an 'eschatological historical monograph'[28] rings true. Certainly, attention to eschatology is warranted by the multiple Isaianic echoes in the baptism scene, and in Jesus' subsequent proclamation of the 'fulfilment of time' (see 1.14–15). As Rowland has reminded us, however, we must not allow apocalyptic eschatology to become a focus that excludes other revealed secrets – and, perhaps more importantly, the act of revelation itself.

Marcus' work on apocalyptic in the second Gospel has by no means ignored its epistemology; he also wrote a perceptive essay on the apocalyptic epistemology at work in a crucial passage, Mark 4.10–12.[29] There, drawing parallels between Mark, the Qumran writings and the Jewish apocalyptic literature, Marcus describes a 'dualism of revelation and concealment'[30] whose source is God himself. In Mark, as in the Dead Sea Scrolls, 'the autonomy that can be ascribed to human beings in matters of perception is severely limited . . . "hearing" is not something that one can simply *decide* to do.'[31] But in his discussion of the baptism of Jesus, Marcus, like Yarbro Collins, demonstrates a tendency to pivot

---

24 So Marcus 2004, 56–7.

25 Yarbro Collins 2007. In addition to Yarbro Collins, see, e.g., Hays 2016, 18; Marcus 2004, 56–7; 1999, 165; Watts 2001, 102–14.

26 Yarbro Collins 2007, 148.

27 E.g. Yarbro Collins 2007, 154–5.

28 Yarbro Collins 2007, 42. Elizabeth Shively has suggested that Collins' designation of Mark as 'eschatological' rather than her earlier use of the adjective 'apocalyptic' represents a significant 'conceptual shift', emphasizing the temporal, rather than vertical-spatial, dimension of the Gospel (Shively 2012, 24).

29 See Marcus 1984, in which he builds on Pauline insights from J. Louis Martyn. On the connection with Paul (and Werner's argument that this revelatory scene is decidedly unPauline), see Marcus 2000, 478.

30 Marcus 1984, 559–61.

31 Marcus 1984, 562.

to eschatology in discussing Mark's apocalyptic theology.[32] Given the important and (to my mind more fruitful) epistemological insights of his earlier essay on 4.10–12, this is something of a shame, and reflective of much discussion of apocalyptic, which often seems to use the terms 'apocalyptic' and 'eschatological' interchangeably.

The crucifixion of Jesus and the torn veil (Mark 15.38–39)

The second of our two architectonic passages is the Markan crucifixion account, and in particular the tearing of the curtain of the Temple from top to bottom in 15.38. Eschatological interpretations of the rending of the veil abound. Perhaps it is a foretaste of the Temple's destruction, or a symbol of the eschatological removal of a barrier between God and humanity, particularly Gentiles.[33] But it is also, and perhaps more centrally, an act of profound cosmological and epistemological importance.

The significance of the Temple as a microcosm is well attested, and much discussed.[34] Moreover, it is nothing new to note the *inclusio* suggested by the verbal and visual parallels between the torn veil here and the rending of heaven in the baptism scene.[35] Marcus notes the repetition of the verb *schizō*, and on this occasion he is clear about the epistemological importance of the removal of the veil as an 'act of revelation'.[36] The torn veil speaks another word in addition to eschatological portents, since 'its ripping is bound to be revelatory as well as destructive: the veil is rent asunder, the glory of God hidden behind it begins to radiate out into the world.'[37] It is not by accident that the centurion's confession in verse 39 is placed immediately alongside this epistemological rupture. This is the third of three structurally important acclamations of Jesus

---

[32] See Marcus 1999, 163–7. Yarbro Collins suggests that 'Mark may be seen as an eschatological and apocalyptic counterpoint to the biblical foundation histories' (Yarbro Collins 2007, 43).

[33] See the informative discussion of these options in Yarbro Collins 2007, 759–64. These are not mutually exclusive interpretations, as Eugene Boring has noted (Boring 2006, 432). See also Hooker 1991, 378 (citing Lightfoot).

[34] See Ulansey 1991, 123–5; Motyer 1987, 155–7; Gurtner 2006; 2007, 292–306.

[35] In addition to Marcus, see, among many others, e.g., Yarbro Collins 2007, 762; Boring 2006, 432, and references therein.

[36] Marcus 1999, 1057. Likewise Gurtner speaks of the 'revelatory function of the *velum scissum*' in Mark (Gurtner 2006, 180).

[37] Marcus 1999, 1067. Note the contrast here with Martyn, for whom *Pauline* apocalyptic is 'not focused on God's unveiling something that was previously hidden, as though it had been eternally standing behind a curtain' (Martyn 1997, 99). Martyn prefers the language of divine 'invasion'. For a fuller discussion of this phrase see Davies 2016a, 117–18, 141–2. Vincent Taylor's suggestion that v. 38 is 'originally a Pauline comment' is an intriguing possibility in this connection (Taylor 1935, 58, cited in Evans 2001, 510).

as 'Son of God' in Mark's Gospel, and the first by a human character.[38] Commentators who either tie themselves in knots trying to work out where the centurion must have been standing in order to face Jesus and still see the curtain torn, or disparage Mark's geography because of that issue, miss the narrative wood for the historical trees and fail to grasp the epistemological point Mark is making by placing these two scenes together.[39] The curtain is torn, heaven is opened, and only now can humankind see who Jesus is.

As it stands, then, it would seem that the 'open heaven' *inclusio* of 1.9–11 and 15.38–39 indicates a Markan epistemology of divine revelation, drawing heavily on apocalyptic imagery, and in particular on the 'open heaven' motif. A purely irruptive revelatory epistemology in Mark's use of the 'open heaven' motif is complicated, however, by an examination of the wider context, and the presence of the language of the 'kingdom of God'.

The 'kingdom of God' and salvation history

The kingdom of God and the fulfilment of time

First, we return to Jesus' baptism. The 'open heaven' scene in 1.9–11 is followed swiftly by Jesus' proclamation, unique to Mark, that 'the time is fulfilled, and the kingdom of God is at hand' (1.15a, ESV). Since these are the first words of Jesus recorded in the second Gospel (a Gospel in which Jesus' words are comparatively few) it seems fair to consider them programmatic for what follows and appropriate to examine them closely.

The word *kairos* can mean a 'decisive moment' as well as a 'span of time', presenting us with an interpretative choice that encapsulates the wider question of apocalyptic eschatology and epistemology. In his translation notes, Marcus recognizes this and argues that 'because of the combination with *plēroun*, "to fulfill", which implies linearity, the meaning "span of time" is to be preferred in the present instance.'[40] (After all, what sense

---

38 The first, 1.11, we have already discussed. The second is the Transfiguration in 9.7, itself also accompanied by the cosmological/epistemological imagery of the cloud. On the first two occasions it is God who makes the declaration that Jesus is *ho huios mou ho agapētos*. There are two more instances of the use of the title 'son of God', spoken by demons, in chs 3 and 5, but these three, being at the exact beginning, middle and end of Jesus' public ministry, are legitimately treated as something of a triptych. Cf. Marcus 2004, 201. Vielhauer argues that this threefold sequence is indicative of an Egyptian coronation ritual. I agree that the three texts can be read as a coronation sequence, but would suggest that they are better seen as a Davidic, not Egyptian, coronation (Vielhauer 1964b, 155–69). See also Marcus 2004, 7.

39 For a survey of some such discussions, see Marcus 1999, 1057–8.

40 Marcus 1999, 172. See too the argument of F. Mussner, supported by Marcus, that 'the

does it make to speak of a decisive punctiliar moment being fulfilled?[41]) However, in his later theological comments on this passage he appears to move away from this linearity in favour of a more disjunctive interpretation of *plēroō*. Insisting, rightly, that Jesus' inaugural proclamation be interpreted 'in the context of apocalyptic eschatology', he goes on to say that 'the *kairos*, the old evil age of Satan's dominion, is now fulfilled, i.e. at an end.'[42] This interpretation requires an interpretation of *plēroō* as 'come to an end' combined with glossing *kairos* as the 'old evil age', resulting in a radically disjunctive interpretation of the statement.[43] While Marcus does not go as far as some in reworking such 'linear' statements in more disjunctive ways,[44] such irruptive interpretations, it seems to me, owe less to first-century Jewish and Christian apocalyptic thought than to contemporary theological commitments to a dichotomy between the punctiliar and the linear, that is to say, between apocalyptic and salvation history. But this is a false dichotomy: both poles of this duality can, and should, be held together in apocalyptic thought, whether in Mark or Paul. The recognition that the time is fulfilled and the kingdom is at hand requires the irruptive revelation of God, to be sure, but it also involves the linear logic of a forward-moving narrative.

Looking forward for the kingdom of God? Joseph of Arimathea's 'prospective epistemology'

Another brief phrase that encapsulates this epistemological and eschatological question is the introduction of the character of Joseph of Arimathea

---

punctiliarity of this concept [viz. *kairos* as 'decisive moment'] contrasts distressingly with the linearity implied in the verb "to fulfill"' (cited in Marcus 1989, 50).

41 As Marcus has asked elsewhere (Marcus 1989, 49).

42 Marcus 1999, 175.

43 Both of which are argued for in Marcus 1989. Space does not permit a full engagement with that article, but briefly, as regards the latter, Marcus has perhaps over-employed the logic of the parallelism in 1.15; regarding the former, in addition to this, too much weight is made to rest on a (to my mind questionable) parallel with the Freer Logion and its mention of the fulfilment of the 'term of the years of the dominion of Satan'. It is not clear why, given his earlier preference for linearity, this argument is to be preferred to the (to my mind) more natural interpretation: a span of time reaching fullness.

44 At this point, Marcus provides a note directing the reader to the similar phrase in Galatians 4.4. There, Paul uses *chronos*, not *kairos*, which should (one might think) lend further support to the linear interpretation. Yet this has not stopped some scholars, seeking to describe a would-be Pauline apocalyptic theology, going to great lengths to avoid such a salvation-historical interpretation of the phrase. Martyn, for example, glosses it as 'a time selected by God' (Martyn 1997, 347–8, 388–9), and de Boer, going still further, takes Paul's *plērōma tou chronou* to mean a 'clean break with the past' (de Boer 2011, 261–2). For further discussion of this see Davies 2016a, 108–12; 2016b, 356–7.

in the crucifixion narrative, a man described as one 'looking for the kingdom of God' (15.43). In chapter 15 references to kingship abound, whether on the mocking lips of the soldiers (v. 18), the inscription on the *titulus* (v. 26) or the scorn of the chief priests (v. 32). Seen in this context, the brief Markan comment about Joseph being one who 'was *looking forward* for the kingdom of God' (*ēn prosdechomenos tēn basileian tou theou*) appears to be far more than a throwaway line. Perhaps this fuller translation of the participle elucidates what is obscured by some translations, rendering it simply as 'looking for', namely a sense of prospective, eager anticipation.[45] Joseph represents many first-century Jews who were waiting expectantly, 'looking forward to the onset of God's reign'[46] and the restoration of the kingdom to Israel in and through the awaited Davidic king.

Now, it is possible that Mark intends a sharp irony in his description of Joseph, brought into the narrative as another imperceptive character, one who was looking forward for the kingdom but did not recognize the king, in contrast to the centurion who, while not looking, experiences the irruptive revelation of the Son of God. If this were correct, then Joseph would stand as an example of the futility of forward-looking epistemology over against irruptive revelation. But Mark gives no indication of this. In this connection it is interesting that Marcus, having earlier argued for the ironic explanation,[47] rejects it in favour of a more positive view of Joseph as one who 'has begun to be grasped by the divine dominion he had been awaiting'.[48]

The second Gospel's interpretation of the OT in its deployment of the motif of the 'kingdom of God' is framed by forward-looking salvation-historical expectations. But to affirm this is not to deny that Mark is a Gospel written in the apocalyptic mode. Rather, it is what we should expect, since apocalyptic, as Hengel has said, 'rests on an Old Testament conception of salvation history'.[49] Mark's understanding of knowledge about Jesus is therefore at once revelatory and salvation-historical. What these features of the crucifixion scene tell us is that while Mark's

---

45 For example, in Luke the word is particularly connected to the coming kingdom and/or restoration of Israel (e.g. Luke 2.25, 38; 23.51). This is also sometimes connected to eschatological expectation (e.g. Luke 12.36; Titus 2.13; Jude 21).

46 Marcus 1999, 1071.

47 Marcus (2004, 67) maintains that the statement is 'probably ironic'. His later commentary, however, argues that 'while it might be possible . . . to take the Markan picture of Joseph "expecting the dominion of God" in a negative, ironic sense . . . it is more likely that Mark means it positively' (Marcus 2009, 1075).

48 Marcus 2009, 1075.

49 Hengel 1974, 251.

apocalyptic epistemology underlines the importance of revelation and the insufficiency of human cognition alone, it does not, however, involve an outright rejection of Joseph's prospective epistemology. The 'open heaven' of the torn veil and Joseph's 'looking forward' are allowed to stand together in relationship, not in dichotomy. In closing I now offer a suggestion of what sort of relationship that might be, and what all of this has to do with the question of 'apocalyptic and history'.

A dialectical suggestion

In his discussion of apocalyptic epistemology in Mark 4, to which I referred earlier, Marcus makes a passing reference to a conversation with J. Louis Martyn in which they discussed how the second Gospel suggests 'a "mysterious interpenetration" between faith and the grace shown in revelation'.[50] A parallel phenomenon is, I suggest, at work in the combination of a 'vertical' revelatory epistemology of the open heaven and the 'horizontal' proclamation of the Davidic king. There is, in Mark's apocalyptic epistemology, a 'mysterious interpenetration' between revelation and expectation, between apocalyptic and salvation history. False dichotomies between these pairs will not do justice to Markan, or indeed Christian, epistemology.

What we need here is the logic not of dualism but of dialectic, by which I mean the speaking of two (seemingly incompatible) words about Christ simultaneously.[51] Jesus is the 'apocalypse of God' and humanity is blind unless God opens eyes through the rending of heaven in revelation. At the same time, Jesus is the long-expected king foretold in the story of Israel who announces and embodies the arrival of the kingdom looked for by many. As Marcus puts it, 'in Mark's Gospel, in other words, a commitment to the "old, old story" is retained at the same time that the story itself is transformed by being read in a new way'.[52] Perhaps we may find in this Markan epistemology a way of transcending the false dichotomies that have come to characterize this discussion?

The last time colleagues and friends were gathered in this way to honour Wright's scholarship was the nineteenth annual Wheaton Theology

---

[50] Marcus 1984, 562 n. 20.
[51] See Boomershine 1989, 147–67. Tilling (2014, 70) has presented a similar challenge to Douglas Campbell's arguments for Pauline retrospective epistemology. Campbell's response to Tilling (Tilling 2014, 74–7) does not (to my mind) sufficiently grasp the importance of this dialectical challenge, but instead essentially repeats the prospective–retrospective dichotomy.
[52] Marcus 2004, 203.

Conference, in April 2010.[53] One of the organizers of that conference was Richard Hays, who closed his own presentation by imagining a dinner party conversation between his friends Tom Wright and Karl Barth.[54] Hays expressed a hope that the two would find much to agree about, perhaps more than Wright would think, but was in no doubt that the question of theological epistemology would remain cause for argument.

Sadly, Hays doesn't tell us much of what he imagined his own contribution to that dinner party conversation might be. Perhaps, as a good host, he simply planned to get his guests talking to each other. Now, I'm sure he and Wright don't need any encouragement from the likes of me to arrange their own dinner-table conversations, but as the dust is now settling on *Paul and the Faithfulness of God* and Wright turns his mind to the Gospels, and (we hope) the next instalment of his Christian Origins and the Question of God, I'd like to suggest that it is in Hays' recent work that a way forward may be found in the matter of 'apocalyptic and the history of God'.

In his recent volume on the Evangelists' use of the OT, *Echoes of Scripture in the Gospels*,[55] Hays has deepened and extended the dialectical thesis begun nearly 30 years ago with Paul.[56] Following Hans Frei, Hays introduces his development of 'figural interpretation' by quoting the German philologist Erich Auerbach:

> Figural interpretation establishes a connection between two events or persons in such a way that the first signifies not only itself but also the second, while the second involves or fulfills the first. The two poles of a figure are separated in time, but both, being real events or persons, are within temporality. They are both contained in the flowing stream which is historical life, and only the comprehension, the *intellectus spiritualis*, of the interdependence is a spiritual act.[57]

In this way, Hays' approach places appropriate emphasis on a retrospective epistemology ('Reading Backwards'), while also affirming a forward-moving narrative continuity.[58] But this emphasis does not lead Hays into

---

[53] Proceedings of which were subsequently published in Perrin and Hays 2011.

[54] Perrin and Hays 2011, 58–9.

[55] Hays 2016.

[56] Hays 1989, 176–7; and see now Hays 2016, 8.

[57] Auerbach 1968, 73, cited in Frei 1974, 28; and Hays 2016, 2. These two 'poles' are interpreted interdependently, in such a way that 'the semantic force of the figure flows both ways' (Hays 2016, 3).

[58] *Reading Backwards* is the title of Hays' earlier short book on the Gospels (Hays 2014a). One of the key insights from Hays' work for the present debate over apocalyptic epistemology, in

a dead-end dichotomy. A preference for retrospective interpretation *over against* a prospective one, or any separation of the two, is to be resisted, as Frei noted:

> The meaning pattern of reality is inseparable from its forward motion; it is not the product of the wedding of that forward motion with a separate backward perspective on it, i.e. of history and interpretation joined as two logically independent factors. Rather the meaning of the full sequence emerges in the narration of the sequence.[59]

Applied to our current themes in Mark, the narrative-figural approach of Frei and Hays allows us to see that the acclamation of Jesus' ministry as the inauguration of the kingdom of God is a salvation-historical claim, made within the stream of time, at its fulfilment. But the perception of this truth requires an open heaven, an apocalypse of God, an event occurring within time, but whose source is without it. Mark's Gospel speaks both words at once. It is vitally important to note here that *both are acts of divine origin*. Such an affirmation of salvation history is therefore not an endorsement of an immanentist or foundationalist epistemology, one which 'derive[s] the New Testament in unilinear fashion from the Old Testament',[60] as if the various 'acts' of the drama of history grew naturally out of each other, but rather expresses a commitment to the history of God's self-revelation to creation in the stream of time.[61] As Barth puts it, in a passage Hays placed on the table at his imaginary dinner party:

> The atonement is history. To know it, we must know it as such. To think of it, we must think of it as such. To speak of it, we must tell it as history. To try to grasp it as supra-historical or non-historical truth is not to grasp it at all. It is indeed truth, but truth actualised in a history and revealed in this history as such – revealed, therefore, as history.[62]

---

that short book and the subsequent larger work, is that the authors of the NT do not merely mine the OT for 'images, stories, tropes and so on' (so Adams 2015, 254) but through *metalepsis* retrieve and reread it Christologically as a salvation-historical narrative.

[59] Frei 1974, 38.

[60] Harrisville 2006, 62, quoted in Adams 2015, 255, in support of his position that such linear epistemological paradigms constitute a denial of transcendence and therefore a significant restriction in Wright's historical methodology. This idea of a smooth 'unilinear' development is sometimes deployed as a straw man in such arguments. See, e.g., the misrepresentation of N. T. Wright's position in Harink 2012, 85. That this is a misreading of Wright is also suggested by Adams 2015, 246.

[61] To put it another way, perhaps the epistemic 'content' is salvation-historical, while the epistemological 'method' is revelatory?

[62] Barth, *CD* 4/1, 157. For Hays' use of this passage see Perrin and Hays 2011, 59. Although, we

There is a marriage of revelation and salvation history in Markan epistemology[63] and any attempt at 'apocalyptic' epistemology, in Mark or elsewhere, must speak these two words at once, reading backwards *and* forwards.[64] In speaking of salvation history, we place a question mark next to the reduction of the 'Christ-event' to an irruptive singularity, but we are also emphatically *not* speaking of anything resembling immanent historical 'development',[65] a mere concatenation of events. It is, rather, *the history of God*, the God of Abraham, Isaac and Jacob, in his providential dealings with humankind and with creation.[66] In Jesus the Messiah, who is himself 'the history of God with man and the history of man with God',[67] the two words of apocalyptic and salvation history are spoken together. All our witnesses to him must be aware of the danger of being pulled towards one pole or the other.

But in speaking in the language of 'two poles', and of the 'horizontal' and 'vertical', am I perhaps choosing the wrong imagery for my purposes? Since it is intrinsic to the metaphor of two axes that they cannot be expressed together, the use of such vectorial metaphors might inadvertently shape the discourse in such a way so as to prevent any possibility of speaking of both apocalyptic and salvation history. In a similar vein, Robert Jenson wrote of his realization that 'the late modern discourse of tangents and perpendiculars and incommensurabilities in general was just Platonism stripped to its geometry'.[68] Others, expressing the same sort of disquiet, have suggested that musical, rather than geometric, metaphors are more suitable. Hays, for example, has written of Paul's dialectical reading strategy in terms of *cantus firmus* and *cantus figuratus*.[69] Likewise, Douglas Campbell has voiced his appreciation for musical rather than vectorial metaphors in tackling difficult theological problems.[70] Wright,

---

should note that, in his response to Hays, Wright thinks that he and Barth might be using the word 'history' differently (Perrin and Hays 2011, 64).

63 Cf. Martyn 1982, 194–8, where Martyn critiques Beker's marriage of salvation history and apocalyptic. Martyn's position was that 'the marriage, as presented in this book, is rather more arranged by Beker than discovered in Paul' (196).

64 See Blackwell, Goodrich and Maston 2016, arguing that a retrospective hermeneutic is 'not simply unidirectional' (11). In this connection, see also Hays 2014b.

65 There is a false dichotomy introduced here, in my view, in some approaches to the question of 'apocalyptic and history'. See, e.g., Kerr 2008, 75.

66 On the possibilities of the doctrine of providence for the 'apocalyptic Paul' debate, see Macaskill 2017.

67 Barth, *CD* 4/1, 158.

68 Jenson 2012, 160.

69 Hays 1989, 178.

70 Campbell 2009, 942 n. 28, citing Begbie 2000; 2007.

too, is no stranger to a good musical illustration.[71] Perhaps he and others will welcome the suggestion, then, that what is needed is a conception of 'apocalyptic and the history of God' not as the intersection of 'vertical' and 'horizontal', but as a polyphonic composition, the chord formed when the two notes of the Christological *novum* and the old, old story of messianic hope are struck at once.

Bibliography

Adams, S. V. (2015). *The Reality of God and Historical Method: Apocalyptic Theology in Conversation with N. T. Wright*. Downers Grove, IL: IVP.

Auerbach, E. (1968). *Mimesis*. Princeton, NJ: Princeton University Press.

Barth, Karl (2004). *Church Dogmatics* IV/1. Translated by G. W. Bromily. London: T&T Clark.

Begbie, J. (2000). *Theology, Music, and Time*. Cambridge: Cambridge University Press, 2000.

—— (2007). *Resounding Truth: Christian Wisdom in the World of Music*. Grand Rapids, MI: Baker.

Blackwell, B. C., J. K. Goodrich and J. Maston (2016) (eds). *Paul and the Apocalyptic Imagination*. Minneapolis, MN: Fortress.

Boer, M. C. de (2011). *Galatians: A Commentary*. The New Testament Library. Louisville, KY: Westminster John Knox.

Boomershine, T. E. (1989). 'Epistemology at the Turn of the Ages in Paul, Jesus and Mark: Rhetoric and Dialectic in Apocalyptic and the New Testament.' In *Apocalyptic and the New Testament*, edited by Joel Marcus and Marion L. Soards, 147–67. Sheffield: Sheffield Academic Press.

Boring, M. E. (2006). *Mark: A Commentary*. The New Testament Library. Louisville, KY: Westminster John Knox.

Campbell, D. A. (2009). *The Deliverance of God: An Apocalyptic Rereading of Justification in Paul*. Grand Rapids: Eerdmans.

Davies, J. P. (2016a). *Paul among the Apocalypses? An Evaluation of the 'Apocalyptic Paul' in the Context of Jewish and Christian Apocalyptic Literature*. Library of New Testament Studies. London: T&T Clark.

—— (2016b). 'The Two Ages and Salvation History in Paul's Apocalyptic Imagination: A Comparison of *4 Ezra* and Galatians.' In *Paul and the Apocalyptic Imagination*, edited by B. C. Blackwell, J. K. Goodrich and J. Maston, 339–59. Minneapolis, MN: Fortress.

Evans, C. A. (2001). *Mark*. Word Biblical Commentary. Nashville, TN: Thomas Nelson.

Frei, H. W. (1974). *The Eclipse of Biblical Narrative*. New Haven, CT: Yale University Press.

---

[71] 'To rule out narrative readings and messianic conclusions in Paul on the grounds that he is an "apocalyptic" thinker is like saying that you cannot include violins and French horns in your composition because you are writing "classical" music' (Wright 2013, 524).

Glasson, T. F. (1980). 'What Is Apocalyptic?' *New Testament Studies* 27.1: 98–105.

Gurtner, D. M. (2006). *The Torn Veil: Matthew's Exposition of the Death of Jesus.* Library of New Testament Studies. Cambridge: Cambridge University Press.

—— (2007). 'The Rending of the Veil and Markan Christology: "Unveiling" the ΥΙΟΣ ΘΕΟΥ (Mark 15:38–39).' *Biblical Interpretation* 15: 292–306.

Harink, D. K. (2012). 'Partakers of the Divine Apocalypse: Hermeneutics, History and Human Agency after Martyn.' In *Apocalyptic and the Future of Theology: With and beyond J. Louis Martyn,* edited by Joshua B. Davis and Douglas K. Harink, 73–95. Eugene, OR: Cascade.

Harrisville, R. A. (2006). *Fracture: The Cross as Irreconcilable in the Language and Thought of the Biblical Writers.* Grand Rapids, MI: Eerdmans.

Hays, R. B. (1989). *Echoes of Scripture in the Letters of Paul.* New Haven, CT: Yale University Press.

—— (2014a). *Reading Backwards: Figural Christology and the Fourgold Gospel Witness.* Waco, TX: Baylor.

—— (2014b). 'Apocalyptic Poiesis in Galatians.' In *Galatians and Christian Theology: Justification, the Gospel, and Ethics in Paul's Letter,* edited by M. W. Elliott, S. J. Hafemann, N. T. Wright and J. Frederick, 200–19. Grand Rapids, MI: Baker.

—— (2016). *Echoes of Scripture in the Gospels.* Waco, TX: Baylor University Press.

Hengel, Martin (1974). *Judaism and Hellenism: Studies in the Encounter in Palestine during the Early Hellenistic Period.* London: SCM.

Hooker, M. D. (1991). *The Gospel According to St Mark.* Black's New Testament Commentaries. London: A. & C. Black.

Jenson, R. W. (2012). 'On Dogmatic/Systematic Appropriation of Paul-According-to-Martyn.' In *Apocalyptic and the Future of Theology: With and beyond J. Louis Martyn,* edited by Joshua B. Davis and Douglas K. Harink, 154–61. Eugene, OR: Cascade.

Käsemann, E. (1969). 'On the Subject of Primitive Christian Apocalyptic.' Pages 108–37 in *New Testament Questions of Today.* London: SCM.

Kerr, Nathan R. (2008). *Christ, History and Apocalyptic.* Eugene, OR: Cascade.

Macaskill, G. (2017). 'History, Providence and the Apocalyptic Paul.' *Scottish Journal of Theology* 70.4: 409–26.

Marcus, J. (1984). 'Mark 4:10–12 and Marcan Epistemology.' *Journal of Biblical Literature* 103: 557–74.

—— (1989). '"The Time Has Been Fulfilled!" (Mark 1.15).' In *Apocalyptic and the New Testament: Essays in Honour of J. Louis Martyn,* edited by Marion L. Soards and Joel Marcus, 49–68. Sheffield: T&T Clark.

—— (1999). *Mark: A New Translation with Introduction and Commentary.* Anchor Bible. New York, NY: Doubleday.

—— (2000). 'Mark – Interpreter of Paul.' *New Testament Studies* 46.4: 473–87.

—— (2004). *The Way of the Lord: Christological Exegesis of the Old Testament in the Gospel of Mark.* London: T&T Clark, 2004.

—— (2009). *Mark 8–16: A New Translation with Introduction and Commentary.* Anchor Bible. New Haven, CT: Yale University Press.

Martyn, J. L. (1982). 'Review of J. Christiaan Beker, *Paul the Apostle: The Triumph of God in Life and Thought.' Word and World* 2: 194–8.

—— (1997). *Galatians: A New Translation with Introduction and Commentary.* Anchor Bible. New York, NY: Doubleday.

Motyer, S. (1987). 'The Rending of the Veil: A Markan Pentecost?' *New Testament Studies* 33: 155–7.

Perrin, Nicholas, and Richard B. Hays (2011) (eds). *Jesus, Paul and the People of God: A Theological Dialogue with N. T. Wright.* Downers Grove, IL: IVP.

Rowland, C. (1982). *The Open Heaven.* London: SPCK.

Shively, Elizabeth E. (2012). *Apocalyptic Imagination in the Gospel of Mark: The Literary and Theological Role of Mark 3:22–30.* Berlin: de Gruyter.

Taylor, V. (1935). *The Formation of the Gospel Tradition.* London: Macmillan.

Tilling, C. (2014) (ed.). *Beyond Old and New Perspectives on Paul: Reflections on the Work of Douglas Campbell.* Eugene, OR: Wipf & Stock.

—— (2016). 'From Adams's Critique of Wright's Historiography to Barth's Critique of Religion: A Review Essay of Sam Adams's *The Reality of God and Historical Method.' Theology Today* 73: 168–77.

Ulansey, D. (1991). 'The Heavenly Veil Torn: Mark's Cosmic Inclusio.' *Journal of Biblical Literature* 110: 123–5.

Vielhauer, P. (1964a). 'Apocalypses and Related Literature: Introduction.' In *New Testament Apocrypha*, edited by W. Schneemelcher and E. Hennecke, 581–642. Philadelphia, PA: Westminster.

—— (1964b). 'Erwägungen zur Christologie des Markusevangeliums.' In *Zeit und Geschichte: Dankesgabe an Rudolf Bultmann zum 80. Geburtstag*, edited by Erich Dinkler, 155–69. Tübingen: Mohr Siebeck.

Watts, R. E. (2001). *Isaiah's New Exodus in Mark.* Grand Rapids, MI: Baker.

Wright, N. T. (2005). *Paul: Fresh Perspectives.* London: SPCK.

—— (2013). *Pauline Perspectives: Essays on Paul 1978–2013.* London: SPCK / Minneapolis, MN: Fortress.

Yarbro Collins, A. (2007). *Mark: A Commentary.* Hermeneia. Minneapolis, MN: Fortress.

'One day as a thousand years': Psalm 90, humility and the certainty of eschatological judgement in 2 Peter 3.8[1]

SCOTT J. HAFEMANN

Introduction

In his recent exposition of Romans 9—11, our honoured colleague pointed out that the references in Romans 11.11, 12, 15 to Israel's 'covenantal "casting away" which was, itself, the strange purpose of election' ultimately 'take us back helpfully, within the larger flow of thought of the letter, to Romans 2. There, the "wrath" of God was to be poured out against all human unrighteousness and wickedness, the Jew first and also the Greek', referring to Romans 2.5–9.[2] Professor Wright then turns back from Romans 2 to Romans 11, this time focusing on the bridge between Romans 2.4 and the argument of Romans 11:

> But in sketching that picture at that point, Paul also built into his narrative the note of God's *makrothumia*, his 'great-heartedness' or 'patience', and God's 'kindness', delaying the final outpouring of wrath so that more will reach repentance. This, too, will be a keynote of his resolution of the question in Romans 11, though again not in the way often imagined.[3]

This is just one example of the countless integrative insights that make N. T. Wright's lifetime of work on the apostle's theology a watershed in the landscape of modern biblical scholarship. In this regard, it is striking that Wright also compares the argument in Romans 2.4 (and later, by extension, Romans 11.28–32[4]) to 2 Peter 3.9, suggesting that the former may

---

1   This essay was made possible by a generous research fellowship at Biola University's Center for Christian Thought through the support of a grant from the Templeton Religion Trust. The opinions expressed in this publication, however, are those of the author and do not necessarily reflect the views of the Trust.
2   Wright 2013, 1194–5 (original emphasis removed).
3   Wright 2013, 1195.
4   See Wright 2013, 1252–8.

be the passage referred to in 2 Peter 3.15 as having been written by 'our beloved brother Paul'.[5] Of course, this is perhaps small solace in reading Romans, since in 2 Peter 3.16 Paul's writings are also acknowledged to be 'hard to understand' and easily 'twisted' by 'the ignorant and unstable . . . to their own destruction'.[6]

But the parallel is nonetheless instructive. It highlights the centrality of God's 'patience' and 'kindness' as a hermeneutical key for understanding the 'strange' divine action set out in Romans 9—11 on the one hand (cf. Romans 11.32), and the apparent delay of the *parousia* in 2 Peter 3.8–9 on the other. This parallel is all the more striking since the declaration of God's 'patience' in 2 Peter 3.9 incorporates an allusion to Habakkuk 2.3, which is also found in one of Paul's programmatic texts as well (cf. Habakkuk 2.4 in Romans 1.17; Galatians 3.11). Here is the text in its own immediate context:

8a Beloved, do not let escape you this one fact,
    that [*hoti*] one day before the Lord is as a thousand years,
8b and, on the other hand, a thousand years is as one day [Psalm 90.4].
9a Therefore, the Lord is not delaying concerning
    the promise [Habakkuk 2.3]
9b as [*hōs*] some consider a delay,
9c but [*alla*] he is showing patience toward you
9d because [adv. ptcp.] he is not willing that any [of you] should perish
9e but [*alla*] that all [of you!] should come to repentance.[7]

Note that in 2 Peter 3.8–9 the theme of God's patience and the use of Habakkuk 2.3–4, which Romans and 2 Peter share, are both based on a principle derived from Psalm 90.4, which is unique to 2 Peter. Of interest here, therefore, is how the maxim derived from Psalm 90.4 in 2 Peter 3.8 functions to support these common Pauline/Petrine motifs.

As a modest token of appreciation for Professor Wright's remarkable

---

5   Wright 2013, 1195 n. 553, pointing also to Wisdom of Solomon 11.23 and to the fact that the motif of God's patience is traditional, as indicated by Wisdom of Solomon 15.1; Sirach 18.11; Prayer of Manasseh 7; *4 Ezra* 7.74, 134.
6   The translations of the biblical texts are my own, though often in close consultation with the ESV.
7   The underlining above indicates my understanding of the logical relationships between the propositions in the text, followed by their underlying Greek formulations when these are explicitly indicated.

achievements and his example of unflagging diligence, the purpose of this essay is to pursue this question by following his own exegetical conviction that scriptural texts, in their larger contexts, were often formative for their NT appropriation.[8] Here this conviction will entail returning to the argument of Psalm 90 as the key to understanding the conclusion in 2 Peter 3.9 that God is not delaying his judgement, but is showing the same kind of patience for the sake of repentance that was at the heart of Paul's understanding of God's ways as set forth in Romans 2.4 and 11.32.

The arrogance of the scoffers

The paragraph of 2 Peter 3.1–7, introduced with a reference to the recipients as the 'beloved' in 3.1, grounds 3.8 as the first of the three imperatives with which the letter concludes, each of which is also introduced rhetorically by the vocative, 'beloved' (see the references to the 'beloved' in 3.8, 14–15a and 17–18a). The main point of this opening paragraph is the statement of the epistle's purpose in 3.1–2. The stated goal of the letter is to remind the 'beloved' of what the prophets had predicted and 'the Lord and Saviour' had commanded through the apostles regarding the Messiah's coming [again] as judge on 'the day of judgement and destruction of the ungodly' (3.7; cf. 1.16; 2.9; 3.10–13). The occasion and urgency of this reminder derive from the anticipated influence of 'false teachers' who, as 'scoffers', deny Christ's 'second coming' in order to support their immorality and to entice others to do the same as a justification for their own actions (2.1–2, 14, 18–19; 3.3–4). For due to the blasphemous and deceptive nature of their judgement-free message of 'liberty' (2.10b–22), the false teachers' condemnation is sure (2.1–10a). The congregation is therefore called to remember what the prophets and apostles have taught regarding the reliability of the promise of Christ's future coming (1.12–21) and its ethical implications for the life of faith in the present (cf. 1.3–11 with 3.10–14).[9] Knowing the certainty of the Messiah's return is the means to keeping themselves from being led astray by the arrogant 'error' of the 'lawless' false teachers (cf. *planē* in 3.17 with 2.18).

---

8 Wright 2013, 176–7: 'even when it often seems obscure to a present-day reader, the context of a scriptural allusion or echo is again and again very important. Whole passages, whole themes, can be called to mind with a single reference.'

9 For the way in which this emphasis on the certainty of divine judgement also counters 'the heart of Epicurean philosophy', which denied the gods' involvement in the world, if they existed in the first place, as well as the more general scepticism in the first century regarding predictive prophecy, see Green 2008, 327–8.

Our purpose is not to examine the nature of the scoffers' support for their rejection of eschatological judgement or its scriptural refutation, both of which are a matter of some debate (see 3.4–8). Of importance here is the assertion in 3.5 that the false teachers' denial of the 'promise of [the Messiah's] coming' (3.4) was only possible because the plain teaching of Scripture regarding the reality of eschatological judgement 'escapes' (*lanthanō*) their notice. Moreover, theirs was no innocent misinterpretation of the biblical tradition and its significance. In accordance with their sinful desires, the 'scoffers' *willingly* fail to take cognizance of the biblical realities (cf. *thelontas* in 3.5 with 3.3 and 16). This reference to their moral disposition as the key to their faulty hermeneutics recalls their character in 2.10b as those who are 'bold' (*tolmētai*) and 'arrogant' (*authadeis*) (NIV), which according to 2.18 leads them to speak 'boastful things of futility' (*hyperonka mataiotētos*). The false teachers' arrogance thus coheres with an *unwillingness* to submit to God's word as creator and judge, whether regarding the past or the future, whether from the prophets or the apostles, whether found in Scripture or commanded by 'the Lord and Saviour' himself (3.2, 5, 7; cf. 2.9, 16, 21).

The antidote to arrogance according to Psalm 90.4

As the counterpart to this ignorance and eisegesis born of arrogance, 2 Peter 3.8 declares the 'one thing' (*hen touto*) that should *not* 'escape' (*lanthanō*) the notice of the 'beloved'. Thus 2 Peter 3.8 is the reversal of 3.5. Here too, significantly, what should not escape notice is also a 'word' taken from the Scriptures, this time from Psalm 90.4, one of two scriptural texts that Second Temple and Rabbinic Judaism commonly pondered when discussing the problem of 'the delay of the End'. The other is Habakkuk 2.3, alluded to in 3.9![10] The two texts are conceptually related. Psalm 90.4, our focus here, provides the principle that must be kept in mind when considering the apparent 'delay' of Christ's *parousia*; Habakkuk 2.3 informs the conclusion that should then be drawn from this truth.[11]

---

[10] For examples of the use of Psalm 90.4 and Habakkuk 2.3 in Jewish and rabbinic texts dealing with the problem of the 'delay of the End', see Bauckham 1980, 3–36.

[11] Though beyond our present investigation, we should not be surprised, therefore, to discover that the allusion to Habakkuk 2.3 in 2 Peter 3.9 likewise deals with the contrast between arrogance and humility. In its own context, those in Habakkuk 2.3 who are not willing to wait faithfully for the vision of God's coming judgement to be fulfilled, thinking it too slow in coming, are said in Habakkuk 2.4 to be 'puffed up', whereas 'the righteous shall live by his [LXX: God's] faithfulness' (cf. Romans 1.16).

In comparing our passage to these other traditions, scholars have observed, however, that the surrounding history of interpretation of Psalm 90.4 does not parallel what we find in 2 Peter 3.8 or its context. The Second Temple, rabbinic and early Christian traditions consequently offer little help in understanding our text. This is largely because the Jewish and Christian literature takes Psalm 90.4 to be a hermeneutical 'rule' for interpreting seemingly difficult OT passages that referred to the time period of a 'day'. For if from God's perspective one human day = 1,000 years, this equivalence could be used to determine the timing and/or length of significant biblical and eschatological events.[12] But there is no such 'eschatological maths' being done in the context of 2 Peter, where no specific 'day' is in view and no conclusions are being drawn about the length of a biblically announced time-period.[13] Hence, the majority of scholars 'conclude that the author has here produced an original argument which has no known precedent or parallel in the literature'.[14] It is surprising, therefore, that scholars have not gone back to the source text itself, Psalm 90.4, *read in its own larger context*, as the potential key to 2 Peter 3.8–9.

Psalm 90 (89LXX[15]), the only canonical psalm attributed to Moses, introduces 'Book IV' of the Psalter (Psalms 90—106), which, in view

---

12 So, e.g., *Barn.* 15.4; Irenaeus, *Haer.* 5.28.3; *b. Sanh.* 97a apply the rule to the creation narrative in order to conclude that the history of the world will last 6,000 years and be followed by a millennial Sabbath. It is also applied to the 'day' or 'days' of the Messiah (Psalm 90.15; Isaiah 62.5; 65.22) in order to conclude that there will be 1,000, 2,000 or even 7,000 years of messianic rule (so Justin, *Dial.* 81; *b. Sanh.* 99ab; *Midr. Ps.* 90.17; *Pesiq. Rab.* 1.7). The earliest and most common application was to Genesis 2.17 to explain why Adam did not die on the same day he sinned, in which it is said that out of God's mercy he delayed Adam's punishment for a thousand years (cf., e.g., *Gen. Rab.* 22.1). For these traditions and their lack of fit in the context of 2 Peter, see Bauckham 1983, 306–7.

13 So now definitively, Vögtle 1994, 230: 'Der argumentative Zusammenhang wird sodann verkannt, wenn man auslegt, "der Tag des Herrn" (V. 10a) = die Messiasherrschaft werde tausend Jahre dauern.'

14 Bauckham 1983, 306. Bauckham himself continues to look to Jewish tradition as the key to 2 Peter 3.8 by adducing several Jewish interpretations of Psalm 90 'not previously noticed' in order to support the conclusion that 'the thought of 2 Pet 3.8 may plausibly be regarded as borrowed from a Jewish apocalypse which made this point' (pp. 308–9; his texts are *Pirqe R. El.* 28 and *Yal.* 76; Sirach 18.9–11; *2 Bar.* 48.12–13; and *L.A.B.* 19.13). Yet these passages establish only that Psalm 90.4 was also used with reference to the contrast between the brevity of human life and God's eternity. This contrast was then applied in apocalyptic contexts to indicate that the period of time until the End may seem long, but in God's eternal reckoning it is actually short. I will argue, however, that a contrast between divine and human perspectives on time is not the point either of Psalm 90.4 or of 2 Peter 3.8–9.

15 The Greek text for Psalm 90 is taken from Rahlfs 1931. 'LXX' as used in this context thus represents this text and the other texts now represented in Rahlfs 2006. 'LXX' is therefore not

of the judgement of the exile, focuses on calling Israel back to its pre-Davidic roots in God's covenant faithfulness (cf. Psalm 89).[16] The canonical structure of the Psalter may of course play no direct role in the way in which Psalm 90 is employed in 2 Peter 3.8. It nevertheless provides a window into its themes and their importance inasmuch as they played a part in its canonical placement. It is widely recognized, therefore, that Psalm 90 was chosen to introduce this section of the Psalter because of its focus on Israel's acknowledgement of her own judgement in view of God's relentless wrath against humanity's sin (vv. 3–11/12), because of its resultant call for YHWH to restore his covenant people (vv. 12/13–17) and because of its recognition of God's eternal and everlasting sovereignty as the basis for both divine judgement and restoration (vv. 1–2).[17] In support of these themes, Book IV begins and ends with a declaration that the Lord is his people's 'dwelling place' as the God who exists from before creation and 'from everlasting age to everlasting age' (Psalms 90.2; 106.48).

Of consequence for our study is the way in which within this broader context Israel's judgement in the exile is seen implicitly in Psalm 90.3 to be an expression of God's universal judgement of humanity. The reality of this judgement is then supported by verse 4, the text in view in 2 Peter 3.8:

v. 3: You return a man to the dust,
    and say, 'Return, children of Adam!'

v. 4: <u>For</u> [MT: *ky*; OG: *hoti*] a thousand years in your eyes
    [are] as a former day when it is past
    or as a watch in the night.

---

to be equated necessarily with the OG tradition. Apart from 89.3, the textual issues in Psalm 90/89 LXX are not significant for our discussion (see below, n. 15).

16 For the concentration on Moses in Book IV, see Psalms 90.1; 99.6; 103.7; 105.26; 106.16, 23, 32 (outside Book IV Moses occurs only in 77.20). The Mosaic backdrop to Psalm 90 is helpfully summarized by Urbrock 1998, 26–9, who notes that Psalm 90 also expands on the plea in Psalm 89 for God's love and faithfulness to be shown in Israel's restoration, 'and extends this picture to include all of Israel (and, by extension, all humankind) in a sweeping portrait of how even those who reach a ripe old age . . . nevertheless spend it all under the anger, wrath and fury of God, so that their entire life-span is but toil and trouble (vv. 7–10)' (Urbrock 1998, 26).

17 For a helpful summary of the role of these themes from Psalm 90 within the five-book structure of the Psalter, focusing on the problem of the ongoing experience of the exile in the life of the community (Psalm 89), even after its apparent end with the return from the diaspora (Psalm 107), see Krüger 1994, 191–219 (esp. 209–12). Krüger's reading of the structure of the Psalter confirms Wright's view of the continuing reality of the exile in the 'post-exilic' period (see pp. 210–12).

In declaring that the God who created them subsequently 'returns' the sinful 'children of Adam' to the 'dust' from which they were created, verse 3 most likely alludes to the curse from Genesis 3.19.[18] The point is to stress divine responsibility for humanity's death as 'the fate determined for humanity by the decree of God'.[19] To that end, Psalm 90.3 affirms that 'human death is as much the result of divine fiat as is creation. Humankind lives under a divine mandate of mortality, which no human being can escape.'[20]

Psalm 90.13 then recapitulates the theme of a divine 'return', now invoking the Lord himself to '(re)turn', this time to his 'servants', not in judgement and wrath, but in his mercy and steadfast love as proclaimed and demonstrated in the books of Moses (cf. Exodus 32.12, 14; 34.6–7; Numbers 14.17–19; cf. Deuteronomy 7.9). God's subsequent return will thus issue forth not in the death that makes all existence toil and trouble (vv. 3, 7, 9–10; cf. Genesis 3.17–18), but in the power and glory of God that recreates a life of joy in one's work (vv. 14–17).

As part of the psalm's opening statement of this divine sovereignty in both judgement and redemption, Psalm 90.4 (89.4 LXX) does not *equate* 1,000 years with a day, contrary to the way in which it was usually taken in the tradition. Rather, it *compares* the passing of 1,000 years in God's sight to the passing of a day or to a watch in the night:

> For a thousand years in your eyes [are] *as* a former day
> when it is past [LXX: *hē hēmera hē echthes* ('yesterday')],
> or *as* a watch in the night.

---

18 So already Delitzsch 1883, 6, though he takes v. 3b, 'Return, O children of man', to refer to the calling of the next generation into being (Delitzsch 1883, 7). Cf. Tate 1990, 432, who considers that the 'dust' in view here could refer to the 'dust of Sheol' as the place of the dead. Hence, vv. 3–11 portray 'life under the wrath of God', which recalls 'of course, the accounts in Genesis 2—3, and also the analysis of sin by Paul in the Book of Romans' (Tate 1990, 441, following Westermann). For the contrary position, see now Goldingay 2008, 26, 30, who argues that the crushing to dust refers 'to putting people down . . . Yhwh has demonstrated the capacity to put down the people from whom the community needed to find shelter' (Goldingay 2008, 26).

19 Tate 1990, 431. He supports reading both clauses in v. 3 to be a reference to the divine judgement of death: 'You turn human beings back to dust, saying . . .' (Tate 1990, 432).

20 Tate 1990, 441. Though it is still implied, this direct link between the divine judgement of death and human sin is lost in 89.3 LXX, which reads the former statement as a plea to God and the latter as a call for repentance by taking *ʾel* ('God') in v. 2 to be the negation, *ʾal*, of a jussive in v. 3a, and by taking 'dust' to refer to 'humiliation' (thus: *mē apostrepsēs anthrōpon eis tapeinōsin*): 'Do not turn man away to humiliation. And you said, "Return, you sons of men . . ."' (Pietersma 2007, 592); for this analysis and its implications, see Hossfeld and Zenger 2005, 425.

This comparison is therefore not a statement about the nature of human reality, since the point of comparison is not between God and humanity, but between two different periods of time 'in God's eyes', one extremely long (a thousand years) and two extremely short (a passing day and a watch in the night). 'In God's eyes' the former is like the latter. This would be true even if humanity did not exist. Furthermore, the force of the comparison is not to establish or highlight the transience of a day or of a night's watch; both are simply assumed for the sake of the argument. Based on this assumption, the argument does not establish a *contrast* between the eternality of God and the transience of humanity, which is now the most common reading of the text,[21] but makes a *comparison of identity or significance* between the long and short periods of time 'in God's eyes'.

If the point of verse 4 were to stress humanity's transience over against God's eternality, it would be difficult to see how such a contrast between the respective *natures* of God and humanity would support the fact that God judges humanity by returning all the 'children of Adam' to the dust of death. God's eternality does not necessarily cause humanity's mortality. Nor is death in Psalm 90 a normal expression of transient human nature per se. In Psalm 90 human mortality is an ongoing consequence of sin under the judgement of God (cf. vv. 7–8, 11). Accordingly, in support of this universal truth, the point of the comparison in verse 4 is neither divine eternality nor human transience, but the irrelevance of the length or passing of time when it comes to God's sovereign commitment to judge. In the Lord's sovereign presence as the God who evaluates all creation, that is, 'in his sight/eyes',[22] the passing of a thousand years is no more signifi-

---

[21] For this traditional reading of the psalm, see, e.g., Dahood 1968, 322; Krüger's summary of the view, which he rejects (1994, 191); and Hossfeld and Zenger 2005, 419, in whose view 'God seems not even capable of grasping this transitoriness of human life', since humanity's experiences of time are so different (Hossfeld and Zenger 2005, 422). For the application of this view to 2 Peter 3.8, ubiquitous in the commentary tradition, see Bauckham's two programmatic studies, for whom the point of Psalm 90.4 is 'to contrast God's everlasting life with the transience of human life' (1983, 307; 1980, 22).

[22] The idiom 'in your eyes' (*beyneyka*) occurs 64x in the MT, usually to refer to a person's or God's evaluation of a person or thing, often leading to a determination to act in a certain way (see, e.g., Genesis 16.6; 18.3; 19.19; 20.15; Exodus 33.13, 16; Judges 10.15; 2 Kings 20.3; Isaiah 38.3; Psalm 51.4; Proverbs 3.7), though it can refer simply to physically seeing something (see below). The LXX equivalents vary between *en ophthalmois sou/mou*, etc. (e.g. besides Psalm 90.4, see Judges 6.17; 17.6; 19.24; 1 Samuel 16.22; Psalm 89.4/90.4MT), *enōpion sou* (Exodus 34.9; Psalm 51.6/51.4MT) and *enantion sou/autou* (Genesis 18.3; Job 11.4). That the idiom refers to an evaluation is represented, e.g., in the LXX of Genesis 16.6, which renders the idiom as *soi areston ē*, and Genesis 20.15, where it is rendered *soi areskē* (cf. too Judges 14.3; 1 Samuel 1.23, etc., and the opposite in 1 Samuel 8.6; 18.8, etc.). When the idiom refers simply to seeing something, it is usually rendered with the dative alone, e.g. *tois ophthalmois sou* (cf.

cant to his continuing determination to judge the world than the passing of a short day or a watch in the night.[23] Read in this way, verse 4 parallels the rhetorical function of the psalm's opening confession in verse 2, which is also a statement about the sovereignty of God in relationship to time. Both verses provide the basis upon which God's judgement in verse 3 is recognized to be unending and unalterable, so that rhetorically verse 3 is the inference from both verses 2 and 4:[24]

v. 2: Before the mountains were brought forth,
       or ever you had formed the earth and the world,
       from everlasting age to everlasting age you are God.

v. 3: <u>Therefore</u>, you return a man to the dust,
       and say, 'Return, children of Adam!'

v. 4: <u>For</u> a thousand years in your eyes [are] as a former day
       when it is past, or as a watch in the night.

The ongoing judgement of humanity in verse 3 thus derives from the Lord's unceasing sovereignty as 'God' from before creation to the never-ending age to come. Verse 4 then supports this unwavering judgement by underscoring that the long spans of time over which the Lord rules as 'God' do not diminish or alter the divine resolve to judge. As the 'dwelling place' of his people 'in every generation' (90.1; cf. Deuteronomy 33.27), God remains as faithful in regard to judgement as he does in regard to showing mercy (cf. again v. 3 with v. 13).[25]

Deuteronomy 3.27; 34.4; 2 Kings 7.2, 19; Ezekiel 44.5; Psalm 90.8), but cf. *en tois ophthalmois sou* in Ezekiel 40.4 (cf. too, e.g., 1 Samuel 12.16). As these examples indicate, the same patterns hold true for the use of the idiom in its other grammatical inflections ('in our eyes', 'in their eyes', etc.).

23 See Schrage 1985, 267–75, 270–1, who argues that 'before the Lord' in 3.8 is not a spatial reference, but a forensic one, as in 1 Corinthians 3.19 and James 1.27, referring to God's evaluation (to be 'before the Lord' as one's judge). The point of Psalm 90.4 and 2 Peter 3.8 is consequently not the same as that in Psalm 84.11 (namely, that one day in God's presence is better than a thousand elsewhere).

24 Cf. too Delitzsch 1883, 7–8, who relates v. 4 to v. 2 and then relates this to 2 Peter 3.8 to show that God 'is raised far above all time, inasmuch as the longest period appears to Him insignificant, and in the shortest period the greatest work can be accomplished by Him . . . A whole millennium appears to God, when He surveys it, just as yesterday appears to us, when . . . it is passing away . . . [like the day or a watch in the night, a thousand years for God] do not last long for Him, they do not affect Him; He is at the close of them, as at the beginning . . . for Him, the eternal One, time is as nothing.' Delitzsch thus concludes that 'the changes of time are for Him no obstacle hindering the realization of His counsel – a truth, which has both a fearful and a consolatory side' (Delitzsch 1883, 8).

25 Cf. too Schreiner 1978, 80–90, who argues that vv. 3–4 have two functions: to direct our view to the theme of the psalm and, at the same time, to create a transitional connection

Hence, though the focus of verses 2–4 is clearly on God's sovereignty, the comparison in verse 4 within its own literary context does not establish a philosophical principle that God exists in a different 'kind' of time than humanity (e.g. that God is 'beyond time' in an 'eternal timelessness'), a general theological statement that God experiences or calculates time differently from humanity (e.g. that a millennium 'feels' or 'appears' to God like a short amount of time from his divine perspective), or a pious confession that God can do with time as he wills, since he is sovereign over the very category of 'time' itself (e.g. that God can 'wait' as long or as short as he wants before judging humanity).[26] Instead, the point of the text is to affirm a truth about God's unwavering commitment to judge regardless of the time-span in view – under God's sovereignty, a thousand years, a day and a watch in the night are all the same.

Looking forward in the psalm, the reality of God's enduring judgement in verses 2–4 leads to a statement in verses 5–6 regarding the implication of humanity's divinely ensured return to dust. Though several elements of the MT/LXX texts are uncertain, the passage is best taken to affirm that God's ongoing and determined judgement means that humanity's life has now become ephemeral.[27] Once again, however, the psalmist views humanity's short-lived life not to be the 'normal' expression of its mortal 'nature', but the consequence of God's condemnation. This is confirmed by the LXX text of 89.5, which refers not to a flash flood but to the sinful character of people's lives: 'their scornful things will be/last years' (*ta exoudenōmata autōn etē esontai*). Their years of scornful acts are then *called upon* to pass away like the early morning blossom or to fall at night like the parched plant (89.6LXX).[28] The fact that death, for the psalmist, is not 'natural', but the result of God's relentless wrath in response to sin,

---

(*Überleitung*) from vv. 1b–2 to vv. 5ff. in that 1,000 years for God is like a small piece, an insignificant fraction of a person's life (Schreiner 1978, 82). 'Was sind schon ein Tag oder eine Nachtwache im Verhältnis zu 70 oder 80 Jahren!' (Schreiner 1978, 82).

[26] So Tate 1990, 440: 'the eternal God is not vulnerable to the passage of time as are human beings, though we should not say that "time has no meaning with God."'

[27] So too von Rad 1980, 210–23, who points out that the recollection of Israel's protective relationship in vv. 1–2, 'instead of expressing consolation, opens the door to a whole chain of exceedingly somber reflections . . . God himself is the cause of bleak transience' (von Rad 1980, 214). Von Rad thus sees the point of v. 4 and vv. 5–6 to be 'a profoundly depressing aspect' and vv. 7–9 to be 'a still more somber horizon' (Rad 1980, 214).

[28] For the MT, see Hossfeld and Zenger 2005, 422: the lament is over 'an end to the life of the individual continually and violently imposed by the creator God himself' (Hossfeld and Zenger 2005, 422). Thus, in vv. 5–6, 'God himself sweeps human beings away because he has decreed mortality' (Hossfeld and Zenger 2005, 422). The image of the grass is 'not a story . . . of a continually renewed life as [a] sign of [an] inexhaustible life force, but a story of

is then further confirmed in the sombre words of verses 7–11, the point of which is manifest in the LXX tradition as well. Yet despite the universal experience of death, Moses wonders, 'Who knows the might of your wrath, and your anger from your fear?' (v. 11, NETS).

So the psalm ends with a call to take God's judgement seriously, remembering that one will soon face God in death ('So teach us to number our days that we may get a heart of wisdom', v. 12[29]), with cries for deliverance from God's wrath ('Return, O LORD! How long? Have pity on your servants!', v. 13; cf. v. 16) and with prayers to live faithfully in the meantime ('Satisfy us in the morning with your steadfast love, that we may rejoice and be glad all our days. Make us glad for as many days as you have afflicted us, and for as many years as we have seen evil', vv. 14–15). These expressions by God's contrite servants climax in verse 17 with an emphatic prayer that the Lord would bless his people in the midst of their affliction by 'establish[ing] the work of [their] hands!' Against the backdrop of God's judgement this prayer becomes a plea that the servants' obedience will be found faithful and approved now and on the day of their death/judgement.

Psalm 90 and the surety of judgement in 2 Peter 3.8, with an eye towards Romans

From the perspective of Psalm 90, the point of 2 Peter 3.8 is not the transience of humanity or the fact that God exists outside time and/ or experiences the duration of time differently from us. Here too, as in Psalm 90.4, the maxim is about God alone and it is again stated in the form of a comparison between two measures of time (. . . *hōs* . . . *hōs* . . .). Contextually, the purpose of the principle in 3.8 is also derived from Psalm 90: the unwavering certainty of God's coming judgement, despite whatever time has transpired (cf. 3.4), should not 'escape' the notice of the 'beloved' (cf. 2.1, 3).[30] To emphasize that the length of time, whether short or long,

---

continual withering, drying, and meaningless dying' (Hossfeld and Zenger 2005, 422). Given that it is an expression of God's wrath, the dying, however, is hardly 'meaningless'.

29 For this point, see now Clifford 2000, 59–66, who argues that v. 12 is not a request for a deeper understanding of one's transience in order to be able to face tribulation and divine wrath (Clifford 2000, 59, 63), 'but of the divine anger causing the community's tribulations' (Clifford 2000, 65). 'To count our days' does not mean, therefore, 'let us know the brevity of human life', but as in Leviticus 23.16 refers to 'numbering or counting days, months, years'; in Psalm 90.12 this refers to gaining 'an accurate knowledge of the time period of the divine wrath behind the distress', which is divinely predetermined (Clifford 2000, 65, 66).

30 Cf. the point of Psalm 90.4, according to Goldingay 2008, 27, that 'even a millennium does not impress Yhwh . . . It does not hold Yhwh back from action, any more than a day does.'

plays no role one way or the other regarding the surety of Christ's 'second coming', the maxim derived from Psalm 90.4, which corresponds most closely to 3.8b, can be reversed in 3.8a. When it comes to the inevitability of God's promise to judge the world in Christ, 'one day before the Lord [is] as a thousand years and a thousand years [are] as one day.' The determining factor in judgement, as it was in creation, remains solely God's word (cf. again 3.5, 7 with the same emphasis on the determining nature of God's word reflected in the question of Romans 9.6, which drives the argument in Romans 9—11).

Hence, given God's relentless commitment to judge in accordance with his word, the Messiah's not yet having returned cannot be considered a 'delay', as even some of the believers consider it to be (3.9a). Instead, it must be an intentional act of the sovereign Lord for whom time, according to Psalm 90, is not a determining factor. And the purpose of that intention is the repentance of God's people (3.9b). For Paul, since God's determination to judge is undeterred, God's *patience* in bringing about the final judgement must also be intentional, being aimed at the repentance of 'the vessels of mercy' (see Romans 2.4; 9.22–24).

Moreover, the focus throughout Psalm 90 is on addressing the Lord directly as the source of both wrath and restoration (God is addressed in the second person in 14 of its 17 verses). This same orientation is reflected in 3.8 in that the impact of the span of time on the realization of 'the promise of [Christ's] coming' (3.4) is said to be irrelevant 'before the Lord' (cf. *para kyriō* in 3.8 with *en ophthalmois sou* LXX // *beyneyka* MT in Psalm 89/90.4). The designation, 'before the Lord' (*para kyriō*), which refers to being in the presence of God, is itself also an appropriate interpretative gloss on Psalm 90.4 (note the move in the psalm from the address to Adonai in v. 1 to YHWH in v. 13, both of which are rendered in the LXX with *kyrios*). Like its equivalent in the MT and LXX of Psalm 90.4, it too can connote a forensic, evaluative sense, signifying the Lord's sovereignty as the one who adjudicates all things in accordance with his righteous character.[31] Thus, as in Psalm 90.4, the surety of Christ's return

---

[31] For the MT and LXX expressions, see n. 20 above. For the use of *para kyriō* in the LXX, see 1 Samuel 25.29; *Psalms of Solomon* 9.5 (being in the presence of the Lord); Judith 11.17 (*para soi, kyrie mou*; being in the presence of the Lord); Psalm 129.7 (mercy and a plenteous redemption being with the Lord); and Proverbs 12.2; 15.11, 28(a); 16.11; 17.3; Job 9.2; Isaiah 49.4; see too Proverbs 12.22 and 15.8 (*par' autō*). All of these references refer to being before the Lord in an evaluative, judicial sense. It is never used in direct address (*para soi*). Proverbs 8.30 refers to wisdom being in the presence of the Lord (*par' autō*); Proverbs 12.13, 16 refer to wisdom, might and strength being 'with the Lord' (*par' autō*); Sirach 35.12 declares that

to judge in 3.8 is based on its 'location' *para kyriō*.[32] That the certainty of Christ's return in 3.4, 9 is a *promise* (*hē epangelia*) anchored 'before the [sovereignty of the] Lord' in 3.8 corresponds to the affirmation in 1.3–4 and 3.13 that the 'divine nature' (*theia physis*) is expressed in the fulfilment of the actual *content* of God's promises (cf. *ta epangelmata* in 1.4 with *to epangelma* in 3.13) as the demonstration of his 'divine power' (*hē theia dynamis*).[33] Of interest in this regard is that *both* mercy *and* wrath are 'with the Lord' in Psalm 90 (cf. too Sirach 5.6; 16.11), which parallels the same confidence expressed in 2 Peter 2.8–9 and in the principles of Romans 11.22 and 32, all of which are derived from the inviolable character of God's promises (see Romans 11.26, 29).

Finally, the adaptation of Psalm 90.4 in 2 Peter 3.8 reflects the eschatological perspective of the latter, in which, in inaugurated fulfilment of the prayer of Psalm 90.13–17, believers know themselves to be living between the two comings of the Messiah. In Psalm 90, prior to the Messiah's advent, the context was the ongoing *wrath* of God, unleashed in the Fall, experienced in death and realized historically in Israel's exile. In 2 Peter, by contrast, the context therefore becomes the ongoing *mercy* of God, poured out through the messianic restoration, experienced in the new life of godliness (1.3) and realized historically in the gathering of the 'beloved' (cf. Psalm 90.16!). Accordingly, if the question in Psalm 90.13 was how long God's *anger* would last before he again had mercy on his people, the question in 2 Peter 3.9 is how long God's *patience* will last before he again judges the world (3.7). And if the concern in Psalm 90 was the death of God's people, in 2 Peter God's judgement now encompasses the entire cosmos, since the 'last thing' yet to be done by God is the establishment of a 'new heavens and earth according to his promise, in which righteousness dwells' (3.13).

The return of the Messiah is thereby 'imminent' in the sense that it is the very next thing to happen in the history of redemption. As an expression of such proximity on a personal level, Psalm 90 turned from the

---

there is no partiality 'with the Lord' (*par' autō*); Daniel 2.22 refers to destruction being 'with God' (*par' autō*).

32 Contrast, e.g., the view of Frey 2015, 339, who extends the idea of the 'incommensurability' of the divine and human evaluations and experiences of time to the meaning of *para kyriō*: 'Der eingefügte Zusatz παρὰ κυρίῳ (*para kyriō*) markiert zunächst, dass es dem Autor um das Zeitmaß geht, welches Gottes Handeln bestimmt: "Vor dem Herrn" gilt anderes als vor Menschen.'

33 For the understanding that the 'divine nature' in 1.4 refers not to God's 'being' or 'essence', but to his dynamic character as that which expresses itself in its corresponding actions, which in 1.3–4 and 3.13 are defined in terms of the content of his promises (cf. *ta tima kai megista epangelmata* in 1.3 // 3.13), see Hafemann 2013, 80–99.

pervasiveness of God's judgement in verses 3–11 to a call to 'number one's days' in verse 12 in order that the righteous might gain a 'heart of wisdom' in regard to the imminence of their own death. In the same way, 2 Peter turns from the certainty of divine judgement in 3.8 to a corresponding call to repentance in 3.9–11 (cf. 3.14–16), which will somehow '[hasten] the coming of the day of God' (3.12). Likewise, in Romans 11.20–22 Gentile believers are called to stand firm in their faith by fearing the severity of God's judgement, thereby resisting the arrogance that considers itself beyond the reach of being 'cut off' from the 'olive tree' of God's redeemed people (cf. Romans 11.18).

Humility and eschatology today

The work of N. T. Wright is characterized by his Christian and ecclesial commitment to move from exegesis to contemporary significance and in so doing to pursue 'theology' in the classic and much-needed sense of always asking the hard questions of appropriation. In this regard, the oft-forgotten and scorned letter of 2 Peter proves to be surprisingly fruitful theologically.

The second letter of Peter reminds us that God's eschatological judge-ment, which will usher in 'new heavens and a new earth in which righteousness dwells' (3.10–13), is a *positive* expectation for God's people. Only this divine judgement, in some still fully incomprehensible way, will 'solve' the 'problem of evil'. At the same time, in the face of the unresolved and rampant evil of this age, the longing for this eschatological resolu-tion creates the 'problem' of 'the delay of the Parousia'.[34] Nevertheless, Christians continue to long for and anticipate the 'imminent' return of the Christ, even as past generations have often expected it in their own time. For rather than doubt and despair, a 'humility of thinking' in *Christian terms* takes place when an eschatological hope for the future (3.13), based on the faithfulness of God's word in the past (3.5, 7), fuels an obedient

---

[34] Bauckham 1980, 7–8, 29, has mapped out this tension well. As he observes, 'Only the over-coming of present evil by eschatological righteousness could vindicate God as righteous, and only the hope of such a future triumph of righteousness could make the evils of the present bearable . . . This universal challenge to the righteousness of God demanded a universal righting of wrongs, an elimination of evil on a universal, even cosmic scale' (Bauckham 1980, 8). Moreover, the 'already' and 'not yet' of early Christian eschatology actually heightens the sense of imminence: 'For if the victory over evil has already been won, it seems even more necessary that the actual eradication of evil from the world should follow very soon' (Bauckham 1980, 29). 'Thus the characteristic tension of imminence and delay in Jewish apocalyptic seems to be, if anything, sharpened by the "already" of Christian faith, since it contributes to *both* sides of the tension' (Bauckham 1980, 29).

life of faith in the present (1.8–11; 3.11, 14, 17–18). Eschatology, in which God's promise for righteousness in the world to come is the object of faith, creates a hope and standard of judgement beyond one's self, and in so doing enables and calls forth an ethic of love for others.

Conversely, the false teachers addressed in 2 Peter evaluate their lives and circumstances from the perspective of the status quo, in which their lawless lives appear to be free from God's judgement. Their arrogant thinking thus regards the present to be the hermeneutical key to the future rather than the divine promise of future judgement being determinative for the present. Their self-validated and self-validating rejection of the return of Christ consequently allowed the 'scoffers' theologically and psychologically to live for immediate gratification as the formative framework of their lives. Such 'intellectual arrogance' expresses itself in an independence from God's word characterized by disobedience to God's commands. 'Presentism', in which one's own potential for satisfaction in this world is the object of faith, creates a hope and standard of judgement in one's self, and in so doing drives a self-directed antinomianism.

'To think humbly' according to 2 Peter 3.8 is thus to evaluate one's life and circumstances from the perspective of God's certain, impending and final judgement of all things, including the systemic injustices of this world. In Psalm 90.12, 16–17 this 'heart of wisdom' was expressed in the prayer of God's 'servants' (itself a humble self-designation) that God would establish the work of their hands. In 2 Peter 3.10, 14 this humility recognizes that when 'the day of the Lord comes like a thief . . . the earth and the works in it will be found' (reading with the NA[27]), with the life of the faithful 'found' to be 'spotless and blameless' through the fire of God's final judgement.[35] When faced with one's own pride in view of the promised return of the Messiah, repentance therefore becomes the expression of Christian humility (2 Peter 3.8–15b; cf. Romans 2.5–11 as the outworking of 2.4). As Paul put it in Romans 11.20 to those believers tempted to be arrogant: 'Do not think proud things, but fear' (cf. 1 Corinthians 10.12).

Bibliography

Bauckham, Richard (1980). 'The Delay of the Parousia.' *Tyndale Bulletin* 31: 3–36.
—— (1983). *Jude, 2 Peter.* Word Biblical Commentary 50. Waco, TX: Word.
Clifford, Richard J. (2000). 'What Does the Psalmist Ask For in Psalms 39.5 and 90.12?' *Journal of Biblical Literature* 119: 59–66.

---

[35] I owe this insight to Darian Lockett in a conversation at the Center for Christian Thought, Biola University, La Mirada, CA, on 2 February 2017.

Dahood, Mitchell (1968). *Psalms II: 51–100, Introduction, Translation, and Notes.* Anchor Bible. Garden City, NY: Doubleday.

Delitzsch, Franz (1883). *Biblical Commentary on the Psalms, Vol. III.* New York, NY: Funk & Wagnalls.

Frey, Jörg (2015). *Der Brief des Judas und der zweite Brief des Petrus.* Theologischer Handkommentar zum Neuen Testament 15/II. Leipzig: Evangelische Verlagsanstalt.

Goldingay, John (2008). *Psalms, Volume 3: Psalms 90–150.* Baker Commentary on the Old Testament: Wisdom and Psalms. Grand Rapids, MI: Baker.

Green, Gene L. (2008). *Jude and 2 Peter.* Baker Exegetical Commentary on the New Testament. Grand Rapids, MI: Baker.

Hafemann, Scott J. (2013). "'Divine Nature" in 2 Pet 1.4 within Its Eschatological Context.' *Biblica* 94: 80–99.

Hossfeld, Frank-Lothar, and Erich Zenger (2005). *Psalms 2: A Commentary on Psalms 51–100.* Hermeneia. Minneapolis, MN: Fortress.

Krüger, Thomas (1994). 'Psalm 90 und die "Vergänglichkeit des Menschen."' *Biblica* 75: 191–219.

Pietersma, Albert (2007). 'Psalms.' In *A New English Translation of the Septuagint,* edited by Albert Pietersma and Benjamin G. Wright, 542–620. New York, NY: Oxford University Press.

Rad, Gerhard von (1980). 'Psalm 90.' In his *God at Work in Israel,* 210–23. Nashville, TN: Abingdon.

Rahlfs, Alfred (1931) (ed.). *Psalmi cum Odis.* Göttingen: Vandenhoeck & Ruprecht.

—— (2006). *Septuaginta.* Editio Altera. Stuttgart: Deutsche Bibelgesellschaft.

Schrage, Wolfgang (1985). 'Ein Tag ist beim Herrn wie tausend Jahre, und tausend Jahre sind wie ein Tag. 2 Pet 3,8.' In *Glaube und Eschatologie. Festschrift für Werner Georg Kümmel zum 80. Geburtstag,* edited by Erich Gräßer and Otto Merk, 267–75. Tübingen: Mohr Siebeck.

Schreiner, Stefan (1978). 'Erwägungen zur Struktur des 90. Psalms.' *Biblica* 59: 80–90.

Tate, Marvin E. (1990). *Psalms 51–100.* Word Biblical Commentary 20. Nashville, TN: Thomas Nelson.

Urbrock, William J. (1998). 'Psalm 90: Moses, Mortality, and . . . the Morning.' *Currents in Theology and Mission* 25: 26–9.

Vögtle, Anton (1994). *Der Judasbrief / Der 2. Petrusbrief.* Evangelisch-Katholischer Kommentar zum Neuen Testament 22. Solothurn and Düsseldorf: Benziger Verlag.

Wright, N. T. (2013). *Paul and the Faithfulness of God.* Christian Origins and the Question of God 4. London: SPCK / Minneapolis, MN: Fortress.

Hope for what we do not yet see: the salvation of all Israel in Romans 11.25–27

RICHARD B. HAYS

> Whenever a long delay casts us into despair, let us remember this word mystery. By this Paul clearly instructs us that the manner of [Israel's] conversion will be unique and unprecedented, and that therefore those who attempt to measure it by their own judgment will be in error.
>
> (John Calvin[1])

Why does Paul tweak Isaiah's text?

In his commentary on Romans, John Calvin observes, with his usual careful attention to detail, that Paul's quotation of Isaiah in Romans 11.26b–27 diverges from the actual text of Isaiah 59.20–21. Having made this observation, however, Calvin dismisses the exegetical difficulty of the citation with a fascinatingly casual assessment:

> Paul, however, does not quote the passage in Isaiah word for word . . . We need not worry ourselves unduly on this matter; for the point which we are to consider is how appropriately the apostles adapt to their purpose the proofs which they adduce from the Old Testament. They desire only to point to the passages, in order to direct their readers to the fountain itself.[2]

In other words, Calvin takes Paul to be gesturing loosely towards the passage in Isaiah rather than attending closely to its wording. Consequently, Calvin proceeds to comment not on what *Paul* actually wrote but on 'the fountain itself', the text of Isaiah 59, observing that the prophet 'says expressly, that a Redeemer shall come to Sion; and he adds, that he will redeem those in Jacob who shall return from their transgression'. Of course, this proclamation differs significantly from what Paul says in Romans: Paul writes that the Redeemer shall come *from* Zion, not *to* it, and that *he* will take away

---

[1] Calvin 1960, 254.
[2] Calvin 1960, 255–6.

the sins of Jacob, with no explicit proviso that they must first repent from their transgression.

Calvin is not unaware of the discrepancies, but he waves them off as a matter of small concern: 'Although the expression used by the prophet, "shall come to Sion" (Isaiah 59.20), suited his purpose better, Paul felt no scruple in following the commonly accepted translation which reads, "A redeemer shall come out of Zion."'[3] Calvin attributes no particular significance to the form of the translation that Paul actually chose to cite. Likewise, mindful that the last part of Paul's citation also does not come from Isaiah 59, Calvin opines that the words found in Romans 11.27 must be derived from Jeremiah (i.e. the promise of a new covenant), even though Paul's actual wording only very indirectly recalls the words of Jeremiah 31.34.[4]

In contrast to the great Reformer's assurance that we 'need not worry ourselves' about the anomalies in Paul's citation of Isaiah, recent NT scholarship has worried a great deal about the peculiarities of Paul's reception and interpretation of Israel's Scripture. Romans 11.25–27 has become an intensely contested *locus* for exegesis – not least because it presents a crucial text for theological reflection about God's faithfulness to Israel and the relationship between the Church and the Jewish people.[5]

Among exegetes who have wrestled with these matters, N. T. Wright holds a place of pre-eminence for the depth and clarity of his engagement

---

[3] Calvin 1960, 256. It is not clear why Calvin assumed that Paul's citation was following 'the commonly received translation', for the OG manuscript tradition of Isaiah overwhelmingly supports the reading *heneken Siōn*. Was Calvin aware of later Greek manuscripts that, under the influence of Romans 11.26, read *ek Siōn*? (For details, see Wagner 2002, 284.) Or was he simply assuming that Paul must have used a source with such a reading?

[4] Calvin writes, 'Although Paul had briefly touched in the last prophecy quoted from Isaiah on the office of the Messiah, in order to advise the Jews of what they were chiefly to hope for from Him, he deliberately added these few words from Jeremiah for the same purpose. The words which he adds do not appear in the former passage.' In Calvin's view, Paul has to supply a reference from Jeremiah to the divine initiative in the removal of sins because otherwise the expectation of conversion of an obstinate people would seem incredible (Calvin 1960, 256). He does not seem to be aware of Isaiah 27.9 as the source of the words cited in Romans 11.27b.

[5] Michael Wolter devoted his Presidential Address at the 2017 General Meeting of the Studiorum Novi Testamenti Societas to the interpretation of this difficult passage (Wolter 2018). Regrettably, Wolter's article appeared in print well after the present essay had been completed and sent to press; therefore, I was not able to engage his arguments in this discussion of the passage. Readers of Wolter's piece will recognize that his interpretation differs significantly from N. T. Wright's and from my own – particularly on the meaning of 'all Israel'. I would, however, note that Wolter's emphasis on the LXX Psalms as the source of Paul's anomalous use of *ek Siōn* in his citation of Isaiah 59.20 is independently convergent with one of my major arguments in the pages that follow here.

with Romans 9—11. From his earliest work in *The Climax of the Covenant* (1991), through his commentary on Romans in the *New Interpreter's Bible* (2002), all the way up to his magisterial *Paul and the Faithfulness of God* (2013), he has consistently highlighted distinctive features of Paul's citation of Isaiah in Romans 11.25–27. His attention to those features has led him to champion an interpretation of Romans 11.25–27 that challenges much modern critical opinion.[6]

It should be noted, however, that in one key respect Wright's reading of the passage aligns closely with the judgement of Calvin about the meaning of Paul's declaration that 'all Israel shall be saved' (11.26a). Thus, Calvin:

> Many understand this of the Jewish people, as if Paul were saying that religion was to be restored to them again as before. But I extend the word *Israel* to include all the people of God, in this sense, 'When the Gentiles have come in, the Jews will at the same time return from their defection to the obedience of faith. The salvation of the whole Israel of God, which must be drawn from both, will thus be completed, and yet in such a way that the Jews, as the first-born in the family of God, may obtain the first place.' . . . In the same way, in Gal 6.16, he calls the Church, which was composed equally of Jews and Gentiles, the Israel of God.[7]

Though Wright makes only glancing reference to Calvin in a footnote,[8] he has arrived at the same destination by a different route. It is a lengthy route, carefully mapped out. Indeed, as far as I am able to judge, in the whole history of Pauline exegesis no one else has developed a more extensive defence of the interpretation of *pas Israēl* in Romans 11.26 as the one people of God composed of Jews and Gentiles together.[9]

In my opinion, as I shall explain below, Wright's reading of 'all Israel' is convincing, and his arguments are both sound and powerful. I believe, however, that several other details of his interpretation of Romans 11.25–27 could be both qualified and amplified. The aim, then, of the present essay will be to carry forward the conversation about Paul's interpretation of Israel's Scripture in the specific *locus* of Romans 11.25–27. I shall query a few aspects of Wright's interpretation and offer some

---

6 Wright 1991, 231–57; 2002, esp. 687–93; 2013, 1231–52. For Wright's concise summary of the points at which his interpretation of Romans 11.25–27 challenges received scholarly opinion, see Wright 2013, 1231–2.

7 Calvin 1960, 255.

8 Wright 2013, 1239 n. 672.

9 I refer here specifically to his treatment of 11.26a, but his interpretation of this verse must be understood in the broader context of his reading of Romans 9—11 as a whole (Wright 2013, 1156–258).

complementary suggestions about this difficult passage.[10] My remarks will fall into three parts: first, a summary of some of the strongest points in Wright's reading; second, an examination of several questions that require additional critical exploration; and finally, a few constructive exegetical suggestions, particularly about the role of the Psalms in the intertextual network of interpretation that underlies Romans 11.25–27.

Wright's reading of Romans 11.25–27: ground gained

Wright's comprehensive exegesis of the passage has, in my opinion, established firm ground on a number of crucial points. Whatever else may be said about these verses – and indeed about Romans 9—11 more broadly – we must acknowledge the force of his reading on at least the following six points. In my judgement the strength of his exegesis has effectively placed the burden of proof on any interpreter who would dispute any of these six findings.[11]

1 The contingency of the argument

Paul is not writing a treatise on election or predestination; he is writing an apostolic pastoral letter. Its particular target audience in Romans 9—11 is a community of Gentile Christians in Rome who may be tempted to claim superior status or to regard themselves as having supplanted the Jewish people within God's special favour (11.13, 17–24, 25, 28–32). Again and again Paul asserts that God is mysteriously at work to bring Jews and Gentiles alike into the sphere of his unfathomable mercy. The Gentile Christ-followers are therefore admonished not to be proud or condescending towards Jews who have, at least in the present time, not believed the gospel.

2 The continuity of the argument

Romans 11.25–27 is not a sudden revelation of a new mystery that contradicts what Paul has said in the preceding chapters of the letter. This is one of the most compelling aspects of Wright's exposition. He demonstrates the carefully crafted continuity of Paul's argument through the entirety of Romans, particularly the way in which 11.25–27 concisely summarizes

---

[10] I am profoundly grateful to Tom for dedicating his magisterial work on Paul to me. In the essay that follows, I trust that my engagement with his reading, while critical at certain points, will be understood as an appreciative conversation between friends who care deeply about getting the exegesis right.

[11] The summary that follows refers to Wright's exposition in Wright 2013, 1231–52.

exactly what Paul had asserted in 11.11–24: branches have been broken off the olive tree (Israel), but they can be grafted back in 'if they do not remain in unbelief' (11.23, *ean mē epimenōsin tē apistia*).[12] The 'mystery' (*mystērion*, 11.25), then, is not a sudden bolt from the blue; rather, it is precisely a disclosure of the insight that Paul has reached through meditation on the course of his apostolic mission in conjunction with his christologically inflected rereading of Israel's Scripture.[13] (Cf. Romans 16.25–26, where Paul's gospel proclamation of Jesus Christ is said to be 'according to the revelation of the mystery [*mystērion*] that was kept silent for long ages but now made known *through prophetic scriptures* to all the Gentiles'.) The *mystērion* is mysterious precisely because it entails a reversal of the narrative order in which Paul, along with his Jewish kinspeople, had expected salvation to come to Israel and to the nations.[14]

3 Gentile believers 'come in' to Israel

When Paul writes of the fullness of the Gentiles 'coming in' prior to the salvation of all Israel, *into what* does he expect them to come? Wright answers that they are to come in to *Israel*, precisely as the olive tree metaphor in 11.17–24 has indicated.[15] As wild olive branches they are grafted on to the tree, which is undoubtedly a symbol for Israel.[16] This image is fully consistent with Paul's well-attested theological conviction that his Gentile converts have been taken up into the story of Israel. Paul insists that Abraham is the father of circumcised and uncircumcised alike (Romans 4). In his view, the non-Jewish Christians at Corinth 'used to be Gentiles' (1 Corinthians 12.2), but now they are to regard Moses and the

---

12 Unless otherwise noted, all quotations from the Bible are my own translation.

13 See Nils Dahl's characteristically incisive formulation: 'Paul introduces this statement as the disclosure of a revealed mystery. Yet the solution draws the conclusion of the preceding arguments. We should probably not think of a sudden, unmediated revelation granted to Paul but rather of a mystery hidden in Scripture until its explanation was unveiled' (Dahl 1977, 152). Wright 2013, 1232, aptly notes Dahl's judgement.

14 Speaking of this reversal and the unexpected way in which the Gentile mission leads to Israel's salvation, Francis Watson, noting the motif of Israel's 'jealousy' in Deuteronomy 32.21, writes: 'If Paul has learned all this through a "mystery" or special revelation (11.25), the revelation has come to him in and through his meditation on the Song of Moses' (Watson 2004, 449). In the light of Romans 11.26–27, we may add that Isaiah 59 and 27 also played a significant role in Paul's scriptural meditation, along with other texts to be discussed below.

15 In support of this interpretation, see also Wilckens 1980, 254–6; Keck 2005, 276, 286; Jewett 2007, 700–1.

16 Against, e.g., Dunn 1988, 680, who joins a line of exegetes including Ernst Käsemann in suggesting that Paul is here dependent on 'pre-Pauline tradition that stems from Jesus'. Dunn therefore suggests an allusion to the Synoptic language of 'entering the kingdom', although Paul does not use that expression anywhere in the present context.

people of Israel in the wilderness as 'our forefathers' (1 Corinthians 10.1–4).[17] As Wright compellingly observes, Gentile believers in Jesus have, in Paul's view, received circumcision of the heart and can now rightly be described as 'Jews' (Romans 2.25–29); accordingly, Paul can encourage his Philippian converts who 'worship in the Spirit of God' and confess Jesus as Messiah to join him in declaring 'we are the circumcision' (Philippians 3.3). In the light of such texts, it also seems highly likely that when Paul invokes a blessing on 'the Israel of God' (Galatians 6.16, NRSV), he is referring to all those, Gentile and Jew alike, who share a common identity in Christ (Galatians 3.26–29).[18]

4 Paul's kinspeople, the Jewish people, can find salvation only through confessing Jesus Messiah as Lord

There is no separate dispensation for Jews apart from Christ. Paul has insistently argued throughout Romans that 'there is no distinction' between Jew and Gentile with respect to God's saving action. This is the whole burden of Romans 1—4. The righteousness of God is revealed through the faithfulness of Jesus Christ for all who trust in him (Romans 3.21–24). And, in case his readers may have forgotten the point, he hammers it home again in Romans 10.9–13: everyone who confesses that Jesus is Lord and believes that God has raised him from the dead will be saved (10.9). Precisely with respect to this point, 'there is no distinction between Jew and Greek, for the same Lord [Jesus] is Lord of all' (10.12). Thus, whatever Romans 11.26–27 means, it cannot mean there is a *Sonderweg*, a separate path of salvation for Israel – or for some part of Israel – apart from trusting in the one whom Paul proclaims to be Israel's Messiah.[19] That is why Paul anguishes over many of his own kinspeople who have not accepted the gospel (9.1–5), and that is why he continues to pray earnestly 'that they may be saved' (10.1, NRSV) – surely meaning that they may not 'remain in unbelief' (11.23).

---

17 On this point, see Hays 1989, 91–104; 2005, 8–12.
18 This reading of Galatians 6.16 and Romans 11.26 is challenged by Eastman 2010a, 147–70; 2010b, 367–95. These two careful essays argue that 'the Israel of God' can only refer to ethnic Israel rather than to a redefined Israel inclusive of both Gentiles and Jews who confess faith in Jesus. For the reasons briefly sketched above, I am not finally convinced by her arguments, but her work must be weighed carefully by anyone seeking to understand the issues.
19 For statements opposing the *Sonderweg* reading, see, for example, Dahl 1977, 152–5; Sanders 1983, 192–6; Dunn 1988, 691; Hafemann 1988, 38–58; Hvalvik 1990, 87–107; Wagner 2002, 297–8; Keck 2005, 285–6; Jewett 2007, 702; Kirk 2010, 81–99.

5 The meaning of *kai houtōs* (11.26a) is 'and thus' – not 'and then'

The phrase *kai houtōs* in Romans 11.26a refers to *manner*, not temporal sequence. In other words, it points back to the events summarized in verse 25 (the hardening of a part of Israel and the coming in of a plenitude of Gentiles to stir Israel to jealousy) as the surprising *manner in which* the salvation of 'all Israel' will occur.[20] As Wright puts it, 'and *that*, the entire sequence of 11.11–24, summed up in 11.25, is *how* "all Israel" will be saved.'[21]

6 'All Israel' means the one people of God, composed of Jews and Gentiles who have come to place their trust in Jesus Messiah

The cumulative force of the previous five points leads almost inescapably to Wright's conclusion that 'all Israel' in 11.26a is Paul's way of describing the whole people of God, the whole body of those who confess Jesus as Messiah and Lord, and thereby find salvation within the christologically reconfigured covenant with Israel's God. Wright's detailed exegesis thus leads him to substantial agreement with Calvin (cited above) and with the classic formulation of Karl Barth:

> 'All Israel' is the community of those elected by God in and with Jesus Christ both from the Jews and also from the Gentiles, the whole Church . . . in the totality constituted by the remnant continuing in and with the original stem Jesus Christ, by the wild shoots added later from the Gentiles, and by the branches which were and are finally grafted in again.[22]

Wright notes that Paul had, significantly, launched this whole train of argument in 9.6 with the declaration that 'not all who are from Israel are Israel [*ou gar pantes hoi ex Israēl houtoi Israēl*]'. And Paul further insists that it is 'the children of promise' who are truly reckoned as the 'seed' of

---

20 The lexical arguments for a temporal interpretation are very slight, and the temporal sense is not attested in Paul.

21 Wright 2013, 1241.

22 Barth 1957, 300. I cannot resist observing with some satisfaction that Tom has been led via his exegesis to concur with Barth – at least on this point. Fitzmyer (1993, 623–4) compiles a formidable list of patristic commentators who advocated this interpretation, including Irenaeus, Clement of Alexandria, Theodore of Mopsuestia, Theodoret of Cyrrhus, and (in some but not all of their writings) Origen and Augustine. Fitzmyer himself judges that such a reading of 'all Israel' cannot be correct. I would suggest, however, that the early prevalence of this interpretation should at least give pause to modern commentators who reject it out of hand. The unpopularity of such a reading in the late twentieth century is surely in part influenced by the laudable desire of exegetes in a post-Holocaust era to interpret Paul in a way they imagine to be more helpful for Jewish–Christian dialogue.

Abraham (9.8). We should not forget that *in Galatians he had argued vehemently that the uncircumcised Gentile believers in Galatia were precisely among the 'children of promise'* (Galatians 4.28), *Abraham's heirs*. Thus, for Paul to include Jewish and Gentile Christians together under the designation 'Israel' is fully consistent with deep currents in his theology. Wright characterizes this locution as a 'polemical redefinition',[23] but I am not sure that is quite the right description. Instead, I would suggest that Paul's designation of Jewish and Gentile believers together as 'all Israel' is simply the *constructive exegetical outworking* of Paul's hermeneutical project, his sustained effort to interpret his mission to the nations through a retrospective reading of Israel's Scripture in the light of the *apokalypsis* of Jesus as Messiah. The redefinition is not so much 'polemical' as it is exegetical and kerygmatic.

Ground still to be explored: open questions

Despite the substantial ground gained by Wright's wide-ranging interpretation, there is still some rough territory remaining to be explored. On several points, there is need for greater clarity. Some of these questions may not be susceptible to definite resolution this side of the eschaton. Nonetheless, it is important to identify them, because they appear to me to represent points of continuing uncertainty (or possible vulnerability) in Wright's position. Once again I offer a list of particular points, coincidentally also six in number, this time in interrogative form.

1 What is the sense of *apo merous* in Romans 11.25?

The meaning of *apo merous* in Romans 11.25 is often left murky by commentaries on Romans. Wright leaves no such ambiguity; he clearly states his preference for a partitive interpretation ('a hardening has come upon *a part of* Israel') as opposed to a temporal one ('a hardening has come *for a while* upon Israel'). He concedes the possibility of a temporal meaning, pointing to Romans 15.24 as an instance, but then writes, 'But it is in my judgment far more likely that Paul is here referring to the "hardening" coming upon *one part* of Israel, as in 11.1–7, especially verse 7.'[24] Insofar as Wright gives reasons for this judgement, they appear to rest on his larger construal of the logic of the discourse, rather than on lexical investigation of the meaning of the prepositional phrase. Perhaps we can advance the

---

23 E.g. Wright 2013, 1242.
24 Wright 2013, 1239 (emphasis original).

discussion, at least a little, by tracking down how *apo merous* functions in other relevant contexts.

Beyond the present passage, Paul uses this expression only four times in his letters. In Romans 15.15, he tells his readers, 'on some points [*apo merous*] I have written to you rather boldly by way of reminder' (NRSV). That is a periphrastic rendering, but the sense here is apparently partitive, and not temporal. The phrase occurs twice more in the opening chapters of 2 Corinthians. In 2 Corinthians 1.14, he tells the Corinthians, 'you have known us *in part*.' And in 2 Corinthians 2.5, he writes, 'But if anyone has caused pain, he has caused it not to me, but to some extent [*apo merous*] – not to exaggerate it – to all of you' (NRSV). Again, these uses of the expression are clearly *not* temporal. In the light of these parallels, I am inclined to doubt that *apo merous* in Romans 15.24 should be taken in a temporal sense – a sense otherwise unattested in either the NT or the LXX. Romans 15.24 could instead be translated literally as follows: 'For I do hope to see you on my journey and to be sent on by you [i.e. given provisions and resources], once I have been *in part* filled up [i.e. supplied] by you.'[25]

It should be observed that in all of these other Pauline usages, the phrase *apo merous* functions adverbially. It does not occur elsewhere in the NT. In the extant Greek versions of Israel's scriptures, the prepositional phrase *apo merous* occurs only seven times. In three of the instances (Numbers 34.3; Joshua 18.15, 20), it is a geographical term referring to an area of land (one thinks of the colloquial English expression 'in those parts' to designate a geographical region). In one other case the term is used to describe a part (the extremity) of a cherub's wings (1 Kings 6.24). But the last three instances offer potentially closer parallels to the sense of this terminology in Romans 11.25. The phrase *apo merous* appears in the rendering of Judges 18.2 in Codex Alexandrinus: *kai exapesteilan hoi huioi Dan ek tōn sungeneiōn autōn pente andras apo merous autōn* ('And the Danites sent from their clan five valiant men from their part').[26] A similar partitive use of the phrase to designate a portion of a larger group of people appears in Nehemiah 7.70 LXX: *kai apo merous archēgōn tōn patriōn edōkan eis to ergon* ('And *some of the heads* of ancestral houses contributed to the

---

25 Interestingly, the KJV renders the relevant clause as 'if first I be somewhat filled with your company'. Most modern translations opt for a temporal rendering, as suggested by BDAG, 633: 'for a while'. It is noteworthy that BDAG offers no other examples of this alleged temporal sense of the phrase.

26 This could, of course, be interpreted as another instance of the geographical sense: '. . . from their territory'.

work'). Finally, in Theodotion's text of Daniel 1.2, we read this: 'And the Lord gave into his hand Joakim king of Judah, *and part of the vessels of the house of God* [*apo merous tōn skeuōn oikou tou theou*].' All three of these examples illustrate the use of *apo merous* to designate one part of a greater whole. Of course, in Romans Paul is not alluding to any of these passages, but they do demonstrate an idiomatic use of the expression *apo merous* in biblical Greek that closely approximates the partitive interpretation given to *apo merous* in Wright's reading of Romans 11.25.

To summarize: a survey of the uses of *apo merous* in Paul and in the Greek versions of Israel's scriptures gives little or no support to a temporal interpretation. The only possible example of such a sense is Romans 15.24, and even that instance is questionable. In all the other relevant comparative passages, a partitive sense is clear. As we have noted, in all of the Pauline passages apart from Romans 11.25 *apo merous* is used adverbially, not adjectivally. Following this pattern in Romans 11.25 would yield a translation such as 'a hardening has partially come upon Israel'. In view of the entire foregoing discourse (branches cut off, etc.) this could hardly mean that individual Israelites were left with only some sort of partial faith.[27] In all likelihood, therefore, even granting the technical adverbial sense, the sentence probably means nothing different from what Wright has suggested: 'a hardening has come upon part of Israel.' The examples cited above from Greek versions of Judges, Nehemiah and Daniel confirm that such a usage of *apo merous* would be idiomatic in biblical Greek in a historical period not far removed from Paul. On balance, I would judge that the evidence favours Wright's interpretation. It should be emphasized, further, that if Wright is correct about the sense of *apo merous*, it follows that *'Israel' in verse 25 might well have the same meaning as 'Israel' in verse 26: the whole body of the people of God made up of Jewish and Gentile believers together.*[28] Part of the totality of *that* Israel is presently hardened, but ultimately, Paul believes, they will come to embrace the saving confession of Jesus as Lord.

---

[27] Wright is probably correct to say that this would, strictly speaking, be nonsensical. From Paul's perspective, either individual Israelites have been hardened, or they have not; either they have believed in Jesus, or they have not. Wright remarks: 'in view of 11.1–10, being "partly hardened" would make as much sense as being "partly pregnant"' (2013, 1239 n. 668). As Keck 2005, 279, observes, the qualifier *apo merous* 'distinguishes nonbelieving Israel from the Christian Jews, who by definition are not among the hardened'.

[28] For slightly different reasons, Wright makes a similar observation about the sense of 'Israel' in v. 25 (Wright 2013, 1244).

2 What is the significance of *achri hou* in Romans 11.25?

A very different judgement applies to the adverbial clause introduced by *achri hou* in 11.25. There is no doubt of its temporal meaning: *achri hou* means 'until', and the translation of the clause is uncontroversial: 'until the fullness [*plērōma*] of the Gentiles has come in'. Paul's articulation of the 'mystery' appears to anticipate a definite future endpoint,[29] at which the full divinely ordained number of Gentiles will have 'come in' to Israel. And Paul's sentence implies that precisely after that definite endpoint the 'hardening' that has come upon 'a part of Israel' will be removed.[30] To most interpreters, the language here strongly suggests an eschatological scenario, analogous to the apocalyptic visions of Revelation. (For an especially interesting parallel, see Revelation 2.25 (NRSV): 'Only hold fast to what you have *until I come* [*achri hou an hēxō*].') Wright, however, has consistently resisted this interpretation of the passage. He believes that Paul, rather than foreseeing a fixed eschatological endpoint, envisages an indefinite period during which the number of believing Jews will gradually increase in 'a steady flow of Jews into the church, by grace through faith'.[31] As he puts it in his most recent extended interpretation of the passage, 'not only will gentiles continue to "come in", but the "remnant" itself will become very much larger, moving towards an eventual "fullness" (verse 12)'.[32]

It appears to me that Wright is (understandably) reacting against an opinion that was briefly popular among some late twentieth-century exegetes but now largely rejected by most recent commentators – namely, the opinion that Paul envisaged no evangelistic mission to the Jewish people prior to the *parousia*, and that God would at the time of the eschaton suddenly save all Jews through some mysterious means unrelated to their placing trust in Jesus as the Messiah. For reasons explained above, I also regard this view as unsustainable as an exegesis of Paul's argument. It is not clear, however, that the only alternative to such a view is Wright's picture of a gradual influx of Jews into the community that confesses

---

29 BDAG (160) describes *achri* as a 'marker of continuous extent of time *up to a point*' (emphasis mine). Wilk (1998, 68) observes that *achri hou* 'bezeichnet in den Briefen des Paulus stets ein konkretes Ereignis der Zukunft als Endpunkt eines Tuns oder Zustands; und zwar entweder das Kommen Christi selbst – sei es "ins Fleisch" (Gal 3:19) oder zur Parusie (1 Kor 11:26) – oder ein Geschehen, das mit ihm eng verbunden ist (1 Kor 15:25)'.

30 It is probably the temporal force of *achri hou* that has (perhaps subconsciously) led some interpreters to inappropriately impose a temporal sense on *kai houtōs* in the following clause.

31 Wright 1991, 249.

32 Wright 2013, 1239.

Jesus as Lord. Paul clearly does hope that in the present time some of his own people will be moved to jealousy by the Gentile mission and brought to faith. The existing 'remnant' (11.5), including Paul himself, already bears witness to such a possibility, and Paul has emphatically agreed that other apostles, such as James and Cephas and John, should continue their mission of proclaiming the gospel message to the circumcised (Galatians 2.9). But such an understanding of a present-time mission to the Jewish people hardly precludes the possibility of a future dramatic event, after 'the fullness of the Gentiles has come in', that will bring many more (*to plērōma autōn*, Romans 11.12) to be 'grafted in again' through coming to acknowledge Jesus as Lord (11.23–24).

Paul's hope for a radical eschatological transformation in the future is amply attested in other passages in his letters (e.g. 1 Thessalonians 1.9–10; 4.13–18; Philippians 3.20–21; 1 Corinthians 15.20–28), including other portions of Romans (13.11–14). Especially pertinent is Romans 8.18–25, which speaks of a hope that the whole creation 'will be set free from its bondage to decay and obtain the freedom of the glory of the children of God' – while acknowledging that in the present time believers continue to groan and wait in hope for that which they do not see. Part of what Paul does *not* see in this 'not yet' time is a large-scale turning of the Jewish people to confess Jesus as Messiah and Lord; hence, his sorrow, anguish and earnest prayers for them (9.1–5; 10.1–4). Yet that large-scale turning is precisely what Paul envisages in 11.25–27 as an event that will not occur '*until* the fullness of the Gentiles has come in'.

3 How does Paul interpret *ho rhuomenos*?

The above line of thought leads on to the citation that Paul adduces in 11.26b–27 as the scriptural confirmation of his foregoing argument. How will the large-scale eschatological turning of unbelieving Israel occur? The answer is given in a blended citation drawn from Isaiah 59.20–21 and Isaiah 27.9, perhaps with wording influenced by echoes of other texts. Here is the quotation as Paul presents it (with words that are not found in Isaiah 59.20–21 in bold type):

> And in this way all Israel will be saved, as it is written:
> '**Out of** Zion [*ek Siōn*] will come the Deliverer [*ho rhuomenos*];
> he will banish ungodliness from Jacob.'
> And this is my covenant with them,
> **when I take away their sins.**

The distinctive form of this composite citation poses several crucial issues.

First, who is 'the Deliverer' and how are we to interpret his 'coming'? In the original context of Isaiah 59, the Deliverer is Israel's God, who sees that there is no justice and 'no one to intervene' (Isaiah 59.15–16); he therefore dons his armour and comes powerfully *to* Zion as Israel's champion and Redeemer (59.16b–20). Paul, reading retrospectively, sees here a figural anticipation of the coming of *Jesus* as Israel's Messiah and Deliverer. (This is a vivid example of the way in which Paul's figural Christological exegesis identifies Jesus as the embodiment of Israel's God.)[33] The identification of Jesus as the Deliverer is confirmed by the strong parallel in 1 Thessalonians 1.9–10, where Paul commends the formerly pagan Thessalonian believers who have 'turned to God from idols to serve a living and true God, and to await his Son from heaven, whom he raised from the dead, *Jesus who delivers us from the wrath that is coming*' (*Iēsoun ton rhuomenon hēmas ek tēs orgēs tēs erchomenēs*). In the light of this Pauline intertext, interpreters of Romans have judged almost unanimously that in Romans 11.26–27 Paul has construed Isaiah 59.20 to prefigure a future coming (*parousia*) of Christ in power to raise the dead, gather all the people of God (including the presently unbelieving remnant) to himself and establish his rightful lordship over all creation (as in 1 Thessalonians 4.13–18; Philippians 3.20–21; 1 Corinthians 15.20–28; Romans 8.8–23).[34] Despite the widespread evidence for this narrative pattern in Paul's thought, Wright has resisted the *communis opinio* that Romans 11.26–27 refers to an eschatological future event of Christ's *parousia*. Instead, Wright maintains, the 'coming' of the Deliverer refers to the proclamation of the gospel to the nations, pre-eminently by Paul himself, whose preaching is 'the fulfilment of the Isaianic promise of the herald announcing God's kingdom (10.15, citing

---

33 Exactly on point is the frequently cited judgement of Sanders 1983, 194: '"The Deliverer," as most scholars agree, is almost certainly Christ in Paul's understanding . . . But for the present question, whether or not Paul thought of the salvation of Israel apart from Christ, it matters little whether he understands "the Deliverer" to be God or Christ; for it is incredible that he thought of "God apart from Christ," just as it is that he thought of "Christ apart from God." . . . To suppose that "the Deliverer" could be for Paul "God apart from Christ" seems to expect of him an unthinkable abstraction.' Capes (1992, 102) notes in passing that Paul interprets 'the Deliverer' christologically in Romans 11.26. Surprisingly, however, Capes does not develop an interpretation of the passage as a significant instance in which Paul considers Jesus 'a manifestation of Yahweh'.

34 Also relevant is Romans 7.24b–25a: 'Who will deliver [*rhusetai*] me from the body of this death? Thanks be to God through Jesus Christ our Lord!' While the timing of the hoped-for deliverance is not specified in this compact outcry, Romans 8 exposits the temporal framing dialectically: deliverance is *both* a present reality (8.1–11) and an urgent future hope (8.18–25).

Isaiah 52.7)'.[35] In the next section, we will consider the question of whether the apostolic proclamation could itself be identified as the coming of the Deliverer. For the moment, I simply want to register the opinion that Wright underestimates the weight of the evidence in favour of the *parousia* interpretation. He does note the parallel in 1 Thessalonians, but brushes it aside a little too casually:

> True, Paul can use the verbal equivalent of the noun *ho rhuomenos*, 'the Deliverer', when referring to Jesus' return and his delivering of his people from the wrath to come. But that does not mean that whenever he uses a cognate word he must always be referring to the 'second coming'.[36]

I offer two rejoinders. First, a technical quibble: *ho rhuomenos* is in fact not a noun but a participle used substantively. And in 1 Thessalonians 1.10 what we find is once again precisely the participial form, this time in the accusative case: *ton rhuomenon*. A good case could be made here for interpreting Paul's construction as a substantive use of the participle in apposition to the proper name 'Jesus', expressing a titular sense identical to that in Isaiah 59.20/Romans 11.26. This would yield a translation such as 'Jesus, our Deliverer from the wrath that is coming'. My point is that in 1 Thessalonians 1.10 Paul uses not 'a cognate word' but exactly the same word in a slightly different grammatical construction, both times in contexts that refer to eschatological salvation.

Second, and perhaps more significantly, this seems to be an unusual instance where Wright has selectively excluded the relevance of a larger dominant narrative structure for the interpretation of a particular local exegetical context. Elsewhere throughout his massive *oeuvre* he emphatically advocates reading individual texts within the context of a larger story, a foundational narrative that unifies and illuminates the individual writings of the Bible as a whole, and of Paul's situationally specific statements in particular. Surely, however, Paul's overall unifying narrative structure points to the consummation of God's saving action in an eschatological future event when the dead are to be raised and Christ's lordship is at last to be made fully manifest. It is not clear to me why that larger narrative pattern should suddenly be ruled out of play in our interpretation of an eschatologically freighted text such as Romans 11.25–27. The connection between Romans 11.26 and 1 Thessalonians 1.10 is not simply a random verbal parallel; both texts appropriate *ho rhuomenos*, Isaiah's descriptor of

---

[35] Wright 2013, 1250–1.
[36] Wright 2013, 1251.

Israel's God, as a title for Jesus in his role as bringer of eschatological salvation.[37] For that reason, the eschatological narrative pattern presupposed by 1 Thessalonians 1.9–10 is directly pertinent to the interpretation of the passage in Romans.

4 Why does Paul say the Deliverer will come *ek Siōn*?

Here we return to the exegetical problem that Calvin sought to sweep under the rug. The textual issues have been exhaustively studied, and can be briefly summarized. The Hebrew text of Isaiah 59.20 says that the Redeemer will come *to* Zion (*lĕṣîyôn*). The LXX renders this, a little broadly, as *heneken Siōn* ('for the sake of Zion'). Paul has altered the quotation to read *ek Siōn* ('from Zion'). Scholars have espoused various opinions on the question of whether Paul's tweaking of the text was deliberate (to further his argument) or unintentional and inconsequential (i.e. he was following a *Vorlage* with a variant rendering).[38] Indeed, those who think Paul is not responsible for the alteration usually contend – as Calvin did – that the wording of the MT or the LXX would actually have served his argument better than the form he does cite. Wright, however, comes down firmly in favour of the view that the change 'cannot be accidental' and that Paul has himself 'adjusted' the text to fit his understanding of what God is surprisingly doing in the events of his own time. This adjustment is part of Paul's 'redefinition of Jewish eschatology around Jesus and the spirit'. Here is Wright's explanation of the textual change:

> [S]alvation is coming *from* Zion to the nations. Paul is not reinscribing the older centripetal tradition [i.e. the pilgrimage of the nations to Zion], but nor is he abandoning the old belief that when Israel's God finally acted to fulfil his promises to his people the gentile nations would come under his rule, whether for rescue or for ruin. Rather, he is transforming the tradition into a centrifugal movement: the Redeemer now comes, with the gospel, *from* Zion to the world, and as a reflex (exactly as in 11.11–15) will 'banish ungodliness from Jacob'.[39]

---

37 In addition to Isaiah 59.20, see also Isaiah 49.7.
38 Koch (1986, 177) opines that the unaltered LXX text would have been more suitable to Paul's argument and that the alteration to *ek Siōn* is for Paul 'funktionslos'. For that reason he concludes that the text-form in Romans 11.26 is taken over from pre-Pauline tradition. For similar positions on the question, see Stanley 1993, 118–42; Wilk 1998, 40. For the contrary view that Paul himself is responsible for the textual alteration, see Shum 2002, 236–9, 280–1 n. 196 (an especially strong refutation of Stanley on this point) and 285–6 n. 208; Jewett 2007, 703; Kirk 2010, 83–6.
39 Wright 2013, 1250.

This account of the textual alteration fits neatly into place alongside Wright's insistence that the coming of the Deliverer is not a future event. Instead, the 'coming' of the Deliverer is collapsed – I find it hard to choose another word – into the dissemination of Christian preaching throughout the pagan world (as perhaps in accord with Romans 10.6–9, 17–18). Wright does not elaborate on this point, but its implications are clearly spelled out by J. R. Daniel Kirk in a lucid essay that converges with many aspects of Wright's interpretation. Kirk recognizes the possible difficulty of identifying *ho rhuomenos* unqualifiedly with the phenomenon of the preached message. Nonetheless, appealing to Romans 10.20 ('I became manifest [*emphanēs egenomēn*] to those who did not ask for me'), he confronts the question squarely:

> Thus, as Paul reads Isaiah, 'the deliverer', be it God or Christ, is *a suitable metonymy for the message that brings salvation*. In interpreting *ho rhuomenos* in Rom 11.26, then, it is highly plausible that the figure indicates Christian proclamation.[40]

On this reading, the apocalyptic future dimension of the gospel is (at least for Romans 11) dissolved, and the hoped-for saving action of Christ is deemed to occur in Paul's immediate present time through the proclaimed word.

What are we to make of this? It must be conceded that Wright's position (likewise Kirk's) has the virtue of consistency. My worry is that the consistency is perhaps purchased at the rather high price of absorbing Jesus into the *kerygma*[41] and excluding the future apocalyptic elements of Paul's eschatology and soteriology, elements that may contribute to a more complex, mysterious and untidy picture of Romans 11.25–27 than the one Wright paints.[42]

---

40 Kirk 2010, 92 (emphasis mine). I take the interpretation that I have cited here from Kirk to be essentially identical to Wright's understanding of the way in which Paul understood the declaration that 'The Deliverer will come from Zion'. Kirk challenges Wright's understanding of *pas Israēl* as the Church of Jews and Gentiles together, but concurs with his rejection of the '*parousia*' interpretation and with his argument that the Gentile mission is the instrument through which the salvation of 'all Israel' will be accomplished.

41 Rudolf Bultmann would no doubt applaud from beyond the grave. (Of course, he would be able to do that only if he was after all mistaken about the mythological character of belief in some sort of post-mortem existence.)

42 I am mindful that Wright is sharply critical of the use of the word 'apocalyptic' as a meaningful descriptive term in characterizing Paul's theology. This problem would require another essay to address. Here I use the term simply to gesture towards Paul's expectation of a dramatic future event that would include Christ's coming in power and glory, the resurrection of the dead, and the creation of a new world in which the powers of Sin and Death are decisively

Wright is no doubt correct to reject the suggestion that 'Zion' in Romans 11.26 refers to the heavenly Jerusalem, as in Paul's allegorical exposition of the story of Sarah and Hagar in Galatians 4.26. Even where Paul elsewhere refers to Christ's coming from heaven (e.g. 1 Thessalonians 1.9–10; Philippians 3.20–21), he makes no reference to Jerusalem, or to any 'heavenly city'. Much more apposite is Robert Jewett's observation:

> Paul's formulation 'from Zion' is consistent with the composite creed that opens his letter concerning Jesus 'descended from David' (1.3) and with the reminder that Christ came from the Israelites (9.5) and that it was in 'Zion' that the stone of stumbling was laid.[43]

In view of these considerations, Kirk concludes that in Romans 11.26 'Zion functions as a metonymy for Jerusalem or the people of Israel' – that is, that Paul's formulation emphasizes Jesus' historical, earthly roots in the people of Israel.[44]

5 Does 'covenant' in Romans 11.27 refer to Jeremiah's 'new covenant'?

In some of his earlier work, Wright seems to suggest that Romans 11.27 contains a quotation from Jeremiah 31.34. In *Paul and the Faithfulness of God*, however, he offers a more qualified formulation: 'Rom. 11.27, affirming that God's covenant will consist of his forgiving his people's sins, while at one level obviously quoting Isa. 59.21 and 27.9, at another level resonates powerfully with Jer. 31.33–34.'[45] Wright is not alone in hearing such a resonance. We have already noted that Calvin connected the 'covenant' of Romans 11.27 to Jeremiah's promise of a new covenant (Jeremiah 31.31–34=38.31–34 LXX). Nor was this reading original with Calvin; it is attested in Thomas Aquinas's commentary on Romans, and no doubt has deeper roots in patristic exegesis. It is also supported, to one degree or another, by several modern commentators.[46]

---

abolished, a world in which God's justice reigns visibly for ever. Despite Wright's disapproval of the term 'apocalyptic' as a descriptor for Paul's theology, he elsewhere affirms all these elements of the story that Paul's theology tells and interprets. This leads to an important point: Wright's resistance to the future '*parousia*' interpretation of Romans 11.25–27 should not be understood as a denial that Paul specifically hoped for the future coming of Christ; instead, it is a more specific and limited position on the meaning of Romans 11.25–27 in its context.

43 Jewett 2007, 703–4. See also Fitzmyer 1993, 624.
44 Kirk 2010, 91. This interpretation was already suggested by Aquinas (1997, 331). Aquinas notes a parallel in John 4.22: 'Salvation is from the Jews.'
45 Wright 2013, 1247 n. 697, acknowledging a corrective offered by Wagner 2002, 290.
46 For example, Barrett, Cranfield, Dahl, Dunn and Fitzmyer.

Despite the antiquity and pervasiveness of this intertextual reading, the actual wording of Paul's citation is drawn almost entirely from the two Isaiah passages, with minor modifications. The words quoted in Romans 11.27a simply continue Paul's quotation of Isaiah 59.20–21; they are taken verbatim from Isaiah 59.21a (*kai hautē autois hē par' emou diathēkē*). And the words quoted in the last bit of Paul's composite citation (*hotan aphelōmai tas hamartias autōn* (Romans 11.27b)) are a slight modification of words drawn from 27.9 LXX: *hotan aphelōmai autou tēn hamartian*. For contextual reasons, Paul's quotation changes the singular *tēn hamartian* to the plural *tas hamartias* and also shifts the possessive pronoun to the plural, in keeping with his focus on the soteriological fate of a large group of people. Apart from the single key term *diathēkē* – which might provide a catchword link between Isaiah 59 and Jeremiah 38 LXX – the only possible traces of allusion to Jeremiah would be the reference to 'sins' in the plural,[47] along with the plural pronoun. That is a slender basis indeed for tracing an intertextual allusion. By contrast, Isaiah 59.20–21 is obviously linked to Isaiah 27.9 by references to God's action of turning away ungodliness (59.20) or removing lawlessness (27.9) *from Jacob*.

Given Paul's concern to affirm the *continuity* of God's covenant relationship with Israel, he might well have chosen for rhetorical reasons to avoid explicitly invoking Jeremiah's image of a '*new* covenant'. Whether that be so or not, my main point here is that, *in defending the proclamation that 'all Israel will be saved', Paul sticks closely to language drawn from Isaiah.* This has two implications worth noting. First, we should be cautious about building our interpretation of Romans 11.25–27 on Jeremiah's picture of a 'new covenant'. Second, when Paul writes that the Deliverer will come *ek Siōn*, his departure from the wording of Isaiah 59.20 becomes all the more surprising and noteworthy.

6 What is the temporal reference of *hotan aphelōmai*?

Here the issue can be sharply stated: does Paul's citation of Isaiah point to an indefinitely repeatable future possibility ('whenever I take away their

---

47 Even here, Jeremiah 38.34 has the genitive *tōn hamartiōn*, in contrast to the accusative *tas hamartias* in Romans 11.27. (The accusative case is of course dictated by the fact that the noun is the direct object of the verb *aphelōmai* from Isaiah 27.9.) The verbal echo of Jeremiah 38 LXX is indistinct at best. Perhaps more pertinent is the echo of Isaiah 59.2: *dia tas hamartias hymōn apestrepsen to prosōpon autou aph' hymōn tou mē eleēsai*. This comes from the Lord's indictment of Israel that introduces the chapter from which Paul has just quoted in Romans 11.26–27a; the verbs *apestrepsen* and *eleēsai* resonate with the immediate context in Romans 11.25–32. See also Isaiah 59.12.

sins') or to a specific future occurrence at some unspecified point in time ('at the point when I take away their sins')? Once again Wright stakes out a definite position:

> What is particularly telling is the exact form of the quotation from Isaiah 27 at the end of 11.27, *hotan aphelōmai*, '*whenever* I take away' their sins. The natural reading of this is not to refer to one single action, a unique, one-off saving event at the end of all things, but to an indefinite future possibility. It could of course mean 'whenever it may be that I perform that single action', but it could equally mean 'at whatever time, however frequently repeated, people "turn to the lord and have the veil removed"', as in 2 Corinthians 3.15.[48]

A good deal is at stake here for Wright. His scenario of a gradual influx of Jewish people drawn over time to confessing Jesus as Lord requires that *hotan* + aorist subjunctive must indicate an indefinitely repeatable future possibility. This grammatical point is, however, like so many other things in this passage, contested. The strongest counterstatement appears in Robert Jewett's Hermeneia commentary. Jewett declares firmly that, on grammatical grounds, God's action of taking away 'Jacob's' sins must be understood as a single action at a future point in time: 'The citation refers to a condition that must be fulfilled before the covenant can be restored: "when I shall have taken away their sins."'[49]

Some of the examples cited in BDAG, to which Jewett appeals, would support his interpretation. It appears to me, however, that passages such as Matthew 5.11 would instead support Wright's case: 'Blessed are you when people revile you and persecute you and utter all kinds of evil against you' (*makarioi este hotan oneidisōsin hymas kai diōxōsin kai eipōsin pan ponēron kath' hymōn*, NRSV). Here it would seem artificial to insist on translating as 'Blessed are you when people shall have [on one definite future occasion] reviled you and persecuted and uttered all kinds of evil against you.' Surely what is envisaged here in Matthew's *hotan* + aorist subjunctive construction is precisely the kind of repeated future action that Wright sees in Romans 11.27b.

I would judge that on this point the strictly grammatical evidence is inconclusive. Wright's position is a possible exegetical option: the construction in Romans 11.27b allows for indefinitely repeated future

---

48 Wright 2013, 1251. Wright's reference to 2 Corinthians 3.15 appears to be a typographical error; 2 Corinthians 3.16 is intended.

49 Jewett 2007, 706, citing in support BDAG, 731. (Jewett also cites BDF § 318, 333, 379, 382. But none of these paragraphs in BDF appears directly relevant to the case at hand.)

action. But this interpretation can be argued (either pro or con) only on contextual grounds, as Wright has attempted to do in *Paul and the Faithfulness of God*.

The ground covered: an overview

Let us pause for an overview of the uncertain terrain we have sought to map. Our exploratory expedition has arrived at these findings:

1 In Romans 11.25, Wright is almost certainly correct to translate 'a hardening has come upon *part of* Israel'.

2 However, his interpretation underestimates the way in which *achri hou* points to a definite future endpoint at which the 'fullness of the Gentiles' will have been grafted into Israel.

3 When Paul cites Isaiah's prophecy of the coming of 'The Deliverer', he is thinking of Jesus, who fulfils and embodies the hope that God would come to rescue his people. Wright recognizes the Christological force of the quotation in Romans 11.26 but underestimates the significance of the parallel in 1 Thessalonians 1.9–10. His resultant reading wrongly excludes possible reference to a future triumphant coming of Christ.

4 Wright is surely correct to insist that Paul's alteration of the quotation of Isaiah 59.20 to read *ek Siōn* must be taken as significant. His suggestion that the coming of the Deliverer 'from Zion' should be interpreted as a reference to the spread of the gospel to the Gentile world is a possible and coherent reading. But this interpretation has the effect of minimizing the unfulfilled future eschatological dimension of Paul's thought and collapsing the person Jesus Christ into the preached word.

5 Despite venerable interpretative precedent, we should be cautious about assuming an intertextual allusion to Jeremiah's 'new covenant' in Romans 11.25–27.

6 The last clause of Romans 11.27 blends Isaiah 27.9 into Paul's citation. The grammatical construction here (*hotan* + aorist subjunctive) refers to something that is to happen in an indefinite future time. On the basis of grammar alone, however, it is not possible to determine whether Paul understands this to indicate a single future event or an indefinitely repeatable possibility.

A path forward: echoes of the Psalms?

Paul's anomalous reading of *ek Siōn* in his citation of Isaiah confronts us with a *crux* for the exegesis of Romans 11.25–27. Our sifting of the evidence so far suggests that much turns on the interpretation of this phrase. What does Paul mean by saying that the Deliverer will come *from* Zion?

Occasionally attempts have been made to identify a single intertextual source for this unexpected wording. One proposed candidate is Isaiah 2.3, with its depiction of the pilgrimage of the nations to Jerusalem to receive instruction: 'For out of Zion [*ek gar Siōn*] shall go forth instruction [*nomos*], and the word of the LORD from Jerusalem' (NRSV).[50] But sceptics have understandably balked at finding such a highly specific allusion on the basis of a single preposition (*ek*), especially since Paul never elsewhere refers to a pilgrimage of the nations to Jerusalem, and never invokes Isaiah 2 as justification for his Gentile mission.[51] Wright, who has himself pointed to Isaiah 2.3 as a possible background to Romans 11.26, has qualified this view in his more recent work by observing that in view of 'Paul's redefinition of Jewish eschatology around Jesus and the spirit . . . it would make no sense to undo this powerful theology by reinstating the earthly Jerusalem as the place to which the nations should go to find salvation.'[52] Therefore, as Wright notes, if there is any possible allusion to Isaiah 2.3 in Romans 11.26, it would require a reversal, or transformation, of Isaiah's scenario.

Commentators on Romans often make passing reference to a few other scriptural passages in which the phrase 'from Zion' appears, chiefly in the Psalms, but rarely do they attribute much significance to these as intertexts.[53] More typically, the commentary tradition takes Paul's alteration of Isaiah as odd but insignificant.

I would propose a different way of proceeding. The phrase *ek Siōn* appears eight times in the Greek Psalter: Psalms 13.7; 19.3; 49.2; 52.7; 109.2; 127.5; 133.3; and 134.21.[54] Reading these psalms cumulatively, one sees that all of them (except the very brief Psalm 133) speak of God's

---

50 See Wright 1991, 250–1, and his reaffirmation of it as a possible echo in Wright 2013, 1249–50. For a more extended exposition of this position, see Bruno 2008, 119–34. The same proclamation that the *nomos* would go forth from Zion appears almost verbatim in Micah 4.2 LXX, lacking the *gar* found in Isaiah 2.3.

51 Donaldson 1997, 187–97. For Donaldson's dismissal of an allusion to Isaiah 2.3 in Romans 11.26, see 329 n. 66.

52 Wright 2013, 1250.

53 Wright mentions Psalm 14.7 but does not explicate its significance for Romans 11.25–27 (2013, 1249–50). Perhaps he regards it as self-evident? He also cites Deuteronomy 33.2, which is of doubtful relevance, since it speaks of the Lord coming from Sinai, not Zion.

54 In the following pages, references to chapter and verse in the Psalms will follow the LXX numeration.

Richard B. Hays

sending help to Israel or coming to save Israel. I think it unlikely that Paul 'intended' in Romans 11 to allude to any one of these psalms in particular. But I think it highly likely that the language of these psalms was embedded in Paul's bones, and that when he was writing passionately to the Romans about the mystery of Israel's salvation the wording of these texts rose spontaneously to his mind. Rather than discussing all eight instances, the following discussion will offer a brief survey of the occurrences of *ek Siōn* in five psalms that offer particularly rich examples of the 'encyclopedia of production' that informed Paul's tweaking of Isaiah.

Psalm 13.7 LXX / Psalm 52.7 LXX

Who will bring the salvation of Israel [*to sōtērion tou Israēl*] out of Sion [*ek Siōn*]?
When the Lord brings back [*epistrepsai*] the captivity of his people,
let Jacob exult, and Israel be glad.

Psalm 13 is particularly significant for our present investigation[55] because *earlier in Romans Paul had quoted it at some length* in a catena of texts that present a withering indictment of human sinfulness (Romans 3.10–18; see esp. vv. 10–12, which draw directly from Psalm 13.1–3). Thus the yearning of the psalm's final verse (13.7), a wish for Israel's salvation, prefigures the movement of Paul's whole letter from indictment to the proclamation of God's action for the salvation of his people.[56] The fact that Paul has previously cited a part of Psalm 13 greatly enhances the likelihood that he knows its concluding expectation that Jacob/Israel will be brought back by the Lord. This is an example of the way in which the criterion of *recurrence* can lend confidence to proposed intertextual readings.[57] It is also highly significant that Romans 3.15–17 includes, within the same catena, material directly quoted from Isaiah 59.7–8 – the same chapter that Paul cites in Romans 11.26–27. Thus, there is a three-way linkage between Psalm 13, Isaiah 59 and Romans (3.10–18 + 11.26–27). One suspects that we are seeing here only a glimpse of a more complex intertexual web.[58]

---

55 I focus my remarks here on Psalm 13 LXX. Almost everything said here is also applicable to the nearly identical Psalm 52 LXX.
56 A fascinating note: the word for 'salvation' here in the Hebrew text (Ps 14.7) is *yeshuah*. Would Paul possibly have been aware of the serendipitous subtextual connection between the Hebrew name of Jesus (*Yeshua*) and the Greek *sōtērion*? If so, he never draws attention to it. But cf. Matthew 1.21.
57 Hays 1989, 30; 2005, 37–8.
58 It should also be noted that allusions to Isaiah 59.17 show up in 1 Thessalonians 5.8 and Ephesians 6.14, 17. Wilk (1998, 239–42) sketches out a whole network of connections between Romans 11.26–27 and intertexts in Isaiah 59.9—60.3, as well as Isaiah 27.6–13.

566

Further, the reference in Psalm 13.7 to *Jacob* as the object of God's saving action provides an additional link to Isaiah 59.20/Romans 11.26, which declares that God 'will turn away [*apostrepsei*] ungodliness *from Jacob*'. Interestingly, one of the minor ways in which Psalm 52 LXX differs from Psalm 13 LXX is that its concluding affirmation of God's restoration of Jacob/Israel shifts from exhortation ('let Jacob exult, and Israel be glad') to future promise: 'Jacob will rejoice and Israel will be glad' (Psalm 52.7 LXX).

Psalm 19.2 LXX

This psalm opens with a prayer that God will come to the rescue of Israel's king:

> May the LORD answer you in the day of trouble.
> May the name of the God of Jacob protect you.
> May he send you help from the sanctuary
> and come to your aid from Zion [*ek Siōn*].
>
> (Psalm 19.1–3)

Because this is a prayer offered for the king, rather than for the sinful people, it has less direct resonance with Romans 11.26. It is noteworthy, however, that the God whose support is invoked is named as 'the God of Jacob'. This is the God who will send help *from Zion*; the synonymous parallelism here suggests that Zion is regarded as the sanctuary, the place of God's dwelling.

Psalm 49.2 LXX

Here the LXX differs from the Hebrew text in a way that suggests an interesting resonance with Isaiah 59.20/Romans 11.26:

> Out of Sion [*ek Siōn*], the excellence of his beauty, God will come visibly [*emphanōs hēxei*].

This 'coming' of God from Zion in a visible manifestation is, we learn as the psalm continues, for the purpose of summoning his people ('who made a covenant with me') to judgement (vv. 4–6). But as the speech of the judge unfolds, it turns from rebuke to invitation and promise: 'Call on me in the day of trouble; I will deliver you, and you shall glorify me' (v. 15). Once again, as in Psalm 13, the movement of the psalm – from judgement

---

To follow his intriguing pointers would take us too far afield from the present purposes of this essay, but his exegesis merits deeper deliberation. Wagner (2002, 287–9) also helpfully observes the many connections between Isaiah 59, Romans 3 and Romans 11.

to the promise of salvation offered by the God who will come *from Zion* – anticipates the narrative shape of Paul's argument in Romans 11.

Psalm 109.2 LXX

The final instance we shall consider offers another example of the import-ance of noting the recurrence of allusion to a highly significant precursor. Psalm 109 LXX (Psalm 110 MT) is of course cited repeatedly in the Synoptic Gospels, in Acts and in the letter to the Hebrews as a prefigur-ation of Christ's exaltation at the right hand of God. Though Paul never quotes this psalm overtly, he clearly alludes to Psalm 109.1 in his depic-tion in 1 Corinthians 15.20–28 of Christ's eschatological triumph over the power of death: 'For he must reign until [God] *has put his enemies under his feet.*' The last enemy to be destroyed is Death. For 'God has put all things in subjection under his feet' (1 Corinthians 15.25–27a).

In view of this distinct allusion, Paul's declaration in Romans 8.34 that the risen Christ is now 'at the right hand of God' should likewise be understood to presuppose Psalm 109 (see also Ephesians 1.20; Colossians 3.1). If Paul's language seems to assume deep familiarity with this chris-tologically freighted psalm, then perhaps we should also follow the Nestle-Aland apparatus in discerning allusions to Psalm 109.5 in Romans 2.5 ('the day of his wrath') and – intriguingly, but more distantly and doubtfully – to Psalm 109.4 ('the Lord has sworn and will not change his mind' (*ou metamelēthēsetai*)) in Romans 11.29 ('the gifts and the calling of God are irrevocable' (*ametamelēta*)). In the light of this scattering of allusions, both certain and less certain, in Paul's letters, it is perhaps not far-fetched to hear also in Romans 11.26 an echo of Psalm 109.2 LXX: ' The Lord will send out from Zion [*ek Siōn*] your rod of power.' In the context of the psalm, the power that goes forth *ek Siōn* is said to subdue and destroy enemies rather than to rescue Israel, though the two things may be closely related. In any case, Psalm 109 LXX is another text that appears to be stored deeply in Paul's memory bank, and his allusions to it in other contexts indicate that he understood it as a prefiguration of Christ's escha-tologically triumphant lordship. If this psalm was one of the subliminal intertexts that caused Paul to modify Isaiah 59.20 by writing *ek Siōn* rather than *heneken Siōn*, then the case is strengthened for interpreting Romans 11.26, alongside 1 Thessalonians 1.10, as a reference to a *future* coming of the Deliverer to turn away the ungodliness of Jacob and accomplish the salvation of all Israel.

To sum up, the Psalms presented Paul with a range of texts in which the expectation of God's help coming *ek Siōn* was associated with the rescue or salvation of Israel. In some of these psalms, the coming of help from Zion was interpreted as God's power issuing forth from the sanctuary – that is, the Temple in Jerusalem, the dwelling place of God (*not* from some other-worldly venue). Further, some of these psalms depict God as a righteous judge who enacts a narrative movement from condemnation of the guilty to a final rescue/salvation of Israel. Exactly that same pattern is present in Isaiah 59, which begins by announcing to Israel that 'your iniquities have been barriers between you and your God, and your sins have hidden his face from you' (NRSV), but concludes by narrating God's decision none-theless to intervene by coming as Deliverer of Israel. Romans 3.10–18 is a key text showing that Isaiah 59 (the key text quoted in Romans 11.25–27) is interwoven in Paul's mind with Psalm 13 / Psalm 52. Further, Paul elsewhere alludes to Psalm 109 in contexts that associate it with the res-urrection of the dead and Christ's final triumph. If Psalm 109.2 is part of the intertextual reservoir from which Paul drew (whether consciously or subconsciously) the words *ek Siōn* and imported them into his citation of Isaiah 59.20, it is more rather than less likely that he interpreted Isaiah's prophecy as a picture of a dramatic future 'coming' of Christ, as in 1 Thessalonians 1.9–10, 4.13–18 – not simply as a portrayal of the Church's preaching of the gospel to the Gentiles.

Conclusion

In the modern era, some NT scholars, seeking to escape the shadow of an ugly history of Christian anti-Jewish bias, have sought to find in Romans 11 a basis for affirming Gentile Christianity and Judaism as separate but equal paths to relationship with God, perhaps through two separate but equal covenants. This interpretative project is, however, doomed to exe-getical failure. Tom Wright, while acutely aware of the vital hermeneutical and ethical issues surrounding Jewish–Christian relations in our time, has charted another course. He has insisted on interpreting Paul within his own historical context as a Jew who believed Jesus to be Israel's Messiah and Lord. Whatever we might wish Paul to have said, or whatever we might think is theologically necessary to say in a post-Holocaust world, we must reckon first of all with what Paul actually said and meant. It is a salutary discipline to distinguish descriptive exegesis from construc-tive theological reflection.[59] (And, I hasten to add, to keep the two in

---

59 Sanders (1983, 192–9) models such a distinction. He argues on exegetical grounds that Paul believed Jews could be saved only through faith in Christ. He indicates, however, that

close, urgent conversation.) Wright's exegesis of Romans 11.25–27 has gone a long way towards clarifying the passage; I am deeply grateful for what I have learned from him. The present essay has sought to engage his exegesis appreciatively, while also suggesting some ways in which it could be sharpened and, in some instances, corrected. It remains for me then to state positively what the text means.

The 'mystery' to which Paul refers (11.25) is the unexpected narrative sequence in which God's saving plan for the world has unfolded and will one day be completed: a hardening has come upon a part of ethnic Israel, with the result that they have rejected the message that Jesus is Lord and Messiah. This hardening has allowed many Gentiles to 'come in', that is, to be grafted into Israel. There will come a day when the 'fullness of the Gentiles' (its number and extent known only to God) will have embraced the faith and been incorporated, through Christ, into the 'olive tree', the people of God. In the meantime, while a 'remnant' of ethnic Israel has believed (and more individuals may continue over time to confess Jesus as Lord), ethnic Israel as a whole remains in the status of being branches 'cut off' by unbelief. But its current status is not its final destiny. There will come a day in the future when Christ will come as the Deliverer and (in some way that we cannot now know) turn 'Jacob' away from its present 'ungodliness' and unbelief. At that time, it will acknowledge him as Lord (as in Romans 10.9 and Philippians 2.10–11). When that happens, the fullness of the whole people of God made up of Jews and Gentiles together in Christ (Romans 11.12 + 11.25) – that is, 'all Israel' – will be saved. (Paul's *kai houtōs* in Romans 11.26 points to the surprising reversal of the eschatological script expected by many Jews in his day: the nations will 'come in' first, with the majority of ethnic Israel later, following a period of 'hardening'). This unfathomable future event is linked with Christ's coming in power, the resurrection of the dead and the final establishment of God's justice. The Deliverer, then, will be seen to have come 'from Zion' in at least two senses: his saving power will come forth from God's own dwelling place (that is perhaps, as Wright proposes, through Jesus himself as the *locus* of God's presence), and from Jesus' specific historical identity as a human being rooted in the people of Israel. In other words, salvation will come not from an alien god but from Israel's own Messiah, whom Paul can describe paradoxically as 'the Messiah *kata sarka*, God over all'

---

he himself would 'vote against' such a theological proposition today, and speculates that perhaps Paul himself might now do the same, in view of the fact that his expectation that the Redeemer would come soon turned out to be mistaken.

(Romans 9.5). But for the present, our appropriate role is one of humility: both soteriological humility about being incorporated by God's mercy into his people Israel and epistemological humility about our capacity to know exactly how the faithfulness of God will finally be consummated.

As Wright observes concerning Paul's olive tree metaphor, 'part of the point of using picture-language is after all to be evocative and not mathematically precise.'[60] My worry about his painstakingly thorough exegesis of the picture-language in Romans 11.25–27 is that he has not sufficiently heeded his own admonition, that he has sought to delimit the force of Paul's open-ended, poetic, intertextual language too strictly: to insist that the coming of the Deliverer from Zion can mean *only* the mission of the Church, not the eschatological *parousia* of the Lord. I would suggest, to the contrary, that we should keep both possibilities open. That would do more justice to Paul's agonized wrestling in Romans 9—11, which seems designed to gesture towards hope for something that we do not yet see.

Bibliography

Aquinas, Thomas (1997). 'Selections from Thomas Aquinas's *Commentary on Romans.*' In *The Theological Interpretation of Scripture: Classic and Contemporary Readings*, edited by S. E. Fowl, translated by E. F. Rogers Jr, 320–37. Oxford: Blackwell.

Barth, K. (1957). *Church Dogmatics* II/2. Edinburgh: T&T Clark.

Bruno, C. R. (2008). 'The Deliverer from Zion: The Source(s) and Function of Paul's Citation in Romans 11:26–27.' *Tyndale Bulletin* 59: 119–34.

Calvin, John (1960). *The Epistles of Paul the Apostle to the Romans and to the Thessalonians.* Translated by R. Mackenzie. Grand Rapids, MI: Eerdmans.

Capes, D. (1992). *Old Testament Yahweh Texts in Paul's Christology.* Wissenschaftliche Untersuchungen zum Neuen Testament 2/47. Tübingen: Mohr Siebeck.

Dahl, N. A. (1997). *Studies in Paul.* Minneapolis, MN: Augsburg.

Donaldson, T. L. (1997). *Paul and the Gentiles: Remapping the Apostle's Convictional World.* Minneapolis, MN: Fortress.

Dunn, J. D. G. (1988). *Romans 9–16.* Word Biblical Commentary 38B. Dallas, TX: Word.

Eastman, S. (2010a). 'Israel and Divine Mercy in Galatians and Romans.' In *Between Gospel and Election: Explorations in the Interpretation of Romans 9—11*, edited by F. Wilk and J. R. Wagner, 147–70. Wissenschaftliche Untersuchungen zum Neuen Testament 257. Tübingen: Mohr Siebeck.

---

60 Wright 2013, 1211.

—— (2010b). 'Israel and the Mercy of God: A Re-reading of Galatians 6.16 and Romans 9–11.' *New Testament Studies* 56: 367–95.

Fitzmyer, J. A. (1993). *Romans.* Anchor Bible 33. New York, NY: Doubleday.

Hafemann, S. (1988). 'The Salvation of Israel in Romans 11:25–32: A Response to Krister Stendahl.' *Ex Auditu* 4: 38–58.

Hays, R. B. (1989). *Echoes of Scripture in the Letters of Paul.* New Haven, CT: Yale University Press.

—— (2005). *The Conversion of the Imagination: Paul as Interpreter of Israel's Scripture.* Grand Rapids, MI: Eerdmans.

Hvalvik, R. (1990). 'A "Sonderweg" for Israel: A Critical Examination of Current Interpretation of Romans 11.25–27.' *Journal for the Study of the New Testament* 38: 87–107.

Jewett, R. (2007). *Romans: A Commentary.* Hermeneia. Minneapolis, MN: Fortress.

Keck, L. E. (2005). *Romans.* Abingdon New Testament Commentary. Nashville, TN: Abingdon.

Kirk, J. R. D. (2010). 'Why Does the Deliverer Come ἐκ Σιων (Romans 11.26)?' *Journal for the Study of the New Testament* 33: 81–99.

Koch, D. A. (1986). *Die Schrift als Zeuge des Evangeliums.* Beiträge zur historischen Theologie 69. Tübingen: Mohr Siebeck.

Sanders, E. P. (1983). *Paul, the Law and the Jewish People.* Minneapolis, MN: Fortress.

Shum, S.-L. (2002). *Paul's Use of Isaiah in Romans.* Wissenschaftliche Untersuchungen zum Neuen Testament 2/156. Tübingen: Mohr Siebeck.

Stanley, C. D. (1993). '"The Redeemer Will Come ἐκ Σιων": Romans 11:26–27 Revisited.' In *Paul and the Scriptures of Israel*, edited by C. A. Evans and J. A. Sanders, 118–42. Journal of the Study of the New Testament Supplement Series 83 / Studies in Early Judaism and Christianity 1. Sheffield: JSOT.

Wagner, J. R. (2002). *Heralds of the Good News: Isaiah and Paul 'in Concert' in the Letter to the Romans.* Novum Testament Supplement Series 101. Leiden: Brill.

Watson, F. (2004). *Paul and the Hermeneutics of Faith.* London: T&T Clark.

Wilckens, U. (1980). *Der Brief an die Römer, 2. Teilband.* Zurich: Benziger Verlag / Neukirchen-Vluyn: Neukirchener Verlag.

Wilk, F. (1998). *Die Bedeutung des Jesajabuches für Paulus.* Forschungen zur Religion und Literatur des Alten und Neuen Testaments 179. Göttingen: Vandenhoeck & Ruprecht.

Wolter, M. (2018). 'Ein exegetischer und theologischer Blick auf Röm 11.25–32.' *NTS* 64: 123–42.

Wright, N. T. (1991). *The Climax of the Covenant: Christ and the Law in Pauline Theology.* Edinburgh: T&T Clark.

—— (2002). 'The Letter to the Romans.' In *The New Interpreter's Bible*, Volume X, edited by Leander E. Keck, 393–770. Nashville, TN: Abingdon.

—— (2013). *Paul and the Faithfulness of God.* Christian Origins and the Question of God 4. London: SPCK / Minneapolis, MN: Fortress.

'Beloved for the sake of their ancestors' (Romans 11.28b): God's covenant love in Romans and some Old Testament backgrounds

STEPHEN I. WRIGHT

Introduction

Near the climax of Paul's argument for the continuing place of Israel in God's purposes comes this key verse: 'As regards the gospel they are enemies of God for your sake; but as regards election they are beloved, for the sake of their ancestors' (Romans 11.28).[1] Amid the debates about the meaning of 'all Israel will be saved' (Romans 11.26a), this assertion of God's love for Israel, with its distinct implications, seems to have been under-explored.[2] However, a long shadow is still cast by the interpretation of Martin Luther, which I cite here in full:

> The word 'enemies' must here be taken in a passive sense; that is, they deserve to be hated. God hates them, and so they are hated by the Apostles and all who are of God. This is shown by the opposite term 'beloved'. They are hated and at the same time 'beloved'. They are hated 'concerning the Gospel . . . for your sakes.' That is to say; As you are loved for receiving the Gospel, so they are hated for rejecting the Gospel. Nevertheless, the lump (*the number of the elect*) is beloved 'for the fathers' sakes, as touching the election.' This means that some of them because of their election until this very hour are being accepted (*saved*). They are beloved for the Fathers' sakes, because they too are friends (*of Christ, as were their Fathers*).[3]

Few Christian scholars today, probably, would seek to pass off such an offensive interpretation as Paul's meaning. Yet not only the anti-Judaism here, but also the characterization of all who reject the gospel as 'hated'

---

1 All English Bible quotations in this chapter are from the NRSV unless otherwise stated.
2 It was, however, a significant text for *Nostra Aetate*, the Second Vatican Council's 1965 'groundbreaking declaration on non-Christian religions'. See Cunningham 2013, 141–2.
3 Luther 1976 (1954), 162–3 (parentheses editorial). See also Reasoner 2005, 126–7.

– strange coming from a Reformer who proclaimed God's free grace! – can still colour some traditional Protestant readings, whether intentionally or not. Luther's interpretation deserves not merely an emotional rejection, but a thorough exegetical response. This chapter aims to offer the beginnings of such a response, though it will naturally be impossible to explore in detail its possible ramifications for the interpretation of Paul more widely, still less the great biblical themes evoked or their reception in Christian theology and practice.

This chapter will seek to shed light on the place of this statement about Israel in Paul's thinking in Romans, elucidating its background in the OT, especially Hosea, with reference to some contemporary Jewish scholarship on the nature of God's love. We will first consider its context in Paul's argument and three immediate questions it raises.[4]

God's love for Israel in Romans 11

The overall thrust of Romans 11 is clear in its positive affirmation of Israel's continuing place in God's purposes: 'God has not rejected his people whom he foreknew' (v. 2). His 'people' here are Israel, God's historic covenant family, among whom Paul numbers himself as 'an Israelite, a descendant of Abraham, a member of the tribe of Benjamin' (v. 1). He declares that though many Israelites are in rebellion against God, there is a faithful remnant, as there was in the days of Elijah (11.2–10). And even the 'stumbling' of those currently antagonistic to God (through their refusal of faith in Christ) is not final, 'so as to fall' (v. 11a). Moreover, a mysterious purpose is at work in them: 'through their stumbling salvation has come to the Gentiles, so as to make Israel jealous' (v. 11c). The fact that many Jews have resisted the gospel opened the door, in practice, for the gospel to go to the Gentiles. Going still further, Paul looks to a time when those who are now in a state of 'defeat' (presumably by the power of sin; cf. ch. 6) will be fully included (v. 12), those who are now in a state of 'rejection' will be accepted (v. 15), when branches that have been 'broken off' the vine will be 'grafted back in' (vv. 17–24).

Thus Paul seems to hold out clear hope not only for a small remnant of Jews, but for Israel as whole, including those who are now resisting God and the gospel. That is underlined in the metaphors of verse 16: 'If the part

---

4   Another is raised by Barrett 1962, 225, but quickly and rightly dealt with: 'his language recalls the Rabbinic doctrine of the merit (*zakkuth*) of the fathers, which forms a treasury on which their sinful descendants can draw; but the resemblance is only superficial, for Paul is not speaking of human merit but of divine election.' Cf. Käsemann 1973, 302.

of the dough offered as first fruits is holy, then the whole batch is holy; and if the root is holy, then the branches also are holy.' In other words, once having set apart Israel's ancestors for himself, once having planted its root, God is not going to declare that any part of Israel is excluded from his special purpose. This confidence comes to a head in verses 25–32. The situation is a 'mystery' (v. 25), but the hope is clear. The hardening upon part of Israel is temporary (v. 25), the Deliverer will banish ungodliness from Jacob (v. 26), and God will fulfil his covenant with the Jewish people by taking away their sins (v. 27). Despite playing the part of enemies of God at the moment, they remain beloved, for the sake of their ancestors; for God will not revoke the gifts he has bestowed on them (vv. 28–29). The state of disobedience in which some now find themselves, because of the coming of the Christ who was a stumbling-block to them (9.33), just serves to place them on the same level as Gentiles who had not received God's revelation at all – that is, as candidates for the mercy of God (11.30–32).

The declaration of God's continuing love for his people in 11.28b thus fits well within a reading of Romans 11 that takes 'Israel' in its plain sense as God's historical people.[5] This has been shown through a detailed exegesis by Matt Waymeyer.[6] Moreover, it can be shown to fit with the whole of Paul's argument in Romans 9—11. John Barclay has elucidated the unity of this argument with reference to 'the paradoxical working of an unconditioned grace'.[7] He has thus effectively answered C. H. Dodd's allegation that Paul was here trying to 'have it both ways', expressing an emotional commitment to his fellow Israelites in chapter 11 that runs (so Dodd thought) against the logic of chapter 9, where Paul acknowledges that Israel has no more of an automatic claim on God's favour than anyone else.[8] However, as I shall argue, the assertion in 11.28b that the (historical) people of Israel are 'beloved, for the sake of their ancestors' opens up a more inclusive vision of God's love than may at first be apparent. Without the need to redefine the term 'Israel', the statement when heard against

---

5 *Pace* N. T. Wright's interpretation of 'Israel' in Romans 9—11 as already redefined by Paul, i.e. as encompassing all who have faith in Christ, whether Jew or Gentile: see Wright 2002, esp. his comments on Romans 11.26a on pp. 688–90. For recent criticisms of Wright's understanding of 'Israel' in these chapters see Vanlaningham 2013; Barclay 2015, 525 and n. 10, 554–5 and n. 79, with other literature cited there.

6 Waymeyer 2005.

7 Barclay 2015, 520–61, quotation at p. 525.

8 Dodd 1932, 182–3.

its Jewish background suggests a broader horizon than Israel narrowly defined.

We shall approach discussion of Paul's claim by way of three stumbling-blocks which it may put in the way of the modern reader (especially a Christian one).

1 Its apparent anthropomorphism can cause a modern reader to stumble. Is Paul suggesting that God does not love individual Israelites for their own sake? It seems to express that human instinct of affection or loyalty to the children or grandchildren of a friend or (as it might be) a brother because, after all, we're quite fond of the old boy himself. It is a natural human tendency – but is it not a somewhat unworthy one, given that God surely loves people individually for their own sake, since he made them all in his image (Genesis 1.26–28)? More significantly perhaps for those who have been taught to read Scripture through an evangelical framework of theology, it may seem to threaten the dictum that 'God has no grandchildren', that is, that one cannot depend on one's parents' or grandparents' faith but needs to have one's own. Of course there is nothing in this verse that negates the importance of a personal faith, yet the assertion that Jewish people can depend on the fact that God loves them simply because they are part of this particular family may jar with traditional Protestant readings of Romans which either emphasize the universal mercy of God to the detriment of his special relationship with Israel, or take Paul's statements about Israel's election as referring to God's election of individuals (including the 'remnant' of Israel) to salvation through Christ.

2 The second problem follows from this. If God loves Israelites because they are part of this family with whom he has had a long-standing relationship, on what basis does he love Gentiles? There can be little doubt that he *does* love Gentiles, according to Paul. Romans is addressed to 'all God's beloved in Rome' (1.7), which surely includes both Jewish and Gentile believers. The inclusion of Gentiles is explicit when Paul turns to focus his address on them in 11.13: 'Now I am speaking to you Gentiles . . .' The great statements of God's love 'for us' in the heart of the letter (5.5, 8; 8.35, 37, 39) most naturally include all those to whom God has extended his power of salvation in the gospel, namely 'the Jew first and also . . . the Greek' (1.16) – for, as Paul says, 'Is God the God of Jews only? Is he not the God of Gentiles also? Yes, of Gentiles also, since God is one' (3.29–30). Is there then a kind of two-tier system of love in which God loves Jewish people because of their ancestry but Gentiles

for themselves alone? This seems like the 'scandal of particularity' at its most scandalous, an unequal arrangement with a strong potential to foster resentment on either side.

3   'They' in 11.28 clearly designates the covenant family of Israel as a whole.[9] But what are the implications of this for how Paul understood God's love for Gentiles? Does God pick and choose which of them to love? If that is the case, is that not a scandalous inequality between Israel and the Gentiles – in which Israel is beloved wholesale, *in toto*, Gentiles loved selectively? I shall float the possibility that the implication of Paul's words may be otherwise: that just as Israelites are beloved 'for the sake of their ancestors', so Gentiles too are loved for the sake of theirs – or perhaps for the sake of one 'ancestor' in particular.

We might summarize these three questions arising from Romans 11.28b thus. Is not the idea of God loving members of a particular family all too human – superseded by the NT idea of the universal love of God?[10] Does it not inevitably raise the spectre of a God who relates to Jews and Gentiles on a different basis, despite all Paul's talk of oneness in Christ? And therefore, if Jews are all loved as members of the Israelite family, can we not say that all Gentiles also are loved not merely on a selective individual basis, but as members of a family? And if so, how does this work?

We should not necessarily imagine that Paul had resolved the tensions between God's purpose for the whole world, which he discerned in Christ, and his particular love for Israel. Romans is a letter which reflects active wrestling with the issue. But perhaps we can better understand the love-language Paul uses if we look back at the nature of God's love as it is expressed in Paul's Bible.

God's love for his people in Scripture

Scripture pictures God as one whose compassion is over all that he has made (Psalm 145.9), but who has particularly set his heart on Israel – not for any reason other than that he loved it (Deuteronomy 7.7–11). This particularity of God's love as it is expressed throughout Scripture (and Jewish and Christian tradition) has indeed been a 'scandal' to many. Yet it can be argued that it is in the nature of love itself to be particular. Love, in

---

9   As pointed out by Moo 1996, 731, it would be exegetically 'unwarranted' to regard 11.28b as referring to a remnant only, as 'they' are clearly the same group called 'enemies' in v. 28a.

10   This was the thrust of the universalizing reading of Paul developed in the nineteenth century by F. C. Baur; on this see Watson 2007, 40–4.

anything like the sense of the full-bodied experience to which we give that name, cannot deal in vague generalities. We might say that it is impossible to love in the abstract; one can only love through meaningful, trustworthy expressions of relationship and care. It is possible, in fact, that a Christian emphasis on the uniqueness of *agapē* as a self-giving and 'spiritual' form of love in the NT has obscured its continuity with the highly earthed, realistic, human-like depictions of God's love in the OT. Its contrast with *storgē*, *philia*, *epithymia* and *erōs*, those supposedly more earthy manifestations of love, may well have been overplayed.[11]

Jonathan Sacks explains that the Hebrew Bible's emphasis on God's care for Israel is a necessary expression of the *particularity* which is integral to love. Drawing on the Jewish tradition of a tripartite division of humanity (elect, anti-elect and non-elect) as opposed to a binary one (elect/damned),[12] he argues that God's choice of Israel does not imply the rejection of others. He shows that even within the biblical story of the covenant, there is a counter-narrative in which figures such as Hagar, Ishmael and Esau who are outside the main covenant line are not rejected by God simply because Sarah, Isaac and Jacob are chosen.[13] The choice of Israel and of certain individuals or family lines within it symbolizes the openness of God to relate in love to any and all. Sacks sees this as the most radical of monotheism's truths: 'that God may choose, but *God does not reject*.'[14] He finds it embodied in the book of Genesis:

> Genesis is the story of two covenants . . . between God and humanity on the one hand, God and Jacob's children on the other. God unconditionally affirms both, the former as his 'image,' the latter as his 'children.' The conclusion to which the whole of Genesis has been leading is *the rejection of rejection*.[15]

Sacks sees this as expressed in the context of the chosen family itself at the climax of Genesis, in the reconciliation between the 'beloved' Joseph and the brothers who have previously rejected him.[16]

One cannot, of course, assume that Sacks' reading of the OT is identical to Paul's. But Paul gives us a clue to his reception of OT love-language

---

[11] See the suggestion of Johnson 1984, 179, that Morris 1981 may have exaggerated the contrast.
[12] On this see also Kaminsky 2012, 119–46, esp. 122–3, 127–30. I am grateful to Dr Zoltán Schwáb for drawing my attention to this chapter.
[13] Sacks 2015, 107–43. See, e.g., Genesis 21.15–21; 33.1–17; Deuteronomy 2.4–5. See also Spina 2005; Kaminsky 2012, 141–4.
[14] Sacks 2015, 124 (italics original).
[15] Sacks 2015, 167.
[16] Sacks 2015, 144–73.

because he has earlier quoted from Hosea, where some of the most striking of such language occurs. He does so in the section of his letter where he is arguing that a mysterious process of selection was going on even within Israel, which makes the present rejection of the gospel by many Jews, and its acceptance by many Gentiles, comprehensible within the narrative of Scripture. So he quotes a Greek version of Hosea 2.23 in Romans 9.25: 'Those who were not my people I will call "my people", and her who was not beloved I will call "beloved".'[17]

There could be no more graphic picture of the particularity of God's love for Israel[18] than that of Hosea being commanded to take a prostitute as his wife and commit himself to her despite her past and future unfaithfulness. It is a picture sustained by the intimate language of marriage and parenthood that occurs throughout the book. It shows us an agonized dialogue of God with his people, and within himself about his relationship with them. In the book as we have received it, presumably in much the same shape as Paul knew it, this accumulates into a dramatic narrative, notwithstanding the fact that its particular prophecies would have been given on separate occasions. Initially God declares that he will no longer have pity on the house of Israel (i.e. the northern kingdom), or save them, or even regard them as his people (Hosea 1.6–9). He grieves over their sin and cannot withhold judgement. At the same time he cannot give them up. Thus 2.14–23 looks ahead to a time beyond his acts of judgement when he will, like a yearning, faithful lover, woo Israel again and 'take you for my wife for ever . . . in righteousness and in justice, in steadfast love, and in mercy' (2.19). This is the prelude to the promise of 2.23 that the earlier verdict will be reversed. In Paul's Greek version: 'Those who were not my people I will call "my people", and her who was not beloved I will call "beloved".'

In Romans 9 Paul takes the promise of God that he will again love the northern kingdom of Israel, whom he had previously turned against, as a word which speaks of God's readiness to love any people with whom he was previously at enmity – and this refers, in Paul, to the Gentiles.[19] In Romans 11, as we have seen, he expresses a similar belief with regard to unbelieving Jews: at present they are enemies of God, but the love God has for them is

---

17 The Hebrew reads 'And I will have pity on [the child called] "Not pitied", and I will say to [the child called] "Not my people", "You are my people."'

18 Indeed, at times for particular groups within Israel (since Hosea's prophecy is directed to the northern kingdom particularly).

19 As pointed out by Tanner (2005, 97–101), however, this should not be taken as excluding the Jews.

enduring. The concept of love enduring beyond enmity has a close thematic parallel in Romans 5, which speaks of God showing his love for 'us' (i.e. both Jews and Gentiles) while we were still sinners (v. 8), and of 'our' being reconciled to God by the death of his Son while we were still enemies (v. 10).

We notice how Paul is ready to take up Hosea's language which pictures God first rejecting, then welcoming back, a people. The Gentiles had previously been 'not my people', but now they are the people of God. The unbelieving Jews are currently 'enemies', but they remain 'beloved for the sake of the ancestors'. The language is redolent of *particular* relationships. We may note two further characteristics of this 'love-language'.

First, it is highly and shockingly personal. As a living visual aid, Hosea is commanded to take a prostitute as a wife, representing the 'whoredom' of the land in forsaking Yahweh (1.2). The names of the offspring which ensue represent God's attitude to the people's behaviour: 'Jezreel' (the site of Jehu's notorious massacre of Ahab's sons, 2 Kings 10.1–14 – the name acting as a reminder that justice was due to Jehu's house too);[20] 'Lo-ruhamah' ('not pitied'); 'Lo-ammi' ('not my people') (1.4–8). This is 'embodied' prophecy at its most scandalous: Hosea is asked to commit himself to a woman who is unfaithful, and have children whose names speak the reverse of the normal blessing associated with a name, so that the truth of God's commitment to his unfaithful people may be exposed. God shows himself as a husband and a father, bound in a paradoxical relationship to his people: Hosea's marriage to Gomer embodies the enduring reality of the covenant, while the children's names appear as a standing contradiction to that reality, and Gomer herself (by implication) continues to have many other lovers (2.2–13). This was precisely Israel's situation. Her God must woo her back (2.14–20), and then the children's names will take on a new colouring, or be changed altogether (2.22, 23). 'Jezreel' will no longer be a reminder of a past atrocity, but the root meaning of the name will come to the fore: God will 'sow' him and make him prosperous in the land. The one who was 'not pitied' will now be known as the one on whom God has had pity. The one known as 'not my people' will be known as the one who belongs to God's people.

Further startling instances of such divine love-language occur through the book. God appears as passionate, totally involved, and subject to dramatic swings of attitude and rhetoric in the way the book in its current final form presents him. 'Every evil of theirs began at Gilgal; there I came to hate them . . . I will love them no more,' reflects Yahweh (9.15). It had

---

[20] Wolff 1974, 18.

not always been so: 'When Israel was a child, I loved him, and out of Egypt I called my son' (11.1). And it might not be so for ever, as he muses again:

> How can I give you up, Ephraim? How can I hand you over, O Israel? How can I make you like Admah? How can I treat you like Zeboiim? My heart recoils within me; my compassion grows warm and tender. I will not execute my fierce anger; I will not again destroy Ephraim . . .
>
> (11.8–9)

Final outpourings of outrage from 11.12 to 13.16 are succeeded by a final reversal: 'I will heal their disloyalty, I will love them freely, for my anger has turned from them' (14.4; cf. MT 14.5). The fact that the book ends on this note suggests that the 'hate' previously expressed is the passionate frustration of the lover when the beloved behaves disloyally, and is strictly temporary.

If we find some of this love-language shocking when used of God, we should note that Hosea is not the only book to use it, though it is one of the most graphic. Jon Levenson discusses how Deuteronomy's account of the renewal of God's covenant with Israel on the borders of Canaan is rooted in the love of God for his people and the love they are to show him in response.[21] Although this is an unequal love, and one which clearly echoes the political language of the day in which an overlord would make a treaty with lesser powers, committing himself to their protection in exchange for their loyalty, Levenson points out that the 'affective' or emotional dimension is not absent. Indeed, he reads Deuteronomy 7.7 as saying that God 'fell in love' with Israel,[22] since the rare verb used here, 'set his heart on', may well have erotic connotations.[23] This connects not only with Hosea who, as Levenson shows, addresses an audience who are in the middle of the ruptured stage of a relationship and need a powerful challenge to return to the response of grateful obedience,[24] but also with the Rabbinic reading of the Song of Songs as an allegory of God's love for Israel.[25] Joel Kaminsky comments: 'The concept of election is itself the deepest articulation of the biblical God's close and merciful relationship toward humanity as a whole in that it is a declaration of the biblical God's profoundly *personal* character.'[26]

---

[21] Levenson 2016, 1–58.

[22] Levenson 2016, 36–42.

[23] Levenson 2016, 40–1. The verb is *ḥašaq*.

[24] Levenson 2016, 113–14.

[25] See Levenson 2016, 143–79.

[26] Kaminsky 2012, 146.

The other characteristic of the divine love-language in Hosea that I want to point to is a counterpart to this. It does not speak only of the *affection* of God for his people. It also speaks of the *effect* of his love in their lives, that is, what it means actually to experience it. In this it is similar to Paul's language concerning God's wrath, which tends to focus on the *effectus* of the wrath, that is, the actuality of judgement, more than on its *affectus*, what God is feeling.[27] In Romans, God's wrath is manifested in the disastrous effects of rebellion by humanity as a whole (1.18–32). Thus Hosea pictures God's love (and its opposite) as something *known in experience*. When it returns after an absence, it is in experience, not as a mere abstract reality to be believed in.

We see this in Hosea 2.14–23 where God speaks of 'wooing' the people of Israel back to himself. He does this through the renewed prosperity he plans to give them. The process starts, to be sure, with the 'wilderness' (2.14) – a place of deprivation, but a place where, as in the past, Israel can learn to trust her Lord once again. Then, however, there will be vineyards (v. 15), and a covenant of peace with the animal world (v. 18a) and protection from war (v. 18c), and answered prayer with a prosperous land (vv. 21–22). Conversely, the experience of God's disfavour is horrible. In the same book, God declares that he is like maggots and rottenness (Hosea 5.12), a rampaging lion that tears apart its prey, a leopard or an enraged bear (5.14; 13.7, 8). Hosea 13.9 says starkly: 'I will destroy you, O Israel'. Such language suggests that we should not automatically recoil from understanding 'enemies' in Romans 11.28a in the sense 'those whom God opposes', without excluding the sense 'those who oppose God'.[28] The other side to this picture is that the experience of his love is almost tangibly good:

> Yet it was I who taught Ephraim to walk, I took them up in my arms; but they did not know that I healed them. I led them with cords of human kindness, with bands of love. I was to them like those who lift infants to their cheeks. I bent down to them and fed them.
>
> (Hosea 11.3–4)

In the context of discussing the experience of God's love it is helpful to turn briefly from Hosea to Malachi. If Hosea represents the experience of Israel itself (indeed, one part of Israel especially), jolting between the love and the enmity of God, Malachi begins with a contrast between the experiences of Israel and its close neighbour Edom: 'I have loved Jacob, but I

---

[27] See Travis 2009, 53–70, esp. 54–6.
[28] For this double understanding see, e.g., Moo 1996, 730–1; Kruse 2012, 445.

have hated Esau' (Malachi 1.3). Paul quotes this verse in Romans 9.13 as part of his cumulative argument that the history of Abraham's descendants shows a division in the bestowal of God's favour from the very beginning, such that it should be no surprise that now many Israelites should be experiencing his rejection. Esau, like Jacob–Israel, was descended from Abraham, yet Jacob and his descendants have been the peculiar objects of God's favour. The broader context in Malachi helps us to understand this shocking verse. Although this 'hate' leads to a devastation of Edom such that they are labelled 'the people with whom the LORD is angry for ever' (Malachi 1.4), the very purpose of mentioning this theme of the distinction between Jacob and Esau is to turn the prophetic fire back on the children of Jacob who are failing to respond to God's love. God now promises to draw near to *them* for judgement (Malachi 3.5). This in turn, it might be argued, retrospectively relativizes the powerful rhetoric of Malachi 1.2–5. If the manifestation of Yahweh's love for Israel in its national history is now under threat from Israel's own behaviour, who is to say that Yahweh's anger against Edom will be as permanent as it seems?

Paul's use of Malachi 1.3 in Romans 9.13 may seem problematic in this light, because he explicitly states that God's election of Jacob over Esau was before they were yet born and 'had done nothing either good or bad' (9.11, ESV). That is, Paul – unlike much of the Rabbinic reception of the biblical material concerning election – emphasized the mystery of God's free choice over against the concrete moral reasons why some might be supposed to enjoy, or not, the privileges of 'election'.[29] Malachi can be naturally read as implying that the experiences of God's love and hatred depend on human responses to God, that the one could in principle give way to the other, and that no one family should presume on a perpetually 'loved' status. Paul, by contrast, seems to stress the arbitrariness of God's choice of the one over the other.

Yet there may not be as much of a tension here as first appears. Paul's conviction, rooted in passages such as Deuteronomy 7.7, is that ultimately God is free to bestow his love on whom he will (Romans 9.14–16). What came upon the Canaanites was due to their wickedness, according to Deuteronomy, but the corollary of this is not that the Israelites have earned the land through their righteousness (Deuteronomy 9.4–6); nor will they be immune from his anger if they turn against him (Deuteronomy 7.10). Thus Paul's use of Malachi 1.3 can be seen as consistent with Malachi's original thrust. Whatever may have been the iniquities which led to

---

[29] See Kaminsky 2012, 134–9.

Edom's current experience of God's 'hatred', God's choice to 'love' Jacob and his descendants was free – though the enjoyment of that love will depend on their returning to and remaining in his covenant. In Romans 9, Paul is emphasizing this fundamental freedom of God's choice which can be seen as lying at the heart of the biblical understanding of his love. And he has, of course, affirmed all through Romans that those previously regarded as 'non-chosen', the Gentiles, have now found their place among the chosen. His use of Malachi does not, then, entrench a division between the chosen and non-chosen, but points to the freedom of God to love whom he wills – in the ironic awareness that those now experiencing that love include many who had seemed previously excluded from it.

It is helpful here to draw attention to the language concerning God's 'mercy' which occurs at significant points of Paul's argument in this section of Romans (9.15, 16, 18, 23; 11.30, 31, 32). In a closing summary of his message, Paul states that Christ became a servant to the Jewish people 'to show God's truthfulness, in order to confirm God's promises to the patriarchs, so that the Gentiles might glorify God for his mercy' (15.8, 9, ESV). For Paul, Israel's calling was to exhibit what it was to be a people which had experienced God's mercy, not for the sake of its own status or the exclusion of others, but for the sake of the world. God's 'kindness' is prior to all human response to him (*pace* the implications of the quotation from Luther with which we began), and it is meant to lead to repentance (2.4; cf. 11.22).[30]

How then does this scriptural emphasis on the particular and personal dimensions of God's love, and its concrete effects, shed light on Paul's comment that Israel are 'beloved for the sake of their ancestors' in Romans 11.28, and on the questions which arise from it?

Light from Scripture on God's love in Romans

The first question identified above as arising from Romans 11.28 was how to take its anthropomorphic implication that God loves a particular family because he loved its parent or ancestor. Even a brief glance at the OT should remind us that God is regularly spoken of in anthropomorphic terms. This does not mean, of course, that such language is meant to be taken with wooden literalism, as if God were able to marry, or have children in the human way, or bare his arm, and so on (any more than

---

[30] Cf. Barclay's (2015, 449–92) emphasis on the responsibilities associated with God's gracious gift.

he is 'literally' maggots, a lion or a leopard). But it does mean that we should allow its force to be felt, as surely Paul did, rather than explaining it away as primitive or a merely dispensable picture of a reality that is much more abstract. Perhaps Christians have been too ready to dismiss quietly such terminology or see it as superseded by (what they think of as) the grander and more universal vision of the NT. This can then become a tacit but illicit reason for asserting Christianity's superiority over against Judaism, insofar as we ignore the fact that Paul's own language continues to be deeply shaped by it.[31] In Barclay's words, for Paul 'the Christ-gift is to be understood not as an impersonal or random distribution of divine benefaction, but as the expression of love . . . a willed and personal commitment from which God will not withdraw.'[32]

We can, however, put the point in a positive fashion. Paul's use of such a concept encourages his hearers (Jewish and Gentile) to recognize that God's love is not less than human love, even though it is far greater. We should not be surprised that Paul asserted God's continuing love for Israel. Having set his love upon the parents, he was not going to turn his back on the children. His claim in Romans 11.28 simply continues the conviction of Hosea that God would never ultimately give up on the family he had chosen, symbolized in the prostitute Gomer and her children. His people might treat him abominably and require stern discipline, but would never be cast off. We should not be troubled by the possible implication of Paul that, apparently, God loved the children for the parents' sake rather than their own. We should rather highlight the fact that God loved the parents so much that he would never reject their descendants. In Wright's words, 'God will not say to Abraham that his physical children used to be welcome in his true family but will be no longer.'[33]

Our second question concerned the implications for the Gentiles of what Paul says about God's love for Israel. Does the fact that God loves the Jews because he loves their ancestors imply an inequality in God's love? What about the Gentiles who have no 'chosen' ancestry? To be sure, it is good that God loves them anyway, but is this love of the same quality?

Here it is relevant to recall the OT emphasis on particularity as an essential feature of God's love. As Sacks and others point out, the overall narrative of the OT by no means implies that God simply rejects those who are not a part of the covenant family. The covenant family, rather, consists

---

[31] Cf. the remarks of Kaminsky (2012, 120) about the tendency in Christianity to underplay the election theology in which, like Judaism, it is indubitably rooted.

[32] Barclay 2015, 450, with supporting literature cited in n. 2.

[33] Wright 2013, 1254.

of those called to embody the reality of God's particular love so that all and sundry may see and experience it.[34] They are precisely those who are weak and insignificant and thus manifestly could not make any claim on God's attention because of any quality they possess (Deuteronomy 7.7). But the love of God for Hagar, Esau and others outside the narrower covenant line shows that this particular love does not exclude the outsider. The background in Hosea, however, suggests even more. If one applies the logic of Hosea 2.23 as Paul does in Romans 9.25 – 'Those who were not my people I will call "my people", and her who was not beloved I will call "beloved"' – then God is not only open to loving Gentiles, but is also open to making them *a people*. In other words, there is perhaps not, after all, a difference in the grounds of God's love as between Jews and Gentiles. Jews are beloved for the sake of the ancestors. Gentiles are not 'beloved' merely as selected, isolated individuals, but as being themselves a people, a family – not now separate from the Jews, but joined to them, all alike adopted sons and daughters of God.

Paul's argument in Romans supports this. In 4.1–25 he argues that the faith shown now by believers in Christ marks them out as members of the same family as Abraham, who trusted in God's promise that he would have many descendants. And in 5.12–21 he presents Christ himself as the new head of a worldwide human family, in which Jew and Gentile alike are included – even as the fundamental identity of both hitherto has been in Adam.

The third question followed on from this. If Paul believes that Israel, *en bloc*, is beloved for the ancestors' sake, does this not imply that the love of God extends also to *all* Gentiles? I believe it does. Recall how Hosea speaks of how the people of Israel had actually experienced and would experience the Lord's love, through his blessing on their land and the delight of intimate relationship. For Paul, too, the love of God is no mere abstract notion. We note Romans 5.5: 'God's love has been poured into our hearts through the Holy Spirit that has been given to us.' This clearly refers to the way in which God's love is made real in Christians' experience,[35] and that despite suffering (5.3). There is an interesting echo of this in Paul's appeal to the Romans to pray for him 'by our Lord

---

[34] This is different from asserting that the Jewish Scriptures advocate an active 'mission' of Jews to Gentiles: as Kaminsky argues, such an assertion lacks evidence (2012, 123–7). He goes on to emphasize that the very concept of election entails the call to be 'a blessing for the larger world' (2012, 145–6), pointing to God's promise to Abraham in Genesis 12.1–3.

[35] This is true whether one takes the word 'God' in the phrase 'God's love' as a subjective genitive ('God's love for us') or an objective genitive ('Our love for God').

Jesus Christ and by the love of the Spirit' (15.30). At the time of Paul's writing, the dominant group among those who are experiencing the love of God in Rome are *Gentile* believers. These people (as well as formerly rebellious Jews like Paul) have grasped the hope held out by Christ (5.4, 5) which gives them joyful confidence in his victory over all evil powers, no matter what hardship they endure (8.31–39). They have known what it is to be 'enemies' of God who have now been reconciled to him (5.10). Now it is noticeable that a substantial part of Israel itself is in a position of enmity towards God (11.28); Paul asserts that these people are nonetheless 'beloved' (11.28), in the confidence that one day they too will experience reconciliation (11.15).

The backdrop of the verse, then, is not (as might first appear) a picture of the Gentiles as those from whom God may select a number to add on to the family of Israel[36] – a family which, by contrast, can rest secure in the love of God for the whole ancestral line. It is rather a picture of the Gentiles as those who are now, precisely, experiencing God's love as a part of his family. Paul is not naive; he well knows how many Gentiles, like Jews, remain alienated from God. But he sees the numbers of Gentiles in the Church, already experiencing God's love, as a sign – a sign that the non-Jewish section of the family is as beloved by God as the Jewish. And if that is the case, there is no reason whatsoever why we should not regard all Gentiles as being within the scope of God's love.

Implications and conclusion

If the main conclusion to be drawn from this study of Romans 11.28 and its background were that Paul believed that God loves everyone as part of his family, that might seem to some disappointingly uncontroversial or even banal. Uncontroversial conclusions are not, of course, to be despised if they follow from a careful investigation of the evidence. Yet given the lingering influence of Luther's comments which seem so restrictive in their view of God's love for Jews *and* Gentiles, I believe that the significance of this exploration for our understanding of Paul goes wider and deeper than that.

First, what is Paul implying here about the continuing role, if any, of historical Israel? Paul's remark about the Jews being 'beloved for the sake of their ancestors' takes on new strength and colouring from the

---

36 The idea of a select number may be suggested to some by the word *plēroma* in v. 25: 'until the full number of the Gentiles has come in'.

Old Testament background we have noted. In particular, the book of Hosea offers a powerful picture of how God's love for his wayward people endures and emerges intact from the most profound trauma and relationship breakdown. Paul sees that breakdown as still continuing in his own time, but he has no more reason than Hosea to think that the relationship will ever end.

Second, what does Paul believe is the scope of God's salvation? If, as we have seen, the statement that Israel is beloved by God does not imply that the Gentiles are *de facto* rejected by him, does that mean that for Paul, salvation is universal? I believe this is indeed Paul's hope. But the notion of being 'beloved' brings into play the issue of human freedom. The history of Israel, like the history of all humankind, shows tragically the possibility of rejecting God's love. In Wright's comment on 11.28, 'They remain "beloved", not in the sense of "automatically saved", but in the same sense that they are "holy" in 11.16'.[37] 'Universal salvation' is thus not a deterministic certainty for Paul. He believes in God's 'universal love' – not as vague benevolence, but as a love that is particular, passionate and known in personal experience. This is not a trivial conclusion, but an important one, given the tendency of some Protestant interpretation that, seeing the link between election and love, denies the reality of God's love for any but a select number. Such a position gives warrant for various kinds of exclusivism that run counter to Paul's vision. Nor should our conclusion about 11.28b lead to complacency by any. Paul leaves no room for that (11.22, 23). Just as he longs for his Jewish contemporaries to return to God, he also fears that repentant Gentiles may fall back into an attitude of rebellion which will inevitably mar or destroy their experience of God's love.

Third, and obviously connected, how does Paul see the nature of God's election? The phrase we have considered implies, surely, that rather than election being a matter of this one or that one picked out here and there to be saved (with the corollary, often, that the others are chosen to be damned), it is a family matter. God's particular love reached into the world to a particular family, so that that family might demonstrate that love and its consequences to all other families. Paul believes that his fellow Jews are loved because they are part of the chosen family on whom God set his love. '[T]hey remain "beloved" in the sense that God continues to yearn over them, as a father for a long-lost son.'[38] Now that Gentiles have come, through Christ and the Spirit, to experience that love too, Paul has seen

---

[37] Wright 2013, 1254.
[38] Wright 2004, 62.

the reality that they also, as a great family, are chosen, and reconciled to the Israel from whom they have been estranged, within the family of the new Adam.[39] Thus our study supports the emphasis of this volume's honorand on the centrality of the community of God's people in Paul's thinking, even if it invites some questions about the precise way that he has construed this centrality in Romans 11 – to which, I have no doubt, he will have some interesting and learned answers.

Bibliography

Barclay, John M. G. (2015). *Paul and the Gift*. Grand Rapids, MI: Eerdmans.

Barrett, C. K. (1962). *The Epistle to the Romans*. Black's New Testament Commentaries. London: A. & C. Black.

Cunningham, Philip A. (2013). 'Paul's Letters and the Relationship between the People of Israel and the Church Today.' In *Paul and Judaism: Crosscurrents in Pauline Exegesis and the Study of Jewish-Christian Relations*, edited by Reimund Bieringer and Didier Pollefeyt, 141–62. London: Bloomsbury/T&T Clark.

Dodd, C. H. (1932). *The Epistle of Paul to the Romans*. Moffatt New Testament Commentaries. London: Hodder & Stoughton.

Johnson, S. Lewis (1984). 'Divine Love in Recent Scholarship.' *Trinity Journal* 5.2 (Autumn): 175–87.

Kaminsky, Joel (2012). 'New Testament and Rabbinic Views of Election.' In *Jewish Bible Theology: Perspectives and Case Studies*, edited by Isaac Kalini, 119–46. Winona Lake, IN: Eisenbrauns.

Käsemann, Ernst (1973). *An die Römer*. 2nd edition. Handbuch Zum Neuen Testament 8a. Tübingen: Mohr Siebeck.

Kruse, Colin G. (2012). *Paul's Letter to the Romans*. Pillar New Testament Commentary. Nottingham: Apollos / Grand Rapids, MI: Eerdmans.

Levenson, Jon (2016). *The Love of God: Divine Gift, Human Gratitude and Mutual Faithfulness in Judaism*. Princeton, NJ: Princeton University Press.

Luther, Martin (1976 (1954)). *Commentary on the Epistle to the Romans*. Translated by J. Theodore Mueller. Grand Rapids, MI: Kregel.

Moo, Douglas J. (1996). *The Epistle to the Romans*. New International Commentary on the New Testament. Grand Rapids, MI: Eerdmans.

Morris, Leon (1981). *Testaments of Love: A Study of Love in the Bible*. Grand Rapids, MI: Eerdmans.

Reasoner, Mark (2005). *Romans in Full Circle: A History of Interpretation*. Louisville, KY: Westminster John Knox.

Sacks, Jonathan (2015). *Not in God's Name: Confronting Religious Violence*. London: Hodder & Stoughton.

Spina, Frank Anthony (2005). *The Faith of the Outsider: Exclusion and Inclusion in the Biblical Story*. Grand Rapids, MI: Eerdmans.

---

[39] Here Paul's thinking in Romans points forward to Ephesians (cf. Ephesians 2.11–22).

Tanner, J. Paul (2005). 'The New Covenant and Paul's Quotations from Hosea in Romans 9:25–26.' *Bibliotheca Sacra* 162.645 (Jan.–Mar.): 95–110.

Travis, Stephen (2009). *Christ and the Judgement of God: The Limits of Divine Retribution in New Testament Thought.* 2nd edition. Milton Keynes: Paternoster.

Vanlaningham, Michael G. (2013). 'An Evaluation of N.T. Wright's View of Israel in Romans 11.' *Bibliotheca Sacra* 170.678 (Apr.–Jun.): 179–93.

Watson, Francis B. (2007). *Paul, Judaism and the Gentiles: Beyond the New Perspective.* 2nd edition. Grand Rapids, MI: Eerdmans.

Waymeyer, Matt (2005). 'The Dual Status of Israel in Rom. 11:28.' *The Master's Seminary Journal* 16.1 (Spring): 57–71.

Wolff, Hans Walter (1974). *Hosea: A Commentary on the Book of the Prophet Hosea.* Translated by Gary Stansell. Hermeneia. Philadelphia, PA: Fortress, 1974.

Wright, N. T. (2002). 'The Letter to the Romans.' In *The New Interpreter's Bible,* Volume X, edited by Leander Keck, 393–770. Nashville, TN: Abingdon.

—— (2004). *Paul for Everyone: Romans, Part 2: Chapters 9–16.* London: SPCK.

—— (2013). *Paul and the Faithfulness of God.* Christian Origins and the Question of God 4. London: SPCK / Minneapolis, MN: Fortress, 2013.

Index of ancient sources

594

Index of modern authors

Index of subjects

adoption 73, 373, 428–9, 431, 435
anthropology 169, 268–70, 295, 341;
  Pauline 34, 364
apocalpytic 12–14, 25, 27, 29, 33, 35,
  40, 42, 114, 211, 217, 260–1, 308,
  368, 442, 463, 467, 494–5, 498–509,
  513–26, 533, 542, 555, 560–1
atonement 12, 41, 421–37, 524
authorship, Pauline 367

baptism 73, 174, 202, 212, 218, 220, 331,
  334–5, 338–9, 501; Jesus' 482, 501,
  516–19
benefaction and patronage 381–2, 394,
  398, 408
biblical theology 5, 35, 48, 266, 287–8
body of Christ 11, 117–18, 120–2,
  174–5, 179–80, 183, 222, 364, 370,
  374–7, 380, 384–5, 424, 476–81, 507

Christology see Davidic Christology;
  Wisdom and Word Christology
circumcision 82, 198–9, 206, 258–9,
  300–2, 335, 339, 372, 379, 452–3, 458,
  550
conversion 27, 92, 153, 169–70, 200–2,
  205–6, 211–13, 219, 224–5, 300, 324,
  334, 338, 351–2, 504, 546, 549–50
covenant 6–7, 9, 13–15, 40, 45–6, 112–15,
  117, 119–24, 148–50, 157–8, 189,
  213, 218, 309–10, 321, 341, 380, 396,
  401–2, 412, 442–3, 494–5, 502–9,
  551, 567, 569, 573–5, 577–8, 580–2,
  584–6; Abrahamic 123, 128–9, 140,
  153–4, 189, 201–2, 219, 260–2, 397,
  427–9, 431, 442, 449–50, 455, 458, 500,
  502–3, 505, 507, 525, 549, 583, 585–6;
  faithfulness 28, 129, 368, 396–7, 402,
  534; Mosaic 123, 321, 327, 483; new
  9, 218, 275, 318, 331, 334–5, 339, 341,
  401, 424–5, 546, 561–4; of works 327–8

creation 10, 36, 39, 62–6, 70, 74, 129,
  135–9, 266–85, 288–9, 304–9, 507;
  God as creator 29, 59, 62–4, 66, 70,
  75, 77–9, 83, 89, 92–3, 114–16, 135–9,
  142, 279, 305–7, 388, 468–9, 471–4,
  477, 479–80, 507
critical realism 2–3, 37, 40, 296–7
critique, imperial 47, 237–9, 258, 263–4,
  322–4, 393, 397–415, 483–6
cosmic powers 5, 11, 65–71, 363–4,
  368–71, 375, 377–80, 383–6, 494–9,
  506–8
coveting 11, 364–70, 375, 379, 411, 413,
  489
cross, crucifixion 21, 27, 29–30, 32, 38,
  44–5, 68, 72, 83, 170, 175, 177–9, 182,
  184, 186–7, 188–9, 227, 493, 506,
  508–9, 517–18, 521

Davidic Christology 7, 9, 72–3, 127–9,
  131, 145–6, 155, 160, 233–53, 521–2,
  561
death 61–2, 65, 68, 70, 269, 273, 333,
  388, 405, 410, 423, 508, 535–6, 538–9,
  541–2, 580; as a power 11, 61, 65, 371,
  375, 377, 506, 560, 568
Decalogue 88–9, 91, 93–7, 100–2, 175,
  275, 489
demythologizing 21–2, 24–7, 29–30,
  32–3, 35, 41
disability 9, 60, 232–53, 414
disjunction 11, 13–14, 112, 494, 506,
  508
disunity 118, 120–2, 168–70, 172–5, 179,
  470; see also unity, ecclesial

election 3–5, 7–13, 16, 40, 46, 48,
  113–14, 120–2, 148–50, 171, 191,
  214, 217, 321, 327, 380, 461, 468, 494,
  503–5, 529, 548, 573–4, 576, 581, 583,
  588